THE ANTIQUE
TOOL COLLECTOR'S
GUIDE TO VALUE

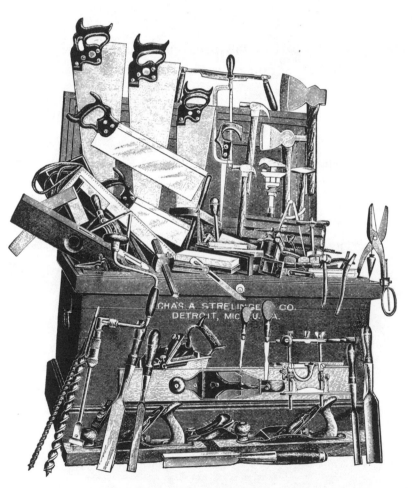

RONALD S. BARLOW

WINDMILL PUBLISHING COMPANY
El Cajon, California 92020

WINDMILL PUBLISHING COMPANY
2147 Windmill View Road, El Cajon, CA 92020

Cover Photo:

Stanley No. 42 Miller's Patent Combination Plane. Circa 1875
From the collection of Roger K. Smith. Photo by Joseph Szasfai.

CONTENTS

INTRODUCTION

Can you imagine being able to buy a real 18th‐century artifact on today's antique market for less than twenty dollars? Does the fragile patina of old iron and brass, coupled with sweat‐stained hardwood make you wax nostalgic? Do you look forward to weekends of tramping through flea markets, or racing from one garage sale to another? Would you rather sit all evening in a cold auction barn than at home in front of the hearth? Do you enjoy working with your hands, and have a genuine appreciation for fine craftsmanship?

Over 4,000 men and women with similar interests belong to half a dozen tool collecting clubs in the United States today. Another six or eight thousand like-minded souls are actively engaged in the hobby, but are not members of any formal organization.

Founded in 1933, The Early American Industries Association, with 3,000 members, is the oldest and largest fraternity of tool buffs. It publishes a quarterly magazine, funds scholarships, provides research grants, and actively supports the preservation and study of antique tools on a national scale.

In 1970 there were fewer than a half dozen tool-related books in print. Today the body of antique tool-related literature exceeds a hundred volumes plus an equal number of old catalog reprints. Collector clubs are springing up from coast to coast and several monthly publications cater exclusively to hobbyists who buy and sell by mail. Widely attended antique tool auctions take place on the East Coast, and in London, two or three times a year. The market is presently as liquid as that of any other specialized collectible.

None of this should come as a surprise because fine tools have much in common with traditional antiques. Beauty, form, function, identifying marks, and historical significance are among the many attributes of these new collectibles.

The supply of old tools is not growing, but collector interest is. Now is the time to study, and carefully accumulate...tomorrow may be too late.

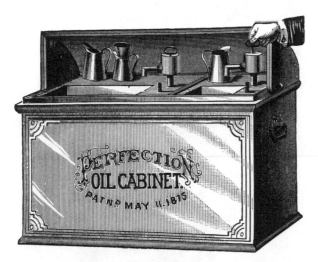

TOOL DEALERS have attempted to establish a uniform set of grading standards for the hobby but not much progress has been made. Each transaction is unique. Every collector has his own set of standards. Many won't touch a tool that has been refurbished (half the joy is in doing the upgrading one's self). Some consider a mint item as one that has never been used. Others say "mint" when they mean "Showing little or no wear". A few dealers actually specify the percentage of original varnish or paint remaining intact.

Generally speaking, a tool in "fine" condition has 90-100% of its original finish and all of its original parts. A "very good" tool might have a trace of light rust, be missing a little paint, and show normal wear. A "good" item could have a minor repair, several dings or scratches, and half of its paint or varnish worn off. "Fair" and "poor" are descriptions that really mean "Buyer beware".

Any of the following defects can seriously affect the price of a collectable tool: Wood checking, chips, cracks, excessive cleaning, severe wire brushing, replacement parts, pitting, rust, stains, broken glass or level vials, missing pinstripes or trademarks, poorly struck maker's names, weak springs, replacement handles or wedges, and a host of other smaller defects that only a specialist might detect.

There must be at least 101 ways to clean and refinish old woodworking tools. The most important thing to keep in mind is that we mortals are just conservators of these artifacts, most of them have already outlived a score of previous owners. Museum curators sum up the restoration game thusly, "Don't do anything that can't be easily undone by the next generation". Years of recorded observation have confirmed the fact that even the best repairs are but temporary in nature. Every chemical compound seems to eventually revert to its original state. Glue shrinks and cracks and finally becomes powder again. Synthetic fillers pop out on cold nights and fall to the floor. Varnish attracts dirt and becomes opaque. Welds tend to corrode surrounding metal and promote rust formation.

Now you can better understand the "Let's leav'em like we find'em" school of thought. (Indeed, this is sometimes the best approach to many situations in life). Common sense tells us that the moderate application of insecticide and a protective coating will prolong the shelf life of any wooden object indefinitely. With just a little care today's tool collections may be passed on for many future generations to admire.

Cleaning Wood. Avoid the use of soap and water. Only the sparest and quickest application will prevent the swelling and rising of surface fibers which takes place after exposure to moisture. Soft, light colored, woods such as pine act as blotters and can't really be cleaned with anything short of bleaching compound. Best to rub with fine steel wool and apply a thin protective coat of floor wax if you do not plan to completely refinish a pine piece. Harder blonde woods, such as box or fruit wood, can be safely cleaned using a rubbing compound such as Dupont's Green Label. Be sure to leave the delicate surface patina intact. Avoid using oil finishes on light colored woods. Rulers may become several shades darker.

On Medium to dark hardwoods one can safely employ turpentine or paint thinner using a fine steel wool pad. Here on the West coast a lot of antique dealers are using a liquid feeder and amalgamator appropriately called Howard Restor-A-Finish, (Howard must be filthy rich by now...my own consumption exceeds a pint a day). The stuff even cleans and polishes brass parts as you rub it on surrounding wood surfaces. Write for a sample from: Howard Finish Restorers, Inc., 411 West Maple, Monrovia, Calif. 91016. (I usually follow up in a day or two with a light coat of low-sheen spray laquer).

Patina Matching is an art indeed. It is usually a lot more trouble to make new wood look old than it is to hop in the car and locate a source of antique lumber. To disguise a large repair part in boxwood bake the new piece in your kitchen oven for several hours before inserting. The coloring of many decades can be duplicated overnight using this method. To turn other light woods a sunbleached, water-stained, grey color you can bury them in a manure pile for a year or two, or use the quicker "ammonia treatment". Place a warm tray of this foul smelling liquid inside a makeshift plastic tent along with the piece of oak you wish to fume. Remove after about 4 hours and set aside for a few days. Direct application of a lye paste also produces a primitive light grey tone in some woods.

Sometimes it is necessary to artificially age a brand new part (such as a moulding plane wedge) to match the ancient dark patina of the original. Wood stains alone don't seem to get the job done. One must somehow simulate the real ravages of time to achieve a pleasing color match. Heat, dirt, oil, grime, sunlight, smoke, fumes and wax are proper ingredients. Before applying them you must simulate a century or so of natural wear. Round off sharp corners which would normally be subject to contact with hands, work piece, other tools, or bench tops. Leave some edges crisp because every surface of a part does not receive equal wear. Add a few short random scratches with a dull knife and maybe even a crooked worm hole or two (straight ones are the mark of an amateur). Smooth the whole thing off with the very finest sandpaper or buffing wheel, perhaps even burnishing some areas to a high sheen. Now we are ready to apply several different colors of alcohol or lacquer-based wood stain (oil stains dry much too slowly). After an hour or two of drying you may want to further enhance your artistry by passing the piece over the sooty flame of a parafin-based candle. Now wipe away any excess lamp black and spray on a light coat of orange shellac or clear matte laquer. Dust the whole thing lightly with residue from your wife's vacuum cleaner and behold what wonders the clever forger hath wrought!

CLEANING & RESTORATION

Metal Processing. Most any gun shop can supply browning or bluing chemicals for recoloring shiny metal parts. I have found that most bright iron or steel will revert to its natural brownish-grey state if left bare for a few months. An annual coating with WD40 or 3 in 1 Household Oil is the only other treatment necessary unless tools are handled often. An important point to remember when cleaning metal parts is to avoid dulling the finely defined edges where wood meets inlaid metal in an almost flawless seam. Too much abrasive on either surface will produce an unnatural gap. Shoe polish or crayons may save the day though....use with heated spatula to fill a crack.

Brass Cleaning can often be accomplished with a simple home-made solution consisting of half a lemon, or a cup of vinegar, and a few tablespoons of salt. Rub it on with a saturated pad of #00 steel wool then rinse with cold water followed by boiling hot water to dry. Buff later #0000 steel wool or a jeweler's rouge impregnated cloth. If a lemon juice treatment seems too mild, try immersion in a 50/50 solution of Lysol liquid toilet bowl cleaner and water. Rub with steel wool and rinse as above. Brass founders use a standard pickling solution of 2 parts nitric acid and 3 parts sulphuric acid with a handful of table salt added to each quart. Castings are dipped and removed at once and water rinsed.

Brass Tinting. You can obtain any color from rose, to green, to blue, and even brown or black by dipping polished brass into various potash and salt solutions described in Henley's Twentieth Century Formulas. Every used book store has a copy for sale.

Rust Removal is easiest if all parts are disassembled prior to cleaning. They can be soaked in kerosene overnight to loosen stubborn particles before steel wooling or soft wire brushing. The idea is to remove only the surface rust which stands away from the old finish. If you use a course wire wheel or sandpaper you will end up with pits and scratches which are more objectionable than the stuff you were trying to eliminate. Purists use a soft knife or dull chisel to remove surface rust. Anything these tools don't get off is best left to preserve the patina. Pits and pores look best when left filled, not cleaned to their shiny bottoms.

Removing Old Screws can be a touchy business. A few are bound to break off no matter how careful one tries to be. Start by cleaning out the screw slot with an X-acto knife or a jeweler's file. Make sure the bottom corners of the slot are well defined so as to match your screwdrivers head. Also be very particular about the size screwdriver you use, regrind to fit if necessary. Add a drop of Liquid Wrench to the screw and let it soak into the threads below. (Protect fresh wood around the head with a preliminary coating of clear linseed oil, also a good precaution before buffing brass inlays.) Now insert the screwdriver and tap it smartly with a hammer blow. Hold your mouth right...and give it a counter-clockwise twist. If you didn't hold your mouth right, the head probably twisted off and you will have to drill it out, or epoxy in a replacement head after removing any trace of oil in the recess.

DANGER! Keep bleaches far away from bowl cleaners, deadly chlorine gas can result from their mixture. Never add water to acid. Always add the stronger solution to the weaker one to avoid a violent eruption. Do not use any paint thinners or restoration products in the same room as a hot water heater or other open-flame appliances. Many a careless refinisher has been blown into the next world or suffered premature loss of the eyebrows from such carelessness.

The Lazy Man's Miracle Cleaner/Restorer. If all of these time consuming conservation processes leave you cold you might be interested in a unique rust-removal method developed by a retired chief petty officer friend of mine. Out behind his barn, he keeps an electric powered cement mixer full of nice round pea gravel. When enough rusty old tools have accumulated, Frank tosses them in and flips the switch. Three or four hours later he checks the load and removes any brass or copper parts for buffing. Back on with the switch and the mixer continues churning for at least a day or two. Frank says his tumbling treatment makes old wrenches, mule bits, horse shoes, rusty keys, and other farm primitives into "valuable antiques".

His "finish feeder" beats any I've ever tried. It is also kept out back, in a stone walled shed. The basic ingredient is filtered crankcase oil from an old Buick. To this he adds 2 gallons of paint thinner, a quart of Old English Black Walnut Scratch Remover, one pint of Lemon Oil furniture polish, a tad of laquer thinner, plus the leavings from whatever cans of oil stain he can scrounge up from around the farm. Any tool too good to go in the cement mixer is soaked in this "snake oil" overnight and rubbed with a pad of #1 steel the next day. With the exception of a few melted, or broken, hard rubber knobs, Frank's restored tools look every bit as good as mine.

Richard Crane and crew conducting the sale of a major tool collection in Nashua, New Hampshire.

Over the latest ten year period average auction prices of old tools have increased at least fourfold. Gains of 1,000 percent are not uncommon, especially among the wider examples of early American moulding planes which are signed by their makers. Just last year a two-bladed crown moulder, 6½ in. wide, by Benjamin Sheneman (a mid-nineteenth century Philadelphia maker) sold for a record $2,050 at a Pottstown Penn. sale conducted by tool & firearm specialist Barry Hurchalla of RD2, Box 558, Boyertown, PA 19512. There were also plenty of bargains for beginning collectors, some 18th-century axes went for $20 apiece.

Secondhand tools have always been a part of the country auction scene, every farm or estate has yielded up its share. The best prices for collectible quality woodworking tools have customarily been realized in the New England area where most early American tools were originally manufactured. In Great Britain it seems that all good antiques eventually gravitate to London area sales rooms. Two U.S. auction firms have made a specialty of antique tools ever since the hobby really blossomed in the mid 1970's. In alphabetical order let me introduce their owners: J.P. Bittner of RFD 3, Putney, Vermont, who was the first to utilize photo illustrated auction catalogs in the sale of old tools. Jack runs a family staffed business with the help of his 13 (count 'em) children and assorted in-laws. A recent one-day antique tool sale conducted by the Bittner clan grossed over $100,000. Mr. Bittner established a world record price for the sale of a single tool: $6,600 for an 1870 vintage carpenter's plane made by C.G. Miller. This prototype plow plane was of gunmetal and ivory. J.P. Bittner retired in 1988.

Richard Crane, president of Your Country Auctioneer, Inc., of Hillsboro, New Hampshire, runs an equally impressive operation with the help of tool expert J. Lee Murray of nearby Warner. Mr. Crane was recently described by the Peterborough Weekly Transcript as "A convincing, fast talking, rolly-polly auctioneer, minus some front teeth and wearing a black derby hat along with bright red suspenders." Mr. Crane is proud of that write-up, and also of a few record tool prices his firm has garnered. Among them is a hefty $8,000 paid for a solid boxwood plow plane. Lee Murray's personal tool collection was auctioned off by Richard Crane last year for $75,000.

Both of the above auction firms issue fully illustrated catalogs prior to important sales and also mail a list of prices realized to subscribers. The average cataloged event features about 450 items and grosses between 55 and 65 thousand dollars. It takes only a hundred or so serious bidders to harvest this cash crop for a top quality collection. Important events are held in hotel complexes near major airports. Well-heeled tool collectors fly in from all over the world to attend these semiannual sales.

At least once a year Christies of South Kensington conducts an important auction of British tools at its showrooms on Old Brompton Road in London. One of the world's largest annual sales of antique craftsman's tools is held by the firm of Tyrone R. Roberts, at Kensington Town Hall on Hornton Street. Collector/ entrepreneur Reg Eaton spends most of an entire year scouring the English countryside in search of at least 600 top quality items for this event. Absentee bids from collectors around the world are encouraged by a profusely illustrated catalog and a prompt shipping policy. You may purchase a catalog from Mr. Eaton at 35 High Street, Heacham, King's Lynn, Norfolk, PE 31 7DB, United Kingdom.

Novice collectors are often unaware of the fact that regular household, estate, and farm auctions are conducted all over the country by at least 8,000 individual firms. Look in the yellow pages of several local and out-of-town telephone books. Write or phone and request that your name be placed on mailing lists for upcoming events.

Once you have homed-in on an auction it is important to attend the "preview" or pre-sale showing, which is usually held an hour or two before the actual event. Walk up and down the rows of goods on display and examine each tool carefully. After a "hands-on" examination, write down the item's number and the price you are willing to pay. In your appraisal you must take into account any broken or missing parts. Knock off about half of "Book Value" for any significant alterations. Heavy rust, hairline cracks, surface skinning, or loss of the original time-mellowed finish, (patina), also call for a discount.

As the auction proceeds, write down the actual prices realized next to your own pre-sale estimates. An erratic pattern will emerge and you may begin to understand the heavy burden we price guide compilers bear.

The prices recorded in this guide were distilled from some 55,000 separate dealer offerings and auction transactions recorded over the past 48 months. Our antique business was a bit slow one week; so I used the idle time to begin compiling a card file. Word got around and local dealers & collectors began asking for appraisals. Three years later our stack of 3x5 index cards had reached over 14 feet in length and the book you are now reading was born. All prices preceeded by the code "Auct." are from post-sale lists. The rest are averaged from dealer catalogs.

18th Century Wheelwright used adze for shaping felloe sections.

AMERICANAX, Glassport, Penn. lip adze Auct. $27

AMOSKEAG WORKS carpenter's adze with 29 in. hickory handle. Auct. $30

AUCTION LOT of 4 old stirrup-type hand adzes, live oak handles. (4) $180

D.R. BARTON with 1832 mark. Lipped adze with tapered poll. Auct. $40

D.R. BARTON, Rochester, NY. 1832 imprint on handle of factory made hewing adze. $25

BEDFORD, Sheffield, No. 3 mark on head of stirrup-type hand adze. Auct. $40

BOWL ADZE hand-forged 5 inch edge, hammer head poll, round eye. Auct $45

BOWL ADZE curved 4 inch wide hand-forged bit, old handle. $50

BOWL ADZE deeply curved 5 inch bit is ready to hone and use. Auct. $75 - $95

BOWL ADZE only 8 inches overall, hand wrought, old handle. $100 - $145

BOWL ADZE fine example with curved cutting edge at least 7 in. wide. $175 - $200 by dealers and auctions.

JAMES CAM, Sheffield. Builder's adze with octagon poll. (rusty) $24

JAMES S. CAM, Cast steel, Sheffield, No. 2 stirrip-type hand adze with closed grip/guard. Auct. $40

CARPENTER'S adze, factory made, 4 in. edge, tapered poll peg. $14

CARPENTER'S adze, hand-wrought, early, 3 in. curved bit. $28

COLLINS label still intact on this 5" lipped shipwright's adze. $35

CONNECTICUT type, unsigned hand adze with pistol grip. Auct. $55

CONNECTICUT type, blade bound to handle with removable iron band. Original oak handle. $89

CONNECTICUT style hand adze, D-handle 4½" wide blade. $110

CONNECTICUT hand adze, museum quality. 5¾" blade has curved shoulders. Short handle, iron strap. $185

COOPER'S notching adze. Thin poll is bent at right angle. $20

COOPER'S adze, hand-forged head is 8" long by 2" wide. Gouge blade. $25

COOPER'S adze, factory made. $23

COOPER'S double bladed adze, early hand forged. Head is almost 11" long. Flat & gouge blades. $35 - $60 - $135 (wide range of dealer offerings)

COOPER'S driving adze, 1 inch poll, 1½ in. wide gouge blade. Shaped handle. $30

COOPER'S bowl adze, early, round eye, no poll. Curved blade, 14 in. handle. $75

CROS AINE/A. BEZIER French cooper's adze. 5¾ in. wide, hand-forged, curved bit drops to bottom of handle. Museum quality. $135

O.H. DENNIS patented American adze has cast head with removable bolted-on cutter housing. (handle missing) $30

DOUGLAS brand, carpenter's long handled adze in usable condition. Auct. $15

DOUGLAS AXE MFG. (Mass., circa 1864) house carpenter's adze with 4 inch wide cutter, flat poll. Orig. hickory handle. $27

E.R.R. & E.R.P. carpenter's adze with extended square head. $20

FENCER'S adze with hand-forged head. Eye socket has lugs or ears at bottom. $42

FRENCH factory made 2¾" adze with round eye, square poll and a nail pulling slot in blade. $14

FRENCH made bowl adze with 6½ in. wide curved blade which extends to bottom of 8 inch handle. $92

FRENCH cooper's hollowing adze with 6 inch long curved blade. $110

W. GILPIN adze head, 4¼ in. cutting edge, rectangular poll. $15

Wm. GREAVES & SONS, Sheaf. Works, No. 2 cooper's hand adze, 3 in. cutter. $25

GUTTER adze, 1¾ in. deep gouge blade is 3¾ in. across. Square poll. $60

GUTTER adze, handwrought concave blade. ¾ size. $85

GUTTER adze, authentic old narrow headed model with ears on eye socket. Curved blade is almost a half circle in dia. $125

HOUSE WRECKER'S adze, 13 in. head is chisel shaped, 2 in. wide. Square eye socket. $25

Connecticut style hand adze (1700-1900) evolved from the Spanish slot or stirrup type which originated in Rome, circa 300 B.C. Blade is removable for sharpening on a wheel.

MOSKEAG AXE CO. cooper's adze with 3½ in. blade. Fine cond. $25

PLUMB adze head. New with paper label. 4 in. cutting edge. $10

PLUMB brand dubbing adze, 5½ in. wide. Fine condition $42

PRIMITIVE flat bitted, square polled adze. 2⅞" bit, square eye socket. $35

RAILROAD type polless adze head with 4½ in. cutting edge. $5 - $8

RAILROAD adze, unmarked factory-made, heavy square poll, short blade. $8 - $15

RELLOTA stamp on this stirrup-type hand adze with ornamental foot. Auct $80

SABOT or CLOGMAKER'S heavy hand-forged adze with slightly curved 7 in. cutting edge. (no handle) $90

SHEFFIELD mark on head of this stirrup type hand adze with flat blade. Auct $50

SHIPBUILDER'S factory made adze, curved blade has peg on poll, square eye. Auct. $25

SHIPWRIGHT'S very large adze, 7½" curved bit, peg poll. Auct. $50- $60

SHIPCARPENTER'S hand-forged, square polled adze with YW 1842 touch mark. Fine. $175

SHOVEL MAKERS lot of 5 old English made hollowing adzes. Auct. $175

SIMMONS HARDWARE CO. Oak Leaf trademark. Shipbuilder's adze. No lip. $35

C.T. SKELTON & CO., Sheffield. Ship carpenter's adze with 13½ in. long head incl. round pin. Like new. $30

A. STAPLES Portland (Maine) cooper's sharp adze with gouge-type blade and square head. $30

UNDERHILL EDGE TOOL CO. long handled gutter or bowl-type adze with 2½ in. deep round bit. Auct. $80

WHALE'S tooth forms the ivory handle of this otherwise conventional cooper's adze. Auct. $160

L.& I.J. WHITE lipped ship adze, 5½ in. razor-sharp bit. Laminated. $75

Carpenter's Adze

Shipbuilder's Lipped Style

Railroad Adze

Bridgebuilder's

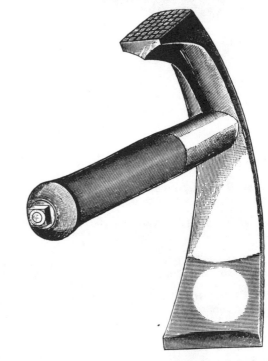

House Carpenter's

Shipcarpenter's

Cooper's Handled & Bolted

Spanish, or Brazilian Trade Adze

Deluxe Scotch Pattern Adze

Factory-Made Adzes, Circa 1880 - 1910

Moulded iron
Swage Blocks and Stands.
100 lb. to 200 lb. sizes. Sold for $5 - $10 in 1903

Round Head
Stake

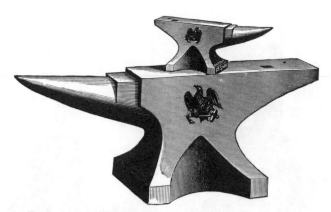

Eagle brand Blacksmith's Anvils, 100 lb. and 800 lb.
First anvil maker in America. Established in 1843.

Horseshoer's Anvil 150 lbs.
(1907 illus.)

Needle Case Stake

Blowhorn Stake

BENCH ANVIL common factory made, 20th Cent., 2½ in. tall by 6 in. long. $15

BENCH ANVIL conventional 21 lb., 3 X 10 inch, has hardie & pritchel holes. $25

BENCH ANVILS, used, factory made anvils in 5 to 7 inch lengths. $10-$25

BLACKSMITH'S mandrel, 48 in. tall cone $300. (36 inch size, $200)

BLACKSMITH'S "Toed" anvil with triangular supports cast into base. 4 X 12 X 14 inches. 118 lbs., flat top, short horn. Early Maine origin. $200 (Another as above, but no horn. $132)

BRASS decorative anvil dated 1897, Odd Fellows symbol on side, 3¼ in. long. $15

BRASS jeweler's anvil, 3 inch. $18

E.W. BUCKLEY, Berlin, Ct., tinners beakhorn stake, 41 in. 45 lbs. auct. $65

EARLY AMERICAN short horn type found in Cumberland, Maine. 148 lbs. auct. $140

EUROPEAN RENAISSANCE architectural style forged iron anvil 18½ x 8¾ x 14 inches. London Auct. $3,700.

FISHER, eagle stamp, 1877 Pat., 160 lb. blacksmith's anvil. auct. $100

FISHER rare sawmaker's anvil dated 1907. 106 lbs. auct. $175

FLEMISH ancient hand-forged T-anvil with gothic moulded collar at base of tanged square shaft, on wooden base. Illus. in Jan. 1981 Connoisseur magazine. auct. $2,400

JEWELER'S brass anvil, 3 inch. $18 (another, 4 in., nice patina. $25.)

JEWELER'S cone. Slotted, 13 in., 3 inch dia. at base, 1½ in. at top. $35

MINIATURE brass anvil advertising Weil Roth & Co. Bonds. $10

MINIATURE cast iron anvils, assorted, 3 to 4½ inch. Auct. $4-$8 ea.

MINIATURE brass, USS XANTHUS stamp on top. 3 in. x 1 in. $20

MINIATURE iron anvil, Concord Axle Co. Extremely well detailed, ground & polished. 3½ inches overall. Auct. $50

NAILMAKER'S anvil, early, hand-forged, 1⅜ in. x 1⅞ in. Auct. $40

NAILMAKER'S anvil, post mounted, 1½ in. square with separate chisel-point cutting hardie. Auct. $100

NEEDLE CASE MAKER'S stake anvil on cast iron bench mount. Auct. $60

RAILROAD track section fashioned into a 12 inch anvil. $8-$12

F. ROYS & CO. Berlin Ct. blowhorn stake, 4¼ in. dia. cone. $85

ROUND & SQUARE HORN combination, 12 oz. anvil for ½ in. hardie hole $32

SAW MAKER'S straight edge, 19 inch long anvil. $25

STAKE anvil, L-shaped steel mandrell, 2½ in. dia., 30 in. long. auct. $30

STAKE anvil, round head for forming sheet metal. 11 lb. auct. $35

SWAGE BLOCKS with multiple openings and edge cutouts. 7 inch to 12 inch sizes. auct. $75 - $200

TINNER'S creasing anvil for sheet metal. 14 inches long. auct. $15 (16 in. $25)

TINNER'S tapered round stake, 2 in. X 22 inch. $22

TINNER'S seaming stake with 4 in. X 7 in. top, weighs 19 lbs. auct. $50

TINNER'S L-shaped, needle nosed, 14 inches in length. auct. $50

TINNER'S beakhorn anvil. $55 (Blowhorn. $40)

T-SHAPE stump mounted anvils, 10 to 14 inches long, one pointed end. auct. $40-$50

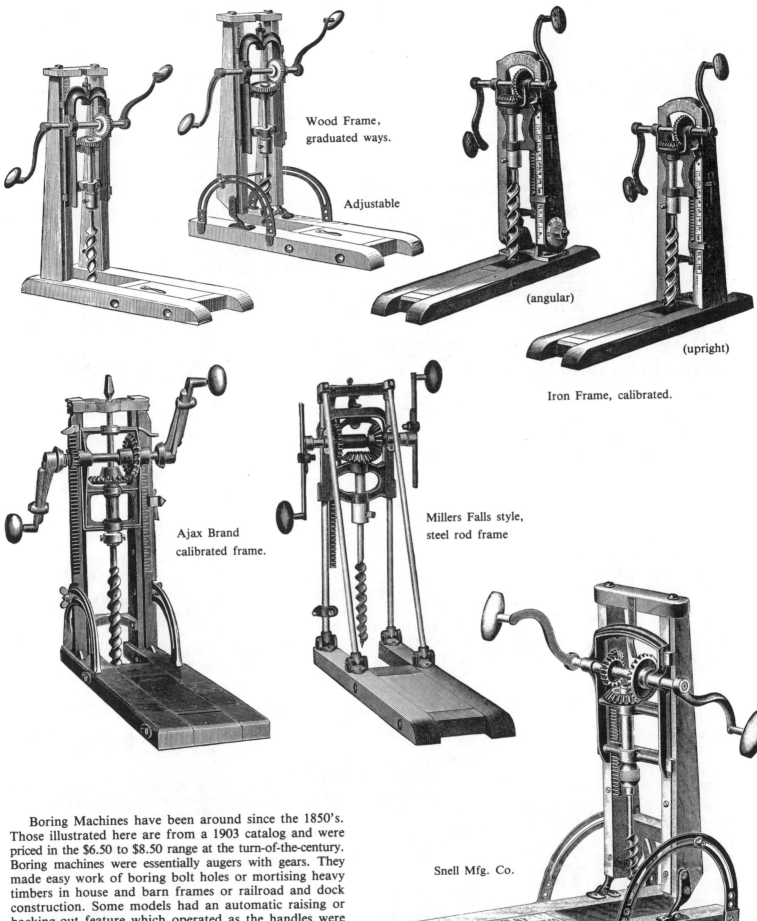

Wood Frame,
graduated ways.

Adjustable

(angular)

(upright)

Iron Frame, calibrated.

Ajax Brand
calibrated frame.

Millers Falls style,
steel rod frame

Snell Mfg. Co.

Boring Machines have been around since the 1850's. Those illustrated here are from a 1903 catalog and were priced in the $6.50 to $8.50 range at the turn-of-the-century. Boring machines were essentially augers with gears. They made easy work of boring bolt holes or mortising heavy timbers in house and barn frames or railroad and dock construction. Some models had an automatic raising or backing-out feature which operated as the handles were being turned in the same direction as when boring. Boring machines frequently sell at auction for $50 - $90. Dealers are currently quoting $125 to $185 for deluxe models with original pinstriping intact.

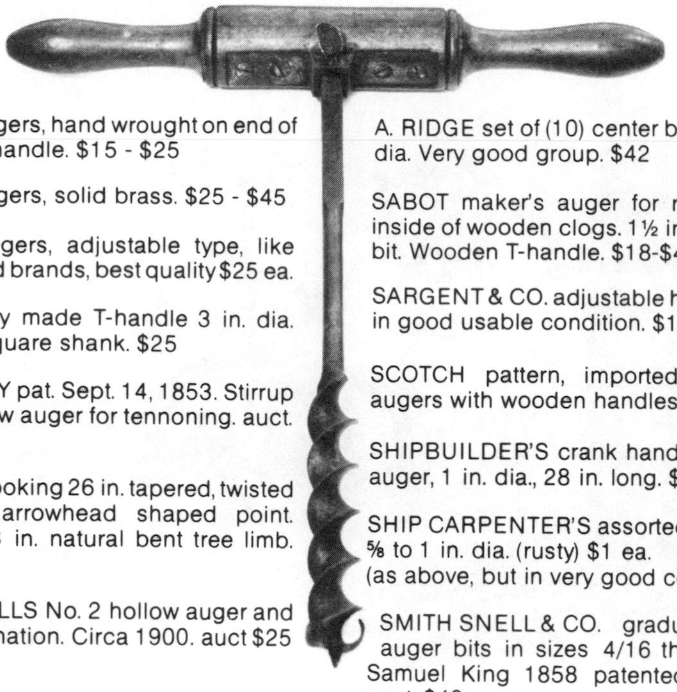

**Auger.
1860 Pat.
Gedge Bit. $35**

16th Century German Wheelright enlarges an axle hub using a tapered reamer. Augers of this basic T-handle style were used in many trades from Roman times until the mid 1900's.

AMES MFG. CO., Chicopee, Mass. pump log auger, nose-type, 1½ in.X 20 in., no handle. $39 (2 inch, auct. $45)

AUCTION LOT common T-handle twist augers in 1 thru 1½ in. dia. (5) $30

B.S.V. CO. adjustable hollow auger with rotating ring. Cuts 8 sizes. $30

AUCTION LOT, T-augers, Ives, N. Bailey, J. Ayers, etc. 1 in.-2 in. dia. (5) $17

BEECHWOOD handle 16 in. long, thumb-screw socket accepts various size auger bits. Includes 1 inch Gedges bit. $35

BREAST auger with fixed spoon bit. Resembles T-handle shipbuilder's, but wooden shaft extends back to end in a breast pad. Up to 30 inches overall. auct. $160 - $350

BURN auger, spear shaped, hand wrought 18 in. with eye handle. $50

CINCINNATI TOOL CO. hollow auger, adjustable with depth stop. 8 in. U-shaped casting. $20

COOPER'S bung reamer, hand-forged, 14 in. long, tang type handle. $20

COOPER'S bung cutter, 3 prongs, T-handle, cuts 3 in. dia. hole. $22

COOPER'S bung tap, tang handled reamer with screw tip. ¾ to 2 in. sizes. $12

C.P. CROSSMAN & CO., Fitchburg, Mass. pat'd Nov. 1850 & 1854. Tapered reamer 21 in long with hardwood T-handles which screw in place. Avg. $35, Fine $65.

W. GILPIN crossed axe trademark. T-auger, ⅝ in nose-type. $35

HOLLOW augers, assorted, non-adjust-able, for cutting round tenons on spokes, etc. auct. $5 - $8

HOLLOW augers, hand wrought on end of shaft with T-handle. $15 - $25

HOLLOW augers, solid brass. $25 - $45

HOLLOW augers, adjustable type, like new. Assorted brands, best quality $25 ea.

HUGE factory made T-handle 3 in. dia. auger with square shank. $25

J. McCREARY pat. Sept. 14, 1853. Stirrup shaped hollow auger for tennoning. auct. $20

MEDIEVAL looking 26 in. tapered, twisted auger with arrowhead shaped point. Handle is 23 in. natural bent tree limb. auct. $150

MILLERS FALLS No. 2 hollow auger and brace combination. Circa 1900. auct $25 dlr. $40

MILLERS FALLS No. 4 ratchet auger handle. Ash. Nickel plated chuck. $28-$50

NOSE auger, hand wrought shell-type with T-handle. Various sizes, ⅞ - 1½ in. $12 - $20

NOSE auger, primitive, 4¾ in. dia. 46 in. long. $50

NOSE bits for drill brace. (5) asrtd. $15

PADDOCK HAWLER IRON CO. felloe borer, pat. May 11, 1880. Large adjustable hollow auger mounted on a spoke clamp-ing jig with an attached crank handle. $40

P.M. CO. USA pat. Feb. 23, 1986. Set of (15) Forstner pattern round shank bits in mahogany rack. $195

POD auger, 25 in. shaft, 1⅝ in bit, (extra fine example) $95

PRATTS PAT. auger handle with 2 piece steel ferrule held by 2 wing nuts. Incl. 2 in. dia. twist auger bit. $16

PUMP BORING auger by I. Coverley, 1 X 2 X 5 in. handwrought shell bit, 19 in long. $25

PUMP auger bits, 2 in. to 4 in. dia., snail and shell types to fit rod shafts. $40-$55

PUMP LOG set. 4 pcs. 11 feet long plus 8 ft. handle and reamers. auct. $125

PUMP LOG set including giant Ram's Head or witchet for turning outside of log taper. Also tapered reamer and twisted cylinder auger bit. All handwrought. $225

PUMP LOG auger/reamer set consisting of 14 bits from 16 to 20 inches long plus 10 other reamers, holders and fixed augers. auct. $300

REAMER handwrought, 3 in. dia. tapered, wooden T-handle. $25-$35

A. RIDGE set of (10) center bits, ⅜ to 1 in. dia. Very good group. $42

SABOT maker's auger for reaming out inside of wooden clogs. 1½ in. dia. spoon bit. Wooden T-handle. $18-$40

SARGENT & CO. adjustable hollow auger in good usable condition. $18-$20

SCOTCH pattern, imported barrel-eye augers with wooden handles. $18-$25

SHIPBUILDER'S crank handle, all metal auger, 1 in. dia., 28 in. long. $30

SHIP CARPENTER'S assorted 26 in. bits, ⅝ to 1 in. dia. (rusty) $1 ea.
(as above, but in very good cond. $2 ea.)

SMITH SNELL & CO. graduated set of auger bits in sizes 4/16 thru 16/16 in. Samuel King 1858 patented T-handle. auct. $40

M. SNELL & CO. screw auger, T-handle, 1 in. dia. $6-$9

R. SORBY deck dowelling auger bit for counter sinking bolt heads. $10

STANLEY No. 49 auger bit depth stop. Nickel plated. $8

STANLEY boxed set of Russell Jennings auger bits, sizes ½ to 1 in., Made in England. $85

STANLEY RULE & LEVEL Foss Pat. 4-22-02 extension bit. 24 in. long. $14

STANLEY No. 1 bit extension, 18 in. long. $15

SUGAR DEVIL, or fruit auger. 20 in. with nicely turned T-handle. $95 (another, dated 1876. $120)

JAMES SWAN boxed set of (13) single twist auger bits from ¼ to 1 in. dia. (Like new cond.) $45

TAP auger with closely spaced, threaded point on end of 17 in. T-handle. $30

D.M. VARNER, Burlington, VT. reamer tapers from ½ in. to 1¼ in., T-handle. Auct $45

WHEELWRIGHT'S hooked reamer. Handwrought, tapers from ⅞ in. to 2 in. 23 in. long (pitted cond.) $55

WHEELWRIGHT'S hub reamer. Huge 5 in. dia. hand-forged blade is affixed to T-handle by 2 tangs. Auct $75

WHEELWRIGHT'S hooked-end hub reamer. Tapers from 1 in. to 3 in. over 28 inch length. Handwrought, (no handle). $135

WHEELWRIGHT'S reamer, 28 in. long with 29 in. carved handle. Wrought shell-type blade 4½ in. wide at top. $175

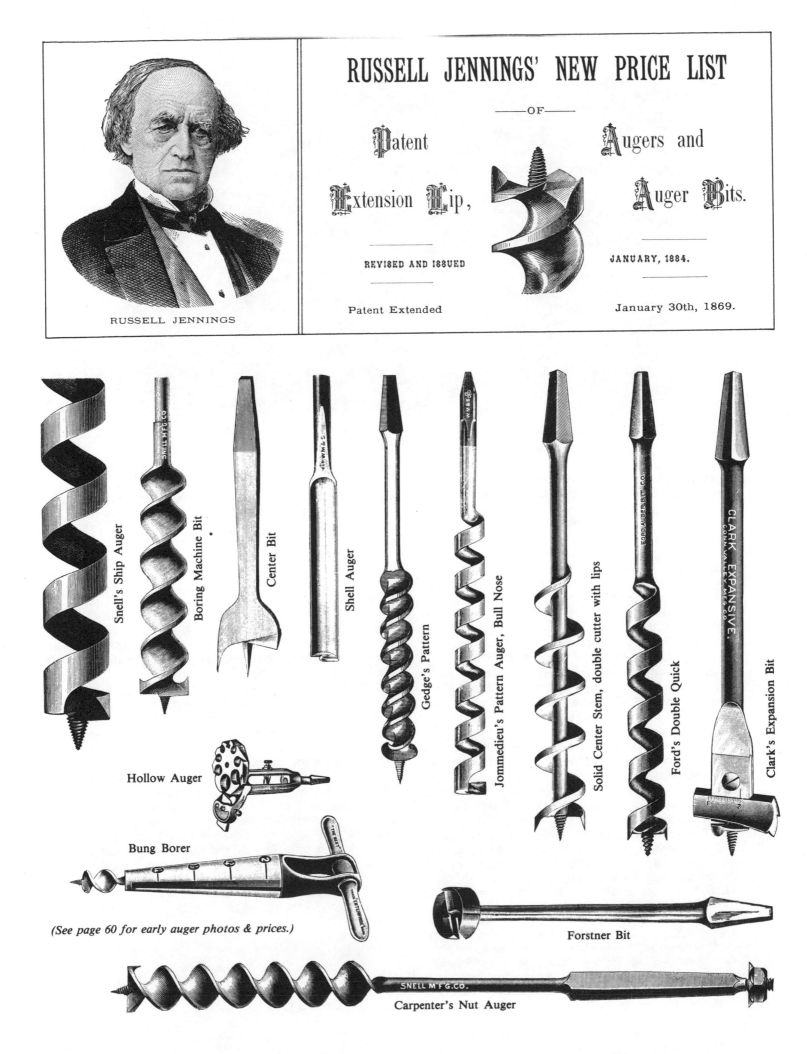

RUSSELL JENNINGS

RUSSELL JENNINGS' NEW PRICE LIST

— OF —

Patent Extension Lip,

Augers and Auger Bits.

REVISED AND ISSUED

JANUARY, 1884.

Patent Extended

January 30th, 1869.

Snell's Ship Auger

Boring Machine Bit

Center Bit

Shell Auger

Gedge's Pattern

Jommedieu's Pattern Auger, Bull Nose

Solid Center Stem, double cutter with lips

Ford's Double Quick

Clark's Expansion Bit

Hollow Auger

Bung Borer

(See page 60 for early auger photos & prices.)

Forstner Bit

Carpenter's Nut Auger

HISTORY OF AXE MAKING

Collins & Company Axe Factory, Collinsville, Conn. 1859

About 6,000 years ago in Europe, Neolithic men began to replace their wooden-handled stone axes with copper ones cast in the same crude shapes. Around 2,500 B.C. the Sumerians started actual commercial production of axes and other implements in bronze.

Sometime around 850 B.C. the wandering Celtic tribes of Central Europe began to settle down in villages. The larger of these settlements could easily support a full-time blacksmith. From a charcoal-fed air-blown fire, the village smithy produced a variety of axe heads, plowshares, swords and jewelry-like trinkets from hammered iron.

Three hundred years later, in Damascus, men began to hammer layers of steel together into much tougher implements and weapons, but until the latter half of the 18th-Century axes were still produced from wrought iron. Most trade and felling axes of the period were not much more than a bow-tie shaped piece of wrought iron folded over an eye mandrel and hammer-welded together at one end to form the cutting edge. After 1744 a steel strip was commonly inserted between the two halves of the cutting edge during this welding process. An additional steel plate was often forged to the flat poll face to make it a more durable hammering tool.

There are two basic catagories of axes: FELLING and HEWING. To chop down, or FELL, a tree, one needed a long handled, light weight, wedge-shaped axe with a cutting edge ground on both sides. To trim, shape, or HEW a fallen tree, one used a shorter handled, heavier & broader axe with a slightly curved blade sharpened on one side only (a side axe). Within the two headings above fall an unbelievably diverse group of sizes, shapes and regional variations. In the United States, local blacksmiths continued to be the primary source for axes until one Samuel Collins of Hartford, Conn. built the first real axe factory in 1826. By 1828 each employee

was hand-forging and tempering about 8 axes per working day. In 1870 the output per man had increased to 50 tools a shift, and total production reached 3,000 items every 24 hours, from a crew of 600 workmen.

Other prominent American manufacturers of axes during the 19th-Century were: D.R. Barton of Rochester, N.Y., Wm. Beatty & Sons of Chester, Penn., the Douglas Axe Mfg. Co., of East Douglas, Mass., Kelly Axe Mfg. Co. of Alexandria, Ind., Thomas R. Mann & Co. of Mill Hall, Penn., A.G. Peck & Co. of Cohoes, New York, D. Simmons & Co. of Cohoes, J.B. Stohler of Schaefferstown, Penn., and The Underhill Edge Tool Company of Nashua, New Hampshire.

Hickory axe handles were made by the user. Each farmer or craftsman owned a favorite wooden pattern and a trusty draw knife with which he fashioned his own handle. Old, and hopefully original handles are important to axe collectors. Replacement handles lower the value.

Closely dating old axes is sometimes an impossible task. Certain styles have been produced without interuption for over 200 years. The entire 1909 line of axes produced by the Austrian firm of John Weiss & Son could easily pass for tools of 1750, if left to rust a bit. Here in the U.S., old European styles existed side by side with the latest Yankee designs for decades on end. The 1865 product line of The Douglas Axe Mfg. Co. (illustrated on page 13) is a good example of this overlapping of styles.

For further reading we recommend Henry J. Kauffman's AMERICAN AXES published by the Stephen Greene Press.

J.P. Bittner Antique Tool Auctions

1. Mortising Axe, 1¾ in. center bit. $50
2. Bearded Axe, early one, IKS stamp. $85
3. Goosewing, left handed, M. Sieger. $325
4. Lot of (4) Mortise Chisel axe heads. $475
5. Early, pitted hatchet $17.50
6. Mortising Axe, 9½ in. head. $40
7. Whats-it? Bill Hook, maybe. $30
8. Goosewing, barely used. J. Bungersohn $350
9. Hewing Axe with lugs, 13¾ in blade. $75
10. Cooper's Hatchet, 8½ in. Fine. $75

11. Early & Huge, 16 in. edge, stamped. $260
12. Ice Axes, lot of (2) Hdwe. stamped. $12
13. Another Goosewing, R. Belzer no. 375. $375
14. W. Kelly Perfect Axe, full inscript. $45
15. Cooper's Side Axe, D. Williamson. $40
16. Timber branding & wedge axes (2) $55
17. Boy's Size Goosewing, Stamped SSS. $100
18. Cooper's Side Axe, extra large. $50
19. Kent style, Douglas Axe Co., W. Hunt. $25
20. Broad Axe, long and narrow variety. $50

Courtesy Dover Publications

German carpenters at work on a riverfront home. Circa 1560. Courtesy Dover Publications

ACKERMAN & JOHNS Mfg., Bangor. Slater's axe with leather handle. $50

ADZE/AXE combination, adze blade cast into top of poll on modern style felling axe. Dlr. $55

ALBERTSON, Poughkeepsie, Kent-style axe with old handle. auct. $17

AYETTER PLUMB early-style broad axe, 9½ in. bit beveled on one side. $75

BARRETTS PATTERN mortising axe with long rectangular blade. $35

D.R. BARTON cooper's side axe, 8½ in. bit. auct. $45
(another, larger, old handle. auct. $105)

B.R. BEARDSLEY, Elmira (1859-1865) 12″ hewing broad axe. Beautiful. Auct. $170.

J.B. BEATTY cast steel broad axe, 11 in. blade, 23 in. overall. auct. $35
(another, circa 1890. dlr $55)

Wm. BEATTY & SON, Chester (Penn.) 11 in. broad axe with imprint of a cow. (some pitting, new handle) $38

Wm. BEATTY & SONS, Chester, Pa., cow imprint, mortising axe with 3 in. X 7¾ in. bit. $45

BEATTY & SONS, cow stamp. Cooper's side axe, only slighty used. auct. $55

W. BEATTY & SON, Phila., cast steel. Chisel edge hewing axe with 11 in. cutting edge. Straight handle $60. Bent . $80

R. BELZER No. 375 classic goosewing with 14 in. blade. Fine. auct. $375

BLACK RAVEN, Kelly Axe & Tool Works of The American Fork & Hoe Co. Charlestown, W. Va. USA. Double-bitted felling axe. $40 - $50

BILL HOOKS, Mostly Collin's brand. New, no handles. Dlr. lots (3) for $10
(many other rusty bill hooks. $3 avg.)

BLOCKMAKER'S axe head, 19th Century, flat top 9 in. head with 6 in. bit. Excellent cond. $125

BRADES Co. Coachmaker's side axe 6 X 7 in. head with beard. (rough) $85

W. BRADY (Lancaster, Penn, circa 1875) Double-bit mortising axe with cutters at right angles $125
(as above, single bit style. $65 - $95)

G.W. BRADLEY with arrow trademark. 9 in. broad axe. auct. $25

P.W. BRAND & C.K. VRISHER, Stahl. Excellent 15 in. goosewing axe. auct. $150

BRAZILIAN trade axe with crossed axe trademark,, rounded poll. (no handle) $6

BREWER, MAINE felling axe, belt carried style, 3 in. bit. $18

BROAD AXE common factory made 20th Century style, 10 - 11 in. blade. (rusty) $25 - $38

H.S. BROWN, Cast Steel, broad hewing axe with orig. canted handle. Bell profile, laid on steel edge and poll. Fine. $90

BROAD AXE hand-forged with 8 in. beveled edge. Good old offset handle. $65

BROAD AXE early American with 14 in. curved cutting edge, hewing style. $175
(another, 12 in., rusty. $65)

BULL or Cattle Felling axe. $38

J. BUNGERSON goosewing axe, shiny bright. auct. $250
(another, 15 in., barely used. auct $350)
(another, 12½ in., rusty, cracked. $100)

J. BUSHER, Cast Steel, mortising axe, square 2 in. poll, 1⅞ in. cuttind edge. $50

CAMPBELLS XXX shipbuilder's broad axe from Nova Scotia. 6 inch blade. $35

CAYUGA, BARKER, ROSE & KIMBLE Inc. Elmira, N.Y. with indian trademark. Double bit felling style, 31 in. handle. $28

COACHMAKER'S early side axe with flat poll and applied steel cutting edge. auct. $65

COACHMAKER'S side axe with bottle-opener beard profile. $78

COLLINS No. 439 round eye export axe. Polless, (no handle, orig. paint) $8

COLLINS AXE CO. No. 296 South American export axe, rounded poll, flat top. (no handle) $9
(another, brand new with label. $12)
(another, extra large, 9½ in. head. $10)

COLLINS hand axe, 4 in. bit, 16 in. handle. New cond. auct. $12

COLLINS Official Boy Scout Axe. $14

COLLINS, Hartford, No. 341 $14

COLLINS AXE CO., Hartford. Legitimus marked hewing axe. Broad style, 13½ in. auct. $65

CONTINENTAL style polless side axe with fan shaped narrow blade and long handle socket. auct. $52

CONTINENTAL polless side axe with wider goosewing-shaped blade. Beard extends below bottom of long handle socket. auct. $75

CONTINENTAL side axe with Penn. German style bearded blade. Stamped with several smith's marks. auct. $98

COOPER'S side axes with short handles and rectangular polless blades from 9 in. to 11 in. wide. auct & dlrs $50 - $75

COOPER'S flat topped hand axe with 4 in. bearded blade and laid on steel edge. $95

COOPER'S stave making axe, French doloire, Bearded rectangular blade with polless octagonal eye socket. $280

DAVIS & CO. broad axe. auct. $25

DOUGLAS AXE MFG. CO. by W. Hunt. Kent style axe with 29 in. handle. auct. $25

DOUBLE BITTED factory made 20th Century felling axe. $8 - $15

DOUBLE BITTED handwrought bow tie style 3½ in. blades. $32 - $55

DOUGLAS AXE MFG. CO. mortising axe. auct. $25

DOUGLAS AXE MFG. CO., W. Hunt & Co. No. 343 cooper's side axe, 10 in. rectangular blade. auct. $75

O. HUNT DOUGLAS, 1817. New York pattern broad axe. Museum quality. $125

EAGLE trademark stamp in circle on American pattern axe head. auct. $50

ELLIOT, Cast Steel, Kent-style broad axe, 6⅝ in. blade, 24 in. offset handle. $35

EDINBURG hand axe with 4 inch edge. $14

ELMIRA marked broad axe. auct. $40

EUROPEAN felling axe, ½ fan-shaped head, 4 deep touch marks, 8 X 16 in. overall. auct. $80

EUROPEAN side axe with 8 in. fan-shaped blade. Polless, socket handle. auct. $100

EUROPEAN as above, 17th Century, auct. $150

EUROPEAN hewing axe, 6 in. symetrical blade, eye socket extends 5 inches. $175

EUROPEAN hewing axe, polless, fan-shape, 10 X 14 in. beveled one side. $185

EUROPEAN 18th Century hewing axe, socket handle, bearded 6½ in. blade. $225

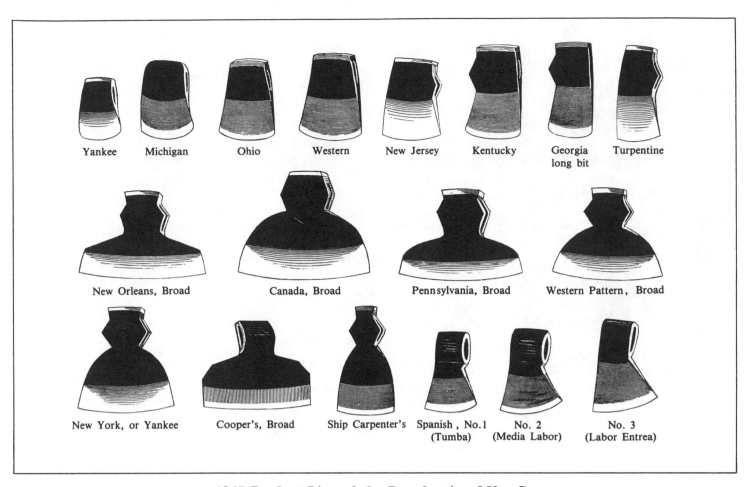

1865 Product Line of the Douglas Axe Mfg. Co.

EUROPEAN decorated goosewing axe with pointed-top 17 in. curved blade. auct. $245

EVANS TOOL WORKS double-bitted mortise axe. $125

D. FERRAUD, A Availles. Fan-shaped hewing axe with half round eye. 15 in. triangular shaped blade is beveled on all 3 faces. $150

FIRE axe, head only, 1920 - 1950 models, $5 - $15

FIREMAN'S axe, dirty, unmarked. $12

FIREMAN'S early, thin, light weight, hand-forged axe with 5 inch edge and a 7 inch curved spike. Star mark. auct. $130

FISK trademark, early wrought hewing axe. $40

FRENCH twibil, hand-forged, 45½ in. head, center-mounted socket handle. $250

FN stamped, Austrian goosewing axe date 1771. Square beard, pointed tip. Auct. $450

GERMAN side axe, dated 1787. Bearded blade, 11 in. cutting edge, decorated with chiseled floral pattern. Flat poll, short socket handle. auct. $481

GIFFORD WOOD CO. No. 602 unusual "house ice axe" with pointed poll and a 6 in. bit. $45

W. GILPIN, Wedges Mill, coachmaker's bearded side axe, 19 in. handle. $125 (another, with goosewing shaped blade $95)

GOOSEWING style hand axe with 10 in. blade. Late 1800's. $125

GERMAN style from Northern Pennsylvania. Circa 1760. 13 in edge. $200 (another, with 14½ in. blade. $275)

GOOSEWING, stamped AR TRANS. 8 in. beard has decorative bracket curve. $350

GOOSEWING, German smith-made axe with punch decorated flower design scattered on cheeks. Triangular socket handle. 24 in. overall. $435

GREAVES & SON cooper's axe. auct. $35 (another, polless, 9½ in. blade. $60)

ISAAC GREAVES shipwright's axe with 14 in. long head, 5 in. edge. auct. $105

C. HAMMOND, Phila. Cast Steel, Broad axe with bent handle. $65

HIBKER with 4 touchmarks, Penn. style goosewing with 11 in. blade. $275

J. HIGGIN, Cast Steel, 68. Left hand side axe with 11½ in. blade. $45

L. HILL common broad axe head. $15

HOLZAXE, 18th Century Penn. with protruding stub. $120

A. HUGHES felling axe head. $10

HURDLE MAKER'S twibil with unusual tang type handle. auct. $85

HURDLE MAKER'S twibil, L-shaped with small wooden socket handle on long leg of L. auct. $90

HYTEST, Sydney, Australia. Best axe made. New cond. auct. $35

HYTEST competition model felling axe with 5½ in. bit. New cond. $60

ICE AXES, various common styles. $10

INDIAN SQUAW, Araucana Hachas, label on this 10 in. wide export axe head, round poll. $16

INDIAN trade axe head. Blacksmith-made, 2¾ in. laid on steel bit. $22

INDIAN trade axe head with round eye. An exceptionally nice one with touch mark. $40

N. JOBIN, Quebec. Hewing style broad axe with 12 in. blade. auct. $60

KEEN KUTTER felling axe head. (worn out) $10

KEEN KUTTER boy's hand axe, shiny clean. $12 - $20

KEEN KUTTER modern style felling axe, 3½ in. edge. $22

French carpenter uses a twybill to clean up joints. Circa 1750.

KEEN KUTTER hand axe with 3 in. blade. $22

KEEN KUTTER unused double edge felling axe. $45

KEEN KUTTER giant hewing axe head with 12 in. cutting edge. auct. $80

(another, in orig. gold laquer finish with paper label intact. dlr. $140)

KELLY True Temper hand axe, 17½ in. overall. Like new. $7

KELLY True Temper land clearing axe with 2 bits at perpendicular angles. $10

KELLY registered axe No. 19690. Good usable tool. auct. $10

KELLY fire axe, red, (no handle) $20

KELLY AXE & TOOL WORKS scarce Black Raven (reground) $24
(another, as above, double bitted, light rust. $40)

KELLY AXE MFG. CO. broad axe with 12 in. bit beveled one side. $35

W. KELLY, Perfect Axe, full inscription, head only (worn) auct. $45

JOHN KING, Oakland, Me. short handled block axe. 12 in. overall. auct. $65, dlr. $125

JOHN KING, Oakland, Me. 6½ lb. axe with 4½ in. bit. auct. $55

MARBLES No. 5 pocket saftey axe. $30

H. MELLINGER (Lancaster, Pa. 1875) mortise axe. $72

H. MELLINS classic center bit Penn. mortise axe with lugs and flat poll. $70

A. MILLER shipwright's axe. auct. $30

T. MILLER No. 80 broad axe. auct. $55

MINIATURE Penn. style broad axe, 2¼ in. cutting edge. Blacksmith made. $45

MORTISING axe, handwrought, 2 in. $38 - $45

MORTISE axe, Penn. style double bit. $70

MORTISING axe, tomahawk-shaped post hole axe with 12 in. long, double-bitted head. $83

NAPANOCH AXE & IRON CO. (circa 1875) hewing axe with 9 in. blade. $85

PARRISH mast, or spar axe, with star trademark. $35

PLUMB Champion, felling axe, head only $22 - $35

PLUMB hewing axe with 11 in. head. Mint, orig. label intact. $85

PRATT marked broad axe. auct. $42

RAZOR BLADE-M, felling axe, American style, square poll. $6

ROOSTER imprint on this early Penn. bearded hewing axe with laid on 7 in. bit. Excellent. $110

ST. GABRIEL WORKS, Montreal. Mast axe. auct. $80

P. SEIB, Penna., classic Germanic goosewing. auct. $275

SHERMAN, Elmira, broad axe. auct. $42

SHIPBUILDER'S American made hewing axe with 6⅝ in. bit, offset handle. $45

SHIPWRIGHT'S English polless masting axe with scroll-shaped swell foot handle. auct. $112

M. SIEGER left hand goosewing. Penn-German pattern, 14 in. edge. auct. $325

SIGMA stamped, early hurdlemaker's twibill. auct. $70

D. SIMMONS & CO., Cohoes, N.Y. 12½ in. broad axe. $85

SNOW & NEALEY, Bangor. Light weight hand axe with orig. cover and label. auct. $20

SORBY coachmaker's side axe, 6 in. blade. $95

SORBY cooper's polless side axe with curved, swell-end handle, 8 in. edge. auct. $96

H.W. STAGER, Rochester, cooper's hand axe with 8½ in. blade. $65

STALLEN Wien. Austrian goosewing with offset handle. Bearded 10½ in. blade is decorated. auct. $105

STALLER, Wein, goosewing axe with trademark. auct. $225

EMERSON STEVENS, Oakland, Maine. Railroad tie axe. $25

J.B. STOHLER, Penn. felling axe with 4½ in. blade. $50

H.H. STRICKER (circa 1880) small plain felling axe by William Brady's apprentice. $55

TOBACCO axe, looks like a hoe with a swivel head. auct. $25

TRADE AXES early American polless handwrought axe heads, avg. 4 in. bit. $25 - $35 ea.

TURPENTINE axe with crescent shaped blade. Polless, 3 in eye. $80 - $175

TWIBILL or TWYBILL, the long narrow chisel-like mortising axe of early carpenters and fence builders.

TWIBILL double bitted, 39 inch. auct. $190 - $220

TWIBILL, European model, 44 in. long with pipe shaped center handle socket. One piece const., handwrought. $225

TWIBILL, French, hand-forged 48 in. marked Bec d' anne. $250

TWIBILL, American, 18th Cent., 22 in. with illegible signature. auct. $425

TYZACK & SONS bearded coachbuilder's axe. Little used. $84

UNDERHILL EDGE TOOL CO. Kent type felling axe. 10 in. X 7 in. $35

UNDERHILL, Nashua, N.H. (circa 1860). 8 in. wide Ohio pattern broad axe. $40

UNDERHILL, Nashua, N.H. boat builder's axe head. auct. $10

R & H VORSTER HAGEN export style hewing axe, flat top, no lugs. $12

WARD wheelwright's small bearded side axe, 4½ in. cutter. auct. $67

WARD & PAYNE English coachmaker's bearded side axe with square poll, curved handle. auct. $80

J.M. WARREN AXE, Troy, N.Y. double bitted felling axe. $30

WERKSCHAFT German goosewing side axe with 9 in. cutting edge. auct. $122

L. & I.J. WHITE narrow symetrical, goosewing bladed hand axe, polless round eye housing. $250

L. WILDER, Cast Steel, broad axe. auct. $15

WINCHESTER Double bitted felling axe, 4⅝ in. cutters. (new handle) $50

WINCHESTER Diamond Edge broad axe. $55

WINCHESTER hunting-style hand axe. $35

Wm. T. WOOD & CO. ice axe. auct. $10

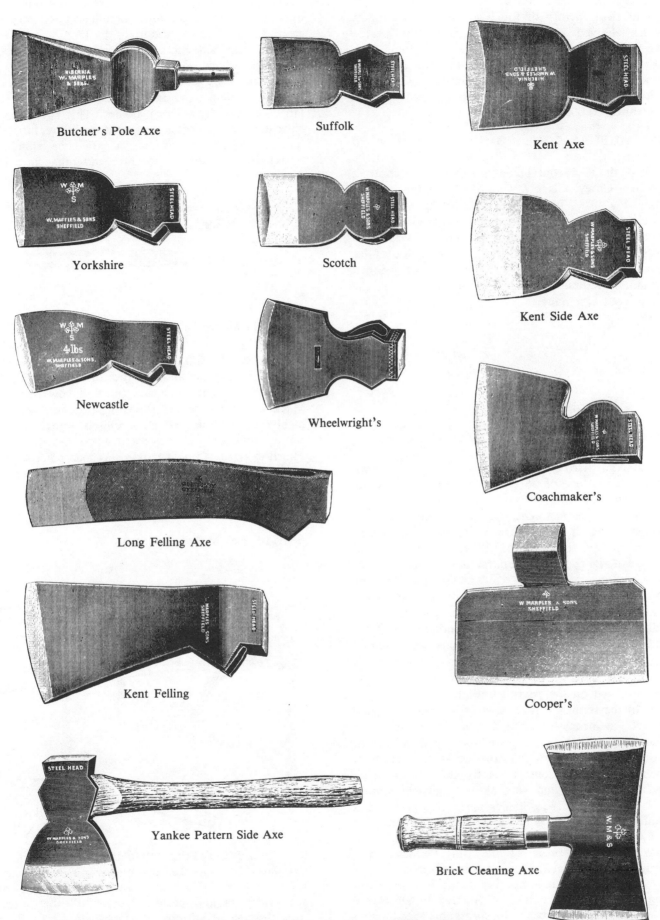

Butcher's Pole Axe

Suffolk

Kent Axe

Yorkshire

Scotch

Kent Side Axe

Newcastle

Wheelwright's

Long Felling Axe

Coachmaker's

Kent Felling

Cooper's

Yankee Pattern Side Axe

Brick Cleaning Axe

English Factory-Made Axes , 1880 - 1910

ARROWMAMMET WORKS was the Middleton, Connecticut factory of the Baldwin Tool Company which derived its trade name from the nearby Arrowmammett River. The firm operated from 1841 to 1857 and later production was continued briefly by the Globe Manufacturing Company. Between 1850 and 1860 the factory produced from 40,000 to 60,000 wooden planes a year.

THE AUBURN TOOL COMPANY was organized in Auburn, New York in the year 1864. It was the outgrowth of an old plane manufacturing contract between Casey, Clark & Company and the Auburn State Prison. Within 24 months of its formation Auburn lost its lucrative labor pool to a higher bidder, but continued on for a number of years with a civilian work force which produced a line of ice skates in addition to over 50 patterns of wooden moulding planes. In 1893 Auburn merged with the Ohio Tool Company.

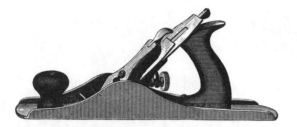

LEONARD BAILEY was granted his first patent at the tender age of 25 (for a scraper plane). Three years later, in 1858, he was awarded a second patent for a cutter adjustment, and soon after, a third patent which is still in use on some woodworking planes today. In May of 1869 Mr. Bailey sold exclusive rights to the manufacture of his patented bench planes, spoke shaves, and scrapers to The Stanley Rule & Level Company on a 5% royalty contract. Just a few days later he also agreed to sell Stanley all of his machinery and inventory for $12,500 in cash. He was given a one year salaried management contract and moved from his home in Boston to Stanley's New Britian, Conn. plant where he remained on the payroll until 1874.

In the spring of 1874 a wiser 49 year old Bailey moved to nearby Hartford and began again to manufacture his own line of tools (which was to later include the new "Victor" plane). Sargent & Company became sole agents for this line in 1876, but Stanley sued and won an infringement suit in 1878. In July of 1884 Stanley again bought Leonard Bailey's machinery and inventory, this time for $30,000. Mr Bailey took part of the cash and went into the copying press manufacturing business, from which he retired at the turn-of-the-century.

The Bailey name has been cast into the iron toe of almost every line of Stanley bench planes since 1902 and appears on brass blade adjusting nuts made from 1867 onward. The names STANLEY and BAILEY are synonymous among collectors of high quality American-made woodworking tools.

BARK SPUD or BARKING IRON. Tannin production was an important home-based industry in early America. Bark spuds or barking irons were used to strip and cut tannin–producing bark from oak trees which was ground and leached in water to produce this leather curing chemical. Most of these tools were handmade which accounts for the large variety of sizes and shapes. This round end, chisel-like tool is often confused with the farrier's buttress (which usually has a rifle-style shoulder stock). Bark spuds are not rare and range in price from $10 to $30.

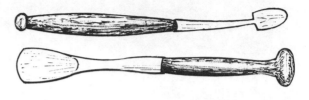

BACK SAW (see Saw section)

D.R. BARTON CO. of Rochester, New York was founded in 1835 as an edge tool and blacksmithing firm. For the next 40 years (until its purchase by Mack and Co., in 1875) Barton produced a very highly regarded line of axes, chisels, draw knives, cutting irons, cooper's tools and wood-bodied planes. The firm's 1835 founding date was incorporated into its trademark and appears on most tools produced.

BEADER (see Router, hand beader)

BEETLE (see Mallet, wooden)

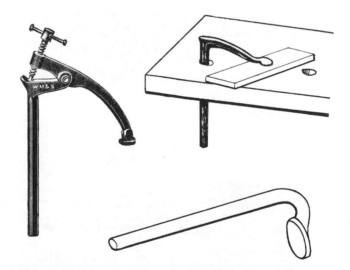

BENCH DOG or British "Holdfast". The origin of this simple lever-type bench clamp is lost in antiquity. It is pictured in the very earliest engravings of shop interiors and hasn't changed all that much over the years. Various wrought iron bench dogs similar to those illustrated here are offered by tool dealers at prices ranging from $15 to $45. Stanley No. 203 bench brackets sell for $20 to $36 each.

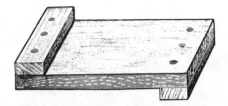

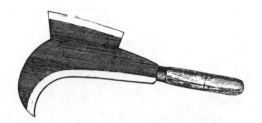

BENCH HOOKS are rectangular shaped hardwood boards with cross cleats fastened or carved into each end. By hooking one end over the edge of a bench, a ledge is provided on the bench top to push, saw, carve or plane against. Nicely shaped old bench hooks of the carved variety frequently are offered for $8 to $20 a pair.

BILL HOOKS were heavy cleavers; used for clearing paths through brush, for trimming hedges and for lopping off small tree branches. Numerous varities remained in British tool catalogs well into the 20th Century. Current value $8-$12.

BITSTOCK (see Brace)

BOLT HEADER blacksmith's wrought iron, closed-end, wrench-type die, used to hot-forge bolt heads. Value, $5 to $10 each, single or double-end.

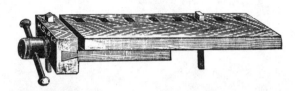

BENCH STOPS are metal bench top inserts which act as blocks rather than clamps, to hold work in place, often in conjunction with a bench vise. Most are either peg of L-shaped and have a serrated head on the end of a 3 to 7 inch shaft. They sell in a broad price range of $9 to $30. Larger or more elaborate styles bring the highest prices.

BONE was used in tool making for handles, wear plates and inlay work. It was most often obtained from the shin bones of beef cattle. When carefully cured it was capable of taking a high gloss finish and wearing quite well. Whale bone was used by coastal tool and knife makers having ready access to beached mammals. Bone differs from ivory in appearance in that it has a flecked or pore marked surface rather than the wood grain pattern of elephant ivory when examined under magnification.

BOXED is a term used to indicate that a tough boxwood wear strip has been inserted by the maker into the sole of a plane to prolong its life. SINGLE BOXED means only one thin insert. DOUBLE BOXED signifys two inserts. SOLID BOXED indicates a thick wear strip, at least as wide as the cutter. DOVETAILED BOXING is dovetailed into the sole for a tighter fit.

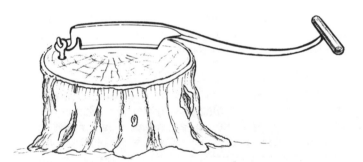

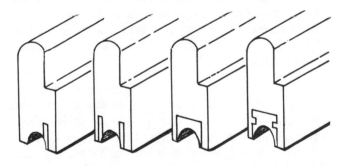

BLOCK KNIFE was originally used by European cloggers to block out wooden shoe blanks and boot lasts. This useful tool later found wide acceptance in early American woodworking shops of all types. Its appearance is that of a cleaver-like knife with an integral forged hook at the front and a long handle extending from the back of the blade. It was mounted on a block, stump, stool or bench by means of an iron screw eye or cleat. Overall length ranged from 26 to 40 inches including handle. Recently advertised prices: Berger, 39 in. with egg-shaped wooden handle $125. Henry Carter, 15 in. cutting edge, incl. eye bolt $87. Graceful 33 in. curved block knife with 8 in. cutter $175. Hand-forged 36 in. model with 7 in. blade $80. Another, marked Steep Falls, Me. $115. Crude butcher knife shape with hook end $25. Saw horse mounted shingle butter, marked R. German $135. Clogger's bench knife, 40 in. long $135.

BOXWOOD was also used occasionally for entire planes, and for most measuring sticks and folding rules. Boxwood is a dense, hard, straight grained, yet flexible wood of blonde to golden tint. The Buxus tree is harvested at an average diameter of only 6 inches, making it too small and too expensive for general toolmaking. It was originally grown in the mountains of Turkey and Southern Russia for export to Liverpool, England and then to the United States. After the turn-of-the-century the Stanley Rule and Level Company began to import Maracaibo boxwood from Venezuela.

Denis Diderot, 1752

Ornamental Ironworkers of 18th–Century France

The first blacksmith to arrive in Colonial America was a fellow by the name of James Reed, who promptly forged an iron chisel for each of his greatful Jamestown shipmates. Needless to say Mr. Reed was sorely missed when a fever took him the next summer. Native American Indians also valued the ironworker's craft. So much so, that many chiefs demanded in their treaties with the Great White Father that a well supplied smithy be settled among them.

Blacksmiths rarely did any finishing or polishing of the charcoal blackened metal which issued from the forge. Some did however, impress their initials or mark upon tools of which they were particularly proud. Not a few smiths went on to manufacture tools on a larger scale. Many founded factories that existed well into the 20th Century.

In addition to a forge, bellows and anvil, a well equipped smithy needed several kinds of tongs and anvil-mounted accessories. Top-surface tools were the set hammer, flatter, fuller, top swage, and chisel. Anvil tools inserted in the hardy hole for working bottom surfaces were, the bottom fuller, bottom swage, hot hardie and cold hardie. Swage blocks and large cone mandrels were floor and stump mounted tools. American blacksmith shops became motorized around the turn-of-the-century.

Power driven hammers increased output tremendously and also eliminated much of the tedious drudgery associated with the trade.

CURRENT VALUES. With the exception of travelers, brass rules, and some drill braces, blacksmith tools are not highly sought after. Sometimes they may be picked up at scrap iron prices by knowledgeable collectors. Complete blacksmiths' shops have been advertised recently at prices ranging from $900 to $2,500. Common tongs, hardies, and bolt headers sell for $4 to $10 each. Good old hammers often fetch from $10 to $20 at auctions. Anvils still can be picked up for a dollar a pound and vises rarely bring more than $50.

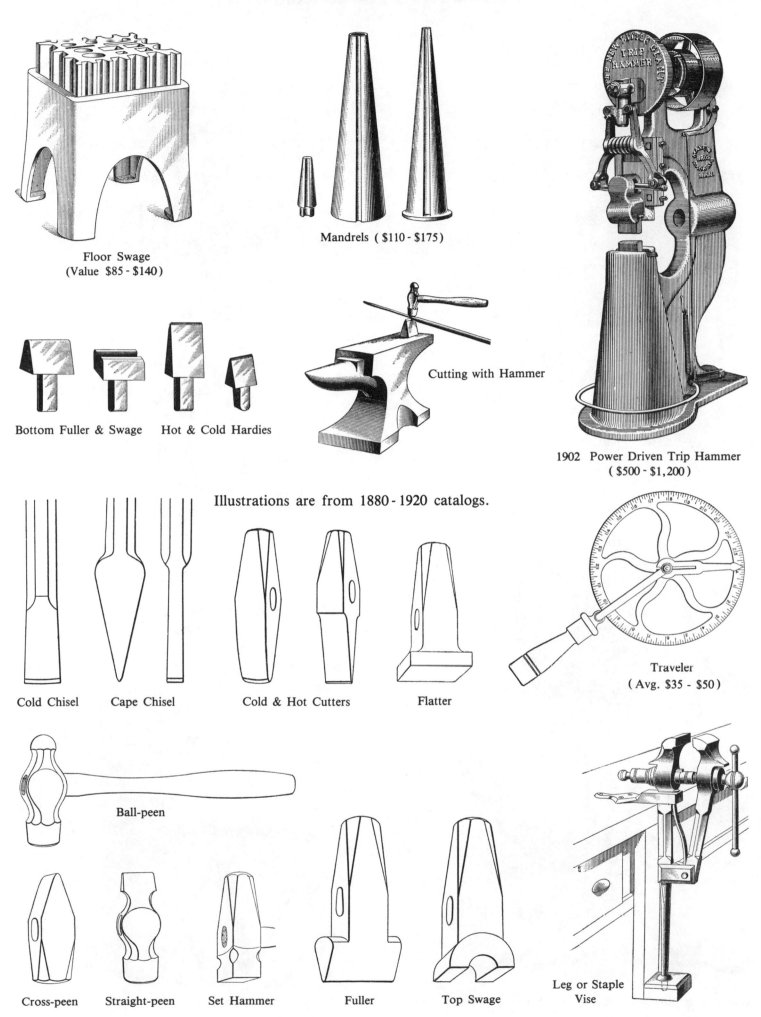

Floor Swage
(Value $85 - $140)

Mandrels ($110 - $175)

Bottom Fuller & Swage   Hot & Cold Hardies

Cutting with Hammer

1902 Power Driven Trip Hammer
($500 - $1,200)

Illustrations are from 1880 - 1920 catalogs.

Cold Chisel   Cape Chisel   Cold & Hot Cutters   Flatter

Traveler
(Avg. $35 - $50)

Ball-peen

Cross-peen   Straight-peen   Set Hammer   Fuller   Top Swage

Leg or Staple
Vise

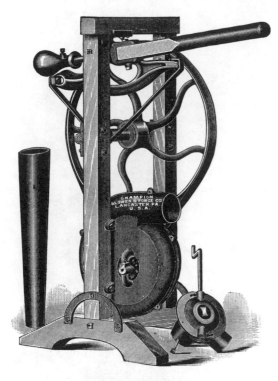

Champion "Leader"
Lever-operated Blower
(1896 - 1903)

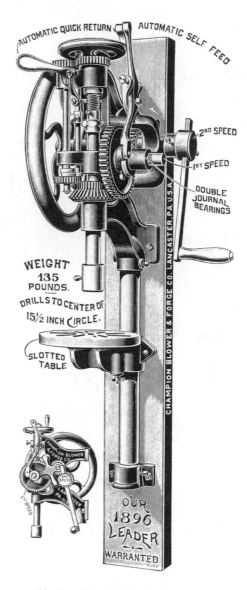

Blacksmith's Self-feed Post Drill
(current value $55 - $95)

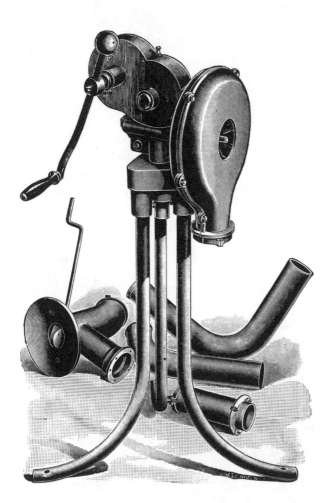

Ball Bearing Blower with Tuyere Iron & Piping. (1903)

(Value $25 - $75)

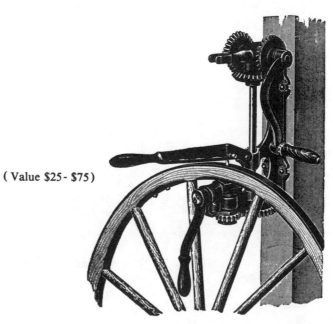

Reynold's Tire Bolting Machine. (1902)

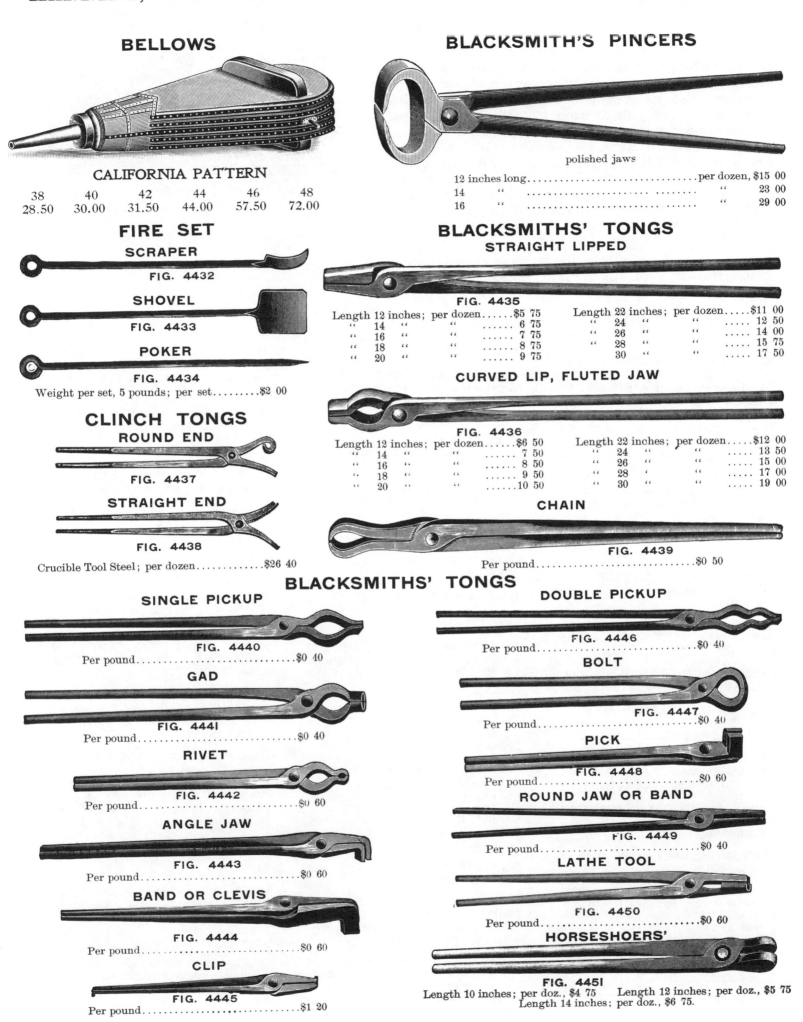

BELLOWS

CALIFORNIA PATTERN

38	40	42	44	46	48
28.50	30.00	31.50	44.00	57.50	72.00

FIRE SET

SCRAPER
FIG. 4432

SHOVEL
FIG. 4433

POKER
FIG. 4434

Weight per set, 5 pounds; per set........$2 00

CLINCH TONGS

ROUND END
FIG. 4437

STRAIGHT END
FIG. 4438

Crucible Tool Steel; per dozen............$26 40

BLACKSMITH'S PINCERS

polished jaws

12 inches long	...per dozen, $15 00
14 "	" 23 00
16 "	" 29 00

BLACKSMITHS' TONGS
STRAIGHT LIPPED

FIG. 4435

Length 12 inches; per dozen.....$5 75	Length 22 inches; per dozen.....$11 00
" 14 " " 6 75	" 24 " " 12 50
" 16 " " 7 75	" 26 " " 14 00
" 18 " " 8 75	" 28 " " 15 75
" 20 " " 9 75	" 30 " " 17 50

CURVED LIP, FLUTED JAW

FIG. 4436

Length 12 inches; per dozen.....$6 50	Length 22 inches; per dozen.....$12 00
" 14 " " 7 50	" 24 " " 13 50
" 16 " " 8 50	" 26 " " 15 00
" 18 " " 9 50	" 28 " " 17 00
" 20 " " 10 50	" 30 " " 19 00

CHAIN

FIG. 4439

Per pound........................$0 50

BLACKSMITHS' TONGS

SINGLE PICKUP
FIG. 4440
Per pound........................$0 40

GAD
FIG. 4441
Per pound........................$0 40

RIVET
FIG. 4442
Per pound........................$0 60

ANGLE JAW
FIG. 4443
Per pound........................$0 60

BAND OR CLEVIS
FIG. 4444
Per pound........................$0 60

CLIP
FIG. 4445
Per pound........................$1 20

DOUBLE PICKUP
FIG. 4446
Per pound........................$0 40

BOLT
FIG. 4447
Per pound........................$0 40

PICK
FIG. 4448
Per pound........................$0 60

ROUND JAW OR BAND
FIG. 4449
Per pound........................$0 40

LATHE TOOL
FIG. 4450
Per pound........................$0 60

HORSESHOERS'
FIG. 4451
Length 10 inches; per doz., $4 75   Length 12 inches; per doz., $5 75
Length 14 inches; per doz., $6 75.

(1896 - 1903 PRICES)

Old books and trade catalogs are wonderful sources for additional research, or just plain entertainment. You can start adding to your accumulation of old tool lore by browsing through the inventory of any used book store. There are also specialist tool book dealers and catalog reprinters who deal with collectors by mail. Send a stamped self addressed envelope for information to: *R. Sorsky, Bookseller 3845 N. Blackstone, Fresno, Calif. 93726* and *Ken Roberts Publishing Co. Box 151, Fitzwilliam, NH 03447.* The Early American Industries Association also issues a book list twice a year. Write *E.A.I.A. P.O. Box 2128, Empire State Plaza Station, Albany, NY 12220.*

Abell, Sir Westcott THE SHIPWRIGHT TRADE. University Press, Cambridge, England, 1948. Hard cover, 6 X 9 in. 219 pages. $25

AMERICAN BUILDER MAGAZINE. Oct. 1927. $5

APPLETON'S CYCLOPEDIA OF APPLIED MECHANICS. A very thick, highly illustrated volume, New York 1898. $30
2 vol. set, 1878. $55

THE ARCHITECTS' & ARTISANS PERMANENT PRICE BOOK and Compendium of Useful Tables, etc. Montreal & N.Y., 1876. 208 pages. $30

AUDEL'S CARPENTERS & BUILDERS GUIDE. 4 vols. 1st edition, 1923. $30-$45
1927 to 1949 editions, $25 - $30

AUDEL'S MASONS & BUILDERS GUIDE. 4 vol. set pub. in 1945, soft cover. $30

AUDEL'S MILLWRIGHTS & MECHANICS GUIDE. 1940 edition, 5 X 6½ in., 1166 pages. $15

Baird, Henry Carey THE TURNER'S COMPANION. Phila. 1872, hard cover, 135 pages. $30

Barnard, John EVERY MAN HIS OWN MECHANIC. Circa 1914, 540 pages. $12

Bergmann, Dr. L. GERMAN BOOK OF TRADES (Dsa Buch der Arbeit) Leipzig, 1854. 182 pages, 85 woodcuts. $42

Bell, William THE ART & SCIENCE OF CARPENTRY MADE EASY. 1883 hard cover. $15. 1858 edition, 7 X 10 in. $16

Bishop, J.L. A HISTORY OF AMERICAN MANUFACTURES, 1608 - 1860. 2 vol., published in 1864. $50

BLACKSMITH'S DAILY LOG BOOK dating back to 1806. $65

BLACKSMITH'S ACCOUNT BOOK, Carnes & Muzzey, Sunapee, New Hampshire, 1888 - 1896. 240 pages, handwritten entries. $50

BOOK OF ENGLISH TRADES, illustrated 1824 edition with workshop scenes. $200

BOOK OF TRADES or CIRCLE OF USEFUL ARTS. 3rd edition, 1837. $120

THE BOY'S BOOK OF TRADES & THE TOOLS USED IN THEM. London & N.Y., circa 1875. 316 illustrated pages. $35

THE BOY MECHANIC 1,000 Things for Boys to do. Published by Popular Mechanics in 1915. 4 vol. set. $50-$70
Single titles. $10-$20 each

THE BUILDER'S DICTIONARY or GENTLEMAN'S & ARCHITECT'S COMPANION. Bellesworth, 1734. $800. 1981 reprint, 2 vols. $50

THE BUILDER & ILLUSTRATED WEEKLY JOURNAL. 1872 building trades advertising. $5

Bryn, M. LaFayette, MD. THE ARTIST & TRADESMAN'S COMPANION. Philadelphia, 1866. 214 pages. $22

Bryant, Ralph Clement, LOGGING, THE PRINCIPLES & GENERAL METHODS OF OPERATION. 1st edition, New York, 1914. $22

Bryant, Seth SHOE & LEATHER TRADE OF THE LAST HUNDRED YEARS. Boston, 1891. 136 pages. $15

Burn, Robert Scott ORNAMENTAL DRAWING & ARCHITECTURAL DESIGN. London, circa 1870. 200 illus. inc. plan views. $22

Butterworth THE GROWTH OF INDUSTRIAL ART. A 200 page history of U.S. art, industry, agriculture. 16 X 20 in., illus. $225 - $275

Callingham, James SIGN WRITING & GLASS EMBOSSING. New York, 1884. 192 pages, illustrated. $32

CARPENTRY & BUILDING MAGAZINE. Bound vol., entire year of 1879. $85
Individual issues. $5 ea.

Day, B.H. AMERICAN READY RECKONER 1866 edition. $15

THE DECORATOR'S & RENOVATOR'S ASSISTANT, 600 RECEIPTS. London, 1929. 164 pages of instructions for making paints and varnishes. $17

Diderot, D. & D'Alembert, J. TOURNEUR ET TOUR A FIGURE. 87 plates & text from The Encyclopedia. Folio size, in paper covered boards. Circa 1772. $315

Disston, Henry & Sons THE SAW IN HISTORY. Phila., 1916. Soft cover, 63 pages. $15

DISSTON HANDBOOK ON SAWS. Phila. April 1914. 6 X 9 in., 209 pages. $25

DYKES AUTOMOBILE & GASOLINE ENGINE MANUAL. Chicago, 1917. $50
1923 edition, 1,226 pages. $20
1943 edition. $14

Ellis, George MODERN PRACTICAL JOINERY. London. Batsford, 1902. 379 pages. $65

Edison, Thomas F. & Westinghouse, Chas. J. THE MECHANICS COMPLETE LIBRARY. 1900. Hard bound, 588 pg. $5

EVERY MAN HIS OWN MECHANIC, A Complete Guide For Amateurs. N.Y. & London, 1900. $27

FLEMINGS LUMBER CALCULATOR. 1908. 9½ X 13 in. 639 pages. $30

Frank, George ADVENTURES IN WOOD FINISHING. Paris & New York, circa 1920. $10

Fisher, George THE AMERICAN INSTRUCTOR or YOUNG MAN'S BEST COMPANION. 1779. $55

THE GREAT INDUSTRIES OF THE UNITED STATES. Hartford, 1872. History and operation of 100's of factories. 1,304 pages. $45 - $65

Godfrey THE HARDWOOD FINISHER. 1902. 109 pages. $9

GROWTH OF INDUSTRIAL ART. U.S. Gov't publication of 1892. 16 X 20 in., 200 pages, illustrated. (poor cond.) $110

GUNTERS SCALE AND THE SLIDING RULE, Treatise On. Published in 1824. $275

Hasluck, Paul WOOD CARVING, PRACTICAL INSTRUCTIONS & EXAMPLES. Cassell & Co., London. Circa 1900. 568 pages. $35

Hasluck, Paul THE HANDYMANS BOOK OF TOOLS, MATERIALS & PROCESSES EMPLOYED IN WOODCUTTING. Cassel & Co., London. Circa 1914. 760 pages. $40

☞ This old establishment is chiefly devoted to the finer and more costly styles of Book-binding in **TURKEY MOROCCO, RUSSIA, ENGLISH, FRENCH** and **AMERICAN CALF,** and especially those unique and economical half Calf and Morocco styles. In all cases the very best of *Stock* and *Workmanship,* with *strength* and *beauty* combined, may be relied upon.

Hodgson COMPLETE MODERN CARPENTRY. 2 vol. set, 1902. Cloth bound, 650 pages. $22
1928 edition, 598 pages. $15

Hodgson, Fred THE STEEL SQUARE. 2 vol. set, 1927. 600 pages. $15
1883 second edition. $30
1913 2 vol. edition. $22

Holtzapffel, Charles TURNING & MECHANICAL MANIPULATION. London 1843 - 1884. Vols. 1 thru 5 in orig. cloth bindings. $220 - $450

Hope, Arthur SORRENTO & INLAID WORK. Chicago, 1876. $30

KNIGHT'S AMERICAN MECHANICAL DICTIONARY plus supplement for complete 4 vol set. 3,700 pages, 7,000 engravings. Circa 1875. $125
1888 edition, 18,000 engravings. $225
1884 edition, 3,000 engravings. $50
1979 reprint of 1884 edition. $20

Lester, G. THE MODERN CARPENTER & JOINER & CABINET MAKER. Suitcliffe, London, 1900. 850 pages, profusely illustrated. $150
1904 edition, 8 vols. $210

LOUDEN HOG HOUSE BOOK. 8 X 11 in. paperback, 1922. $6

Meloy, D.H. PROGRESSIVE CARPENTRY, 50 Years Experience in Building. Waterbury, Conn. 1890. 55 pages, illustrated. $22

Meyer, Franz Sales HANDBOOK OF ORNAMENT. 300 plates, 3,000 illustrations. 1915. 548 pages. $24

THE MODERN CARPENTER & JOINTER. 3 vol. set of English manuals. $80

Nicholson, Michael Angelo THE CARPENTERS & JOINERS COMPANION. 1826. Quatro size, calf binding. $46

NICHOLSON'S PRACTICAL CARPENTRY JOINERY & CABINET MAKING. Revised edition of 1854. 9 X 11 in., 168 pages, 88 plates. $110

Nicholson, Peter THE CARPENTER'S NEW GUIDE. 9th edition, 1827. 84 plates. Full calf binding. $100
1890 edition of 240 pages. $70

Nicholson, Peter THE MECHANIC'S COMPANION or The Elements & Practice of Carpentry, Joinery, Bricklaying, Smithing, Turning, etc. Philadelphia, 1859. 362 pages. $60

Paine, Wm. PRACTICAL HOUSE CARPENTER. London, 1789. $85

Pallett, Henry THE MILLWRIGHTS & ENGINEER'S GUIDE. Phila., 1878. 10 plates, 24 pages of ads, 286 pages. $32

Phin, John HINTS & PRACTICAL INFORMATION FOR CABINENTMAKERS, UPHOLSTERERS & FURNITURE MEN GENERALLY. New York, 1884. Includes 30 pages of ads. $30

Plumier, Charles L'ART DE TOURNER, ou de fair en perfection toutes sortes d'ouvrages du tour. 62 plates with text in French and Latin. 187 pages. Lyon 1701. $444. Second edition, 1749, with copy of English translation. $650

THE RADFORD AMERICAN HOMES, 100 House Plans. Riverside, Ill., 1903. 255 pages. $20

RADFORD DETAILS OF BUILDING CONSTRUCTION. 1911. 200 pages. $18

RADFORDS ARTISTIC BUNGALOWS. Chicago, 1908. 218 pages. $10

RADFORDS CYCLOPEDIA OF CONSTRUCTION, Carpentry, Building, Architecture. 12 vol. set in ¾ leather bindings. $50

Richardson, M.T. PRACTICAL BLACKSMITHING, ILLUSTRATED. Vol. 3, N.Y. 1890. 307 pages. $15

Riddell THE CARPENTER, JOINER, STAIRBUILDER AND HANDRAILER. Circa 1875. 10 X 13 in., 125 pages plus diecut foldout models. $155

Rose, W. THE VILLAGE CARPENTER. Cambridge Univ. Press, 1937. 146 pages. $40

Ross, George Alexander WOOD TURNING. Textbook for Highschool & College. Ginn & Co., Boston, 1909. $15

RUSSELL ON SCIENTIFIC HORSESHOEING, For Leveling and Balancing the Action & Gait of Horses. Cincinnati, 1895. 279 pages $60

Ure, Andrew A DICTIONARY OF ARTS, MANUFACTURES & MINES. New York, 1842. 1,340 pages. $85

Vaux, Calvert VILLAS & COTTAGES. A Series of Designs. Harpers, N.Y., 1857. 1st edition. 300 engravings. 321 pages. $175

Wall, William GRAINING, ANCIENT & MODERN. 2nd edition, published by the author in 1924. 143 pages. $40

Ware, I.D. THE CARRIAGE BUILDERS REFERENCE BOOK. Philadelphia, 1877. 286 pages. $40

AMERICAN TRAINING SCHOOL EQUIPMENT. Rochester, N.Y., 1915. 6 X 9 in. soft. cover. 60 pages. $12

AMERICAN SAW MILL MACHINERY CO. 1925 soft cover. 192 pages. $25

Arnold & Walker Ltd. BRITISH ANTIQUE TOOL DEALERS catalogs bound into one volume. $55 - $75

ATHOL & STARRETT VISES, MACHINERY & TOOLS Catalog No. 32. Circa 1915. 62 pages. $7

Atkins & Co. SAWS, SPOKESHAVES, SCRAPERS. Catalog No. 21. Circa 1935. 151 pages. $30

AUBURN TOOL COMPANY. 1868 price list of Planes, rulers & cooper's tools. $30

The Baker, McMillen Co. AKRON ECLIPSE PLUMB & LEVELS. 1909 soft cover. 15 pages. $25

BARNES WOODWORKING MACHINERY 1901 catalog of foot-powered machines. 40 pages. $35

H.S. Bartholmew, Bristol, Ct. DRILLS & BRACES. 1890 paperbound price list. 23 pages. $20

Belcher & Loomis Hardware Co. MANUAL TRAINING SCHOOL SUPPLIES. 1915 catalog, paperback. 210 pages. $25

C.L. Berger & Sons, Boston, ENGINEERING INSTRUMENT CATALOG. 1912, 400 pages. $45

Billings & Spencer, 33rd edition. 1915 catalog of TOOLS & WRENCHES. 182 pages. $20

W. BINGHAM HARDWARE CATALOG. Cleveland, Ohio, 1894. 1,476 pages. $110

R. Bliss Manufacturing Co. Cat. No. 27 MILL SUPPLIES, TOOL CHESTS FOR MACHINISTS & CARPENTERS. 1907. 30 pages $15

Braunfels Browning & Co. BLACKSMITH, LUMBERING & CARPENTER TOOLS catalog. 1919 edition. 323 pages. $16

BROWN & SHARP TOOLS No. 137. Hard cover, 4 X 6 in. 609 pages. $20
1925 catalog No. 138. 637 pages. $ 8
1938 catalog No. 33. 480 pages. $ 10

BURHANS & BLACK HARDWARE JOBBERS. 1922 catalog, hardbound, 979 pages. $55

CENTRAL MANTEL CO. Science of Mantle Making. 1900 era 48 page 9 X 12 in. catalog. $45

The Cincinnati Tool Co. 1923 soft cover catalog of WOODWORKING TOOLS, SHAVES, HOLLOW AUGERS, etc. 55 pages. $30

The Collins Co., Collinsville, Conn. 1926 catalog of AXES, HATCHETS, MACHETES. 8 pages. $25

Commercial Sash & Door Co. Pittsburgh. 1917 catalog of COLONIAL COLUMNS, BALUSTERS, RAILS, NEWELS, etc. 48 pages. $15

P & F Corbin Co. 1895 hardcover cat. of LOCKS, KEYS, DOOR PULLS, etc. 790 pages. $48

F.W. Devoe & Co., New York, circa 1870. ENGINEER'S SUPPLIES & MATHEMATICAL INSTRUMENTS. Hardcover catalog, 262 pages. $75

Henry Disston & Sons, Jan. 1899 SAW, TOOL, FILE & KNIFE CATALOG. Hard bound, 7 X 10 in. 145 pages. $50

HENRY DISSTON & SONS, Saw Catalogs:
1909 Edition. $30
1910 Saw Catalog. 50 pages. $20
1912 Hardcover cat. 86 pages. $35
1914 Hardcover, 7 X 10 in. 237 pages. $35
1918 Hardcover, 4 X 6 in. 240 pages. $35

DODGE HALEY CO. 1912 Hardbound catalog of items for farrier, blacksmith, cement worker, carriagemaker, wheelwright & carpenter. 310 pages. $25
1887 Edition, 290 pages. $35

Empire Manufacturing Company, Quincy, III. THE FARMER'S HANDY WAGON. 32 pages, 8 in. color. 1898 edition. $60

J.A. FAY & Egan Co., Cincinnati, Ohio, 1920. 5 X 8 in. soft cover catalog. WOODWORKING MACHINERY. 225 pages. $15

SS. Forsaith Machine Co., WOODWORKING MACHINERY CATALOG No. 55A. Printed in 1891 on 11 X 13 in. stock. 190 pages. $35

R. Hoe & Co. SAW CATALOG OF 1893. $30

Goodell Pratt SMALL HANDTOOLS & MACHINISTS ITEMS. 400 page, 3½ X 5½ in. catalog. 1905 to 1926 editions. $7 to $15 each.

Greenlee Bros., Rockford, III., No. 27 paperbound catalog of AUGER BITS, CHISELS & DRAWKNIVES. 108 illus. pages. $12 - $19

Gurley, W. & L. E. , MANUAL (CATALOG) OF PRINCIPAL INSTRUMENTS USED IN AMERICAN ENGINEERING & SURVEYING. 23rd edition, Troy, 1878. 234 pages. $60

A. Hammacher & Co., New York. TOOL & HARDWARE CATALOG of 1884. 296 illustrated pages, hardbound. $70

HAMMACHER, SCHLEMMER & CO. Ct. No. 355. 1,147 pages. Circa 1900. $85
1915 Edition, 320 pages. $40
1915 Edition, 1,000 pages $40
1929 Edition, inc. Stanley $16

INTERNATIONAL HARVESTER. Dealer catalog of 1910. 20 lines of farm machinery 500 pages. $75

KEEN KUTTER (see E.C. Simmons)

Keuffel & Esser Co., New York. Cat. No. 35. DRAFTING & SURVEYING SUPPLIES. 1916 edition. 566 pages. $35
1927 Edition. $25
1936 Hardcover. $18

Lane Mfg. Co., Montpelier, Vt. SAW MILLS & COMPONENTS. 40 page catalog of the 1880's. $55

LUFKIN RULE CO., Saginaw, Mich. 1948. Cat. No. 8. Hundreds of Machinists measuring tools. $6
Cat. No. 11, circa 1911. 166 pages. $70

Machinery Co. of America, Grand Rapids, Mich. SAW & KNIFE FILING MACHINERY & TOOLS. 1925 catalog. 80 pages. $10

Maher & Grosh, Toledo, Ohio. 1929 CATALOG OF POCKET KNIVES. 175 illustrations. $30

Manning, Maxwell & Moore, N.Y., 1902. HUGE CATALOG OF FARM, FACTORY, BLACKSMITH & RAILROAD TOOLS & SUPPLIES. 1,000 illustrated pages. $95

MARPLES EXPORT TOOL CATALOG No. 3. Sheffield, England, 1954. 110 p. $45

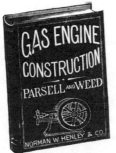

MARTIN CARRIAGE WORKS, Cat. No. 27 217 glossy pages of exceptional illustrations. 1913 edition. $175

THE DAVID MAYDOLE HAMMER CO. Catalog of 1922. 31 pages. $30

DAVID MAYDOLE "A Captain of Industry" catalog/book. 68 pages. $18

MILLERS FALLS TOOLS Catalog No. 35. Braces, drills, foot-operated saws. 1915 softcover, 183 pages. $25
1949 Edition. 176 pages. $15

Montgomery & Co., New York, 1910. PIPES, VALVES, ENGINES, TOOLS. 392 page, softcover catalog. $15

Mosers Limited, England, 1910 hardcover catalog. WOOD & METAL-WORKING MACHINERY, FORGES, HANDTOOLS, etc. $15

NICHOLSON FILE CO. Providence, R.I. 1937 softcover catalog. $15

NORRIS PLANES, 3 British Plane catalogs 1914-1928. $130

OLIVER MACHINERY CO. CAT. No. 22 1915 hardbound, woodworking mach. $30
1917 Edition, 301 pages. $35
1922 Hardcover, 320 pages. $15

Peck & Mack Co. 1932 HARDWARE CATALOG 280 pages. $10

Peck, Stow & Wilcox Co. TINSMITH TOOLS & MACHINES & CARPENTER'S TOOLS. 1898 hardcover catalog. 486 pages. $135
1927 Edition, 95 pages. $25
1933 8½ X 11 in. softcover. $25

Edward Preston & Sons, circa 1901 catalog of RULES, LEVELS, PLANES, TOOLS, etc. 6th edition. Cloth covered. $333

Reading Hardware Works, Phila. 1868. Small 84 page catalog of BUILDER'S HARDWARE & HOUSEHOLD ITEMS. $85

O.S. Rixford SCYTHES & AXES. Vermont, 1887. 68 page catalog. $25

George Roberts & Bros. ENGINEERING SUPPLIES FOR HOTELS & FACTORIES, RAILROADS & APARTMENT HOUSES. 1920 hardbound, 517 pages. $15

Russell & Erwin Mfg. Co. LOCKS & BUILDER'S HARDWARE 1897 cat. $75

RUSSELL JENNINGS MFG. CO., Chester, Conn. 1925 softcover catalog. 32 pages. $10

Russell Manufacturing Company 1915 catalog of SCREW PLATES, TAPS & DIES. 54 pages. $10

SARGENT & COMPANY, 1910 hardbound catalog of the complete lock, tool and hardware line. 1,320 pages. $70
1926 Edition. $70

Searls & Starr Co. 1894. CARRIAGE RAILS & MOUNTS. 48 pages, priced & illus. $25

The Seneca Falls Mfg. Co. Cat. No. 16A FOOT-OPERATED SAWS & MOULDING MACHINES. Circa 1898. 24 pages of engravings. $18

Shapleigh Hardware, 1942. KEEN KUTTER Brand Tools & Hardware. $125

A.H. Shipman, Rochester, N.Y. FOOT TREADLE LATHES, JIG SAWS, & SHUTE BOARD PLANE. Circa 1880. 5 X 7 in., 25 pages. $15

Simmons Hardware Company, St. Louis, 1880. 1,140 pages, hardbound 9 X 12 in. catalog with some early KEEN KUTTER items. $300

E.C. Simmons No. 487 KEEN KUTTER tool catalog. 30 pages, 6 X 8 in. Airbrush illus. $50

E.C. Simmons KEEN KUTTER Cutlery. Pocket Pal, 3 X 6 in. catalog of 1920. $15

E.C. Simmons KEEN KUTTER YEARBOOK A "Sears" size catalog of 2,776 pages, 1920. $150
1930 Edition. $250

Simonds Mfg. Co., Fitchburg, Mass. SAWS & ACCESSORIES. 1916 softcover catalog. $25
Leather bound edition, No. 27. 168 pages. $35

Smith & Hunt, CHILDREN'S CARRIAGES. Mfgd. in 1876 by Guilford in Brattleboro, Vt. 9 pages. $55

STEWART SPIERS, METAL WOOD-WORKING PLANES Catalog of 1930. $55

STANLEY TOOLS, set of 15 wall charts, circa 1936. 14 X 18 in. $50

STANLEY RULE & LEVEL CO. Pocket catalog of 1902. 3½ X 6, 18 pages. $15
1904 catalog No. 34 (torn cover). $42
1907 pocket catalog. 3 X 6 in. 24 pg. $15
1914 pocket catalog 3 X 6 in. 24 pg. $15
1926 catalog No. 34 soft cover, $25
1927 catalog No. 34 soft cover, 191 pg.$25
1939 edition, 5 X 7 in., 240 pages $27
1950 - 1963 copies sell for about $20

L.S. Starrett Cat. No. 25., 1935 edition, MACHINIST'S & OTHER HANDTOOLS. 370 pages. $5 - $15
No. 26 Deluxe hardbound edition. 1938. $37

Chas. A. Strelinger, Detroit, Mich. 1895 CATALOG OF HANDTOOLS, MACHINERY & SUPPLIES. $30

SWEETS ARCHITECTURAL CATALOG. 20th Annual, 1925-26 hardcover, 2,855 pages. $25

H.E. Taylor Co., N.Y. COFFINS & CASKETS of the 1800's. Rosewood, Mahogany, etc. $45

TUCK'S TOOL CATALOG. Brockton, Mass. circa 1910. 48 pages of screwdrivers, chisels & razors, etc. $10

Union Mfg. Co., New Britain, Conn. PLANES, SCRAPERS, SPOKE SHAVES, etc. 3 X 5 pocket catalog, 1905. $15

Union Tool Co. 1910 catalog of QUALITY MACHINIST'S TOOLS. 64 pages $8

UNIVERSAL DESIGN BOOK. Official prices of moulding, balusters, stair work, columns, leaded glass, etc. 416 pages. $45

VONNECUT HARDWARE CO., Indianapolis, 1907. 1004 illustrated pages of tools & machinery. $65

Adam Waldner, Ashland, Penn. Circa 1901 FRONT DOORS, FANCY LEADED GLASS, PORCH COLUMNS, GABLE ORNAMENTS, etc. 94 pages, 4 X 8 in. $22

J.M. WARREN HARDWARE CATALOG OF 1919. Hardbound 8½ X 11 in., 1,353 pages. $135
1920 Edition, 1,353 pages. $50

YALE & TOWNE MFG. No. 20 catalog of Locks & Keys. Stanford, Conn., 1910. 915 pages. $18

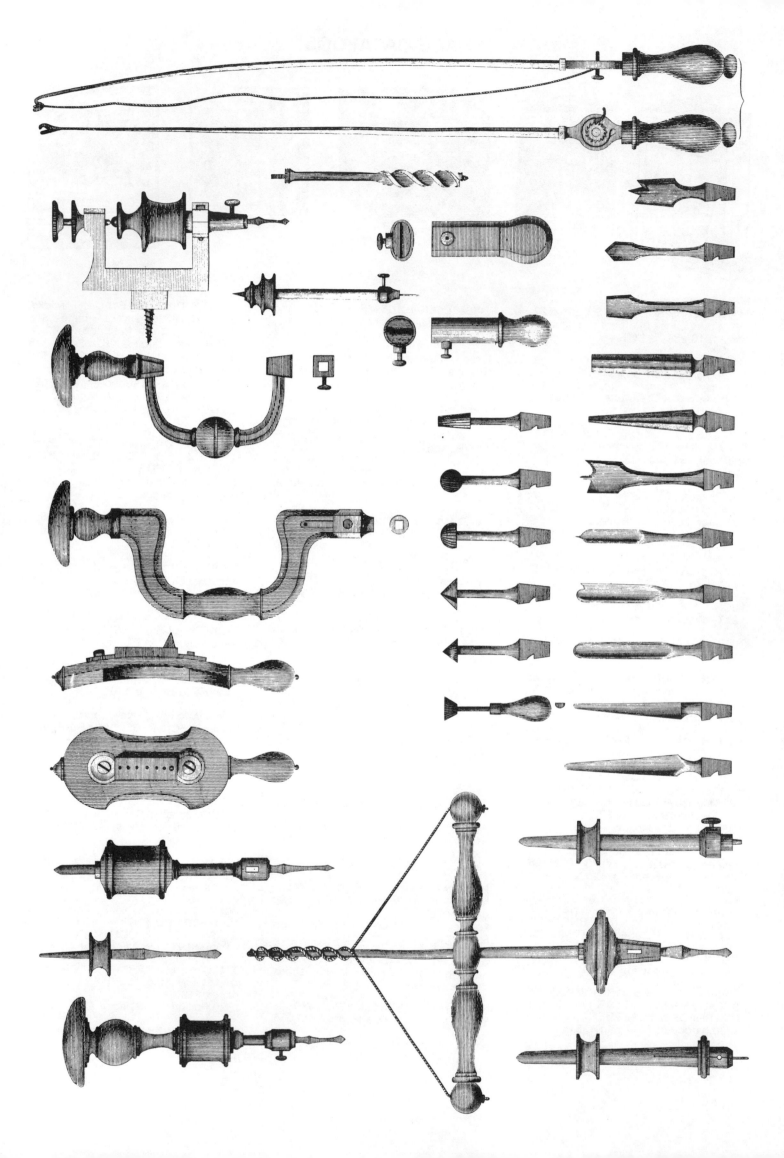

Courtesy The Mechanick's Workbench.

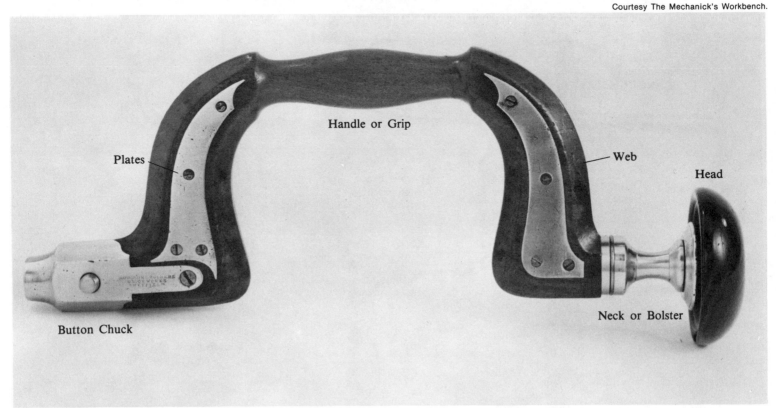

Plates

Handle or Grip

Web

Head

Button Chuck

Neck or Bolster

Plated Sheffield braces by British makers of the late 1800's sell in a very broad price range depending upon the manufacturer, material, workmanship, age and condition. Photo is of a registered model with a brass trademark medallion surrounded by an ivory ring disk. It could bring anywhere from $200 to $400.

A SHORT HISTORY OF THE BRACE, OR BITSTOCK

The Chinese are credited with inventing the double crank brace in about 100 A.D. Europeans did not have ready access to this useful tool until the 15th century. The wooden bitstock, with its small button-like top, remained virtually unchanged for the next 300 years. These early braces were made complete with fixed-bit in place. If you customarily drilled 3 different sized holes in the line of chairs you made - you would own 3 separate bitstocks. A 17th Century craftsman, who did a lot of hole drilling, apparently grew tired of carrying a dozen bulky braces to his place of employment and invented removable bit pods (pads). These first interchangeable bit pads were held in the drill brace only by the pressure of the tool upon the workpiece. Sometime later, thumbscrews were added to the crude chucks and by the early 1800's fancy button-operated lever-release mechanisms began to appear.

Exact dating of unmarked braces is difficult because all three forms of wooden bitstocks mentioned above, along with several metal types, existed side by side for over a century. The unbraced, beechwood-framed bitstocks of Europe were gradually refined to include brass reinforcement plates on their fragile elbows. In 1850 Mr. William Marples, of Sheffield, England, developed the "ultimate" brace. It had a cast brass frame with exotic hardwood infill. The "Ultimatum" as it was called, could be purchased in basic beech, finer rosewood, or exotic ebony. A few were made with animal horn filling.

About the same time that Marples was introducing his new tool in Great Britain, several different all metal braces were being developed in the United States of America. These braces incorporated a shell-type chuck which was designed to accommodate a wider range of bit sizes than had previously been used. By the turn-of-the-century the new American Pattern had captured the entire world market. It featured ball bearing construction, alligator jaws, a ratcheting drive shaft and sold for $1.50 in the year 1896.

◄ **Engraving from Manuel du Tourneur, 1816 Edition.**
Boring tools used by 18th-Century European craftsmen.

BRACES (continued)

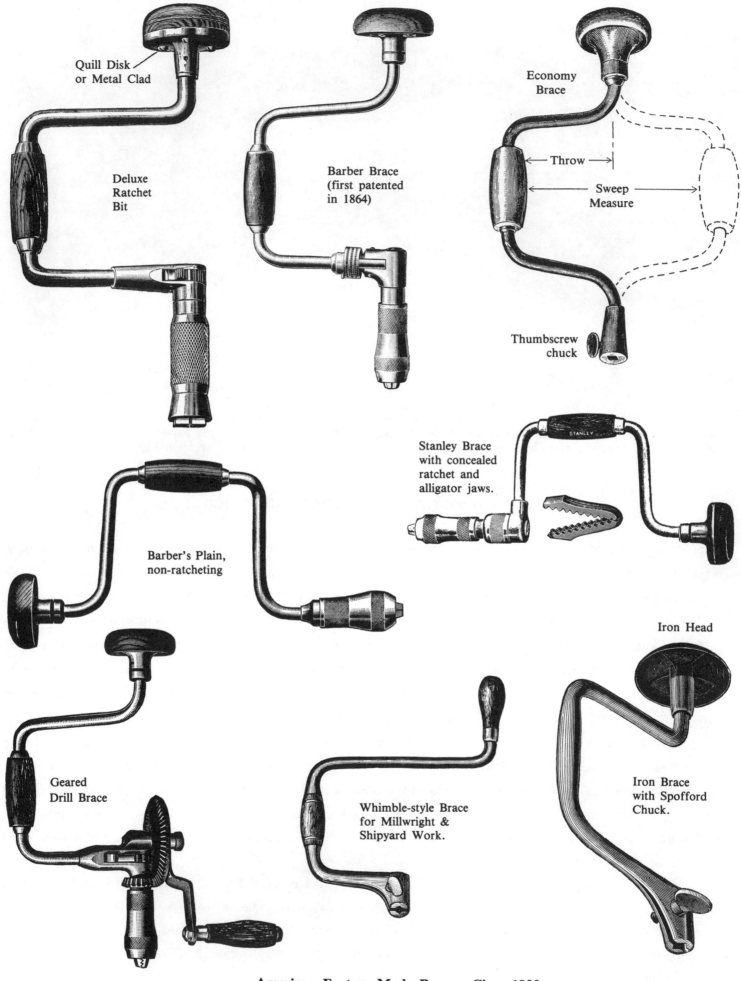

Quill Disk or Metal Clad

Deluxe Ratchet Bit

Barber Brace (first patented in 1864)

Economy Brace

Throw

Sweep Measure

Thumbscrew chuck

Stanley Brace with concealed ratchet and alligator jaws.

Barber's Plain, non-ratcheting

Iron Head

Geared Drill Brace

Whimble-style Brace for Millwright & Shipyard Work.

Iron Brace with Spofford Chuck.

American Factory-Made Braces, Circa 1900

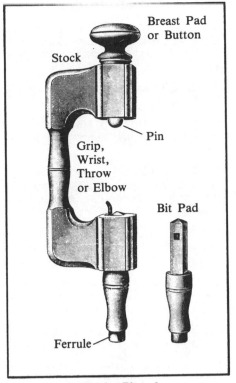

Wooden Bitstock

AMERICAN PATTERN BRACES

AMERICAN PATTERN BRACES (Modern, Barber Patent & Shell Chuck Type. Usually metal framed with wooden head & grip)

AMIDON'S PAT. July 20, 1880 by Amidon & White, 137 Main St., Buffalo, N.Y. $10

ATHOL MACH. CO. Manufacturers, Athol Depot, Mass. Pat'd Feb. 1, 1870. All metal brace with R.S. Hildreth pat. chuck. Find cond. $80

AUCTION LOT of (12) American factory made metal bit braces with wood trim. $144

O.S. BACKUS, Winchendon, Mass., Pat. Nov. 5, 1872. Carpenter's brace. Rosewood grip has brass flanged stops. Lignum vitae head. $35

BARBER'S PATENT of 1868. Plain metal brace with brass ferrules on wood wrist. Non-ratcheting. $15

BELL SYSTEM No. 2101 Yankee-made modern ratcheting brace. auct. $25

BUGGY WRENCH brace with adjustable jaws. Metal grip. 3 inch throw. auct. $55

W.M. CALDWELL "This brace is made of superior steel manufactured expressly for me and I warrant every brace". Rosewood grip and head. $32

DAVIS LEVEL & TOOL CO. patent 1864 (and later). Carpenter's brace with wooden head and decoratively turned grip. $60-$95

FRAY'S PATENT Jan. 8, 1889. Rosewood pad and handle with inset pewter rings. $40

JOHN S. FRAY & CO. Bridgeport, Conn. Spofford type chuck, all metal. $6 - $9

JOHN FRAY, Joiner's brace with pewter rings inset in throw. Spofford chuck. $14

JOHN FRAY & CO. No. 110 with 12 in. sweep. Rosewood handle & head. Excellent cond. $25

JOHN FRAY, wimble style brace. $39-$60

JOHN S. FRAY, coachmaker's brace with rosewood pad & handle, pewter rings. $50

S.W. HILDRETH, Athol Depot, Mass. Pat. Feb. 1, 1870. Chuck collar slides back to insert bit. $45

HOLT MFG. CO., Springfield, Mass. Pat. Dec. 12, 1880. American style with unusual ball-shaped chuck. $35

HSB CO. Mfg., very small, short throw brace. Fray's patent chuck. $60

KEEN KUTTER Nos. KA10, 12, 14 & 18. $15-$30 No. KA6. $25-$35. T-style Corner Brace. $45

P. LOWENTRAUT'S wrench brace, 1894 patent brace . Auct. $60 - $89

MILLERS FALLS No. 1 brace fitted with adjustable hollow auger. $55

MILLERS FALLS No. 2 carpenter's brace, 1867 patent. Wooden head & throw. $50

MILLERS FALLS No. 34 bit brace with unusual 3 inch sweep. $30

MILLERS FALLS No. 36 ratchet brace, 6 in. sweep. $9

MILLERS FALLS No. 182 ratcheting brace with geared drill in addition to conventional throw arm. $55 - $100

MILLERS FALLS No. 771 brace with cocobolo head and rosewood handle. $26

MILLERS FALLS No. 7312 wimble brace with 95% or orig. nickel plate. $25-$45

MILLERS FALLS assorted carpenter's braces circa 1900 - 1930. $8 - $15 each

MILLERS FALLS Pat. 1866 - 1868 braces with brass trimmed chucks. $30 - $40

NOBLES MFG. CO. Pat. Dec. 12, 1866 metal brace with rosewood head. Slip-ring over split chuck secures bit. $24

NORTH BROS. No. 2101A "Yankee" 10 inch brace with black compo handle & pad. $45

PECK, STOW & WILCOX, Sampson ratchet brace No. 8008A. Nickel plated frame, rosewood pad and wrist. $25

PECK, STOW & WILCOX braces of the 1890's with most of nickel gone. $10-$15

S.E. ROBINSON wrench-type brace identical to Lowentraut's. Pat. Dec. 25, 1877. $80

STACKPOLES Pat. Sept. 23, 1862. All metal brace with alligator chuck, brass collar & an octagon grip. $75

STANLEY No. 12W, S.H. Fray wimble brace. $75

STANLEY No. 813 nickel plated, box-ratchet brace. Circa 1929. $35

STANLEY No. 921 concealed ratchet brace. $25

STANLEY No. 923 box ratchet brace. Mint cond. in orig. box. $75

STANLEY No. 965N nickel plated ratchet brace with alligator jaws. $14

STANLEY No. 2101A heavy duty brace with 14 in. sweep. $35

STANLEY No. 8136 ratcheting brace. $38

A.W. STREETER, Shelburne Falls, Mass. Pat. Jan. 8, 1867 $20 - $45

A.W. STREETER, Pat. Jan. 23, 1855. Iron frame, pad and sleeveless grip. $85

J.H. WESTOTTS modern brace with king-size double-grip chuck. Pat. Mar. 7, 1874. $125

WINCHESTER carpenter's brace. 8 in. $60, 10 in. $40

EARLY BITSTOCKS

AMERICAN bitstock, circa 1770. Tiny button pad has pewter ferrule. Chuck held in place by wrought iron strap and wire cotter pin. $225

AUSTRIAN bitstock 19 inches in length. Egg-shaped wooden head, clothespin bit pad, wrought iron ferrules. auct. $150

BEECHWOOD cooper's brace with wide shoulders & large diameter head typical of this tool. auct. $150 - $250

BENTWOOD or natural curved brace, 14 in. long. Birch head and neck. $325

BRITISH cooper's brace with 4 in. dia. head and fixed spoon bit. $275 - $375

CHAIRMAKER'S primitive bitstock 12 to 15 inches long. Fixed bit and small button-style head. $135 - $175

CLASSIC British chairmaker's bitstock with fixed spoon bit. $175 - $225

CLASSIC French form chairmaker's brace with fine patina. $345

CHERRY wood, early American bitstock. 16 in. overall. Wooden thumbscrew chuck accepts a square tapered bit pad. Very fine. $325 - $375

CHERRY bitstock with early handgrip instead of pad-type head. Extra wide chamfers on arms terminate in dowell-shaped throw. auct. $450

CONTINENTAL STYLE beechwood brace with clothespin bit pad. auct. $130 - $210

OTHER EARLY BITSTOCKS

AMERICAN bitstock 19 in. long. Top button is doweled into gently curved stock. Comes with 4 original pad bits. Not a blemish. $325

BEECH bitstock of basic Sheffield shape. 15 in. long including copper plate on end of chuck. $350

BEECH bitstock 15 inches long. Metal bolt holds head in frame. Square chuck holds pad. $280

BLIGH, Whitechapel, signed cooper's brace. All wood with iron chuck. $350

BUCK & CO. beechwood cooper's brace with brassbound wooden chuck. auct. $227

DARK BEECH early American cooper's brace, 10 in. sweep, 4 in. head. Brass ferrule. $295

D-SHAPED fruitwood brace of same thickness overall. auct. $300

DUTCH bitstock (Booromslagen) of darkened beechwood with finial-shaped bit pad. Neck, chuck and pad have brass ferrules. $420

DUTCH ash bitstock with ball-shaped head. 8⅝ in. to 11½ in. lengths. auct. $165 ea.

DUTCH gimlet brace or Spykerboor. 9½ in. long with fixed bit & round head. $225

DUTCH pod brace 12½ in. long with parrot-nosed bit. $375

18th-CENTURY primitive wooden braces with the usual iron strap repairs. $180-$250

HEADLESS ash brace, probably used with a bib. 20 inches long, square socket, horn ferrule. auct. $200

HEADLESS French bib brace, shaped like a question mark. Has tapered horn pivot point instead of a head. $240

MAPLE bitstock in ornamental bracket shape. Nicely turned head. 4 original square pad bits. auct. $600

MAPLE bitstock, artistically shaped, fixed spoon bit, octagon pewter ferrule. auct. $250

OAK bitstock with tall neck and knob. Brass collar and ferrule. Square pad socket. auct. $100

OAK bitstock of the 18th Century. Button head. $375

SWEDISH primitive all wood brace. Wooden chuck pad has tapered threads which screw into iron reinforced round chuck. $275

WALNUT 17th-Century pad brace with curved webs and turned grip. Illustrated on plate K2 of Hooper's "Handcraft in Wood". Auct. $650

BLACKSMITH'S BRACES

BLACKSMITH'S beam brace, 18 inches long. $65

BEAM BRACES, 17 in. handwrought. $48 - $75

BRACE & CLAMP combination. 30 inch C-clamp with sliding bottom jaw. Headless brace (included) fits against bottom of screw shaft. $125

LEVER DRILL 11½ in. U-shaped forging with pointed end bearing and square chuck. $85

BRASS BRACES

BRASS powder or gas works brace. Plain rounded disk head, sleeveless grip, thumbscrew chuck. auct. $85

HEAVY solid brass 10 in. to 11 in. blacksmith style braces with thumbscrew chuck. $100 - $175

BRASS wimbel style brace with oak handle and grip. auct. $165

BREWER'S solid cast brass brace, 10½ in. long with square chuck hole. $150

BRONZE powder works brace, 9 inches in length, auct. $95 - $115

DOWN BROS. London, chrome plated brass medical brace. 11 inch. $295

CAGE HEAD BRACES

TWO SUPPORT iron cage head coachmaker's brace. Chamfered edges, 15 in. overall. $295

TWO POLE plain cage head brace. auct $100 - $200

THREE POST cage head braces, 10 in. to 14 in. long. $165 - $275 - $350

FOUR POST primitive English cage head brace. $595

FOUR SPOKES on 3 in. dia. pad, 5 inch throw, 12 in. overall. Swollen grip. $200

FOUR CURVED spokes support an open ring style head on this unusual cage head brace with spring-loaded square chuck. $250

PENNSYLVANIA made, 4 post cage head brace. Early handwrought piece. $275

CLASSIC 4 POST cage head brace with 4¾ in. dia. thick disk head and thumbscrew chuck. 15 in. overall. auct. $200

TWISTED SUPPORTS on 5 in. dia. head. 13 inches long, 6 in. throw. auct. $575

SCANDINAVIAN cage head brace with 4 iron struts secured to brass disk head with screws. Much knurling and forged decoration, rarely found on early iron braces. $850

SIX POLE iron cage head brace. $475

CORNER BRACES

ALLIANCE MFG. CO., Aliance, Ohio. a 6 foot long telescoping brass-headed angle boring tool. Ratchet action, leather belt. $65

JOHN S. FRAY CO., Bridgeport, Conn., No. 80 corner brace. $35

GOODELL PRATT CO. No. 85 universal ratchet handle. Iron handle with lignum vitae head. $32

GOODELL PRATT No. 215 universal corner brace. Two handles with encased gear drive at elbow. Pat. Sept. 9, 1905. $125

C.J. HAEBERLI & H.E.O. SCHMIDT of Buffalo, N.Y., Pat. No. 859,059 convertable corner brace. auct. $150

L.M. & K. Wks., Lancaster, N.Y., corner brace with removable wood handled crank. $45

MILLERS FALLS No. 502 corner brace in unused condition. $30 - $65

MILLERS FALLS Pat. Feb. 18, 1890 corner brace with 2 crank handles. $50 - $75

J.H. RUSBY Pat. straight stocked, iron framed extension corner brace with see-thru shaft housing, telescoping. $25 - $45

STANLEY No. 982 corner ratchet bit brace. $22 - $38

STANLEY No. 984 corner ratchet bit brace. $40 - $45

STANLEY No. 993 deluxe, geared corner brace. $50 - $100

UNMARKED Modern corner brace with triangular frame, 2 wooden wrists and a wooden pad. $20 - $30

GENTLEMAN'S BALL GRIP or SIX PENNY BRACES

AUCTION LOT of 5 common English made six penny braces. $60 all

AMIDONS PAT. May 21, 1867. Gentleman's brace with sleeveless grip and unusual chuck. $32

H.K.R. BOKER gentleman's brace with decorative details. $28

FRENCH made gentleman's brace with 7 in. sweep. Ball grip. Extra decorative touches. $40

KIRCHBAUM gentleman's brace with egg-shaped head and a spring-loaded chuck. auct. $35

MILGER & SONS gentleman's brace with push-button spring latch. auct. $45

H.W. SPECRENBACH gentleman's brace with ivory screw-plug head insert. $40

UNDERTAKER'S folding iron gentleman's style pocket brace. Wooden head hinges at base of neck. auct. $910

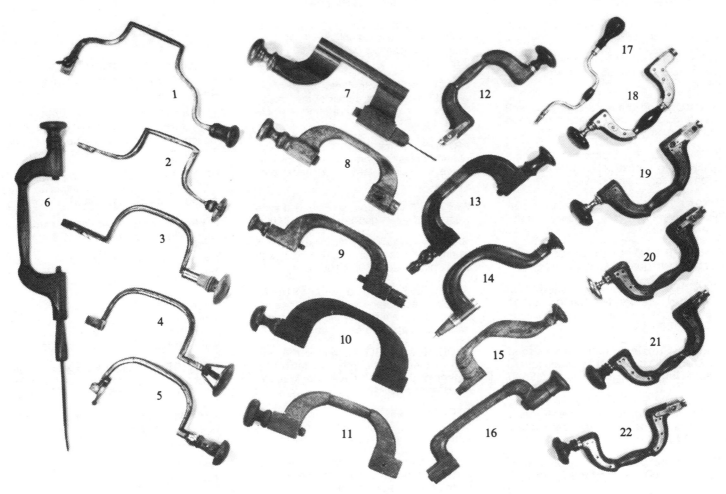

A selection of braces sold at antique tool auction in New Hampshire.

J.P. Bittner Antique Tool Auctions

1. BLACKSMITH-MADE brace 19 in. long. Wrought frame, turned wooden head, rams horn nut on chuck. $160

2. EARLIER, smaller version with burl head. Chuck holds flat bits which are included. $187

3. BEAUTIFUL handcrafted metal brace. Beechwood head, brass ferrule, spring loaded thumblatch bit lock. $275

4. 4-POST Cage Head Brace. Early hand-forged piece with threaded take-up wear nut. $200

5. HIGH QUALITY but unsigned brace stamped No. 8. Elm head, fancy brass ferrule and clever spring bit-release lever. $225

6. INCREDIBLY LONG 32 inch, early beechwood brace with bit pad. $475

7. ASH brace with clothespin-style lock pad. $575

8. 18th-CENTURY birch brace with wooden thumb-screw, pewter socket ring, and a square pad hole. Little used. $275

9. OLD REPAIR in wrap around sheet metal on this maple brace with square pad. $160

10. MASSIVE old working brace with glue repair. $225

11. EARLY ASH brace of pleasing design. Rough. $225

12. SLATER, Sheffield. Unplated beechwood brace with lignum vitae head. $55

13. HANDLE REVOLVES on this refined early wooden brace with horn chuck ring. $300

14. BELLY BRACE, beautifully made, with 3 brass rings. $350

15. DELICATE light-duty brace made of elm. Finely crafted. $275

16. SHALLOW THROW Oak brace in excellent cond. $275

17. TREPANNING brace for skull work. Ebony head & handle. $65

18. WILLIAM MARPLES, Hibernia Works. Ebony-filled Ultimatium brace. $400

19. JOSEPH COOPER Patent brace with turned brass neck and ebony pad. (screws & latch missing) $125

20. R.M. MARPLES, Oct. 15, 1846 Safety Pat. Fine old brass-headed brace. $150

21. BOWER, Sheffield plated brace with lignum vitae head. (some checking) $95

22. BARTON BROTHERS, Clossop Road, Sheffield. Utile dula plated brace. $90

OTHER IRON BRACES

T. BRADBURN & SONS, Scotch iron wagon maker's brace. $75

CARRIAGE MAKER'S all metal brace. Bit release lever protrudes above arm. Sleeveless grip. $20

COMMON iron brace 12½ in. long with chamfered stock and nicely turned wood pad. 3½ in. throw, no grip. $35-$50

B. DARLING, Pat Oct. 20, 1868. Fine quality all iron construction. Very fine condition and rare maker. $895

EXTRA LONG SHANK, all metal brace. 34 inches overall, 4 in. dia. head, thumbscrew chuck. $160

C. FOSTER & CO. metal brace of superior factory made quality. auct. $70

FRENCH wrought iron brace dated 1735. Ball shaped grip. Pewter bearing in turned head. Similar examples in the Louvre. auct. $1,850

FRENCH 18th Century decorative forged iron brace with tall tapered wooden turned head having a floral iron cap. auct. $590

MUSHROOM PAD 4 in. tall surmounts this 16 inch handwrought iron brace with 4 in. throw and small square thumbscrew chuck. $40 - $60

MUSHROOM head on this iron brace with unusually short 2½ inch throw. auct. $85

HANDWROUGHT iron brace with C-shaped stock. Fancy tall turned head. 17½ in. overall. Thumbscrew chuck. $125

HEBRON CO. No. 3 patented carriage maker's metal brace. Plain. $20

S.W. HILDRETE Manufacture, Athol Dept. Pat. Feb. 1, 1870. Tubular spring-loaded chuck. All iron brace. $48

W. MARPLES Scotch-pattern metal brace with lignum vitae head. Lever chuck. auct. $45

Wm MARPLES & SONS iron wagon builder's brace. Nicely turned neck & head, butterfly thumbscrew chuck. Included are 26 vintage bits. $225

MINIATURE ancient handwrought and turned iron brace 9½ in. long with 3 in. throw. Dragon head design where frame meets chuck. Initialed J.V. auct. $700

MINIATURE common iron brace with brass head. 1½ in. throw. Thumbscrew chuck. auct. $129

UNSIGNED common factory made iron brace with Spofford type chuck. auct. $10 dlr. $18

WHIMBLE-type wrought iron brace with wooden head. $25 - $40

WILSON MFG. CO., New London, Conn. Solid iron brace with tapered spring lever chuck. $30 - $40

SHEFFIELD BRACES

Repaired, reglued, chipped, parts missing. Various brands of Sheffield type braces with brass side plates & chucks. $38 - $95

J.H. ANDREWS, Sheffield style brass plated brace by the owner of the Toledo Steel Works. (dented, scratched & cracked) $125

ARTHUR, Edinburgh (1793-1844). Unplated Scottish button-chuck beechwood brace with brass ferrules at neck joint. auct. $75

Wm. ASH & CO. Unplated Sheffield style wooden brace in good cond. $85-$100

BARTON BROTHERS, Clossop Road, Sheffield. Utile dula wood brace with brass plates. auct. $90-$100

JAMES BEE, Sheffield (circa 1814-28). Plated beech brace with ebony head & brass neck. Henery Brown, Patentee, with eagle mark appears on medallion. $150

BLOOMER & PHILLIPS with lion & unicorn emblem. Sheffield style, plated brace. Patented 10-12-1847. Lever chuck, ebony head. auct. $185-$250

BLOOM & SON German Silver plated ebony brace with gunmetal neck. Button chuck. Fine. Auct. 1984. London. $1,092

BRASS HEAD, button chuck, neck & plates. Mahogany stock. Unmarked. auct. $600. Beech stock. auct. $125

HENRY BROWN, Sheffield. "The Mechanics Patent Brace", brass plated beechwood with ebony head. Excellent. auct. $120 Dlr. $200

BROWN & FLATHER brass plated beech stock with lignum vitae head. $75-$140

As above, but with ivory center plug. $175

BUCK & HICKMAN brass framed ebony brace with lever chuck. auct. $166

COLQUHOUN & CADMAN brass plated beechwood with brass neck and lever chuck. auct. $175

COLQHOUN & CADMAN brass framed ebony brace with lever chuck and set of 18 bits. Auct. $262

Another, similar to above sold at 1983 Auction $600

JOSH. COOPER, Patentee, Birmingham. Plated beech brace with beaded brass neck. Rosewood head has ivory ring and disk. $275

Another, as above but hollow brass head. Light colored beechwood. auct. $400, dlr. $600

Unplated version. auct. $95-$110

J. FENN, Newgate St. Lady's style brace with beechwood frame and cocobolo head. $325

FENTON & MARSDENS Registered Head Design No. 986 (Pat. Mar. 4, 1847). Unique steel spindle head bearing on this ebony, brass and hardwood brace. $365

FENTON & MARSDEN ebony framed, brass plated, registered brace with lever chuck. Fine. $695

D. FLATHER & SONS, Solly Works, Sheffield, Improved, Registered. Brass plated beech brace with ebony head. Includes 12 signed bits. $215

FREETH (Benjamin, Birmingham, 1770-1824) stamped on chuck of this unplated elm wood brace. auct. $400

J. FROST, Norwich. Plated beech brace with hollow brass head. Auct. $184

GABRIEL plated beechwood brace with button chuck, wooden neck & head. auct. $367

W. GREAVES & SONS rosewood brace with brass neck and plates. Ebony head has brass button and ivory ring. Complete with 29 matching bits. Dlr. $1,250

IOHN GREEN Sheffield style unplated beech brace. Chuck engraved with owner's name and dated 1816. auct. $592

H. HAWKE, Solly Works. Sheffield plated beech brace with lignum vitae head. auct. $100 - $125

Another, with cocobolo head and eagle emblem $135

JAMES HOWARTH, Broom Springs Works, Sheffield. Brass framed Ultimatum with ebony infill. auct. $375 - $500

JAMES HOWARTH, Broom Springs Works, Sheffield. Beechwood brace with trefoil ends on brass web plates. Lignum vitae neck & head, brass center button. auct. $130

IBBOTSON & CO. brass framed brace with ebony infill. Ring chuck and 6 bits. auct. $280

IMPROVED Brass Framed Brace, only mark on this ebony filled Ultimatum with disc in head. auct. $375

KENDALL, York. Beechwood brace with brass button chuck. auct. $85

LADY'S size Sheffield brace, unplated. 12 in. long with 3 in. sweep. Cocobola head has plain brass medallion. $475

LION & UNICORN seal on head medallion of this ebony & brass framed patent brace, "Warranted Superior". $300

ROBERT MARPLES, Reg. No. 3954 heavy brass framed, beech filled brace. auct. $500

ROBERT MARPLES, Hermitage Works, Sheffield. Cooper's Patent, beech brace with arrowhead shaped ends on brass web plates (trfoil), and a parabolic brass-necked ebony head with ivory ring. auct. $720 Dlr. $1,200

Photo Courtesy The Mechanick's Workbench.

Left to right: A factory-made wrought-iron Scotch brace with wooden head and heart-shaped lever spring chuck, $25 - $45. 2nd from left: 19th-Century Sheffield brace in beechwood with no brass plates (unplated), made by Moulson Brothers, $95 - $120. Top center: 18th-Century style cooper's brace of solid beech with removable neck and head measuring 4 inches in diameter. The brass-ferruled chuck has a fixed spoon bit. $200-$275. 2nd from right: another Moulson Brothers Shef-field-style brace. This one has brass reinforcement plates (plated) and a lignum vitae head with typical brass center plug, $165 - $185. Far right: circa 1880 six penny, or gentleman's, or common ball brace. Handle and head are beechwood. Frame has a bit more decoration than most, so it might be worth from $35 to $45. (common ones sell in the $20 - $30 range) Bottom: Lady's size ball brace 9 in. long. Signed P.L. Schmidt, $65 and up.

ROBERT MARPLES "Ultimatum brass framed brace" with ebony head and infill. auct. $315   Dlr. $450 - $550

ROBERT MARPLES, circa 1857 double-bound beechwood carpenter's brace with wrap-around brass plating and neck auct. $475   Dlr. $900

W. MARPLES & SONS, Sheffield, Hibernia. Brass plated beechwood with ebony head & ivory ring inset. $165

WILLIAM MARPLES Ultimatum in brass framed ebony with Hibernia stamp on head seal. auct. $350 Dlr. $425 - $525

WILLIAM MARPLES "By Her Majesty's Royal Letter Patent". Ebony filled brass Ultimatum. auct. $450 Dlr. $600

Wm MARPLES Horn filled Ultimatum brace. Ebony head and handle. auct. $800 - $1,380 Dlr. $2,400

Wm MARPLES boxwood filled Ultimatum with Hibernia trademark on plug. Large coat arms stamp. Auct. $850 Dlr. $3,400

MARSDEN BROTHERS, Bridge Works, Sheffield, imprinted on chuck of this Reg. Mar. 4, 1847 Brass plated beech brace with necked ebony head. auct. $275

A. MATHIESON & SON plated Sheffield brace with large button chuck, brass bolster, ebony head. $165 - $300

A. MATHIESON & SON, Glasgow. Unplated boxwood brace with brass necked ebony head. Ivory ring & button. auct. $500 Dlr. $850

MAW & STALEY brass plated hardwood brace. $125

JOHN MORRISON, Manufacturer, marked on ring chuck of this brass framed ebony brace. auct. $210

MOSELEY & SON, Covent Garden. Pre 1891 Sheffield style beech brace with brass plates & neck. Ebony head. $165 - $185

PIANO MAKER'S German silver plated beechwood brace. Fine condition. $595

PIANO MAKER'S Sheffield style 8½ inch long unplated brace with ivory head 2½ in. dia. Circa 1850. auct. $800

PILKINGTON PEDGOR & CO. "Made for Stanley, Morton & Davis". Elaborately plated beech brace with brass neck and cupped head. auct. $1,240

G. SCHOFIELD Reg. April 20, 1848. Brass plated beechwood brace with lever chuck. auct. $400

SCHOFIELD, Warranted brass plated beechwood brace with rosewood head and brass balustrade neck. $215

SIMS Patent, registered ebony brace with brass plates on inner surface of webs. Also has inlaid brass dots and elbow rings. auct. $1,050

SLATER (1822-1844) brass plated beech brace with lignum vitae pad. auct. $55 Dlr. $150

R. SORBY unplated Sheffield style brace with brass bolster & ebony head with brass button. $115

THOMAS & CO. brass framed ebony brace. auct. $375

THOMPSON, Sheffield, Patent. Rare "Sims" type button-chuck center-framed brace with rosewood web plates attached to brass frame with large saw handle screws which bear a coat of arms. auct. $1,443

T. E. WELLS American made Sheffield style plated with beech stock. $65 - $135

Courtesy Dover Publications

At left, a 16th-Century nobleman admires the inventory of a Nuremburg toolmaker whose stock in trade consists largely of calipers and dividers.

Calipers are ancient measuring devices similar to compasses and dividers but with curved legs not intended for scribing or plotting. The most collectable calipers are early handwrought pieces, especially those with extra decorative touches such as chamfered legs. Brass calipers often command a premium and extra large or very tiny pairs are also desirable. Lumber calipers are often displayed with ruler collections and we have listed them in the rule section on page 170.

BELCHER BROS. cross caliper barrel gauge. Sliding L-square jaws with brass corner reinforcements. 24 in. long when closed. auct. $100

BEMIS & CALL outside wing caliper. 18 inches overall. $20

BRASS HANDLED blacksmith's double jaw wrought iron calipers with fancy turned handle terminating in swivel ring. $65

BROWN & SHARP No. 826 ice tong shaped outside caliper, 24 inches long. $20

CAST IRON double outside calipers with center wing. Ring-top handle. Very graceful & rare cast iron piece. auct. $225

CLOCKMAKER'S brass outside caliper. Forms a 2 in. dia. half circle. $30

Same as above only double end, hinged in middle. 4 in. $40

CLOCKMAKER'S double-yoke type dated 1860. 2 legs pivot on wishbone arm ends. Calibrated scale at foot. auct. $50

COACHBUILDER'S huge iron wing caliper. 26 inches from top to end of sickle-shaped legs. Chamfered brass top hinge is 5 layer type. Museum quality. $350

DOUBLE END figure 8, handwrought 12 inch bow tie caliper with brass washer. $36

DANCING LEGS caliper in black finish, 2¼ in. long. $45

DANCING MASTER handwrought 7 in. caliper. $60 - $80

DANCING MASTER sheet iron inside outside double calipers, 8½ inches in length. $80

Another, as above, 10 inches $125

DANCING LEGS, 4 inches long with copper hinge. $85

DANCING LEGS shiny old metal, male legs, 8 inches overall. $110

DOUBLE, Blacksmith's factory made 20 inch calipers with slotted sheet steel handle and ice tong claws. $35

DOUBLE hand-forged, loop handle, 14 inch calipers. Curved outer arms are hinged at different points on center shaft with double hook end. auct. $70

DOUBLE outside calipers, sheet iron, ice tong shape. Ring-end handle. $70

ELLIOTT BROS., London, 1892. Heavy brass vernier caliper with steel jaws. Calibrated to 10½ inches. Fitted mahogany case. auct. $125

EROTIC calipers, formed female legs 3½ in. long, complete with garters. auct. $120

HANDWROUGHT double blacksmith's 21 inch calipers. Auct. $55 - $95

ICE TONG shaped, heavy-duty factory made wing caliper with half round legs. 20 in. overall. auct. $55

M. J. JAQUIS finest quality French made double wing calipers. Chamfered steel with turned wooden handle. Circa 1840. Rug beater shape with center wing. $225

KIMBALL & TALBOT, Worcester. Watchmaker's simple 2 inch outside caliper. $10

KIMBALL & TALBOT, patent 1863, registering calipers. $50

LADY'S LEG plated calipers, 5¾ in. long, large pivot. $48

LADY'S LEG miniature calipers, 3 in. overall. Large round brass joint. $50

LADY'S LEG voluptuous profile. 4 in. $90

LADY'S LEG pregnant, full, fat-figured 4 inch calipers. Unique. $140

LOG CALIPER (see rule, log)

MACHINISTS' factory made outside caliper. Spring steel, 7 in. $4

MACHINISTS' assorted styles, small factory made calipers, circa 1900. $5 ea.

MAISIN: PASSAGER & HUTANT French sculptor's proportional 32 in. caliper. Steel with brass center adjustment. $195

OUTSIDE wing caliper, circa 1850. Each rod shaped 15 inch leg makes a half circle. $40

PATTERN MAKER'S bronze caliper with scissor-style handles. 12 in. $75

PECK, STOW & WILCOX outside wing caliper. 8½ in. long. $18

PROPORTIONAL sculptor's caliper. Twin end, slotted wooden legs. 28 inches overall. French. auct. $130

W. SCHOLLHORN, New Haven, Ct. No. 35 outside caliper. Pat. 1866. auct. $12

SCHULTHEIS, Strasburg. 23½ inch conventional outside caliper. (pitted) $18

L. S. STARRET set of (3) pat. May 1895. Friction lock machinists' calipers. $40

L. S. STARRET, Athol, Mass. Pat. Jan 6, 1885. Outside caliper, fine adjust type. Straight legs, 6 in. overall. $16

L. S. STARRET CO., Athol, Mass. No. 34 screw adjusting outside caliper, 30 in. overall. $25

R. TURNER inside/outside calipers in solid brass. Hook and leg style, 5 inches long. $95

VERNIER calipers, 10 in. long. Steel monkey wrench style. Circa 1860. $25

VERNIER calipers, 10 inch, unmarked. Mint. $50

VIOLIN-MAKER'S hand-forged thickness gauge. Indicator-type calipers on end of screwdriver style handle with pointer on protractor scale. 14 in. overall. $45

VIOLIN MAKER'S thickness caliper with registering dial & gauge. U-shaped brass frame with wooden handle. 12 in. long. auct. $14

WATCHMAKER'S caliper, brass wing on plier type handles has calibrated scale. $10

WATCHMAKER'S figure eight shaped, double caliper. 3½ inches. $12

Another as above, but jaw tips are made to grasp ends of a balance staff. Larger center hinge. $45

WHEELWRIGHT'S early hand-forged wishbone shape with 22 inch legs. Multiple layer friction top joint. $85

WHEELWRIGHT'S early hand-forged wing top caliper in giant onion shape. 45 in. tall. auct. $145

WRIGHT MACHINE CO. Worcester, Mass. Patented Sept. 24, 1867. Bow spring top machinists' caliper. $18

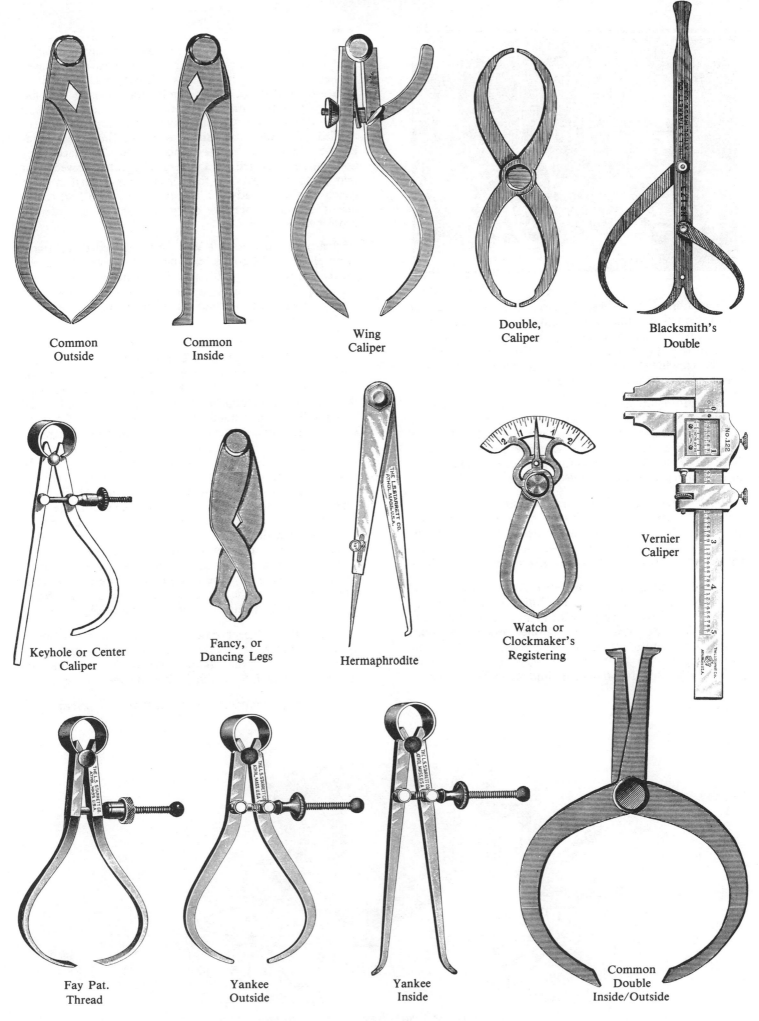

Common
Outside

Common
Inside

Wing
Caliper

Double,
Caliper

Blacksmith's
Double

Keyhole or Center
Caliper

Fancy, or
Dancing Legs

Hermaphrodite

Watch or
Clockmaker's
Registering

Vernier
Caliper

Fay Pat.
Thread

Yankee
Outside

Yankee
Inside

Common
Double
Inside/Outside

American Factory-Made Calipers, Circa 1895 - 1915

The Biblical two wheeled chariot had no springs and was obviously a rough riding contraption on the best of roads. Little progress in carriage design was made from those early days until the mid 16th-Century when an enamored Dutchman presented Queen Elizabeth with a fine heavy coach for her personal use.

English nobility and other rich folks of the day quickly adopted this new form of transport and a new British industry was born. About a century later a Mr. Obadia Elliot invented the elliptic spring and someone else added leather shock absorbers. The cumbersome early coach soon evolved into a much more comfortable and graceful vehicle.

With these and other improvements came a more factory-like approach to carriage building. Blacksmiths were housed in one room and wheelwrights in another. The wood-working department was sealed off and a special dust free area was set aside for painting & varnishing.

Woods used in coachwork were Ash, for frames, and Basswood, Cherry, Poplar, and Tulip for body panels. Wheels were hickory spoked with gumwood hubs and oak felloes. All of this lumber was seasoned at least five years before any shaping was done. A first class Philadelphia body shop of the 1870's kept at least eighty thousand board feet on hand in its curing and seasoning rooms.

Painting, varnishing, and hand rubbing the finish was standard procedure on even the least expensive carriages. First the body was covered with a sealer coat of oil-based primer then any open pores which remained were filled with a thinned putty, lightly sanded and covered with another coat of oil primer. After drying, five coats of ochre pigment and japan varnish, mixed with turpentine, were applied. This was hand rubbed to a fine finish with pumice stone and again coated and sanded. The last color application consisted of 3 layers of paint followed with two protective coats of fast drying copal varnish. The coach was now ready for the customer, who had to repeat the whole procedure every year or two in order to protect his investment.

Just prior to the Civil War machinery covering nearly every phase of the coach-building process was introduced. Power-cut mortises, hydraulic tire-setting machines, and self-oiling junction boxes were but a few of the inovations by American carriage making firms who now led the world in production.

The topless sporting rigs and spidery wheeled Yankee phaetons actually frightened European visitors who were used to much more substantial looking coaches. Before the war of the Union it took half a year's wages to purchase one of these vehicles. Even an economy model was priced well over one hundred dollars. The term "Carriage Trade" had come to denote the wealthiest customers of local merchants, those who did their shopping from liveried carriages. However, by the turn-of-the-century almost any farmer could afford a factory made vehicle. Census figures for the year 1900 showed nearly one hundred thousand pleasure rigs a year coming off the production lines. Just a month's wages could now put a tradesman "in the buggy seat." By 1895 one could purchase any part of a wagon or carriage's running gear from Sears & Roebuck or any large hardware house. Factories had become assembly lines, components were no longer primarily made on the premises but were purchased from outside specialist firms in wholesale quantities.

The tools of the carriage maker run the entire spectrum of handicrafts. Generally speaking they are often more curved or refined than those of the carpenter or cabinet maker and are much in demand by collectors.

(See plane, router, and shave sections for prices)

Brewster Calash Coach. New Haven, Conn. 1860

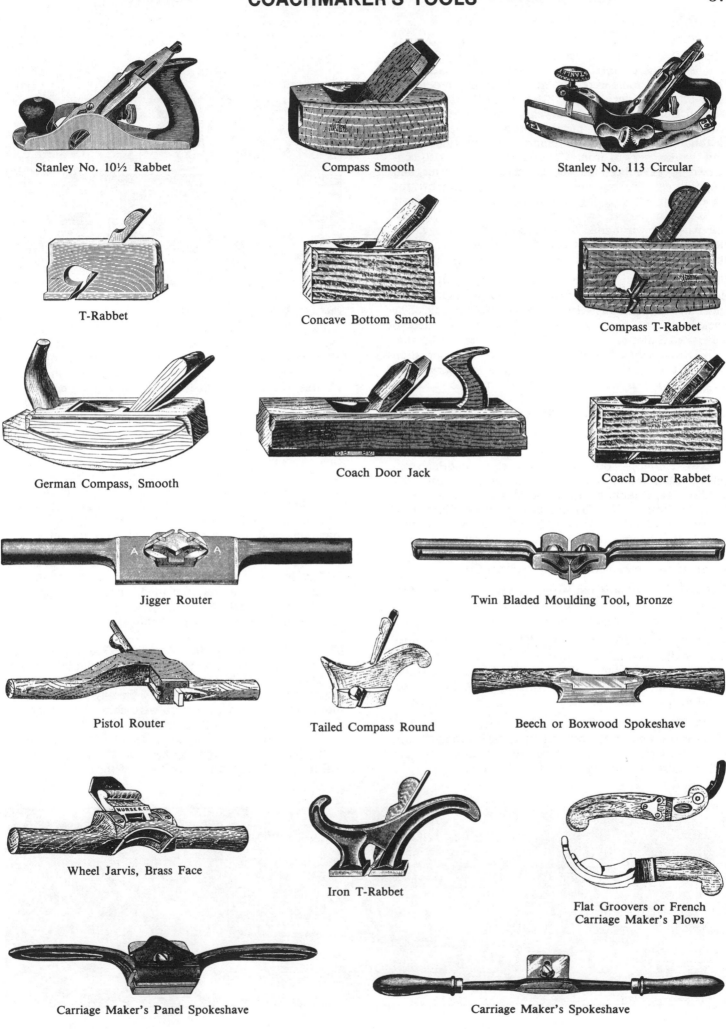

Stanley No. 10½ Rabbet

Compass Smooth

Stanley No. 113 Circular

T-Rabbet

Concave Bottom Smooth

Compass T-Rabbet

German Compass, Smooth

Coach Door Jack

Coach Door Rabbet

Jigger Router

Twin Bladed Moulding Tool, Bronze

Pistol Router

Tailed Compass Round

Beech or Boxwood Spokeshave

Wheel Jarvis, Brass Face

Iron T-Rabbet

Flat Groovers or French
Carriage Maker's Plows

Carriage Maker's Panel Spokeshave

Carriage Maker's Spokeshave

BRASS is made by adding one part zinc to two parts copper. Zinc and copper occur naturally together in India so it is supposed that brass was first made by accident. The first metal tools were hammered from native outcroppings of almost pure copper. Men began to cast copper tools in Europe almost 7,000 years ago. Bronze did not become the predominant metal for tools and weapons until about 3,500 B.C. but it remained so for 1,600 years until the discovery of iron. The earliest bronze is also considered to have been an accidental alloy, (arsenic and copper occur side by side). Later, imported tin became the common alloying ingredient. Approximately 4 parts tin to 96 parts copper produced a suitable bronze for tools. One part zinc was added to the mixture for coinage. Tin melts at 450 °F., Lead at 600 °F., Copper at 1,900 °F., and common Iron becomes molten at about 2,100 °F.

BUCK is a name almost synonymous with fine tools. At least ten different British firms engaged in tool making under this surname between the years 1826 and 1898. The Buck brothers, John, Charles and Richard emigrated to the United States in the mid 1800's and, after a brief stint with D.R. Barton, began their own edge tool operation in 1853. Charles Buck branched out with a separate factory in 1873 and won many awards on his own. Buck Bros. produced one of the finest lines of carving chisels and plane irons available in 19th-Century America.

CHAPIN-STEPHENS Co. was founded by Hermon Chapin at the Union Factory in Pine Meadow, Conn. in 1826. The concern flourished for over a hundred years before selling out to the Stanley Rule & Level Company in 1929. Mr. Chapin added a line of wooden rules to his plane business in 1834 by purchasing an existing manufacturer's machinery. The plane & rule manufacturing firm became H. Chapin's Sons in 1868. At the turn-of-the-century Chapin purchased L.C. Stephens and the new conglomerate was renamed Chapin-Stephens Co.

COCOBOLO, a hard red wood of very fine grain. Obtained chiefly from the Isthmus of Panama. Widely used in drill brace making for heads and handles.

COMBS, PAINT-GRAINING. Thin, flat, rectangular metal combs used to simulate wood grain on freshly painted surfaces. Originally sold in sets of 12 and occasionally offered today in antique shops for $15 to $30 in their original metal containers.

CORMIER or Service Wood is the preferred close grained hardwood used in the production of finer quality French woodworking tools. It is related to the Mountain Ash and is a fruitwood who's produce is edible.

CHAIR-MAKING did not exist as an industry in the United States until after the close of the Revolutionary War. Lambert Hitchcock established a parts factory in 1818 which evolved into a 1,000 chair a month operation by the time he sold out 22 years later. Prior to Hitchcock's success with mass production most chairs were made by country craftsmen. All of the lathe turning work was done as close to the timber source as possible, to save on shipping costs. Some assembly was done in suburban city shops for the same reason; a fully assembled chair took up too much room on a shipping barge or railroad for the comparitively small wholesale price it might fetch in a distant city. The specialized tools of the American chairmaker were: braces with small button-like heads and fixed spoon bits, palm-held wooden shaves for scooping out seat depressions, and the hook bladed chair-maker's knife.

CORNERING TOOL. Stanley No's. 28 & 29 flat metal 5½ in. long can opener-shaped scorp for rounding off the sharp edge of a freshly planed board. First appeared in 1909 catalog, sold for many years. Offered by dealers recently in the $10 to $20 price range.

CLOGGER, or Sabotmaker. As late as 1750 wooden shoes remained the working man's footwear of choice in much of Europe. In early France only the middle class could afford sabots, the entire peasantry literally went barefoot most of the year. English clogs were cheap leather-topped shoes, or sandals, with thick wooden soles. The word clog is derived from *clogge:* a stump or log, an impediment. In the 18th-Century engraving below we find French Sabot makers employing most of the tools of their trade.

Denis Diderot, 1752

COPELAND & CO. was owned and operated by four brothers whose plane-making experience dated back to 1820 Hartford, Connecticut. The Copeland brothers came to Norwich, Mass. during the 1840's. According to census records the firm employed 15 workers in 1855. Production for that year was $12,000 worth of wooden planes and the company ceased to operate thereafter.

DAVIS TOOL & LEVEL CO. (see page 90)

DENGELSHTOCK, a four piece scythe sharpening kit sometimes worn on the waist and carried into the field by workmen at harvest time. In Pennsylvania the pick-shaped anvil was called a dengle. It was carried in a cow horn along with the dengle hammer and a whetstone. Average price for a set in good condition is about $40.

J. DENISON of Saybrook, Connecticut operated a small but efficient tool-making shop employing about 6 workers who produced from 1,500 to 12,000 high quality wood-working planes a year between 1845 and 1866. G.W. Denison brought in outside partners in 1868 and ran the firm under his name until 1890.

HENRY DISSTON, an Englishman, came to this country in 1833 with his father (who died just three days after their arrival). A destitute 14 year old, Henry soon bound himself over as a saw-maker's apprentice. By the time he had reached eighteen he had been promoted to factory foreman. In 1840 Henry began producing his own line of saws in a rented cellar room. By the year 1856 "Henry Disston & Son" was winning gold medals in world wide competition with other saw manufacturers. The works had grown to cover eight acres at the original 30 by 60 foot Philadelphia, Penn. site. In the 1870's six hundred workers were employed at Disston's Keystone Saw Works and sheet steel production for saw blades totaled over thirty tons a week. By 1914 the plant had grown to cover fifty acres with sixty buildings housing 3,600 employees.

DOWELLING TOOLS take on a number of different forms. (also consult the plane section)

Edward Preston & Sons, Dowel Plate. ½ in. thick steel plate, 5½ in. long with 5 holes in sizes ¼ thru ½ in. dia. Dowels were made by driving square peg stock through successively smaller openings. This tool was recently offered at $18. Handwrought Sizing Plates sell for $15 - $25.

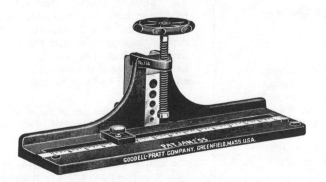

Goodell Pratt No. 114 Doweling Machine. A 10 lb. jig for accurately boring dowel pin holes. Patented Jan. 2, 1906. Auct. $35, Dlr. $65.

Stanley No. 77 Dowel & Rod Turning Machine. Black metal finish, weighs 14 lbs. These are scarce and sell for $175 to $225 each.

Stanley no. 59 Doweling Jig. Nickle plated clamp on tool with 5 guides. Dealer prices range from $15 to $25. Stanley No. 60 Same as above but has 9 guides.

Stanley No. 22 dowel Sharpener is a nickel plated cone that fits on the end of a drill. About 3 inches overall. Miniature Spoke or Dowel Pointers, similar to the Stanley model above, sell for $12 to $25 each and occasionally a brass one will bring more.

Spoke Pointers in larger sizes are usually factory made of iron, cone-shaped and up to 5 inches in length. Average dealer price is about $8.

FAKES. The same week that Leonard Bailey's new iron plane hit the market in the 1870's, a number of poor but skilled mechanics began to cast copies working directly from the originals. If one had access to a foundry and a machine shop it was far cheaper to make your own brass or iron woodworking plane than buy one at the going retail price of $5. Spiers Norris, a British plane making concern, offered finished iron or gunmetal castings of plane bodies and lever caps for sale to craftsmen in the early 1900's. Many beautiful copies were made using these factory provided components. When we are all dust as the Egyptians, who is really going to care? Probably no one, but today's tool collectors keep a sharp eye out for reproductions and avoid them like the plague.

Stanley's No. 1 smoothing plane is one of the most often copied examples. It's current $500 to $700 price range encourages both the evil and the innocent to try their hand at duplicating the scarce original. Solid wood squirrel-tailed carriage maker's planes are often reproduced, as well as tiny boxwood thumb planes.

Hand-forged broad axes and strap adzes are currently being produced for the antiques trade. They are of Spanish origin but have Germanic touch marks exactly like the originals of two centuries ago.

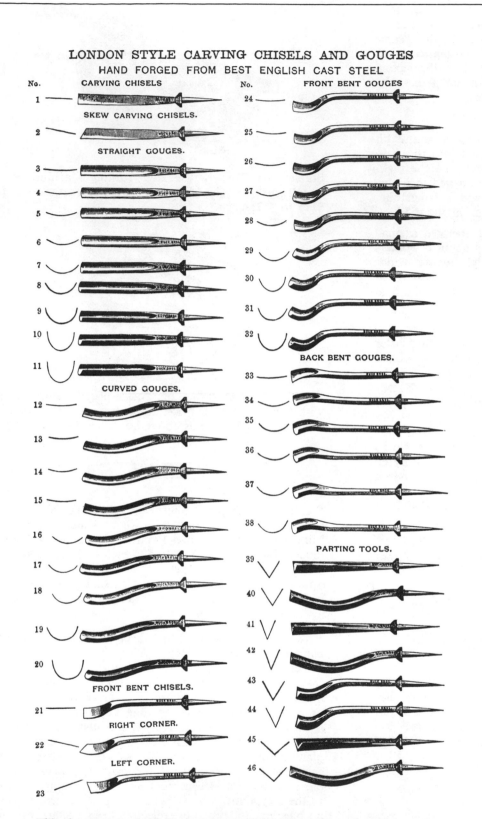

LONDON STYLE CARVING CHISELS AND GOUGES
HAND FORGED FROM BEST ENGLISH CAST STEEL

CARVING CHISELS
No. 1

SKEW CARVING CHISELS.
No. 2

STRAIGHT GOUGES.
No. 3, 4, 5, 6, 7, 8, 9, 10, 11

CURVED GOUGES.
No. 12, 13, 14, 15, 16, 17, 18, 19, 20

FRONT BENT CHISELS.
No. 21

RIGHT CORNER.
No. 22

LEFT CORNER.
No. 23

FRONT BENT GOUGES
No. 24, 25, 26, 27, 28, 29, 30, 31, 32

BACK BENT GOUGES.
No. 33, 34, 35, 36, 37, 38

PARTING TOOLS.
No. 39, 40, 41, 42, 43, 44, 45, 46

This chart was (and still is) used internationally by craftsmen ordering carving chisels by mail. They simply specified a size and pattern number. American artists and craftsmen generally preferred English brands of carving chisels and domestic brands of the heavier socket-type chisels and gouges. Popular British labels sold in the U.S. before 1900 were: *W. & S Butcher, Spear & Jackson, J. Howarth, I. Sorby, Ward & Payne* and last, but not least, *S.J. Addis* of London, which outsold all the others. The best American chisels of the 19th-Century were: *D.R. Barton, Buck Brothers, L.& J. White, Charles Buck, A.W. Crossman, Merrill & Wilder,* and *James Swan.*

BUTT CHISELS are stubby, beveled, straight-bladed, pocket-sized, all purpose carpenters chisels with sturdy socket handles. They are the same style as the plastic handled chisels sold in supermarkets today.

SOCKET FIRMER chisels have plain flat blades approx. 6 inches long. Often equipped with leather-tipped handles. They were the best selling style at the turn-of-the-century. Socket firmers could also be ordered with beveled edges or gouge blades, from $1/8$ to 2 inches wide.

PARING chisels with tang-type handles were used by craftsmen who needed a lighter weight, thinner-bladed tool. They could be ordered with socket handles in either straight or gouge style.

MILLWRIGHT chisels fall between socket firmers and framing chisels, with blades running from $7\frac{1}{2}$ to 10 inches in length.

SOCKET FRAMING chisels have rounded or thick bevel backs and are $7\frac{1}{2}$ to 10 inches long. They were a short-handled heavy-duty tool used in house and barn framing.

CARPENTER'S SLICKS are the largest of all chisels, often two or three feet long and up to 4 inches wide. These razor-sharp tools were made to be pushed with the arms or shoulder rather than struck with a mallet. The wooden socket handle terminates in a swollen-end knob.

CORNER or **PARTING** chisels were the most difficult to fabricate and most makers would not warrant them past the front door. The V-shaped cutting edge was available in $\frac{1}{2}$ in. thru $1\frac{1}{2}$ inch widths. The earliest corner chisels were of all-metal construction, but are not rare.

MORTISE chisels came in 3 styles: The common short-handled joiner's mortise with its straight, almost square ended blade. The Swan, or Goose-necked, lock-mortise-style that looks like a pry bar. The Twibil, a pick-like straight-bladed tool with a right angle socket handle at its center.

CARVING chisels are pictured at left and came in dozens of sizes and shapes, many with peculiar names like bent spoon, fish tail, etc. They are the lightest of the chisels above, only hobby, or wood-block chisels are smaller.

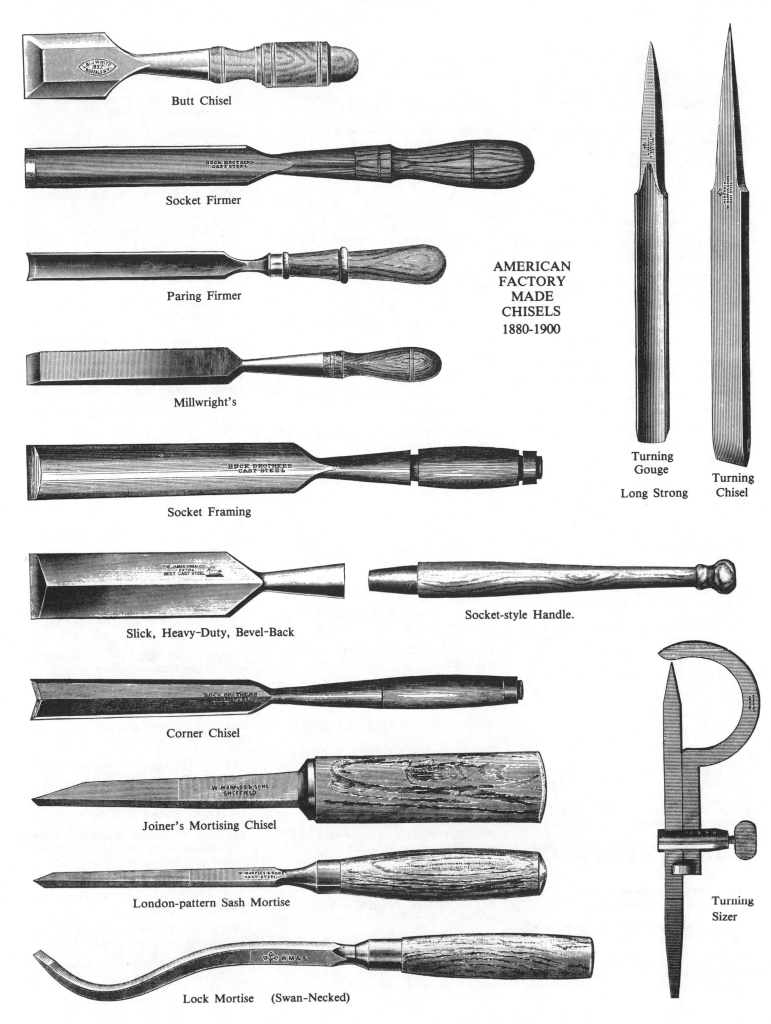

Butt Chisel

Socket Firmer

Paring Firmer

Millwright's

Socket Framing

AMERICAN
FACTORY
MADE
CHISELS
1880-1900

Turning
Gouge

Turning
Chisel

Long Strong

Slick, Heavy-Duty, Bevel-Back

Socket-style Handle.

Corner Chisel

Joiner's Mortising Chisel

London-pattern Sash Mortise

Lock Mortise   (Swan-Necked)

Turning
Sizer

This Stanley No. 96 plane-shaped Chisel Gauge was made to raise a shaving for blind nailing. It sold for 20 cents in 1907. Today's collector might pay $200.

ADDIS No. 40 curved V parting chisel. Octagonal handle, brass ferrule. $18

ADDIS set in canvas roll, 40 extra nice carving chisels. auct. $300

J. B. ADDIS fine set of 13 spoon bit & curved gouges. Boxwood handles. auct. $130

ADDIS set of 14 pattern maker' gouges with tear shaped handles. auct. $122

S. J. ADDIS set of 20 carving gouges with Masonic emblem marking. auct. $136

S. J. ADDIS, London. Set of 8 long-bent carving gouges with hickory handles. $100

ASSORTED BRANDS flat bevel edge chisels, ⅛ to 1 in. wide. Buck, Douglas, Parr, Witherby, Hobson, Tillitson, and others. Half are socket type. 26 pcs. $135

AUCTION LOT of early British made chisels. W. Weldon (1774-1788), P. Law (1787-1833), J. Cam (1781-1838), Manners & Cam etc., 6 chisels. auct . $140

W. C. BAILEY, Sag Harbor Tool Co. Carpenter's slick, 3 in. wide. $35

D. R. BARTON set of 17 matched carving chisels with fruitwood handles. Bent spoon, fish tail, & gouges. auct. $272

Set of 13 as above, some straight. $75

D. R. BARTON Shipwright's slick, 3 in. wide. Original cherry handle. Fine. $60

BUCK BROS. Cast Steel. No. 8 carving chisel. $14

BUCK BROS. wood turning sizing chisel, 21 in. overall. $65 18 in. $25 to $50

BUCK BROS. framing chisel, 1½ in. laid on steel edge, socket handle. $18

BUCK BROS. unused set of 12 paring gouges, from ⅛ to 2 in. widths. auct. $180

BUCK BROS. carpenter's slick 3½ in., orig. handle. 32 in. overall. $60

Another as above, 2½ in. no handle. $35

BUCK BROS. socket firmer chisel with 2 in. bevel edge. $20 Socket gouge, inside bevel. $20

BUCK BROS. set of assorted gouges with inside bevels. ⅝ to 2 in. wide. $120

BUCK BROS. paring chisel with step down handle. ¾ in. x 13 in. $16

BUCK BROS. socket paring gouge with inside bevel, ⅛ in. width. $12

BUCK BROS. outside bevel 2 in. gouge, tang handle. $18 1 inch. $14

BUCK BROS. Excelsior No. 4 butt chisel, 1¾ in. auct. $20

BUCK BROS. turning chisels, set of 8 with tang style handles. $65

Same as above, 20 assorted turning chisels. $75

CHARLES BUCK socket firmer, straight beveled. $10

JOHN BULL, Sheffield. straight 1 inch chisel with brass ferruled maple handle. $12

W. BUTCHER heavy socket handled framing chisel, 1½ in. wide. $15

JAMES CAM joiner's mortise chisel, ⅜ in. $12 ⅝ in. $15

CARPENTER'S SLICKS assorted, with replacement handles. auct. $45 – $65

COLQUHOUN & CADMAN, Sheffield. Improved style lock mortise, heavy duty, ½ in. x 21 in. $40

CORNER CHISELS by various makers, all with socket handles. Powell & Co., Buhl & Sons, Ohio Tool Co., McIntosh-Heather, etc. 1 inch size. $25 to $30 ea.

CORNER CHISELS auction lot of 4 very good ¾ to 1¼ in. tools. $90

CORNER CHISELS, early all-metal, up to 1 inch wide. auct. $20 - $30 ea.

CORNER CHISEL all brass. Unusual. auct. $50

A. W. CROSSMAN cast steel slick, 2 in. solid metal handle. auct. $50

Another, 3 in. maple handle. Dlr. $55

DIAMIC by Aaron Hiblock. Unused set of bent shank paring gouges in labeled box. ⅛ thru 1 in. widths. auct. $112

DASCO all steel bevel-edge 1 in. chisel with decorative shaft. $9

P. DICKENSON cast steel slick, 4 in. wide, orig. handle. $45 - $65

DISSTON lathe turning chisels, 16 in., set of 8 assorted. $40

DOUGLAS MFG. CO. parting tool, ½ in., socket handled. $30

DOUGLAS MFG. CO. carpenter's 3 in. wide slick. auct. $35 - 4 inch, Dlr. $75

GEO. FARR socket handled corner chisel, 1¼ in. framing size. $42

FIRMER CHISELS, assorted brands of socket handled gouges. $5 ea.

FULTON TOOL CO. corner chisel, 1¼ in. with socket handle. $20 - $25

ISAAC GREAVES common joiner's mortise chisel with ½ in. blade. $14

ISAAC GREAVES paring chisel, 2 in. straight blade, octagon handle, 20 in. overall. $56

ISAAC GREAVES set of 10 tang-handle bench chisels from ⅛ to 2 in. wide. $250

IOHN GREEN (1781-1800) straight flat 2⅛ in. blade with tang (no handle). auct. $46

GREENLINE socket paring chisel, ⅜ in. x 12½ in. $9

S. HADCOCK, Watertown. Rugged 1⅛ in. corner chisel. $30

HANDWROUGHT all-metal chisels, mostly home-made gouges, ½ to 2 in. $8 - $20

HASBORN, South Hampton. Swan-neck lock mortise, 16 in. long. $56

HAYDEN handwrought 4 inch wide slick. $65

HINSDALE MFG. CO. socket mortise, ⅝ in. $12

HORTON & ARNOLD carpenter's slick, 4 in. $55

JAMES HOWARTH swan neck lock mortise with laid on steel cutting edge. $45 - $55

J. HOWARTH, Sheffield. Set of 6 pattern maker's gouges, ¼ to 1¼ in. auct. $112

THOS. IBBOTSON & CO. (1837-1879) swan-neck lock mortise, 23 in. long. $50 - $65

Wm. JACKSON set of 6 paring chisels with Masonic emblem. Auct. $28

C.E. JENNINGS NO. 191 boxed set of firmer chisels, ⅛ to 2 in. $85

KEEN KUTTER bevel edge butt chisel, unused. 1¾ in. width. $20

KEEN KUTTER corner chisel with ¾ in. V-blade, socket handle. Mint. $45

KEEN KUTTER socket firmer, ¾ in. beveled blade is shiny new. $12 Another (rusty) $6

KEEN KUTTER bevel edge socket firmer chisels in sizes 1 in. to 2 in. Unused. $25 ea. (slightly pitted) $18 ea.

KEEN KUTTER, rare 3½ inch wide carpenter's slick. Brand new, never sharpened. Asking $175

Wm. MARPLES goose neck 19 in. lock mortise with long sweep. $50

W. MARPLES & SONS swan-neck lock mortise chisels in 18 to 22 inch lengths. $45-$65

MARPLES paring gouge with octagonal handle. ¾ inch. $17

MARPLES set of 10 turning chisels & gouges. Auct. $90

MARPLES carving gouges, ⅜ to 1 in. $15 ea.

W. MARPLES pattern maker's trowel-shank paring chisels. Set of 14, up to 2 in. wide. $250

MARSDEN BROTHERS, Sheffield. Swan-neck lock mortise, approx. 20 in. overall. Perfect $75

A. MATHIESON, Glasgow & Edinburgh. Swan-neck socket mortise, 23 in. overall. $50

MAW & STALEYS common short straight bladed joiner's mortise chisels. Set of (7) $100-$150

P. MERRILL & CO. socket firmer gouge, 2 in with outside bevel. $15

P. MERRILL Cast Steel. Socket mortise chisel, 14 in. long incl. hickory handle. $12

P. MERRILL & CO. corner chisel, 13/16 size. $30

MILLERS FALLS Hobby carving set of 5 small lino chisels with palm grip handles. Circa 1950 in orig. wooden box. $15

MILLERS FALLS set of 6 rosewood handled carving chisels in box. $35

C.I. MIX & CO. carpenter's slick. Auct. $35

MORTISE CHISELS common short straight joiner's heavy bladed style. Various makers, Underhill, Sorby, etc. $8-$16

MOULSON BROS. set of 7 long paring gouges, each with a unique inlaid exotic wood handle. Auct. $180

MOULSON BROTHERS giant turning gouge, 18½ in. long. $12

P.H. NEISS set of 4 framing chisels, ½ to 2 in. wide. $60

NEW HAVEN EDGE TOOL CO. socket mortise chisel. Pat. 1891. ½ in. by 14 in $11

NEW HAVEN EDGE TOOL CO. carpenter's slick, 3 in. wide. Auct. $35–$55

OHIO TOOL CO. socket handled parting tool. V-shape, 1 in. $25

OHIO TOOL CO. NO. 501 set of 6 bevel edge socket firmer chisels, size ¼ thru 2 in. Excellent, in orig. wooden box. $125

OHIO TOOL CO. socket mortise chisel, ⅜ in. wide. 14¾ in. long. $7

ONIONS & CO. swan neck socket mortise. 20 in., cast steel edge. $40

PATTERNMAKER'S paring gouges, group of 8 inconel type with step down shank and brass ferruled boxwood handles. Sizes ⅛ thru 1⅛ in. by various makers. $175

PATTERNMAKER'S set of 60 assorted ⅛ in. to 2 in. gouges, fishtail, spoon, straight & bent. By Buck, Greaves, Sorby, Moulson, etc. Includes 4 drawer chest, 32 in. wide, 22 in. deep and 17 in. tall. $850

PEXTO carpenter's slick, 3 in. wide, 30 inches long. $55

PEXTO socket mortise chisel, ¼ in. wide x 15 in. long. $6

P.S. & W. fine old cherry handled carpenter's slick 3½ in. wide. Auct. 1984. $125

P.S. & W. socket handled corner chisel, ¾ in. size. $20 1½ in. $32

H. PORTER & STROBRIDGE shipbuilder's shallow handwrought, tapered gouge. 2 7/16 in. wide. $35

ROCKFORD BIT CO. Kokomo, Indiana. Carpenter's slick, 3½ in. wide. $45

G. RYAN, 312 Euston Rd. Set of 12 English carving gouges with octagon boxwood handles. ⅛ in to 1 in. $325

SHIPBUILDER'S Block and tackle making gouges. 1½ in. to 2½ in. wide, socket handles. $24 to $30 ea.

SHIPWRIGHT'S huge 4 in. socket gouge, 16 inches long, no handle. $28

SLICK, in solid brass. 4 in. wide by 14 inch long blade. Mahog. handle. $90

SLICK CLAPBOARD. From Upper Maine. One piece wrought iron with 6 in. by 6 in. cutting blade. $60

Another with T-handle and 5 in. x 5 in. blade. $40

Others with hickory handles and 3 in. to 4 in. blades. $40-$45 ea.

SLICK, Penn. type with D-style shovel handles and 4 inch cutters. $40-$60 ea.

STANLEY No. 20 socket firmer 2 in. $20

STANLEY No. 40 bevel edge pocket chisel. ¾ in. x 9⅝ in. $18

STANLEY No. 60 butt chisel, ¾ in. with plastic handle. $5 1½ in. $6

STANLEY No. 96 blind-nail chisel gauge. $170-$225. Auct. & Dlrs.

STANLEY No. 450 butt chisel, socket style, leather capped hickory handle. $4

STONEMASON'S set of 8 assorted solid chisels with serrated edges. $40

JAMES SWAN carpenter's slick. 3 in. $50 4 in. $65

I. SORBY firmer chisel with octagonal boxwood handle. 1 in. wide. $17

I. SORBY Joiner's straight, short, 7/16 in. mortise chisel. $20 ½ in. $12 ⅜ in. $15

I. SORBY with jester mark (circa 1810) Swan neck socket handled mortise chisels $35-$55

I. SORBY paring chisels, ¾ in. to 1¼ in. $17 ea.

D. TAFT hand-forged clapboard slick with shovel style handle. Auct. $80

HENRY TAYLOR, Sheffield, set of 6 bevel edged paring chisels, ¼ in. to 1½ in. Like new. Auct. $147

M.B. TILDEN, Warranted. Early hand-wrought socket handled corner chisel. 1 in. by 12 in. $45

TILLINGHAST all metal shovel-handled slick $50

TILLOTSON, Sheffield. Common joiner's mortise. $10

T. TURNER & CO., Sheffield. Socket handled swan-neck lock mortise chisel. Auct. $35

TURNER'S SIZING CHISELS with hook end, assorted brands. $40-$55 ea.

UNDERHILL EDGE TOOL CO. carpenter's slick. 3½ in. Auct. $55-$75

UNDERHILL shipbuilder's gouge. Socket handle. 2⅝ in. (rough) $20

G.W. UNDERHILL & CO., Nashua, N.H. 4 inch carpenter's slick. $80

UNION HURD "Sampson" short handled 3 inch slick. Auct. $15-$35

WARREN EDGE TOOL set of 10 Blue Brand socket firmer chisels with bevel edge blades. ⅛ in. to 2 in. wide, original box. $110

T. H. WITHERBY, Jessops Patent, master socket handle which accepts 9 accompanying straight and gouge shanks. Set $125

T. H. WITHERBY No. 882 set of 12 bevel edge socket firmer chisels in orig. box. auct. $155

WARD, (11) chisels & gouges with London pattern boxwood handles. auct. $210

WARD (2) mortise chisels, one is swan necked. auct. $68

L.H. WATTS, curved 3 inch slick-sized gouge, long handle. auct. $85

L. & I.J. WHITE set of 10 matching patternmaker's gouges, 18 inches in length. Brass ferrules and fancy handles. Fine cond. Auct. $300

Stanley No. 28 cornering tool, used by patternmakers and woodworkers to round off sharp corners. Sold for decades at 40 cents. Today's price range $10-$20.

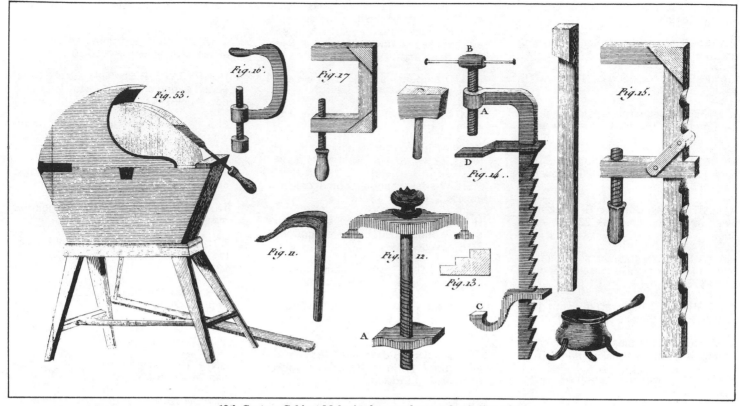

18th-Century Cabinet Maker's clamps, glue pot & grinding wheel.

M. ALDRICH, Lowell, Mass. Cabinet maker's wooden screw clamp. $14

COLT, Batavia, N. Y. pair of 2 ft. bar clamps in iron with cam lock slide. $20

CRAMP BOX, early dovetailed rectangular box, all wood construction, with a handled, threaded wood screw at one end. auct. $25

18th-Century type giant wood clamp with duck's head profile. Handscrew at end forces jaws shut. 23 in. long. $28

18th-Century type chamfered maple cabinet maker's clamp. $17

FLOOR CLAMP, lever-action iron bar 18 in. long, pulls tongue and groove flooring into position. $15-$18

FLOORING CLAMP, arch-framed, clamp-shaped like a wine press with a wooden T-handle screw. Auct. $70

H. E. HATCH, Dexter, Me., 1884 Pat. floor clamp in original red and black paint. Auct. $55

SAM L. WINSLOW, Worcester, Mass., Pat. May 15, 1866. Flooring clamp with two hooks and a ratchet handle on screw shaft. $40

HANDSCREW, brass handles and screws with conventional mahogany jaws. Auct. $75

HANDSCREW, unmarked wooden clamp with 6½ inch throat. $14

HANDSCREWS, small solid wood variety with 3 to 8 in. capacity. $5 to $10 ea.

BLISS MFG. CO., Pawtucket, R. I. No. 4 handscrew clamp. Opens to 13 in. $25

HARTFORD CO. all metal furniture clamp with a 4¾ in. throat. Opens to 12 inches. $10

HOOD & RICE, Makers, Valley Falls, R. I. No. 12 wood screw clamp for 5 in. stock. $11

INSTRUMENT MAKER'S pair of 21 inch wooden screw clamps. 2 Cylindrical disks are threaded on a wooden shaft. Dark red patina. $65

JORGENSON handscrew, wood jaws, steel screws. 6 in. throat. $10

N. LYON MFG., Albany, N.Y. Wheelwright's cast iron felloe clamp with turnscrew shaft and yoke base. $22

MITRE JACK: A triangular-jawed, wooden screw clamp which allows mitres to be trued by shooting a hand-held plane across the face of the angular jaws. Auct. $50 - $95

MITRE JACK, in Bird's-eye Maple. 24 in. long with metal screw shaft. $135

MITRE JACK, beechwood body is 17 in. long by 6 in. high. Mint cond. $140

MITRE JACK in solid mahogany, 28 in. overall. $98 As above, in dark beech $98

Another with rosewood base, brass screw. $75

Another maple, 3 feet long. $150-$190

Another, oak and walnut, 17 in. $125

CINTI. TOOL CO. huge metal C-clamp. 10 x 14 inch capacity. $15

REDMAN'S PAT. Feb 8, 1885. Long handled flooring jack. Auct. $30

SARGENT & CO. wooden screw clamp for 5 in. stock. $7

W. F. TARBELL, Milford, N.H. Pat. July 17, 1888. Cabinent amker's bar clamp, wooden double screw. Auct. $25

SAW CLAMP (see Vise, saw)

J. STAMM, Mount Joy, Lan. Co. PA. Instrument maker's dowel shaped wooden clamp with wooden disk jaws on threaded shaft. Auct. $130

STANLEY No. 203 bench clamp. Black japanned triangle frame with wing nut screw. $18-$20

E. A. STEARNS pair of door clamps on notched steel bars. 32 inch capacity. Cranks have wooden handles. $25

E. C. STEARNS floor board jack. $22

UNIVERSAL STYLE combination clamp with metal jaws and central screw having a wooden handle. $27

VIOLIN MAKER'S single post, knob top, hardwood screw clamp. $6

Double and Triple post types. $12 ea.

Set of 13 Violin makers clamps. $85

WHEELWRIGHT'S felloe clamp. Huge U-shaped handwrought frame. Thumbscrew top. $22

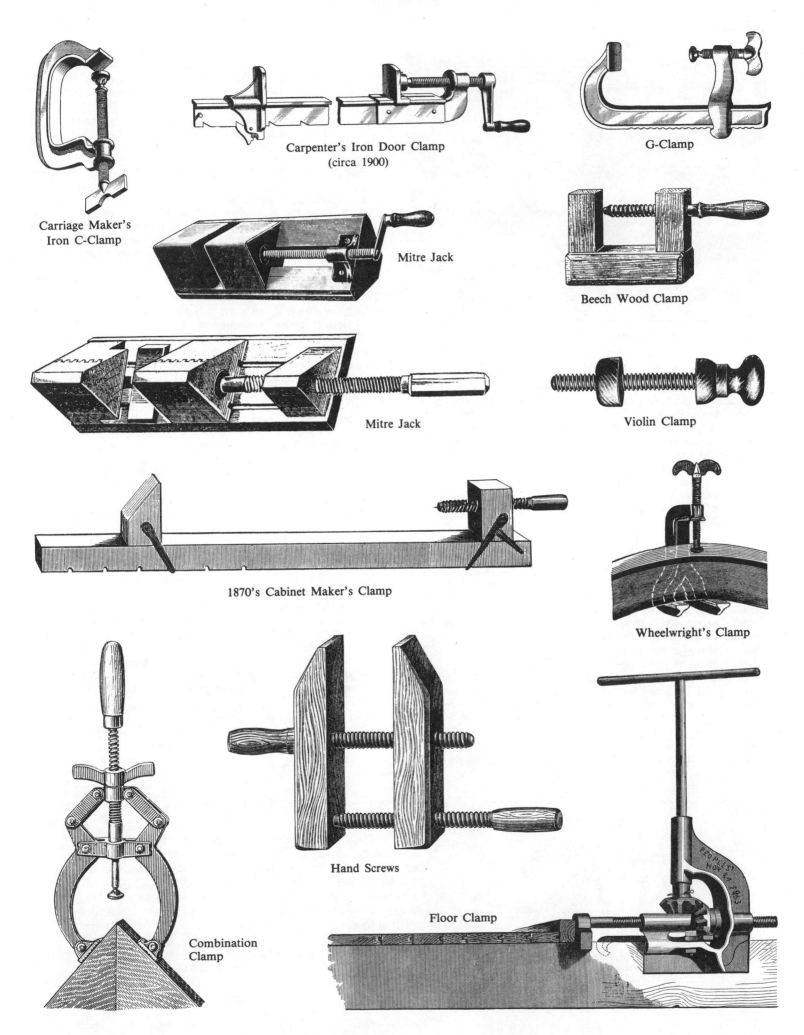

Carriage Maker's
Iron C-Clamp

Carpenter's Iron Door Clamp
(circa 1900)

G-Clamp

Mitre Jack

Beech Wood Clamp

Mitre Jack

Violin Clamp

1870's Cabinet Maker's Clamp

Wheelwright's Clamp

Combination
Clamp

Hand Screws

Floor Clamp

Cobblers at work. An American cottage industry of the early 1800's.

In early America it was common for farmers to trade room and board to itenerant shoemakers in exchange for the family's annual footwear. (If you wore out a pair of shoes in less than a year's time you literally went bare-foot). A cobbler following this line of work was said to be "whipping the cat". His set of tools was called a "kit".

Shoemaking began with the leather tanning process. Salted down hides were purchased by tannery agents from farmers and cattlemen and placed in large vats filled with lime water to cure until hair and loose skin could be easily scraped off with a long dull fleshing knife. (Not a pleasant task because of the odor and accompanying hordes of flies.) After a subsequent cleaning by soaking in saltwater the hides were tanned in an acid solution made from the ground-up bark of oak or hemlock trees. In early America bark gathering was an important source of cash income for the rural population. Special tools called barking spuds were fashioned to make quick work of stripping felled trees, which were often left to rot after removal of their bark. After soaking in tannic acid the hides were dried in the open air and softened with special oils to complete the curing.

The actual shoemaking process could have begun in any of several common locations. In a colonial cordwainer's cottage, at a cobbler's shoe repair shop, in the back room of an uptown bootery, on the second floor of a large New England shoe factory, or on a farmer's porch. Tongue and toe pieces called *vamps*, along with rear quarters and insoles were cut to fit the customer's personal last using a half circle-shaped leather knife. (In factories dies were used to stamp out these pieces by the thousands.) Before the invention of the sewing machine shoe tops were stitched together using a hog bristle "needle" with a thread of waxed linen. Assembled "uppers" were stretched over the wooden last and around its bottom to cover the edges of the primary insole. Short wooden pegs were hammered through both layers of leather into the underside of the form. In factories automatic nailing and pegging machines were employed. The cobbler used a pair of stretching pliers with with a built-in tack hammer to accomplish this task with one hand. (Shoemakers hammers with their quaintly-shaped large flat heads were employed mostly to flatten seams and beat soles into shape.) Temporary tacks which held the insole in position on the last were then removed and the outer sole and heel were either nailed or pegged thru the whole assembly with longer willow pegs. After a final trimming and shaping with various knives and shaves, the wooden last was removed and pegs were filed flush with a long handled peg cutting rasp which reached inside the assembled shoe or boot. An eyelet-installing tool or machine completed the manufacturing process which was followed by the liberal application of a beeswax and beargrease waterproofing compound.

Shoe lasts were not widely used in the making of boots and shoes until about 1785. Prior to their invention one's "fit" was largely a matter of trial and error. In the early 1800's an employee of the Springfield Armory invented a lathe which could turn gunstocks, duck decoys, and shoe lasts.

Anyone who has ever mended a sock using an old-fashioned darning egg can appreciate how wooden shoe lasts make easier the task of stitching together a pair of leather shoe tops and soles. Maple, Persimmon and a few other rock-hard fruitwoods are the only varieties suitable for making these forms. Shoe lasts often were discarded long before they wore out. These hard-rock maple forms usually outlasted production of any one style. Fashions have changed almost daily in the American shoe industry since the mid 1850's. Each different shoe design required a complete set of about 2 dozen pairs of lasts in size variations of 1/3 of an inch, starting with the smallest standard infant last which is 4 inches long.

A cord of wood (usually from New Hampshire) was enough to make 1,000 shoe lasts. The timber was sawn into 12 inch lengths and seasoned under cover, in the open air, for two full years. The use of artifical heat by kiln drying was thought to destroy the "life" of the wood and caused lasts to crack under constant use. When properly seasoned the rough blocks were put in a lathe-like machine which carved each last exactly to the form of a "model" (which had been skillfully hand-made by a master craftsman who specialized in this art). The duplicating lathe worked like an engraver's pantograph, enlarging or reducing any number of sizes from the foot sculptor's model. As each last left the machine it was finished by hand with heels rounded and toes shaped to conform to the fashion of the day. A final polishing was performed by workmen employing high speed wooden wheels covered with quartz dust glued to a flannel covering. After polishing the lasts were dipped in linseed oil and packed 20 pairs to a bag for delivery.

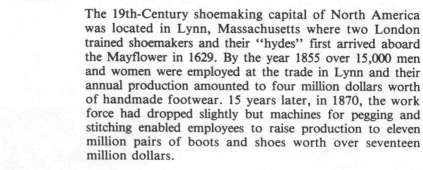

The 19th-Century shoemaking capital of North America was located in Lynn, Massachusetts where two London trained shoemakers and their "hydes" first arrived aboard the Mayflower in 1629. By the year 1855 over 15,000 men and women were employed at the trade in Lynn and their annual production amounted to four million dollars worth of handmade footwear. 15 years later, in 1870, the work force had dropped slightly but machines for pegging and stitching enabled employees to raise production to eleven million pairs of boots and shoes worth over seventeen million dollars.

AUCTION LOT of 20 assorted old shoe-maker's tools including many brass ferruled and a lignum vitae burnisher. $45

AWLS and trimming knives. Lot of (20) assorted with brass ferrules. Dlr. $45

AWLS, wrench chuck type. Pegging and sewing. $2 - $3 ea.

BELCHER BROS. & CO., New York. Sliding foot measure, boxwood. auct. $25

BENCH, primitive plank seat & back with hooded top drawer section and 3 large drawers under bench. auct. $440

BENCH, European clogger's short 26 inch bench plus (3) hook-end block knives and (24) cobbler's tools. Dlr. $435

BENCH, pulpit-shaped top section has arched opening, 1 drawer and 2 shelves. Backless carved plank seat. 3 large lower drawers. Full assortment tools. Dlr. $1,350

BENCH, beautiful, Shaker-made, chair-seat-style, 3 legged cobbler's bench from New Lebanon brethern's shop. 7 drawers in top section, one under bench. Includes 18 tools. auct. $3,300

BENCH, working cobbler's bench and complete set of tools including several iron last stands. Round leather bottom seat, 2 open shelves, dowel legs. Dlr. $445

BENCH, plank-style straddle bench, no seat. 3 legged with 5 spice drawers on low top section. auct. $85

COBBLER'S HAMMERS, common shapes, factory made, $9 to $18 each. Unique shapes, $20 to $50 ea.

HAMMER, "Giant" German-style cobbler's hammer with 3 inch head and short side straps on handle. Dlr. $32

HAMMER, leather softening hammer with round and square faces. Very softly rounded corners. Dlr. $50

HAMMER, museum quality cobbler's hammer of the early 1800's. Initialed and decorated head, original handle. Dlr. $75

HEAD KNIFE, C.S. Osborne & Co. with half-moon blade. $18

LONDON MADE cobbler's kit. Includes awls, cutters, edgers, burnishers, punches and hammers. (51) items. Dlr. $225

C. S. OSBORNE & CO., Newark, N.J., Est'd 1826. Leather knife, half moon 5 inch blade. $16 - $20

OSBORNE & Co., Newark, N.J. Est. 1825. Rosewood and brass pistol-handled leather cutting gauge, or slitter. Dlr. $48

PEGGING AWLS, wrench chuck type. $2 - $3 ea.

PLIERS & HAMMER, cobbler's combination tool. $12

SNELL & ATHERTON iron leather shave with adjustable fence and 4 cutters. $18

Lathe for turning shoe lasts. Circa 1850. Invented by Thomas Blanchard.

SHOELAST JACK, H-shaped wooden frame 23 inches tall by 11 in. wide. Iron pin on end of leg holds top of shoe last. Center wratchet winding shaft tightens leather strap around last. $25 - $40

SHOE STRETCHER Patented Oct. 30, 1917. Hand sized oval-shaped iron frame has an end ball which is forced thru a wrought ring to stretch leather. Plier-type hand grip. $20

Shoemaker as pictured in Prang's "Occupations & Trades" series of 1874.

The terms *compass* and *dividers* have been used interchangeably for over a hundred years. The modern definition of dividers is that of a small compass used for measuring purposes. A compass is most often thought of as a scribing or drawing tool. Calipers are really curved-legged dividers, and are only used for measuring objects. (see page 34)

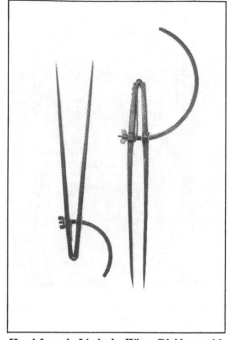

Hand-forged 24 inch Wing Dividers with Ram's Horn nuts. $100 each at auction.

ASSORTED factory made compasses and dividers, by the following makers: Sargent, Peck Stow & Wilcox, H&R Boker, John Parson, Starret Tools, & Goodell Pratt. Most are wing type, 6 in. to 12 in. tall. $4 to $8 ea.

ASSORTED metal wing dividers with round copper or brass hinge tops. auct. $8 ea.

ASSORTED lot of 6 steel dividers from machine shop. All under 6 in. $15 lot

BEAM COMPASS, ebony bar is 26 in. long, has block shaped brass trammel points. $30

(see Trammel Point heading on page 213 for more examples)

BENTWOOD early primitive compass, approx. 12 inches tall with points driven into bottom of each carved leg. Wedge adjusted center wing or rod. (Top is splintered) $65

BENTWOOD 22 in. compass with wedge thru one leg against top of 15 inch cross bar. auct. $175

BRASS pencil compass dated Dec. 19, 1871. Wing type with thumbscrew adj. 5 in. long. Dainty. $25

BRASS dividers with 7 inch long sliding steel points. Wing curves to above top. 14 in. tall. $40

BRASS wing compass, 8½ in. long, steel points. Nicely made English piece. auct. $55

BRASS wing dividers with 16 inch legs. Very fine, showy item. $185

BRITISH made iron wing compass. 14 inches long, traditional shoulder notches and chamfers. $35

CHERRY wing dividers, 16 in. tall with wrought thumbscrew and points. Wooden pinned top joint. Extra wide 1¾ in. wing. $135

COOPER'S bentwood oak bow compass, 12 in. tall. Wood threads are well worn auct. $90

COOPER'S compass, European, circa 1730. Square legs, turned wooden center turnbuckle. Typical bentwood construction. $240

Another as above, but with finer turned details and ferruled leg tips. $360

FRENCH cooper's compass, all wood, bent type, small size. auct. $135

FRENCH carpenter's decorated iron compass made from flat sheet stock with twisted legs starting midway up and terminating in long fine points. 33 inches tall. Dated 1737, "Jesus Maria, Joseph" inscription. auct. $592

Another pair in the same twisted sheet stock style, 22 in. long. auct. $157

Wm FRIEDRICKS metal dividers, 11 inch. $10

HAND-FORGED 18th-Century iron wing dividers with heart shaped wing nut. 11 in. overall. $25 16 in. $45

HAND-FORGED 19th-Century iron compasses. Standard wing thru leg with thumbscrew. 3 layer top hinge, chamfered legs. 10 in. $35 12 in. $40 14 in. $45 22 in. $55

HANDWROUGHT from buggy top frame and joint. 21 in. long wing divider. $25

HILGER & CO. hand-forged wing dividers. 13 inch legs, 5 leaf top hinge. $25

HANDWROUGHT wing dividers, 17 in. long. Wing-tip ends in a round knob finial, well past the top of compass. Auct $30

HANDWROUGHT dividers, (not wing type). 18 in. long. Head has 5 layer friction disk with brass spacers. Finely made. $60

HANDWROUGHT iron wing dividers, American, dated March, 1870. Thumbscrew adj., 12 in. long. Square shoulders, small leaf hinge. $70

Wm. JOHNSON CO., Newark, N. J. factory made iron wing dividers with 23 inch square-topped rod legs. $25 12 inch size, steel. $12

MANNBACH BROS. massive wooden cooper's dividers. auct. $350

PRIMITIVE solid walnut wing dividers, 13 in. Finer quality. auct. $95

PRIMITIVE wooden dividers, 25 in. to 30 in. length. Plain, no chamfers. $25 - $50

PRIMITIVE wooden wing compass with spike tipped 28 inch legs. Fine patina. $90

PRIMITIVE dark hardwood dividers in wishbone shape (not wing type). Bark still on backs of legs. 26 in. long, iron ferrules. $150

W. SCHOLLHORN & CO., New Haven, Ct. "Excelsior" 9½ inch wing dividers with unique locking feature. $16

SHIPBUILDER'S compass dated 1878. Square steel with chamfered edges, blending to round lower legs, 24 in. overall. $95

SIECO brand solid cherry compass with brass wing and trim. 24 inches long. $85

STANLEY No. 30 angle divider. Nickel plated iron T-square with 2 angle dividing arms linked to center. Auct. $25 - $40

STANLEY No. 31 angle divider in rosewood. $65

STANLEY No. 57 nickel plated 8 inch wing compass/divider. $10

L. S. STARRETT No. 90 nickel plated wing divider. 8 in. long with extra set of long and curved style legs. (circa 1915) $30

L.E. STIMMEL stamped. Forged wing dividers 18 inches long. Superb workmanship & condition. auct. $30

O. STODDARD, Pat. Aug. 27, 1872. Boxed set incl. brass wing compass with both style legs. $30

WALNUT wing compass, 24 inches long. Hinge is 2 inches down the side of the offset left leg. Superior workmanship. auct. $100

WHEELWRIGHT'S iron wing dividers with 22 inch legs. Thumbscrew adjust. $75

WHEELWRIGHT'S huge hand-forged wing compass with chamfered top and rounded legs. 30 inches overall with 18 inch curved wing. $125

WOODEN wing dividers a full 38 inches in length. Chamfered legs, handwrought trim. Clean and shiny. $95

Others as above, in cherry, mahogany, etc. 20 in. to 33 in. long. $90 to $100

W. & C. WYNN (Birmingham, England, 1796-1887). Highly decorative dividers forged with concentric rings on hinge and 6½ inch moulded detail legs. $35

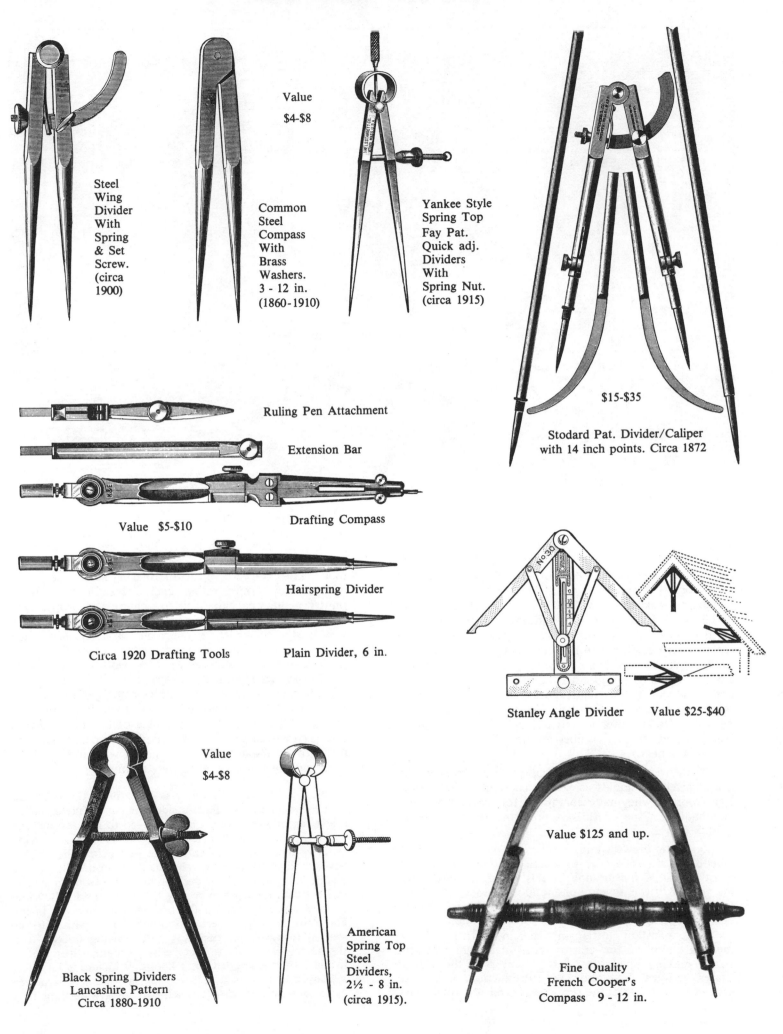

Steel Wing Divider With Spring & Set Screw. (circa 1900)

Common Steel Compass With Brass Washers. 3 - 12 in. (1860-1910)

Value $4-$8

Yankee Style Spring Top Fay Pat. Quick adj. Dividers With Spring Nut. (circa 1915)

$15-$35

Stodard Pat. Divider/Caliper with 14 inch points. Circa 1872

Ruling Pen Attachment

Extension Bar

Value $5-$10

Drafting Compass

Hairspring Divider

Circa 1920 Drafting Tools

Plain Divider, 6 in.

Stanley Angle Divider

Value $25-$40

Value $4-$8

Black Spring Dividers Lancashire Pattern Circa 1880-1910

American Spring Top Steel Dividers, 2½ - 8 in. (circa 1915).

Value $125 and up.

Fine Quality French Cooper's Compass 9 - 12 in.

Denis Diderot, 1752   Courtesy Dover Publications

As illustrated in the circa 1750 engraving above, early coopers needed only a few basic tools to ply their craft. Many European cooperage concerns operated in open-air city markets or under the archways of municipal buildings. American coopers most often worked in sheds or barn-like structures.

Barrel making was a 3,000 year old trade at the birth of Christ. Pliny, the Roman naturalist, gives the Piedmontese credit for inventing wooden wine casks which replaced their earthenware jars and animal skin containers. Early Egyptian merchants shipped grain in hoop-bound wooden containers and since then nearly every product under the sun has been transported in barrels. Southern plantation owners shipped their produce to Northern cities in casks. Other states moved apples, nails, beef, pork, fish, flower, sugar, cranberries and laundry soap in these containers.

There were two kinds of coopers: *Wet Coopers* who made barrels for liquids using oak, chestnut or beech; and *Dry Coopers* who made containers for transporting dry merchandise. Pine or fir was preferred for these lesser quality barrels.

Domestic brewers and distillers employed thousands of coopers. In 1866 beer production alone required the construction of five million barrels. Whiskey output for the year 1870 was seventy-one million gallons. The West India rum and sugar trade kept both British and Yankee based cooperages going full-time for several decades.

This constant unflagging demand finally led to mechanization of the entire trade. Over 400 different barrel making inventions were patented in the United States between 1844 and 1883. Production became so efficient that by 1880 the cost of a barrel was only 32¢.

The best barrel staves were those cleft with a curved **froe.** The process of splitting the wood naturally along its grain made staves much less likely to warp at some point after assembly. A **side axe** was used to narrow the ends of rough staves before a trip to the shaving horse where they were further refined with a curved **draw knife.** Next a **jointer plane** was employed to achieve the proper side angle on each stave, for a watertight fit. **Stave gauges** were used as templates for the radius curve and edge pitch on large storage vats and other containers where an exact measure of liquid was specified. Most work on stave joints was however, done strictly by eye. After the jointing process the staves were set up in an assembly jig and various sized truss hoops were used to pull the whole thing together tightly. Next came a steaming of the inside surface with a **cresset,** or crude stove, fueled by woodshavings and sprinkled with water. The truss hoops were further tightened and the still open ends were sawn off.

Next a chime, or bevel, was cut around the inner lip with a **cooper's adze.** Then a sideways-curved plane, called a **leveling** or **sun plane,** was employed to run around the top edge and level it off for another process. A wide shallow depression was cut inside just below the chime-beveled edge, using a **howel plane.** In the middle of this scooped out area, a V-shaped (or sometimes square) groove was cut with a **crooze** to receive the barrel head. The same process was repeated on the bottom and then the inside and outside seams were smoothed down with various **scorps, inshaves, downshaves** and **drawing knives,** and the barrel was ready to receive its permanent iron hoops in place of the wooden truss hoops. With heads in place, a **hoop dog** was used to force the last band (which was called a chime hoop) over each end for a watertight fit.

Barrel Crozing Machine Patented in 1883

1. DOUGLAS MFG. CO. No. 343 side axe. $75
2. HOOP DOG, or crank. $15
3. BUNG BORER, auger. $8
4. LEVELING PLANE or sun plane, maple. $55
5. SUN PLANE, as above but in fruitwood. $60
6 HOWELL with brass wear plates. $40
7. COMBINATION howell & croze. Fine. $100
8. CROZE, sliding post type, chestnut. $35
9. D.R. BARTON fruitwood croze. $30
10. STAVE GUAGES, pair of radius type. $40

11. DRAW KNIFE by D.R. Barton, curved. $28
12. DRAW KNIFE, deep bellied style. Fine. $40
13. CHAMFER KNIVES, cooper's. Pair. $30
14. FROE, cooper's curved type. $60
15. SPOKE SHAVE, Bailey, Boston. 18 in. $20
16. HOOP DRIVERS (3) $37
17. TRAVELERS, wooden, (3) $75
18. BARREL SHAVE by G.L. Anderson. $50
19. JOINTER plane, 5 ft. beechwood. Fine. $200
20. HEADING SHAVE by L. & I.J. White. Iron. $65

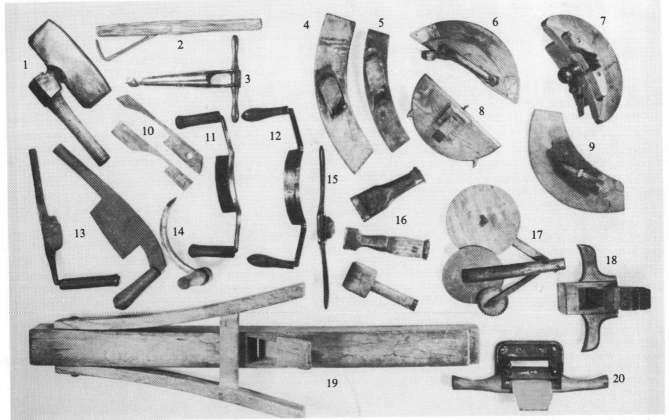

Shaving the bottom of a dry barrel.

ADZE cooper's bowl, with deeply curved 4 inch bit. $45 to $95

As above, with curved handle and 5 to 7 inch cutting edge. $100 - $190

ADZE, driving or nailing adze with claws. $30

ADZE, cooper's notching, no claw. $20 - $35

AUGER, cooper's bung reamer, hand-forged, $10 - $30

AUGER, cooper's trident-shaped bung cutter. $20 - $24

AUGER, Combination bung borer and tapered reamer, 2 in. bit. Deluxe. $45-$55

(see Auger section for additional examples.)

AXE, Cooper's side axes sell for from $50-$100 each. (see pages 11 to 15)

BLOCK HOOK, cooper's 8 to 10 inch spike-footed, serrated hook which was driven into a tree trunk to clamp a barrel stave in place for shaving. auct. $25 to $35

BRANDING IRON, 30 in. long wrought iron rod with barrel owner's name on 2 in. x 8 in. head, $22.   Smaller examples to $15

BRACE, cooper's beechwood bitstock, auct. $150 - $250 Dlr. $295 - $395

(more braces on pages 27–32)

Before 1850 most coopers owned a separate fixed-spoon-bit brace for each size hole they wished to drill. These very heavy duty braces were usually made of thick beechwood with extra wide webs or arms and 4 or 5 inch dia. heads or breast pads.

BUNG EXTRACTOR, T-handle with sliding weight on 12 in. shaft. $60

Others with cam joints or threaded shafts $30 - $50

BUNG SPIGOT, factory made wood with cork insert $8 to $15
Terra Cotta version, usually marked with a stoneware factory name. $32

Boxwood type with metal spout. 24 in. long $25

BUNG START, cooper's square headed mallet with long flexible handle. $30 to $35

CHAMFER KNIFE, cooper's L-shaped draw knife with one handle of wood and a 5 or 6 inch cutting blade on up to 18 inch shaft, the end of which was smooth and served as second handle. auct. $25 - $40 Dlr. $30 - $50

CHINCING IRON used to drive rush into the crooze groove around the edge of the barrel head. Shaped like a modern 6 inch wide brick cutting chisel. $12 - $25

COMPASS, cooper's early bentwood style. $175 to 250 (see pg. 49 for illus.)

COMPASS, iron with notched shoulders and chamfered legs. 19th Cent-type, 7 inches long $15

CRESSET, an 8 in. dia. cage-like heater made from hoop iron. Held burning shavings or wood for steaming barrel interiors. $40 - 60

Heavier, wrought iron type. $100 up

CROZE groove cutters are usually mounted on beechwood slabs 14 to 19 inches wide. (see page 109).

Assorted cooper's crozes from England Auct. $30– $55

American-made examples from $30-$60.

Highly–grained, exotic woods sell best.

DRAWING KNIVES, factory-made for the coopering trade. $12 to $25 ea.

With S-curved blade. $35 - $45

Jigger style or Chamfer knife, (one wooden handle). $30– $50

FLAGGING IRON, a yoke shaped pry bar with horseshoe end. Used to force barrel stave joints apart for inserting rush where needed to make watertight. $25 - $35

FROE, cooper's cleaver-like tool with right-angle, handle eye. Curved blade examples run from $50 to $80 ea.

HEAD VISE, or giant iron screw-eye used to pull barrel head into place. $22 - $50

HOOPING DOG was used to pull the last hoop into position over end of barrel head. Wooden handle with L-shaped iron hook hinged in its center slot. $15 - $30

HOOP DRIVERS or socket handled chisels for forcing hoops down to a tight fit. $6 - $15 ea with wooden handles.

Bent iron version in pick shape. $20 - $40

Notched end Nantucket type $18

Scotch driver with steel neck ring and grooved nose. $6 to $12

HOOP LOCK CUTTER, Penney's Monitor brand, small, table-mounted metal cutting device. auct. $40

HOOPER NOTCHER $10 - $20

HOOP SPLITTER, an iron maul with a tapered V notch running the length of its head. Used to split saplings in thirds for hoop stock. 9 to 10 inches long. $45 - $65

HOWEL (also see cooper's planes, pg. 109). Assorted unmarked English made cooper's howels in good condition. Auct. $30-$45 each.

Large and early American cooper's howels of almost museum quality. $65 to $75

HEADING SWIFT or FLOAT was used to plane flat the seams on a peg-assembled barrel head. (also see shave, cooper's, page 192).

Assorted cooper's floats & pluckers of British make. 3 in. to 5 in. cutters. $30-$40

Extra large of finer quality. $45-$65

INSHAVE (see pages 192-195).

JOINTER planes used by cooper's often have two throats, some as many as four. American made cooper's planes sell in a very wide price range of from $100 to $400. Carved and dated European jointers have sold at auction for as high as $700. (please see page 109 for additional listings).

LEVELING or SUN PLANES generally bring from $50 to $125 each. Few exceed 14 inches in length. (more data on page 109).

SCORPS were one or two-handled circular bladed pull-shaves for inside smoothing chores. They sell for $20 to $40 each. (see page 184 for more examples).

SHAVES made of cast iron became popular in the late 1800's. Stanley/Bailey cooper's style spoke shaves bring from $20 to $40. (see page 193).

STOVES made of cast iron replaced cressets, but few are ever offered for sale.
A 3 ft. tall, fluted column, 230 pounder by J.W. Ruger Mfg. Co. was offered last year at $250.

STAVE TEMPLATES still are available for $12 to $20 ea.

TRUSS HOOPS are often found in sets of graduated sizes. Wooden ones start at $5 each and large hickory hoops with wrought fittings have gone for as much as $25 apiece at auction.

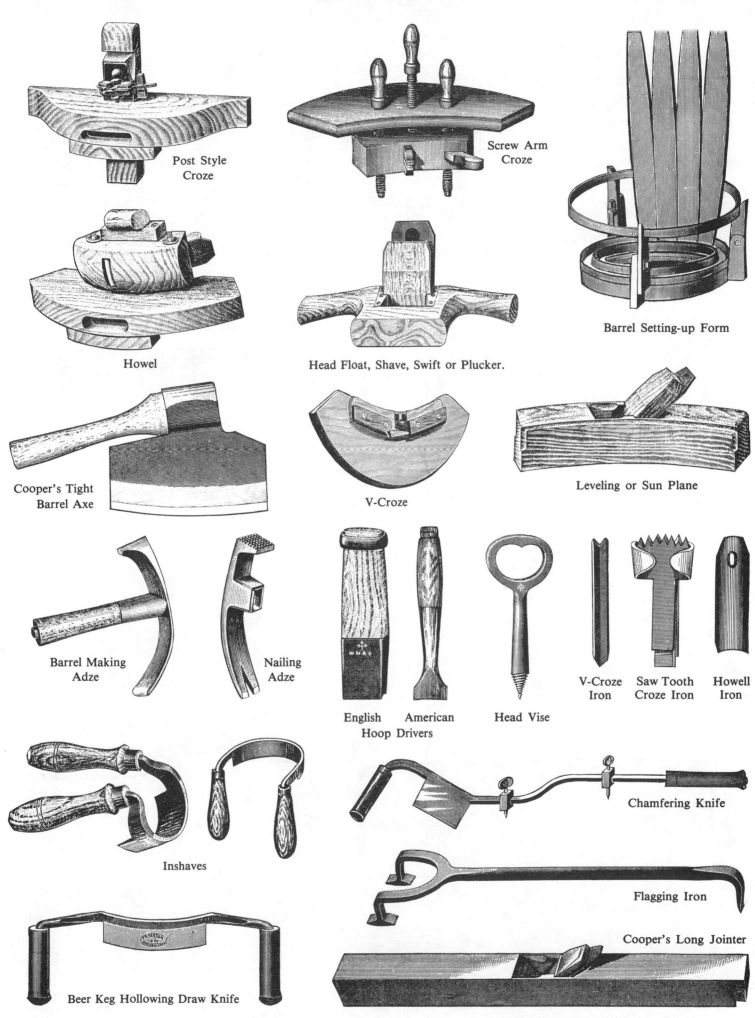

Post Style Croze

Screw Arm Croze

Barrel Setting-up Form

Howel

Head Float, Shave, Swift or Plucker.

Cooper's Tight Barrel Axe

V-Croze

Leveling or Sun Plane

Barrel Making Adze

Nailing Adze

English American
Hoop Drivers

Head Vise

V-Croze Iron

Saw Tooth Croze Iron

Howell Iron

Inshaves

Chamfering Knife

Flagging Iron

Cooper's Long Jointer

Beer Keg Hollowing Draw Knife

Factory-Made Cooper's Tools, Circa 1880 - 1910

COOPERS' TOOLS.

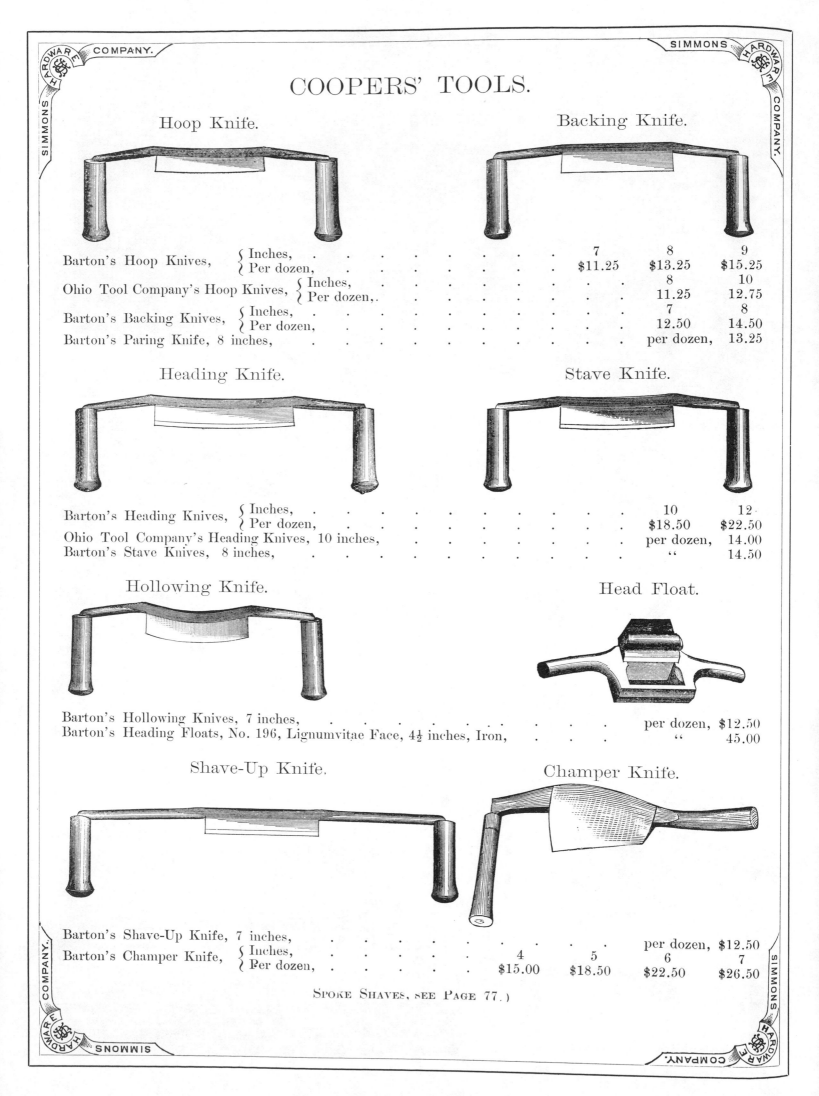

Hoop Knife.

Backing Knife.

Barton's Hoop Knives,	Inches,	7	8	9
	Per dozen,	$11.25	$13.25	$15.25
Ohio Tool Company's Hoop Knives,	Inches,		8	10
	Per dozen,		11.25	12.75
Barton's Backing Knives,	Inches,		7	8
	Per dozen,		12.50	14.50
Barton's Paring Knife, 8 inches,			per dozen,	13.25

Heading Knife.

Stave Knife.

Barton's Heading Knives,	Inches,	10	12
	Per dozen,	$18.50	$22.50
Ohio Tool Company's Heading Knives, 10 inches,		per dozen,	14.00
Barton's Stave Knives, 8 inches,		"	14.50

Hollowing Knife.

Head Float.

Barton's Hollowing Knives, 7 inches,		per dozen, $12.50
Barton's Heading Floats, No. 196, Lignumvitae Face, 4½ inches, Iron,		" 45.00

Shave-Up Knife.

Champer Knife.

Barton's Shave-Up Knife, 7 inches,					per dozen, $12.50
Barton's Champer Knife,	Inches,	4	5	6	7
	Per dozen,	$15.00	$18.50	$22.50	$26.50

Spoke Shaves, see Page 77.)

With the exception of the folding handled styles introduced in the 1870-1880 period, draw knives have not changed appreciably over the past 500 years. This basic shaping tool of nearly every woodworking trade does not yet command high prices on the collector market. Perhaps because so many sturdy specimens have survived in such good condition.

AUCTION LOT of cooper's curved bladed draw knives. 4 for $40

D.R. BARTON cooper's chamfer knife. L-shaped with one handle. auct. $20-$25 dlr. $35-$50

D.R. BARTON conventional 10 in. draw knife with beechwood handles. $15

A.K. BELKNAP, St. Johnsbury, Vt., cooper's curved draw knife. auct. $30

I.G. BOLTON cooper's chamfer knife with cast iron handle. $40

I.G. BOLTON, Portland. Cooper's S-curved draw knife. $40

C.W. BRADLEY huge mast knife with 14 in. cast steel blade. auct. $40

BROWN, LEIGHTON & UNDERHILL (New Hampshire) cooper's chamfer knife. auct. $25

CHAS. BUCK miniature draw knife with 4 inch wide blade. auct. $85

BUCK BROTHERS small 6 inch draw knife. $20

BUTCHER brand, 12 inch draw knife. $12

B.W. stamped hand-forged 23 inch draw knife with 15 in. blade. Horn handles. $30

J.S. CANTELO folding handle draw knife with 7 in. blade. Deluxe quality. $28-$35

COACHMAKERS offset drawing knife with 2 in. blade mounted in center of graceful S-curve handle bar. auct. $80-$95

COACHMAKER'S double-bladed yoke-style draw knife, handwrought, 16 in. wide. $72

COACHMAKER'S or shovel maker's style draw knife with 2 in. dia. half circle blade at center of 12 in. bar. Outside bevel ground. Dlr. $65 - $75

COOPER'S shallow S-curve drawing knife. $40

DATED 1731 draw knife with 15½ in. cutting edge. Blurred touchmark. auct. $55

COOPER'S CHAMFER knife or Jigger. 14 in. to 18 in. sizes $30-$45

COOPER'S Circular heading knife. Lot of 30 from various British makers, circa 1900. 12 in. $12 ea.

COOPER'S hollowing knife. British made 12 in. draw knife with bent blade. $15-$20

BARTON'S No. 88A CARRIAGE BODY KNIVES.

Sizes.   Net price each.
No. 88A, with three blades, 1, 1½ and
    2 inch $3.60

H.N. DEAN, eleven lb. draw knife with 5 in. X 10 in. cutting edge on 18 in. bar. $68

DOUGLAS MFG. CO. (New York City, circa 1870) American pattern curved blade draw knife with brass ferruled walnut handles. $45

FRENCH COOPER'S hand-forged 14 in. draw knife with 8 in. straight blade. Egg shaped handles. $12-$15

GILPIN, with hammer trademark. Large mast shave 26 in. overall. Thumb impressions deeply worn into handles. auct. $66

No. 9L57606 A practical compact tool for the carpenter's outfit. Handles fold to protect cutting edge. Forged from best steel. Tangs extends through handles. Warranted.
Size cut, inches...... 8   10   12
Price **73c   84c   95c**

HANDLE-MAKER'S drawing knife with U-shaped bend in center of its broad blade. $25-$40

JAMES HOWARTH gentleman's drawing knife with 6 in. cutting edge and nicely turned handles. $52

JENNINGS & GRIFFIN draw knife with folding handles. $12-$18-$28

C.E. JENNINGS small patternmaker's draw knife. 6 inches wide. auct. $25

KEEN KUTTER draw knife 8 in. $18 - $25

Wm. MARPLES gentleman's little-used draw knife with boxwood handles. 6 inch cutting edge. auct., London $75

MAST SHAVE with laid on 19 inch steel cutting edge. 26 inches overall. Hand-forged. $45 Chestnut handled 30 inch. Dlr. $75

MELHUISH "Gents" deluxe British boxwood handled draw knife. Auct. $69

NEW HAVEN EDGE TOOL CO. Conventional draw knife with clamp-on guide. Pat'd July 19, 1887. $28

NOBLESMAN F.G. Co., swivel handled draw knife with 5¾ in. cutter. $18

PEXTO folding hand. draw knife $22 - $35

RABBETING or boxing type draw knife with 13/16 in. router (chisel-like blade) in center of handlebars. $28-$35

ROBERSON BROS. chamfer knife. $25

S. SANDERS, curved S-blade cooper's draw knife. $35

J.M. SHEFFIELD, Stamford, Ct. Extra large mast knife, 26 in. overall. $28

H.D. SMITH & CO. Perfect Handle. Conventional 16 inch draw knife with the exception of its sandwich-style wooden half section handle grips which resemble those of a mechanic's screw driver handle. $25

SPRING & ROBINSON, Hyde Park, Mass. Pat. Mar. 11, 1879. Finest quality folding handle draw knife. 5¾ inches wide. $40

JAMES SWAN folding handle draw knife, Patented in 1888. 9 inch cutter. auct. $15 dlr. $28- $35

UNDERHILL, Boston (circa 1840) mast knife with 16½ in. blade. auct. $35

Another, 30 in. overall. $35

W. WALKER, Burton, cooper's jigger with short curved center cutter. $30

WARD & PAYNE Ltd., Sheffield. Circa 1900 cooper's circular (curved) heading knife. A draw knife for final smoothing. $12 - $18

Another, straight bladed, common. $14

WEST POINT draw knife, 10 in. $10

L. & I.J. WHITE cooper's chamfer knives in sizes 4 to 6. auct. $15-$20 ea. dlr. $30-$38

L. & I.J. WHITE, Buffalo, N.Y. Mast shave, 23 in. overall. $18-$22

L. & I.J. WHITE huge draw knife with step down trowel-type handles, straight blade is 2¾ in. X 12½ in. $45

A.J. WILKINSON folding handle draw knife. Patented in 1895. $35 up.

Another, unused cond. with chamfer guides. auct. $90

Another, (light rust & pitting) $20

WITHERBY conventional draw knife. $15

Drawing Knife Chamfer Guides, or Gauges, prevented the blade from taking too deep a bite and also regulated the width of chamfer cuts. The pair above is from an 1890's catalog and were available in sizes to fit 3 different blade widths for 50¢ each. Dealers offer them today at about $25 to $35 a pair.

N. H. Edge Tool Co.'s Drawing Knives.

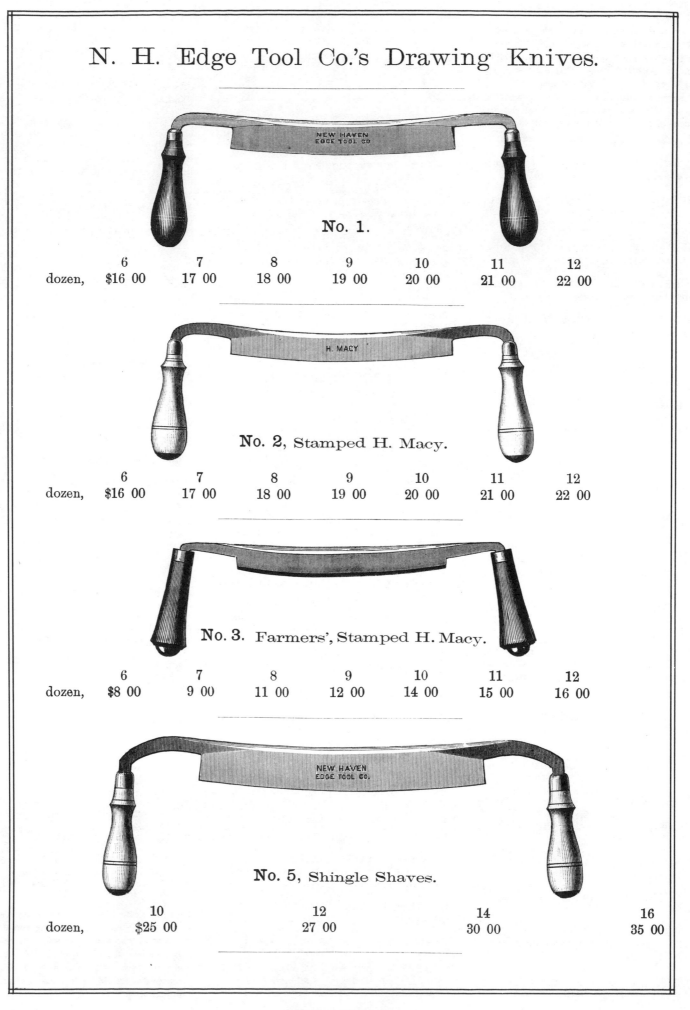

No. 1.

	6	7	8	9	10	11	12
dozen,	$16 00	17 00	18 00	19 00	20 00	21 00	22 00

No. 2, Stamped H. Macy.

	6	7	8	9	10	11	12
dozen,	$16 00	17 00	18 00	19 00	20 00	21 00	22 00

No. 3. Farmers', Stamped H. Macy.

	6	7	8	9	10	11	12
dozen,	$8 00	9 00	11 00	12 00	14 00	15 00	16 00

No. 5, Shingle Shaves.

	10	12	14	16
dozen,	$25 00	27 00	30 00	35 00

(Page from 1884 Catalog)

N. H. Edge Tool Co.'s Drawing Knives.

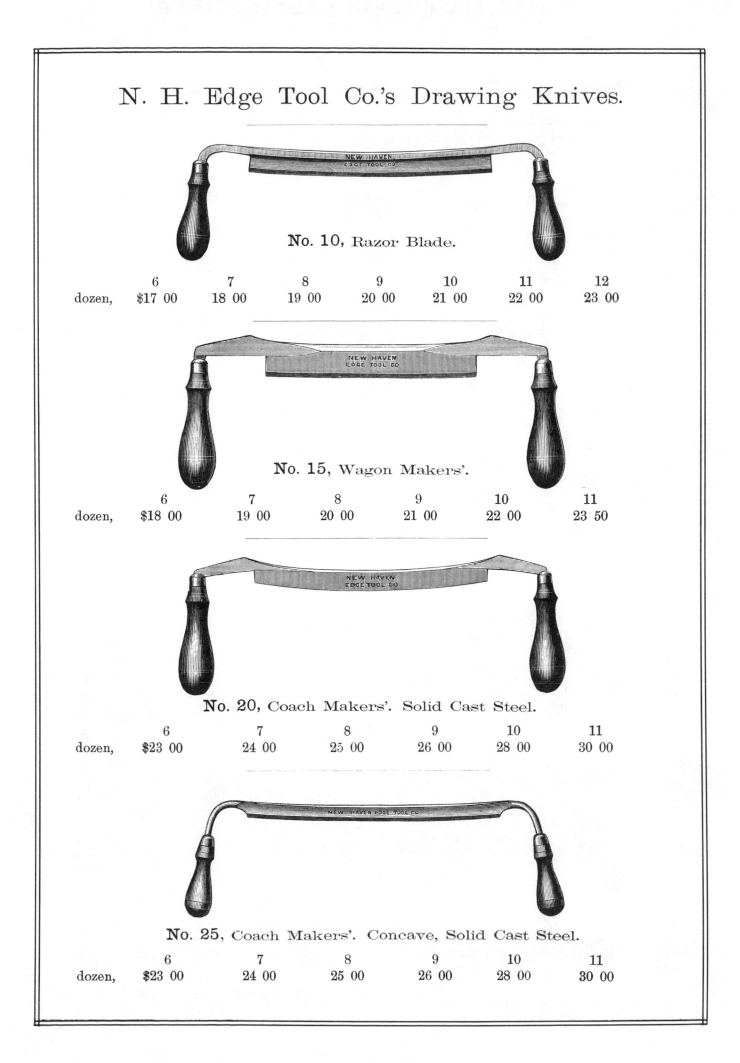

No. 10, Razor Blade.

	6	7	8	9	10	11	12
dozen,	$17 00	18 00	19 00	20 00	21 00	22 00	23 00

No. 15, Wagon Makers'.

	6	7	8	9	10	11
dozen,	$18 00	19 00	20 00	21 00	22 00	23 50

No. 20, Coach Makers'. Solid Cast Steel.

	6	7	8	9	10	11
dozen,	$23 00	24 00	25 00	26 00	28 00	30 00

No. 25, Coach Makers'. Concave, Solid Cast Steel.

	6	7	8	9	10	11
dozen,	$23 00	24 00	25 00	26 00	28 00	30 00

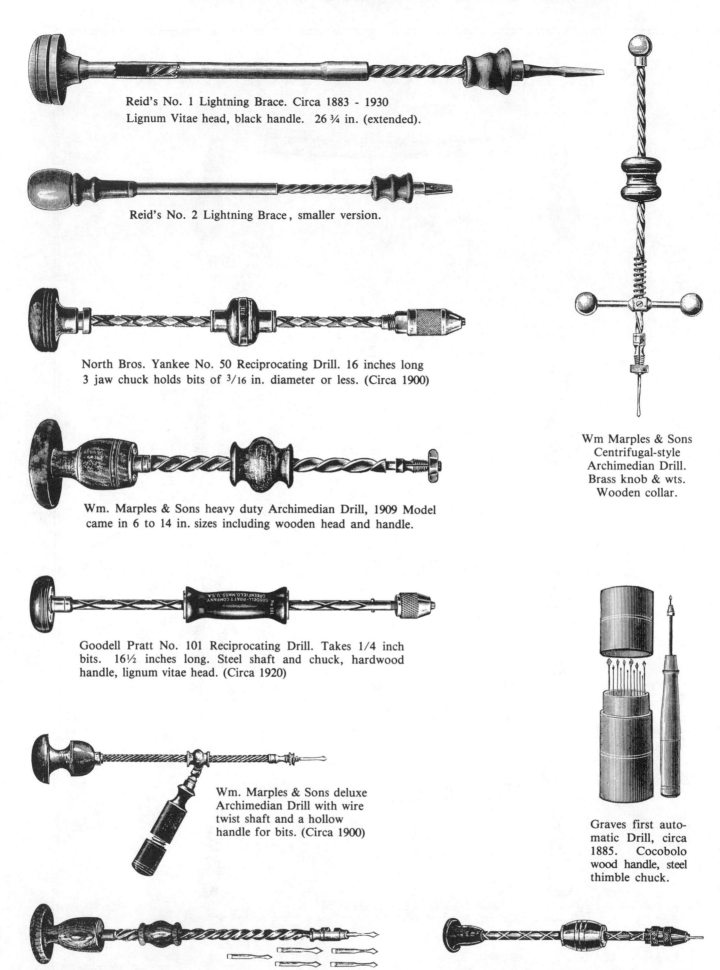

Reid's No. 1 Lightning Brace. Circa 1883 - 1930
Lignum Vitae head, black handle. 26 ¾ in. (extended).

Reid's No. 2 Lightning Brace, smaller version.

North Bros. Yankee No. 50 Reciprocating Drill. 16 inches long
3 jaw chuck holds bits of ³/16 in. diameter or less. (Circa 1900)

Wm. Marples & Sons heavy duty Archimedian Drill, 1909 Model
came in 6 to 14 in. sizes including wooden head and handle.

Goodell Pratt No. 101 Reciprocating Drill. Takes 1/4 inch
bits. 16½ inches long. Steel shaft and chuck, hardwood
handle, lignum vitae head. (Circa 1920)

Wm. Marples & Sons deluxe
Archimedian Drill with wire
twist shaft and a hollow
handle for bits. (Circa 1900)

Sheffield-style English Archimedian Drill with
typical diamond shaped bits. (Circa 1880)

Wm Marples & Sons
Centrifugal-style
Archimedian Drill.
Brass knob & wts.
Wooden collar.

Graves first auto-
matic Drill, circa
1885. Cocobolo
wood handle, steel
thimble chuck.

Chicopee brand, American-made double spiral
13 in. Archimedian Drill with maple head and
handle. (Circa 1895)

Archimedian Drills first appeared in American tool catalogs of the mid 1880's and were followed shortly by the introduction of the popular "Yankee" style push drill with a concealed double-spiral shaft. Archimedian drills made quick work of boring holes in ivory, wood and soft metals where space limitations prevented the use of conventional hand drills.

Push drills were advertised as "A perfect tool for dentists, piano & organ builders, jewelers, artisians and cabinet makers." Even today, push drills are still preferred by many craftsmen engaged in household and remodeling tasks. A drapery installer could hardly get by without one. (Please see page 60 for prices).

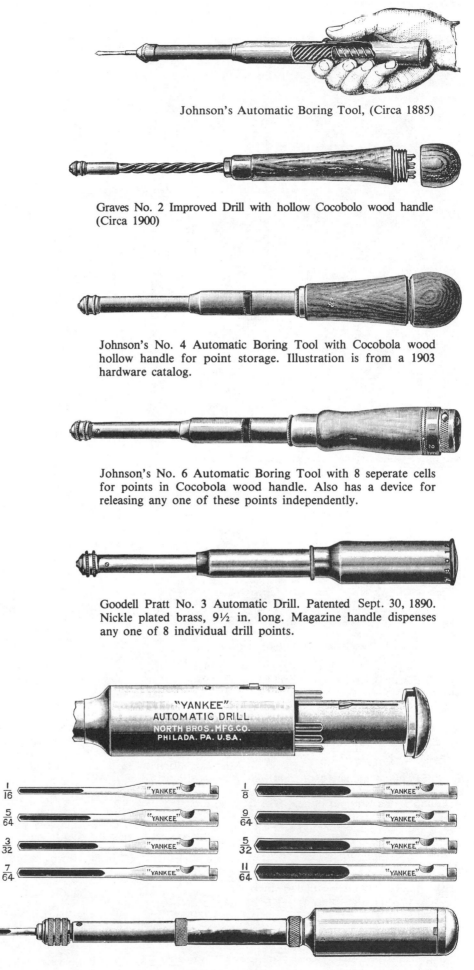

Johnson's Automatic Boring Tool, (Circa 1885)

Graves No. 2 Improved Drill with hollow Cocobolo wood handle (Circa 1900)

Johnson's No. 4 Automatic Boring Tool with Cocobola wood hollow handle for point storage. Illustration is from a 1903 hardware catalog.

Johnson's No. 6 Automatic Boring Tool with 8 seperate cells for points in Cocobola wood handle. Also has a device for releasing any one of these points independently.

Goodell Pratt No. 3 Automatic Drill. Patented Sept. 30, 1890. Nickle plated brass, 9½ in. long. Magazine handle dispenses any one of 8 individual drill points.

Millers Falls Finest Quality Automatic Boring Tool of 1915. Sold for $2.00 with 8 drills.

No. 180

Yankee No. 41 Automatic Drill. Smooth handle, 1900 style. Complete with 8 drills.

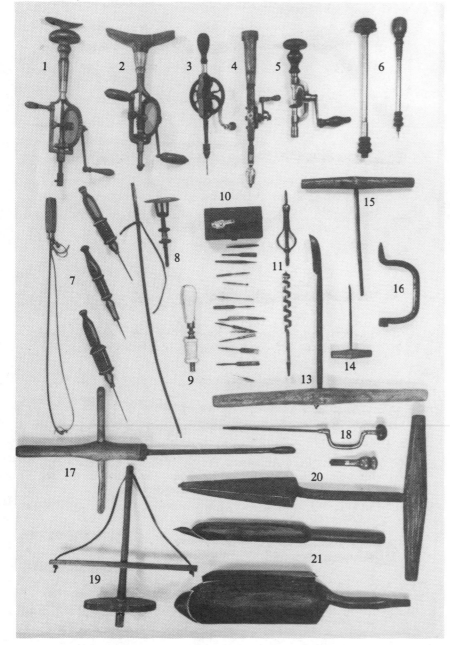

1. **BRASS FRAMED** breast drill with shoulder pad on head. $150

2. **IRON DRILL** with shaped wooden pad. $35

3. **IRON HAND DRILL** with brass crank and a 3 jaw chuck. $50

4. **MILLERS FALLS** high posted hand drill pat. 1883. 2 jaw chuck. $10

5. **EARLY IRON FRAMED** hand drill. $95

6. **A.H. REID** pat Dec. 12, 1883. Lot of 2. Archemedian and screw driver push drill. $40

7. **BOW DRILL** in forged steel with 3 crude tropical wood spools and bits. $185

8. **BOW DRILL,** hand-forged with 2 post head. Matching wood bow. (as found) $225

9. **IVORY DRILL** chuck and spindle, (no bow) $500

10. **TOOL HOLDER** in rosewood. Unmarked Sheffield type with 12 bits in orig. walnut box. $150

11. **ACCESSORIES** by Leland & Co. pat Dec. 17, 1859. Single twist bit and spring-loaded screw driver bit. $20

12. **SHEFFIELD BITS,** box of 50 assorted makers, (not illustrated) $95

13. **SPOON AUGERS,** lot of 2 with wooden T-handles. 1 in. and 1¾ in. $25

14. **GIMLETS,** lot of 3 large size, from 8 to 24 in. in length. Wood T-handles. $30

15. **NOSE AUGERS,** lot of 3 hand-forged, ¾ in. to 1¼ in. signed. $30

16. **BLACKSMITH'S BRACES,** lot of 2 headless iron braces, 9½ in. & 16 in. $90

17. **BREAST AUGER** with beechwood handle and cross-bar. 7/8 in. spoon bit. $115

18. **ORGAN-MAKER'S** brace & screw driver. $40

19. **PUMP DRILL,** primitive all wooden const. $80

20. **WHEELWRIGHT'S REAMERS,** lot of 2 hooked style with massive 28 in. handles. $250

21. **PUMP LOG AUGERS,** (lot of 2) $85

BRASS-BODIED archimedean drill with ball-end flywheel. 10½ in. long incl. threaded chuck. $65

CHICOPEE archimedean, or reciprocating, drill circa 1895. Maple head and slide. 13 in. overall. $25

ENGLISH made archimedean drill with beech head and center runner. 15 inches including brass wingnut chuck. $35

FENN, signed, ebony handled archimedean drill, 9¼ in. long. File style handle, ebony runner. German silver trim. Delicate and beautiful. $110

GOODELL-PRATT nickel plated automatic push drill with rotary bit storage handle. Pat. 1891. $8-$12

GOODELL-PRATT No. 0 reciprocating 16 inch automatic drill with cherry slide and lignum vitae head. 1895 pat. 3 jaw chuck. auct. $35

HAND-FORGED iron archimedean drill with flat disk head, iron runner. 16 inches long. $35.

HOBBIES brand (circa 1930) steel archimedean drill with steel flywheel balls. $42

C.E. JENNINGS & CO. wood handled push drill. $8

JOHNSON & TAINTORS, Pat. Oct. 5, 1869. Automatic drill with 3 stepped brass cylinder-shaped body. Complete with 8 bits in orig. tin box. $25-$45 (mint)

MILLERS FALLS No. 5 nickel plated . $12

MILLERS FALLS No. 61A nickel plated push drill with wooden handle. $10

MINIATURE finely made 7¾ inch archimedean drill with wooden handle, brass ferrule and runner. $45

A.H. REID spiral push drill, 16 inches long. lignum vitae head. $25-$35

REID'S Lightning Drill Brace & Screwdriver No. 1 Pat. 1882. Lignum vitae head, tubular brass frame. 17½ in. long. $15

Another with lignum vitae head and nickel plated tubular enclosed shaft. auct. $20 dlr. $35

YANKEE No. 41 by North Bros. Nickel plated brass push drill with 10 bits. $15

YANKEE No. 50 reciprocating drill, $25

YANKEE No. 75, North Bros. push brace, enclosed mech. Will drive a ⅜ in. auger bit into hardwood. $40

UNMARKED small 8 inch arch. drill with wooden pad and sleeve. $12

Another, small unmarked drill with knurled brass sleeve and ferrule, beech head. $35

Unmarked flywheel type, 12 inches long with brass balls and chuck. Wood handle & slide. $65 - $75

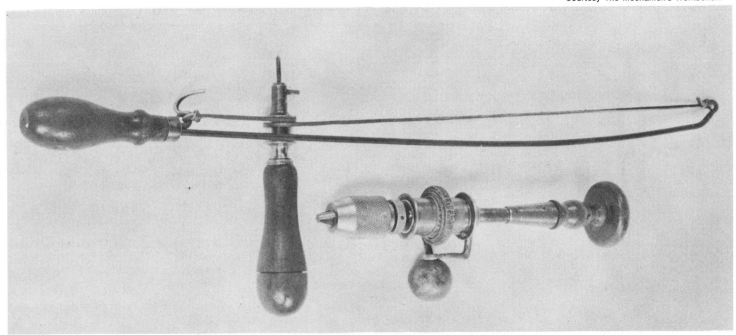

The interesting bow drill above has a thumbscrew chuck. It's walnut handle compartment hold 7 bits, each in a seperate cell. Dealer prices for comparable quality tools run from $200 to $250. Ebony examples are worth more.

This pull-cord ratchet drill is marked Auto Hand Drill, Pat'd June 11, 95. Best Tool Co., Boston. We've seen these offered in a wide price range, from $150 at auction to $600 for a perfect example in mint condition.

BOW DRILLS have been around in one form or another for over 10,000 years. They undoubtedly evolved from primitive hand twirled fire making sticks. Some scholars believe that the hunter's bow was also utilized as a drill turning tool.

GEO. BUCK, Tottenham Ct. Rd. (1835-63) Ebony and brass bow drill with maker's name engraved in top ring. auct. $270 dlr. $375

G. BUCK, Maker, 242 Tottenham Court Rd. Ebony spool and handle on this drill with a brass chuck and cap band. (no bow) $460

G. BUCK, Maker, 242 Tottenham Ct. Rd. Brass and rosewood handles on bow and drill. (replacement bow) $350

BUCK, Tottenham Ct. Rd. brass trimmed ebony drill a full 11¾ inches long. Bow is forged steel with turned ebony handle. Engraved steel ratchet tension key and plate. Truly a museum piece with the quality and workmanship of a fine firearm. Asking $2,750

BUCK, Tottenham Ct. Rd. ebony and brass bow drill with the numbers 8, 23 and 162 on underside of brass cap band. A smooth working drill with a few minor nicks on brass chuck. $400

G. BUCK, Maker, 242 Tottenham Ct. Rd. signed in brass band on handle. Fine ebony, (no bow). $450

Another with steel bow. auct. $350

Another with brass bow. auct. $375

BUCK, Tot. Court Rd. (circa 1877) grooved rosewood spool, brass fittings and spacer in rosewood handle. Beautiful . $650

CAST IRON bow drill in small size with cherry handle and home-made walnut bow. $165

HORN HANDLED bow drill with matching 26 in. bow. Drill measures 5¾ in. long incl. brass shank and steel spool. Adjustable pivot bearing. Dlr. $700

H.S. & CO. N.Y. (agent), probably Erlandson make. Ivory spool bow drill with octagon brass ends & rosewood handle. Bow has beechwood handle. handle (does not match). Asking $975

IVORY reel and handle ends on ebony stock with brass fittings. Very fine and rare gut strung bow, knock-out chuck & 12 bits. auct., London. $1,950.

LA MOTTE, Paris. Bow drill with rosewood head and brass spool. Bow, 3 drill holders & bits. auct. $450

LIGNUM VITAE stock and handle. Ratchet tightened bow. Complete with 18 bits. auct., London. $500

MAPLE & IRON bow drill. Nicely turned with thumbscrew chuck and original wooden bow. auct. $125 -$350

UNMARKED smaller size bow drill with brass fittings. Inc. bow. auct. $150

UNMARKED bow drill with lignum vitae handle, brass spindle, original steel bow. Ratchet type adjustment. auct. $200

WALNUT bow drill with storage compartment in handle. Plain, turned. $235

WATCHMAKER'S brass bow drill with 10 inch long bow made of horn. $105

PUMP DRILLS were used in Roman times for drilling hard substances and in making on-the-spot repairs where a craftsman needed a tool he could operate with just one hand. The motion of the flywheel serves to rewind the cord after each downward stroke.

BEECHWOOD cross bar is 9½ in. long on this early pump drill with iron flywheel on 13 in. shaft. $65

BRITISH made 12 in. pump drill with brass flywheel and steel collett chuck. Auct. $55 - $95

IVORY pump rod on unmarked brass and rosewood pump drill with 4 extra pads. auct. $525

JEWELER'S pump drill with brass disk flywheel and turned finial on iron shaft. Wooden cross bar. $75

J. NEILL & CO. Eclipse No. 3 pump drill made in Sheffield England. $78

PRIMITIVE pre-1800 hand-forged pump drill with 5 flywheel weights on square hole shaft. 16 in. iron cross bar. $180

PRIMITIVE pump drill with large wooden ball which acts as flywheel and chuck. 12 inch turned spindle slides on 18 in. metal shaft. $160

PRIMITIVE pump drills with weighted wooden flywheel disks. $60-$190 ea.

(Decorative inlay work brings top prices)

UNMARKED small pump drill with wood cross bar, brass disk flywheel and tiny 4 jaw chuck. auct. $110

CHAIN DRILLS consisted of a shaft, chain & chuck unit made to fit heavy-duty breast drills. The chain tightened with each turn of the shaft to provide constant pressure when operator could not.

B.S.V. Co. Cleveland, Ohio. Small sized chain drill. $8

CHICAGO No. 0 made by Chicago Pneumatic Tool Co. Heavy duty chuck. $12

DUFF MACHINE CO. Lowell, Mass. Excellent nickle plated chain drill. $12

GOODELL-PRATT No. 327 automatic chain drill approx. 3 in. by 9 in. (circa 1910) $12 - $20

KEEN KUTTER pat. Aug. 14, 1900. Chain drill with spring loaded rod attachment. (no chain) $35

MILLERS FALLS CO. No. 62 Barber's patent ratchet brace with chain drill attached. $30

MILLERS FALLS early heavy duty chain drill in excellent cond. $20

NORTH BROS. Yankee No. 1500 chain drill pat. July 30, 1912. $8 - $15

NORTH BROS. Phila. Pa. pat 1910. T-handle chain drill with accessories. $40

AYERS high speed breast drill with huge hand-cranked flywheel/drive gear. Pat. June 1868. $165

BRASS FRAMED breast drill with iron gears and fittings. 2 rosewood handles, rectangular flat brass breast plate. auct. $50-$100

BRASS FRAMED breast drill with iron gears. Tall, turned cherry neck and mushroom pad. Wooden side and crank handles. auct. $70

BRASS & STEEL breast drill featuring a 5½ in. brass crank wheel which engages 2 brass bevel gears. Steel main frame. Large brass breast plate. $125

BRASS FRAMED and geared breast drill with polished hardwood handles and a Jocobs chuck. Top wood handle has pedal shaped brass plate affixed. 15 inches overall. auct. $170

BRASS FRAMED breast drill, 17 inches long. Tall wooden mushroom handle. Iron spoked crank, gravity chuck. $195

BRASS FRAMED and geared breast drill 18 in. long. 3 hardwood handles. auct. $175

BRASS PLATED and geared breast drill of museum quality. auct. $1,750

BRONZE FRAMED breast drill circa 1840. Large wooden mushroom-shaped pad. Iron spoked gear wheel. 17 in. overall. $195-$225

J. CARTER iron-framed egg beater-style breast drill with brass crank handle. 12 inches overall. $80

CHICAGO No. 0 heavy duty iron breast drill with extension handle. $15

DUNLOP iron rod stocked, 2 speed breast drill. $12

GANG DRILLS consisting of 4 bits extending from a metal box housing, with a single drive shaft, were used for mortising sash pulley frames, etc. $50-$100

GOODELL-PRATT No. 477 breast drill. auct. $5-$10

GOODELL-PRATT extra heavy duty breast drill with leather strap chest pad. $20

GOODELL-PRATT pat 8-18-95. Finest breast drill ever made. Enclosed gears. auct. $75

GOODELL-PRATT No. 219 red & black 2 speed breast drill. $24

GOODELL-PRATT No. 57 breast drill. Nickel plated, 14 inches long. $25

GOODELL-PRATT Pivoting breast drill with provision for chain. $35

GOODELL-PRATT No. 6 solid wheel breast drill with orig. paint & decals. $35

E. HALBACH iron breast drill made in Germany. Nicely chamfered, decorative. auct. $35

INTERNATIONAL MFG. CO., Worchester, Mass. Metal framed breast drill with circular ring spoked drive gear. Reversible, ratcheting. $40

Wm. MARPLES & SONS, LTD. No. 6045 all metal, 2 speed breast drill. $30-$50

Mc CLELLAN, Sound Beach Conn. Pat. Nov. 6, 1900. Pivoting iron-framed breast drill with chain attachment. $75

MILLERS FALLS No. 10A budget priced breast drill, 17½ inches overall. $10-$15

MILLERS FALLS No. 87 open iron-framed breast drill 17 in. long. Deluxe Model. 5 positions, 2 speeds, hinged crank handle. $35

MILLERS FALLS No. 96 ratcheting drill. Pat. Oct. 23, 1900. $45

MILLERS FALLS No. 97 breast drill. Pat. Aug. 4, 1911. ½ inch chuck. $35

MILLERS FALLS enclosed gearbox and crank breast drill made of steel and aluminum. $45

MILLERS FALLS pat. 1877 iron rod-shaped breast drill. Large main gear has curcular cutouts. Turned wooden head. 20 in. overall. auct. $60

PECK, SMITH & CO., Southington, Ct. large brass-framed breast drill with Barber chuck. auct. $75

STANLEY No. 731 iron-framed breast drill with built-in level vial. 16½ in. overall. $28

STANLEY No. 733 two speed iron breast drill with level bubble. 16½ inches overall. Dlr. $18

STANLEY No. 742 two speed metal breast drill. Solid style gear drive. $8-$12

STANLEY No. 743 breast drill with level bubble. auct. $15

STANLEY No. H1220 "Handyman" hollow handled hand drill. $8

J.B. TOWNER solid brass, egg beater-style, breast drill, 11 inches long. Fine. $175

A.W. WHITNEY circa 1855 iron breast drill, (no chuck). $46

YANKEE No. 555 breast drill with 2 jaw chuck. $30 - $45

YANKEE No. 1455 iron rod-framed breast drill with rectangular metal pad. $22

YANKEE No. 1555 by North Bros. multiple speed breast drill. Main shaft has 4 gears. $35-$50

UNMARKED iron breast drills, pre-1880. $40 - $60

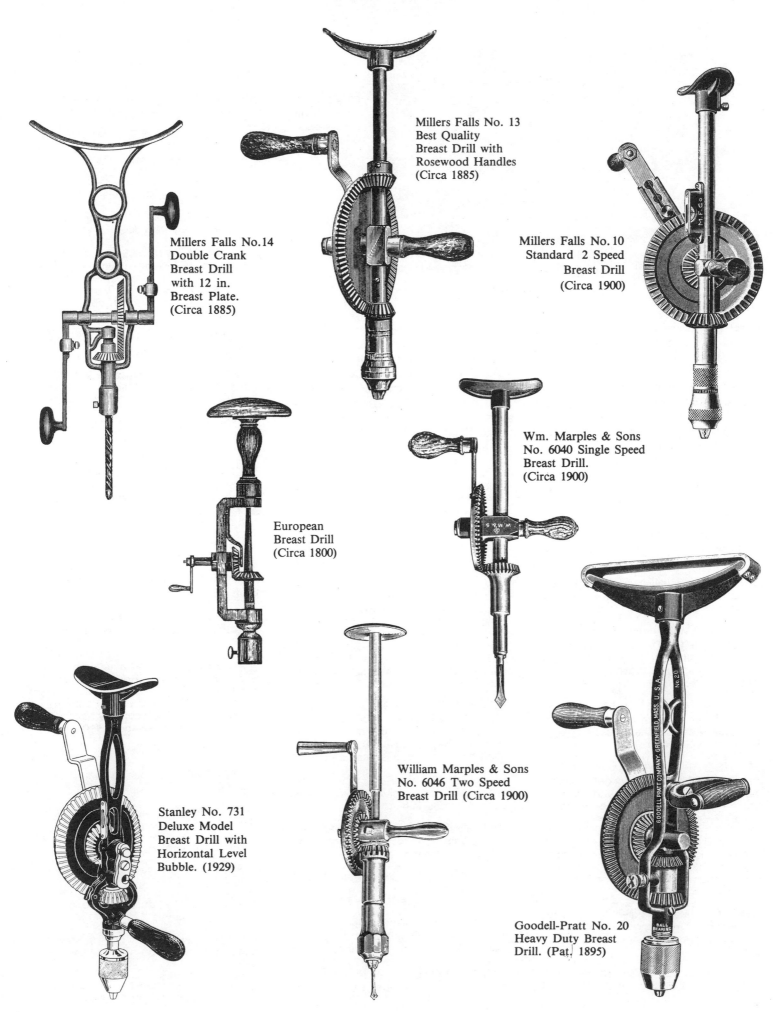

Millers Falls No.14
Double Crank
Breast Drill
with 12 in.
Breast Plate.
(Circa 1885)

Millers Falls No. 13
Best Quality
Breast Drill with
Rosewood Handles
(Circa 1885)

Millers Falls No. 10
Standard 2 Speed
Breast Drill
(Circa 1900)

European
Breast Drill
(Circa 1800)

Wm. Marples & Sons
No. 6040 Single Speed
Breast Drill.
(Circa 1900)

Stanley No. 731
Deluxe Model
Breast Drill with
Horizontal Level
Bubble. (1929)

William Marples & Sons
No. 6046 Two Speed
Breast Drill (Circa 1900)

Goodell-Pratt No. 20
Heavy Duty Breast
Drill. (Pat. 1895)

Circa 1890 Advertisement For Jeweler's Drill Set.

Whitney's Hand Drill in Box, per set, $1.00.

Bevel geared braces, drill stocks, breast drills, or hand drills appeared in Europe in the very late 1700's. The first models had gravity chucks and 1 to 1 gears. Their chamfered, hand-forged frames were usually less than a foot long. Between 1820 and 1850 thumbscrew chucks and 3 to 1 gear ratios became popular. In the 1860's larger cast steel rod-shaped frames with curved breast plates appeared in American catalogs. During the 1870's Millers Falls and other domestic makers introduced the modern style hand drill with its long hollow wooden handle and alligator-jaw chuck. In 1914 Duncan Black and Alonzo Decker added an electric motor and revolutionized the hand tool industry.

BRASS FRAMED eggbeater-style hand drill with 3 jaw chuck. Walnut head. auct. $50 - $75

BRASS hand drill circa 1850. Brass disk head. Straight spokes on crank gear. 10½ in. overall. $250

BRASS tiny headless hand drill with open frame of the 1880's. Curved spokes in gear wheel. auct. $85

BRASS FRAMED American-style hand drill of the late 1880's. Tall hollow wooden handle. 15 in. overall. Modern chuck. Spoked brass gear drive. auct. $100. dlr.$185

CONTINENTAL STYLE drill brace, circa 1820. Mushroom turned wooden head. Brass crank and side handles. 13 in. long. $175

CONTINENTAL STYLE gearing brace, circa 1820-50. 10½ inch decorative brass frame. Mahogany head and handle. Square hole, thumbscrew chuck. Museum quality. $600

CONTINENTAL STYLE nickle-plated iron-framed hand drill with polished steel gear drive, no spokes. Square shank thumb-screw chuck. Beechwood head and handle. $245

GLASGOW patented pull-chain drive reciprocating drill with gyro trademark. Storage compartment in hinged breast plate. auct. $225

GOODELL-PRATT, Toolsmiths, No. 655 iron framed 12 in. hand drill. Hardwood handle. $10

GOODELL-PRATT No. 54 nickel plated hand drill. Pat. 1891 & 1895. Hardwood handle holds 8 bits. 3 spoked gear wheel. 11½ in. long. $18

GOODELL-PRATT CO., Greenfield, Mass. Pat. Mar. 31, 1896. Black iron frame, 14½ in. overall. Hollow rosewood handle. $27

GUNMETAL & BRASS continental-style hand drill with long necked teakwood handle. $157

E. HALBACK signed 19th-Cent. iron framed hand drill. Tall turned beech head and crank handle. Solid bevel gear and drive. $85

INTERNATIONAL MFG. CO., Worchester, Mass. Ratcheting hand, or breast drill with straight lever handle, not side crank type. Horizontally mounted main gear on round shaft that terminates in a small pad. $30

KEEN KUTTER hand drill with spoked gear wheel and nickel plated hollow storage handle. $28

MILLERS FALLS No. 1 iron framed hand drill 12½ in. long. Rosewood handle has drill compartment. $12 - $22

MILLERS FALLS No. 2 iron framed hand drill. Spoked gear drive, hollow rosewood handle. 14½ in. overall. $18 - $25

MILLERS FALLS No. 2B (circa 1916) iron framed hand drill with solid hardwood handle. Red gear, black frame. $20

MILLERS FALLS No. 4 Jeweler's size hand drill 8 in. long. Open style cast iron frame. $25 - $30

MILLERS FALLS No. 5 iron framed hand drill with extra wide red gear drive plus idler gear. Hollow rosewood handle. $12-$20

MILLERS FALLS No. 38 solid gear hand drill 14⅞ in. long, ⅜ in, capacity. $9-$18

MILLERS FALLS No. 77 hand drill. Sold new for $2 in 1935. 12½ in. long. Solid handle and gear wheel. $6-$8

MILLERS FALLS No. 98 large hand drill with spoked drive wheel gear. $25

MILLERS FALLS No. 198 two-speed iron hand drill 15 in. long. $20

MILLERS FALLS No. 666 enclosed gear-type hand drill with aluminum frame. $28

MILLERS FALLS No. 980 hand drill 16 inches long. Hollow rosewood handle and 5 bits. $22

MILLERS FALLS No. 981 hand drill, converts to breast style. $25

I. PETER, Lenz. Swiss made iron framed hand drill with turned head, neck and handle. Circe 1850. auct. $277

PROTO MFG., U.S.A. No. 370 modern jointed hand drill, adjusts to any angle. $25

RUGER CORP., Southport, Conn. Hand-gun shaped drill with geared crank sitting horizontally on top of barrel (drive shaft). Storage compartment in pistol grip handle. $45

E.C. SIMMONS Keen Kutter, nickel plated hand drill with brass storage handle. $45

STANLEY "Defiance" No. 1221 economy hand drill. $7

STANLEY No. 618 iron hand drill with spoked drive gear and a wooden handle. $12

STANLEY No. 624 iron framed hand drill with 2 pinion gears. Hollow hardwood handle $14 - $20

STANLEY No. 1220 economy hand drill with wooden storage handle. $10

STANLEY No. 1221, ditto.

J.B. TOWNER solid brass drill with nicely chamfered frame. $175

YANKEE No. 1430 solid gear wheel type. $20

YANKEE No. 1431-A. hand drill. $25

YANKEE No. 545 hand drill by North Bros. $25

YANKEE No. 1530 solid gear hand drill with wooden handle. $20

YANKEE by North Bros. No. 1545 wood handled drill with 5 position transmission $30

UNMARKED continental-style iron-framed hand drills, pre-1870. $50 - $90 ea.

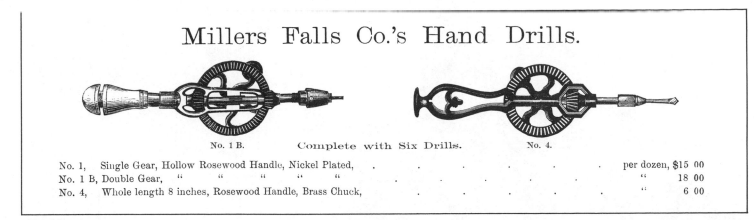

Millers Falls Co.'s Hand Drills.

No. 1 B.   Complete with Six Drills.   No. 4.

No. 1,	Single Gear, Hollow Rosewood Handle, Nickel Plated, ...	per dozen, $15 00
No. 1 B,	Double Gear, " " " " "	" 18 00
No. 4,	Whole length 8 inches, Rosewood Handle, Brass Chuck, ...	" 6 00

1884 Advertisement

(Most of these factory-made drill presses can still be purchased for $50 to $95 each)

DRILL PRESSES

GOODELL-PRATT No. 8 bench top drill press. Pat. Aug. 13, 1895. Clamp-on type, 13 inches tall. $35

GOODELL-PRATT No. 90 clamp on drill press, ⅜ in. capacity. auct. $40

BLACKSMITH'S 24 inch factory made drill press with direct drive horizontal-mounted crank wheel on top of L-shaped frame. $25 – $45

O.W. BURRITT & BROS., Weedsport, N.Y. small post mounted cast iron drill press with faucet-handled power feed and direct hand crank drive. $38

COLUMBIA, ASA Goddard, Worchster, Mass. Post mounted hand, or belt-powered crank drill press with feed wheel at top of cast iron frame. $75

MILLERS FALLS No. 22 combination hand drill/drill press, 15½ in. tall. $45

MILLERS FALLS No. 21 Universal Hand Drill Press. Bench mounted clamp-on type. Hand cranked with screw pressure feed and a universal vise table. auct. $75

MONROE MFG. CO., Fitchburg, Mass. Pat. April 19, 1859. Wood framed drill press with large decorative crank and thumbscrew top feed. 16 inches tall. auct. $225

POST DRILL, heavy-duty pipe type with hand crank and a 6 in. dia. flywheel/pulley. Automatic top ratchet feed. $50 – $75

E.C. STEARNS & CO., Syracuse, N.Y. bench-top drill press with hand crank and a large top-mounted flywheel. Feeds via a smaller wheel just above gear drive. Accepts work up to 7 inches tall. $95

YANKEE No. 1105, North Bros. Mfg. Co., Philadelphia, Pa. Very nice iron-framed bench top drill press with solid-type drive gear wheel. $125

UNMARKED tiny table top drill press with hand drill on upright rod. Top has horizontal flywheel. $22

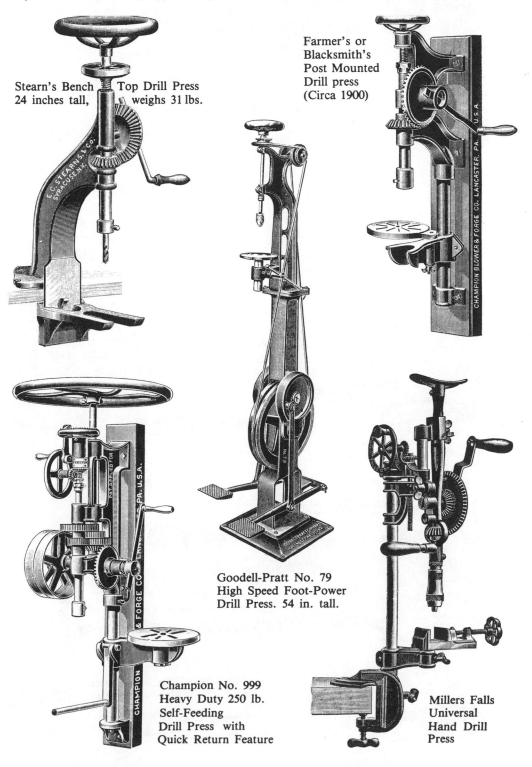

Stearn's Bench Top Drill Press 24 inches tall, weighs 31 lbs.

Farmer's or Blacksmith's Post Mounted Drill press (Circa 1900)

Goodell-Pratt No. 79 High Speed Foot-Power Drill Press. 54 in. tall.

Champion No. 999 Heavy Duty 250 lb. Self-Feeding Drill Press with Quick Return Feature

Millers Falls Universal Hand Drill Press

In the early 1800's the Farrier was as well known for his veterinary skills as he was for his horseshoeing expertise. By 1850 vertinary surgery had become a separate profession and blacksmith shops had begun making and fitting horseshoes.

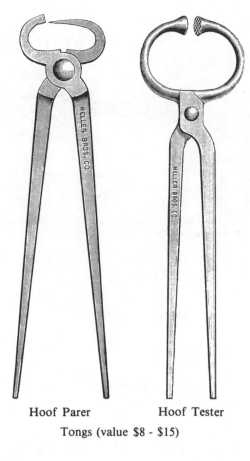

Hoof Parer   Hoof Tester

Tongs (value $8 - $15)

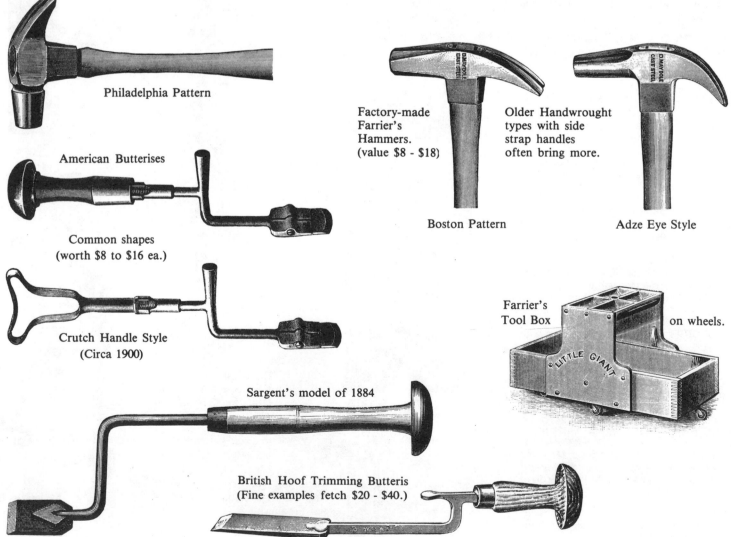

Philadelphia Pattern

American Butterises

Common shapes
(worth $8 to $16 ea.)

Crutch Handle Style
(Circa 1900)

Factory-made Farrier's Hammers. (value $8 - $18)

Older Handwrought types with side strap handles often bring more.

Boston Pattern   Adze Eye Style

Farrier's Tool Box   on wheels.

Sargent's model of 1884

British Hoof Trimming Butteris
(Fine examples fetch $20 - $40.)

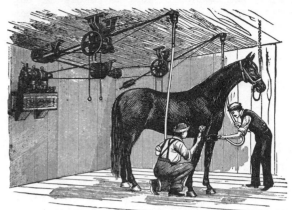

Cowboy
Style Shoe

Hoof Knife, Iron Handle   (current value $6 - $10)

Steel Toe
Racing Shoe

Farrier's Hoof Filing Rasp

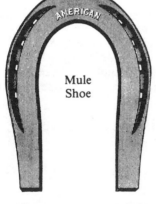

Mule
Shoe

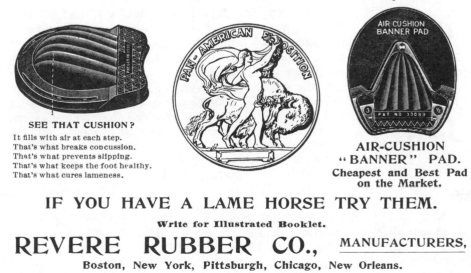

Burden
Horseshoe

FILES and FLOATS. Cavemen made rough files from flint. Early Greeks tried imbedding fish teeth in wooden paddles. Most Bronze age cultures also had files made of the new alloy. Iron files are cut in their softened state and then tempered in cold water.

Leonardo de Vinci designed the first file-cutting machine in 1490 but it didn't catch on for several centuries. Sheffield, England remained the world's primary source for hand-chiseled files until the American File Company at Pawtucket, Rhode Island, installed a French designed file-cutting machine and began mass production in 1870.

The most collectable files are those which can be associated with a particular trade. Gunsmith's and Planemaker's floats are good examples. Floats are very course files, almost saw-like, with only 5 or 6 parallel lines of teeth per inch. The most refined floats are those with trowel-like stepped-down handles and polished brass ferrules. Common factory made files are purchased by collectors only for their utilitarian value.

The four gunsmith's floats pictured above, are worth about $175. A Graille, or horn worker's float, 2 inches wide, sold recently at auction for $50. A set of 23 oval, straight & riffler pattern Gunsmith's files with matching step-down handles was offered this year for $650 by a well known dealer. A set of 6 assorted cabinet maker's floats by Mathieson, 3/8 to 2 inches wide, sold for $166 recently. Exceptional examples of planemaker's floats have brought in excess of one hundred dollars each.

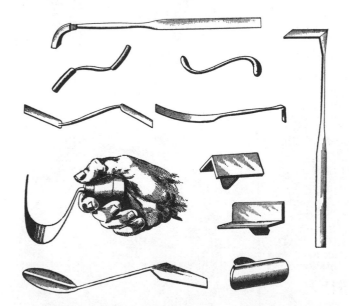

FOUNDER'S tools have attracted a small band of collectors who pay from $50 to $100 for complete sets of these steel and brass, spatula-shaped, sand moulding tools. Individual items are usually priced at under $8 each.

FORGES are not exactly collectable but they do show up at auctions of blacksmith's equipment and are often knocked down for less than $100. The Champion Blower & Forge Company of Lancaster, Pa. was the nations largest producer. Their catalog of 1896 listed over 50 pages of forges for farmers, jewelers, blacksmiths and miners.

FROE, a wedge-like knife with an integral forged eye for its right angle handle. Captain John Smith, of Jamestown fame, referred to it as a "split pole". Its wedge-shaped, thick blade was struck on the top edge by a crude wooden maul, after being positioned parallel with the end grain of a sawn log. The driven blade was then rived back and forth until a shingle or rough clapboard was produced.

Barrel staves were roughed out with froes because they were less likely to split or warp after being assembled if cut along the natural grain using this tool. From its absence in old engravings, we must assume that the froe is a more recent invention than the axe, drawknife, or carpenter's chisel. Hand-forged froes, (with curved blades) often bring from $40 to $65 at auction. Recent factory-made examples go for half as much. Straight-bladed froes are the most common. Cleaver-like knife froes, with metal handles, are scarcer than either of the above; but do not bring higher prices. Hooked-end grafting froes commonly sell in the area of $12 to $25 each. Exceptional examples of any of these splitting tools, including finely curved cooper's froes, are offered by dealers at $75 & up.

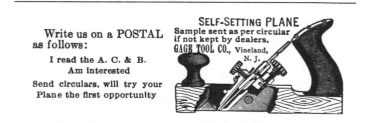

GAGE TOOL CO. John P. Gage was a 37 year old New Jersey farmer and real estate investor who developed and promoted a new plane design patented by a cabinet maker named David Bridges in 1883. Gage planes were widely advertised in carpenter and woodworking publications until the end of World War I and had achieved a respectable level of sales prior to selling out to the Stanley Rule & Level Co. in 1919. Stanley added iron-bodied planes to the line, which they continued to produce until the Second World War. Numbers on early Gage-produced models do not correspond with the later Stanley numbering system. No wood bodied planes were made after 1934.

GERMAN SILVER is a variable proportion alloy usually consisting of approximately 20% nickle, 20% bronze and 60% copper. There is no silver in German Silver, that is why it made a good non-tarnishing trim (hinges, tips, or inlay) on finer tools made from about 1850 onward.

GIMLETS are miniature versions of the auger, often used by cabinet makers and other tradesmen for sinking small screw holes, especially in hard to reach spots. Most common gimlets do not command more than $2 or $3. An elaborate, exotic, or dated handle would up the value considerably. Iron handles are not too unusual.

GLASS CUTTERS were loose industrial diamonds in the 1850's. You simply bought one and glued it into the end of a stick or rod to make your own tool. Lovejoy's combination glass cutter and putty knife was an instant success when introduced in 1870. It employed a tempered steel wheel and wrench-like notches and sold for 50 cents. The many subtle variations of Lovejoy's basic design which have come onto the market over the ensuing century make glass cutters interesting and inexpensive collectables. European brass-handled glass cutters with half-moon heads command the upper range at $15 - $25. Common rosewood-handled varieties can still be picked up for a dollar or two.

GLUE POTS have been around as long as glue. Somewhere in history some hardy soul discovered that if you boiled a horse's hooves, hide, and tendons long enough, you would come up with a powerful smelling concoction that stuck to anything. The double boiler principle employed in glue pot construction maintains a constant steam-heated temperature and allows the workman to concentrate on the job at hand without constantly monitoring the consistency of the glue. Some recent prices quoted by antique tool dealers for these charming little kettles are: Cast Iron, sizes 000 to 3 pint, (some have porcelain liners) $9 to $18 each. Copper, Double Boiler type, Handmade, 4 in. dia. $30, 6 in. $40 and 8 in. $75.

GOODELL-PRATT CO. was founded in 1888 and incorporated in 1895 at Greenfield, Mass. By the year 1915 the company's line of machinists' and carpenter's tools exceeded 1,500 different items. Many were obtained through a series of acquisitions including: Richardson & Sons (metal levels), & Wells Brothers (farrier's butterises). In 1931 Millers Falls Co., also of Greenfield, Massachusetts, acquired the company and incorporated its best selling lines into their own catalog.

GREENFIELD TOOL COMPANY. A fire was responsible for both the birth, (in 1852) and death (in 1887) of this producer of high quality wooden planes. Several residents of the Mass. village of Greenfield formed a corporation to rebuild the nearby Conway Tool Co. which had been destroyed by fire. Alonzo Parker founded the company just 10 years earlier and it had grown to employ 80 workmen prior to the disaster. In spite of its limited capitalization, Greenfield Tool Company shortly ranked among the top plane producers in the nation. In 1886 a Mr. Henry Watson purchased the Company and its 200 foot long factory building, which burned to the ground shortly thereafter. Wooden planes were rapidly being outmoded at that time and no attempt was made to rebuild after the second fire.

GUNMETAL was first used for cannon barrels. It is an alloy of copper & tin, best known for its resistance to corrosion by saltwater. The mixture for naval bearings was 83% copper, 12% tin, 2½% zinc and 2½% lead. The percentage of tin varied according to the end use, up to 20% for the hardest grades. The mixture employed in the brownish-yellow bodies and trim of woodworking planes was 8 to 10% tin. Gunmetal melts at 2,000° F.

HARNESS MAKER'S Tools consist of those generally employed in other leather-working crafts. Most often they appear at auctions in box lots. A few representative pieces from recent auction sales are: Lot of 6 dozen small leather-working tools, floats, burnishers, awls, etc. $125. Osborne brand harness maker's tools, 75 pcs. with hardwood handles and brass ferrules. Awls, knives, scribes, pricking wheels, creasers, edgers and ticklers. $225. 100 pc. assortment of harness maker's tools in fitted wooden box. Most have rosewood handles with brass ferrules. $295. Harness maker's benches with wooden upright clamps go for $35 to $75 at auction.

HORN for knife handles, inlays, etc., was chiefly obtained from Buffaloes of Siam and India.

HORNBEAM is an Old World hardwood of almost white coloration. Used in plane making.

HORNBILL also was chiefly an Old World product. Related by leaf type to birch, alder and hazel trees, it is a white hardwood with smooth grey bark.

IRON. Europeans got off to a late start in the iron business but have been smelting the grey metal now for about 3,000 years. All an early iron monger needed to produce a batch was, an outdoor oven, a charcoal fire and a pile of crushed ore. With the help of a crude bellows the fire would exceed 2,000 degrees F. and after a few hours a small stream of iron would trickle out and run along the ground into hollowed out depressions where it puddled and cooled into piglet-shaped ingots (pig iron).

From these humble beginnings grew the industrial base of both France and England, who had blast furnaces going day and night by the year 1550. American iron production had several false starts before finally achieving commercial production at the Saugus River mill in Lynn, Massachusetts in 1644. George Washington's father was part owner of a Virginia firm called the Principio Company, which became the largest iron works in this country prior to the Revolution.

A typical U.S. iron foundry of the early 1800's was run by a waterwheel-powered blast bellows and could produce the following articles during an 18 week run from an 8 by 20 foot furnace: 360 tons of hollow ware plus additional large potash kettles, stove parts, fire backs, door jambs, plates, gudgeons, anvils, hammers, cannon balls and various pieces of mill machinery. The total expense for the above undertaking was recorded as having been exactly $10,750.32 which included: 2,130 cords of wood for charcoal, 726 tons of iron ore at $6 per ton, two sets of stones to build the hearth, and $2,600.00 to pay a foreman and his crew 4 months wages. Not a bad price for 360 tons of saleable iron castings!

Before the mass production of steel was made economical in 1865, wrought iron was king. Blacksmiths had always preferred the use of wrought iron because of its easy welding characteristics. Wrought iron was produced from cast iron by a puddling process that boiled out most of the carbon and other impurities by extreme heat and by the introduction of magnetite or hematite which attracted unwanted silicon and manganese to form a slag which could be drawn off by hammering and rolling. In this fashion a commercial wrought iron was produced which would not melt at under 3,000 degrees F. and which was used to make rails, locomotives, bridges, buildings, pipes, axles, wheels, tools and countless other items before the Bessemer steel-making process was introduced.

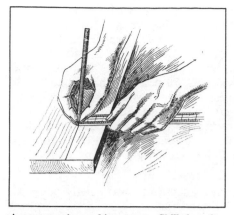

An amateur's marking gauge. Skilled crafts-men frowned on pencils, preferring a cut or scribed line.

GAUGES came in many styles and sizes. They were used to mark, measure or cut to predetermined measurements. Among the most sought after by collectors are those exotic rosewood, ebony and brass marking and mortise gauges produced from 1830 to 1930. MARKING GAUGES are used to scribe a parallel line along the edge of a board and usually have only one cutting point. MORTISE GAUGES were used to layout a mortise and tenon joint so they have 2 or 3 scribe points. The terms are often overlapping in usage. PANEL GAUGES are much larger than the average 8 inch marking gauge. They are found in up to 30 inch lengths and usually lack the brass fittings of the shorter gauges. Their single spur was used for marking off furniture and door panel material. VENEER slitting gauges resemble the marking or mortise variety but are heavier and usually longer than 8 inches. They have a flat cutting blade instead of a scribe-like point and often have a handle attached.

A & E BALDWIN, New York (1830-41) Boxwood mortise gauge with brass thumb-screw and adjustable stem. Inlaid parallel bands on face. $42 - $60

A.H. BLAISDELL'S, Newton Corners. Scarce marking gauge with brass extension collar and concave fingers. Rosewood stem. Pat. June 22, 1868. auct. $150-$250 ($300 mint)

M.M. BRAINARD, Green River, N.Y. Boxwood and brass mortising gauge. auct. $40 - $80

E. BRIGGS, Foxboro, Mass., boxwood marking gauge with redish patina. $65

H. BROWN & SONS, Sheffield. Veneer slitting gauge in ebony with brass plate on head and full end-cap on stem. $50-$80

BROWNS PAT., 1881, cherry stairbuilder's gauge with telescoping shaft and T-ends. 24 in. long when closed. auct. $200

E.W. CARPENTER, Lancaster (circa 1859) Beechwood marking gauge 11 in. long. Scale on side, wooden thumbscrew. $20-$50

E.W. CARPENTER panel marking gauge, 27 in. long. Ruled markings on side. Scribe inset in rosewood block. Mint cond. $50

H. CHAPIN, Union Factory No. 260. Fruit-wood and brass mortising gauge. auct. $175

CIRCLE CUTTER for leather. Beam compass style. Turned wooden T-handle center post slides on 14 in. rule. $16

CIRCLE CUTTING GAUGE in brass with slotted 6 in. blade holder on rod arm. auct. $30

CIRCLE CUTTER in mahogany with brass wear plates. 19 in. long with carved handle at each end. For cutting privy seats. English, circa 1857. auct. $110

Another, in mahogany, 14 in. auct. $145

CIRCLE CUTTING GAUGE, or router, in fruitwood. 18 in. long including turned handles at each end. Full brass bottom plate. For cutting holes in wash stand tops. $110 - $160

CIRCLE CUTTER, gunstock shaped mahogany handle and stem has wedged-in blade, plane style. Fence slides on chamfered stem, 18 in. overall. Highest quality. auct. $170

CLAPBOARD MARKING GAUGE, metal frame has wooden file-type handle with brass ferrule. Large conical metal thumb-screw. $25

CLAPBOARD GAUGE, Unmarked oak with steps for measuring board overlap. 9 X 5 in. with 5 inch handle. $45

CLAPBOARD GAUGE, beechwood triangular prism shape with 15 stairsteps. $50

COACHMAKER'S Grasshopper-style wooden T-shaped marking gauge. auct. $12 - $25

Another with brass trim and steel rod passing through mahogany stock. $30

COMBINATION Marking Gauge and Trammel Points. Pair of round rosewood heads with knurled brass adjusting screws. Brass trimmed beam. auct. $330

CRAWFORD & SAUERBI, Newark. Pistol handled leather slitting gauge in rosewood and brass. $35

HENRY DISSTON & SONS No. 93 mortise gauge in rosewood and brass. $47

HENRY DISSTON & SONS No. 96 boxwood marking gauge with heavy brass trim and two knurled adjusting screws. $75

DISSTON & MORSE boxwood marking gauge with brass faced fence. $45

J. DIXON leatherworker's plow style cutting gauge with file-type handle & rod shaped arm. auct. $53

Wm. DODD & CO. No. 4 leather slitting draw gauge. $20

R. FAIRCLOUGH & CO. 72 Byrom St. (Liverpool). Rosewood and brass mortise gauge. $48

FENTON & MARSDENS, Bridge Street, Sheffield. Rosewood mortising gauge 6⅝ in. long with full brass face plate. Mint cond. $85

FLATHER BROTHERS, Sheffield. Rosewood veneer slitting gauge 10½ in. long. Brass trimmed square stem and head. auct. $95

D. FLATHER & CO. rosewood and brass mortise gauge. Square head and stem. $50

H.G. FULTON'S Patent, July 17, 1888. Solid wooden butt gauge made from two flush mounted rectangles. $25

GERMAN—STYLE twin-stem marking gauge in beechwood. $20-$30

Another, with hornbeam head and iron face plate. auct. $30

GOODELL-PRATT No. 222 triple beam roller gauge. Nickel plated, 8 in. long. $20

GOODELL-PRATT No. 227 nickel plated butt gauge with 2 rod shafts and 3 scribers Patented Dec. 18, 1894. $10

GOODELL-PRATT No. 340 nickel plated clapboard marker 8 in. long with 6 beveled disk scribes and a hardwood handle. $10 - 25

L.B. HASKINS rosewood and brass mortise gauge. $45

JAMES HOWARTH, Sheffield. Oval headed ebony mortise gauge with inlaid brass ring on face and screw surround. $60

HUMPHREY TOOL CO., Warren, Mass. Pat. Sept. 7 & 14, 1886. Unusual T-head metal marking gauge on 12 in. rod. $25

W. JOHNSON, Newark, N.J. standard rosewood and brass mortising gauge. auct. $25. Another in boxwood. $25

JOHNSON'S PATENT iron framed clapboard gauge with cherry handle. $35

S.A. JONES & CO., Hartford, Ct. (circa 1842) rosewood marking gauge. auct $40

LEATHER SLITTING GAUGE very plain style with file handle. $12

LEATHER SLITTER in rosewood and steel. Early pistol grip style. $45

LEATHER SLITTER, deluxe quality rosewood and brass pistol handle with two decorative thumbscrew adjustments. auct. $80

LEATHER SLITTING GAUGE in open style, see-thru pistol handle, all brass frame. Circular trigger guard. Mint. Asking $150

S.E. LEONARD signed boxwood marking gauge conventional style with screw adj. auct. $25. Brass-trimmed

(Above, left to right) AMERICAN PATTERN rosewood marking gauge. Brass trimmed rectangular stem and fence. Brass is attached with concentric ring rivets. $25 - $35

PATENTED May 30, 1871 stamped on this rosewood marking gauge with curcular stem and brass ferrules. Round blade on one end and scribe point on other. $35

A.H. BLAISDELL, Newton, Corners (Mass). Pat. June 23 stamped on circular brass thumbscrew of this rosewood mortise gauge. Concave fingers on sliding fence are connected to beam on brass slide block with brass rods. $150 - $250

UNMARKED rosewood and brass mortise gauge in as found condition. Cast brass face. $20

(2nd from right) VENEER SLITTER, ebony with cast brass end. Cutter held with set screw. $35 - $50

(far right) BRASS circular stemmed ebony mortise gauge with plated round head. Near new cond. $45 - $65

Photo Courtesy The Mechanick's Workbench.

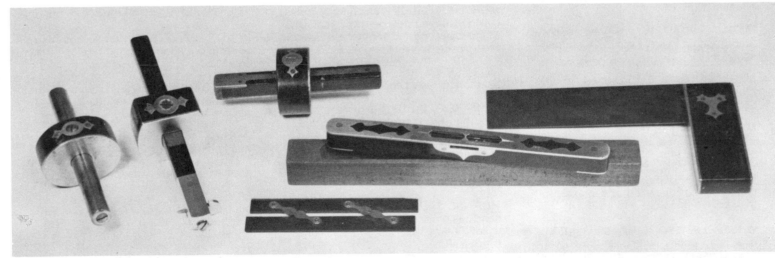

(far left) TYZACK & SONS, LTD. ebony and brass mortise gauge with oval head. Round stem has sharp scribing points. Little used. $40 - $70

(2nd from left) MATHIESON & SON Glasgow & Edinburgh Mechanical Tool Manufacturers. Ebony and brass veneer slitting gauge, adjusted by key and screw. $56 - $85

(3rd from left) UNMARKED Ebony and brass mortise gauge with rectangular stem and oval face with brass face plate. $35-$60

(center) BENNET B. BURLEY, Glasgow, Warranted. Decorative 12 inch level in ebony and brass with mahogany case. Ebony is flush with top of plate through cutouts. Circa 1880-1900 $90 - $150

(right) C.G. BALLARD, Ipswich. Ebony and brass trysquare, 7¼ in. blade. $35 - $60

(bottom) UNMARKED Ebony parallel rule with beveled edges and brass hinges, 6 inches overall. $24

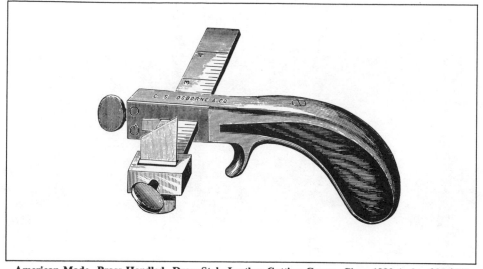

American Made, Brass-Handled, Draw-Style Leather Cutting Gauge. Circa 1880 (value $35-$50).

LOCKWOOD BROS., Sheffield. 6 inch rosewood and brass marking gauge. $50

MINIATURE mahogany marking gauge. 2 inch long brass stem held by wedge. Head is 1 X 1½ in. Craftsman made. $50

MARKING GAUGES. Common beechwood with ruled stems and boxwood thumbscrews. $5 - $7

With wedge locking devices. $4 - $6

MARKING GAUGE, British made with threaded 9 inch wooden stem and circular head. $15

MARKING GAUGE, unsigned boxwood with brass trim. $30 - $45

MARKING GAUGE, unsigned ebony, 11 inches long with wedge running in groove on stem. $25

MARKING GAUGE, unsigned ebony, round head and stem with brass thumbscrew. $45

MARKING GAUGE, unsigned ebony, cross shaped with wedge thru stock. 12 in. $65

MARKING GAUGE, rosewood and brass, deluxe, unsigned, 8 in. Conventional square head. $45

MARKING GAUGES, conventional 8 in. factory made rosewood and brass. Unmarked. Normal wear. $14 - $25

W. MARPLES & SONS, Hibernia. No. 2096 oval head ebony cutting gauge 10½ in. long. Brass face plate, arm tip and wedge. auct. $45, Dlr. $65

MARPLES ebony mortise gauge with heavy brass trim. $50

MARPLES & SON, circa 1900. Oval head rosewood mortise gauge with cylindrical brass stem. $58

W. MARPLES oval head ebony mortise gauge with brass face plate. Mint condition. auct. $79

MARPLES & SONS, Hibernia. No. 2155 round head ebony and brass combination marking and mortise gauge with brass rule inset in stem. Scarce London pattern. $150

A. MATHIESON & SON, Glasgow. Round head ebony mortise gauge with brass face and cylindrical shaped stem. Fine. $80

MATHIESON & SON, Glasgow & Edinburgh, Mechanical Tool Manufacturers. Ebony and brass veneer slitting gauge. $95

MORTISE GAUGE unmarked boxwood with brass stem slide insert. Unplated. $40

MORTISE GAUGE unmarked boxwood. Cast brass rectangular stem has boxwood infill. $65

MORTISE GAUGE unmarked brass cylinder shaped stem has two heads. One round rosewood and another in boxwood. Multiple adjustment features. $150

MORTISE GAUGE solid ebony, round head on threaded ebony shaft. $55

MORTISE GAUGE unmarked ebony, oval head has two brass bands inlaid. Brass stem insert. auct. $40, Dlr. $60

MORTISE GAUGE, unmarked ebony, arch-topped head has no brass trim other than thumbscrew. $40

MORTISE GAUGE unmarked ebony oval head has brass plate on both faces. Stem is solid brass rod. Heavy, professionally made. $70

MORTISE GAUGE unmarked square mahogany head on solid brass rod stem. Matching knurled brass adj. knobs set points. $100

MORTISE GAUGES auction lot rosewood and brass, conventional factory made type with full brass face plate. Square stems have end screw adj. slide. Normal wear. $20 - $30 ea.

MORTISE GAUGE circa 1820, British

made rosewood with arch topped head and round shaft held by half-round wedge. $30 - $50

MORTISE & SLITTING combination rosewood gauge 7½ in. long. Normal brass trim. Round head, square stem. auct. $90

NESTERS PATENT 1867 clapboard marker in the shape of a 12 in. shoe measure. Hardwood with built-in level vial and lavish brass trim. $200-$250

S.S. NORTON, Colchester, Conn. Exceptional quality rosewood and inlaid stem rule. auct. $35, dlr. $55

NURSE, Maidstone, England. Ebony mortise gauge with sliding brass inset scribe. $55

PANEL GAUGE unmarked beechwood 20 inches long. Conventional T-shape with wrought iron hdwr. $22

PANEL GAUGE, unmarked boxwood T-head, 12 in. long. Heart-shaped thumbscrew. Roman numeral calibrations. $30

PANEL GAUGE. British made, rosewood with 20 inch oval stem. Decorative curved T-head. $25

PANEL GAUGE Patented Aug. 3, 1873. Rosewood with brass fittings. 21 in. long. auct. $40

PANEL GAUGE rosewood, shaped head has thumb indent, boxwood wedge. 30 in. overall. $55

PANEL GAUGE walnut, 14 in. wide T-head, 22 in. shaft. $40

Other Walnut and brass panel gauges from $50 to $60 offered by dlrs.

PANEL GUAGE, British made from bog oak and boxwood. Wedged T-head. Auct. $60-$120

PANEL GAUGE ebony, with thumb cutout in sliding head. 30 in. length. Boxwood wedge. $65 - $95

PANEL GAUGE mahogany, 24 in. long with captive wedge. $14 - $20

Another, with pallete shaped head. $20

PANEL GAUGE birdseye maple, 21 in. with 10 in. head. Brass thumbscrew. $40

PANEL GAUGE tiger maple, Beech T-head has ivory wear plate. Fine. $60

PANEL GUAGE with 5 bone wear plates in sole and a bone scribe-holder tip. Auct. $130

PECK, STOWE & WILCOX. L-shaped clapboard gauge with turned handle. Large wingnut adj. $15

PHILLIP'S Patented Marking Gauge pat. Jan. 15, 1867 by Russell Phillips. Rosewood stem has 2 adjustable bronze fences. auct. $195

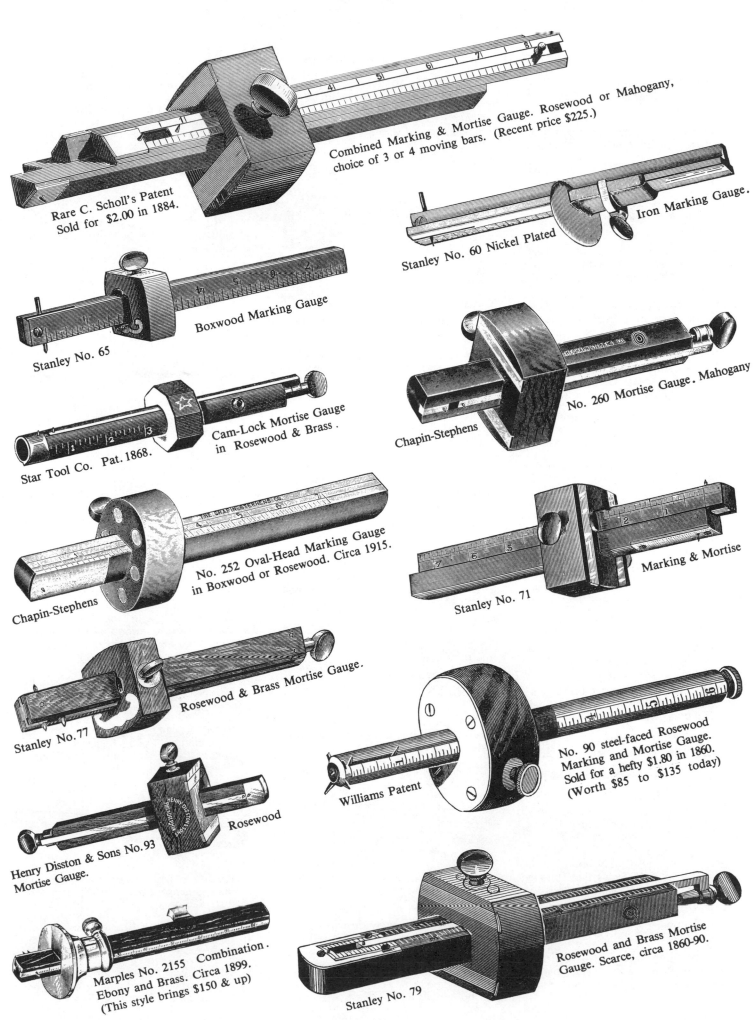

Combined Marking & Mortise Gauge. Rosewood or Mahogany, choice of 3 or 4 moving bars. (Recent price $225.)

Rare C. Scholl's Patent Sold for $2.00 in 1884.

Stanley No. 60 Nickel Plated Iron Marking Gauge.

Boxwood Marking Gauge

Stanley No. 65

No. 260 Mortise Gauge. Mahogany

Cam-Lock Mortise Gauge in Rosewood & Brass.

Star Tool Co. Pat. 1868.

Chapin-Stephens

No. 252 Oval-Head Marking Gauge in Boxwood or Rosewood. Circa 1915.

Chapin-Stephens

Marking & Mortise

Stanley No. 71

Rosewood & Brass Mortise Gauge.

Stanley No. 77

No. 90 steel-faced Rosewood Marking and Mortise Gauge. Sold for a hefty $1.80 in 1860. (Worth $85 to $135 today)

Williams Patent

Rosewood

Henry Disston & Sons No. 93 Mortise Gauge.

Marples No. 2155 Combination. Ebony and Brass. Circa 1899. (This style brings $150 & up)

Stanley No. 79

Rosewood and Brass Mortise Gauge. Scarce, circa 1860-90.

THOMAS RICE pat'd. Sept. 9, 1873. Rosewood & brass T-head panel gauge with brass wheel cutter. (repaired) auct. $115

L. SAUNDERS signed ebony marking gauge with brass stem insert. Screw adj. head. auct. $25

SCOTCH style ebony and brass oval head marking gauge with brass face plate. $65

W.H. SEYMOUR & CO., New York. Rosewood and brass marking gauge. auct. $35

A.B. SEYMOUR, Newark, N.J. Slitting gauge 5 in. long with brass faced head. auct. $45

SHEFFIELD type mortise gauge with heavy cast brass disc head on 9 in. ebony stem with inlaid brass rule. $120–$150

STANLEY No. 0 early beechwood marking gauge 8 in. long. Boxwood thumbscrew. $25

STANLEY No. 1 "Odd Jobs" pat. Jan 25, 1887. Nickel plated iron casting with built-in level bubble, scribe, depth gauge and straight edge attachment. $40 – $55

STANLEY No. 60 nickle plated iron marking and cutting gauge. Pat. May 12, 1874. $50 – $65

STANLEY No. 61 plain beechwood marking gauge. $5 - $7

STANLEY No. 62 adjustable point beechwood marking gauge. $6 - $12

STANLEY No. 64½ oval head beechwood marking gauge with brass thumbscrew and face plate. $25 - $30

STANLEY No. 65 boxwood marking gauge with brass thumbscrew and face plate. Like new. $10 - $20

STANLEY No. 66 rosewood marking gauge. Pat. Aug. 5, 1873. Brass plated bar, oval head and thumbscrew. $35 - $48

STANLEY No. 71 double marking & mortise gauge in beechwood with 1862 pat. date. Full brass wear plate on head. (fair) $20

As above, with 1872 pat. date. auct. $35

STANLEY No. 73 standard boxwood and brass mortise gauge. $15 - $25

STANLEY NO. 74 double stem marking & mortise gauge in boxwood with full brass plate on head, 1862 Pat. $30 - $40

STANLEY No. 85½ rosewood panel gauge. 20½ in. long. Brass plated head. Pat. Oct. 22, 1872. $40-$60

STANLEY NO. 88 sheetmetal sawtooth-blade clapboard marker with wooden handle. Circa 1900. $8 - $15

STANLEY No. 89 clapboard marker, circa 1888-1900. Consists of 2 steel blades mounted on an adjustable metal stock with wooden handle. $12 - $18

STANLEY No. 77 best quality rosewood mortise gauge. First patented in 1872. Sold for over half century. $15 - $35

STANLEY No. 90 nickel plated all metal marking gauge with oval head. $5 - $10

STANLEY No. 91 metal marking and mortise gauge with 6½ in. long double bars. $12 - $18

STANLEY No. 92 rosewood butt & rebate gauge, Pat. Aug. 23, 1892. auct. $50-$85

STANLEY No. 93 nickel plated butt gauge. Hollow rectangular shape with 2 in. slide. auct. $35, dlr. $60 (fine)

STANLEY No. 94 butt, mortise & marking gauge made of nickel plated iron with 2 sliding steel rods, graduated for 2 inches. Pat. 1911. $5 - $10

STANLEY No. 95 improved model of No. 94, nickel plated with calibration on top of slotted frame. Approx. 3 in. long. $5-$10

STANLEY No. 97 nickel plated marking gauge with double-faced machined head and a roller cutter. 6½ in. ovrall. Circa 1930. $10 - $15

STANLEY No. 98 duplex marking & mortise gauge. Same config. as No. 97 but has two shafts. $10-$15

STANLEY No. 165 boxwood and brass marking gauge with shoe plate on head. $10 - $15

STANLEY No.198 scarce oval head rosewood mortise gauge with twin nickel plated stems. auct. $20, dlrs. $45 & $64

STANLEY No. 281 butt gauge in orig. box. $20

STANLEY No. 373½ butt marker, new in plastic case. $6

STANLEY No. 374 butt marker, 4 in. wide. New in plastic case. $4

STANLEY "Defiance" No. 1291 promotional quality beechwood marking gauge. (like new) $24

STAR PATENT beechwood marking gauge with twist-to-lock feature. Incised scale. dlrs. $20 - $70

STAR TOOL CO. pat. 1888 rosewood with octagon head. $22-$45.
1868 model. auct. $140

L.S. STARRETT No. 429 carpenter's steel scratch gauge with octagon head. $5

STEARNS No. 85 butt gauge, rectangular 3 inch nickel plated type. auct. $5

G.W. TINSLEY'S Sept. 19, 1871 patented clapboard gauge with coil-end spring steel blade on turned wooden handle. 14 in. overall. $20-$25

THUMB GAUGE primitive solid birch 2 in. X 8 in. stick with fixed tongues extending from rectangular head. $15

U.S. LOCK CO. No. 63 rectangular shaped butt mortising gauge in exotic wood and brass. $85

TURNER & CO. rosewood mortise gauge with brass trim. Circa 1850. $30

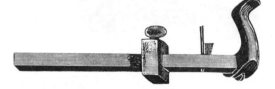

VENEER slitting gauge in beechwood, with saw handle mortised into shaft. Sliding wooden head has wrought iron thumbscrew. $38

VENEER slitting gauge in ebony, 10½ in. long. Brass wear plate and end piece. Elegant looking tool. $65

VENEER SLITTING gauge, craftsman made of rosewood. $18

VENEER slitting gauge, British factory made of rosewood with plain arch topped head and stem. No brass except thumbscrew. $45

VENEER slitting gauge, British factory made, deluxe rosewood and brass with full face plate and 9 in. long square stem. Brass wedge holds cutter. $68

VENEER slitting gauge in solid L-shaped beechwood, 15 in. long. Sliding head has thumbscrew. $28

VENEER slitting gauge in boxwood, 12 in. long. Sliding T-head has built-in brass cutter wheels. Stem has pallete shaped butt plate with thumb hole. $30

WEDGE LOCKING early marking gauges in various exotic woods, 10 to 12 in. long. auct. $25 ea.

GEO. WHEATCROFT, Newark, N.J. Solid boxwood marking gauge. auct. $30, Rosewood $45

WINSLOW'S Pat. Oct. 23, 1900. Nickel plated, adjustable protractor faced, marking gauge with 2 fences. $35 - $50

Hammering out horseshoes. Circa 1560.

HAMMER. A subtle clue to the origin of the hammer is furnished by its derivation from early Icelandic and Russian words meaning "stone". The iron or steel claw hammer of modern times is a Roman invention dating from the time of Christ. Bronze hammers had been around for 3 or 4 thousand years before iron was discovered. Many of today's specialized hammer-head shapes were developed in the middle ages. A Continental favorite, the strapped hammer, (with side straps extending down the handle from the head) appears in engravings dated as early as 1514.

Nails were chiefly handmade prior to 1800 and were very expensive in the United States. Early American craftsmen preferred to make their own nails using native woods. These trenails were driven with wooden hammers — iron hammers were late in arriving here. It was not until after the war between the states that factory made, cast steel hammers became cheap and plentiful. Prior to that time most folks used the back of an axe head or a hard-wood mallet. (Please turn to page 78 for additional hammer listings)

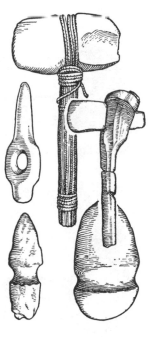

ADAMS & HAMMOND, Boston, 1845. Stonemason's bush hammer. Rectangular head is made up of laminated sharpened plates held together by 4 large bolts with nuts. $35

J. AHERN, Barre, Vt. Maker. Another stone hammer with inserted teeth. auct. $30

SOLOMON ANDERSON rare patented carpenter's hammer with claw attached to handle. (very pitted cond.) auct. $110

ATHA TOOL CO. railroad maul, 3½ lb. $8

E.C. ATKINS sawmaker's hammer. $75

H.A. AYVAD, Hoboken, N.J. Rare unsplit claw hammer with barbed outside claw edges and a center cutout hole for larger nails. $175

BALL PEIN, Machinists heavy duty hammer with 18 in. handle. auct. $40

BELDEN MACHINE early slater's hammer with flat shaft and laminated round washer grip. $20 - $35

BERLYCO No. H60 brass-headed claw hammer. auct. $22

BILL POSTER'S take-down style 3 section tack hammer with nickle plated ferrules at joints of hickory handle. auct. $125-$185

BLACKSMITH'S assorted style hammers. $10 - $20

B-R MFG. CO. Chicago. "Compliments of Kellog Toasted Corn Flake Co." solid iron crating hammer with arrow-head pry bar handle. $25

(BRASS HEADED hammers were used in powder mills & gas works to avoid sparks.)

BRASS ball pein hammer. $12

BRASS hammer with round & flat faces. $20

BRASS cylinder-shaped 1¼ in. X 3 in. head on hardwood handle. $18

BRASS claw hammer of conventional shape. auct. $35   Single claw type, $70

BRASS Goat's Head figural cast hammer with red handle. auct. $55 - $85

BRASS square head hammer with 2 leather faces. 2 lb. size. auct. $50

BRITISH factory made strap-handled hammers in assorted styles. $20-$30 ea.

BRONZE SLEDGE, 10 lb. (head only) auct. $34

BROOM-MAKER'S hammer, resembles a dull meat cleaver with a turned wooden handle. auct. $40

C.H. BROWN "Steel Face" early factory-made claw hammer. $15

BUSH HAMMERS for millstone work. Sharpened steel plates are bolted together leaving round eye. $15 - $30

BUFFALO HORN head on this factory-made jeweler's hammer. $25

CAULKING Hammers (see Mallet, caulking) Iron-ringed oak mallets used by shipbuilders. $35 - $55

CAVALRY, combination farrier's hammer and nail puller in tent peg shape, iron, 14 in. long. $32

CHENEY, Little Falls, N.Y. claw hammer with ball bearing nail holder. 16 to 20 oz. size. $25

CHENEY No. 777 adze-claw hammer with orig. handle. $35 - $40. Replacement handle. $25

CIGAR BOX opener, tiny claw hammers less than 5 in. long. Usually embossed with an advertisement. $20 - $25

CLAW HAMMERS in various early forms without straps. $18 - $25 Exceptional examples $35

CLAW HAMMER hand-forged with iron straps riveted to front and back of original hickory handle. 5¾ in head. $35

CLAW HAMMER, strap handled Kent style. $40

CLAW HAMMER, Wrap around style Pat. 1843. Claws continue around to fasten on handle just below head. auct. $110 Dlr. $165

DOUBLE CLAW. Most of these bear a 1902 patent date and sell for $145 to $185

TRIPLE CLAW, each regular claw has a miniature claw cut in its tip. Circa 1905. $185

COLLINS dynamicut ball pien hammer. Like new cond. auct. $7

COLLINS Legitimus 2 lb. blacksmith's hammer. Unused. auct. $10

CONN. ARMS MFG. CO. nail holder style. $36

COBBLER'S shoe hammers. Common styles. $9 - $20
Rarer forms. $30 - $50
(see Cobbler, page 47)

COOPER'S hammer, London pattern. $11

CRATE OPENERS without advertising. $3

C. CULVER "Cast Steel Warranted" early factory made claw hammer. $15

DAVID DOMINIGUS multiple spoked timber marking hammer with 1 in. characters on end of ea. spoke. auct. $40

FARRIER'S hammers in various styles without straps. $8 to $15 ea.

FARRIER'S hammer, claw type, hand-wrought with side straps. $35

FIGURAL HEADED ceremonial hammers in goat's head and other cast and embossed motifs. $35 - $85

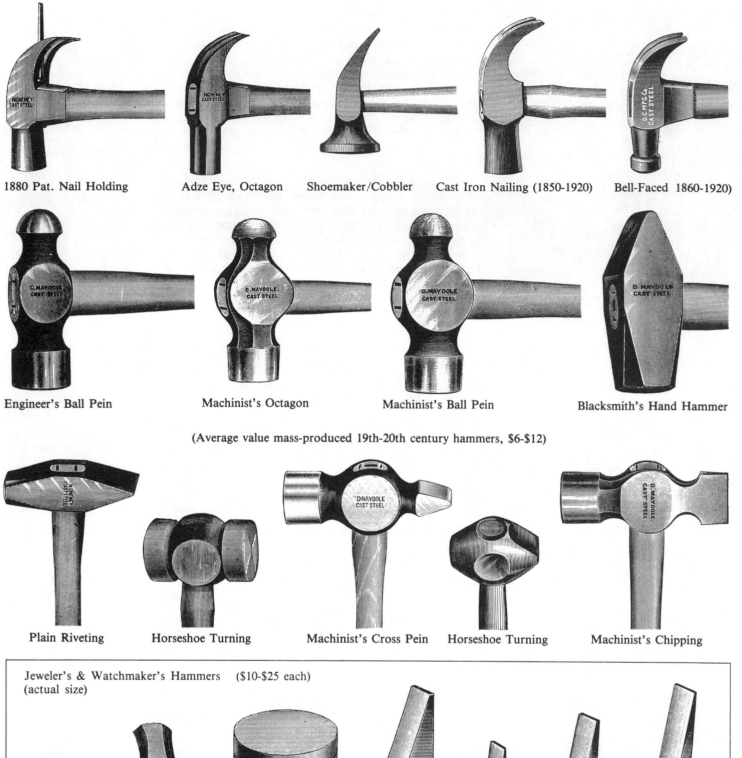

1880 Pat. Nail Holding   Adze Eye, Octagon   Shoemaker/Cobbler   Cast Iron Nailing (1850-1920)   Bell-Faced 1860-1920)

Engineer's Ball Pein   Machinist's Octagon   Machinist's Ball Pein   Blacksmith's Hand Hammer

(Average value mass-produced 19th-20th century hammers, $6-$12)

Plain Riveting   Horseshoe Turning   Machinist's Cross Pein   Horseshoe Turning   Machinist's Chipping

Jeweler's & Watchmaker's Hammers   ($10-$25 each)
(actual size)

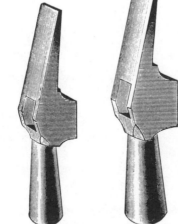

Small Case   Large Case   Metal Chasing   American   Swiss Style, Stubb's pattern, Watchmaker's
                                             Style
Repouss'e

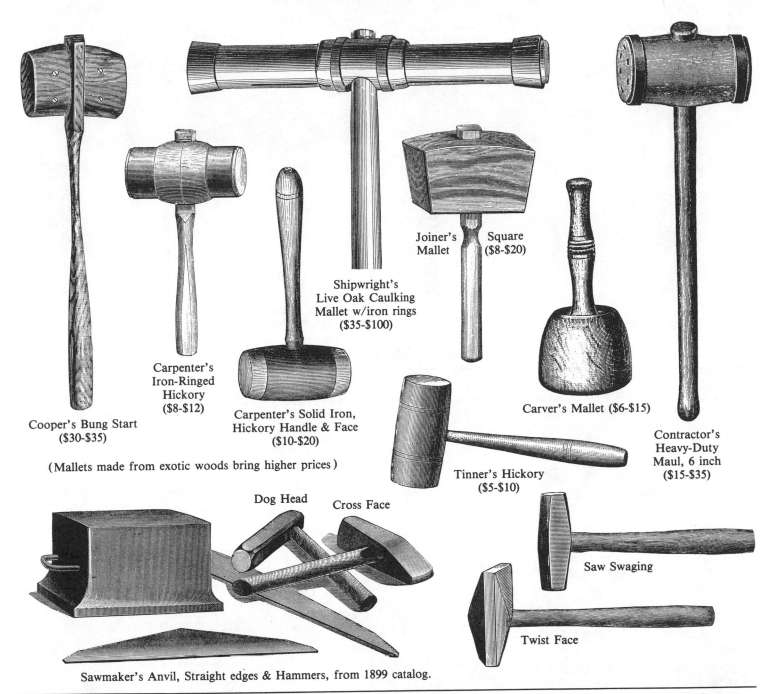

Cooper's Bung Start
($30-$35)

Carpenter's
Iron-Ringed
Hickory
($8-$12)

Carpenter's Solid Iron,
Hickory Handle & Face
($10-$20)

Shipwright's
Live Oak Caulking
Mallet w/iron rings
($35-$100)

Joiner's
Mallet

Square
($8-$20)

Carver's Mallet ($6-$15)

Contractor's
Heavy-Duty
Maul, 6 inch
($15-$35)

Tinner's Hickory
($5-$10)

(Mallets made from exotic woods bring higher prices)

Dog Head

Cross Face

Saw Swaging

Twist Face

Sawmaker's Anvil, Straight edges & Hammers, from 1899 catalog.

Circa 1860-1920 (Average value $8-$10 ea.)

Carriage Ironer's
Framing Hammer

Boiler Maker's
Riveting Hammer

Cooper's Hoop
Driving Hammer

Ship or
Bridge
Builder's
Riveting

Brick
Mason's

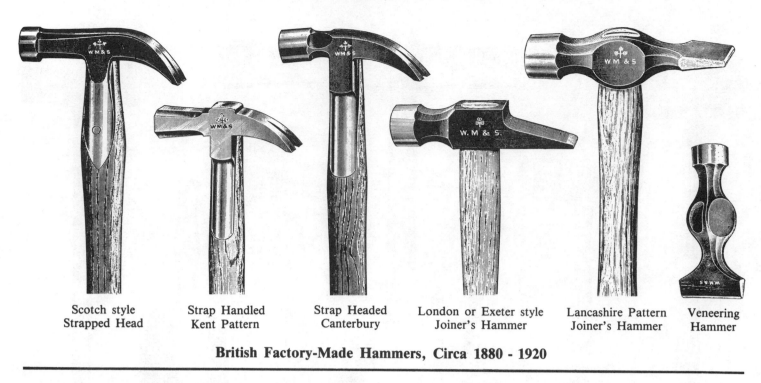

| Scotch style Strapped Head | Strap Handled Kent Pattern | Strap Headed Canterbury | London or Exeter style Joiner's Hammer | Lancashire Pattern Joiner's Hammer | Veneering Hammer |

British Factory-Made Hammers, Circa 1880 - 1920

FILE-MAKER'S hammer with 5½ in. head. Curved handle is set well to the back of head length. $50 - $150 (Hand-forged examples in largest sizes bring top dollar).

JOHN ROTHERY (circa 1835) filemaker's hammer with some files and accessories. auct. $300

FLAT PIEN machinist's hammer. $12

FRENCH carpenter's solid-claw type with 4 inch head. 17th century. $50

GEORGIA PACIFIC log marking hammer. 8 in. head has G.P. on both ends. $39

GOAT'S HEAD in brass figural style. auct. $55 - $85

IMP. Pat. Nov. 1, 1902. Double claw hammer with minor dents & scratches. $185. Others from $125 to $165.

JEWELERS hammer. auct. $20

JOINER'S hammer from England, circa 1900. $15

Another, with octagon face and chamfered neck. $20

Wm. H. JORTH & CO., Jamestown. Combination wrench, hammer and wire cutter. $14

JwG claw hammer. Asking $100

KEENKUTTER Hammers. $12-$25 ea.

LOG MARKING hammers sell in a broad range between $20 and $40 depending upon the initials and style. Some are double-end, others have a point or spike in addition to the raised initials. Four sided and multiple spoked models run $50 & up.

MAYDOL claw hammer, modern 13 oz. $8 (16 oz. ripping style. $12)

MILL PICK double end stone mason's hammer $15 - $20

NAPPING or Knapping hammer, stonemason's with thick rounded disk head. $20 - $25

NELS LUND & CO., Minneapolis, Minn. Combination nail puller, plier, and hammer. Pat. Apr. 1909. $28

PAVING HAMMER pick-like tool with 15 to 18 in head and chisel ends. $18-$25

P.F. PETE, Pat. Jan. 25, 78. Coil spring around prong-like pane. $35

A.R. ROBERTSON, Boston, Mass. Bill poster's tack hammer. 3 section hickory take-down-handle has nickel plated ferrule joints. Tack remover is fastened at side of neck. $125 - $185

ROOFER'S hand-forged 2 lb. square-faced hammer with extended claw and seperate strap-handle. auct. $80

SAW MAKER'S hammer, 8½ lbs. auct. $35

SAW MAKER'S hammer, early hand-forged example. Extra fine. auct. $80

SILVERSMITH'S light weight planishing hammer with swollen end handle. $10-$25

SILVERSMITH'S early double-faced chasing hammer with square eye and 2½ in. dia. faces. Orig. handle. auct. $55

SNOW KNOCKERS or snow-ball hammers come in many hand-forged styles. Open metal handles, wooden handles, some with chains and harness snaps. They were used to remove hard packed snow from the inside of horses hooves. They are 5 to 10 inches long with round bell and pick end. $18 - $34

STANLEY No. 100 plus "Golden Hammer of Merit" in velvet lined box with presentation plaque. These deluxe polished steel presentation quality hammers were advertised in Stanley's 1929 catalog for $2 each. Many were boxed or mounted and gold or brass plated before presentation. $100 - $125.

STONE CRANDLE, all metal tool for millstone dressing. Made from 12 double end steel spikes, stacked and welded into a rectangle with an iron handle. $35

P.S. STUBS, England, Silversmith's hammer with swollen end handle. $15

TACK HAMMER, novel fish-tail pulling-claw type. $18

THAYER PATENT June 24, 1862 tack hammer. $40

UNMARKED factory made U.S. claw hammers circa 1850 - 1870 $8 - $12 ea.

VENEERING hammer in solid walnut. auct. $30

VENEER hammer with 3½ in. wide heavy brass blade. $32

VENEERING hammer, early handwrought iron head with 2⅛ in. wedge shaped pane. $20 - $30

J. VIGEANT, Marlbo, Mass. Pat. 1-7-1869. No.2 double-faced 2 lb. hammer. auct. $25

WINCHESTER brand claw hammer. $35

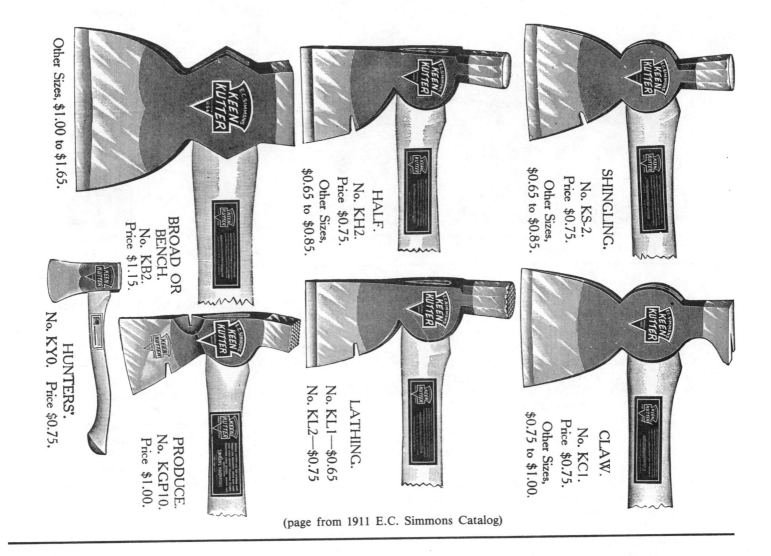

Other Sizes, $1.00 to $1.65.

BROAD OR BENCH. No. KB2. Price $1.15.

HALF. No. KH2. Price $0.75. Other Sizes, $0.65 to $0.85.

SHINGLING. No. KS-2. Price $0.75. Other Sizes, $0.65 to $0.85.

HUNTERS'. No. KY0. Price $0.75.

PRODUCE. No. KGP10. Price $1.00.

LATHING. No. KL1—$0.65 No. KL2—$0.75

CLAW. No. KC1. Price $0.75. Other Sizes, $0.75 to $1.00.

(page from 1911 E.C. Simmons Catalog)

AIRCRAFT emergency, or rescue hatchet. All metal with hooked poll. Some have jagged fuselage cutting edge. 14 in. overall. $8-$14 Scalloped edge, flat poll. auct. $40

D. R. BARTON No. 4 Kent style hewing hatchet. Nearly new cond. auct. $20

BOY'S HATCHET, factory made toy shingling hatchet 8 in. long. Better quality. $15

BOY SCOUTS OF AMERICA, Genuine Plumb. Camping hatchet. $18

BRIDGEPORT HDW. MFG. CO. Tomahawk Junior No. 9. Cast steel crating hatchet with claw extending from top. $16

BROAD AXE-SHAPED hatchet with 6 inch edge beveled one side. $12

CEREMONIAL TYPE hatchets in various styles of Indian-looking weapons, etc. Usually nickel plated and embossed with a message. $20-$35

COACHMAKER'S bearded hatchet with round hammer type poll. 8 in. blade has some asterisk type decoration. 18 in. overall. Auct. $75

COLLINS half hatchet with original paper label on head & handle. Mint, unused condition. $12

CRATING HATCHET with wooden handle riveted to metal shaft. Pry claw top. $12

FARMER'S Ever Ready Tool Kit. Combination hatchet, pliers, wire cutters, screwdriver, etc. $18

GERMAN made hand-forged carpenter's bearded side hatchet with fir tree smith's mark. Clove-shaped slot cutout in side of long rectangular blade. auct. $65

GOOSEWING style hatchet with 9 inch iron blade. Touchmark. 13 in. handle is wormy. $100

GOOSEWING hewing hatchet decorated blade has nail pulling cutout near flat top. Heavy poll is flared out on each side for larger striking surface. 5 x 6 in. bearded blade. $120

C. HAMMOND, Phila. No. 1 square head lathing hatchet. $15

ICE HATCHETS with round profile cutting edges. Various factory marked styles with lugs on eye bottom. $7 ea.

KAKADAM tobacco hatchet. Embossed with black lady, water barrel and jugs. Barrel acts as eye for handle. $60

KEEN KUTTER hatchets. $15-$25 (used & worn condition)

KEEN KUTTER broad axe shaped hatchet with 5 in. hewing blade. $35

KELLOGG TOASTED CORN FLAKE CO., Compliments of. Embossed crating hatchet with arrow head handle. $35

MARBLES Safety Pocket Axe. 12 inch hatchet has gutta-percha handles with name stamp. Swinging blade guard is hinged to middle of handle. $35-$95

JOHN RILEY'S Trianax. Heavy sheet steel hatchet with triangular profile head. $25

SHINGLING HATCHETS in various modern factory-made styles. $8 - $10 ea.

TOMAHAWK No. 99, by Bridgeport Mfg. Co. Crate-opening hatchet & pry-claw. Wooden grips riveted to shaft. $12-$16

TRADE HATCHET early handwrought, flat topped type, 2 inch cutting edge. $30

UNDERHILL EDGE TOOL CO. flat topped lathing hatchet with thatched square poll. $12 Mint example. $24

WINCHESTER hatchet head only. Flat top $18. Full blade style, 6 in $25

WINCHESTER broad axe style hatchet with raised lettering. $35 - $50

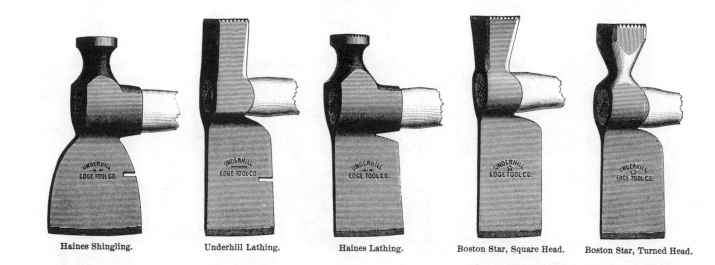

Haines Shingling.   Underhill Lathing.   Haines Lathing.   Boston Star, Square Head.   Boston Star, Turned Head.

1884 Advertisement

HATCHETS are, of course, small axes with hammer head polls. "Hache" is the French word for axe and "Axette" the first term for hatchet used in the New World. Sam Collins of Hartford, Conn. was the first American to mass produce hatchets, circa 1830. George Underhill followed with his factory in Nashua, New Hampshire in 1841. The output of these two Yankee factories soon dominated the world market for hatchets and trade axes.

IVORY was used in rule making and also as a trim or inlay material on finer hand tools made prior to the turn-of-the-century. The very appearance of genuine ivory on any tool should tip off a novice collector to the possibility of an important find. Elephant ivory found on the west coast of Africa was considered vastly superior to that of the east coast or Asian sources.

Unlike the flecked or pore-marked surface of bone, ivory has a delicate wood-like grain. To test for imitation material, heat a needle to red hot with a candle and press it firmly against an inconspicuous area. If the test material is not real bone, or ivory, the red hot needle will sink in like it were going through butter.

JAPANNING. Japan varnish or lacquer was originally a natural resin obtained in Japan by tapping the Rhus vernicifera, or varnish tree. Various pigments were added to the dried sap for specific applications. An all-purpose formula used in the 1890's consisted of: 2 lbs. gum shellac, one gallon oil, 1 pound each of red lead and litharge, and ¼ lb. of amber. "Melt the gum in a small quantity of oil (Linseed) and then add it gradually to the rest of the oil while it is boiling. Boil the whole receipe until Stringy".

Another early process for protecting iron consisted of coating the object very uniformly with a thin layer of linseed oil varnish, and burning it off over a charcoal fire. The process was repeated several times until a deep black color had been achieved. Finally this covering was wiped off with a dry rag and moderately heated again. The article was taken from the fire and rubbed with a linseed oil varnish soaked rag. The black turned completely dull and formed a rust proof coating.

A 20th-Century formula for japanning metal consisted of fusing 12 ounces of amber and 2 ounces of asphaltum by heat and adding ½ pint of boiled linseed oil and 2 oz. of rosin. While the mixture was cooling you added 16 ounces of turpentine to complete the black varnish.

Any vintage formula book will provide the reader with a half dozen more ways to create Japan varnishes for everything from carriage tops to bicycle fenders. Those who say that the early methods of Japanning tools are lost forever have simply never bothered to look.

KEENKUTTER was a trademark of the Simmons Hardware Company, organized in 1873 as a corporation by E.C. Simmons. Mr. Simmons began his hardware career in 1859 at the age of 19 when he secured an office boy's job with Wilson, Levering & Waters. Simmons bought out the widow of the founder, with the help of two partners, in 1870 and the business grew at a rapid pace under his stewardship.

By the beginning of the 20th-Century the E.C. Simmons Keen-Kutter hardware catalog contained no less than 4,200 pages of goods; a total of 79,000 items and 21,000 illustrations. The 25,000 catalogs published for Keen Kutter dealers in 1906 weighted in at the post office at half a million pounds. They had consumed 16 railroad car loads of paper and 2,500 lbs. of printer's ink.

In 1925 the Winchester Repeating Arms Co. merged with Simmons to take the burden of an ill-fated venture into hardware distribution off their own shoulders. At that time the combined hardware dealer outlets shared by both firms had dwindled to only 6,000 stores nationwide. In 1940 the Winchester-Simmons firm was puchased for $2,750,000.00 by the venerable Shapleigh Hardware Company of St. Louis, Missouri. Shapleigh continued the Keen Kutter trademark line and prospered during the booming wartime period and on into the 1950's. Finally a combination of escalating costs and a declining market share put an end to the company. After a lengthy labor walkout in 1960 the owners decided to close the doors forever.

Pre-1940 tools and knives with the Keen Kutter logo are actively collected, both for the unique trademark they bear and for the high quality production standards Simmons imposed upon its suppliers; among whom were the Stanley, Sargent, and Ohio tool companies.

LIGNUM VITAE is one of the heaviest, hardest, and oiliest hardwoods used in toolmaking. The source is Central and South America. Color varies from yellow to deep sepia, sometimes on the same piece. Lignum Vitae was also used in boat bearings for its toughness and self lubricating qualities.

– 2640 –

INFORMATION
REGARDING *KEEN KUTTER* POCKET KNIVES.

It is our aim to furnish, under the *KEEN KUTTER* Brand, the Highest Quality of Pocket Cutlery which can be produced. That we have accomplished this is shown by the Awards for the Highest Quality, granted to this line at the Louisiana Purchase Exposition, held in St. Louis, Mo., in 1904, and the Lewis & Clark Exposition, held in Portland, Ore., in 1905, illustrations of which are shown on pages 2634 and 2635. We believe this result cannot fail to follow from the method which we use in the manufacture of the goods.

It is our constant aim to see that everything about the line is of absolutely the Highest Quality, from the selection of the Raw Material to the Wrapping and Packing of the finished product.

Workmanship—Nearly 90 per cent of the men who manufacture this line were schooled in the art of making Fine Cutlery in the best English factories, where they learned their trade, and where their fathers and grandfathers spent their lives in the manufacture of Pocket Knives. The men are liberally paid for their work, and are constantly reminded that the item of quality is of much more importance than quantity.

Blades are made from the Highest Grade of English Crucible Steel imported especially for the purpose. They are Forged by hand from the Bar, and not stamped out from sheet steel (the method employed by many makers of Knives). They have an absolutely Uniform Temper, and are Whetted by Hand on an Oil Stone to a Sharp Cutting Edge, Ready for Use.

As specified in the description, the Blades are either Full Crocus Polished (i. e., each Blade Polished on Both Sides) or Half Polished (i. e., Large Blade Polished on One Side and other Blades Glazed Finish).

Patterns of Blades—The line contains every possible shape of Blades which is at all practical, as is shown by the following illustrations:

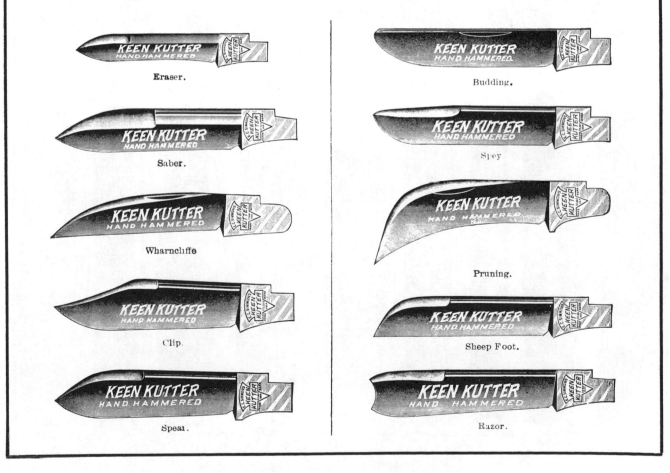

Eraser.

Budding.

Saber.

Spey

Wharncliffe

Pruning.

Clip.

Sheep Foot.

Spear.

Razor.

(page from 1906 E.C. Simmons Hardware Catalog)

KNIVES (continued)

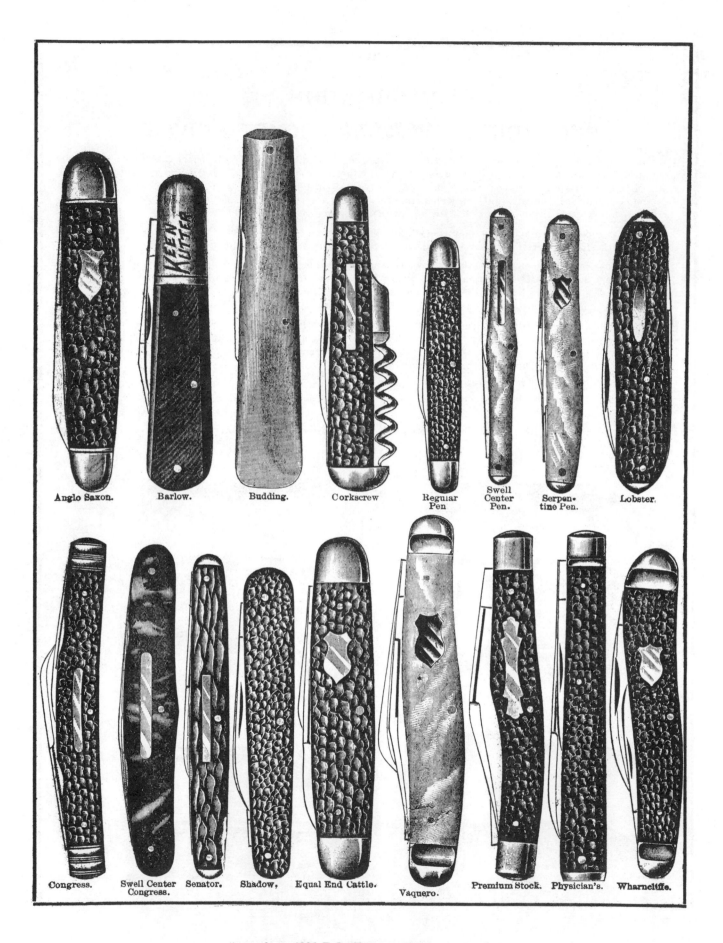

Anglo Saxon.   Barlow.   Budding.   Corkscrew   Regular Pen   Swell Center Pen.   Serpentine Pen.   Lobster.

Congress.   Swell Center Congress.   Senator.   Shadow,   Equal End Cattle.   Vaquero.   Premium Stock.   Physician's.   Wharncliffe.

(page from 1906 E.C. Simmons Hardware Catalog)

Information regarding *KEEN KUTTER* Pocket Knives (Continued).

Patterns of Handles—A great variety of shapes and designs of Handles are used in this line, the principal ones of which, with the names by which they are most commonly known are given below:

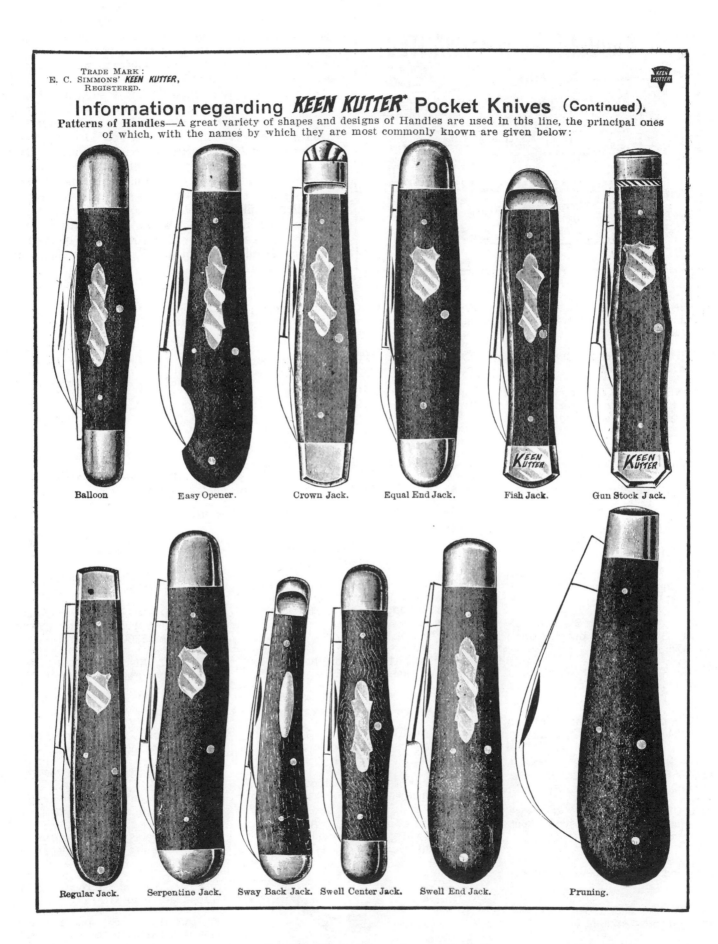

| Balloon | Easy Opener. | Crown Jack. | Equal End Jack. | Fish Jack. | Gun Stock Jack. |

| Regular Jack. | Serpentine Jack. | Sway Back Jack. | Swell Center Jack. | Swell End Jack. | Pruning. |

(page from 1906 E.C. Simmons Hardware Catalog)

KNIVES, like axes, evolved from prehistoric flint, to copper, to bronze, to iron, and finally into today's carbon-steel-bladed product. Folding knives were owned by early Romans but the small pocket knife, as we know it, was not invented until sometime in the 1600's.

Solingen, Germany and Sheffield, England have been important knife manufacturing centers since the Middle Ages. The first large scale cutlery manufacturer in the United States was founded by a wealthy 37 year-old cotton broker named John Russell. Mr. Russell pioneered the use of the trip hammer for forging blades and bolsters, thus increasing the average production of two men from 150 blades a day to 3,000. Russell's sales for the year 1871 exceeded a million and a half dollars. Pocket knives of the period wholesaled anywhere from thirty cents to a dollar each and were available in dozens of styles and patterns. Handles were made of ivory, horn, bone, cocobolo, ebony and stag.

N. AIKEN, eagle stamp, race knife, 2 prongs, turned applewood handles, brass ferrule. Auct. $60

ARTIS, Brighton. Folding race knife with stag horn handles. $40

O. BARNETT TOOL CO., Newwark, N.J. (1900-1915) combination pliers, punch and 2 bladed knife with stag handles. $115

BEMIS and CALL race knife in like new cond. Turned handle, brass ferrule. $50

BEVIL DEVIL bevel cutter in jointed oak box. $10

BLECKMAN, Superior Cutlery. Bone handled switchblade with release button on bolster. $190

H. BOKER & CO. Cutlery, Germany. Boker's corn kinfe printed on yellow handles. $35

H. BOKER & CO., Solingen. Staghorn lock back with 2 blades, saw, punch & corkscrew. $75

BOWL-MAKER'S hooked hand-forged knife with long shaft and wooden handle. $50

BLEEDER or Fleam. Veterinarians brass 3-bladed, key-shaped knife. $75

E. BRUCKMANN, Solingen, Germany. (1922-1956) pearl-handled pocket knife. Mint cond. $60

CAMILLUS CUTLERY jack knife-style folding race knife or timber scribe. Auct. $25

CAMILLUS CUTERLY CO. Babe Ruth signed one blade style in baseball bat shape. $57

CASE XX two bladed pen knife with cracked-ice handles. Mint. $25

CASE XX Muskrat pocket knife. $65

CASE Tested, rough black handled Stockman's pocket knife. $85

CASE TESTED XX Grandaddy Barlow style single blade with smooth bone handles. $80

CASE TESTED XX office knife with white composition handles. $55

CASE XX Scout knife. Bone handles have reddish tint. Mint cond. $40

CASE XX M279 two bladed metal pen knife. $20

CASE TESTED XX No. 561 axe/knife combination in original leather sheath. (circa 1920-1940) $215

CASE Circle C. No. M 1217 pat. 11-9-37. pull-ball type switch-blade. $150

CASE TESTED XX No. 4257 office knife (circa 1920-1940) Perfect. $65

CASE TESTED XX No. 5171 (pre 1915) rare early switchblade with green tinted stag horn handles. Oval trademark on bolster. $800

CASE BROS. CUT. CO. TESTED No. 83088 (1900-1912) pearl handled 2 blader with french file. $150

W.R. CASE & SONS "Coke Bottle" pocket knife in green bone. $250

CATTARAUGUS CUTLERY CO., Barlow type 2 blade pocket knife with brown bone handles. $60

CHAIR-MAKER'S hand-forged, hook-bladed, knife with 4 inch horn handle. $40

CHALLENGE CUT. CO., Bridgeport, Conn. (1891-1928) fly-lock double switch-blade with bale. Mint cond. $165

CROOKED KNIFE with carved bent-limb handle and wire-wound ferrule. Used by Northwestern Indians for woodcarving and basket making. $39-$49

CROOKED KNIFES in plain primitive, undecorated styles. $15-$30

CROOKED KNIFE with birch handle and string wrapped ferrule. Rich Patina. $45

CROOKED KNIFE from Maine with circular shaped handle. auct. $55

CROOKED KNIFE with scroll carved handle. $45

Another, with inlaid pewter. $50-$75

CROOKED KNIFE decorated with carved hearts. auct. $75

Another, with raised heart on handle. $65

CROOKED KNIFE found in Maine, carved human hand for handle. auct. $100

CROOKED KNIFE, left hand style with whale bone handle. auct. $150

CROOKED KNIFE ornately chip carved with tiny mirror and ladies picture inlaid in handle. auct. $200

CROOKED KNIFE elaborate scroll, carved finger groove. auct. $200

CROOKED KNIFE figural style, male torso and head for handle. auct. $300

Another, with nude woman in figurehead style. Old file blade. auct. $400

Another, bust of Naplolean? Asking $750

L.P. HYDE turpentine knife with scorp-end blade and plain wooden handle. $8

HYDE rosewood and brass utility, or mat cutting knife, also used by patternmakers. $15 - $20

JIM DANDY black handled 3½ in. three bladed jack knife. $10

KA-BAR (1923-1951) fork and spoon knife with one blade. Yellow handles. $90

KEEN KUTTER, E.C. Simmons, St. Louis. Bone handled, 2 blade, easy-open style with bale. $65   Other styles $30-$150

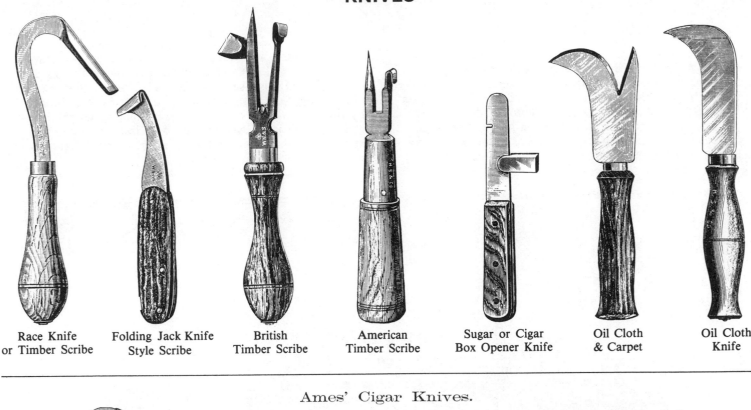

Race Knife or Timber Scribe   Folding Jack Knife Style Scribe   British Timber Scribe   American Timber Scribe   Sugar or Cigar Box Opener Knife   Oil Cloth & Carpet   Oil Cloth Knife

Ames' Cigar Knives.

Cincinnati Pattern, Square Point.   Cincinnati Pattern, Sharp Point.

1884 engraving

PAL BLADE CO. Made in USA. Scout knife with clip, pen blade, screwdriver, etc. $18

PAL CUTLERY CO. (1935-1953) Cattleman's long-pull style 3 blader with rough black 3¾ in. handles. $35

RACE KNIVES or Timber Scribes. Fixed blade variety avg. $25 Folding cutter and extra blade. $50-$65

REMINGTON (circular mark) pearl handled 2⅞ in. pen knife. $45

REMINGTON (circle mark) single-blade jack knife with swell-end green swirl handle. $55

REMINGTON No. R7925 pen knife, 2 blades, white celluloid handles. (mint) $60

REMINGTON pocket knife, 3 blades, multi-colored flakes in handles. $75

REMINGTON advertising knife with Kelly Tire and Boy on yellow celluloid handles. $80

REMINGTON letter opener/pen knife combination. Pearl handles. Mint cond. $95

REMINGTON, Barlow style 3½ inch pocket knife with bone handles. $100

REMINGTON gentleman's pen knife etched Bissels 1876-1926. Gold handles. $175

REMINGTON No. R645 (1920-1939) Fish-tail switchblade 4 in. long. Red & cream candy striped handles. Mint. $200

REMINGTON No. 1613 toothpick-style 5 inch knife with bone stag handles and round end bullet shaped shield, stamped Remington UMC. $395

ROBESON Suredge, Rochester. Scout knife, Pat. 1905. Bone handles. $60

J. RUSSELL & CO., Green River Works. Grandaddy Barlow style, lock-back single blade, stag handles. $175

SCHRADE CUT. CO., Walden, N. Y. (1904-1948). 4 bladed congress with 3¼ in bone handles and inlaid shield. $25

SCHRADE CUT. CO. advertising switchblade, 3¼ in. yellow handles. "Radio-Art Cabinets." $65

SCHRADE CUTLERY CO. Peanut-style., p.s. bone handles. $65

SCHRADE CUT. CO. large 4 in. pocket knife with candy striped cream colored handles. Mint cond. $165

SHAPLEIGH HDW. CO., DE (1843-1960). Brown bone handled knife with pen and sheepsfoot blades. Inlaid shield. $35

SHAPLEIGH HDW. CO. double-bladed pen knife with rough black handles and inlaid shield. $40

UNION CUT. CO., Coke bottle shape with 5¼ in. bone stag handles. KA-BAR inlaid shield. $175

VAN CAMP, Indianapolis (circle logo). Equal-end 2 bladed jack knife with stag handles. $50

W. & H. CO., Newark, N.J. advertising pen knife. "Ex-lax a friend in need" (worn cond.) $25

WESTERN STATES, Boulder, Colo.(1911-1951) Jack knife with 3 in. rough black handles, 2 blades. $40

WINCHESTER, Trademark, Made in USA (1919-1942). Pen knife 3 in. long. Multi-colored celluloid handles. $35

WINCHESTER, Trademark, Made in USA. Cattlerman's 3 blade pocket knife with brown bone handles. $210

WINCHESTER jack knife with inlaid shield on black swirl handle. $65

WINCHESTER, Trademark, Made in USA. Jack knife with a punch and 2 blades Swirled brown and cream handles. $85

WINCHESTER, Trademark, Made in USA No. 3365 pearl handled whittler, 3⅝ in. long. 3 blades. $160

I & XL, GEORGE WOSTENHOLM, Sheffield, England. Gentleman's 3 in. pearl handled pocket knife with a file and 2 blades. $50

LATHES, TURNING

The word LATHE comes to us from the Danish "drejelad" and the Old English "lade", meaning to load. Simply put, a lathe is a machine which holds and rotates an object which is to be changed by some form of cutting. This function may be performed with a series of hand-held turning chisels or by an automated cutting tool programmed to trim stock to a given shape. The ancient potter's wheel was actually a vertical lathe. Horizontal lathes, utilizing the bow and spindle principle, came into being about 740 B.C. The most popular turning projects of Cicero's day were elaborate wooden vases. So many were produced that Cicero named their makers "Vascularis". In 1818 an American named Thomas Blanchard invented the first lathe capable of turning irregular forms. By tracing a pattern or model, a workman could produce gunstocks, duck decoys, wooden shoe lasts, furniture legs and many other non-symetrical shaped items that previously had been handcarved.

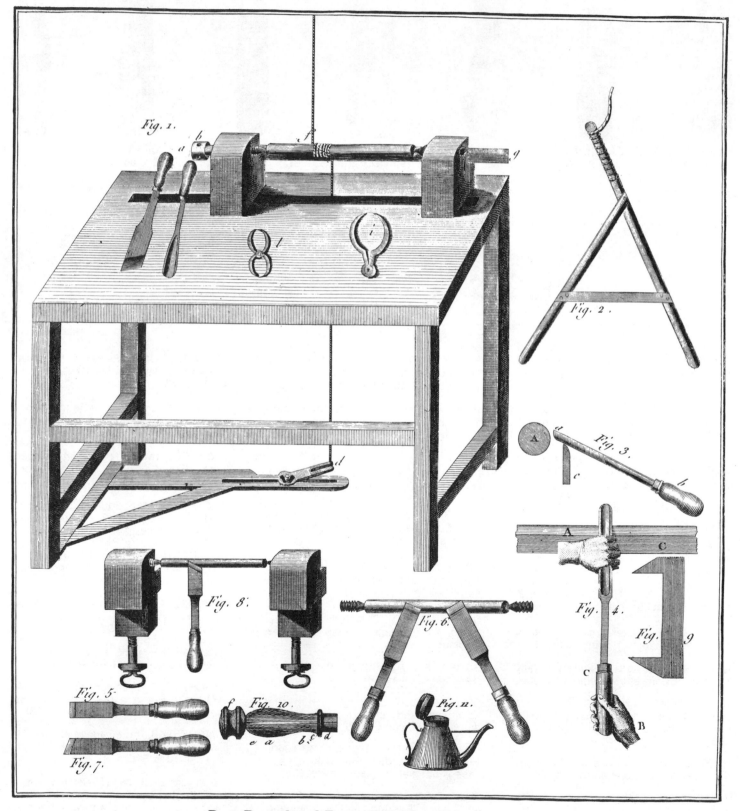

Page Reproduced From 1816 Manuel du Tourneur

Apprentice Turns Long Wooden Poles in a Two Man Shop of 1775

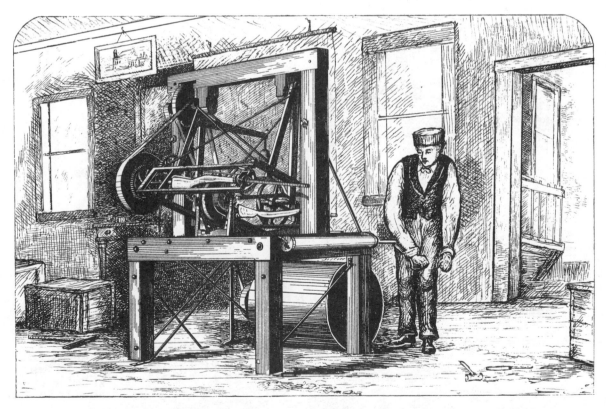

Crank Action Traces Pattern on U.S. Patent Gunstock Lathe of 1818

Completing a finish cut with the skew chisel.

Cutting-in Tool
for rapid cutting
of multiple grooves.

Bead Chisel

Sizing chisel for
cutting pilot grooves
to exact depth.

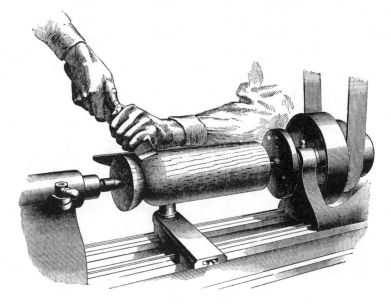

Preparing to cut a bead using the heel of a skew chisel.

Gouge for
roughing in
& hollowing.

Parting Tool
for separating
finished work
from stock.

Round Nose
Chisel for
safer, slower,
scraping out.

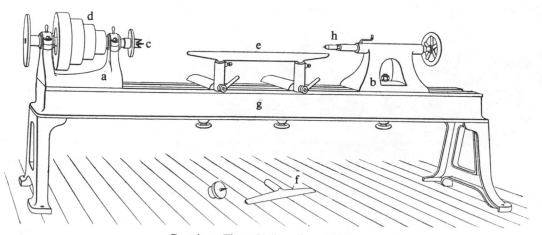

Cast iron Floor Lathe, circa 1900.

a. Headstock
b. Tail-stock
c. Headstock Spindle
d. Cone Pulley
e. Double Rest
f. Single Rest
g. Bed
h. Tail-stock Spindle

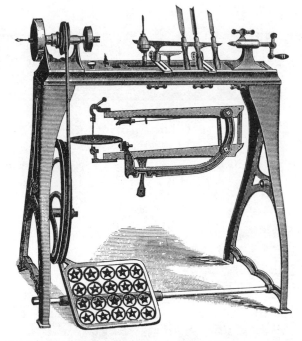

This GOODELL Lathe & Jigsaw combination was designed by A.D. Goodell, a master mechanic at the Millers Falls Factory. It appears in an 1886 catalog priced at $10. A similar lathe & saw outfit named the COMPANION was manufactured by Millers Falls for the "Youths Companion Magazine". It was offered as a subscription premium to young salesmen. Both models were very popular overseas as well as in the United States. They remained a staple item in mail-order catalogs well into the 20th century.

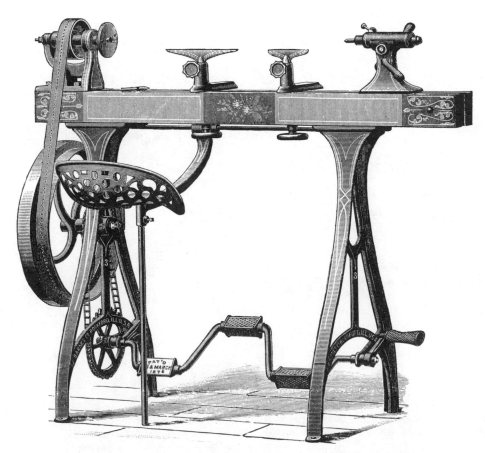

J. Barnes Co., Rockford, Ill. No. 3 Pedal-Powered Lathe. Circa 1876.

RECENT DEALER & AUCTION PRICES

BRASS MANDREL lathe, hand cranked, 13 inches overall. Ebony handles, helical cut gears. Mounted on chamfered mahogany block base. auct. $425

GOODELL "The Companion" foot treadle lathe with jig saw attachment. auct. $170

HAND-FORGED 18th Century all iron construction. Portable wood turning lathe, 30 in. long. All parts have thumbscrew adjustments. Takes up to 2 in. dia. stock, 16 in. long. 2 speed pulley drive. $345

JEWELER'S Brass lathe, 19th Century. 10 in. overall including tailstock. Has adjustable hand rest, table clamp and 4 speed pulley. auct. $200

MACHINIST'S Iron lathe from the Waltham Watch Factory tool room. 24 inch bed with compound feed. Spindle grinding attachment, idler pulley, face plate and assorted accessories. Auct. $425

MAHOGANY FRAMED ornamental 5 inch dia woodturning lathe with wooden treadle and flywheel. Holtzapffel headstock and tailstock No. 1868. Bed length is 40 inches. Complete with hand-rest and six drawer chest of accessories. Auct. $1,050

C.A. MANN, Prov., R.I. 38 in. long red and black cast iron bench lathe. 125 lbs. (legs have weld repairs) $125

MILLERS FALLS foot treadle powered woodturning lathe. 27 in. long x 31½ tall, 15 inches between centers. Combines drill chuck and emery wheel on left side of head stock. 98% of original black paint remains intact. $240

JOHN MUCKLE (British, 1830-1840) Ornamental woodturning lathe with mahogany frame, treadle & flywheel. Iron bed. Complete with accessories. auct. $765

OAK FRAMED foot operated overhead wheel lathe with 48 in. bed. Complete with rest, pulleys, drive rod & belt. Beautifully made. auct. $600

PRIMITIVE Hand-powered lathe 4 feet long. For turning spokes and tool handles. Wrought iron crank resembles automobile type in shape. $45

SPOKE TURNING lathe with mortised & tenoned hardwood frame, 4 feet long. Handwrought crank and holder slides in slotted 4 x 4 base. $50

UNMARKED wood or metal turning lathe of good quality. Nuts, collars and all brackets are brass 42 in. long, 16 in. tall, 22 in. between centers. Has 28 in. flywheel for conversion to foot power. $275

WATCHMAKER'S Lathe in solid brass Swiss quality, circa 1875. 8 inch headstock and mandrel are mounted on a 20 inch long iron bed plate. $975

DAVIS LEVEL AND TOOL CO.'S
Patent Adjustable Iron Plumbs and Levels.

No. 1.

Nos. 2, 3 and 4.

Davis' Patent Iron Level, Plumb and Inclinometer.
Adjustable, with Graduated Scale for working at any angle.

No. 1, 6 Inch, For Machinists, etc., . . . per dozen, $24 00	No. 3, 18 Inch, For Machinists, etc., . . . per dozen, $36 00
No. 2, 12 " " " " . . " 30 00	No. 4, 24 " " " " . . " 42 00

· One-twelfth dozen in a box.

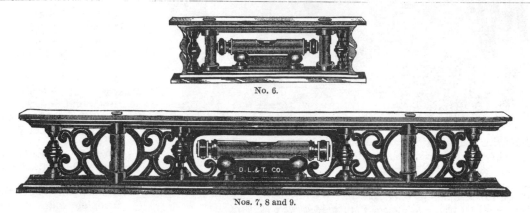

No. 6.

Nos. 7, 8 and 9.

Davis' Patent Double Plumb and Level.
All Iron, Adjustable.

No. 6, 6 Inch, For Carpenters, etc., . . . per dozen, $24 00	No. 8, 18 Inch, For Carpenters, etc., . . . per dozen, $30 00
No. 7, 12 " " " " . " 27 00	No. 9, 24 " " " " . " 36 00

One-twelfth dozen in a box.

Nos. 6, 7, 8 and 9 are also furnished with Extra Quality GROUND GLASS for Surveyors' use.

Nos. 10 and 12.

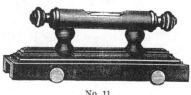

No. 11.

Davis' Patent Iron Bench Levels.

No. 10, 4 Inch, Adjustable Iron Bench Levels, For Machinists, etc., ... per dozen, $6 00
No. 12, 6 " " " " " " " " . . . . " 9 00
No. 11, 4 " Can be used on a Square on Straight Edge, Adjustable Iron Bench Levels, ... " 8 00

One-twelfth dozen in a box.

Nos. 14 and 15.

Davis' Patent Iron Pocket Levels.

No. 14, 3 Inch, Polished Brass Top, Ball Tips, ... per dozen, $2 50
No. 15, 5 " " " " " . . . . . " 3 50
No. 17, 3½ " " " " " Can be used on a Square or Straight Edge. . . " 3 00

1884 catalog page featuring the iron level line of the DAVIS LEVEL & TOOL CO., (established by Leonard Davis in 1867 at Springfield, Massachusetts). Mr. Davis, a former blacksmith's apprentice, and 25 loyal employees manufactured a small but popular line of levels, planes and handtools which were marketed both here and abroad. Prior to 1875 the firm was known as the L.L. Davis Co. Levels produced between 1875 and 1892 have no gold painted decoration on their filigree openwork. Mr. Davis sold out at the turn-of-the-century and went into the electric lamp business.

Masons at work. Circa 1750. Diderot's Encyclopedia.

Standing water is always level and a free-hanging weighted cord is always perpendicular to level. These two principles enabled the earliest masons to produce very accurate work, even by today's standards. The 18th-Century stone masons (at left) are pictured using the same kind of wooden A-frame level that Egyptian pyramid builders employed. A weighted string hangs from its apex and crosses a plumb mark in the center of the bottom bar.

Early American carpenters often made their levels in the shape of an L-square. A plumb bob was suspended from the top of the stem to a beet-shaped cutout near the base. Spirit levels, as we know them today, were invented in the late 1600's but not adopted by craftsmen in general until another two hundred years had passed.

Millions of spirit levels have been manufactured since the early 1800's but not all of them are necessarily collectable. Large, long levels, present a display problem. Softwoods and synthetic materials are not desirable, however filigree & cast iron is. Collectors esteem small sizes, exotic woods, and lots of brass trim. The most valuable levels look expensive; the craftsmanship will be apparent. Condition is a prime factor also. Levels showing much wear are best left for novice collectors or interior decorators.

ACME LEVEL CO. 30 inch mahogany level with 2 large brass porthole covers. 1 dial is marked in degrees, both are adjustable. $35

ACME LEVEL CO., Toledo, Ohio. Pressed steel 26 in. level with 3 bubbles and brass porthole surrounds. $20 - $25

ACME LEVEL No. 4½ sheetmetal level, 20 in. long. Diamond Edge Brand imprint of Shapleigh Hardware, St. Louis. Copper center section has star cutouts. Inclinometer in center. $22 - $27

AMERICAN COMBINED Level & Grade Finder (see Edward Helb listing, levels)

ATHOL MACHINE CO., Athol, Mass. 6 in. steel level with 3 bubbles. $10

AKRON LEVEL by Baker McMillan Co., Akron, Ohio. 12 inch long laminated mahogany level with brass trim. $15

AKRON ECLIPSE Level. Pat. 12-20-04 Baker McMillen Co., Akron, Ohio. Plain, untipped, unlipped, mahogany level with unusual double tubed vials. $25 - $45

BAKER & McMILLEN CO., Akron, Ohio, Pat. 12-20-04 Hardwood 48 inch level with maltese cross logo under old red paint. 4 portholes, 6 vials, 2 oval plumb bob cut outs. No brass. $75

BAKER McMILLEN completely brassbound 12 inch level in box. auct. $115

W. BALES tapered mahogany level 30 inches long. Nearly new cond. auct. $35

BENNETT & BURLEY, Glasgow. Ebony spirit level with full length 12½ inch ornamental brass top plate. Includes mahogany shoe. auct. $91

BEDORTHA BROS., Windsor, Conn. cherry levels in 18 to 28 inch lengths. No brass. $15 - $20 ea.

BRASS TRIANGULAR STOCKED 19 inch level with twin vials and horizontally mounted compass. Walnut case. auct. $210

BRONZE Level/Inclinometer with hand-stamped scale and 1841 date. Consists of 100 degree protractor with vial, pivoting at end of 7 inch rule. auct. $300

BROWN'S PATENT gradient level, inclinometer with 2 curved tubes. Full length 10 inch brass plate on boxwood. In orig. case. auct. $70 Dlr. $115

BUCK & HICKMAN combination rule and level. Boxwood with brass trim. 2 vials. $125

J. BUIST, Edinburgh. Heavy rosewood 11 in. level with thick top & bottom plates. $50

Another, 12 inch, brassbound, with integral sight. $100

Another, in ebony, 10 inch, brassbound. $148

BENNET B. BURLEY, Glasgow, Warranted 12 in. mason's boxwood rule & spirit level with increments on sides at base. Plain brass bubble cover. $60 - $80

BENNET B. BURLEY, Glasgow. Brassbound 10 in. ebony level with arrow-end top plates. auct. $91

Another, in ebony, 12 inch long with decorative cutouts in brass top plate. $140

E. M. CHAPIN, Pine Meadow (1868-1897) cherry level, 22 inches in length. auct. $25

H. CHAPIN, Union Factory (circa 1826-1860) 26 inch cherry level. Plain with brass ends. $20 - $30 Another, 12 inch. $30

H. CHAPIN, Union Factory. Combination rule and level 28 inches long. Brown mahogany with 2 vials. $60

C. S. CO., Pine Meadow, Conn. (circa 1901-29) Hardwood level 28 in. long with brass ends and large round dial marked off in degrees. $75 With pop-up sights $175

CHAPIN STEVENS CO., Pine Meadow, Conn. Vogel patents May 18, 1919, 1923 & 1926. Aluminum 30 inch level with 3 portholes and brass center pane. $30

CHAPIN STEPHENS CO. cherry plumb and level 28 inches long. Brass ends and side view lips. Circular boxwood inclinometer. $55

COGHILL PAISLEY unusual rosewood spirit level with 9⅝ in. full length brass top plate. $58

COLQUHOUN & CADMAN rosewood level 7 in. long with brass top plate. $40 10 inch. $48

COOK'S No. 4 patented 30 inch cherry level (circa 1886). auct. $30 26 inch with case. $50 No. 6 $60

G. S. CROSBY "Boss" 12 inch mahogany level made in Brooklyn, N.Y. Heavy brass plates. Mint in original box. $150

J. M. DAVIDSON, New York. Early 30 inch level with 3 different brass bubble mounts. $80

DAVIS No. 4 japanned iron filgree level 24 inches in length. $150 - $200 Mint $400

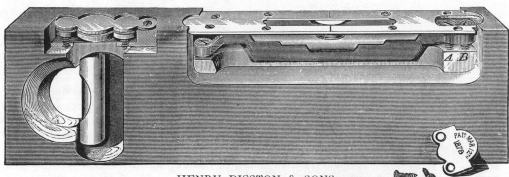

HENRY DISSTON & SONS

In presenting this level to the Trade, we would say that it is superior to any other adjustable level now in use. The adjusting is done by screws, and when adjusted forms a perfectly solid plumb and level, and therefore cannot get out of order. The adjusting screws are covered by the protecting shield *C*, thereby securing its accuracy at all times. Mechanics can rely on it.

(From 1899 catalog)

DAVIS & COOK, Watertown, N.Y. Pat. Dec. 7, '86. Hardwood plumb & level with twin portholes set near center of stock on either side of nickle plated brass center divider. 28 in. and 30 in. Dlr. $35 - $55 Cast iron 18 in., sloped ends. Auct. $325

L. L. DAVIS, No. 2 cast iron machinists level, plumb and inclinometer. 12 inches long. Rail shape with filigree web. auct. $75 - $160

DAVIS No. 3 iron machinists level in rail shape with filigree surrounding inclinometer housing. 18 inches long, 1867 patent date. $95 - $140 Mint cond. $220 Another, unlisted 7inch model. $135 - $200

DAVIS PATENT, made for M.W. Robinson Co. No. 8 duplex plumb and level, fancy iron openwork pattern with 3 vials. 18 in. long. $65 - $90. No. 3 Auct. $35

DAVIS No. 14 Mahogany inclinometer, plumb & level, with 2 portholes. One houses a brass inclinometer and the other view is unplated. Top vial has arch-end top plate and side view lips. 1867 patent date. 24 and 30 inch sizes. auct. $125 Dlr. $225 Worn cond. $75

L. L. DAVIS No. 22 plain mahogany level, 30 in. long. Brass bubble plate, no side plates or butt plates. Single unlined porthole. Circa 1880. $35

L. L. DAVIS, Springfield, Mass. Pat. March 17, 1867. No. 34 mason's double plumb and level with brass lipped side views and butt plates. $25 - $40

L. L. DAVIS No. 36 iron pocket level, 2½ in. long with ball ends and a straight edge clip. auct. $75

L. L. DAVIS mahogany level 36 inches long. Clean and perect. Unplated, plain model. $60

DAVIS LEVEL & TOOL CO. No. 37 rectangular iron pocket level with ball ends, 3 in. overall. Full brass trim and top plate. Circa 1880. auct. $50 6 inch model $85

DAVIS LEVEL & TOOL CO. pat. 1877 & 1883 fancy 24 inch iron filigree level with long horizontal center tube and round framed vial at each end. $85

T. F. DECK LEVEL CO., Toledo, Ohio. patented 1905. Cherry level, 24 in. long with large round spring-loaded gravity type mechanism. Brass corners and trim. $175

DECLEVITY type level. Unmarked, rosewood and brass. Rod is raised to desired angle as marked on support. auct. $220

HENRY DISSTON & SONS, Keystone Tool Works, Phila. Pat. Oct. 29, 1912. No. 27 plumb & level 18 inches long. Cherry with brass trim. $22 - $30

DISSTON & SONS, Phila. No. 55 plumb & level, 24 inches in length. Fully brass bound, arch top plate, lipped views. $55

HENRY DISSTON mason's plumb & level with cutout and a lead plumb bob. 42 inches in length. auct. $25

H. DISSTON & SONS 12 inch rosewood level, brassbound on all edges. Single unplated porthole at left end. auct. $95

HENRY DISSTON & SONS Master Mechanic. 16 inch cherry level. auct. $16

DISSTON & SONS, pat. Oct. 29, 1912. Brassbound 24 inch mahogany level in narrow, thinner style with single porthole. auct. $55

HENRY DISSTON & SONS, Pat. Oct. 29, 1912. Single porthole 24 inch cherry level with thumb grooves. This model had no end plates. $20

DISSTON & MORSE beechwood 26 inch level with brass end plates. $20

E. A. DODGES PATENT, Saratoga Springs New York. "Elastic Spring Needle" birchwood plumb & level. 38 inches long with N. P. Sanborn trademark stamps on either end. Auct. $250-$400 (1985)

EBONY unmarked 4 inch brassbound pocket level in metal case. $40

EBONY unsigned, decorative brass plated, 12 inch level. Angular cutout top plate. $75 - $85

EBONY British made, unsigned 10 inch level with elaborate scrolled brass plates covering 30% of the surface area. $100

FEDERAL TOOL CO. patent 1912, inclinometer level with 28 inch hardwood stock. 3 portholes, brass tips. $60

FENTON & MARSDEN rosewood level with full length brass top plate. Circa 1841, fine. $95

D. FLATHER & SONS, Solly Works, Sheffield. Boat shaped 12 in. rosewood level with short brass top plate and bottom tips. $35

J. R. FLETCHER, 348 W. 37th St., New York inscribed on brass bubble plate and sides of mason's 5 foot long wooden level with 2 portholes and a plumb bob cutout. $35 - $55

P. L. FOX, Pat. Sept. 20, '87. Unusual flat steel level with 3 portholes and 3 bubble covers. $85

C. H. FRECH with eagle stamp. Mahogany 30 in. level with single unlined porthole, brass lipped side view. auct. $25

P. FARLEY No. 183 Triangular shaped rosewood and brass level, 3 vials. $450

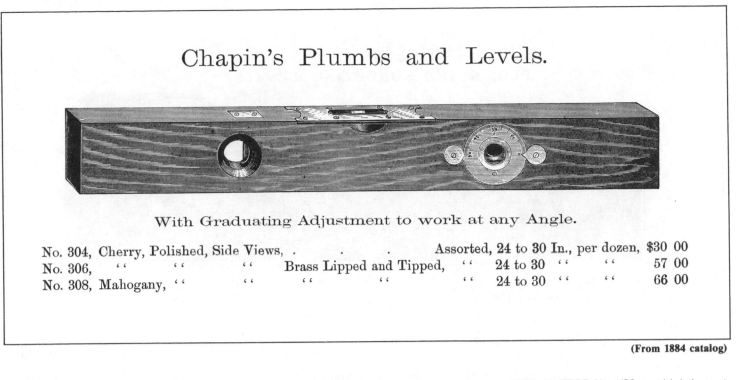

Chapin's Plumbs and Levels.

With Graduating Adjustment to work at any Angle.

| No. 304, Cherry, Polished, Side Views, | | | Assorted, 24 to 30 In., per dozen, | $30 00 |
| No. 306, " " " Brass Lipped and Tipped, " 24 to 30 " " 57 00 |
| No. 308, Mahogany, " " " " " 24 to 30 " " 66 00 |

(From 1884 catalog)

GOODELL-PRATT CO. fully brassbound 24 or 28 in. plumb & level. 1 in. x 2 in. auct. $45 - $80 Dlr. $70 - $95

GOODELL-PRATT CO. iron 12 in. duplex plumb & level. $15

GOODELL-PRATT No. 510 iron level 24 inches long. $10

GOODELL-PRATT No. 4326 brassbound mahogany 26 inch, Near new. auct. $50. Plain style 26 in. mahogany level. $20

GOODELL-PRATT CO. Greenfield, Mass. No. 612 pocket level. Brass hexagonal tube 3½ in. long, nickle plated. $10

W. GREAVES & SONS, Sheffield. 10 in. rosewood level with full brass top plate. $45 - $55

R. GROVES & SONS, Sheffield. 8 in. rosewood level with full top and bottom plates. $95

HALL & KNAPP, New Britian, Conn. with eagle and shield imprint. 29½ in. mahogany level, circa 1853 - 1858. $30 - $45

HALL & KNAPP with eagle trademark. Heavy exotic hardwood level 26 inches long. Single plain porthole, brass rectangular side view plate. auct. $55

J. W. HARMON, Boston, circa 1870 - 80. Mahogany level, 30 inches in length. Brass top plate and side views . $30

J. W. HARMON, Boston. Patented telescope plumb level in mint condition. Pat. Nov. 23, 1880. Including orig. box. $145

EDWARD HELB "American Combined Level And Grade Finder" Manufactured by Edward Helb, Railroad, York Co., Pa. U.S. July 12, 1904. Cherry 24 in. stock with sight inside and square-framed round inclinometer. auct. $125 - $210 Dlr. $225

JOSEPH HIBBERT tubular brass end pocket level on walnut base. Dovetailed oak box. auct. $160

HOME-MADE various hardwood levels, mostly mahogany with brass bubble covers on top. 20 in. to 30 in. long. $10 - $15 each.

C. E. JENNINGS & CO., New York. iron filigree level with 3 bubble vials. 24 inches overall. $32

W. JOHNSON, Newark, N.J., beechwood 28 inch level. $15

KEEN KUTTER No. KKO single porthole, plain hardwood level in 24 to 30 inch lengths. Only brass trim is top bubble cover plate. auct. $12 - $15 Dlr. $20 - $30

KEEN KUTTER No. KK1 cherry plumb & level 30 in. long. E. C. Simmons appears in logo on brass top plate along with pat. dates of 6-2-91 & 6-23-96. $20

KEEN KUTTER No. KK13 non-adjustable 12 inch cherry level with no porthole (refinished). $20 Mint cond. $40

KEEN KUTTER No. KK30 duplex 28 in. cherry level with 2 large porthole frames and brass butt plates. Fine. $35 - $50

KEEN KUTTER Nos. KK40, KK45 & KK50 Brassbound mahogany levels with brass trimmed portholes and side views. 24 in. to 30 in. lengths. $55 - $75 Mint $95 - $175

KEEN KUTTER No. KK104 level in avg. cond. $25

KEEN KUTTER, E. C. Simmons, double enclosed vials. Patented 12-2-04. Brassbound some red paint remaining. $60

KEEN KUTTER cherry plumb & level 12 inches long. Brass top plate and tips. Mint. auct. $40

KEEN KUTTER No. K69 machinist's cast iron 9 inch plumb & level with 3 vials. $50 - $65

KEEN KUTTER No. K618 cast iron 18 inch machinist's or carpenter's plumb & level with 3 vials. $65 - $95

LAMBERT, MULLIKEN & STACKPOLE mahogany 24 inch level with eagle stamp and short brass top plate. auct. $15. 29 inch model. $22. 26 in. early type. $30

LAMBERT, MULLIKEN & STACKPOLE (Boston 1852-1855) mahogany 24 inch level with brass end corners and side view plates. auct. $30 Rosewood model 25½ long. auct. $45

M. LENNON, Boston, Mass. 42 in. mahogany mason's level with inscribed hammer & trowel on brass plate. $50

D. M. LYON & CO. (Newark, N.J., 1846-1862) Mahogany stairbuilder's 30 inch level in original wooden carrying case. 2 adjustable vials set under round brass viewing plates. auct. $160

D. M. LYON & CO. 24 to 30 inch mahogany levels with no side plates. Plain with brass tips. $20 - $35

MACHINIST'S unmarked 7½ in. cast iron pocket level with turned round end knobs and full length brass top plate. $18

MACHINIST'S tiny 4 inch rail-shaped cast iron pocket level with tube running the full length on top. $25

MACHINIST'S 12 inch cast iron rail-style level with 45 degree angle slope at each end, (shorter top length than bottom). Heavy brass bubble cover. $40

JAMES McCOSKRIE & CO. black mahogany level 24 x 1½ inches. Rectangular brass side views. Mint cond. $85

ALEX. MATHIESON & SONS, Ltd.
PLUMB AND SURVEYING LEVELS.

No. 46 D. —Plumb and Surveying Level, Rosewood, Full Plated, Best, ...

	12	14	16	inch.
	10/3	10/9	11/	each.

(From 1899 Catalog)

W. MARPLES No. 2280 square end rosewood level with full brass top plate. auct. $46

Wm. MARPLES & SONS No. 2316 rosewood tapered pocket level with arrow head-end top plate and tips. No porthole. $30 - $35

W. MARPLES No. 2331 tubular brass 6 inch engineer's level with bubble cover. auct. $32

Wm. MARPLES & SONS ebony pocket level 10 inches long with brass top plate and sliding cover. Fine. $95. 9 in., good. $55

W. MARPLES Blonde hardwood 10 in. spirit level with round ends & full brass top plate. auct. $32

W. MARPLES & SONS, Hibernia, Warranted Correct. Round end rosewood level 10 in. long with solid brass top plate and tips on bottom ends. $65

W. MARPLES & SONS, Hibernia. No. 2290 brass topped ebony level with sliding guard plate over tube. Circa 1900. Fine. $100

MARSHALL rosewood & brass torpedo-shaped 9 inch level. $30 - $35

Another, as above. Ebony, porthole. $32

ALEX MARSHALL, Glasgow. Brass topped ebony torpedo level 12 in. long. Made for Marsden's of Preston on brass top. Fine. $100

MATHER & SON, Solly Works, Sheffield. Heavy brassbound ebony level. 8 inches long. auct. $60

A. MATHIESON & SON No. 7C Brassbound rosewood level 9 inches long. Normal wear. auct. $45

ALEX MATHIESON brass topped mahogany level 12 inches long. Top boldly engraved with bricklayer's name and dated Ipswich 1841. auct. $95

MATHIESON & SON ebony level plain with brass top plate, 10 inches in length. auct. $75

MATHIESON No. 011C ebony 10 inch level with ornate cut-outs in full length brass top plate. $95

MATHIESON, Glasgow, No. 014D ebony level with scalloped fancy brass side view. Ornate brass top and tip plates and full length 12 inch bottom plate. Circa 1899. $140

MATHIESON, Glasgow, No. 18A ebony & brass spirit level. 12 inches long. Rotating tube cover. auct. $220

MATHIESON, Glasgow, No. 20C rosewood torpedo level 10 inches long. Arrow head ends on top plate. Brass tipped bottom. $32

A. MATHIESON & SON, Glasgow. No. 44D Warranted. Proved Tubes. Brassbound 12 in. rosewood surveyor's level with peep sight in butt plate. auct. $200

W. B. MELICK, Pat. Dec. 3, 1889. Mahogany 30 inch inclinometer level with nickle plated cast iron dial frame. $195

MILLERS FALLS CO. No. 24 iron level with 85% of original japanning intact. 12 inches long, circular cut-outs. $20

MILLERS FALLS tiny 8 inch rosewood brassbound level of the Stratton Bros. style. Brass half circle view at right end plus brass lipped side views. No full porthole. auct. $250

MILLERS FALLS No. 1 Mahogany level full brass top plate & trim. 26 in. Auct. $80

MULLIKEN & STOCKPOLE, Boston, Mass. Plain 18¾ in.rosewood level with plumb bubble set inside an angled side opening. $50

MULLIKEN & STACKPOLE, Boston, Mass. (1856-1860) small 22 in. mahogany level with brass top plate and no porthole or side views. $42 29½ inch model with single unlined porthole. $35 - $55

MULLIKEN & STACKPOLE rosewood level 29½ in. long with brass corners, top plate and side views. $115

A. J. MURRAY, Warranted. Rosewood boat-shaped 9 inch plumb and level with brass trim. $35

HENRY NICHOLSON & SONS, New York. cast iron 14 inch level, later model. $25

Wm. T. NICHOLSON, Prov., R.I. pat May 1, 1860. Cast iron 14 inch level. auct. $150

H. M. POOL, Easton, Mass. 24 inch mahogany level with brass trim. auct. $30

H. M. POOL, Easton, Mass. 30 in. mahogany level with eagle imprint. Brass top plate. Excellent cond. $40 27 inch model, circa 1850. $60 8 in. Auct. $145

H. M. POOL, Easton, Mass. with eagle trademark. Heavy 26 in. mahogany level with thick brass end corners and a double aperture rectangular side view. auct. $80 30 inch, mint cond. $95

EDWARD PRESTON & SONS (1889-1933). Brass pocket level only 3 inches long. $35 Tubular brass, 6 in. Auct. $42

PRESTON Wood's pat. cat's eye level. 4 inch rectangular pocket level. $35

PRESTON rosewood 6 in. pocket level with full length brass top plate. $18 - $30

Ebony Spirit Level, Scotch Pattern, Marples No. 2286

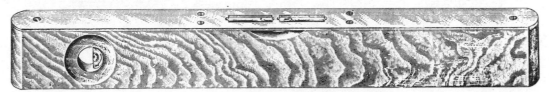

William Marples & Sons No. 2300 Walnut Plumb & Level. Sold in 8 to 18 in. lengths.

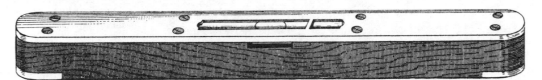

Edward Preston & Sons No. 1242S Rosewood Level With Brass Top. 8 to 12 inch.

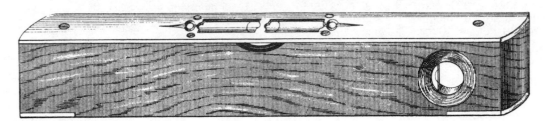

Edward Preston & Sons No. 1053 Plumb & Level With Brass Top Plate. 10 inches long.

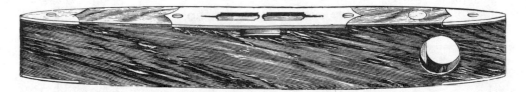

Torpedo-Shaped Rabone No. 1628 Rosewood Plumb & Level. 9 & 12 inch.

Rabone No. 1354 & 1355 Brass Adjusting Level. Sold in 4 thru 14 in. sizes.

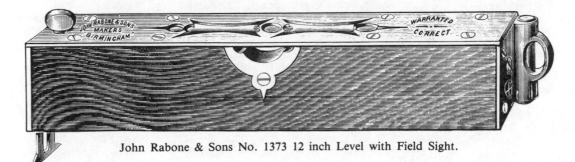

John Rabone & Sons No. 1373 12 inch Level with Field Sight.

A Selection of British Made Spirit Levels. Circa 1890-1910.

EDWARD PRESTON & SONS No. 1053 mahogany 10 in. spirit level with full length top and bottom plates. $58

E. P. trademark on 12 in. ebony level with full length brass top plate and tipped bottom ends. $45

EDWARD PRESTON & SONS fancy brass-trimmed ebony 9 inch level. auct. $35 Dlr. $65 10 in RD No. 300723. $75 No. 100 w/porthole, 18 in. Auct.$180

EDWARD PRESTON & SONS boat-shaped rosewood plumb and level 12 in. long. Pointed end top plate and brass tips. Single porthole is plain. $40–$55

E. PRESTON & SONS No. 1209 brass topped ebony level with round ends. No side views. 9 inches in length. auct. $35 - $60 10 inch $35

PRESTON & SONS No. 1243 brass trimmed ebony level 8 inches long. Heavy full length top plate and lipped side views. auct. $75 Dlr. $95

P.R.R. CO. oak railroad grade level. Adjustable, 5 feet long, steel trim. auct. $40

JOHN RABONE & SONS No. 1327 rosewood level 12 inches long. Full length brass top plate, tipped bottom. Circa 1890. $70 8 inch. $35

J. RABONE & SONS, Birmingham, No. 1354 brass cylindrical shaped 4 inch level with flat bottom. Circa 1890. $39

RABONE No. 1621 economy grade mahogany level 8 inches long. Made in Birmingham, England. Brass top. $20

J. RABONE & SONS, Birmingham, No. 1625 rosewood & brass torpedo level 6 in. long. (one dry bubble) $40

JOHN RABONE & SONS No. 1627 rosewood torpedo level with brass trim. 9 inches in length. $30 - $35 Another, 12 in. $45

JOHN RABONE & SONS No. 1628 rosewood plumb & level in torpedo shape with tapered ends. 12 inches over all. Brass plate in center of top has pointed ends, tips have notched end. Single porthole. $35 - $45

J. RABONE, 10 in. rosewood level with pierced brass top and a brass plumb vial side plate. $50

JOHN RABONE & SONS, Makers, Birmingham. Rosewood level with brass end caps and full length 10 in. top plate. 2 vials. Original finish. Fine. $100

J. RABONE, Makers, Birmingham. 10 in. boxwood rule with level set in brass top plate. $35 - $60

RABONE & SONS, Birmingham, Warranted Correct. Solid brass rectangular 6 in. pocket level. $48

C. F. RICHARDSON, Athol, Mass. (circa 1887) Decorative black cast iron double plumb & level 24 in. $35. 6 inch. Auct. $20

R. J. SANFORD, Worcester, Mass. Pat. Nov. 8, '87. Iron level with adjustable protractor arm which holds bubble at any angle to horizontal base. Most of orig. black japanning remains. $60

SARGENT & CO. early cherry mason's plumb & level with cut-out for plumb bob. auct. $60

SHOFIELD'S ANGLE INDICATOR cast iron mantle clock shaped level. Pat. June 23, 1885. Black japan finish with brass bezel around dial. $170

S. G. SHERMAN, New York. Cast iron line level 3½ in. long. $12

SIBLEY'S PAT. 6-23, 1868 cast iron 11½ in. level with detachable brass peep sights. auct. $160

SIGHTING LEVEL in folding brass, 8 in. long ruler shape with vial attached to edge of horizontal leaf. auct. $130

SIGHTING LEVEL, French made, 1½ in. x 9 in. with raised rectangular sights at each end of a boxwood spirit level/scale/rule combination. $63

I. & D. S. SMALLWOOD, Birmingham, England. 12 inch rosewood level with full length brass top plate. $35

SORBY ebony pocket level, 8 in. $55

STANDARD TOOL CO. Athol, Mass. Cast iron level with V groove in bottom for piping. $35

STANDARD RULE CO., Unionville, Ct. Plain cherry level 12 in. long with one porthole. $10

STANLEY RULE & LEVEL CO.

Dating levels made by The Stanley Rule & Level Company presents a problem unless one consults old catalog reprints.

Brass side view plates were rectangular in shape between 1859 and 1870. In the 1874 catalog we find them becoming lip-shaped with fat ends. By 1909 side views on all models had evolved into streamlined concentric half circle bands. The familiar sweetheart logo was adopted in 1920 and phased out after 1935. Brass butt plates which covered only the corners of some models in 1909, had become full end plates in the 1929 catalog.

For the first 60 years even the least expensive levels were made from solid cherry or mahogany, but by 1929 aluminum bound "lightwoods" and "softwoods" (sugar pine) had begun to creep into the line. Orange lacquer also reared its ugly head to displace the handrubbed polish of turn-of-the-century models. The 1939 catalog featured such exotic fare as laminated walnut & redwood with aluminum tips in addition to the traditional cherry or mahogany with brass.

STANLEY RULE & LEVEL CO. Wm. T. Nicholson, Prov, R.I., Pat. May 1st, 1860. Iron level 19½ in. long with 6 circular cutouts in web. Opening in bottom rail for overhead reading. $150. 24 in. Auct. $35

STANLEY Nos. 01, 02, 03, & 04 non-adjustable hardwood mahogany or cherry plumb and levels first appeared in 1879 catalog, offered in 24 to 30 inch lengths. Nos. 02 and 03 were still in production in the 1930's. We assume that these economy grade levels are so common that they are not advertised by tool dealers, as no prices are recorded. A well worn, but decorative, non-adjustable level by Stanley might fetch $15 to $20 in an antique shop. No. 010 cherry 25 inch. Auct. $25

STANLEY No. 011 rosewood level 30 in. long. Brass tips, side view lips and square-end top plate. Circa 1900. auct. $45

STANLEY No. 00 non-adjustable hardwood plumb and level with arch-end top plate, but plain tips and porthole, with no side view lips. Appears in 1870 - 1939 catalogs. 18 - 24 in. long. $20

STANLEY No. 0 non-adjustable hardwood plumb and level Pat. 6-23-96. Offered in 24 to 30 inch lengths. Brass arch top plate but plain ends, porthole, and unlipped side views. Near Mint. $15 - $20 With detachable peep sights. $35

STANLEY No. 1 "Odd Jobs" nickle plated cast iron tool. This 4 inch long combination level, plumb, tri-square, depth and mortise gauge first appeared in Stanley's 1888 catalog and was not phased out until the combination square made it obsolete in the early 1930's. Beginning in 1898 it was sold with a one foot rule but would fit most any folding pocket ruler. $45 - $85

STANLEY No. 2 cherry level, in 24 to 30 in. lengths. Brass trim varies with year of production. Early models had brass lipped side views and arch top plate. 1929 model had no tips or lips and might fetch $12 - $15

STANLEY No. 2 Level Sights. Pair of clamp-on iron peep sights introduced at the turn-of-the-century. $10 - $15

STANLEY No. 3 adjustable hardwood plumb and level is another model whose features changed from time to time. The 1867 catalog offered them in 26 to 30 inch lengths but 18 inch models were available in 1898. Normally sold with lipped side view plates but offered plain in 1909. $15 to $25 for 1898 - 1925 levels in fine to mint condition.

STANLEY No. 5 laminated level 3 piece cherry stock with brass arch top plate, tips & lipped side views. auct. $20 - $30

STANLEY No. 6 adjustable mahogany level. Plain unplated ends. Brass square top plate and side view lips on 1859 - 1870 models. 24 to 30 inch lengths. Phased out prior to 1929. $30 - $40

STANLEY Nos. 7, 7½ & 8 non-adjustable hardwood Masons plumb & level. Circa 1874-1939. Nos. 7½ & 8 have no brass trim except bubble cover. No. 7 was 36 in. brass tips. No. 8 is 42 in. Dlr. $15-$20

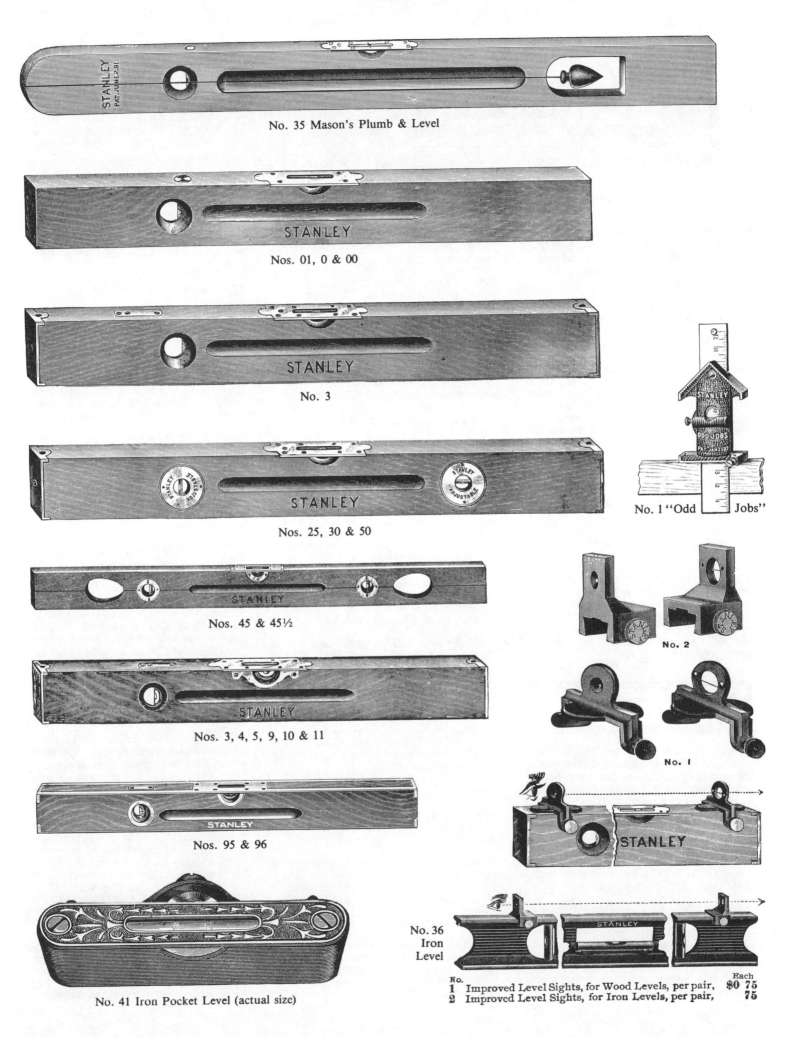

No. 35 Mason's Plumb & Level

Nos. 01, 0 & 00

No. 3

Nos. 25, 30 & 50

No. 1 "Odd Jobs"

Nos. 45 & 45½

No. 2

Nos. 3, 4, 5, 9, 10 & 11

No. 1

Nos. 95 & 96

No. 36
Iron
Level

No. 41 Iron Pocket Level (actual size)

No.		Each
1	Improved Level Sights, for Wood Levels, per pair,	$0 75
2	Improved Level Sights, for Iron Levels, per pair,	75

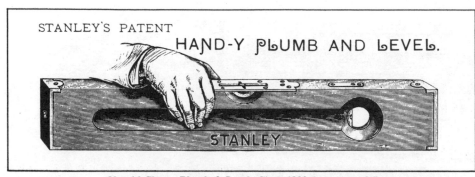

STANLEY'S PATENT
HAND-Y PLUMB AND LEVEL.
STANLEY

No. 16 Cherry Plumb & Level. Circa 1892 (scarce model).

STANLEY No. 9 adjustable mahogany plumb and level patented in 1862 & 1872. Sold in 24 to 30 inch lengths. Brass arch top plate, tips & lipped side views. $40 Appears in 1929 catalog.

STANLEY No. 10 adjustable 24 in. to 30 inch mahogany level with laminated triple stock. Brass tips, lips and top plate. First offered in 1859, appears in 1907 catalog but phased out before 1929. (No examples offered for sale recently)

STANLEY No. 11 adjustable rosewood plumb and level with brass arch top plate and side view lips. The single porthole is plain. Offered in 24 to 30 in. lengths. 1869 pat. date, rough cond. $70 1872 model, excellent. $110 1872 model, dirty. $50 Pat. Feb. 1890 $75 Well used 6-23-96 level. $50

STANLEY No. 12 Machinists rosewood plumb and level. Super-deluxe, brass-bound 4 sides, 20 inch. Offered from 1855 thru 1877. (no sales recorded by our sources)

STANLEY No. 13 Nicholson's Patent Iron Level. 14 inches long with oval holes in web. Sight opening in base as well as top view. First appeared in 1867 catalog. Phased out before 1890. Dlr. $175 No. 14 model 20 inches long. Asking $200. Auct. $60

STANLEY No. 15 Nicholson's 1860 patent 24 inch iron level. Auct. $105-$140

STANLEY No. 19 "Victor" plumb and level, pat. 6-23-96. Adjustable rosewood 28 inches long. Square brass top plate and end corners. Brass lipped side views, plain porthole. auct. $120 Dlr. $160

STANLEY No. 25 mahogany duplex plumb and level. Extra wide brass porthole rims. Brass arch top plate and end tips. Sold in 24 to 30 inch lengths. 1896 pat. $55 1872 pat., excellent cond. $95 Good. $55 auct. Fair. $20

STANLEY No. 30 adjustable hardwood duplex level. Brass lips & square top plate, no tips. 24 to 30 inch lengths. 1898 model with arch top plate. $30-$40 26 inch level with orig. label. $90. 1920 type. $30

STANLEY No. 31 hexagonal nickel plated machinists' 2 to 4 inch. $20 - $24

STANLEY No. 33 machinists' level same as No. 31 but with detachable base for mounting on a square. Pat. 8-4-96. $65

STANLEY No. 34 "Eclipse" tubular nickel plated level on iron base. Circa 1898 - 1940. Sold in 4, 6, 8 or 10 inch lengths. $21 - $38

STANLEY No. 35 mason's 42 inch cherry plumb and level. These appear in Stanley catalogs as early as 1867 and also in our 1939 edition. An undated 48 inch model was offered recently for $50. An 1892 dated 42 incher for $35. Both have cut out window for plumb bob on string.

STANLEY No. 36 adjustable cast iron plumb and level with nickel plated trim. These replaced Nicholson's product in the 1898 catalog and sold for at least another half a century. 1909 catalog offers 6 thru 24 inch lengths. Plain rail-shaped level with rectangular center cutout and half circle ends. Center web is scored with horizontal line decoration. 3 bubble vials. Black japanned finish. $14 - $30.

STANLEY No. 37 adjustable cast iron level, same as No. 36 above, but entire frame is nickel plated and center vial has a sleeve cover. (No sales reported)

STANLEY No. 37G as above but with grooved bottom for pipe work. $15 - $25

STANLEY No. 38 Oil Burner Level in 6 inch long doorstop shape. Cast iron with flat bottom and bowed top. Circa 1937. Orange lacquer finish. $6 to $15

STANLEY No. 38 cast iron Leveling Stand 4½ x 3½ inches with 4 adjustable screw-end feet. Circa 1910. $30

STANLEY No. 38½ nickel plated machinists' 4 inch rectangular iron pocket level. 1898 model has scroll relief design on sides. 1910 level has STANLEY lettering. $25

STANLEY No. 39½ machinists' iron pocket level is a 6 inch version of No. 38½ and is much more commonly found today. 1890 patent, pitted condition. $15 1896 patent, excellent cond. $20 - $30 Plain example, no lettering. auct. $10

STANLEY No. 40 machinists' iron pocket level. Rectangular with round ends. 3¼ inches long, iron top plate. Japanned sides. Appears in Stanley catalogs from 1855 onward.

STANLEY No. 41 brass topped version of No. 40 iron machinists' level with screw on clamp to affix to steel square. Top plate is plain on 1867 model, embossed floral design until 1909 when brass plate is again plain, but with the words Stanley, Pat'd. Recent dealer price $18

STANLEY No. 42 solid brass edition of Nos. 40 & 41. Circa 1855 - 1910. (No sales reported)

STANLEY No. 44 Bit and Square level attachment. Circular brass bubble holder with clamp for drill bit or steel square. 1¾ x 1½ inches overall. Sold for over a half a century after introduction in 1888. Good cond. except for broken bubble vial. $10 Very good cond. $22 - $30 Mint, as new. $35 - $40

STANLEY Nos. 45 & 45½ are soft wood mason's plumb and level with (2) cutouts for plumb bobs.
Brass porthole rings 48 inches overall. (No transactions reported)

STANLEY No. 46 improved version of No. 40 machinists' iron pocket level. Circa 1870-1910. Approx. 3 in. long, has slot for straight edge cast into base. Brass top plate. (No transactions reported)

STANLEY No. 50 duplex plumb & level. 3 piece laminated construction in both cherry and mahogany versions. 1986-1907 has arch end top plate. 1910-1929 has square end top plate and butt plates. All models have side view lips and wide brass porthole surrounds. 24-30 in. Good $40 Fine $55

STANLEY No. 93 mahogany brassbound adjustable plumb and level. Has square brass top plate and end pieces but no side view lips or collar on its single porthole. Sold in 24 to 30 inch lengths from 1908 to circa 1929. Much heavier than model 1093. Stock measures 2³/₁₆ in. 1908 model in mint cond. $120 refinished. $95 Circa 1920 26 in. Auct. $40 Dlr. $88

STANLEY No. 95 mahogany level as above but more expensive model with brass side views and porthole surrounds. auct. $50-$85 Dlr. $45-$95

STANLEY No. 96 deluxe brassbound rosewood plumb and level, with full brass trim and single porthole. First patented in 1896. Sold in 24 to 30 inch sizes till circa 1910. Does not appear in 1929 catalog. auct. $70 $115 Dlr. $125

STANLEY No. 98 deluxe rosewood machinists' brassbound level with complete brass trim. First sold in only 12 inch size. 1909 catalog featured 6 in. thru 18 in. lengths. Discounted during the Depression of the 1930's. Worn but sound 12 in. $60 Pat. Feb. 19, '95. Fine. $150. 18 inch size with sweetheart logo. $78 - $120. 6 inch length, asking $275

STANLEY No. 102 inexpensive non adjustable hardwood level with no plumb vial. Brass arch top plate plain ends and no side view plates. Sold from 1867 thru 1939 in 10 to 16 inch lengths. $10-$29

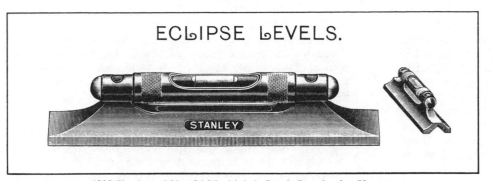

ECLIPSE LEVELS.

1898 Version of No. 34 Machinist's Level. Popular for 50 years.

STANLEY Nos. 103 to 107 are also inexpensive non-adjustable hardwood levels of similar value.

STANLEY No. 138 clamp-on Level Sights. Black finished brass peep sights circa 1929. $15-$35

STANLEY No. 187 aluminum line level. 3¼ in. long, ¾ in. dia. tube. In orig. box. $8

STANLEY No. 259 torpedo shaped 9 inch walnut plumb and level with rounded ends. Single unlined porthole and side views. First offered in 1939. (No current sales reported)

STANLEY No. 260 rosewood plumb and level with round ends. 2 plain unlined portholes. Brass vial cover. Circa 1939. (No transactions reported)

STANLEY No. 323 cherry level with recessed dial channel. 3 portholes. Auct. $30

STANLEY No. 338 iron leveling stand. Nickle plated fixture made to hold an iron level fitted with peep sights. Circa 1930. $35-$50

STANLEY No. 1093, later, lighter version of the deluxe brassbound rosewood No. 93 level. Offered in 12 thru 24 inch lengths. Circa 1930. Mint cond. $85

L.S. STARRETT adjustable iron bench level. 10 sec.± .00058 in. per ft. Nickel plated spirit tube on cast iron base. Like new in orig. mahogany box. $30

L.S. STARRETT No. 96 machinists' adjustable iron bench level 18 in. long. Nickel plated tube on japanned iron base $35-$42

L.S. STARRETT No. 98 Machinist's adjustable bench level, 12 inch. Mint. Auct. $60

L.S. STARRETT No. 132 iron bench level in fancy filigree pattern. 9 to 18 inch lengths sell in the $5 to $15 range.

STARRETT No. 133 engineer's and plumber's 15 in. iron level with movable incline tube. $20-$25

L.S. STARRETT No. 133A iron incline level with movable tube. 10 inches long, 3 bubbles. $40

L.S. STARRETT No. 132 cast-iron bench level only 6 inches long. 3 vials mounted in open rail type frame. $20-$28

L.Y. STEELE, Hudson, N.H. script signed on large brass side plate of this 28 in. mahogany level with slotted porthole covers and retractable sights. In pine case with owners stamp. Auct. $175

L.C. STEPHENS & CO. Jan. 12, 1858 pat. Combination folding boxwood level, rule, square and bevel, with protractor arm. Auct. $125 - $150 Dlr. $150-$175

STRATTON BROS. LEVELS

Stratton levels are especially sought after by collectors. We have cataloged more of this brand than any other, except Stanley. The Stratton Bros. Level Company began production in about 1870 and was purchased by Goodell-Pratt in 1912. Many Stratton levels are brassbound on all 4 edges. Their best grades were of laminated 4 pc. rosewood construction with solid mahogany cores. The 2nd grade was a 5 pc. mahogany lamination. The 3rd grade down was made from a solid stick of seasoned mahogany with brass binding rods dovetailed along the entire length of all 4 edges. Its portholes were unlined. A fourth grade in price was a narrow model ade from a solid stick of rosewood and bound in the same fashion. Budget priced hardwood levels without brass edges were also offered. Goodell-Pratt lists 145 different sizes and styles of Stratton Bros. levels in its 1917 catalog.

Stratton Bros. Unnumbered, fully brass bound mahogany levels with 1872 to 1887 patent dates, single unlined porthole and scalloped brass side view lips sell in 26 to 30 inch lengths for: Worn $40-$60. Good $65-$90. Fine $95-$140

Plain, unbound mahogany Stratton Bros. levels of the 1880's in 24 to 30 inch lengths sell for $20 to $35 each in retail shops.

STRATTON BROTHERS, Greenfield, Mass. No. 3 Cherry level 28 in. long. Single unlined porthole. Auct. $25

STRATTON BROS. No. 1 brassbound 24 inch mahogany level with original paper label. Nearly mint. Auct. $90 Dlr. $140 Others in varying degrees of wear. $45-$100

STRATTON BROS. No. 2 stamped July 16, 1872. $50-$75

STRATTON Bros. No. 4 mahogany level. 28 inches long, (scratched) $28

STRATTON BROS. No. 10 Pat. July 16, 1872. Brassbound 8 inch rosewood level with circular cut-out see-thru plumb vial and half circle side views. $200-$300 Less scarce 22 in. model. $130

STRATTON BROS. No. 11 brassbound mahogany 26 inch narrow, thin model with single porthole and no side view lips. Auct. $100

STRATTON No. 11½ brassbound mahogany level with 2 portholes. Normal wear. $60

STRATTON No. 1406 brassbound 6 inch rosewood level 1 inch wide x 1⅝ in. tall. Pat. May 22, 1888. Mint Cond. $275

STRATTON "The Dandy Level" cherry, 24 inch model. $45

STRATTON BROTHERS 1870 patent rosewood level, 8 inches long with end-mounted plumb vial. Brassbound. $350
10 inch Auct. $225 - $275
12 inch Auct. $225 Dlr. $300

STRATTON BROS. 18 inch brassbound mahogany level with one porthole. Near mint. $60

STRATTON BROS. rosewood 22 inch brassbound level, pat. 1887. $125

T. UNDERHILL, 2 Corporation St. Manchester. Rosewood level with 10¾ inch brass top plate. Auct. $75

UNION GRAVITY LEVEL CO. Inc., Sioux City, Iowa. 42 inch aluminum level with long brass inclinometer. Pat. 1/9/23. $65

UNIVERSAL MFG. CO. sheet metal mantle clock-shaped 6 inch wide inclinometer with brass dial. $15

UNMARKED ebony & brass 10 in. British made level w/4 arrowhead cutouts in full length brass top plate. Auct. 1985 $170

P.H. VOGEL MFG. CO., New Britain, Conn. Pat. May 13, 1919. Aluminum framed 24 inch level with flat center pane of brass. 3 views, 4 bubbles. $85

WILLIAM WARD, 513 8th Ave., New York. 28 inch Cuban mahogany double plumb and level. Slotted brass porthole covers and scalloped rectangular side view plates. Auct. $105

L.B. WATTS (Cambridge circa 1851-1860) 16 in. level with eagle trademark stamped in large square top plate. Brass vial cover disk. $75 - 24 inch version with brass side view and end tips. $45. 28 inch brass-trimmed mahogany, Auct. $20-$25

WILLIAMSBURG MFG. CO., Williamsburg, Mass. 24 inch iron filigree level with 3 vials. $35

WINCHESTER No. 9806 cherry level with single porthole. 16 inches overall. $20

WINCHESTER Trade Mark USA No. 9802 stamped on brass top plate and original paper label of this 12 inch plumb and level. $35 No. 9813 cherry level 26 inch. $35

WILLIAM MARPLES, the son of a skate and carpenter tool maker, was born in Sheffield, England in 1807. At the age of 21 he left his father's employ to start his own tool making business. His venture was soon profitable enough for him to live away from the factory building; unusual for those times. In 1850 Marples announced that he had refined the brass-framed joiner's brace of the day to its ultimate perfection. He called his version the "Ultimatum" and it outsold all of the competition. Soon William and his three sons moved their booming business from its Broomspring site (called the Hibernian Works) to a much larger Westfield Terrace plant which he called the Hibernia Works. Mr. Marples died in 1877 and his sons continued to further expand the business. In 1892 they acquired the stock and trade of the venerable John Moseley and Son, London plane makers since 1730. Marples also purchased Turner, Naylor & Co. who produced fine edge tools under the I. Sorby trademark, and Thos. Ibbotson & Co. (founded in 1814).

The turn-of-the-century trade catalog of William Marples & Sons featured virtually every tool of every trade. Also illustrated were razors, pocket knives, horse clippers, motor tool kits, ice skates and garden tools. This period probably represented the zenith of hand tool manufacturing for Marples and 174 other small Sheffield firms engaged in the business.

In 1932 the company began competing with Stanley Tools, U.S.A., by manufacturing a similar line of Bailey-style iron-bodied planes for the British market. In 1962 William Marples & Sons was sold to the predecessors of Record Ridgway Tools Ltd., thus completing a century and a half of continuous family ownership.

ALEXANDER MATHIESON began his tool making career in 1792 at Glasgow, Scotland. Joined by a son Thomas in 1853, Mathieson soon became the largest tool manufacturer in the country. Quality was always foremost in the Mathieson family operation. Prize medals were awarded at the London Exibitions of 1851 & 1862. The firm took away gold medals in Melbourne in 1880 and Edinburgh in 1886. Tools of all woodworking trades were represented in the company's 1899 catalog. William Ridgway & Sons purchased what was left of the business in 1962, hoping to capitalize upon the strength of the Mathieson trademark in foreign markets.

MILLERS FALLS COMPANY began operations in 1861 as a clothes wringer manufacturer, owned by Levi Gunn & Charles Amidon of Greenfield, Mass. Both of these gentlemen were veteran tool makers and immediately recognized the market potential of the new "Barber" brace. In 1864 Gunn and Amidon purchased patent rights for the new brace, and within 12 months were in full production. Two fires and two factories later Millers Falls had a fresh line of products and several new faces among the owners. They had begun to use their well placed New York sales office to represent other small New England tool manufacturing firms and this front line experience enabled them to make many wise acquisitions.

By the year 1885 the company's products dominated the domestic drill brace market and had gone into world wide distribution. Between 1872 and 1931 Millers Falls acquired The Backus Vise Company, George Rogers Co. (metal mitre boxes), Goodell-Pratt (1,500 hand tools), Stratton Level, and the Ford Auger Bit Company. In 1978 Millers Falls Co. was purchased by a division of Ingersoll Rand Corp. and continues to make fine hand tools today.

MITRE TRIMMER. Various floor and bench-model lever-operated moulding choppers or trimmers have been produced for the picture frame and moulding trade since the turn-of-the-century. Most of these machines are valued for thier use as functional tools rather than as collector's items. Current prices for Lion brand trimmers range from $100 to $150.

MORTISING MACHINES are also useful as well as decorative. Lion-pawed, cast iron floor models have sold recently for $100 at auction and up to $300 in dealer show-rooms. A wood framed, foot-operated mortising machine by J.S. FAY & CO. of Keene, N.H. with an original paper label dated 1846, & "World Prize For Best Design", sold for $450 in New Hampshire. Stanley No. 280 Butt Mortisers, for door jamb hinge cuts, have been offered recently for $45 - $50.

NAIL PULLERS come with exotic names such as "Red Bull", "Tiger", and "Sampson", Most of these iron shoe-footed, lever-operated, nail-pullers sell for $15 to $20.

T. NORRIS & SON. Thomas Norris began his plane making career in London about 1860. Joined by a son in 1873 he rapidly expanded the business and apparently purchased the rights to manufacture Stewart Spier's famous dove-tailed metal plane line. Norris and Son continued production of these rosewood and ebony-filled metallic woodworking planes until 1941. Lessor quality tools bearing the Norris trademark were produced by an aircraft instrument firm until 1952.

THE OHIO TOOL COMPANY was founded in Columbus, Ohio in 1823. For a forty year period, commencing in 1841, it used prison labor supplied under contract from a nearby state penitentiary. In the late 1880's Ohio Tool employed a civilian workforce and in 1891 bought out the Auburn Tool Company. Quality was vastly better than in the prison contract years and in 1900 Ohio Tool was presented with the highest award for woodworking hand tools at the Paris Exposition. After the expiration of Stanley Rule & Level Co. patents, Ohio Tool began to duplicate nearly the entire Stanley metallic plane line, (even using a similar numbering system). The company ceased operations in 1920.

OIL CANS will brighten any tool collection. Gleaming brass or copper examples from the 1850 to 1915 period can be purchased in all shapes and sizes at prices ranging from $5 to $35. Those with long snouts and built-in pumps command the highest prices. Trademarks and patent dates also add to value.

EDWARD PRESTON & SONS (1889-1933). The high quality tools of this British firm are avidly collected on both sides of the Atlantic. Edward Preston, senior, started his planemaking business at the tender age of 20, in Birmingham, England in the year 1825. He was joined by a talented son, Edward Jr., in 1850 and later by another son, Henry. The Preston family prospered individually at a number of different locations, finally combining all of their tool making operations at Whitehall Street in the late 1880's under the name Edward Preston & Sons. By the time of the Great Depression of the 1930's the business was being run by a third generation of Prestons and succumbed to the fate of many other hand tool firms of the period. The rule & level manufacturing portion of the business was sold to Raybone and Son and the plane line went to a predecessor of Record Ridgway Ltd.

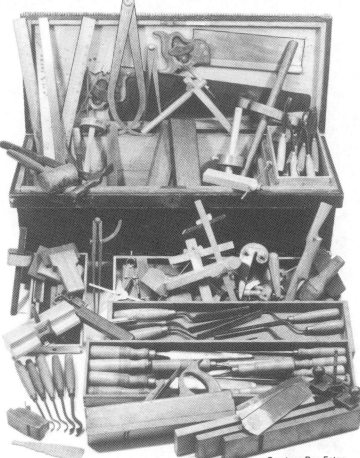

Courtesy Reg Eaton

A very good chest of pattern maker's tools comprising:—(7) trowel shanked gouges, (12) long chisels & gouges, (11) spoon bit & other gouges, a round plane with (4) interchangeable soles & irons, (6) contraction rules, (3) old woman's tooth routers, (2) spokeshaves, (4) miniature planes, (2) saws, (14) wooden spider & other gauges, rawhide mallet, oil stone & numberous calipers, compasses, patterns, scrapers etc., approx. (100) items. Auction, London. $500

PATTERNMAKER'S tools are generally those used in other branches of close-tolerance woodworking. His rule is calibrated to allow for the shrinkage of metal in the mold, for which he makes a master pattern or model. His chisels may have stepped-down handles and pattern-maker's planes usually come with a wide variety of curved soles that fit one body. Core box planes were developed expecially for this trade. They are designed to quickly and accurately carve a half–cylinder depression in a solid block of wood. A sand and clay core is formed in this mold. The core serves as a space filler in cylindrical molds and eliminates much wasted time in machine finishing pipe-like castings.

The Patternmaker's knowledge, skill, and responsibility far outweighed that of other woodworkers. He had to have a firm grasp of metallurgy, the skill of a cabinet maker, know the art of wood turning, possess the ability to make accurate drawings to perfect scale, and thoroughly understand the work of the founder. Each wooden pattern had to have built-in provisions for ease of removal from wet sand molds. Even the amount of shaking or tapping required to loosen a small part had to be figured in its pattern design. Draft, or taper, was a necessary feature for angular patterns. Finish allowances for the machinist also had to be figured in. Finally, warpage of castings during the cooling process had to be compensated for in pattern design.

WOODWORKING PLANES are far and away the most popular tools being collected today.

Some scholars feel that the Hebrews developed the first woodworking planes, using a stone chisel inserted through a wooden block. Other experts credit the early Egyptians with its discovery. The removable metal adze blade of the Ptolemaic period could be reversed to form a bullnose plane. Iron plated planes with wooden cores were found in the ruins of Pompeii which date from 79 A.D. Roman carpenters used a variety of hand-held planes including grooving, moulding and rabbeting types. The Romans also produced the first cast iron planes, complete with front and rear knobs.

Early Americans used mostly English made woodworking tools prior to the year 1800. Between 1810 and 1840 about two dozen planemakers were engaged full time at the activity, mostly around Philadelphia and New York City. The first planemaking factories were founded in the 1840's and 50's, primarily in Connecticut where industrial leadership had already been established. The average sized firm was capitalized at about $10,000 and employed 15 workmen, who produced from 5 to 20 completed tools per day. These were of course beechwood, with few if any metal parts.

Wooden plane production peaked a couple of decades later and then plumeted when Stanley began to mass-produce Leonard Bailey's iron-bodied planes starting in 1870. A massive advertising program, coupled with aggressive pricing and a nationwide distribution network, soon eliminated most of the competition. By the year 1900 over 3 million Stanley "Bailey" planes had been sold.

Stanley Rule and Level Company went on to manufacture over 250 different models of woodworking planes.

In order to prepare readers unfamiliar with the terminology used by tool dealers and auctioneers, when referring to Stanley planes, we list the following definitions:

EAGLE TRADEMARK appears on most prelateral models of the wood-bottom type made from 1869 to about 1887.

LIBERTY BELL emblem appears on the lever caps of some models made for the 1876 Centennial and continued on through World War I. (not a rarity)

PRELATERAL models without a lateral blade adjusting lever, made prior to 1884.

BAILEY name was cast on the toe of iron planes starting in 1902.

LOW KNOB refers to the lower height front-knob design of planes produced prior to 1922.

KIDNEY CAP is a term describing the kidney-shaped hole in lever caps made after 1933.

SWEETHEART trademark adopted in 1920 and discontinued circa 1935.

TRANSITIONAL PLANES are wood bodied planes with metal tops or blade housings. They were a transition between all-wood and all-metal planes. Most of them were out of production by 1920.

STANLEY ADJUSTABLE PLANES.

PATENTED.

These Planes are adjusted by the use of a Lever, and are equally well adapted to coarse or fine work.

Wood Planes.

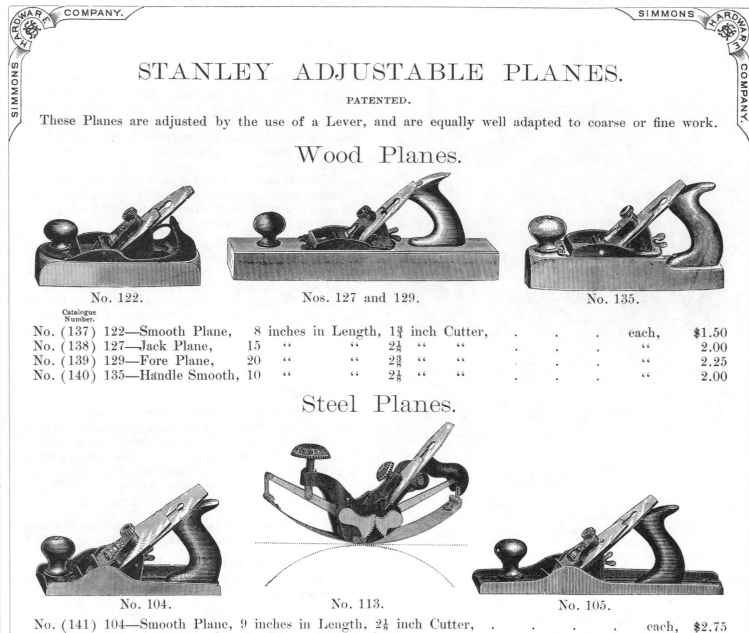

No. 122. Nos. 127 and 129. No. 135.

Catalogue
Number.

No. (137) 122—Smooth Plane,	8 inches in Length,	1¾ inch Cutter,	.	.	.	each,	$1.50
No. (138) 127—Jack Plane,	15 " "	2⅛ " "	.	.	.	"	2.00
No. (139) 129—Fore Plane,	20 " "	2⅜ " "	.	.	.	"	2.25
No. (140) 135—Handle Smooth,	10 " "	2⅛ " "	.	.	.	"	2.00

Steel Planes.

No. 104. No. 113. No. 105.

No. (141) 104—Smooth Plane, 9 inches in Length, 2⅛ inch Cutter, ... each, $2.75
No. (142) 113—Adjustable Circular Plane, 1¾ inch Cutter, . . . " 4.00
No. (143) 105—Jack Plane, 14 inches in Length, 2⅛ inch Cutter, . . . " 3.50

No. (142) 113, Adjustable Circular Plane, has a Flexible Steel Face, which can be easily shaped to any required arch, either concave or convex, by turning the Knob on the front of the Plane. The Knob is attached to a double-acting screw, which moves two levers properly connected by gears, thus controlling accurately both ends of the flexible Face. By the peculiar construction of the Plane, a smaller arch, either concave or convex, can be obtained by this Plane than by any other similar tool.

No. 101. No. 110. Nos. 102 and 103.

No. (144) 101—Block Plane, 3½ inches in Length, 1 inch Cutter, ... each, $ .20
Valuable to mechanics in all the lighter kinds of wood working, and so useful about offices, stores, and dwellings, for making slight repairs of windows, doors, furniture, etc., that it seems likely to be wanted in every household.
No. (145) 102—Block Plane, 5½ inches in Length, 1¼ inch Cutter, ... each, $ .40
No. (146) 103—Block Plane, Adjustable, 5½ inches in Length, 1¼ inch Cutter, . . . " .60
No. (147) 110—Block Plane, 7½ inches in Length, 1¾ inch Cutter, ... " .60

COMBINED PLANES.

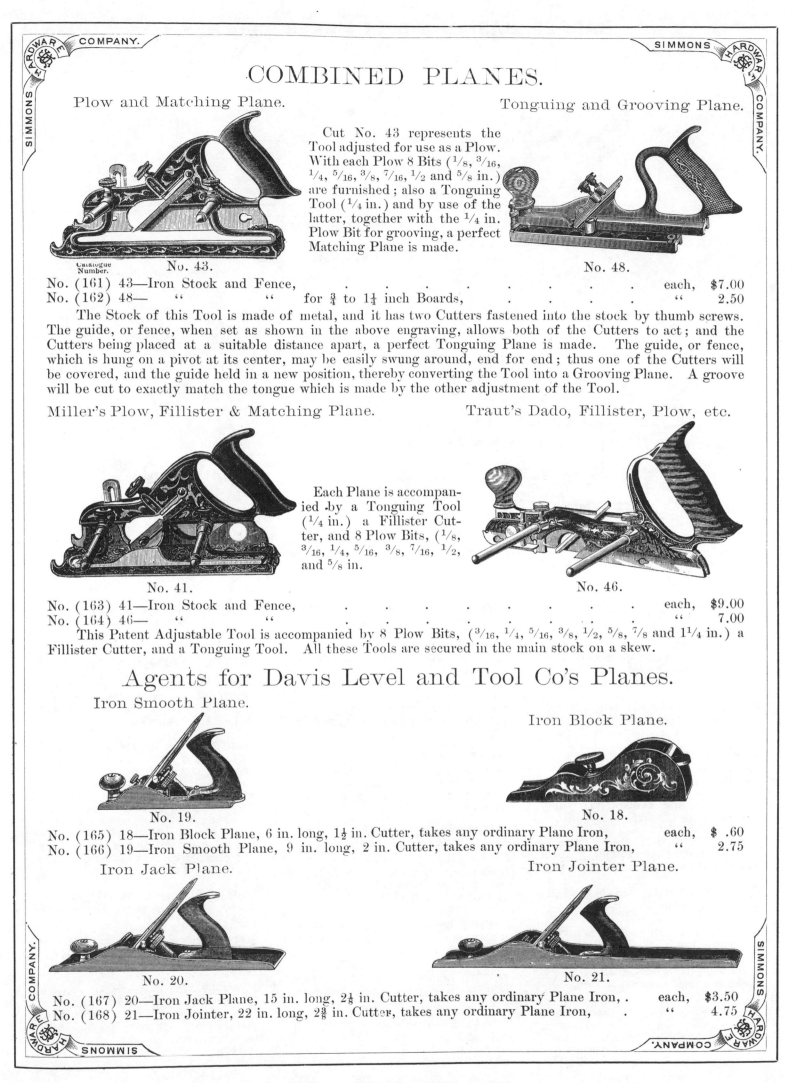

Plow and Matching Plane.

Tonguing and Grooving Plane.

No. 43.

Cut No. 43 represents the Tool adjusted for use as a Plow. With each Plow 8 Bits ($\frac{1}{8}$, $\frac{3}{16}$, $\frac{1}{4}$, $\frac{5}{16}$, $\frac{3}{8}$, $\frac{7}{16}$, $\frac{1}{2}$ and $\frac{5}{8}$ in.) are furnished ; also a Tonguing Tool ($\frac{1}{4}$ in.) and by use of the latter, together with the $\frac{1}{4}$ in. Plow Bit for grooving, a perfect Matching Plane is made.

No. 48.

No. (161) 43—Iron Stock and Fence, ... each, $7.00
No. (162) 48—   "   "   for $\frac{3}{4}$ to $1\frac{1}{4}$ inch Boards, ...   "   2.50

The Stock of this Tool is made of metal, and it has two Cutters fastened into the stock by thumb screws. The guide, or fence, when set as shown in the above engraving, allows both of the Cutters to act ; and the Cutters being placed at a suitable distance apart, a perfect Tonguing Plane is made. The guide, or fence, which is hung on a pivot at its center, may be easily swung around, end for end ; thus one of the Cutters will be covered, and the guide held in a new position, thereby converting the Tool into a Grooving Plane. A groove will be cut to exactly match the tongue which is made by the other adjustment of the Tool.

Miller's Plow, Fillister & Matching Plane.

Traut's Dado, Fillister, Plow, etc.

No. 41.

Each Plane is accompanied by a Tonguing Tool ($\frac{1}{4}$ in.) a Fillister Cutter, and 8 Plow Bits, ($\frac{1}{8}$, $\frac{3}{16}$, $\frac{1}{4}$, $\frac{5}{16}$, $\frac{3}{8}$, $\frac{7}{16}$, $\frac{1}{2}$, and $\frac{5}{8}$ in.

No. 46.

No. (163) 41—Iron Stock and Fence, ... each, $9.00
No. (164) 46—   "   "   . . . .   "   7.00

This Patent Adjustable Tool is accompanied by 8 Plow Bits, ($\frac{3}{16}$, $\frac{1}{4}$, $\frac{5}{16}$, $\frac{3}{8}$, $\frac{1}{2}$, $\frac{5}{8}$, $\frac{7}{8}$ and $1\frac{1}{4}$ in.) a Fillister Cutter, and a Tonguing Tool. All these Tools are secured in the main stock on a skew.

Agents for Davis Level and Tool Co's Planes.

Iron Smooth Plane.

Iron Block Plane.

No. 19.

No. 18.

No. (165) 18—Iron Block Plane, 6 in. long, $1\frac{1}{2}$ in. Cutter, takes any ordinary Plane Iron,   each, $ .60
No. (166) 19—Iron Smooth Plane, 9 in. long, 2 in. Cutter, takes any ordinary Plane Iron,   "   2.75

Iron Jack Plane.

Iron Jointer Plane.

No. 20.

No. 21.

No. (167) 20—Iron Jack Plane, 15 in. long, $2\frac{1}{8}$ in. Cutter, takes any ordinary Plane Iron, .   each, $3.50
No. (168) 21—Iron Jointer, 22 in. long, $2\frac{3}{8}$ in. Cutter, takes any ordinary Plane Iron, .   "   4.75

(page from Simmons Hardware catalog of 1880)

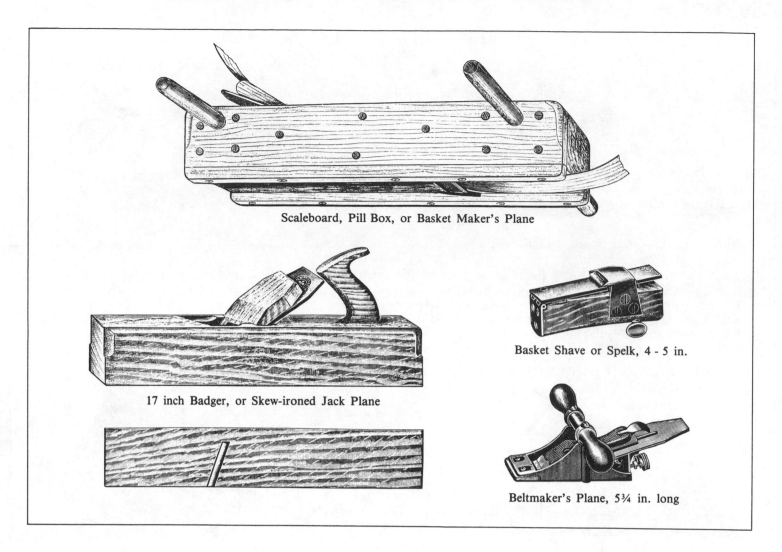

Scaleboard, Pill Box, or Basket Maker's Plane

17 inch Badger, or Skew-ironed Jack Plane

Basket Shave or Spelk, 4 - 5 in.

Beltmaker's Plane, 5¾ in. long

BADGER PLANES are essentially Jack planes with skew angle cutting irons. They are used for cross grain and panel work. Badgers often have a sole-mounted fence. We did not find any Badger planes listed as such in American catalogs. They are usually of British manufacture.

AUCTION LOT of 5 British badger planes by Nurse, Maidstone, King and others. 5 pcs. $66

ATKINS & SONS, Birmingham. 8½ in. smooth style badger with 2¼ in. skewed iron. $90

W. GREENSLADE beechwood badger plane with closed handle. 3 x 16 in. Dlr. $20 - $40

HIELDS, Nottingham. Coffin shaped badger 8½ in. long with 2¼ in. cutter. $40

KING & PEACH, Hull. 9 inch smooth-style badger with fence attached. $95

D. MALLOCH & SON, Perth. Skew ironed jack plane 17 in. long by 2½ in. wide. $52

A. MATHIESON & SON, Glasgow. Skew ironed smoother. Beech, 9 in. long. $80

J.W. PEARCE, Prov., R.I. fancy beech badger 15½ in. with mahogany wedge and diamond shaped strike button. $40

BASKET SHAVES or SPELK PLANES were either vise-held tools with hinged soles which adjusted the thickness of their thin willow shavings, or a much larger and heavier plane with 4 or more dowel shaped pull handles. The latter type often had a recessed sole up to 2½ inches wide.

ANCIENT and worn 24 inch spelk with 7 udderlike handles at several angles. Auct. $325

BASKET SHAVE from the collection of R.A. Salaman. 4½ x 1½ inches overall with hinged sole. Sold at auction for $75. Another unmarked basket shave only 4 inches long. Auct. $90

CHERRY WOOD spelk with twin handles on a 3½ x 7 in. stock. $150

Another cherry spelk, 4 in. wide by 19 inches in length. Hand-forged wing nuts on iron rods. auct. $175

SPELK or basket maker's plane, a full 28 inches long. Double bar handles, hinged at chute. auct. $300

MASSIVE crudely hewn 5 x 22 inch spelk with 2 large wing nuts on tang ends. auct. $325

TOP EJECTING style spelk, 22 in. long. auct. $85

SCALEBOARD or PILL BOX PLANES used by basket makers as well as pharmacy owners. The term seems to have been used interchangeably with Spelk in describing a large plane with tug handles.

EARLY PILL BOX plane, 18 inches in length by 3½ in. wide. Closed handle, 4 scoring spurs for various widths of box making stock. Auct. $400

NEW YORK area pill box maker's plane. Hollow plane with low angle blade and scoring spurs. Auct. $475

PILL BOX variety of the spelk. Probably the least found of all American planes. This one came from Knox, N.Y. area years ago. 3 in. wide x 18 in. long. Metal plate covers area in front of tote where wedge and escapement on a regular plane are found. Auct. $450

UNMARKED scaleboard, 3 x 3 x 22" with shallow rebated sole. Several handles. $350

BELTMAKER'S PLANES were used to chamfer down the laps of machinery belt ends before fastening them together.

STANLEY No. 11 Beltmaker's plane. Made from 1870 - 1943. 5¾ in. japanned iron body with one piece maple cross handle. 2⅜ in. wide blade. $60 - $85 (less if sole is scored)

Rare Knowles Pat. Block Plane. **Mr. Knowles informed the Patent Commission, in 1827, that wood was an outmoded material in plane construction.**

BLOCK PLANES are usually under 7 inches in length. Used for cross-grain work and other one-handed trimming chores, the low angle blade makes a shearing cut not apt to follow the grain.

AMERICAN BOY block plane, iron, 6½ in. long. Wooden knob. $7 - $15

AMERICAN TOOL & FOUNDRY cast iron block plane, 4½ inch. auct. $15

BAILEY TOOL CO., Woonsocket, R.I. 7⁷/₁₆ iron block plane with rosewood front knob. auct. $60 - $90

BAILEY TOOL CO. "Defiance" No. B iron block plane, 7½ in. long, 1¾ in. cutter. Circa 1876 - 1880. auct. $60

L. BAILEY'S "Victor" No. 00 iron block plane with nickel plated trim. 7 inches long. Circa 1858 - 1888. $75 - $150

No. 0 Non adjustable, no nickel trim. Model of 1880 - 1888. Auct. $100 – $175

No. 0½ (page 44 of 1884 catalog.) This model in production for 48 mos. auct. $200 - $300

No. 1 with adjustable mouth & cutter. 6 in. long. Pat. 1876. $100 - $175

L. BAILEY'S "Victor" 4½ in. pocket block plane with 1¼ in. cutter. Circa 1879-1888. auct. $325 Dlr. $200.   3¼ in. auct. $70

BAILEY No. 19 adjustable iron block plane, 7 inches long. Nickel trim. Circa 1897 - 1912. $17 - $35

BIRMINGHAM PLANE CO. solid iron block plane, 5⅝ in. long. Distinctive blade cap. 1¾ in. cutter. Auct. $55

BOSTON METALLIC PLANE CO. iron block plane 6¾ in. long. Hook shaped palm rest, rosewood wedge. Auct. $40 - $100

BRATTLEBORO TOOL CO. iron block plane 5¼ in. long with flower petal blade cap configuration. Circa 1885. Auct. $70 Dlr. $135

CASEY & CO. solid boxwood block plane, coffin shaped (mint) $83

O. R. CHAPLIN'S Pat., Tower & Lyon, New York, May 7, '72. 6⅝ in. iron block plane. $30 - $60

DAVIS chariot shaped iron block plane 6 in. x 1½ inches. Circa 1880. No gold floral. $100 - $125

HERCULES low angle iron block plane. $15

KEEN KUTTER No. K15 adjustable throat iron block plane. $50

KEEN KUTTER No. 103 adjustable 5½ in. iron block plane. $16

KEEN KUTTER No. K140 iron block/rabbet plane with removable cheek plate. $38

KEEN KUTTER No. K220 adjustable iron block plane 7 inches long. $25

M .C. MAYO stamp on cutter of this 7¾ in. iron block plane with large brass blade cap screw. $85

METALLIC PLANE CO., Auburn, N.Y. iron block plane 5½ in. long.   auct. $75

MILLERS FALLS No. 5 iron block plane in excellent condition. $30

MILLERS FALLS No. 07B (comp. to Stanley No. 140) combination rabbet & block with nickel plated lever cap and a skew angle cutter. $65

MILLERS FALLS No. 16 iron block plane 6 in. long. Excellent. $25

MILLERS FALLS No. 17 with lateral adjustment. $10

MILLERS FALLS No. 56 low angle type, 1⅜ in. wide x 6 in. long. $20

MILLERS FALLS No. 700 block iron plane with rosewood knob. (mint) $12

OHIO TOOL CO. Auburn, N.Y. No. 09½ adjustable iron block plane 6 in. $25 - $35

BLOCK PLANES (continued)

OHIO TOOL CO. No. 0100 iron block plane 1 x 3½ inches, plus squirrel tail handle. $40 - $80

PRESTON No. 118 Same as Stanley No. 18 Knuckle joint lever cap. Auct. Lond. $115- $238

SARGENT No. 105 squirrel tailed iron block plane with 3½ in. bed, 1 in. cutter. (sold for 60¢ in 1926) $24

SARGENT No. 106 with T-shaped cap screw. 5⅜ in. long. Dlr. $25-$35 (excellent).

SARGENT No. 206 adjustable iron block plane pat. 1893. $20 No. 207 7¼ in. $25

SARGENT No. 217 japanned iron block plane with mahogany front knob. 7½ in. length. Pat. Mar. 21, 1893. $10 - $20

SARGENT No. 227 double-end iron block plane 7¾ in. long. Mahogany knob. $18

SARGENT No. 317 tailed block plane with rosewood handle. Auct. 1985. $550

SARGENT No. 507 rabbet/block plane 7 inches long. 1⅞ in. wide cutter extends thru sides of bottom. Auct. $80 Dlr. $150

SARGENT No. 5206 low angle block plane 6 in. long. Dec.1915. $15 - $25

SARGENT No. 5306 adjustable iron block plane with knuckle joint cap $20

STANLEY BLOCK PLANES

STANLEY "Bailey" No. 9 cabinet makers 10 inch block plane with 2 in. cutter. Rosewood ball-shaped rear knob and hot dog style detachable side handle. 1870-1943. auct $900 - $1,400 (photo, pg. 108)

STANLEY "Bailey" No. 9½ Excelsior model. Early type no throat adj. lever. $30
1867 dated plane. $50
1895 model, worn badly. $19
1875 model. Auct. $25
Late version. $12 to $22

BAILEY No. 9¾ japanned iron block plane with round rosewood rear handle. (Sold from 1873 - 1934). Early model $325. 1894 pat. Auct. $288 1930 model, fine. $125

STANLEY "Bailey" No. 15 general purpose block plane 7 inches long. Japanned with polished sides. Early 1869 - 1872 version $40. Circa 1910 model, $12- $25

STANLEY "Bailey" No. 15½ iron block plane 7½ in. long, 1⅞ in. wide blade. Round rosewood handle. Discontinued in 1935. Avg. $125. 1881 Model. Auct. $250

STANLEY "Bailey" No. 16 adjustable iron block plane, 6 in. long with 1¾ in. cutter. Same as No. 9½ but has nickel plated trim. $15 - $25

STANLEY No. 17 all purpose iron block plane. Circa 1892 - 1942. $11- $22

STANLEY "Bailey" No. 18 iron block plane with knuckle joint steel lever cap. 6 in. x 1⅝. $15 - $25

STANLEY No. A18 rare aluminum block plane. (Circa 1925 - 1934). 6 in. long with nickle plated knuckle-joint lever cap. $95 - $150

STANLEY No. S18 steel block plane designed for trade school. Auct. $30-$75

STANLEY No. 019 7 inch block plane with knuckle joint lever cap. Sides have thumb indentations. $25 - $35

STANLEY No. 0H20 Two-Tone colorful block plane made for Special Promotion in 1941. $15 - $30

STANLEY "Bailey" No. 25 transitional wood bottom block plane 9½ inches in length. (Sold from 1870 - 1923). $125

STANLEY No. 60 low angle metal block plane 6 in. long with nickel plated trim. $25 - $35

No. 60½ polished metal instead of nickel plate. $18- $32

STANLEY No. 61 low angle iron block plane 6 inches long with nickel plated trim. No throat adj. Introduced in 1914. $30 and up.

STANLEY No. 62 scarce 14 inch low angle block plane with rosewood handle and knob. $175 - $325 (photo, page 108)

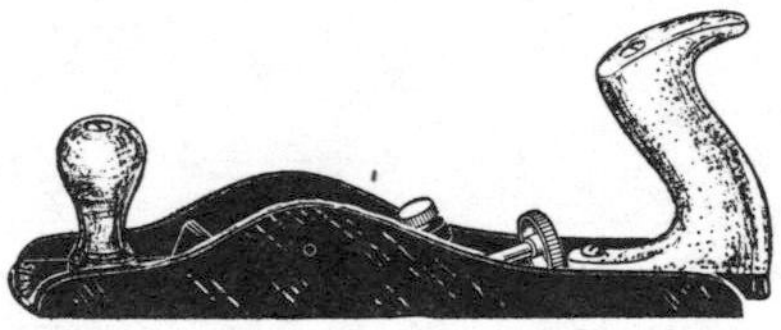

STANLEY No. 64 butcher's block plane. Japanned iron low angle type 12½ in. long. Beechwood knob and tote. (Made only from 1915 to 1924.) $500 – $950

STANLEY No. 65 all metal low angle block plane with nickle plated, knuckle-joint lever cap. $25 - $30

STANLEY No. 95 edge trimming block plane 6 inches long. $1^1/16$ in. cutter is placed vertically at skew angle. 1912 pat. $65 - $150

STANLEY No. 100 toy-sized iron block plane 3½ inches in length. Japanned black with squirrel tail handle. First sold in 1898 with slotted screw lever cap. Discontinued 60 years later. $25 - $40

STANLEY No. 100½ with curved and convex bottom. Squirrel tail handle. $50 - $85

STANLEY No. 101 3½ inch block plane. Similar to No. 100 but no tail. $20 - $30

STANLEY No. 101½ bull nosed version of the No. 101. One of the rarest Stanley tools. Auct. $900 (photo, page 108)

STANLEY No. 102 non-adjustable block plane 5½ in. long. Worn cond. $10 Excellent $20

STANLEY No. 103 inexpensive japanned iron block plane 5½ x 1⅜ in. Sold from 1877 thru 1950. $7 - $15. (Very early models bring $25 .)

STANLEY No. 110 all metal block plane with 6 point star on lever cap. (5 point star was introduced on Nos. 110 & 120 in 1876 and continued for two years, then changed to a six point emblem in 1888.) These seem to sell in a very broad range, from $15 - $50. The very earliest model with a fancy cap once sold at auction for $250. Other early examples avg. $115 Discontinued in 1972

STANLEY No. 118 low angle iron block plane produced from 1933 to 1973. A 6 inch long student quality tool. $20-$32

STANLEY No. 130 double-end iron block plane with rosewood handle. 8 in. long, 1⅝ in. cutter. Made from 1892 to 1955. $25 - $45

STANLEY No. 131 double-end adjustable iron block plane with japanned trim. Ground metal sides and thumb indentations. $45 - $65

STANLEY No. 140 Rabbet/block plane comb. 7 inches in length. Auct. $55 - $85

STANLEY No. 203 school quality iron block plane 5½ in. long with rosewood front knob. Sold from 1912 to 1962. Dlr. $45

STANLEY No. 220 iron block plane 7 inches long with 1⅝ in. cutter. Rosewood knob. $10 - $15

STANLEY No. 1120 Four Square household block plane. (Circa 1934-1937) $15 - $35

TOWER & LYON, New York. Chaplin's improved iron block plane, (circa 1902-1914). 6½ inches overall. $60. Another with 1876 patent. $75

UNION No. 102 iron block plane 5¼ in. long. $12 - $18

UNION No. 137 double-end non-adjustable 8 inch iron block plane which appears in 1929 Stanley catalog. Like new cond. $30 Auct. $20

WHALE SHAPED Dutch block plane 5 inches long. Hardwood with steel sole plate. Auct. $165

A. L. WHITING chariot shaped block plane, iron, 6 inches long, 1½ in. blade. Worcester, Mass. Circa 1875. $45

A. L. WHITING & CO., Worcester, Mass. 7 inch block plane with 1½ inch rosewood wedge. $125

WINCHESTER No. 3068 low angle 7 in. adjustable iron block plane. $50

WINCHESTER No. 3090 highly polished iron block plane 7¼ in. long. $35

Bailey "Victor" Nos. 1, 1¾,
2 & 2¾ (Circa 1880)

Bailey "Victor" Nos. 12, 12¼ & 12½
(1880-1888)

Bailey "Excelsior" Nos. 9½, 9¾,
15 & 15½ (1879-1884 model)

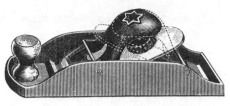

Stanley No. 130 (1883 patent)

Sargent No. 227 (1926 model)

Stanley No. 131 (1907 illus.)

Sargent No. 206 (Circa 1880)

Sargent No. 206 (1893-1926 version)

Sargent Nos. 5306 & 5307 (1926 model)

Stanley No. 140 (1907 model)

Sargent No. 507 (1926 illus.)

Sargent No. 107 (Circa 1880)

Stanley Nos. 110 & 120 (1884 illus.)

Ohio Tool No. 09½ (Circa 1910)

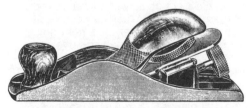

Millers Falls No. 07 (1935 model)

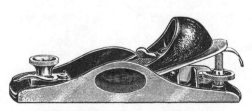

Millers Falls No. 17 (1935 model)

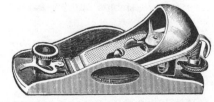

Bailey Nos. 9½, 15, 16 & 17 (1909 type)

Stanley Nos. 60, 60½, 65 & 65½ (1905 illus.)

Sargent Nos. 316 & 317 (1884 version)

Bailey "Victor" Nos. 1¼ to 2½ (1879 illus.)

Stanley "Bailey" No. 9¾ (1907 style)

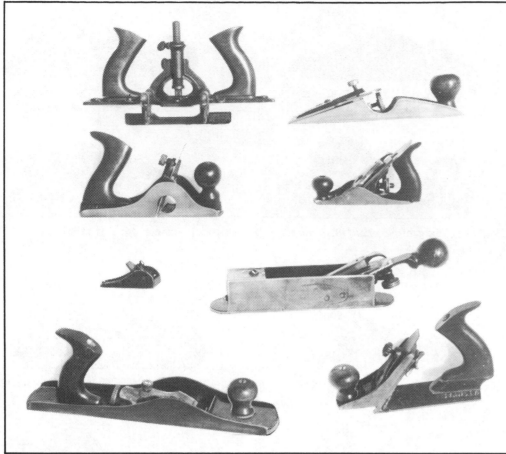

J.P. Bittner Antique Tool Auctions

RECENT AUCTION PRICES

(Row 1) STANLEY No. 171 Door Trim & Router Plane, circa 1911 - 1934. $150 - $200

STANLEY No. 97 Cabinet Maker's Edge Plane, 10 in. long, circa 1905 - 1940. $250 (London $450)

(Row 2) STANLEY No. 85 Cabinet Maker's Scraper Plane, circa 1905 - 1934. $650 - $700

STANLEY "BAILEY" No. 1 Smooth Plane, 5½ in. $450 - $600 (London, mint in box $1,500)

(Row 3) STANLEY No. 101½ Bull Nosed toy-size Block Plane, 3½ in. long. Circa 1906. $800 - $900

STANLEY No. 9 Cabinet Maker's Block Plane 10 inches in length. Was sold intermitently from 1870 to 1943. $900 - $1,200

(Row 4) STANLEY No. 62 Low-Angle Block Plane, 14 inches overall. Circa 1905 - 1942. $175 - $325

STANLEY No. 72 Chamfer Plane, 9 in. long. Circa 1886 - 1938. $170 - $320

CARRIAGE MAKERS or COACHBUILDERS planes will be found alphabetically under the headings of Moulding, Rabbet, Router and Smoothing Planes.

CHAMFER PLANES (with the exception of Stanley) are usually short beechwood planes with V-soles. Their purpose was to cut a 45 degree bevel on a right angle edge. A removable box, which serves as a depth adjustment, fits inside throat in front of the wedge.

AUCTION LOT of (12) assorted wooden chamfer planes 5 - 6 inches in length. $25 - $45 each.

BUCK, 242 Tottenham Rd. beechwood chamfer plane 2 in. wide by 6 in. long. Brass plates on sides. $90

LIGNUM VITAE chamfer plane 6½ in. long with adjustable sole box. Auct. $65

EDWARD PRESTON No. 360 stop-chamfer plane in polished beech. $63 - $135

STANLEY No. 72½ chamfer plane, as above but with beading and moulding attachments. $350 - $500 London. $625

GARDNER & CO., Makers, Bristol. 6 inch wooden chamfer plane with box type depth adjustment and brass side screw plate. $85

LEE'S PATENT, Feb. 13, 1883. Iron chamfer plane with slide arms and closed handle. Auct. $150 -$300

MANDER & DILLON, Man'fr., Phila., Pat'd. Mar. 24, '85. Adjustable beechwood chamfer plate 3 x 7 in. Auct. $100 Dlr. $250

MELHUISH, Fetter Lane. Wooden chamfer plane, resembles Mander Pat. Auct. $40

JOHN MOSELEY & SON, London. Wooden chamfer plane. Auct. $35 - $50 Another with cast iron sole, 6 inches long. Dlr. $160

C. NURSE & CO., London. With horse trademark. Beechwood chamfer plane 6½ in. long with brass side plate. $75

CHARIOT PLANES are so called because of their distinctive profile. The term is used in referring to any of several small chariot-shaped planes, usually block or bullnose-types of British manufacture.

BRASS bodied chariot plane 3 inches long with wooden wedge. Owner's name engraved on side. Auct. $125 Dlr. $195

BRONZE chariot plane only 2¾ in. long. Dovetailed steel toe, rosewood wedge. Auct. $222

D. LYON, London (circa 1875). Gunmetal chariot plane with turtle back wedge of ebony. 3 in. x 1⅛ in. overall. Dlr. $225

NORRIS, London. No. 28 iron chariot plane with gunmetal wedge bar. 3½ x 1½ inches overall. $150 -$250

NORRIS No. A28 gunmetal chariot plane with steel sole and rear adjustment knob. Absolutely mint, unused cond. Auct. $1,130

H. SLATER, Meredith St., Clerkenwell, London. 3¾ in. malleable iron framed chariot plane with mahogany wedge. $112 - $175

SLATER fine gunmetal chariot plane with steel sole & ebony wedge. Auct. $290

IRON chariot plane 3 inches long with walnut wedge. Brass cross bar, detachable sole plate. Auct. $85

COOPER'S CROZE cuts a crooze qroove (for barred head) in the center of the previously cut, wide, shallow, howell depression. Different styles are used for wet or dry casks. Some blades are saw-toothed, others are V-shaped gouges. They can be either post-mounted or affixed like router blades.

BEECHWOOD curved slab-back coopers croze. 2 tooth lance crooze and hawks bill style cutter. $35

BRITISH MADE assorted coopers crozes in good condition, 8 at $30 each.

D. R. BARTON fruitwood V-croze with cast iron blade holder. Auct. $30

J. BRADFORD, Portland. Excellent old coopers croze. Auct. $35

FRENCH MADE rectangular coopers croze with post mounted saw tooth cutter mounted in brass sleeve with double spur and wooden wedges. $48

GERMAN MADE coopers croze. Screw arm style with rectangular fence. Carved decor with eagle. Circa 1783. $277

A. HEALD & SON, Milford, N.H. common maple coopers croze. Auct. $45

A. McKENZIE, Aberdeen, croze with 3 bladed cutter and 3 metal wear plates on standard half moon back board. $60

A. McKENZIE, Aberdeen. Matched pair handled howel & croze. Auct. $65

SANDUSKY TOOL CO. coopers croze with rosewood wear plugs in backboard. $95

S. WEATHERBEE sawtooth coopers croze 7 x 18 in. birch backboard. $38

L. & I.J. WHITE No. 10 birch coopers croze like new cond. Auct. $45

UNMARKED primitive old sawtooth croze made of fir with 20 in. backboard. Auct. $25

UNMARKED curly maple coopers croze with hand-forged fittings & V cutter. $50

UNMARKED curly grained oak coopers croze with cutter made from old file. Conventional shape. Auct. $50

UNMARKED coopers croze made from cherry slab with solid cast iron croze block. Long V cutter for dry barrel. $65

UNMARKED huge old 19 inch croze with closed U-shaped handle bolted to plane. $75

UNMARKED saw handled coopers croze of unusual configuration. Auct. $80

UNMARKED rare cross-shaped oak coopers croze with pivot hole in end and copper wear plates. Auct. $120

COOPER'S HOWEL or CHIV forms the wide, shallow, gouge-shaped, cut inside the barrel end in preparation for the croze groove which receives the tapered edge of the head.

D. R. BARTON massive coopers howel on 7½ x 17 in. maple board with 3 inch wide cutter. Auct. $65 Dlr. $89

BRITISH made assortment of coopers howels in good condition. (7) at $40 each.

J. BRADFORD, Portland. Excellent old coopers howell. Auct. $45

C. F. CLOSE "So Easy" cast iron coopers howel. Auct. $40 Dlr. $48 - $65

J. DOLMAN, Burton. Very fine beechwood howel. Auct. $140

HORTON, New York impressed on cutter of this exceptional howel with blacksmith made fittings. Museum quality. $78

LANGLEY No. 85 patented rosewood and aluminum coopers howel. $35

MASSIVE 21 inch fruitwood coopers howel. Early and fine. Auct. $60

UNMARKED small beer howel for tight work. Conventional shape. $40

UNMARKED Birdseye maple medium coopers howel. Fine early piece. Auct. $110

COMBINATION HOWEL & CROZE

A. HEALD & SON, Milford, N.H. exceptional birchwood howel and croze. Auct. $100

UNMARKED combination howel and croze with handle on top. Auct. $65-$80 for common shapes and wood. Up to $150 for exceptional shapes and exotic materials.

COOPER'S JOINTER differs from a regular jointer plane in that it is much longer and is mounted in an upside down position on 2 to 4 legs or an A frame.

AUSTRIAN MADE coopers jointer 6 feet long, dated 1707. Ornamental throat cut, carved scroll & leaf decor on top of block. Nose has 2 holes for legs. Rounded heel has deteriorated. Auct. $700

BIRCH double-throated coopers jointer 52 in. long by 8 in. wide. 2⅜ in. cutting irons. Attached fence for each side. Auct. $160

J. BRADFORD, Portland, Me. double throated 35 inch coopers jointer. Twin side by side irons and wedges. 3 x 6 inch stock. Swale in bottom for working curved staves. Asking $375

J. BRADFORD, Portland, Me. coopers 45 inch bench jointer with 2⅛ in. iron. Very fine cond. Auct. $80

SANDUSKY TOOL CO. beechwood coopers jointer 32 inches long with 2½ in. iron. $95

UNMARKED late model cast iron coopers jointer 6 feet long with 3 inch wide cutter marked Briggs Engineers, Burton on Trent. Cast iron A frame supports front. $395

UNMARKED common coopers jointer 43 inches long with curved bottom. Some worm holes. $75

UNMARKED beautiful 58 in. applewood coopers jointer with single throat. Saw set marks on all sides from use as an anvil. Auct. $225

UNMARKED Maple double-throated coopers jointer 56 inches long. Side by side cutting irons are marked W. Butcher, cast steel. $300

UNMARKED double throated 50 inch coopers jointer, 7 inches wide. Auct. $125

UNMARKED, tongue & groove cutting coopers jointer with adjustable fences. One side cuts a V groove on stave edge, the other cuts a V tongue. Rare. Auct. $360

UNMARKED 4 throated coopers jointer, 4 feet long. Nice Patina. Auct. $230

UNMARKED 4 throat maple coopers jointer with brass screw- down lever caps. $325

UNMARKED sliding carriage type coopers jointer. 16 inch jig holds 2 curved staves on this 40 inch single throat plane, made for mass production. Auct. $360

LEVELING or SUN PLANE was one of the first tools employed by the cooper after the barrel was assembled. The leveler was run around the top & bottom stave ends so that the inside cuts that followed would be parallel, (or level) with the top.

AUBURN TOOL CO. stamp on cutter of this 14½ in. maple sun plane with steel sole plate. Auct. $30

D.R. BARTON No. 241 coopers leveling plane. Low profile type. Auct. $50

D.R. BARTON fruitwood sun plane 13 in. long. Very fine cond. Auct. $105

J. BRADFORD coopers leveling plane with revolving fence. Auct. $80

J. DYSON left hand sun plane with James Howarth iron. (dirty) $52

BENJ. F. HORN, St. Louis, Ill. No. 240 sun plane in dark beech with steel sole plate. $75

J.G. MADDIN 204 St. John Street. Worn but sound 13 in. left-handed beechwood sun plane. Auct. $70

C.W. MANNING solid cherry coopers leveling plane with brass thumbscrews. Auct. $150

REED & AUERBACHER New York. Leveling plane in solid cherry. Excellent. $90

SORBY, Sheffield. Left handed sun plane with punched trademark. $78

L. & I. J. WHITE fruitwood sun plane. $45 $75 with metal sole plates.

UNMARKED cherry sun plane, 11 inches long. Auct. $45

UNMARKED banana-shaped birchwood sun plane. $55

UNMARKED sun plane with rounded front and heel. Outstanding piece. $110

TINY BRITISH PLANES: (Left to right) Bullnose signed Eastwood, York. Beechwood, 4 inches long, 1½ in. wide, $65-$100. **(2nd from left)** pair of compass rabbets with R. Dix stamp on toes. Boxwood, 4 inches long, 1 inch wide, $125-$150 pair. **(2nd from right)** Adjustable 5 inch compass plane in boxwood with ebony depth stop, $150-$175. **(Far right)** 4 inch Beech compass plane by unknown maker. 1½" wide cutter, $65.-$95.

COMPASS PLANES (also called circular planes). Any of a number of adjustable and non-adjustable curved-bottom wood or metal planes made for working curved surfaces such as coach door panels, wheels, arches, etc. (Also see Rabbet planes, compass bottom.)

ADDISON & HEALD, Milford, N.H. beechwood shipbuilders 9 in. compass plane with wooden wedge and 2 in. cutter. Seasoning checks. $15

BAILEY TOOL CO., Woonsocket, R.I. "Defiance" adjustable circular metal plane with flexible steel sole. Circa 1875. $150-$260

BAILEY No. 13 iron circular plane. Yoke-shaped with flexible steel sole. $75-$95

J. BRADFORD (Portland, Me. 1849-1875) circular bottom 7 inch stair rail moulding plane with 1½ in. wide complex curved blade. Matched pair. Auct. $300

BUCK, Edgeware Rd. wooden compass plane with screw adj. plate in sole. Auct. $28

DUTCH Shaaf, black jack or whale-shaped 8 inch wooden compass bottom plane with wedged iron having crossed axes imprint. $270

G. EASTWOOD, York, coffin-shaped hardwood compass smoother 7 in. long by 2½ in. wide with boxwood depth adjust. slide dovetailed into nose. $55

EVANS unique iron framed compass plane with pair of flexible steel soles. Brass cap screw bears patent date of Jan. 28, 1862. Auct. $650

A. B. HOYT Patented 1848, stamped on toe of this beechwood compass plane with flexible steel sole. Auct. $350

J. KELLOG, Amherst, Mass 2⅛ x 8 in. coffin-shaped wooden compass plane. $12

JOSIAH KING wooden compass plane 8 inches in length with adjustable front shoe built into toe. Auct. $75

KING & COMPY, Hull. Internal stop compass plane with brass plate & thumbscrew on top of toe. 7 in. long x 2¾ in. wide. $65

KUNZ modern metallic circular plane, similar to Stanley No. 113. Nearly mint condition. $75

LAMB & BROWNELL unhandled 9 in. wooden compass plane. Auct. $25

LEMAINQUE, PARAS, forge royale stamp. Finest quality fruitwood 6 in. compass plane. Auct. $85

D. MALLOCK, Perth, wooden compass plane 7½ in. long with steel sole and adjustable front shoe. Auct. $105

A. MATHIESON beechwood compass plane with adjustable boxwood nose mounted depth stop and another in the sole behind the mouth. Auct. $140

R. H. MITCHELL & CO., Hudson, N.Y. Pat. Jan. 28, 1862, Mar. 22, 1864 on oval brass plate on front adjustable iron compass plane with flexable steel sole 10 9/16 x 2⅜ in. $65-$95

MOIR, Glasgow, compound compass plane in beechwood half circle profile with flat top. Auct. $69

J. MOSLEY coffin shaped compass plane with flexible iron sole. Auct. $65

MOCKRIDGE & FRANCIS coffin shaped compass plane in beechwood with screw adjustable nose piece attached to metal sole plate. $35

C. NURSE & SONS coffin shaped beechwood compass plane with brass toe top plate and thumbscrew adjust. $78

W.H. POND, New Haven, carriage makers compass plane in beechwood, 6⅜ inches overall. $28

E & T RING CO. (Worthington, Mass. circa 1849) 8½ inch compass smoother. $45

I. SLEEPER beechwood 1 inch wide compass round. Auct. $55

STANLEY "Bailey" Victor No. 20 metal circular plane manufactured from 1879 to 1958. $75 - $100

No. 20½ Same as number 20 but with japanned finish. Made prior to 1918. $85

WILLIAMS, 4 Long Acre, London, Beech coffin shaped bottom, compass smoother with adjustable steel sole plate. Auct. $170

STANLEY "Bailey" No. 113 iron framed adjustable circular plane with flexible steel sole. $70 - $90 (1880) Sold for 62 years.

UNION No. 411 adjustable metal compass plane, identical to Stanley No. 113 of 1898. $75 $95 UNION No. 311 Dlr. $40

COPING, COREBOX & DADO PLANES

COPING PLANES are essentially reverse window sash moulders. Each sash plane needs a coping plane to match its blade pattern.

JOHN BELL, Philadelphia. ¾ in. wide coping plane. $20

P. BROOKS, E. Hartford. Beechwood coping plane with Ovolo cutter. $22

J. KELLOGG, Amherst, Ma. beechwood L-shaped sash coping plane. $22

J.F. & G.M. LINDSEY, Huntington, Mass. ⅞ in. coping plane. $18

C. PRESCOTT, Lowell, dble. coping plane. L-shaped. $30

TILESTON, Boston. Wooden sash coping plane. $60

COREBOX PLANES were used by foundry patternmakers to cut one half of a cylinder shaped mold. The finished hollow cylinder was used to construct sand cores used in metal castings.

ALUMINUM core box planes, (3) 6 to 9 inches long with ebony knobs. $40 ea.

BRASS core box plane 6½ inches long body plus palm shaped wooden handle. Auct. $140

BIRDSEYE Maple core box plane with cast brass braces. Walnut handle. Auct. $60

PATTERN MAKERS type core box plane. Coffin shaped 6½ in. with set of 7 convex and concave soles. $95

PRIMITIVE wooden core box plane, 12 in. overall. Comes with 5 & 7 in. wings. Auct. $75

JOHN ROBINSON pat. Dec. 18, 1855. V-shaped wooden core box plane. Auct. $220

N. SPAULDING, McLEAN stamped on this beechwood core box plane with clever, beautifully crafted, wings. Pegged and bracketed construction. Auct. $100

STANLEY No. 56 core box plane. 4 inch long metal trough-shaped bed with a short rosewood dowel handle. Sold to pattern makers 1909 – 1923. Auct. $875 -$1,150

UNMARKED Beechwood 15 in. long core box plane with open handle. $110

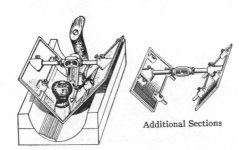

Additional Sections

STANLEY No. 57 core box plane with side wing extensions, 10 inches long. Sold from 1896 to WWII. $200-$325

DADO PLANES used to cut grooves across the grain. They have a forward mounted nicker iron to score the edges of the groove ahead of the main blade, to avoid splitting and lifting the grain.

THOMAS APPLETON wooden dado plane in mint condition with ¼ in. brass depth stop. $60

ASSORTED British dado planes. Dealer lot of (43) at $10 each. (17) better quality at $12.50 each.

AUBURN TOOL CO. No. 177 dado plane with ⅝ in. iron. Knurled brass screw stop. $18 Another in unused, mint condition. $40

D.R. BARTON No. 259 dado plane with top screw depth adjustment. $14-$18

BRASS framed dado plane with rosewood handle grip. Factory made appearance but unmarked. Auct. $150

CHAPIN STEVENS No. 136 dado plane with brass screw adj. depth stop. $25

H. CHAPIN No. 139 dado plane with ¾ in. cutter. $25

CHAPIN STEPHENS No. 139 with top screw stop. ⅜ in. cutter. $15

D. COPELAND (hartford, 1820) Beechwood ⅞ in. dado plane with original price tag intact. $35

A. CUMMINGS, Boston. Excellent ½ in. adjustable dado plane. Auct. $25

MARTIN DOSCHER & CO., N.Y. pair of dado planes in mint condition. $85
As above but average wear. Auct. $12.50 each.

DUVAL'S PAT. adjustable dado plane. 9½ in. long. Birch & beech. Auct. 1985 $1,100

GREENFIELD TOOL CO. adjustable ⅞ in. dado plane. Circa 1870. Auct. $25

IOHN GREEN ¼ in. dado plane with brass adjusting screw and depth stop. $95

W. GREENSLADE, Bristol. Narrow 5/16 in. dado with top mounted brass thumbscrew depth stop adjustment. $45

J. KELLOGG. Amherst, Mass. ⅞ in. beechwood dado plane with slotted brass depth stop, 2 wedges, 2 irons. $15

JOSIAH KING, 373 Bowery, N.Y. Handled dado plane. Auct. $30

MARLEY, N.Y. (1820-1856) Scarce close-handled razee-style dado plane with 1¼ in. cutter. Near mint. Auct. $75

JOHN MOSELY & SON. 54-55 Broad St., Bloomsbury, London. ½ in. beechwood dado plane with brass depth stop adjustment. $28

F. NICHOLSON, Living in Wrentham, Very early birch dado plane, 10 inches long. Replaced wedge. Very good cond. $450

OHIO TOOL CO. No. 47 beechwood dado plane with brass side plate. $15-$25

SANDUSKY TOOL CO. No. 62 ½ inch dado plane with top screw depth stop. Auct. $17

SARGENT No. 32 japanned iron dado plane with depth gauge. 8 inches long. $35

STANLEY No. 39 iron framed dado plane. Sold in 8 widths. Auct. $35-$90

STANLEY No. 239 all metal special dado plane 7½ inches long. $65-$150 (mint cond. ⅛ inch size brings top price.)

H. WETHERAL (Jr.) Chatham, 3/16 in. dado plane (missing irons and knicker wedge) Auct. $145

ISRAEL WHITE (circa 1835) various sized dado planes in very good cond. $20-$50

STANLEY No. 144 Corner Rounding plane. Sold from 1925 thru 1943. $140 - $250

STANLEY No. 444 Dovetail plane with 5 cutters. Complete in orig. box. Auct. $1,250 Another, missing fence, no blades. Auct. $350 Others in average condition. $500-$700

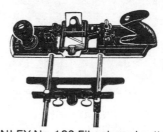

STANLEY No. 193 Fibre board cutter with 6 blades for cutting, slitting, grooving or mitre work. Original and complete. Auct. $75-$175 Dlr. $135-$150

STANLEY No. 194 Fibre board beveler. Circa 1936-1958. Japanned iron frame 8⅜ in. long. Red hardwood handle. Holds razor type blades. Auct. $35-$65 Dlr. $30-$40

STANLEY No. 195 Hard board beveler. 8½ inches long. $35

STANLEY No. 1951 Hard board beveler. Circa 1938-1952. 10½ in. long. Japanned iron frame with red stained hardwood handle and knob. Uses razor blade type cutter. $60-$125

FILLETSTER PLANES are highly refined versions of the rabbet plane equipped with a spur for cross grain cutting and also a depth adjustment feature. MOVING FILLETSTERS have an adjustable fence, usually attached to the sole. SASH FILLETSTERS are of plow plane configuration. They cut rabbet grooves or steps on the outside of window sash bars to provide a flush surface for window panes to be puttied against. All filletsters have skew angle cutting irons and usually an outside-mounted brass shoe-type depth stop, while conventional plow planes generally have straight cutters and an internal depth adjustment shoe. Filletsters were handy tools for panel raising and other small shop projects requiring an adjustable cross-grain plane.

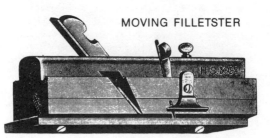

MOVING FILLETSTER

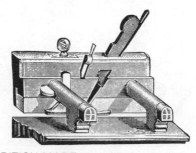

BRITISH MADE sash filletster. 1890's

AMES, London, wedge arm sash filletster with full brass trim. Double dovetailed boxwood wear inserts. Crisp and completely original. $115

ARROWMAMMETT WORKS, Middletown. Filletster with brass side stop. $20

ASSORTED English makers, common sliding arm sash filletsters in good working condition. $60 each.

AUBURN TOOL CO. Beechwood filletster with boxwood insert. auct. $30

J. BUCK, London, beechwood sash filletster with brass tipped wedge arm. $75

E. & C. CARTER, Troy, N.Y. Screw arm filletster with boxwood threads. Great condition, extra body included. $195

L. CASE, Watertown N.Y. (circa 1850) filletster with corner boxing. $40

CASEY & CO. Auburn, N.Y. (circa 1857) moving filletster. $35

H. CHAPIN/UNION FACTORY No. 149 beechwood filletster with boxed shoulder and brass stop. $45

A. CUMMINGS, Boston, screw arm type moving filletster with boxwood arms & nuts. Perfect condition. auct. $425. Another, repaired throat. $98

CUMMINGS & GALE (Providence, 1832) side stop filletster, as found. $30

MARTIN DOSCHER, moving filletster plane. auct. $45

J.W. FARR & CO., N.Y. nearly new 3 inch filletster with adjustable fence and depth stop. auct. $125

GABRIEL, moving filletster plane with boxwood insert & brass trim. auct. $40

GLADWIN & APPLETON moving filletster plane. auct. $25

IOHN GREEN (1774-1807) wedge arm sash filletster with church window depth stop. $40-$80

GREENFIELD TOOL CO. No. 272 moving filletster, beech w/brass depth stop. $36

GREENFIELD TOOL CO. very rare, handled rosewood, moving filletster with rosewood fence and box wood screw arms. Nearly mint. auct $350

J. KELLOGG screw arm sash filletster with boxwood arms. $90

J. KELLOGG, Amherst, Mass. (circa 1865) common beech filletster with brass side stop. $40

D. KIMBERLEY & SONS sash filletster, wedge arm, brass trimmed beech with boxwood inserts. $125

D. KIMBERLEY & SONS patented self-regulating screw arm sash filletster. 3 metal arms, wooden body & fence, closed handle. Auct. $250 Dlr. $450-$650

HILLS & WINSHIP screw filletster plane with wide fence. auct. $100

J.P. & CO. beech sash filletster with brass tipped arms. Brass trim. $70

A. KELLY & CO., Ashfield, Mass. Handled beech filletster with moving fence and brass depth stop. Fine. auct. $95

OHIO TOOL CO. No. 54 moving filletster. Boxed edge, brass depth stop. $38

OHIO TOOL CO. screw arm filletster. Stock is 2 in. wide, fence is 4 in. $80

D.P. SANBORN, Littleton, brass trimmed moving filletster 2¾ in. wide. $75

SARGENT No. 70 adjustable japanned iron bullnose filletster & rabbet plane. $20

STANLEY No. 78A aluminum duplex rabbet & filletster with fence. $125-$175

STANLEY No. 78 japanned iron duplex rabbet & filletster, 8½ inches in length. $20-$35

MATHIESON No. 10 brass trimmed wedge-arm filletster with fence. auct. $85

McMASTER & CO., Auburn, N.Y. sash filletster with wedge arm fence, brass trim. auct. $130

METALLIC PLANE CO. filletster with skew cutter 2 in. wide. 10½ in. long including closed rosewood handle. (embossed fence missing). $425

Wm. MOSS (1775-1800) sash filletster wedge arm fence. Brass trim. auct. $80

NURSE & SON, Mill St., Maidstone. Beech wedge arm filletster with brass trim. $80

STANLEY No. 11½ Scraper-style floor plane. 7 inches long with cross-bar handle. $125 - $300

STANLEY No. 74 Floor Plane with 10½ in. bottom. Maple handle is 45 inches long and has 2 pistol-style hand grips. Pat. Dec. 15, 1885. Sold til 1920's. $250-$450

FLOOR PLANE

FORE PLANES are the American version of the English Trying plane. They are used to smooth joints for gluing or to generally clean up rougher work done by the shorter Jack Plane. Wooden fore planes range in length from 18 to 22 inches, with an occasional 24 inch example to be found. Metal models are almost always a uniform 18 inches in length. The fore plane is a workhorse-type tool and does not often command the high-flying prices paid for many more exotic special-purpose planes.

ATKIN & SONS, Birmingham, 22 inch beechwood fore plane with matching name on its 2½ inch iron. Fine cond. $50

L. BAILEY'S "Victor" No. 6 adjustable iron fore plane 18 inches long. Cast iron rear handle, embossed front knob. Circa 1880-1888. Auct. $100 -$200

BRATTLEBORO TOOL CO. 1885 Steer's Pat. No. 406 metallic fore plane. $105

P. CHAPIN, Maker, Balto. (circa 1840) rosewood fore plane 22 in. long. ½ in. thick boxwood sole has rosewood wear plugs. Replacement handle. $200

CHAPIN STEVENS CO. Pine Meadow, Ct. (Circa 1880, mfg'd. for Sargent Co.) 20 inch iron fore plane with corrugated bottom. Hardwood handle & knob. $225

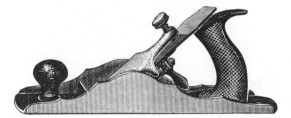

CHAPLIN'S PATENT, Tower & Lyon Co., New York, circa 1888. Iron fore plane 18 inches long with corrugated bottom. Checkered hard rubber rear handle. Non-adjustable throat. $125

DUTCH VOORLOOPER, or fore plane dated 1783. Heart-shaped throat carving 24 in. long by 2½ in. wide. (Some worm holes & restoration). Auct. $1,480

GAGE TOOL CO., Vineland, N.J. transitional 18 inch wood bottomed fore plane. Auct. $50

THE GOODALL CO., Phila., Pa. No. 29 transitional for plane. $95

HAZARD KNOWLES type fore plane, (circa 1827). Mahogany-filled iron frame 19 inches long. Closed rear handle, (front knob missing). asking $450

D. KIMBERLY & SONS, Warranted, "Highest Awards, 3 Gold Medals" heavy beech fore plane 22 inches long. Excellent cond. $35

MILLERS FALLS No. 18C corrugated bottom iron fore plane 18 in. long, 2⅜ in. cutter. Rosewood handle and knob. Black body, red frog. Mint condition. $60

NORRIS No. 72 all wood trying plane with patent adjustment and a metal lever cap. Auct. $260

OGONTZ No. 19 wooden fore plane with closed handle, 22 inches overall. $20

OHIO TOOL CO., beech fore plane 22 inches long with 2½ in. iron. $18 - $26

OHIO TOOL CO. No. 06 adjustable iron fore plane 18 inches long. $45

SARGENT No. 718C corrugated bottom iron fore plane 18 inches long. Circa 1915. Nearly new cond. auct. $105

PALMER & STORKE'S Patent, Metallic Plane Co., Auburn, N.Y., Nov. 28, 1871. Iron fore plane with 20½ in. corrugated bottom. Beech handle and knob. Auct. $75

SIEGLEY No. 6 corrugated bottom iron fore plane 18 inches long. Pat. 1893. Auct. $45

STANLEY No. A6 aluminum bodied fore plane, (sold for 12 years after 1925 introduction). Rosewood handle and knob. $175-$225

STANLEY "Bailey" No. 28 transitional fore plane in beechwood with iron top. 18 inches long, 2⅜ in. cutter. Auct. $25 Dlr. $35-$45

STANLEY "Bailey" No. 29 transitional fore plane 20 inches long. $20-$40

STANLEY No. 129 transitional wood bottom fore plane 20 inches long. $20-$40

STANLEY "Bed Rock" No. 606 iron fore plane 18 inches long. Rosewood handle and knob. Auct. $35 Dlr. $45-$65

STANLEY "Gage" No. G6 self-setting iron bottom fore plane 18 inches long. 2¼ in. cutter, rosewood handle and knob. $75

No. G6C with corrugated bottom. $90 up.

STANLEY "Bailey" No. 6 iron fore plane 18 inches long, 2⅜ in. cutter. Rosewood handle and knob. Auct. $35-$50. Dealers asking up to $95 for earliest models, circa 1870. In production for 100 years.

No. 6C corrugated bottom. Auct. $40-$60

STANLEY "Gage" No. 28 self-setting wood bottomed fore plane with metal throat, frog and handle cap. Circa 1919-34. $35-$55

STEER'S PATENT Sept. 11, 1883 iron fore plane 17⅞ in. long, 2¼ in. cutter. Rosewood handle and inlaid sole strips. Auct. $225

UNION corrugated bottom iron fore plane 18 in. long. Circa 1930. Mahogany handle and knob. $18-$25

UNION No. 6C metallic fore plane, pat. Dec. 8, 1903. $95

JOHN VEIT, Phila. beechwood fore plane 24 inches long. Fine cond. $35

W. WARREN, Nashua. Wooden fore plane 21½ x 3⅜ x 3¼ inches overall. $28

WINCHESTER No. 6 corrugated bottom iron fore plane with wooden handle. $70

WORRALL'S PATENT applied for. 22 inch wood bottom fore plane with decorative iron top plate which holds closed wooden handle and metal cutter assembly. Auct. $250

UNMARKED Beechwood factory-made fore planes. $20

UNMARKED Lignum Vitae wood fore plane 20 inches in length. Razee back. Auct. $85

UNMARKED Razee style in dense oak $45. Other more exotic woods, up to $120 at auct.

Chapin-Stephens and Greenfield Tool Co. style Gutter Plane. Circa 1866 - 1900.

GUTTER PLANES have a round bottom and blade for hollowing out gutters and other wooden pipe-like troughts of 1½ to 2 inches in diameter. They were often home-made with skew angle blades. Only 2 American tool makers featured gutter planes in catalogs of the late 1800's.

PUMP PLANES (see profile above) are a form of the gutter plane made specifically for cutting 1 to 1½ inch chain pump grooves. In England these gutter forming tools were called spout planes.

S.H. BIBIGAUS handled gutter plane 2½ x 3 x 14 inches with round bottom. $89

BUTLER, Phila. 12¼ inch gutter plane, open handle, single boxing. Auct. $75

DWIGHT & FOSTER imprinted cutting iron on 14¾ in open tote gutter plane. $30

DUTCH Blokschaaf with round gutter plane bottom. Top is carved with date 1730 inside a scroll. $1,780

GREENFIELD TOOL CO., 14 in. pump plane. Dlr. $175

18th Century handled pump plane 15½ inches long including fence. $75 - $260

FURRING PLANE the STANLEY No. 340 iron topped furring plane illustrated below is a rare tool made only from 1905 thru 1917. It is 10 inches in length with a 2 inch cutter. The stock, handle, and knob are beechwood. Furring planes were design-ed for the purpose of quickly removing fur and grit from rough sawn mill lumber to prepare it for fine finishing by smoothing planes. We have only seen two examples offered at auction. They brought $750 and $900. Dealers have offered this scarce tool at prices ranging from $1,200 (with a cracked handle) up to $1,500 for an example with 80% of its original finish intact.

FURRING PLANE

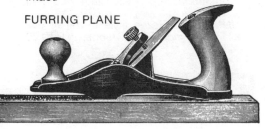

Factory-made Halving Plane. Circa 1860 - 1900

HALVING PLANES cut a fixed width stair-step rabbet for shiplap board joints. These scarce planes have cutters up to ¾ in. wide and range in length from 8½ to 10 inches overall.

CUMMINGS & GALE (Providence, 1832) beechwood halving plane for ¾ in. board. $28

GOLDSMITH, 18th century halving plane, stair-stepped 1 inch rebate cutter, com-pass bottom type. Scarce. $150

I. JONES, Living in Holliston, birch halv-ing plane 9⅞ in. long. (repaired). Auct. $700

JOSHAH KING, N.Y. 373 Bowery. Very good beechwood halving plane. $28

UNMARKED 18th century halving plane. Heavily chamfered beech, 9½ in. long. $35

HANDRAIL PLANES come in a variety of 2 inch wide rail or banister moulding shapes including the common half-round. Most of these planes are by English makers.

J. BRIDGE, Liverpool. Ogee handrail plane with attached fence. 6⅞ in. long. $115

BUCK 247 Tottenham Ct. Road. 7¼ in. concave bottom rail-type plane with 2 in. iron. $45

T. GOLDSMITH banister moulder with fillester type fence and depth stop. Auct. $65

S. KING, Hull (England, 1776-1806) Ogee stair rail moulder with moveable fence on sole. $95

JOSIAH KING 373 Bowery, N.Y. little 6 inch wooden handrail plane with adjust-able fence. Auct. $140

P. SARGENT, Concord, N.H. stairmaker's handrail moulding plane 6⅝ in. long with brass sole. Auct. $55

SIMS, Queen Street, Westminster. Pair of English handrail planes. Auct. $140

German made Horn-style Finishing Plane, circa 1900. Lignum Vitae Sole.

HORN PLANES are still being manu-factured today. They are patterned after their German counterparts and come in several horned styles including Smooth, Scrub, Jack and Toothing planes. Consult these headings for more data.

COMPASS STYLE Horned planes from Europe. Set of 4 stubby little curved bottom planes with root-shaped horns. 5½ inch blocks have extended front bibs and skew irons. set $230

ENGLISH Made fruitwood horned tooth-ing plane 8 inches long with 90 degree set wide-angle blade. $45

EUROPEAN radius curved horned smoothing plane in sun-plane-style, but only 7½ inches long. $65

1853 DATED horned smoothing plane with chip-carved decor on sides of block. Auct. $155

1754 DATED coffin shaped smoother with ram's horn front knob. Heart-shaped throat has scroll & clover leaf carving. Other tooled decorations. $1,550

FRENCH Made horn plane 3 x 8 inches with laminated rosewood sole. $28

FRUITWOOD horned plane 10 inches in length. $35 - $50

M. HIESSINGER in Nurnsberg. Unusual horn plane with iron cutter seat and lever cap. Adjustable block at mouth. $45

JOSIAH KING 373 Bowery, New York. "Kellett's" patent cutter on this hornplane dated Sept. 16, 1884. $40

LIGNUM VITAE wood horned smoother 9½ in. long. Unsigned. Auct. $45

ULMIA Doppel Hobel No. HW2 beech & boxwood horn plane with instruction sheet. Auct. $38

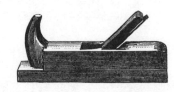

:UNION FACTORY Chapin Stevens, with Hammacher Schlemmer overmark, com-mon beech horned smoother. $45

JACK PLANES were made for the hardest and roughest work. The 1¾ to 2 inch cutter was slightly convex for rapid removal of excess stock. Wooden Jack Planes range in length from 14 to 18 inches. The newer all metal variety are usually a uniform 14 inches long.

ASSORTED ENGLISH makers. Common 12 to 18 inch wooden jack planes in dealer lots. $10 each.

J. P. BACHELDER, N. Danville (Vt.) 16 inch beechwood jack plane. Auct. $90

L. BAILEY'S "Victor" No. 5 adjustable iron jack plane 14 in. long, 2 in. cutter. Cast iron handle and embossed front knob. Circa 1880-1888. Seldom offered. $100 up.

BAILEY TOOL CO. No. 15 iron jack plane, 14 in. cap embossed all over Auct. $500

BIRDSILL HOLLY iron jack plane 14¼ in. long. Unmarked 1852 model with open wooden handle keyed into plane stock. Lever cap is iron sleeve surrounding cutter. Low wooden front knob. Auct. $100

BIRMINGHAM PLANE CO. "B" plane, patented Oct. 22, 1883. 15 inches long wood bottom, iron top plate. $75 1889 model $25

BIRMINGHAM PLANE MFG. CO. solid iron jack plane 14 inches in length with openwork type rear tote and ring style front knob. Circa 1887. Auct. $425

CHALLANGE PAT. cast iron jack plane, 15 in. Blade holder sides embossed. Auct. $1,300

CHAPINS IMPROVED corrugated bottom iron plane with synthetic black checkered rear tote. 50% of finish remains. $50 No. 1277 (smooth sides) $145

CHAPLIN PATENT Apr. 17, 1888, Feb. 14, 1890. 18 inch iron jack plane with hardwood handle and knob. $60
Another with no markings. 15 inch iron jack with hard rubber handle. $125

U. CLAP, 18th century maker. Beechwood open handled jack 15½ inches in length. $60

DIAMOND EDGE iron jack plane 14 in. long. Circa 1930. Made by Stanley for Shapleigh Hardware Co. $35

MARTEN DOSCHER 15¾ inch wooden razee jack with Butcher brand iron. $15

DOUBLE ACE brand Korean made jack plane. Slotted German made iron. Like new. $40

FALCON No. F5 plane. A Pope Product, made in Australia. Auct. $30

FIRESTONE No. 5 cast iron jack plane with conventional handle and knob. $25

GABRIEL (1770-1816) handled jack plane. Auct. $114

L. GARDNER, Green St., Boston. Nearly mint closed handle jack rabbet with double spurs, depth stop and fence. Auct. $55

A. HEALD & SON, Milford, N.H. wooden jack plane 16 inches in length. $15

Another, "jack rabbet" style, 19 inch length with closed tote and double spur pockets. Auct. $35

KEEN KUTTER No. K5 iron jack plane with perfect rosewood handle and knob. $35 KK5½C, low knob, 98% orig. Dlr. $175

KEEN KUTTER No. 5½C corrugated bottom iron jack plane with rosewood handle and knob. 99% of finish remains. $95

KEEN KUTTER transitional wood bottom, iron top. Restored jack plane. $30

KEEN KUTTER solid beechwood jack plane. $35

KEEN KUTTER No. 5065 iron jack plane. (Handle reglued). Auct. $20

J. KELLOGG, Amherst, Mass. A perfect 16 inch jack plane that shows little use. $18

JOSIAH N. KING 373 Bowery, New York. Beechwood jack plane 16 inches long. $16

S. KING imprint on this 18th-Cent. 14 inch jack plane with offset tote. Auct. $25

LAKESIDE TOOL CO. (made by Union) 15 inch transitional wood bottom jack plane. $30

LIGNUM VITAE auction lot of 6 damaged jack planes. $90

METALLIC PLANE CO., Auburn, N.Y. Palmer & Storke's patent Nov. 28, 1871. Iron jack plane 15 inches long. Beechwood handle & knob. Non-adjust cutter. $125

METALLIC PLANE CO., Auburn, N.Y. adjustable throat iron jack plane 15 inches in length with corrugated iron bottom. Open spoked adjusting wheel. $150

METALLIC PLANE CO., Auburn, N.Y. pat. Mar. 14, 1876 by E. G. Storke. 15 inch iron jack plane with rosewood handle and iron mushroom-shaped front knob. $185

MILLERS FALLS No. 14 iron jack plane in new condition. $45 Average cond. Auct. $15

MILLERS FALLS No. 714 Buck Rogers style metallic jack plane, circa 1950. Auct. $40

MOHAWK, Shelburne, metal jack plane 14 inches long with wood handle and knob. $25

NEW YORK TOOL CO. No. 12 (Auburn Tool Co. circa 1864) open tote beechwood jack plane 16 inches long with 2⅛ in. cutter. $16

NEW YORK TOOL CO. razee style jack plane with closed saw-style handle. $20

NORRIS No. A71 wooden jack plane 17 in. long with patent adjustment & 2¼ in. iron. Auct. $240 - $393

OGONTZ TOOL CO. No. 13 wooden jack plane. $15

OHIO TOOL CO. No. 5 corrugated bottom 14 inch iron jack plane, 2 in. cutter. $16

OHIO TOOL CO. No. 05¼ iron jack plane with corrugated bottom. Auct. $25

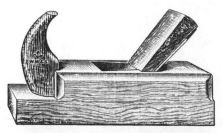

William Marples & Sons No. 2821
German-style Jack Plane. Circa 1910.

Sargent Transitional Style Jack Plane No. 3415.
Circa 1895 - 1925.

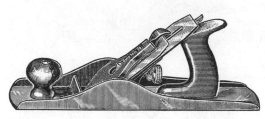

Ohio Tool No. 05 Iron Jack   Circa 1900 - 1920.

Stanley "Bedrock" No. 605. Model of 1902-1913.

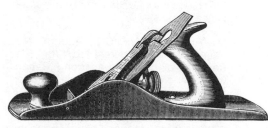

Stanley "Bailey" No. 5 Iron Jack
Prelateral, 1870 - 1884.

Steer's Patent Iron Jack Plane with rosewood inlaid sole.
Circa 1883-1888

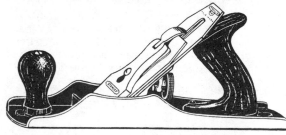

Stanley No. S5 Steel Bottom Jack Plane.
Sold from 1926-1941.

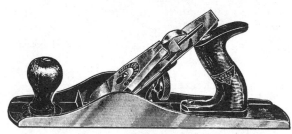

Millers Falls No. 14 Iron Jack Plane of 1935.

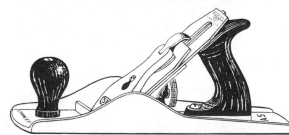

Stanley No. A5 Aluminum Jack Plane.
Offered from 1925-1935.

Morris Patent 16 inch Jack Plane, Circa 1870-1887.
Manufactured by Sandusky Tool Co.

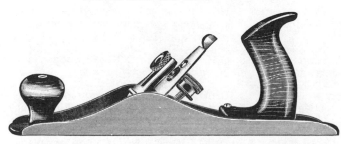

Sandusky No. 13S "Semi-Steel" Jack Plane. Circa 1925

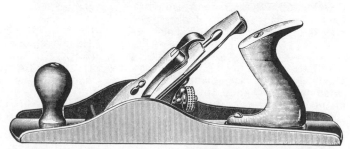

Sargent "Hercules" No. 1414. Low priced line, circa 1925.

Common Jack Plane (1850-1925)   **Panel Plane**   **Badger Plane**   **Fore Plane**

OHIO TOOL CO. transitional wood bottomed jack plane. $15 – $20

C. PRESCOTT, Lowell, Mass. (circa 1832) jack rabbet plane 15 inches long. $35

ROCKFORD TMP No. R5 metal jack plane 14 in. long. Rockford, Ill. Auct. $35

RODIER'S (1879 patent) iron jack plane 14½ inches long. Sides have vertical grooves cast in them over the entire length of the plane. Auct. $550

SANDUSKY TOOL CO., Morris patent iron 16 inch jack plane with floral decorated top and diamond pattern corrugated sole. Dealers asking $750-$1,000

SANDUSKY No. 13S semi-steel jack plane 14 inch (circa 1925) $15 - $25

SARGENT No. 414 adjustable iron jack plane 14 inches long with 2 in. cutter. Mahogany handle and knob. $16

SARGENT No. 714 iron jack plane 14 inches long, mahogany handle and knob. Auct. $25

SARGENT No. 3415 VBM transitional wood bottom jack plane 15 in. long. Auct. $22

SCIOTO TOOL WORKS wooden jack plane with open tote and E. W. Carpenter wedge assembly. $40

SIEGLY transitional wood bottom jack plane comp. to Stanley 27½. Like new cond. $40

SIEGLY No. 5½ iron jack plane. $50

SPEIRS AYR metal jack plane with mahogany handle & infill. (Refinished in ugly orange shellac). $170

STANDARD RULE CO. (1883-1886) Razee style wooden jack plane with metal lever cap. Blade marked Unionville, Conn. (repaired split) $100

THE STANDARD RULE CO., Unionville, Conn. Pat. Oct. 30, 1883 stamped on blade. Iron jack plane with rosewood handle and knob. 14⅜ in. overall. Mint cond. $225

STANLEY No. A5 Aluminum bodied 14 inch jack plane, sold from 1925 to 1935. Auct. $150-$175 Dlr. $185-$225

STANLEY "Gage" No. G5 self-setting iron jack plane 14 inches long. $75 - $100

STANLEY No. OH5 Two-Tone jack plane mfg'd for National Hardware promotion in 1941. $40 - $75

STANLEY "Bailey" No. 5 iron jack plane, 14 inches long. Rosewood handle and knob. $18-$35. Prelateral models made prior to 1885 $40-$55

STANLEY No. S5 jack plane, nearly identical to Bailey type but with steel bottom. $120-$155

STANLEY "Bailey" No. 5¼ Manual Training type jack plane. $40 - $70

STANLEY "Bailey" No. 5¼C iron jack plane as above, but corrugated bottom. Scarce item, made from 1922 to 1942. $165-$200

STANLEY "Bailey" No. 5½ iron jack plane 15 inches long with rosewood handle & knob. $35-$55

STANLEY "Bailey" No. 5½C corrugated bottom iron jack plane. $50-$60

STANLEY "Bailey" No. 26 transitional wood bottom jack plane 15 inches long with 2 inch wide cutter. $20-$30 Earliest models bring slightly more.

STANLEY "Bailey" No. 27 wood bottom jack plane made from 1870 - 1917. 15 inches in length with 2⅛ in. wide cutter. $15-$30 . No. 27½ $20-$35

STANLEY "Gage" No. 27½ self-setting wood bottom jack plane. $50

STANLEY "Bailey" No. 37 Jenny wood bottom smoothing or jack plane 13 in. long. Iron top plate holds wooden handle and knob. 2⅜ in. cutter. Discontinued in 1923. $175 and up.

STANLEY No. 105 pressed steel jack plane 14 inches long with rosewood handle and knob. Wide price range $150-$325

STANLEY No. 127 beechwood transitional model, sold from 1877 to 1918. Some have Liberty Bell lever cap. $30 - $40

STANLEY "Bed Rock" No. 605 iron jack plane. Rosewood handle and knob. $45-$75. No. 605C sells in same price range.

STANLEY "Bed Rock" No. 605½ iron jack plane 15 inches long with 2¼ in. cutter. $50-$95

STANLEY "Defiance" No. 1205 (circa 1932-1953) Japanned iron jack plane 14 inches long with hardwood handle and knob. $15-$25

STEER'S PATENT iron jack plane with 14 inch composite bottom formed with strips of inlaid rosewood. Auct. $100 Dlr. $195 to $275.

J. J. STYLES, Kingston, N.Y. (1820-1876) razee style jack plane 16 in. long. $28

TABER PLANE CO., New Bedford, Mass. Pat'd Feb. 28, '65. Beechwood jack plane with closed handle and no front knob. Auct. $45

TOWER & LYON, N.Y. transitional wood bottom jack plane 15 in. long. Toe and blade stamped Chaplins patent. May 7, 1872. $75 - $100

TOWER & LYON, New York, May 7, '72 & July 4, 1876. Iron bottom jack plane with corrugated sole. Black wood knob and checkered hard rubber tote. $100

UNMARKED common factory made beechwood jack plane 15 inches long. $15– $25

UNMARKED earlier birchwood jack planes 15 to 17 inches long. $20 - $35

UNMARKED Lignum Vitae wood jack planes, razee style. $50 - $100

WINCHESTER No. 3010 iron jack plane in good condition. $90

WORRALL'S Patented May 27, 1856 jack plane 16 in. long wooden stock has some age checks. Auct. $75 - $165

JOINTER PLANES are the longest members of the plane family. Their extreme length levels out the "hills" and "valleys" left by preliminary shaping and smoothing with shorter tools. This absolutely true surface is necessary when joining boards in side-by-side fashion for flooring, table tops, barrel staves, and case work. English trying and panel planes are also used for jointing work and the terms often overlap. (Cooper's Jointer's page 109)

ASSORTED American factory made jointers. Beechwood 22 to 28 in. long. $15-$35

ASSORTED English made trying planes up to 24 inches long, beech. (150) at $12

ARROWMAMMETT WORKS, Middleton, Conn. (circa 1857) beechwood jointer 30 inches long. Tiger maple handle. $35

BAILEY'S "Victor" No. 7 adjutable iron jointer, 22 in. long. Iron handle and embossed front knob. 1893 model. Auct. $55. 1883 type $150. No. 8 (1867-1876) 23½ in. Auct. $330

BOSTON BAILEY No. 11 transitional style beech jointer 24 in. long. Iron marked pat. Dec. 24, 1867. $187

BALDWIN TOOL CO. dense mahogany razee style jointer, 17 in Auct. $55

A. BARNES, S. Orange, Mass. figured applewood jointer 23 in. long. Auct. $35

BARTON cooper's jointer 34½ in. long with 2⅛ in. iron. $100

BIRMINGHAM PLANE CO., Birmingham, Conn. No. 6 iron jointer, 21½ in. long. Beechwood handle and knob are grained to resemble rosewood. $125-$150

BOSTON METALLIC PLANE CO. (Boston, Mass. 1872-1874) 22 inch iron jointer. Openwork iron bottom has 8 see-thru slots. Wooden handle & knob. $215

J. BRADFORD, Portland, Me. razee style ships jointer in rosewood with dark contrasting handle and strike pin. Auct. $195

BUCK Scottish style patent metal jointer with rosewood handle, infill. Auct. $297

H. CHAPIN, Union Factory "Extra" 28 inch beech jointer in perfect condition. $45

N. CHAPIN & CO. Eagle Factory. 26 to 29 inch beechwood jointers. $35 - $50 ea.

P. CHAPIN, Baltimore. Rare and unusual rosewood jointer with beech handle. $150

DUTCH Reisschaaf, or jointer, dated 1753 Initials WVV are part of throat carving. Some worm holes. Auct. $3,330

1825 DATED jointer 28 inches long. Chip carved with heart, tulip and cross decor. Vertical file-type dowel shaped handles at each end. Auct. $400 Dlr. $695

GAGE TOOL CO. No. 16 wood bottom 20 in. jointer. Auct. $35 Dlr. $55 & up. No. 18 24 in. Dlr. $125 No. 30. Auct. London. $95

EDWIN HAHN, Wilkes-Barre, Pa. (circa 1908-1918) Nos. 8 & 9 corrugated bottom iron jointer planes with checkered hardwood totes. $225 ea. No. 6 $150

HOLLY'S PATENT iron jointer 20⅛ in. x 3⅛ in. Pat. July 6, 1857. Dlr. $495-$695

KEEN KUTTER No. 8 corrugated bottom iron jointer with rosewood handle and knob. $85

J. KELLOGG beechwood jointer 3½ x 30 inches. Auct. $15

LOWELL PLANE & TOOL CO. Worralls's 1857 pat. 22 inch wood bottom jointer with cast iron top. Excellent cond. Auct. $250

MATHIESON steel dovetailed jointer 20½ inches long. Side plates are screwed into rosewood infill. Square front knob. Auct. $280

METALLIC PLANE CO., Auburn, N.Y. Palmer & Storke's patent corrugated bottom iron jointer 20 in. long. $290 Later model 20½ inches long. $200

MILLERS FALLS iron jointer plane 24 inches in length. Circa 1935. $35

NORRIS No. A1 dovetailed steel jointer, sold in 10 different lengths. Gunmetal lever cap. rosewood infill and closed handle. Auct. 22 in. $500. 28 in. $1,120

RODIER Pat. 1879 iron jointer 21½ in. long. $375 - $500

M. M. SANDERS & CO. Boston, Mass. solid rosewood 22 inch jointer with brass end caps and mouth plate. Auct. $95

SANDUSKY TOOL CO. No. 925 beechwood razee style 22 in. jointer. Auct. $50

SARGENT No. 422 Iron jointer 22 inches long. Mahogany handle and tall front knob. $30 - $50

SIEGLEY No. 8 corrugated bottom iron jointer 24 inches in length. $50 -$100

SSS SIEGLEY transitional jointer approx. 24 in. long. Comparable to Stanley No. 31. $35 - $60

A. SMITH, Rehoboth (Mass) 18th Cent. yellow birch jointer 30 in. long. $140

SPIERS, AYR No. 2 dovetailed steel jointer 20½ in. long, 2½ in. cutter. Bronze lever cap, rosewood infill. Auct. $350 - $450. 23 inch. Auct., London, $600

STANDARD RULE CO. No. 30 transitional wood bottom jointer 24 in. long. Metal frog, knurled brass adjust. knobs. Circa 1883-1888. $100 - $175

STANLEY "Gage" No. G7C self-setting corrugated bottom iron jointer 22 inches long. $85

STANLEY "Bailey" No. 7 iron jointer plane 22 inches in length. $35 - $65 (earliest pre-lateral models in fine condition bring more.)

STANLEY "Bailey" No. 8 iron jointer 24 in. long. Rosewood handle & knob. Auct. $70 Dlr. (mint cond.) $85

No. 8C Corrugated bottom version. Dlr. $65 - $85

STANLEY "Gage" No. 30 self-setting wooden jointer plane with metal throat, frog & handle cap. $35 - $65 Lond. $95

STANLEY "Bailey" No. 30 wood bottom jointer 22 in. long. Circa 1870-1918. $20 - $35. Early & fine pre-lateral. $65 up.

STANLEY "Bailey" No. 33 beechwood jointer with iron top plate. 28 in. long. $30-$35 Earliest prelateral models bring up to $75 in fine cond.

STANLEY "Bailey" No. 34 transitional wood bottom 30 inch jointer plane. $45 - $75. Prelateral model with eagle touchmark, brass adj. screw. Auct. $145

STANLEY RULE & LEVEL CO. No. 132 transitional jointer plane, circa 1877-1918. Auct. $30 Dlr. $60

STANLEY No. 386 Jointer Gauge (Fence) nickle plated adjustable angle guide. $35 - $65

STANLEY "Bed Rock" No. 607 iron jointer plane 22 inches. $50 -$75 Lond. $95

STANLEY "Bed Rock" No. 608 iron 24 inch jointer plane, rosewood handle & knob. $65 - $125 London Auct. $169

JOHN M. TABER, New Bedford, honey colored 30 inch jointer, full handle. $40

TOWER & LYON, New York. Chaplin's Patent May 7, '72 & July 4, 1876. Iron jointer with hard rubber handle and wooden front knob. 21½ inch corrugated bottom. $100

TOWER & LYON transitional wood bottom model. $75

UNION No. 7 iron jointer 22 inches long, circa 1929. Auct. $35

UNION TOOL X No. 8 Pat 12-8-08 japanned iron jointer 24 in. long. Auct. $56 Dlr. $150 (Mint)

UNMARKED Bird's eye maple jointer plane 31 inches long. Auct. $75

UNMARKED Shipwright's Lignum Vitae jointer 32 inches in length. $145

THE UPSOM NUT CO. japanned iron jointer with mushsroom-shaped front knob and large brass adj. screw nuts. Mint cond. $200

WINCHESTER No. 3050 wood bottomed transitional 18 inch jointer. $28

WINCHESTER No. 3055 jointer plane 24 inches in length. $45

WORRALL'S PATENT transitional wood bottom jointer. Metal top bracket holds blade and closed style handle. Circa 1857. $225

Alex. Mathieson & Sons, Glasgow, Scotland. Circa 1899 Wrought Steel Jointer, 20½ to 26½ in.

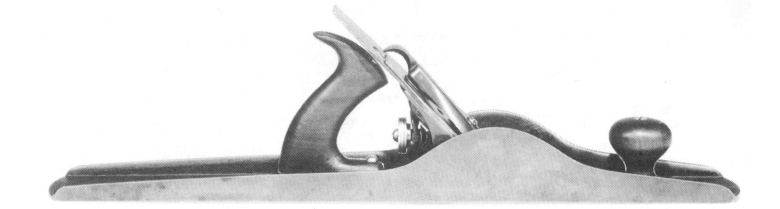

Bailey's Patent Aug. 6, 1867. No. 7 Iron Jointer, $21^5/_{16}$ inches long. Rosewood handle and knob.

Holly's Patent Iron Jointer Plane, $20^1/_8$ inches overall. Made by Casey, Kitchel & Co., circa 1852.

Roger Smith "Patented Transitional & Metallic Planes In America, 1827-1927"

MATCH PLANES were commonly produced in matched pairs for the purpose of cutting a tongue on the edge of one board and a matching groove on another. The object was to achieve an absolutely straight, tight fitting joint for hardwood flooring, table tops and other applications.

Some wooden plow planes came with tongue & groove cutters as an optional feature. Metallic match planes were introduced by Stanley in 1870.

Pair of Grooving Irons

Tongue
Groove

ASSORTED Sizes, English match planes by popular makers. $25-$40 pr.

ARROWMAMMETT WORKS, Middletown, 1870. Matching tongue & groove planes. $24 pr.

AUBURN TOOL CO., Auburn, N.Y. Nos. 71 & 72 combination (unhandled) match planes with both tongue & groove cutters set in same block at opposing angles. $25 - $50 ea.

AUBURN TOOL CO. full handled combination tongue & groove match plane with opposing cutters and closed handle at each end. Auct. $450

D. R. BARTON 1832, No. 13 matching tongue and groove planes. Auct. $20 pr.

BARRY & WAY No. 48 pair of matching plank planes. Auct. $35

GEO. BURNHAM, Amherst, Mass. pair of wedge-arm plank-match planes in fine cond. $80

R. & L. CARTER, Troy, 14 inch long plank match with fence screwed to sole. $30

CASEY & CO., Auburn, N.Y. one inch tongue plane. $12

N. CHAPIN & CO. Eagle Factory. Pair of No. 87 closed handle tongue & groove match planes. Auct. $80

J. COLTON, 379 Market St., Phila. matched pair of screw arm 14 inch T & G plank match planes. Auct. $125

CHAPIN STEVENS, Union Factory No. 171 combination tongue & groove plane. Double or twin style, opposing blades, unhandled. Auct. $20 No. 172 $30

H. CHAPIN, Union Factory, pair of open handled screw arm T & G match planes. $165

CHILD. PRATT & CO., St. Louis, Mo. Pair open tote 14 inch plank match planes with screw arm fences. $80

MARTIN DOSCHER pair of handled tongue & groove ½ inch match planes. Auct. $65

EUROPEAN screw arm match plane dated 1774. Huge heart-shaped throat. 3 arm fence (missing 1 arm) is also decoratively carved. Worm holes. Auct. $462

JO FULLER, Providence. Wedge arm tongue plane 14 inches long. Open tote. Auct. $225

P. A. GLADWIN & CO. Patented June 9, 1857. Double style match plane with both cutters facing in same direction. Closed handle, 12 inches long. Auct. $150

IOHN GREEN (3) pairs of T & G planes. ½, ⅝ & ⅞ inch sizes. (6) planes. $75

GREENFIELD TOOL CO. No. 327 matching tongue & groove planes. Auct. $35 pr.

GRIFFITHS, Norwich. Pair of unhandled ⅝ in. tongue & groove planes. $20 Another pair, with fences. $40

HIELDS, Nottingham (circa 1830) beechwood tongue plane with pass-thru shavings window. Auct. $15 - $20

W. HOFFMAN, N.Y. matched pair of T & G planes in nearly mint condition. Auct. $75

KEEN KUTTER No. K76 metallic swing-fence tongue & groove match plane. $45

J. KELLOGG, Amherst, Me. No. 24 pair of T & G match planes 11½ inches long with steel wear plates on fences. pr. $45

L. KENNEDY, Hartford (1809-1842) unhandled beechwood match planes, pair $25

JO: FULLER, Providence (1773-1822) with the N backwards and intertwined USA also on toe. 10 inch tongue plane in birch with original wedge and iron. Auct. $1,600

LAKESIDE (Montgomery Ward) nickle plated swing-fence match plane, identical to Stanley No. 48. $20

J. H. LAMB, New Bedford (1869-1874) pair of unhandled beech ⅞ in. match planes. $25

J. E. & G. M. LINDSEY unhandled beech, twin match plane with opposing cutters. Auct. $25

T. J. M'MASTER & CO., Auburn, N.Y. pair of matching tongue & groove planes. $40

P. H. MANCHESTER (Prov. 1843-1857) slide arm beechwood groove cutting match plane with brass thumbscrews. Has depth stop. $40

A. W. MARSH, Cleveland, Ohio. combination tongue & groove match plane. Auct. $65

CHARLES E. MARSHALL, Boston, Mass. Gunmetal framed match plane with closed rosewood grips at each end. 11½ inches overall. Pat. Oct. 8, 1872. asking $800

F. NICHOLSON, Wrentham (1683-1753) birchwood grooving plane 9⅞ in. long. Earliest documented American planemaker. Damaged and restored. Auct. $500

Another with "Living in Wrentham" stamp. Auct. $300

I. NICHOLSON yellow birch 1 inch tongue match plane with applied fence. $500

OHIO TOOL CO. No. 82 pair of open handled screw-arm tongue & groove plank planes 14 inches long. Auct. $55 pr. Dlr. $150 pr.

PHOENIX CO. Hitchcockville (Conn.) pair of shiny clean ¾ in. T & G unhandled match planes. $40 - $50 pr.

D. P. SANBORN closed handled tongue match plane in perfect condition. $58

SANDUSKY TOOL CO. No. 100 tongue plane ⅜ inch, like new cond. $30 Double end style. $25

SANDUSKY No. 106 screw-arm-style match plane. $40 - $60 ea.

SARGENT No. 1067 iron bodied reversible tongue and groove match plane. $85 No. 1068 all metal reversible ⅞ in. match plane. Auct. 1985, $110. Mint in box. Dlr. $200.

P. SARGENT, Concord, N.H. handled set of matching T & G planes. Auct. $65

SHERMAN, New York, nicely matched pair of handled tongue & groove planes with brass soles. Auct. $35

A. SMITH, Reheboth, grooving plane with open tote, 12 inches overall. Auct. $100 Unhandled version. $30 per pair.

STANLEY No. 48 nickle plated tongue & groove match plane. $25 - $45 (early examples bring more if near mint cond.)

STANLEY No. 49 Swinging fence tongue & groove match plane 8 in. long. $25-$50

STANLEY Nos. 146, 147 & 148 all metal match planes in sizes ⅜, ⅝, & ⅞ in. Auct. $45 each. Dlr. $95 ea. in mint cond.

J. M. TABER (New Bedford, Mass., circa 1820) beechwood unhandled ⅞ inch tongue plane with rounded chamfers. $40 Pair of 1 inch planes 13½ in. long. $60 pr.

ROBERT WOODING (British, 1710-1739) un-handled tongue match plane, 10¼ in. long. Auction, London, 1985. $650

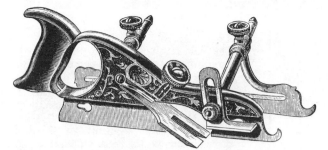

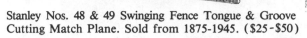

Stanley No. 43 Miller's Patent Iron Plow Plane of 1870 with stock reversed and tongue cutter in place for use as a Matching Plane. (Value $175 - $250).

Stanley Nos. 48 & 49 Swinging Fence Tongue & Groove Cutting Match Plane. Sold from 1875-1945. ($25-$50)

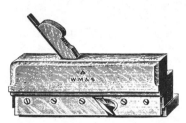

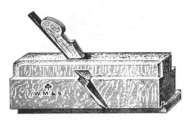

British-Made Grooving Plane with movable fence attached to bottom.

Matching Moving Tongue Plane with fence. (circa 1909)

Stanley No. 148 Double-End Match Plane. Manufactured from 1905 to 1959.

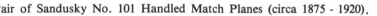

Pair of Sandusky No. 101 Handled Match Planes (circa 1875 - 1920).

Screw-Arm Match, Grooving type.

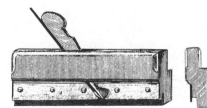

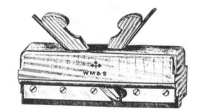

Pair of Scottish-Style Match Planes (circa 1899).

Double or Twin-style Match Plane.

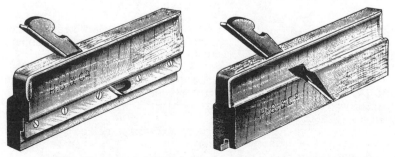

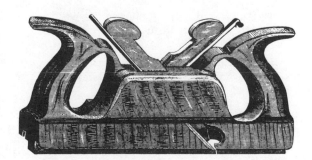

American-Made Board Match Planes (circa 1895) Came in 9 sizes.

Scarce Double-Ended-Style. Scottish, Circa 1890.

Courtesy Christies, South Kensington

A RARE 16th Century IRON PLANE. Made in Nurembug, circa 1550. This 5½ inch Plane brought $7,000 at a Christie's South Kensington sale.

The baluster-handled plane at left is a forerunner of most 18th-century British mitre planes. Constructed of decorative etched iron plates, with brazed joints, it is typical of those made in Nuremberg in the 16th-century.

The Elector Agustus of Saxony owned a number of these tools according to a 1580 inventory. The furniture maker, Freidrich Finkhauer is shown using one in his 1571 portrait appearing in the Landauer Monastery Book. Only a few other planes of this type have survived, all are slightly different. They are in museum collections in Vienna, Dresden and Rouen. Hence the $7,000 price tag, even with a 19th-century cutting iron replacement.

MITRE PLANES come in the same sizes and shapes as wooden smooth planes but their blades are pitched at a lower angle and usually do not exceed 1¾ inches in width. Stocks were made from any of a number of exotic woods and rarely exceed the maximum 10½ inch length. As the name implies these planes were designed for end-grain work on picture frame and other decorative mouldings. Larger mitre planes mounted in stationary jigs or fixtures are called shooting board planes. British mitre planes resemble early Roman metal carpenter planes in design.

ADDISON HEALD, Milford, N.H., low angle wooden mitre plane. Auct. $30

AXE & HIELDS (Nottingham, England. Circa 1832) wooden mitre plane 12 inches long by 3⅛ in. wide. Adjustable boxwood mouth stop. $320

BARNES, Worcester (England) beechwood mitre plane with boxwood mouth adjustment at front of throat. Auct. $546

D. R. BARTON & CO., Rochester. Rare American made beech mitre plane 9½ inches in length. $60

J. BRADFORD, (Portland, Me. 1849-1875) solid boxwood mitre plane with steel wear plate. Auct. $25

BUCK, 245 Tottenham Court Road (1838-1852) Dovetailed iron cased mitre plane 6¼ in. long including front bib. Comes with slip-on mahogany sole guard. Auct. $370

CHAPIN STEVENS, Pine Meadow, Conn. No. 434 wooden mitre plane 9 inches long. Mint. $30

BRASS BODIED British mitre plane 9¾ in. long with dovetailed iron sole. Crossbar is double tenoned into sides which are comb-jointed. Finest quality and craftsmanship. Rosewood wedge. Auct. $520

Another brass mitre plane, 8 inches in length. Brass crossbar is flat on top, scalloped at base. Auct. $475

MATHIESON & SON, Edinburgh. Dovetailed wrought steel mitre plane with gunmetal lever cap and correct snecked iron. Bibbed front, plain heel. No raised foregrip or palm rest, hidden infill. Auct. $425

MATHIESON, Glasgow, fine cast iron mitre plane with gun metal cap. Improved version with raised rosewood fore grip and heel infill. Auct. $375

H. L. NARRAMORE, Goshen, Mass. (1865-1872) beechwood 9 inch mitre plane with slotted cutter bearing clover leaf trademark. $15

ROGERS MITER PLANER by Langdon Miter Box Co. Dark green cast iron bed with 2-bladed, single-handled sliding plane approx 4 in. wide. Perfect. $950

G. RUTHERFORD (Ayr, Scotland) dovetailed steel mitre plane with brass bridge. 10½ X 2⅝ in. overall. Auct. $300

B. SHENEMAN, Market Street, Philadelphia. Low angle wooden plane. $15

W. SIMPSON, Leeds (British, 1807-1819) Beechwood rectangular mitre plane 13 in. long, 2¾ in. wide. Arch top boxwood insert at front of throat. $275

SPIERS, AYR stamped on brass bridge of this early dovetailed steel mitre plane with rosewood infill. 10½ X 2¾ iches overall. Auct. $271 - $333

SPIERS "improved pattern" dovetailed steel mitre plane. Rosewood filled. Original Ward snecked iron 2¼ in. wide. 10¾ in. overall. Auct. $280

Another, fine "improved" model in dovetailed steel with extra wide 2½ in. special ordered cutter. 12 inches long, filled with rosewood. Auct. $665

J.R. TOLMAN, Hanover, Mass. beech mitre plane 10 inches long. Coffin shape. $22

Rt. TOWELL, London. Early dovetailed mitre plane of approximately same size and style but with rosewood wedge & infill. (pitted cond.) Auct. $364. Another in fine cond. 2 x 10 in. Dlr. $590

C. WARREN, Nashua, N.H. (1857-1872) coffin-shaped beechwood mitre plane 9 in. long with steel faced sole. $18

WILLIAMS early dovetailed steel bib-front mitre plane with mahogany infill. (pitted) Auct. $140

UNMARKED cherry wood low angle mitre plane 1¼ X 5¼ in. overall. Seasoning cracks. $55

UNMARKED cast iron mitre plane with scroll-shaped front and raised rear palm rest. Rosewood wedge and infill. $200

UNMARKED Brass-bodied mitre planes with wooden wedges have sold at auct. for $175-$500

Courtesy Reg Eaton

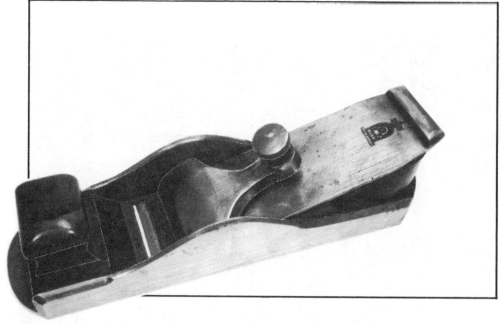

(At left) A rare "special order" mitre plane by Spiers, Ayr, Scotland. Rosewood filled, dovetailed iron body is extra wide 3 inch size by 12 ¼ inches long. This plane was sold at a recent London tool auction for $665.

(Below) Lot 111 is a fine Dovetailed Mitre Plane by Mathieson & Son, Edinburgh. It has a gunmetal lever cap, rosewood infill and a snecked-end iron. It brought $427 in U.S. funds.

Lot 112 is a Cast Iron Mitre Plane marked Mathieson, Glasgow. Also with gunmetal lever cap, it brought $375.

Lot 113 is a Dovetailed Steel Thumb Plane also by Mathieson of Glasgow. It is rosewood filled and features a brass lever cap. This rarity brought $735.

Courtesy Reg Eaton

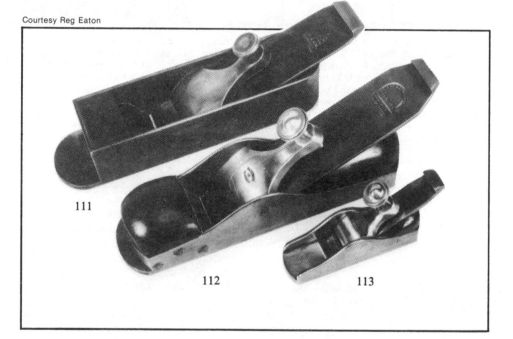

111

112   113

UNMARKED British dovetailed steel mitre plane with rosewood infill. Conventional bib front and round heel. 9¾ in. long, 2 in. wide. Dlr. $395

UNMARKED English mahogany mitre plane with Ward & Payne snecked iron. Stock is 16 inches in length and 2½ inches wide. Gunmetal sole. No handles. $290

UNMARKED British cast iron mitre plane with flush mounted boxwood infill, beech wedge. Gunmetal bridge is scalloped V shape. 3 x 10½ inches overall including short front & rear bib. Auct. $120

UNMARKED English made mitre plane No. 0011. Shaped in form of a 3 in. X 11 in. metal box with a mahogany wedge and stuffing. Flat metal sole extends an inch beyond the front of box and is rounded off. Auct. $790-$1,000

Plain style Mitre Plane of the late 19th Century.

Alex Mathieson & Sons No. 847 Improved Mitre Plane, circa 1899. Came in 2 in. X 8½ inch and 2½ in. X 10½ inch sizes.

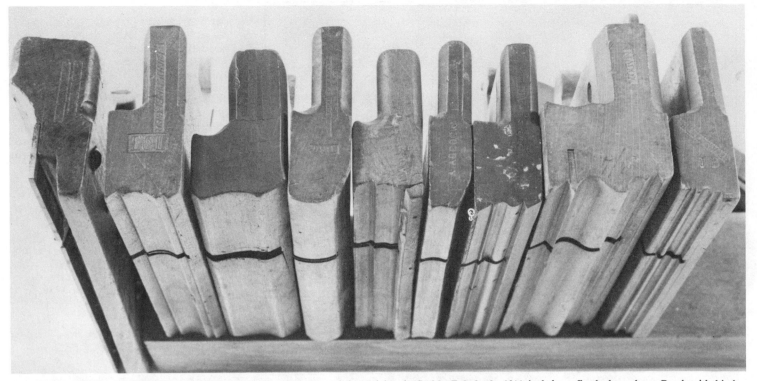

A SELECTION OF 18th CENTURY MOULDING PLANES, From left to right: **A. Smith, Rehoboth.** 13½ inch long fixed plow plane. Beech with birch handle. Heavy skate rivets and original stepped iron are by maker. Smith died in 1822. (2nd from left) **I. Lindenberger,** ovolo pattern complex moulder in birch, 10 inches long. John Lindenberger died in 1817 in Providence. (3rd from left) **Ion: Ballou, Providence,** hollow moulder of 18th Century. Birch with heavy chamfers and straight wedge. 9¾ inches overall. Jonathan Ballou lived from 1723 to 1770. Examples of his work are rare. (4th from left) **T. Morse, Stratford-upon-Avon,** no. 10 round plane 9⅝ in. long. Morse worked in Shakespear's home town in the 1770's. (Center) **I. Briscoe,** ovolo moulder 9⅜ inches in length. Rounded chamfers. Hildick stamped iron of the 1780's. (4th from right) **J. Switsur,** ½ inch hollow. Switsur worked in Winchester, England from 1774 to 1800. (3rd from right) **Mutter,** quirk ogee with single boxing. A narrow moulder 9⅜ inches in length. George Mutter worked in London from 1766 to 1812. (2nd from right end) **Madox,** quirk ogee with astragal. 9¾ in. long, single boxwood insert. Very wide chamfering. William Madox was in London from 1748 to 1765. This is a good usable plane. (Far right) **John Rogers,** astragal moulder with faint York stamp. 3/16 size, 9⅝ in. long. Another good useable tool from London, circa 1734 - 1765.

MOULDING PLANES have been used to cut ornamental profiles in wooden trim since early Roman times. Picture frames, casement and ceiling mouldings, furniture embelishments, clock and coffin trimmings and a host of other decorative touches all owe their development to the inventor of the moulding plane.

Prior to 1700 skilled craftsmen usually made their own cutting tools, often to accommodate the requirements of a specific moulding or beading task. At the beginning of the 18th Century there were less than half a dozen plane makers in and around London. The trade had been concentrated in Europe where highly refined woodworking tools had been produced since the beginning of the 16th Century. However by the year 1850 a pent up demand for ornate Renaissance and classical Greco-Roman moulding had encouraged the establishment of at least 150 plane makers near London.

The distinctive American style of moulding plane that evolved by the mid 19th Century was probably the result of several factors. Among them were Shaker design influences, the use of unskilled prison labor in tool factories, and our chronic need to get things done in a hurry.

The yellow birch used by early domestic plane makers was gradually replaced by beechwood and the favored length became a standardized 9½ inches (a good tool chest fit). The wide, well defined chamfers on the tops and shoulders of earlier planes became narrower and often rounded. Hand-forged blades by local blacksmiths were gradually replaced by those bearing the imprints of well known edge tool makers who produced extra quantities of "irons" for the trade.

A victorian era carpenter or cabinet maker might have owned several dozen simple narrow moulding planes as well as a few more complex styles for cornice work. By the turn-of-the-century factory-milled moulding sticks had suddenly made millions of beechwood moulding planes obsolete. Our friend the carpenter now carried a metallic combination-plane in his new smaller tool box and road to work on a trolley car with the tools of his trade tucked under one arm.

SIMPLE MOULDING PLANES are just what the name implies...simple shapes...portions of circles or rectangles that can be described with a compass and straight edge. COMPLEX MOULDING PLANES are usually wider, with irregular curved cutters, and sometimes have handles. The most sought after are Cornice, or Crown moulding planes in 4 to 6 inch widths. These larger moulders often came equipped with thru-the-stock tow bars (dowels) so that two workmen could exert the push and pull necessary to cut a very wide profile.

Fractional numbers stamped on the heels of these planes do not denote actual blade width, but rather the minimum size stock required to accomplish a cut. Names and initials on heels, toes and sides might be those of various owners. Trademarks can also be in the form of initial stamps but will be more formal and thought out in design, often surrounded with a border. In some cases hardware dealers overstamped original manufacturer's marks with their own logos. All of these bits of "tool box trivia" combined with the often interesting biographies of early makers are what make Rhykenology (the collecting of planes) such an absorbing hobby.

ASSORTED sizes of common English-made simple moulding planes. (76) at $8 each.

ASSORTED 18th Century British moulding planes, mixed makers. (145) at $18 ea.

ASSORTED hollows and rounds by Barton, Casey Clark, Howland, Ohio Tool & Sandusky. $8 - $10 ea.

ASSORTED hollows and rounds, unmarked. Dealer lot $5 each.

ASSORTED narrow moulders by 19th Century English makers in very good condition. (49) available at $12 each.

AUCTION LOT of (30) different simple beech moulding planes, various sizes and styles. (Some missing wedges or cutters.) $150

AUCTION LOT of (4) unmarked early birch moulders with 18th Century lines. $40

AUCTION LOT of (15) 18th Century style moulding planes. $120

S. ABBOT, birch moulding plane, ⅝ in. round, 9⅞ in. length. Auct. $45

L. AMES, London (circa 1800-1850) 1¼ in. round. Auct. $6 -$12

ANDRUSS, extra large one inch bead plane, single boxing. Dlr. $14

THOS. L. APPLETON, Boston. Double boxed ¼ in. center bead. $12 - $14 Larger bead planes in near mint cond. by same maker. Dlr. $25 - $35 ea.

ARROWMAMMETT WORKS, Middletown. Fully boxed ¾ in. bead plane 1¾ inches wide. $20 Single boxed, by same maker, ⅝ inch bead. $12

G. ASHLEY, Little Falls, No. 108 hollow moulding plane with metal strike point in heel. $22

ATKINSON, Baltimore, size ⅞ in. side bead in mint condition. $28

AUBURN TOOL CO., Auburn, N.Y., beechwood beader, ⅛ inch, perfect. $12 ⅜ in., solid boxed bead. $10 ½ in. single boxed bead. $8

AUBURN TOOL CO. complete set of (16) moulding planes in mint factory finish. $250 No. 155½ quarter round in like new condition. $35 Set of (4) No. 182 double reeding planes with triple boxing. Mint, unused. $155

G. AXE, No. 2 round plane in good condition. $11 Pair hollow & round. $28

A & E BALDWIN (1830-1841) No. 352 bead with ⅜ in. cutter. $10 No. 6 round. $10

E. BALDWIN, No. 83 double-bladed ⅜ in. beading plane. Auct. $42

JON BALLOU, Providence (1723-1770) birch moulder, astragal. $185 Round. Auct. $600

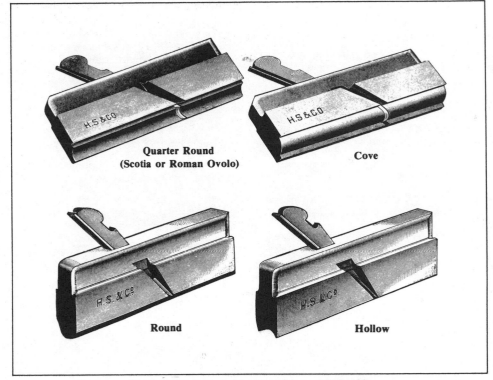

Quarter Round (Scotia or Roman Ovolo)

Cove

Round

Hollow

Simple Factory Made Moulding Planes (1860-1920)

R. BARNES beechwood moulding planes, ⅜ and ¾ in. irons. $15 -$18 ea.

H. BARRUS & CO., Goshen, Mass. (1854) ¼ in. single boxed bead. $12 No. 10 round. $15

N. L. BARRUS, Warren, R. I. (1849) beechwood ⅜ in. side bead. $22

S. S. BARRY, N.Y. No. 14 hollow. $10-$12

D. R. BARTON, Rochester, N.Y. beaders, moulders, hollows & rounds. $12 - $17

I. S. BATTEY, Prov. (1841-1855) beechwood reeding plane 1¾ in. wide (rough, worn bottom) $22

BELCHER BROS., Prov., R. I. No. 105 bead plane, ⅞ inch. $12 1¼ in. round. $20

JOHN BELL (Phila.) table-leaf moulding plane. $15 Double reeding plane, mint. $35

BENSEN & M'CALL, Albany (1842) ½ in. bead in like new condition. $20

DAVID BENSEN, Albany (1832-1847) 1 in. wide hollow moulder. $10

BENSEN & CRANNELL, Albany (1844-1862) beechwood 1¾ in. round. Near new. $15

S. H. BIBIGHAUS, Phila. Single oblique boxed ⅜ in. beader. $16

HOMER BISHOP & CO., Boston, No. 20 round 1⅜. $12

J. BRADFORD, Portland, Me. (1849-1875) pair of beading planes. Auct. $20 pr.

I. BRISCOE, British (1785) common moulder, 9⅞ in. Auct. $8 – $12

P. BROOKS, E. Hartford (circa 1850) hollow with owner's name brand burned in. $12 Another with raised mark, fully boxed, 3/16 in. bead. $14 1 inch snipe bill. Mint. $30

BUCK No. 16 pair of hollows and rounds in nearly mint cond. $26

G. H. BUCK, 1824, London. Single boxed ⅞ in. bead in mint cond. $26

J. BUCK, Holborn Viaduct, London. Triple bead reading plane with 2 boxwood inserts. Mint. $50

J. E. BUCK, 2 Russell Street, Landport. Simple moulder in good condition. $16

J. BUDD, London, ⅛ in. bead. $12 Side round, 1 in. radius. $26

C & S BULKLEY, Saybrook, Conn. (1850) matched pair of 2 in. wide beech hollows and rounds in near mint condition. $75 pair.

GEO. BURNHAM, Jr., Amherst, Mass. (circa 1849) No. 21 hollow moulder. $12

H. BUSH, Rochester, No. 12 hollow with impressed logo. $16

BUTLER, Phila. (1795-1835) 1⅝ in. round by one of 2 brothers. $21

MIGUEL CABOT, Rivadavia 2085, Buenos Aires. Set of 8 South American rounding planes in heavy tropical wood. Auct. $130

B. CALLENDER & CO., Boston, ½ inch single boxed bead. $16

CAM, hand rail moulder of the 18th century, 2½ inches wide by 15 in. long. with James Cam blade. $40

EDWARD CARTER, Troy, N.Y. set of 24 matched hollows & rounds in a box. Like new. Auct. $432 set

R. CARTER, Troy (1831-1861) ⅝ in. bead. Excellent shape. $14

C. CARY (circa 1800) beechwood round, size 3/32 in., 9¼ in. long. $15

CASEY CLARK & CO., Auburn, N.Y. ¼ inch round in mint condition. $12

CASEY, KITCHEL & CO. pair of hollow & round moulders. $18

A. CAUGHTER & CO., Louisville, Ky. hollow moulder, size ½ in. Auct. $25

CAYUDUTT FACTORY, New York, Extra Cast Steel, is the unusual 3 line imprint on this 1½ inch wide round moulder. $32

CHAPIN STEVENS round moulding planes sell in the $10 to $12 range. Beading planes are offered for from $12 to $24 each.

CHARLES & CO. No. 18 hollow with dividers & arrow trademark. $12

CE. CHELOR, Wrentham, ¼ in. beading plane in beautiful condition. Auct. $800 Fine ½ inch hollow moulder by this freed black man who died in 1784. Auct. $1,100 ¼ in. beader with hanging hole bored thru nose. $525 Hollow moulder. Auct. $600

CE. CHELOR, Living in Wrentham is the 3 line imprint on this 1¼ inch round in birch with ⅜ in. wide flat chamfers. $750 Same stamp. 1⅜ in. birch round in exceptional, as found, condition. Auct. $650 Same imprint, very strong impression on this 1¼ inch Scotia moulder. Auct. $2,600

J. E. CHILD (Prov. 1852-1875) ½ inch bead, as found. $14 ¾ inch cove moulder. $14

J. CLAP, 18th century style ⅝ inch hollow moulder in birch. Auct. $65

I. CLARK beading plane. Auct. $25

E. CLARK, Milwaukee, No. 10 round moulder. $13

E. CLARK, Middleboro. Rare 18th century hollow moulder. Auct. $650

JAS. CLARKE, Liverpool. Pair of snipesbills. Shoulder boxed, fine condition. $54

I. COGDELL (1750-1765) bead plane. Auct. $45 Hollow moulding plane. Auct. $56

COLLINS & ROBINS, Utica (circa 1830) No. 16 round in excellent condition. $25

D. COLTON, No. 327 Market Street, Phila. (1839-1875) ⅝ in. cove moulder. $15

I. COOMBS, ½ in. bead, beautifully boxed, exceptionally grained. $35

COPELAND & CO. Warranted. Beechwood ¾ in. bead with single boxwood insert. $12 - $15

A. COPELAND, Columbus, Ohio, No. 15 hollow. $22

D. COPELAND, Hartford. Beechwood snipe bill in mint condition. $30

M. COPELAND, ⅛ in. beader, perfect condition. $12 Pair Hollows & Rounds. $22

I. COULSON, British 18th century moulding plane 9¾ inches long. Auct. $20

I. COX, Birmingham, England (1770-1801) beechwood bead, ⅝ in. $15 Round. $8 - $14

BENSEN CRANNELL, Albany, No. 18 hollow, in need of cleaning. $10

A. CUMINGS, Boston (circa 1850) ⅞ inch Cove Moulder. $17 Handrail, 8 in. $60

S. CUMINGS, Providence (1828) No. 17 hollow. $12 ⅞ inch Astragal $25

S. DAVID washboard moulding plane, 9½ in. long with ⅝ groove cutter & 2nd parallel groove guide to follow previous cut. $60

S. DALPE, Roxton Pond, P.Q. (Canada) ¼ in. center bead. dble. boxed. $9

DARBY & COX, British moulder in beechwood. Auct. $8

G. DAVIS single boxed bead plane, $10

I. DAVIS, Birmingham (1770-1781) common moulder. Auct. $6 Hollow moulder, 10 in. Auct. $38

B. DEAN 18th century style ¾ inch round. Auct. $25

C. P. DEAN beechwood 1¼ in. round. $20

DE BANK, Bath. British moulding plane. Auct. $8 - $16

DE FOREST, Birmingham. (Conn. circa 1850) pair hollows and rounds. Auct. $17 ⅜ inch side beader. $12

JOHN DENISON, Saybrook. ⅝ in. hollow moulder. $10 1/16 in. bead. $16

G. W. DENISON & CO., Winthrop, Conn. (1868-1890) single boxed ⅝ in. bead. $12 -$23

W. DIBB, York (1800-1845) simple British moulder. $16 Hollow & Round, pair. Auct. $10

MARTIN DOSCHER, New York, ¼ in. side bead. $14

EASTWOOD, York, quarter round beech moulder with brass wear plate. $22 Facing moulder. Auct. $9

EDWARDS, Manchester. Common British moulder. Auct. $6

EDGERTON, Buffalo double boxed 1 in. bead, 2 inches wide. $15

G. EASTWOOD hollows and rounds (9) pairs. $200

18th CENTURY reeding plane, Phila., no maker. $45

18th CENTURY birch bead plane 10½ in. long. "Wrentham" features. $40

1828 DATED round, owner marked. Auct. $35

E. & J. EVANS, Rochester, No. 12 round. $12

J. W. FARR, New York (1832-1851) fully boxed ⅞ in. bead. $24

S. FELCH stamped, early 2⅛ in. wide reeding plane with heavy rounded chamfer. $65

JOEL FENN CO., Wallingford, 1849. Pair of hollows and rounds. $22

ISAAC FIELD, Providence (1828-1857) round, only 2½ inches tall. $40 ⅜ in. bead. $35 Bead & Cove, flame birch. $215

FOX & WASHBURN, Amherst, Mass. (1840-1842) ⅜ in. bead plane. $15

G. FISTER (unlisted 18th cent.) ¼ in. center beading plane, boxed. Auct. $50

FOX & WASHBURN, Amherst, Mass. (1840-1842) ⅜ inch beader. $15

B. FROGATT (1765-1790) English moulder, 1⅛ in. round. Auct. $15 Dlr. $25

FULLER & FIELD, Prov. (1842) birch bead, wedge and boxing gone. $85

C. FULLER, Causeway St., Boston (1852-1856) quarter round. $12 Right and left curved ¾ inch beading planes with boxwood inserts. Auct. $200 pair.

D. FULLER, Gardner, Me., ½ in. beader. Auct. $35

JO FULLER, Providence (1773-1822) round moulder. Auct. $100 - $225 Reverse astragal by same maker. Near mint. Auct. $400

GABRIEL, London (1770-1795) No. 15 hollow moulder. $15 (110 common moulding planes. Auct. $88 No. 6 round. Dlr. $29 5/16 bead. Dlr. $27

GARDNER & MURDOCK, Green Street, Boston. Cove moulder 1⅜ in. wide. $19

E. GERE with rooster stamp. Beechwood round. Auct. $20

J. GIBSON, Albany. No. 18 round. $11

J. GILMER, New Albany (Indiana) ½ in. moulding plane. $10

P. A. GLADWIN & CO. No. 24 round. $11

GLADWIN & APPLETON (1873-1877) quarter round. Auct. $22 Side bead. $12

GLEAVE, Oldham St., Manchester. (1854-1868) ¾ inch round. $12

GOLDSMITH, Corner Market & Green Street, Philadelphia. ½ inch side bead. $15

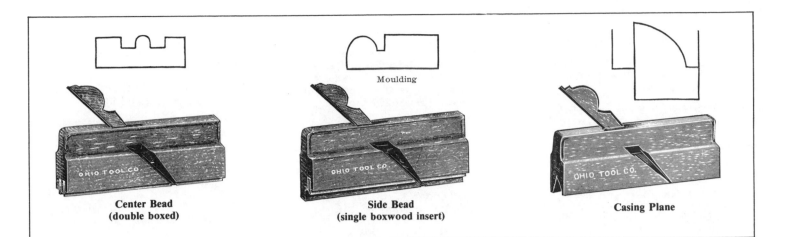

Center Bead
(double boxed)

Moulding

Side Bead
(single boxwood insert)

Casing Plane

GLADWIN & APPLETON, Boston. ¼ in. fully boxed bead plane. $11

GONZALEZ, HEROS, Buenos Aires. Set of 8 tropical wood moulding planes. Auct. $160

GOODMAN & HUSSEY quarter round moulders. Auct. $15 ea.

F. J. GOUCH, Worcester, No. 6 hollow. $14

THO: GRANT, N.Y. 18th century beech 1½ in. round 10¼ inches long. Auct. $350 1¼ in. hollow. Auct. $200 Another round, dented and saw cut mark. $85

JOHN GREEN, York, England (1774-1807) No. 4 hollow. $15 1 inch beader. Auct. $25 6 inch long hollow. Dlr. $38 Snipe bill. $40

S. GREEN, Bristol (1774-1801) No. 21 round. $35

GREENFIELD TOOL CO., Greenfield, Mass. fully boxed bead plane 1¾ in. wide. $22

W. GREENSLADE, Bristol, double reeding plane 1⅜ inches wide. $40 - $50

GRIFFITHS, Norwich, single boxed astragal, ¾ in. $12 No. 18 hollow. $9 Matched pair of snipe bills. Auct. $55

IOHN HAZEY (British 1766-1771) astragal moulding plane 9½ inches long. Auct. $39 Same maker, common mouldr. $16

HIELDS, Nottingham, matched set of (18) hollows & rounds, owner stamp. Auct. $200

D. HEIS (18th cent. Penn. maker) side bead plane. $50

A. HIDE, Conn. (circa 1780) birch ⅜ in. round. Heel cut to 9½ inch length. Auct. $200

A. PICK HIGGS, London (1821-1827) fully boxed snipe bill plane. $20 Matched pair in beechwood by same maker. Perfect. $75 No. 3 hollow. Fine. $15 Double reeder. $22 Boxed bead. $27

J. HILLS, Springfield, Mass., ⅜ in. bead plane. Auct. $15

HILLS & RICHARDS, Norwich, Mass., ⅝ in. bead, single boxwood insert. $15

HILLS WINSHIP, Springfield. ⅝ in. bead, 1½ inches wide, fully boxed. $22

HILLS & WOLCOTT, Amherst, Mass. (1829) ¼ inch bead plane. (dirty) $24

HOLBECK (British 1730-1770) round moulding plane, 9½ inches long. Auct. $96

HOLBROOK side beader in mint condition. $20

C. W. HOLDEN, Norwich, Conn. (1850-1875) unusual 1¼ in. wide hollow with curved compass bottom. Double iron. $15 3/16 in. side bead. (worm holes) $14

HOPKINS pair of 1½ in. skew-ironed hollow and round moulders. $32

S & R HOWDEN, Manchester, England, matched pair of snipe bills, boxed. $75 pr.

W. HOWE matched set of early hollow and round moulders. Auct. $20 pr.

A. HOWLAND & CO. pair of hollows and rounds. ¾ inch. $24 pr.

C. JACOBSEN, Copenhagen, ⅝ in. quarter round. $12

H. L. JAMES, Wmsburg, Mass. (circa 1855) ¼ in. bead plane. $10 - $14 Hollow & Round, pair $17

J. N. STAMP with CROWN (J. Nooitgedagt & Zonen, Yest) set of 29 assorted red beechwood, Dutch moulding planes. Auct. $270 Another J. N. Dutch made set of 24 hollow and round moulders. $275

JENNINGS & CLARK, pair No. 16 hollow & round moulding planes. $22

GEO. RUSBY KAYE, Leicester, England, matched set of 18 skew-ironed hollows & round. $270

KENNEDY, Hartford (1809-1842) No. 10 round moulder. $11

I. KENDALL (Mary Kendall 1765-1814) simple beechwood moulder. Auct. $8 Dlr. $16

KENDALL, York (William 1818-1830) astragal moulder, ⅜ inch. Auct. $9

L. KENNEDY, Hartford (1809-1842) ⅜ in. round, beechwood. $15 Reeding plane. $45

J. KELLOGG, No. 8 round moulder. $8 Pair of No. 18 hollow & round moulders. Auct. $20 3/16 in. bead. mint cond. $12 1¼ in. bead, perfect. $18

KELLY & CO., Ashfield, Mass., 3/16 in. center beading plane. $12 -$14

J. KILLAM, Glastonbury, Conn. (1822-1860) ½ inch cove moulder. $25 Side bead. $10 -$18

D. KIMBERLEY matched set of 9 pairs of hollows and rounds. (18) pcs. $200

JOSIAH KING, 373 Bowery, N.Y. (1835-1837) No. 18 hollow. $12 5/16 in. center bead. $15

KING & PEACH, Hull. Common British moulding plane. Auct. $9

S. KING, 18th century simple moulder. Auct. $9 Dlr. $16 1⅛ in. round. Dlr. $22 Cockbead. Dlr. $30

J. H. LAMB, New Bedford (1869-1874) right & left side bead with 2 wedged irons. $58 Single boxed ⅝ inch beader. $12

E. LEONARD 18th century style hollow moulder. Auct. $50

J. LINDENBERGER, Providence, R. I. (circa 1800) Beech hollow, perfect. $75 Birch center bead, sharp maker's mark. Auct. $250 Sash moulder in birch, mint. Auct. $600

J. E. & G. M. LINDSEY, Huntington, Mass. Single boxed ⅜ in. beader. $11

J. LOVELL, Cummington, Mass. No. 14 round. $10

MANNERS, Rare ivory soled 7½ in. side bead moulding plane. auct. $115

T. J. McMASTERS, Auburn, N.Y. ⅜ in. bead plane. $12 ¾ in., fully boxed. $60 ⅝ inch applewood bead with single boxwood insert, circa 1825. $30

MADOX, London (1748-1775) No. 13 round in new cond. $45 Hollow, No. 18. Auct. $50 Side bead with astragal. $25

D. MALLOCH, Perth, ⅝ in. side beading plane. $12 Unusual 1 inch wide moulder. $28 Set of (18) hollows and rounds. $200

P. H. MANCHESTER, Providence (1843-1857) beechwood beader. $11

MANNERS (British) simple moulder with clear maker's mark. $16

MARLEY, 40 Elm St., New York. ⅝ in. beading plane, fine. $14

W. MARPLES & SONS, Sheffield (1860) No. 18 round with 1⅜ in. cutter. $8 -$12

JOSEPH MARPLES, York, matched set of (18) hollow & round moulding planes. Auct. $130

MARSHALL, Glasgow, 1¼ in. wide side bead. $11 3/16 in. moulder. $20

MARTIN & SHAW, Birmingham, England (1845-1854) matched pair of snipe bills, mint. $65

A. MATHIESON, Glasgow, set of 18 hollow & round moulding planes. Auct. $130

MATHIESON & SON, Glasgow & Edinburgh. Narrow moulding plane with tall brass wear plate on side. $20

McVICAR, Perth, side bead 1¾ in. wide. $11

MELHUISH, Fetter Lane (England) 1½ in. wide triple beader. $45

MOIR, Glasgow (1843-1874) ⅝ in. side bead. Usable. $12

A. C. MORE, Goshen, Mass., No. 10 round. $12

MOSELY & CO. (English circa 1800) 9¼ inch long bead with fillet. $18

MOSELY & SONS, London. Pair of side rounds, ½ in. radius. Usable. $52 pr. 18 hollows and rounds. $175

JOHN MOSELY & SON, 54-55 Broad Street, Bloomsbury, London. 1¼ in. wide beader. $28

MOSELY LATE MUTTER No. 16 round. $15

E. MOSES (New York circa 1850) beech moulding plane, size 1 in. round. Perfect. $30

WILLIAM MOSS (1775-1800) ¾ in. round. $25

Wm. MOSS (England 1812-1843) auction lot of 8 moulding planes. $52

Wm MOSS, Birmingham. Matched set of 18 hollows and rounds. Auct. $120 Pair snipe bills. Auct. $65 Masonic emblem on No. 1 round. $14

MULTIFORM MOULDING PLANE CO.

Patented Aug. 29, 1854. Pair of solid boxed moulding planes with slot in stock behind wedge for master handle (not included) $110 pr. Single boxed ⅜ in. bead, as above. $30-$50 Set of 4 wooden planes all slotted. Includes handle and 4 cutters. Handle has brass base. Auct. $225 Set of (8) Dlr. $625

G. MUSGRAVE, Lincoln. Set of 3 simple ovolos in nearly mint cond. $110

MUTTER auction lot of 11 British moulders. $105

MUTTER (London 1776-1812) 9½ inch side bead. $16 No. 8 round. $18

H. L. NARRAMORE, Goshen, Mass. (1865-1872) No. 4 round in mint condition. $9

H. L. NARAMORE, G. Plant, ⅛ in. single boxed bead plane. $10 ¼ in. side bead. $14

NAZRO & KING, Milwaukee, 3/16 inch boxed fruitwood beading plane. Auct. $50

R. NELSON, 122 Edgeware Rd., London. Single boxed 5/8 in. beader. $12

F. NICHOLSON, Wrentham (circa 1760) Hollow moulder with rough bottom edges. Auct. $550 1 inch ogee moulding plane. Auct. $525 1½ inch quarter round (with severe heel chipping). Auct. $160

I. NICHOLSON, birch hollow moulder 9⅞ in. long. Auct. $250-$275

P. C. NORTHUP birch bead plane 10 inches long. (Fence repaired.) Auct. $75

C. NURSE & CO., 182 & 184 Walworth Road, London. Matched set of 9 beading planes. Like new cond. $140

OHIO TOOL CO. Auction lot of 11 assorted simple moulding planes. Auct. $85 1⅛ inch round. Dlr. $11 Set of 18 hollows and rounds in mint cond. Dlr. $225 No. 43½ inch quarter round. $15 No. 43 cove moulder in mint cond. $20

OKINS (London 1740-1835) round moulder 9⁷/₁₆ in. long. Narrow chamfers. $55

OSWALD, English moulding plane 10 inches in length. Auct. $20

OWASCO TOOL CO., New York, ⅜ inch center bead, double boxwood inserts. $12

PARKER, HUBBARD & CO. (Conway, Mass., 1850-1851) ½ in. side bead, beechwood. $15

R. A. PARRISH, Philadelphia. ¾ in. side beading plane. $15 Mint cond., boxed. $16 - $20

J. W. PEARCE (Fall River, Mass.) ⅞ in. wide. Fine. $25

P. M. PECKHAM, Fall River. Double boxed bead plane. $12 - $16

W. PENNELL, No. 225 Arch St., Philadelphia. ⅜ in round. $15

W. H. POND, New Haven. ½ inch bead. Straight & perfect. $15

POND & WELLS, New Haven, No. 16 round moulder. $16

L. T. POPE, Boston (1841) beech beader, ⅝ in. (Some boxing gone.) $17

PRATT & CO., Buffalo (1836-1850) No. 6 round moulding plane. $11 Fully boxed bead by same maker. $20

D. PRESBREY (Norton, Mass., 1785-1856) beechwood cock-bead. $40

C. PRESCOTT, Lowell, fully boxed ¼ in. bead plane in excellent cond. $14

PRESTON & SON, No. 5 Boro Road, London. Single boxed ¾ in. bead plane. $13

PRESTON & SONS pair of snipe bills with boxwood inserts. $55

RANDALL & BENSON No. 8 round with raised lettering (1827-1829) $13

RANDALL & COOK, Albany (1835-1839) ¾ in. bead plane. $12 Rare gunstock inletting plane by same maker, 8 inches long with brass wear plate on front. $32

W. RAYMOND (Beverly, Mass. 1762-1836) beechwood ⅝ in. hollow $50 Another moulder with heavy chamfer. Auct. $75

M. READ, Boston (1842-1844) fully boxed ¾ inch bead plane. $20

REED, Utica, New York (1820-1868) ⅜ in. single boxed beader. $12

M. REED, Boston (circa 1844) fully boxed ⅞ in. bead plane. Fine. $24

P. B. RIDER, Bangor, Maine (1834-1848) ⅝ in. beader. $18

E & T RING CO., Worthington, Mass. (1849) rounder. $10 Side bead, near new. $15 Double bead. $30

ROCK SONS & CO. British-made round with ½ inch cutter. $13

Iohn Rogers (1734-1765) No. 8 round, heavy chamfers. $28

S. ROWELL, Troy & Albany, N.Y. (1820-1832) ¼ in. side bead. $10

ROWELL & GIBSON, Albany (1824-1828) beechwood ⅝ in. round. $12

E. SAFFORD, Albany (1813-1821) early round with 1¼ in. cutter. $13-$16

D. SAMPSON, Portland. Beechwood quarter round moulder, 1 inch. Auct. $40

JER. SAMSOM, 18th cent. stamp, ⅜ beech bead. (stained & boxing gone) Auct. $50

SANDUSKY TOOL CO. simple moulders $12 - $18 Set of 24 matched. $310 Triple reeding plane 2¼ inches wide. Fine cond. $65 Set of 15 hollows and rounds. $227

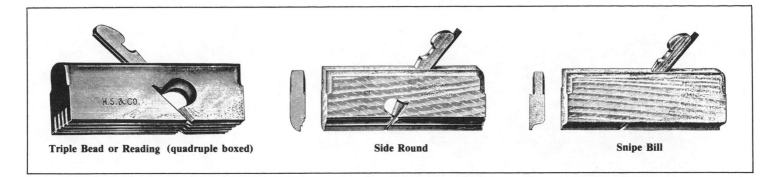

Triple Bead or Reading (quadruple boxed)   **Side Round**   **Snipe Bill**

D. P. SANDBORN, Littleton, N.H. (1856) No. 8 round moulder, 1½ in. iron. $15

SARGENT ½ inch single boxed beader. $9 With double boxwood inserts. $10 No. 5 round. $8 Mint examples bring more.

I. SCHAUER (circa 1776) beechwood moulding plane, ⅝ in. deep hollow. Auct. $20

N. SCHAUER (1755-1829) beechwood hollow, ⅝ in. Auct. $30 (Side beader 9⅜ inches long. Dlr. $45)

W. SCOTT, Pittsburgh (18th cent.) ½ inch side bead with insert wear blocks of lignum vitae placed fore and aft of cutter. $30

A. B. SEIDENSTRICKER, 90 W. Balto. Street, Balto. ½ inch hollow. $15 - $28

B. SHENEMAN 735 Market Street, applewood moulding plane, round. Mint. $45

ARAD: SIMONS (circa 1800) 10 inch long bead plane with wide flat chamfers. $45

I. SLEEPER.(John Sleeper, Newburyport, Mass., circa 1775-1825) beechwood hollow with heavy chamfer and orig. wedge. (chipped body). $60 Quarter round by same maker, 9½ in. Auct. $75 - $125. Beader. Auct. $90

A. SMITH, Lowell (1853-1856) No. 5 round. $15 Low profile hollow with wide flat chamfer. $25

A. SMITH, Rehoboth (1769-1822) ½ inch beader with boxwood insert. Auct. $45 1½ inch round. Auct. $35 1½ inch hollow. Dlr. $55

A. M. SMITH, New Bedford (1834) ⅜ in. beechwood beading plane. $15

E. SMITH, hollow with 1⅛ in. iron. $9 Side beader. $15 Twin cutter bead. $30

N. SPALDING, McLeane, N.Y. (1824-1850) 3/16 beader, full boxing. $13

W. H. SPALDING, Elmira, N.Y. ¼ in. hollow in mint condition. $15

P. SPOONER (18th cent. American) 10 inch beech hollow. Auct. $170

J. J. STYLES, Kingston, N.Y. (1820-1876) No. 8 round with shoulder. $25

A. SMITH, Reboth, cove with bead. Rounded chamfers. Beautiful. $60 Another complex moulder by this 18th century maker, size ¾ inch. Auct. $325

J. M. TABER, New Bedford, Mass. (1852-1875) 3/16 inch double beading plane. Auct. $20 Another John Taber moulding plane, unusually large, with handle, cuts 1⅞ in. bead, 13½ inches overall. Beautiful. $95 Hollow moulder, 1 inch. $13 Pairs of hollows and rounds $15-$18 pr. ⅜ inch side bead. Dlr. $2 Pair of snipe bills. Auct. $60

N. TABER (1790-1839) beechwood side beading plane with boxwood insert, 10 in. Auct. $125

TABER PLANE CO., New Bedford, Mass. (1866-1892) beech ½ inch beader. $12

WING H. TABER, Fairhaven (1833) ¼ inch side bead (worn) $10 Matched pair of hollows and rounds, ¾ inch. $25

THOMAS TIDD, marked TIDD, (circa 1744). Beechwood hollow, 9¹¹/₁₆ in. long. 1½ in. cutter. Wide flat chamfers. Decorative owner's mark. $85

T. TILESTON, Boston (1820-1865) ½ inch side bead with dovetailed solid boxing. $15 ¾ in. bead, dovetailed inserts. $24 ⅜ In. round. $25 Coping plane. Mint. $45

J. R. TOLMAN, Hanover, Mass. ⅞ in. bead with Tolman double iron. $28 Shipbuilder's round with 1½ in. Moulson Bros. cutter. $58 1¼ inch wide round with chamfered bottom edges and corner flutes. Like new. $25

VARVILL & SONS, York, England (1862-1904) single boxed 1 inch bead plane. Excellent. $24 Complete set of (18) skew-ironed common moulding planes to 1½ inches wide. $260

I. WALTON in Reading, Mass. (circa 1764) clearly marked hollow moulder. Auct. $425 Another (wedge damaged) Auct. $175 Yellow birch moulder with inverted V sole. ¾ in. wide by 10⅛ in Dlr. $600

WILLIAM WARD 513 8th Ave., N.Y. ¾ inch beader. $16 Fine quality stair rail moulder. $160

C. WARREN, Nashua, N.H. (circa 1860) ¼ in. bead. Auct. $15 Cove moulder. $16 Nice beading plane. Auct. $35

WAY & SHERMAN, N. York (1849-1852) 1¼ inch side bead. $20

WARNER & DRIGGS, Phoenix Factory. ¾ inch single boxed bead plane. $22

WEBB BAKER, Pitsfield. Single boxed ⅜ in. bead plane. $16

M. H. WEBSTER, Detroit. No. 4 hollow moulder. $15

H. WELLS, Wmsburg, Mass. No. 8 round in very nice cond. $13

R. WELLS (Trenton) 1½ inch wide round moulding plane. Auct. $35

H. WETHERELL, Chattam (circa 1790) faintly marked 1 in. hollow. $45

H. WETHERALL, In Norton (circa 1764) fine beading plane. Auct. $600 ⅜ inch beader. Auct. $750

T. WHEELER (1790-1826) British made round. Auct. $20

HENRY G. WHITE, Philadelphia (circa 1812) 3/16 in. side beader. $15

G. WHITE (circa 1820) 1¼ inch round with 2 boxwood insert wear strips. Auct. $20 ¾ inch side bead with lignum vitae boxing. Dlr. $30

L. & I. J. WHITE, Buffalo No. 16 round in excellent condition. $12 Set of (22) hollow & round moulding planes. $175

WILSON (Glasgow) astragal moulder with dovetailed ivory sole, 7 inches long. Auct. $75

W. WINSCOMB in zig-zag border. 18th century moulding plane 9½ in. long. Auct. $20

ROBERT WOODING (London 1710-1728) 10 inch round, 3 inches tall. Cuts 1¼ inch. $200 Clearly stamped astragal moulder (some worm holes in heel). Auct. $315 ⅞ inch hollow with 2 line imprint on heel. One of the earliest documented makers. Auct. $600

Wm. WOODWARD, Taunton (1810-1850) Nice ⅞ in. astragal moulder. $25 ¼ in. side bead. $20 1⅞ inch bead plane with raised impression. $48 Round, with decorative embossed border. $45

YOUNG & McMASTER, Auburn, N. Y. No. 12 round moulding plane. $14

Circa 1856-1870 4-ironed moulder by Mathieson & Son, sold at T.R. Roberts Auction for $446.

C. ALLEN (Troy, N.Y. circa 1800). ½ in. Grecian ogee complex moulding plane in beechwood. Auct. $40

AMES No. 2 reverse ogee 2½ inches wide. (Some worm holes). $25

J. ANDRUSS complex moulder. Auct. $32

THOS. APPLETON, Boston. Complex moulding plane 1¾ in. wide. $15-$20

ARROWMAMMET WORKS, Middletown, Conn. (circa 1858) 2½ in. wide beechwood moulder. Perfect. $28-$34

ARTHINGTON, Manchester (England) complex moulding plane 1¾ in. wide. Mint. $35   Grecian ogee and cove moulder, 4¼ in. wide with Scottish-style rear-mounted handle. $190

ARTHUR, Edinburgh (1793-1844). Scotia moulding plane with 2 irons, 2 inches wide. $30

ASSORTED English made complex moulders in sash ovolo style. $15 each. Dlr. lot.

ATKIN & SON, Late W. Moss, No. 1 single-boxed scotia and ovolo moulding plane 1⅝ in. wide. Fine cond. $28

AUBURN No. 128 beechwood complex moulder in excellent condition. $18-$22

BAILEY, Sunderland, auction lot of (3) 2 inch wide moulders. $60

A & E BALDWIN (N.Y. 1830-1841) 1¾ inch wide complex moulding plane. $20-$24 Handled crown moulder by same maker. 14½ inches long, 5½ in. wide. Auct. $400 Gothic bead plane with right & left shaving exits. ⅞ in. dble. iron. Auct. $140

E. BALDWIN (1817-1850) fine Grecian ovolo with bead. Double boxed, 1¼ in. wide. $15

BARRY & WAY, N.Y. (1842-1847) beechwood complex moulder, 2¼ in. wide. $25-$30 2⅞ inch wide Grecian ogee with quarter round. $45 Unusual razee-style open handled quirk ogee with bevel, 3½ inches wide by 14½ inches in length. $200

D. R. BARTON & CO., Rochester, N.Y. (1832-1875) Grecian ogee with bevel. Fine. $30

J. BASSET ⅞ inch moulding plane with heavy chamfer. Auct. $75

I. O. BEATTLE Middletown, N.Y. (1861-1872) beechwood complex moulder 9½ inches long. $40-$60

JOHN BELL, Philadelphia (1829-1851) 2¼ inch wide complex moulding plane. $25-$35 Crown moulder by same maker, 3 inch cutting iron. Fine condition. Auct. $350 5 inch crown moulder in excellent cond. Auct. $700   4 x 14 in. Auct. $225

D. BENSON, Albany (1827-1850) 1¾ in. wide complex moulding plane. $25

BENSEN & CRANNELL, Albany (1844-1862) 2 inch wide complex moulder in fine cond. $35   Reverse cabinet ogee. $90

BENSEN & PARRY, Albany. Complex moulder 2 inches wide. Auct. $50

G. A. BENTON, Boston (1858-1876) Grecian ogee with bead. Open handle, 2½ in. iron. $135

BEWLEY, Leeds, 18th cent. English made complex moulder, 2 inches wide. $20-$25

B. G. aux Mines de Suede, Paris. Fruitwood complex moulding plane with 3 separately wedged cutting irons. $185

S. H. BIBIGHAUS, Phila. closed handled crown moulder 2⅞ in. Like new. $165 Another, 3½ x 14 in. Sharp. Auct. $525

F. B. STAMP (FERDINANDO BOTTLE, 1739) fruitwood ogee moulder made by British church builder and furnisher. Auct. $740

J. BRADFORD (Portland, Me. 1849-1875) crown moulding plane 16 inches long x 5 in. wide including applied fence. (Replacement handle) Auct. $400

P. BROOKS, E. Hartford. Beechwood ogee 1 inch wide. $12 Fine Grecian ogee moulder 3¼ inches in width. Auct. $70

H. BROWN (1812-1843) Bilection moulder with 1 inch cutter and single boxwood insert. $15

BUCK 245 Tottenham Ct. Rd. 19th century single-boxed cove and ogee moulder, 3 in. wide. Usable tool. $95

EDWARD CARTER, Troy, N.Y. (1848-1897) beech complex moulder 1¾ inches wide. $35 Another 3 inches in width. $45

CASEY & CO., Auburn, N.Y., fine complex moulding plane 3½ inches wide. $135 Another by same maker, 2¾ inch. $25 Crown moulder 16 inches overall. $145

CASEY, CLARK & CO., Auburn, N.Y. (1864) large beechwood moulding plane 2¼ inches wide. Clean & shiny cond. $40

CB mark in zig-zag border on 16 inch long crown moulder with open handle, 3½ in. cutter marked Brown. Auct. $450

CHAPIN STEPHENS CO. (1901-1929) common ogee moulder 1⅝ inches wide. $15-$25

H. CHAPIN (1826-1860) complex moulding plane. $20 Another, 2¾ in. wide. $45

H. CHAPIN, Union Factory, Warranted. No. 127 ovolo. $25

N. CHAPIN & CO. Eagle Factory (Westfield, Mass. 1849) reverse ogee, 2 in. wide. $22

P. CHAPIN, Balto. (1842-1860) Grecian ovolo, 1 in. cutter. $20. Crown moulding plane by same maker, 3 inch Butcher iron. Asking $400

C. E. CHELOR, Living in Wrentham. 18th century Bilection 1 inch moulder in birch. Auct. $550 1¼ inch ogee with astragal by same maker, perfect condition. Auct. $2,600   Unblemished nosing plane, Auct. $2,600 Crown moulder. Auct. $1,625

J. E. CHILD (Providence 1852-1875) complex moulder 2 in. wide. $22-$45

C K mark in zig-zag border on 14 inch long crown moulding plane with 4½ in. wide cutter. Offset handle, rounded wedge and iron. Hole in nose for tug rod. Auct. $650

E. CLARK, Middleboro. 1½ inch compound moulder with axe-shaped iron. Auct. $650

I. COGDELL (London 1750-1765- beechwood ogee 10 inches long, 1 in. iron. $50 9⅞ inch version. Auct. $75

CROWN MOULDING PLANES BRING $2,850.

At a recent tool auction conducted by Richard Crane strong local interest ran the bidding up rapidly as affluent tool collectors vied for this pair of 5 inch wide complex moulding planes. They were made by C. Warren of Nashua circa 1864. Commonly called cornice planes in the 19th century, and now complex moulders, they sold in pairs when two cuts were necessary to complete a very wide moulding profile. A pull rope was attached to the thru-the-nose tug bar for two man operation.

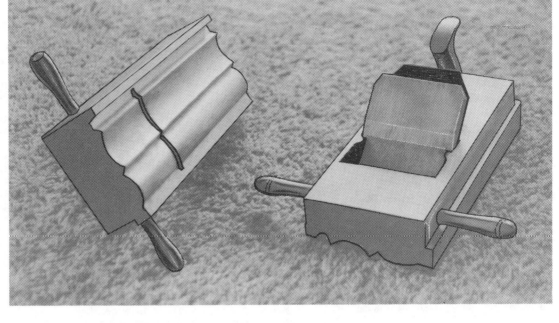

D. COLTON, Phil. (1835-1875) handled complex moulder 12 inches long, 3 in. iron. $160

J. COLTON 247 South 2nd St., Phila. Double rosewood inserts, cove with bead moulder, 1¼ in. iron. $40 Double-ironed complex moulding plane, 2¾ in. $75 Another, 2 inch width. $55

COPELAND & CO. (Huntington, Mass. 1856) beautiful beechwood complex moulder in perfect condition. 2⅜ inches wide. $40 3 inch version, mint. $70

M. COPELAND (Hartford, Conn. 1831-1842) 2 inch wide complex moulding plane in excellent cond. $45 Grecian ovolo with fillet. $35 Crown moulder 3½ in. Grecian ogee with bevel. Tug bar in nose. Auct. $350

I. COX early 18th century moulder, primitive $28 1⅞ in. complex cutter. $39

M. CRANNEL, Albany (1862-1892) ½ inch reverse ogee, 1½ in. wide. $16-$18

N. CURTISS, Boston. Complex moulding plane 2 inches in width. Auct. $135

A. CUMMINGS, Boston (1848-1851) complex moulder 2¼ in. wide. $22 With attached fence and 1¾ in. cutter. Auct. $35 Another beechwood moulder, near new. $50 Crown moulding plane 14 inches long with 3 in. blade. Closed tote. Auct. $300 5 inch wide crown moulder in original cond. with 4 in. iron. Auct. $450

B. CUMMINGS radius moulder, no description given. Auct. $350

S. CUMMINGS (Providence 1828) beechwood complex moulding plane. $25-$35

S. DEAN (early Mass. maker?). Beautiful architectural crown moulding plane with 3¾ in. iron, attached fence. Auct. $450

DARBEY (Thomas, 1767-1785) ovolo moulder 9⅞ in. long. $55

J. & L. DENISON, Saybrook. Complex moulder 1¾ inches wide. Auct. $30

DETER, Phila. narrow moulding plane. Auct. $170

S. DOGGETT, early birch reverse ogee & bead, 10⅛ x 1½ inches. Auct. $300

DM mark in zig-zag border, 16 inch crown moulder, 5⅝ inches wide. Tug dowel thru stock, offset handle. Auct. $500

G. EASTWOOD, York. Complex moulding plane with twin-wedged irons. Grecian ogee. $65

JOHN ELSWORTH pair of British tandem-ironed sash ogee & fillet moulders. Auct. $64 pr. Three-ironed moulder by same maker, two shoulder style, 3½ inches wide. Auct. $115

J.W. FARR, N.Y.C. (1832-1851) beechwood complex moulder 2⅜ inches wide. $30 - Another very clean ogee moulding plane by same maker 14½ inches long. $165

A. FOSTER, ogee crown moulder, 4½ x 15 in. (with some age checking) Auct. $575

JO FULLER, Providence (1797-1817) yellow birch moulder 1¼ in. wide by 10 inches long. Heavy chamfers. $75-$100. Fine ½ inch birch ogee with very clear mark. 10 inches overall. $150. 1½ inch complex moulder in prime, "as found" condition. $200. Beautiful birch crown moulding plane by Fuller with 4½ inch iron. Short blocky body and offset tote. Auct. $800

GABRIEL (London 1775-1790) ogee moulding plane stamped 5 on heel. 9 in. x 1½ in. $34 Scotia sash mould. Auct. $75 Double boxed ovolo by same maker, 1⅞ inch wide ovolo with astragal. $65

GARDNER & MURDOCK (1825-1845) complex moulding plane 2⅜ in. wide. $60
Grecian ogee with James Cam cutter 2½ in. wide. $150
Handled Cornice moulder 14½ inches long. Auct. $230
Extra nice Gardner & Murdock, Boston-made crown moulding plane with top-mounted tow bar. 3¾ inch cutter. Auct. $450

GIBBS & CATON, New York (1834) complex moulding plane 2⅛ inches wide in mint condition. $40 - Another 1¾ inch model. $20

J. GIBSON, Albany (1823-1852) fine Grecian ogee moulder 1¼ inches wide. $16-$32

GLADWIN & APPLETON, Boston (1873-1877) very nice Grecian ovolo, 2¼ inches wide. $26

T. GOLDSMITH complex moulding plane (no description) Auct. $22

THO. GRANT complex moulder, sold at auction for $275

JOHN GREEN (England, circa 1774) plain ogee 1⅜ inches wide. $25-$40 Another with many delicate beads and curves, 2 inches wide. $85

GREENFIELD TOOL CO., Greenfield, Mass. (1851-1887) beechwood complex moulder, reverse ogee, 2¼ inches wide. $25-$35 - Another, near new 2½ inch model. $45 No. 228 3 inch ogee cornice moulding type. Auct. $200

W. GREENSLADE, Bristol (1826) complex moulder, marked "Exhibition Medal" on nose. 3 inches wide. $40 - Double curved ovolo only 7 inches long for sash work. $65 - Set of (4) moulders with same owner's stamp. Auct. $120 all. Pair of compass bottom ovolo moulding planes with convex soles. Like new. Pair $135

MOULDING PLANES, COMPLEX (continued)

Courtesy "Your Country Auctioneer, Inc."

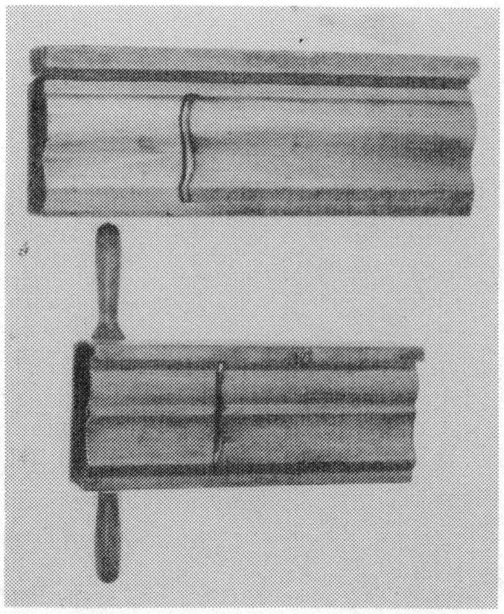

Top: Unmarked 5½ in. wide crown moulder, 18 inches long. Sold for $650 at auction. Bottom: A. Adams, yellow birch moulding plane, 4½ in., brought $1,600 winning bid.

GRIFFITHS, Norwich (19th Century family of British plane makers) 1½ inch wide quirk ovolo with astragal. $28 - Grecian ovolo 1⅞ in. width. $35 - 3¼ inch wide grecian ogee with astragal, boxing. $50 No. 78 bead with cove, 2¼ inch wide complex moulder. $60 - Grecian ogee 3⅜ in. wide. $100 - Beechwood stair rail moulder with complex curves. Asking $275

I. HAMMOND, New Haven (1840-1845) double boxed complex moulder 2 in. wide. $45 - Another 2¾ inches in width. Fine cond. $75

J. HARRIS crown moulding plane 16 inches long with 3⅜ in. blade. Auct. $225

ADDISON HEALD with star and sunburst imprint. Complex moulding plane. $18

C. HEBERLING, Kneass & Co., Philadelphia. Complex moulder. $45

D. HEISS, Lan' (Lancaster 1769-1814) beautiful unhandled 18th century moulding plane. Auct. $225

S.&.H. HILLS, Amherst, Mass. (1829-1830) 1⅝ in. wide complex moulding plane. $25

HOFFMAN, Edinburgh. Two ironed complex moulder with handle. 3½ in. wide. (some worm holes) Auct. $105

S. HOLBECK (1730-1770) ovolo moulder. Auct. $125

HOLBROOK ovolo with cove, 2⅛ in. wide. $38 - Reverse ogee. $40 - Picture frame profile cutter, 2 inches wide. $50

A. HOWLAND & CO., Auburn, N.Y. (1869-1874) No. 106 reverse ogee moulder with ⅞ in. cutter. $15 - No. 140 Grecian ogee moulder, 2 inch. $35 - Others, $20

JOHN JENNION (apprentice to Robert Wooding in 1724) ovolo moulder 10 inches in length, 3½ in. tall. $170 - Another with replacement wedge. $125 (Jennion ceased production in 1757.)

J. KELLOG, Amherst, Mass. Ogee moulding plane 2⅛ in. wide. $30

KENNEDY & CO., Hartford (1845) 1¼ in. complex moulder. $40

L. KENNEDY single boxed ⅞ in. quirk. $21 Another with astragal, 1¾ in. $35

KENNEDY & WHITE, N. Y. (1822-1840) 2 inch wide complex moulder. $40

JOSIA KING, 373 Bowery, N.Y. Beechwood stair cove moulder, very nice cond. $95. - Common moulder. $30

S. KING, Hull (England 1776-1781) ¾ inch Grecian ogee with wide flat chamfers. $28

J.H. LAMB, New Bedford. 2 inch wide complex moulder, ⅞ in. ogee. $17

T. LAMSON (with tiny stars around the T) beech cove with bead. Late 18th cent. $75

J.F. & G.M. LINDSEY (1856-1879) Roman reverse ogee, ⅝ in. with applied fence. $12 Another complex moulder with concave cutter. $18

N. LITTLE complex moulding plane. $170

JAS. LUMSDEN, Dundee. Two cutting irons on 3¾ in. wide complex moulding plane. Auct. $73 - Another moulder by Scottish maker, 3 separately wedged irons in L-shaped stock cut a 1⅝ in. quirk ovolo with bead and fillet. Dlr. $175

I. LUND, London. 2⅜ in. wide quirk ogee moulder with single boxed ⅞ in. cutter. $45

T.J. McMASTER & CO., Auburn, N.Y. Complex moulding plane 2⅜ in. wide. Auct. $35

MADOX (British 1748-1775) wide profile moulder. Auct. $38

D. MALLOCH, Perth. Double-bladed complex moulding plane 1½ inches wide. Auct. $55 - Three-ironed quirk ogee with cavetto and cove. 3 wedges. 9⅜ in. overall. $150 - Scottish-style handled cornice plane 3⅝ in. wide. $165

Wm. MARPLES & SON, Sheffield, Hibernia Air-tight type joint moulder. Mint cond. $40

M. MARTIEN late 18th century style complex moulding plane. Auct. $45

MARTIN & SHAW narrow Grecian ogee moulder. Single boxed, 1⅜ in. wide. Fine. $34

MATHIESON, Dundee. (6) fine architectural moulding planes, avg. 2½ in. wide. Auct. $300

ALEX MATHIESON & SON, Dundee. Ogee & double fillet with 4 irons. Auct. $450

A. MATHIESON & SON, Glasgow & Edinburgh (1853-1954) single boxed Grecian ogee with bevel, 2⅝ in. wide. $32 - Another with twin irons and single boxing. $58 Three-ironed complex moulder 2¼ inches wide. Auct. $75-$95, Dlr. $145

MELHUISH, Fetter Lane (London 1828-1925) excellent beechwood moulder 1¾ in. wide. $20

MELVILLE (Aberdeen, circa 1820) two iron Grecian ogee 2¼ inches wide. $100

J.P. MILLENER & CO. Kingston (Ontario, Canada) ogee moulder 2¾ in. width. $45

MOCKRIDGE & FRANCIS, Newark, N.J. (1845-1870) beechwood moulder 2½ in. wide. $25 up. - Another by same maker. Handled cornice moulder 5¼ inches wide. Auct. $500

MOIR, Glasgow. Complex moulding plane 1½ inches wide. $18 - Handled moulder with two wedged cutters. Auct. $67

A. MONTY, Roxton Pond, P.Q. (Quebec) complex moulding plane 2¼ in. wide with oles thru nose for pull rope. $40

MOORE, N.Y.C. (1856-1861) beechwood complex moulder 2⅛ in. wide. $22

MOSELEY & SON, New Oxford St., W.C. (London 1878-1888) beechwood complex moulding plane 1½ inches wide. $17 - Roman ogee, ⅞ in. size. $22 - No. 5 ovolo 1½ inches wide. $20

JOHN MOSELEY & SON, 54-55 Broad St., Bloomsbury, London No. 2 sash ovolo 1½ inches wide with heavy dovetailed boxing. Mint cond. $38 - Handrail plane 7 inches long with adjustable fence on sole. Auct. $78 - Dlr. $95

MOSELEY LATE MUTTER one line imprint on 1⅝ in. wide complex moulder. $22

Wm MOSS, Birmingham (England 1775-1800) 1¼ in. wide plane, cuts ½ in. ogee. $32 - 1¾ inch wide complex moulder in beechwood. $35 - Sash ogee. $45

H.P. MUCHMORE handled cornice plane with 2½ inch iron. Asking $195

MUTTER (London 1766-1812) delicate belection moulder 9½ inches long. $45

THO. NAPIER in zig-zag border on 9¾ inch ogee moulding plane. Auct. $280

R. NELSON, 122 Edgeware Road, London. Grecian ovolo and cove 2 in. wide. $40 Cove and ovolo 1¾ in. width. $30

E. NEWELL, Lanesboro. Beechwood ogee moulder 1¼ inch with boxed V-quirk. Auct. $210

F. NICHOLSON, Living in Wrentham. Complex moulder with replaced wedge. Auct. $475-$700

C. Nurse & Co. 181 & 183 Walworth Rd., London S.E. 2⅜ in. wide ovolo with cove. $40

OHIO TOOL CO. (1851-1913) 3 inch complex moulder. $35 - No. 59 moulding plane. Auct. $35 - No. 61½ ogee with bead. $35

THOMAS OKINES with crown trademark (London 1740-1770) 1¼ in. wide ogee. Dlr. $70. ½ in. ogee moulder. Auct. $25

OWASCO TOOL CO., New York. Complex moulding plane 2¼ inches wide. $24

H. PALMER beautiful 1¼ inch wide complex moulder in mint condition. $30

R.A. PARRISH, Philadelphia (1807-1845) 1¾ in. wide moulding plane with exotic wood boxing insert. $20

PHILLIPSON (British 1740-1775) ogee moulding plane 10 inches long. Auct. $148

PHOENIX COMPANY, Hitchcockville. Single boxed complex moulder 2 in. wide. Listed as Barkhamstead (1853-1864). $40

POND & WELLS, New Haven. 2½ inch wide moulding plane. $25

S.F. PRATT, Buffalo. Single-boxed complex moulding plane 2 inches wide. $24

E. PRESTON (1833-1863) delicate little ogee only ¾ in. wide. $25 - Another with Litchfield St. address. 3 inch plane cuts wide shallow ogee. $39

EDW. PRESTON & SONS (1894-1933) complex moulding plane 2 inches wide, cuts quirk ogee with cove. Like new cond. $48

P. PROBASCO (Philadelphia) complex moulder 1¼ inches wide with exotic wear strip. $25

RANDALL & COOK, Albany (1835-1839) Grecian ovolo with fillet, 2⅝ inches wide. $30 - 1⅞ inch complex moulder. $40

W. RAYMOND interesting complex moulding plane 2 in. wide by 9½ inches long. $60

W. RAYMOND (with crown and T.S. stamp) Beverly, Mass. circa 1800. Unhandled complex moulder. Auct. $150

Another W. Raymond Crown moulder sold at auction in 1983 for $700 (no description given).

M.H. READ, Wilmington, Vermont. Open handled 3 inch wide crown moulding plane. Auct. $225

REED, Utica, N.Y. 2⅜ in. wide complex moulder. $24 - Grecian ogee with bevel, 1⅝ in. wide. $32 - Outstanding crown moulder 4½ inches wide by 16 inches long. Original wedge and iron. $475

P.B. RIDER, Bangor (Maine 1839) Grecian ovolo with fillet. 1¾ in. iron. Auct. $40 - Complex moulder with 2 wedges, 2¼ inch blade. Auct. $130

JOHN ROGERS (London 1734-1765) ⅞ in. wide ovolo. $35

WILLIAM C. ROSS, 44 Light Street, Balto. Handled ogee 3 inches wide. $65

S. ROWELL, Albany (1810-1828) Belection moulder size ⅞. $20

S. ROWELL, Troy (1828-1832) 1¾ in. wide complex moulding plane. Mint cond. $48

H. RUSSELL, Cabot, Vt. Double-boxed 2 inch complex moulder. Auct. $115

D.P. SANBORN, Littleton. Crown moulding plane body (no blade or wedge). Auct. $250 - Another Sanborn moulder, circa 1866, side-by-side double throat 5 inch wide, handled, fancy profile with original hand-written price list from maker. Auct. $2,100

SANDUSKY TOOL CO. No. 74 common ogee moulder made for Chas. Strelinger Hardware Co. $20 - 1¼ in. ogee. $35 - Brand new unused No. 82 reverse ogee, size 1¾ in. $75 - Rare Sandusky handled cornice plane, 4 inches wide with attached fence. Near mint. Auct. $500

E. SARGENT, Concord, N.H. Ogee cornice moulder with original 3 inch iron. Auct. $250

P. SARGENT, Nashua, N.H. Beechwood crown moulding plane with attached fence and 3 in. Greaves blade. $185

MICHAEL SAXBY (Biddenden, Kent 1730-1775) reverse ogee moulder. Auct. $158

BENJAMIN SHENEMAN, mid 19th-century crown moulder 6½ inches wide. This Philadelphia made, 15½ inch, 2-bladed side-by-side style, complex moulding plane, sold at auction for a record $2,050.

I. SLEEPER (Newburyport, Mass., circa 1895) cove with bead moulder 1¾ inches wide. $55 - Another with wide flat chamfers. Auct. $70 - Another, more intricate pattern. Auct. $100 - Complex moulder sold at auction, no description. $375 - Crown moulding plane 18 inches long x 6 in. wide. Tow bar in nose. $1,300

STEWART No. 154 script-signed Grecian ogee moulder (circa 1840) 2⅝ inches wide. $30
Twin-ironed ovolo and scotia 1⅜ in. wide. Fine cond. $48

J. STEVENS, Boston, ⅞ in. cove with bead. $35

STOKOE No. 5 double-boxed 2 inch Grecian ovolo. $25
No. 6 solid-dovetail-boxed Grecian ovolo complex moulder 2¼ inches wide. $75

STOTHERT, Bath (1785-1841) quirk ogee 1¾ inches in width. $38

STOTHERT & WALKER 2⅛ in. wide complex moulding plane. $18

SUMMERS VARVILL, Ebor Works, York. Single boxed No. 4 Grecian ogee with bevel. $34

I. SYM. (London 1753-1802) 1⅛ in. $45

J.M. TABER (New Bedford 1820-1872) Assorted narrow complex moulders. $25-$40 each.
No. 7 bead with cove, 2⅛ in wide. $55
Cornice moulder 4 inches wide. $225

T. TILESTON, Boston (1802-1808) narrow complex moulding plane with rosewood boxing. Auct. $100 Beautiful 2⅜ in wide complex moulder. $45 1⅞ in $34 Huge 6½ inch width O.A. crown moulder with 5 inch iron. Tug bar thru nose. Auct. $700

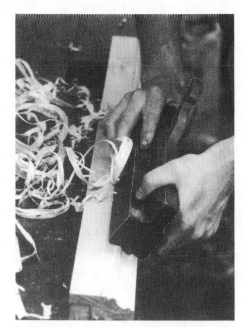

The proper use of a 19th century moulding plane is demonstrated by professional furniture restorer John D. Cushing in his Essex, Mass. shop.

UNMARKED birchwood crown moulding plane with 3½ inch iron. 5 x 18 in. overall. Auct. $275

UNMARKED crown moulder 4½ x 15 in. Auct. $325

UNMARKED 18th-century yellow birch 4¼ in. crown moulder with hole thru nose for pull rod. Handwrought 3⅜ in. cutter. Dlr. $300

UNMARKED 19th century sliding-arm ogee 3¾ inches wide. Trenails in thumbscrew adjusted fence. Auct. $450

UNMARKED handled beechwood crown moulding plane 15 inches long by 5½ in. wide. Toe has diamond-shaped start pin. Tug handle rods intact. Crisp and clean. Auct. $800

I. WALTON, In Reading (Mass., circa 1764) low profile birch moulding plane, size 1 in. ogee. Auct. $450 Crown moulder 4½ in wide with diamond patch on fore end. Auct. $1,700

ISRAEL WHITE, Philada, Warranted. (1831-1839) Grecian ovolo with brace, axe, mallet & plane trademark stamped in heel. Mint cond. $85. ⅝ scotia moulder. $22

S.F. WILLARD, Roxton Pond (Quebec 1876-1884) Matched pair of dust proof or air tight joint moulders. Auct. $75 pr.

Wm. WOODWARD, Taunton (Mass. early 19th cent.) complex moulding plane with 3 inch cutter. Excellent cond. Auct. $175 Another open-handled 3 inch wide crown moulder 13½ inches long. Auct. $225

ROBERT WOODING (1710-1728) unhandled ogee moulding plane 10¼ in. long. Auct. $260

YOUNG and McMASTER, Auburn, New York. Complex moulder 2⅝ in. wide. $35

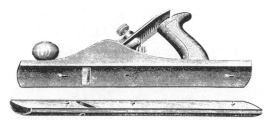

NOSING PLANES were used to cut the half-round fronts of stair treads. Average diameter ranged from ¾ to 2 inches. All are of wooden construction.

THOS. L. APPLETON, Boston. 1¼ inch nosing plane. $12

AUCTION LOT at recent tool club event. Nosing planes averaged $20 each

AUBURN TOOL CO. 1⅛ in. twin ironed nosing plane 9½ inches long. $16-$20 Set of (3) No. 189 sizes 1⅛ to 1½ inch. Like new condition. $33 each.

CHAPIN-STEVENS No. 13 nosing plane. Auct. $15. No. 138½ with double bit. $35. No. 133 unhandled nosing plane with two cutters. $16. Pair of handled-type marked Union Factory. $80 pr.

GREENFIELD TOOL CO. Large double-bladed variety. $14

J. KELLOGG, Amherst, Mass. Beechwood noser with single 1 inch cutter. $16

J.F. & G.M. LINDSEY, Huntington, Mass. (1856-1879) twin-ironed beechwood Average. $12-$16. 1½ in. Exceptional. $30

A. MATHIESON & SON 2-ironed nosing. Auct. $130

F. NICHOLSON, Living in Wrentham. 18th century yellow birch plane with wide chamfers. ⅝ inch cutter. $750

OHIO TOOL CO. No. 91 Double-bladed 1⅜ in. nosing plane. $12-$20

A.M. PIPER, Wolfboro, N.H. half round nosing plane with 2 inch iron. Auct. $85

SANDUSKY TOOL CO. double-ironed 1⅛ in. nosing plane in mint cond. $20 Razee handled type. $40

SARGENT & CO. nosing planes. $12-$14

PANEL PLANES (Metallic) See Planes, "Raising" for wooden variety

BUCK, 247 Tottm. Court Road. Dovetailed steel panel plane with high scalloped-top sides. Full rosewood handle, square knob & infill. Auct. $140

D. GALLOWAY & CO., Edinburgh. 13¼ in. iron panel plane with mahogany infill. Auct. $210

MATHIESON, Glasgow No. 845 dovetailed steel panel plane with closed-style rosewood handle and infill, square front knob. Gunmetal lever cap. 14½ in. long. (pitted, circa 1899 model) Auct. $100. Another in better cond. $275. 12 inch model. Auct. $75. 15½ in. x 3 inch example in fine cond. $495

NORRIS No. 1 dovetailed steel panel plane 14½ inches long. Rosewood infill. Auct. $195
No. A1 model with 2½ inch wide cutting iron and gunmetal lever cap. Dlr. $325, Auct. $230
18 inch example with beechwood infill $335 Later model in original grease packing, never used. Auct. $560

SPIERS, Ayr No. 1 dovetailed steel panel plane 13½ inches long, 2½ in. cutter. $200-$300 Later model with sides raised only at midsection and a modern round rosewood front knob. Auct. $98 Old style 16½ inches long. Auct. $332

UNMARKED Brass cased Norris-type panel plane 15 inches long. Auct. $225

SEIGLY PATENT (circa 1893) iron patternmaker's plane 14½ inches long with 6 detachable wooden soles or shoes, 2½ in. wide. This model has sold at auction in the $120-$140 range. Dealer prices are higher.

PATTERNMAKERS used planes made with a variety of interchangeable curved and convex soles, to produce wooden patterns for sand cores & forms used in metal foundry casting.

ALUMINUM bodied pattern maker's plane with beechwood filling which forms English style handle and square knob. 4 beech soles. $125 Another with round beech front knob and infill. Auct. $45

BRASS pattern maker's plane 10 inches long with squirrel tail handle. Detachable maple sole, maple handle. Auct. $55 Another only 7 inches in length. Mahogany handle. Auct. $65 Another with walnut pistol grip and 6 birch soles. $235

BRITISH Gunmetal patternmaker's plane with 8 curved wooden soles. 8 inches overall including wooden squirrel tail handle. Auct. $175 Another gunmetal plane made by an unknown craftsman. Graceful mahogany handle and infill. 8 interchangeable beechwood soles. 9 inches overall. Dlr. $255

PHELPS, Oakland, Calif. Round bottom aluminum bodied patternmaker's plane with 10 extra soles and cutting irons. Perfect condition. $125 – $175

PANEL PLANES, Not to be confused with raising planes, are British made truing and finishing planes 12½ to 17½ inches long. They are steel or iron framed and have exotic wooden handles and infill. This style was popular from 1850 until World War II.

The walnut filled Scottish panel plane at right has typical ovolo curves. It sold at a recent London tool auction for $300 in U.S. funds.

Courtesy Reg Eaton

PLOW PLANES date back to the time of King Tut. This sophisticated grooving tool made quick work of preparing drawer sides to receive bottoms and cutting panel grooves in door and chests frames.

The very first plow planes did not have fences. Fancy Continental screw-arm models appeared late in the 16th Century, as did the simpler wedge-arm and thumbscrew-adjusted types. All three versions were popular at the same time and remained in production for over 300 years.

The earliest recorded British and American makers seemed to have preferred the wedge-lock style of sliding arm adjustment. However, some domestic plow planes of the period had wooden thumbscrews threaded thru the top of the stock.

Between 1800 and 1840 many elaborate new screw-arm plows were developed in a frantic race by inventors hoping to find an ideal system for automatic parallel alignment of fence and body.

Metal plow planes came into widespread use between 1870 and 1880. The traditional set of 8 cutting irons used in wooden plows was replaced by a vast array of over 50 assorted blades.

Handled Bridle Plow Plane by Mathieson. Sold at auction for $490.

ASSORTED American & English screw-arm and wedge-style planes in poor condition with missing thumbscrews, arms cracked, screw arm threads chipped or stripped, gouged finish and/or other serious defects. $12-$24 each.

AUCTION LOT of (6) American made screw arm plow planes with broken or missing parts, but with good possibilities for repair. $160 all.

ASSORTED common wedge-arm or sliding-stem style British-made wooden plow planes in good condition, but not show pieces. (19) at $55 each. Dlr.

G. AHRENS, Hamburg. Screw arm plow with turned nuts on heavy concave bottom fence. $75

AMES, London. Wedge arm plow plane with boxwood fence & wedges. Brass trim. Auct. $77

ANDERSON & LAING, W. VA. Unhandled boxwood screw arm plow with ivory tips. Auct. $1,000

THOS L. APPLETON, Boston. Unused beechwood screw arm plow, boxwood arms and nuts. Includes 7 extra irons. Dlr. $155 Rosewood version in nearly mint cond. Includes set of Moulson irons. Auct. $800

ARNOLD, 3 High St., Bloomsbury (London circa 1840) Bridle style plow plane. Clamp-like fence top is adjusted by single brass thumbscrew. $285

ARROWMAMMETT screw-arm beechwood plow (with some thread chips.) $85

ARTHUR, Edinburgh (Late 18th cent.) wedge arm plow with brass plate. Auct. $80

ATKIN & SONS script stamp on beechwood wedge arm plow. $25

AUBURN TOOL CO. Auburn, N.Y. No. 90 threaded arm beechwood plow with closed handle. $190-$225 No. 88 same maker. Auct. $30 No. 92 with boxwood arms and nuts. Dlr. $100 No. 96 handled rosewood plow with boxwood arms. Auct. $420

AUGENIE, Paris. Cormier wood plow with metal screw arms, brass nuts. Auct. $65

BABSON & REPPLIER, Boston (circa 1870) Phillips Pat. iron-framed plow plane with rosewood handle. Harp-shaped top. (some repairs) Auct. $150 Another with 1867 patent date. Single slide rod for fence. Dlr. $245

A&E BALDWIN, New York. Unhandled boxwood screw arm plow plane. (worn cond.) $125

E. BALDWIN beech wedge arm plow of simple design. Dlr. $35 Another with brass depth stop and plate on skate. $50

A.C. BARTLETT Ohio Planes No. 123 Probably made by Sandusky. Closed handle. $125

D.R. BARTON boxwood plow. (repaired crack in nut) $225 Rosewood plow by Barton. $295 Another in fine condition, with extra cutters. $450

JOHN BELL, Phila. unhandled beech plow with mahogany screw arms. Auct. $45 Handled style by same maker. $125

BENSON & CRANNELL, Albany (1844-1862) beechwood screw arm plow with boxwood arms and fence. $78 Another in applewood. Fine cond. $155

L.B. BIGELOW (Providence 1852) handled plow plane in boxwood with extra course threads. Charles Hall patent. Auct. $750

S.H. BIBIGHAUS, Phila. Unhandled rosewood plow plane with curly grained boxwood screw arms and knobs. $495

BLIZZARD (British 1805-1824) unhandled wedge arm plow. Auct. $65

BOOKBINDERS British-made open-handled style plow plane. Auct. $122 Plainer style maple plow with 2 metal guide rods and plain-handled maple center screw. Dlr. $75 Bookbinder's plow with square maple arms and nicely turned center screw. 10 in. x 23 in. Auct. $80 Dlr. $175

BRIGHT & CHAPPEL, 1837. Short, light colored plow with long threaded arms and a boxwood fence. Auct. $150

J. BUCK, Waterloore, London. Beech wedge arm plane with brass trim. Auct. $55

BUCK & HICKMAN beechwood plow with boxwood screw arms. Auct. $98

GEORGE BURNHAM Jr., Amherst, Mass. (1849) Boxwood screw arm plow. Dlr. $250 Unhandled version. $180

E.W. CARPENTER'S Improved Arms, Lancaster, (Penn., 1838) unhandled boxwood plow with rosewood handle, wedge, and fence. Screw arms pass clear through the female threaded stock. Dealers have offered in $2,000 to $4,000 range.

CARRIAGE MAKER'S fixed-style, scroll-handled, palm-held plow. Made of one layer each wood, brass and steel, held together by 6 slotted wood screws. French. $750

CONTINENTAL Carriage Maker's closed Saw handle-style, 10 inch fixed plow with round side handle. Auct. $450

C.M. CARTER, Hyde Park, N.Y. Book-binder's wooden plow plane with large wrought wing nut. Used to trim book pages. Operated in a clamp-like jig. $210

EDWARD CARTER, Troy, N.Y. (1847-1848) beech wedge arm plow. Auct. $50

I.M. CARTER, Hyde Park, N.Y. Bookbinder's plow with identical hickory fences. $125

CASEY, KITCHELL & CO., Auburn, N.Y. Sliding 11 inch arms with captive boxwood wedges, depth stop, and thumbscrew. $75 Screw arm version. Auct. $105 Ebony-bodied plow by same maker. Boxwood fence and nuts with ivory tipped arms. Auct. $1,000

H. ·CHAPIN, Union Factory. Unhandled beechwood plow with boxwood screw arms and nuts. $55 No. 232 screw arm plow by same maker. $65 No. 236 $45 No. 237 full-handled beechwood plow in perfect condition. Auct. $125 No. 238 $75 No. 239 Auct. $90 Same plane in Applewood with slotted metal fence slides and threaded wooden center adjustment. Minimum bid considered. $600 No. 239½ $325 Another with slotted metal slides and ball end wooden center screw. Asking $3,500 No. 240 solid boxwood screw arm plow with closed tote. Auct. $235-$350 Mint. $500 No. 245 curly grained boxwood screw arm plow. Auct. $125

N. CHAPIN, Eagle Factory. Beechwood slide arm plow plane. $70-$90

P. CHAPIN, maker, Balt. Beechwood screw arm plow with brass plate on skate. $85-$115

CHARLES & CO. Slide arm plow with inlaid ruled ivory scales. Dlr. $175

CHILD-PRATT CO., St. Louis, Mo. solid boxwood plow plane with ivory tipped screw arms. $1,150

COCKBAIN CARLISLE scarce screw arm plow with graduations on boxwood fence. Brass indicators are attached to main stock which is beech. $450

COPELAND & CO. beechwood screw arm plow in beech with boxwood arms. $80-$100 Nearly new boxwood plow by same maker. $195

D. COPELAND unhandled-style beechwood screw arm plow. Auct. $75

M. COPELAND plow planes in both styles offered in the $60-$100 price range.

COTMAN'S PATENT sash filletster-type plow with inlaid ivory rule. $250

COX & LUCKMAN, London (circa 1865) brass trimmed beechwood slide arm plow. $55

I. COX 18th-cent. wedge arm plow, transitional style with brass tips. $175

CRAFTSMAN metallic combination plane. Sears version of Stanley No. 45. Mint. Dlr. $175

M. CRANELL, Albany. Plows by this maker are frequently offered in the $100-$160 range.

A. CUMMINGS, Boston. Beech slide arm plow cuts V groove. Plain. Auct. $75

CUMMINGS & GALE beech slide arm plow with brass skate plate. $65

CURRIE, Glasgow (1833-1844) very heavy wedge-arm plow with church window lock plate depth stop. Brass trim. $75

G. DAVIS, Birmingham (1832-1872). Nicely shaped beech plane with boxwood arms and nuts. Fancy finials. $65-$80

J. DEARBORN fruitwood slide stem plow. Superior style, quality, and condition. Auct. $300

DeFOREST, Birmingham. Boxwood screw arm plow plane, unhandled. Excellent. Auct. $180

G.W. DENISON, Winthrop, Conn. Solid boxwood screw arm plow. Auct. $200-$400

J. DENISON (Winthrop, Conn. (1840-1876) unhandled beech screw arm plow. $50 Another with brass skate plate and depth stop. $185-$200 Another in boxwood with closed handle. As found cond. Auct. $200-$300. Rosewood version, boxwood screw arms and nuts. $300-$385

MARTEN DOSCHER, N.Y. handled boxwood screw arm plow plane. (slight damage) Auct. $275

DUTCH Ploeg, or Plow Plane. Unhandled slide arm style with ornamental wing nuts. Maker's mark FM with fleur-de-leis. Dated 1750. (worm holes) Auct. $650

EASTBURN wedge arm plow in beechwood with riveted skate and arms. $100

F. ELKINS RUNYON & BARTLETT, Chicago, No. 97 handled beechwood plow with applewood screw arms. (minor repair) Auct. $100

JOHN ELSWORTH, Glasgow. Handled plow with skate front. Boxwood arms & nuts. Auct. $135

FALES PATENT unusual metal framed plow plane with broom-stick-shaped rosewood handle. Was advertised in 1880's as a tool that combined the functions of 80 woodworking planes. (No accessories remain). $225-$350

FOX & WASHBURN, Amherst, Mass. screw arm plow. Auct. $50 Dlr. $85

FREIMANN, Pat. Appl. for. Model No. L414 solid brass grooving plow with cam-action fence and depth adjustmants. Auct. $300

JO. FULLER, Providence (Rhode Island, 18th-Cent.) Sliding arm beechwood plow with wooden thumbscrews. (replaced). Auct. $150-$200. Dlr. $450 with orig. wedge.

GABRIEL (1770-1795) unhandled style beech wedge arm plow with brass trim. Orig. & fine. Auct. $100-$150 In average worn condition $55 and up.

GARDNER & MURDOCK, Green Street, Boston. Sliding arms held by wooden thumbscrews. Fence is tiger-striped boxwood. $285-$400

P.A. GLADWIN & CO. solid boxwood screw arm plow. $175 Rosewood plane by same maker with boxwood screw arm. Auct. $380-$500

GLADWIN & APPLETON, Boston. Handled boxwood screw arm plow with brass plate. Orig. $265

GLADWIN & PLATT, Wallingford, Ct. Yankee-style wedge-arm plow. (replaced wedge & thumbscrew) Auct. $45

IOHN GREEN, British beechwood sliding stem plow with conventional brass trim. Auct. $65

GREENFIELD TOOL CO. No. 540 beechwood plow with boxwood arms. Auct. $55 No. 513 (circa 1875) with 8 blades. Auct. $65 No. 518 solid boxwood unhandled plow. $175 No. 530 closed handled beechwood model, boxwood fence. $70-$135 No. 532 boxwood with closed applewood handle. Auct. $175 Dlr. $350 No. 534 boxwood model. Auct. $150-up. No. 536 rosewood plow with boxwood screw arms and knobs. Auct. $280 No. 910 unhandled beech plow with boxwood arms. $55 Unhandled rosewood screw arm plow, plain arms. Auct. $425 With ivory arm tips and in very fine condition. Auction. $1,300

GRIFFITHS, Norwich. Unhandled beechwood wedge arm plow with lots of brass trim. Auct. $55 up. Another with ivory inlaid arms and wedges. Auct. $350 Stirrup fence-type by same maker. Auct. $150-$250. Rarer compass bottom circular coachmaker's plow with brass tipped sliding arms, 5⅝ inches overall. Auct. $860

HALL CASE & CO., Columbus, Ohio (circa 1850) Boxwood plow with ivory arm tips. Auct. $500

A. HAMMACHER & CO. (Hardware dealer) applewood screw-arm plow plane. $125

W.O. HICKOCK, Harrisburg, Pa. Bookbinder's plow plane in dark beechwood with center screw arm. 25 inches overall. $150 Another with vise-like fixture. $345

HILLS & RICHARDS, Norwich, Mass. Beechwood slide arm plow with brass arm tips and skate plate. $45

JAMES HOWARTH, Sheffield, Slide stem beechwood plow with boxwood arms. $125

HOWKINS Model A brass-stocked, steel-soled, combination plane with 5 pairs of cutters. Auct. $140 Another with extra fences, cutters, soles, etc. $236 Model C with all original accessories. Auct. $300 No. 46 in orig. box (only 50 made) $600

A. HOWLAND & CO. (Auburn, N.Y. 1869-1874) handled boxwood plow. $150-$250 Another Howland plane in rosewood with boxwood screw arms. $375-$575 Another in rosewood, No. 98, nearly mint condition with ivory tips. Auct. $700-$800

H.L. JAMES, Williamsburg, Mass. Beechwood screw arm plow with boxwood arms. $65 Another with fruitwood screw arms and brass teim. Beautiful cond. Auct. $200

CHAPIN Nos. 236, 237, 238, 239 (Beech Handled). 239½ (Applewood Handled), 240 (Solid Boxwood), 240½ (Solid Rosewood).

CHAPIN Nos. 242, 243, 244 (Beechwood). 244½ (Applewood), 245 (Solid Boxwood), 245½ (Solid Rosewood).

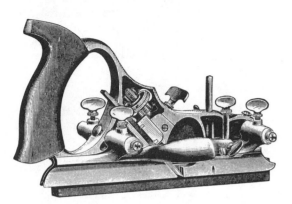

SIEGLEY'S 1881 Patent Combination Plow (1923 Model).

STANLEY No. 45 Traut's Adjustable Plow (1884-1887 style)

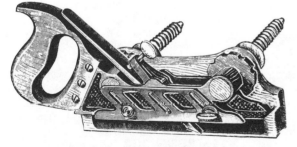

GERMAN Iron Framed Plow with wooden handle, fence and arms. (Circa 1900)

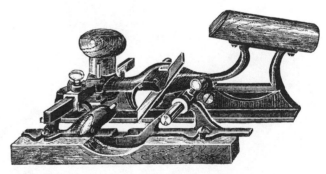

FALE'S Patent Combination Plow Plane (1884-1917)

CHAPIN Pat. V-Slide Arm Plow Nos. 236¼, 238¼ (239¼. (1884 illus.)

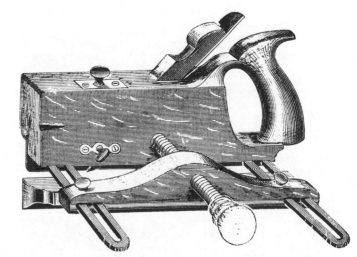

CHAPIN Pat. Adjusting Plow Nos. 236½, 238½ & 239½.

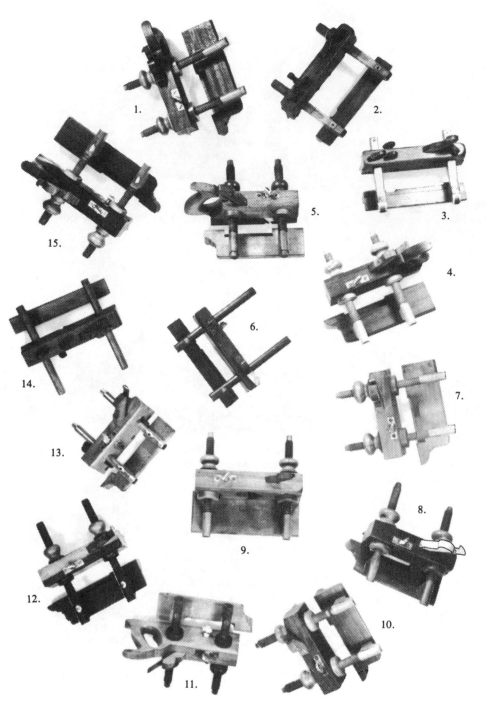

J.P. Bittner Antique Tool Auctions

AN IMPRESSIVE COLLECTION OF PLOW PLANES SOLD AT AUCTION

1. J. KELLOGG wavy mahogany plow plane with boxwood screw-arms & nuts. Near new. $300
2. 18th CENTURY birch plow, plain & simple with steel plated fence & brass washers. $225
3. DATED 1820 important plane with thick brass fence plates and arm trim, plus other decorative brass touches. $425
4. UNION FACTORY No. 240 rosewood handled plow with boxwood fittings. Like new. $500
5. F. ELKINS, RUNYON & BARTLETT, Chicago, No. 97 handled beechwood plow with applewood screw-arms & nuts. Minor repair and roughness. $100
6. SOLID EBONY early slide-arm plow with hand-forged thumbscrews which convert plane from wedge-lock style. $300
7. J. KELLOGG beechwood plow plane with boxwood screw-arms & nuts. $110
8. GREENFIELD TOOL CO. No. 536 rosewood plow with boxwood arms. $280
9. FILLETSTER by J. Kellogg. Beechwood with boxwood screw-arms & nuts. $90
10. UNION FACTORY No. 245 rosewood plow with boxwood arms, nuts & wedge. Has minor repair and thread chips. $170
11. SANDUSKY TOOL CO. No. 124 beech-bodied plow with rosewood screw-arms. Shaped handle. $225
12. LIGNUM VITAE plow with ebony screw-arms and fence. Ivory tips. Unmarked. $900
13. VARVILL & SON, Ebor Works, beech wedge-arm plow with graduated ivory arm inserts. $325
14. A. CUMMINGS, Boston, slide-arm V-groove plow with wooden locking screws. $75
15. ROSEWOOD crotch-grained large plow with boxwood arms, ivory tips, brass trim. No maker's mark. Magnificent. $1,400

JENNION (John, 1732-1757) sliding arm plow with boxwood wedges. Auct. $315

JN mark (Jan Nooitgedagt of Ylst) 19th Cent. Dutch plow plane. Auct. $120

J. KELLOGG (circa 1850) red stained beechwood slide arm plow with spring lock depth adjust screw. Auct. $50 Slightly used beech slide arm plow with brass skate plate. Dlr. $75 Top of the line unhandled beechwood plow with boxwood screw arms, brass trim, etc. Auct. $125, Dlr. (Mint cond.) $195. Another Kellogg, Amherst, plane in solid rosewood. Auct. $250-$550 Another in wavy grained mahogany. Auct. $300

KEEN KUTTER No. K64 iron plow plane, (style of Stanley No. 45) long rods only. Dlr. $225

KENNEDY, (Hartford, Ct. 1809-1842) early unhandled beechwood slide arm (damaged) $45

J. KILLAM (Glastonbury, Conn.) Early 19th Cent. beech slide arm plow with wooden thumbscrews for locking arms. $90

D. KIMBERLY & SONS Patent plow plane (Birmingham, England 1887). Closed handled beechwood plane with 2 steel slide rods ¼ inch diameter. Faucet handled center-arm-screw is heavier. Steel skate, brass trim. Auct. $275-$365 Dlr. $400-$550

KING & COMPANY wedge arm plane with brass fittings. Short 7⅝ in. block. $68

J.H. LAMB, New Bedford (Mass, circa 1869) beechwood plow with closed handle, boxwood screw arms and nuts. $100-$125 Rosewood version. Auct. $275

LAMB & BROWNELL, New Bedford, Mass. Handled beech plane with boxwood screw arms. Brass plate on skate. (as is cond.) $65 Solid boxwood plow with brass trim. $265-$375

I. LUND, London. Nice wedge arm plow with brass trim. Auct. $65

PETER MACKAY & Co., Glasgow. Large handled skate front plow. Auct. $125

I. LINDENBERGER (circa 1800). Birch slidearm plow 10 in. in length with wooden thumbscrews in top. Auct. 1985. $900

D. MALLOCH, Perth. Handled ornamental screw arm plow with ball-end tips. Auct. $130 Beechwood bridle plow plane with brass tipped ebony arms, closed handle. Auct. $645

MARLEY, N.Y. (1820-56) wedged slide arm plow, brass tips and skate plate. Dlr. $75

W. MARPLES & SONS beechwood wedge arm plow with brass tips and skate plate. $65 No. 2912 beechwood plow with boxwood screw arms and acorn finials. $125

MARSHALL, Glasgow. Skate-nosed beechwood screw arm plow. $125

MARTIN & SHAW from H. Moss's. Beechwood wedge arm plow with brass trim. $65

MATHIESON, Edinburgh, No. 5B unhandled plow with prowed skate, crossboxed wedge arms have brass tips. Auct. $70 A. MATHIESON No. 9 plow with boxwood screw arms. $95-$135 No. 9B handled beechwood plow, circa 1899. $185-$275 No. 96 screw arm plow. $150 Bridle style Mathieson plow with rosewood side handle. Auct. $350 - $490 Another rare handled-plow with additional center bead and double bead moulding planes to fit on boxwood screw arms. Auct. $400 Unhandled No. 5B wedge arm plow. Auct. $80 No. 9B skate-front screwarm with handle. Auct. $125 No. 10 handled beechwood plow with slotted brass cylindrical arms. Complete with set of irons. Auct. $665 Another bridle plow with boxwood arms. Auct. $490 No. 12 ebony arms, brass lined bridle. Auct., London. $1,690

M.C. MAYO'S Improved Plane, Patented Sept. 14, 1875, Boston. "The Boss Plane" cast in right side. Cast iron plow with single steel rod for sliding fence, which is rosewood faced. Auct. $375-$500. Dlr. $850 Without fence. $150-up

J.M. McCUNE & CO., Columbus, Ohio. Beechwood screw arm plow with boxwood arms and nuts. Auct. $45 Deluxe rosewood model with closed handle and ivory tipped screw arms. Auct. $2,350

T.J. McMASTER, Auburn, N.Y. (1825-1829) solid cherry wedge arm plow. $85

CHARLES G. MILLER Pat. June 28, 1870. Gunmetal carpenter's plow plane. Single arm with ivory nut tips and handle inserts. Auct. $6,600

PLOW IRONS sets of assorted brands in 8 graduated sizes. $25-$50 per set depending upon rarity of maker and condition of irons.

J. MILLER, 37 Clayton St., handled plow with wedged arms and brass trim. Auct. $130

MOCKRIDGE, handled boxwood plow plane sold at auction for $200

MORRIS PATENT Iron plow plane, circa 1871. Unmarked example with scissor or X type adjustable fence arms having 5 pivot points. Wooden handle. Auct. $700

MOSELEY, London (1819-1862) unusual side-handle beechwood plow with brass plate. $175 Common wedge arm style with brass tips. $25-up

MULTIFORM PLANE CO., Pat. Aug. 29, 1854. Beechwood screw arm plow with brass handle. Dlr. $1,200 Others with steel & wood handles, extra bodies, etc. Auct. $350-$600 per partial set. Boxwood with dark hardwood handle. Auct. $3,400

MUTTER (George, London 1766-1812) Beechwood sliding stem plow with rounded wedge and handforged thumbscrew. (well worn cond.) $55

NELSON in zig-zag border on mellow beechwood wedge arm plow with brass trim. $95

HENRY J. NAZRO, Milwaukee. American wedge arm plow, unhandled. $75

F. NICHOLSON, Living in Wrentham. Rare 18th Cent. sliding arm plow approx. 10 inches long. Sold at auction in 1981 for $2,200

NURSE & CO. Master, 1943. British government war issue wooden plow plane with steel fittings, incl. 8 cutters. $95 Earlier skate front screw arm plow with boxwood arms and brass fittings. Auct. $65

E. NUTTING boxwood screw arm plow with closed handle (repaired). $200

OHIO TOOL CO. early beech screw arm plow (with some age cracks) $45 No. 97 handled style with applewood screw arms and round nuts. $75 Unhandled beech plow with boxwood arms. $75 No. 97 improved style handle and metal wear plate. $125 No. 100 closed handle beech plow. $135 No. 102 rosewood screw arm plow in mint condition. $300 No. 104 boxwood handled screw arm plow with brass depth adj. $235-$350 No. 105 rosewood plow with ivory tipped boxwood screw arms. Auct. $650-$1050 Another with chipped threads. $400 Another in boxwood. Dlr. $950 No. 110 self-regulating boxwood 3-armed plow. Auct. $550 Ohio Tool 3-armed fruitwood plow plane with closed handle, 2 arms have ivory tips. Center screw arm is boxwood. Asking $3,000

P.M. PECKHAM, Fall River (Mass) slide arm plow with brass skate plate. $85

PHILLIPS PATENT Improved Iron Plow plane with Babson & Repplier trademark on skate. M.C. Mayo's improved Jan. 1, 1872 stenciled on side of japanned fence. Auct. $350-$400. Dlr. $400-$800

PRATT & CO., Buffalo, N.Y. boxwood plow plane, handled. (old repair) $195

SANDUSKY TOOL CO. No. 119 close handled beechwood screw arm plow plane. Dlr. $100 No. 120 handled beech plow with brass adjusting screws. $60 No. 123 handled beechwood plow with boxwood screw arms. Shaped right-hand handle. Auct. $185-$250 No. 124 beech plow with rosewood arms, shaped handle. Auct. $225 No. 126 $75 No. 128 apple wood model, closed handle. $200 No. 129 fruitwood $85-$150 No. 130 boxwood $195 No. 132 dark hardwood with boxwood arms and fence. $260-$400 No. 133 dark rosewood Sandusky screw arm plow plane, ivory arm tips. Auct. 1985. $1,534 No. 137 solid ebony plow with ivory tips. (sold in 1929 catalog for $26) Sold at auction in 1980 for $900. Very rare No. 140 rosewood model with boxwood arms and fence. Has brass center wheel for self-regulating. Unused model from estate of company's manager. Asking $6,850. Another sold at auction in 1983 for $3,500 A well used example sold in 1980 for $1,300 No. 141 boxwood center-screw-arm plow with 6 ivory arm tips. Auction, 1985 $8,000

SARGENT "Fulton" combination metal plow plane with long rods only. $30 Sargent & Co. No. 738 handled beechwood screw arm plow plane with brass fittings. Auct. $75 No. 1080 metal combination plane in nickel plate. $80-$135

P. SARGENT, Concord, N.H. Yankee-style slide-arm plow plane with wooden thumbscrews in top. Brass arm tips. Auct. $95 (Fine)

I. SCHAUER (Eastern Penn., early 1800's) unhandled beechwood plow with long arm wedges. Brass plate on skate and inlaid fence rivets. $90

SHIVERICK handled boxwood screw arm plow plane. Auct. $175

SIEGLY PATENT, Mar. 11, 1884, combination plow plane, iron with beechwood closed handle. Steel slide-arm-rod, maple and rosewood fence plate. Auct. $75-$150 Dlr. $175-$275. With 8 irons. Dlr. $350

A. SMITH, Rehoboth (18th Cent. Mass.) yankee style plow plane. Auct. $350-$400

E. SMITH plow planes in both screw-arm and slide-arm styles, beechwood. Auct. $50-$75 Unhandled, all boxwood version with 7 irons. Auct. $175

OTIS SMITH & CO., Rockfall, Conn. (circa 1882-1886) Fale's No. 1 Patent iron framed combination plow plane 10¼ in. long with beechwood fence and rosewood handle & front knob. Steel slide arms, one square, one round. Auct. $175 With 18 shoes and 10 irons $550-$700

STANLEY No. 41 Miller's Patent combined filletster and match plane. First patented in 1870, sold thru 1894. Early model, non-slitter, (filletster and depth stop missing). $195   Another (with chipped handle) $140   1892 model with perfect filletster bed, 95% orig. finish intact. $400-$500   Another with (6) cutters Auct. $375   With one fence, (no filletster) fine. Auct. $175

STANLEY No. 42 Miller's patent plow. Same as No. 41 except that body and fence are made of yellow gunmetal. Has iron filletster bed attachment and rosewood handle. Several have been sold at auction for $1,000 and up.

STANLEY No. 43 Miller's patent plow plane was sold without filletster bed. Otherwise same as No. 41. Auct. $175-$250 (if all 9 cutters in orig. box)

STANLEY No. 44 Miller's Patent plow. Issued without filletster bed and cutter. Cast in gunmetal including fence. Auct. $750-$1,100. Dlr. $1,275

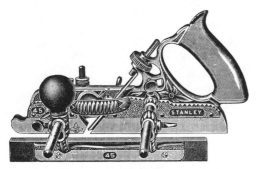

STANLEY No. 45 combination beading, rabbet, slitting, match, and plow plane was the most popular model offered. Sold from its inception in 1884 to the final year of 1962. First models were japanned black with floral & vine design in casting. In 1892 the vines disappeared fom the fence. In 1896 all of the parts became nickel plated. In 1897 the round thumbscrews were changed to flat and the knob was moved to outside fence position. A cam rest was added on 1905 models and in 1909 a stippled pattern replaced the old floral design. By 1921 a total of 22 cutters were offered.

In 1922 the word STANLEY was embossed on curved part of center section. Another cutter was added in 1935 for a total of 23. No other major changes took place for the next 40 years except the retail price, which had risen from $8.00 in 1887 to about $50 in 1960.

A 1913 nickel plated No. 45 with 21 cutters and orig. box sold at auction in 1983 for $120. Another with a set of scarce hollow & round bottoms and a stair nosing attachment sold for $225. Dealer prices vary according to date, condition and accessories, $50-$150 is current range. The rarest model is the No. A45 aluminum bodied version. In 1983 a fine example with all attachments and cutters sold at auction for $1,800. Dealers have offered this plane at prices approaching $3,000.

STANLEY No. 46 Traut's Patent Adjustable Dado, Filletster and Plow Plane. Differs from No. 45 in that all cutters are skew angle. An original 1874 model with added guard plate and 9 cutters sold at auction in 1982 for $520. Dealer offerings fall in the $50-$150 price range.

STANLEY No. 50 Adjustable Beading plane weighed only 3½ lbs. Auct. $55-$125 . In worn condition with some parts missing these planes bring only $35

STANLEY No. 141 Bullnose Plow, Filletster and Matching planes were sold from 1887 to World War I. They rarely appear at auction and dealers ask from $200 (for damaged examples) to $400 for prime specimens.

STANLEY No. 143 is the same plane as above but without a filletster attachment. Dealer offerings are in the $200-$300 range.

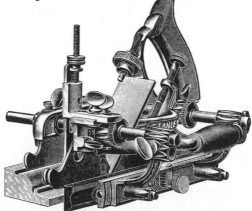

STANLEY No. 55 was the fanciest and most complete combination plane ever offered. First patented in 1893 it sold well into the 1960's. All parts are nickel plated and this 15 lb. plane has a rosewood handle and fence. By 1925 (55) cutters had evolved for use in this "portable wood mill." Recent auction price range for mint condition sets, $300-$475. Dealer offerings range from $150 - $350.

STANLEY No. 238 Weatherstrip plow was designed to cut a ⅛ to ⅜ inch groove in a window sash. These little planes weigh less than 2 lbs. The body is jappaned and parts are nickel plated. Auct. $100 Dlr. $135. In production for 8 years starting in 1930.

STANLEY No. 248 Grooving Plow was also designed for weather stripping work. It was sold from 1936 to World War II. Mint examples have brought as much as $85 at auction. Dealers asking from $55 to $125. No. 248A (aluminum) Auction, 1985. $130-$160.

J.S. STEPHENS, Boston (1836-1860) also marked H.M. Foss. Sliding arm plow with brass trim. Auct. $55. Dlr. $125.

SUMMERS VARVILL, Ebor Works, York. Beech plow with boxwood nuts. Dlr. $95 Handled version with ivory scale in. $350

TABER PLANE, New Bedford, Mass. (1866-1892) applewood screw arm plow plane. $165

J.M. TABER, New Bedford, Mass. Beechwood slide arm plow. $65

WING H. TABER, Fairhaven, Mass. (circa 1833). Solid boxwood const. brass skate plate. $250

T. TILESTON, Boston. Early wedge-lock slide-stem plow. Auct. $40

TUCKER & APPLETON, Boston (1868-1871) Handled rosewood plow plane with boxwood screw arms. Auct. $325

VARVILL & SON, Ebor works (1862-1904) beechwood wedge arm with graduated ivory inlay strips in arms. Brass trim. Auct. $325

EDWIN WALKER, Erie, Pa. Pat. May 19, 1885. Plow plane made of laminated iron plates. Rosewood grip & fence. Dlr. $650

JOHN WEISS & SON, Gergrundet, Wein. Wooden curved-style plow with double spurs and screw arm type fence. Auct. $140

A. WALLACE, Dundee. Bridle plow with round side-knob. Iron fence clamp. Auct. $390

C. WARREN, Nashua. Beech slide arm plow with boxwood fence. Brass trim. $85 Another with plain trim and brass skate plate. $55
Screw arm version. $68   Handled-type with boxwood screw arms and round nuts. Auct. $325

HENRY WHITE (Philadelphia 1851-1858) self-regulating plow plane with pair of smooth outside arm rods and a large threaded wooden center screw. 8 inches long by 11½ in. wide. Auct. $2,600. Dlr. $5,500

ISRAEL WHITE, Corner Callowhill & Fourth St., Philada. Unhandled-style screw-arm plow . Auct. $120-$225 (1985)

RECORD SETTING TOOL AUCTION IN NASHUA, NEW HAMPSHIRE

Richard Crane of Your Country Auctioneer, Inc. hammered down some unbelievable prices at this record setting sale.

Row 1
MILLER'S PATENT gun metal plow plane $1,100

SQUIRELL TAIL T-rabbet (middle) $150

Row 2
(3) BRONZE T-RABBETS (incl. top right) $1,475

Row 3
F. NICHOLSON "Living in Wrentham" unhandled 18th Century plow plane. $2,200

MULTIFORM MOULDING PLANE CO. pat. 1854 solid boxwood plow plane with removable handle. $3,400

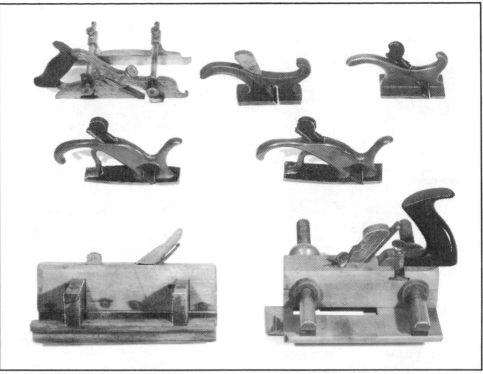

Courtesy "Your Country Auctioneer, Inc."

RABBET is the American word for the English verb "Rebate" which in turn was derived from the French "Rabattre", (to reduce). A rebate is the stair-step-cut made on the edge of a board to form an overlapping joint or to cover a panel edge. Some types of rabbet planes are made for cutting rather wide flat-bottomed grooves.

The Jack Rabbet is a handled plane 1½ - 2½ inches wide and up to 16 inches long. It has forward mounted spur cutters on either side of the stock to make preliminary knife-type scoring cuts which prevent splitting on wide grooves.

Most all rabbet planes have skew angle blades which are exposed on both sides of the mouth. A stopped-rabbet cut stops just short of the end of a board to hide the joint from front viewing. Bull-nosed rabbets have their blades mounted at the extreme front of the toe, under a rounded bull-like nose. The most exotic members of the rabbet plane family are the curved bottom variety.

This STANLEY No. 196 nickle plated Curved Rabbet plane was manufactured from 1912 to 1935. It was designed to cut a rebate on either side of a curve or circle, as in a window arch or door panel. The tool pictured at right sold in 1983 at a London tool auction for $1,120 in U.S. dollars.

One of the world's largest annual sales of antique woodworking tools is conducted by auctioneer Tyrone R. Roberts at Kensington Town Hall on Hornton Street in London. Collector/entrepreneur Reg Eaton spends most of an entire year scouring the English countryside in search of 600 top quality items for this event. Several new record prices for "Stanley" brand tools were realized at the March 26th, 1985 sale. (A photo illustrated catalog is available from Mr. Eaton at 35 High St., Heacham, King's Lynn, Norfolk, England, PE 31 7DB)

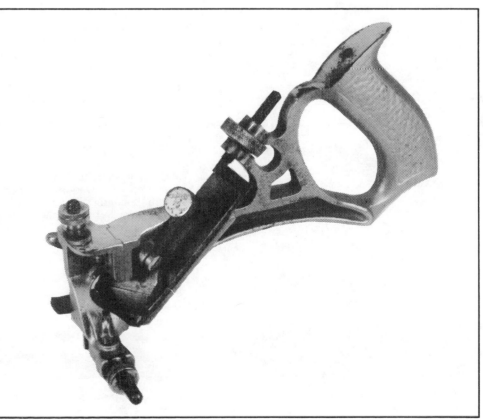

Courtesy Reg Eaton

FACTORY MADE American Rabbet Plane with hardware dealer's imprint. (1895 catalog).

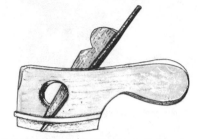

CARRIAGE MAKER'S Tailed Rabbet with compass bottom ($35-$95). Exotic woods & graceful shapes bring highest prices.

Wm Marples Coach Maker's T-Rabbet (from 1909 cat.).

GERMAN STYLE compass Rabbet. (1880-1920 era).

OHIO TOOL No. 119 Jack Rabbet, or handled Skew Rabbet.

ASSORTED British made compass-bottom carriage maker's T-rabbet planes in beechwood 6 in. - 8 in. lengths. Auct. $20-$30 each. Dlr. $30-$45 ea.

I.H. ANDRIES, Dutch rabbet plane in hardwood. Rectangular with hump on toe. 1½ in. wide x 14 inches long. Dlr. $25

O. ANDRUS, Glastonbury (Conn. 1840-1871) 1¼ inch beechwood skew rabbet. $75

THOS. APPLETON, Boston. ⅞ in to 1¾ in. rabbets with slitters sell in the $10 to $20 range.

AUBURN TOOL CO. side-handled rabbet plane 1½ in. x 15 in. with 2 cross knickers. Auct. $20. Dlr. $40   Common 1 in. beechwood rabbet by same maker. $10-$15

A & E BALDWIN side rabbet. Auct. $12

BARRY & WAY, N. York. Beechwood 1¾ in. skew rabbet, (shiny clean) $10

D.R. BARTON beech skew rabbet ½ inch width. $8   2 inch size. $35

C. BAYFIELD, Nottingham (England) cast iron shoulder rabbet with rosewood wedge and infill. Auct. $84

DAVID BENSEN beech skew rabbet, 1 inch. $8

BENSEN & CRANNELL, Albany (1844-1862) beech skew rabbet 2 inches wide. $12

J.B. BIGELOW handled beech rabbet. Rectangular, 15 inches long, (slitters gone) $35

BIRMINGHAM PLANE CO. Derby, Conn. (1862-1889) carriage maker's iron T-rabbet plane, 2 in. x 8 in. Open cast frame has ring-type front finger grip. $195   Another 9 inches overall. $250   Unmarked 6 inch model. $240   8 inch size (with lateral adjust. missing) $130

J. BRADFORD (Portland, Me. 1849-1875) good side rabbet plane. Auct. $15

BRANDELL'S PATENT (circa 1989) iron shoulder rabbet with 10³/₁₆ in. open sided iron frame. Fine cond. $275

BUCK, Tot. Court Rd. Iron shoulder rabbet, 7⅜ x 1½ in. with rosewood wedge and infill. Auct. $55-$95 depending upon cond. Magnificent ebony-filled brass shoulder plane by same maker, 1½ x 7¾ inches. Auct. $195-$237   Dovetailed steel rebate with rosewood wedge & infill, 9 x 1 in. (pitted) $50

BOXWOOD coffin-shaped rabbet 5¾ x 1 x 2¾ inches. Very well made. Unmarked $65

CASEY, CLARK & CO., Auburn, N.Y. (1864) beech 2 in. skew rabbet. Perfect. $10

H. CHAPIN compass-bottom T-rabbet. Auct. $15   Union Factory 1 in. wide. $12

C.E. CHELOR, Living in Wrentham. Birch skew rabbet 9⅞ inches long. (sole rejointed many times). $750   Another in old blue painted finish. $1,200. Chelor was an ex slave apprentice of America's earliest documented plane maker. Became his own master in 1753 and married in 1758.

J.E. CHILD Prov. 1852-1875) Right hand side-rabbet. $15   Jack rabbet with offset handle. 2 x 16 inches. $35-$45

I. CLARK beechwood coachmaker's rabbet plane 7 inches long. $28

I. CLARK, Middleboro. Birchwood 1 in. skew rabbet 9¾ in. long, wide chamfers. Fine. Auct. $300

M. COPELAND skewed rabbet plane 2¼ in. wide. $16

COPELAND & CO., Warranted. Simple rabbet plane with fancy scroll stamp. $22

I. COX (Birmingham, England, 1770-1801) skew rabbet with wide chamfers, 1½ in. cutter, crude attached oak fence. $18

CUMMINGS & GALE (providence, 1832) open handled 15 inch rabbet plane with skew iron. (slitter gone, finish worn) $18

CURRIE, Glasgow (1833-1844) Unusual bi-directional side rabbet. Resembles a 9½ inch moulding plane with 2 vertical wedged cutters about 3 inches apart. Auct. $115

DEFOREST, Birmingham (Conn.) wooden side rabbet plane. Auct. $22

S. DOGGETT, Dedham (circa 1750-1800) narrow rabbet with cut-out depth stop. Auct. $237   Another ⅞ in. square rebate in birchwood 9¼ in. long. Auct. $360

EASTBURN stamp on early 19th Cent. beech rabbet 1⅜ in. wide by 9⅝ in. long. Auct. $50

EASTWOOD, York. brass-soled bullnose rebate. Auct. $50

EBONY wood, side rabbet 5¾ in. long by 2⅞ in. wide. Looks like a moulding plane laying on its side. 1 inch iron, boxwood wedge. Dlr. $160

Courtesy Christies, South Kensington

FRENCH Carpenter's Rabbet. Hand-carved and dated 1752, over 45 inches long.

NORRIS No. A7 dovetailed steel Shoulder Rabbet with "patent adjustment" and rosewood infill, 1¼ in. wide. Sold at recent Tyrone R. Roberts tool event for $420.

EIGHTEENTH-Century birchwood side rabbet with 1778 scratched on side. 10 inches overall. Auct. $75

ISAAC FIELD (Providence, R.I.) beech skew rabbet with 2 slitter irons. 9½ in. $50

A. FISH, Lowell. Unusual full-handled beech rebate with slitter grooves (blades missing) $45

FRENCH Carpenter's 45 inch long carved rabbet plane with 1752 boldly carved in side. Intregal carved closed-handled at rear of stock. Scroll-shaped foregrips and wedge. Much floral carved detailing. Auct. $400 Modern French - made 20 inch long square rebate with 1⅛ in. iron and flat-topped wedge. $65

JO FULLER, Providence. Yellow birch rabbet, (Modified by user) $60 - $75

GERMAN factory-made rectangular shaped rabbet with adjustable throat and dovetailed sole. $24

GLEAVE, Manchester. Pair of coachmaker's tailed, radius-bottom and compass-bottom rebate planes. Auct. $87 pr.

THO: GRANT with crowned initials R.L. on toe. (New York circa 1716-1786) 9⅞ inch rabbet with 1¼ in. skew cutter. $125

GREEN, Pimlica. British gunmetal shoulder-rabbet with steel sole. 8 inches long. Auct. $175

GREENFIELD TOOL CO. beechwood factory-made rabbet planes sell in the $30-$40 range.

GREENSLADE, Bristol. Auction lot of (4) unusual rebate planes. $35 all. 1¼ inch skew rabbet with exhibition medal imprint. $16

GRIFFITHS, Norwich, No. 5 side rabbet. Auct. $13 Skew rabbet, 1 inch. $10 Matched pair of beechwood side rabbets in fine condition. Dlr. $65 Brass-soled bullnose by same maker. Auct. $80 Compass bottom T-rebate in dark rich beech. Dlr. $45 Coachmaker's tailed-style radius rebate with curved sides. Auct. $98

GUNMETAL shoulder plane 1⅛ x 8⅛ inches. Round ears on top at each end. Rectangular ebony wedge. Auct. $225-$297 Another unmarked gunmetal British made rabbet, 3⅞ x ⅜ in. Auct. $135 Another 4 x ½ inch size. $115

HIELDS, Nottingham. Miniature compass-bottom rabbet plane. Dlr. $40 - $65

S & H HILLS, Springfield, Mass. (1829-1830) beechwood rabbet 1 in. wide with slitter $15

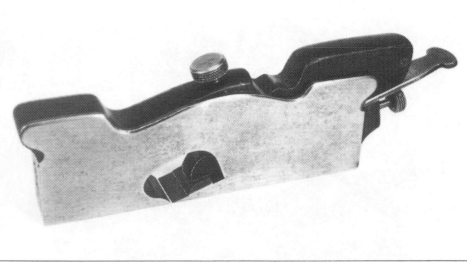

Courtesy Reg Eaton

HOLLAND Marked dovetailed steel ¾ inch rebate with rosewood infill. Auct. $100 Another little rebate by this London maker (1862-1869). Bronze with steel sole, 5 inches. $114 8 inch gunmetal shoulder plane with "Rino" shaped rosewood infill. Steel sole. Auct. $185

THOS. IBBOTSON gunmetal bullnose rebate 3¹¹/₁₆ inches overall. Iron sole. $115

H.L. JAMES, Williamsburg, Mass. Skewed rabbet, 1½ in. wide. $10

KEEN KUTTER No. 10 Carriage maker's rabbet plane. Auct. $90 Dlr. $110

J. KELLOGG, Amherst, Mass. 1½ in. skew rabbet. Auct. $10

D. KIMBERLY pair of excellent side rabbet planes. $56

D. LOVEJOY & SON, Lowell, Mass. Cast iron skew rabbet with offset handle. 8½ inch long frame has wooden front knob. Auct. $500

I. LUND, London. Matched pair of side rabbets. Auct. $30

T.J. McMASTER side rabbet plane. $15

P.H. MANCHESTER (Prov. 1843-1857) ⅞ in. rabbet plane with dual slitters. $10 Unusual 2 inch wide skew rabbet with brass depth stop & twinscoring cutters. Sliding fence (not included). $48

W. MARPLES pair of radius curved coachmaker's tailed rebate planes. Auct. $63

W. MASSEY, Philada. (1808-1830) 1 inch rabbet plane. $20

MASTER DUPLEX all metal rabbet plane made for Montgomery Ward by Stanley in the 1930's. $16

A. MATHIESON & SON, Glasgow. T-bottom beechwood rabbet plane. $28

MATHIESON, Edinburgh. 5 inch gunmetal bullnose rebate with scalloped top and square ebony wedge. Good cond. Auct. $120

MILLERS FALLS No. 07 combination rabbet & block plane identical to Stanley No 140. $70 Another bullnosed rabbet 4 inches. Comp. to Stanley No. 75 . $25 No. 85 (style of Stanley No. 78) Mint. $60

MOSELY & SON, London. Iron shoulder rebate 8 in. long with 1½ in. infill. $125

MULTIFORM PLANE CO. Pat. 1854 wooden rabbet plane with slot in top. Auct. $65

I. NICHOLSON, Wrentham (1760-1790) rabbet plane (no descript.) Auct. $150

F. NICHOLSON, Wrentham (Mass. circa 1750) birch rabbet plane with unstopped chamfering. 9⅞ inches long, ½ inch cutter. Crisp name stamp & fine patina. America's earliest recorded planemaker. Dlr. $650

NORRIS No. 7 dovetailed steel shoulder plane with rosewood wedge and infill. Avg. cond. $135 Fine to mint. Auct. $225-$335 (more with ebony infill)

NORRIS No. A7 adjustable shoulder plane with knurled adjusting knob on top which passes thru rosewood infill. Auct. $400-$475

NORRIS No. 8 dovetailed steel rebate, small version 6 in. long. Auct. $157 Dlr. $275 Larger 8 inch size. $140-$165

NORRIS steel soled gunmetal shoulder plane with stag's horn ebony infill. Auct. $333

NORRIS No. A20 gunmetal shoulder rebate with 1¼ in. wide steel sole, ebony infill, knurled adjustment rod at heel. Auct. $875

NORRIS No. 22 "Unbreakable" steel shoulder plane with rosewood infill. 7¾ x 1¼ in. Auct. $114-$150 Mint cond. $220

NORRIS No. 25 bullnose rabbet in orig. box with label. Fine cond. Auct. $238

NORRIS, London, No. 27E gunmetal rebate 3⅞ inches long x 1¼ in. wide. Ebony wedge, steel sole. $165-$185

Courtesy the Mechanick's Workbench

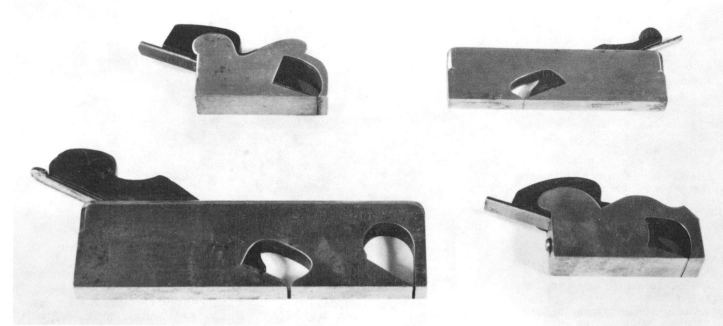

(Pictured above, top left) British bull nose rebate in gunmetal with ebony wedge. 3⅝ inches long X 1 inch wide. (Top right hand) Miniature dovetailed steel shoulder rebate, signed Buck, 249 Tottm Ct. Rd. With rosewood wedge and infill. 6 inches long, ½ inch wide cutter. (Bottom left) Rare ¾ inch dovetailed steel double-throat rebate marked Mathieson, with star & crescent trademark. Combination shoulder and bull nose rabbet. (Bottom right) Cast iron bull nose rabbet. H. Slater, maker, Meridith St., Clerkenwell, London. 3¾ in. long with 1⅛ in. iron and original ebony wedge.

OHIO TOOL CO. beechwood skew rabbets sell in the $8 to $14 price range. No. 010 iron bench rabbet with wooden handle and knob, 13 inches overall. $105

A. PEARCE brass side rabbet, duck bill or pistol-shaped wooden tote. Dlr. $250

R. PIPER, Dublin, N.H. skew rebate with 1½ inch cutter sold at auction for $85

S. POMEROY, N. Hampton (Mass. circa 1790) birch ½ in. rabbet with intregal fence and relieved wedge. Auct. $300

W.H. POND, New Haven, Ct. (circa 1850) 1½ in. wide curved T-rabbet. $50   6½ inch long wooden rabbet plane with brass re-inforcing straps. Auct. $25   Carriage maker's T-rabbet. Auct. $35

EDWARD PRESTON & SONS No. 2 coachmaker's wooden T-rebate 6½ inches long x 1½ in. wide. Near new. Dlr. $45

EDWARD PRESTON & SONS, LTD. gunmetal bullnose rebate curca 1910. 3½ inches long x 1⅛ in. wide. concave side grip, ebony wedge. Dlr. $245

PRESTONS PATTERN No. 1347 iron bullnose rabbet plane 3¾ in. long with 1 inch cutter. Knurled brass thumbscrews. $65

PRESTON dovetailed steel rabbet plane in the rectangular shape of a moulding plane. 9 in long x 1⅝ in. wide. Rosewood wedge and infill. Auct. $70

EDWARD PRESTON & SONS No. 1351 malleable iron smooth-sided shoulder rabbet with rosewood infill. 8 x 1½ inches overall. Auct. $130

No. 1353 gunmetal shoulder rabbet. Smooth sided, 8 inch model with ebony wedge and infill, Auct. $250

No. 1355 adjustable iron bullnose rabbet plane 4 inches long. $40-$50   5½ inch model. Auct. $56

No 1363 green-finished bullnose rebate 3¾ inches long. $60   Another ¹¹/₁₆ in. wide. Fine. Auct. $114

W. RAYMOND wooden rabbet plane with integral fence. Closed handle. $65

E & T RING & CO., Worthington, Ms (1849) 1½ inch rabbet plane. $8

ROWELL & GIBSON (1824-1828) ¹¹/₁₆ in. wide rabbet plane. $16   Matched pair of side rabbets by same Albany maker. Beautiful. $55 pr.

D.P. SANBORN beechwood skewed rabbet 1⅝ in. wide. $35

SANDUSKY TOOL CO. No. 146 beechwood rabbet plane with 1 in. cutter. $8

SARGENT & CO. (New Haven Conn. 1864 onward) No. 79 iron rabbet and filletster plane 8½ inches long. Complete with fence & arm. $20 Like new, in orig. box.$38 No. 81 side rabbet, nickel plated, 4¼ in. long. $50-$75 Mint. $100 No. 196 japanned iron rabbet similar to Stanley No. 190. $53 No. 198 adjustable iron rabbet plane 8 in. long. $25   Aluminum, same shape . $85 No. 505 adjustable bullnose style, 4 inches long by 1 in. wide. $35 No. 1506 Cabinetmaker's beetle-shaped nickle plated rabbet, Auct. 1985. $220

H. SLATER, Maker, Meredith St., Clerkenwell, London (1873-1877) iron bullnose rabbet plane 3⅝ in. long x 1½ in wide. Rosewood wedge. Auct. $45. Dlr. $90   Another by same maker, 8 inches in length, 1½ in. cutter. Auct. $90. Dlr. $160   Another in solid brass with rosewood infill. Auct. $125-$225

SPIERS, Ayr. No. 3 dovetailed steel rabbet plane 9 in. x ¾ in. Rosewood wedge and infill. Dlr. $125-$175 No. 4 combination rebate & bullnose with 2 wedged cutters in tandem. Dovetailed steel frame with rosewood infill. Auct. $175-$210 No. 8 dovetailed steel shoulder plane 8 in. x 1⅛ inches. $135-$157 No. 11 gunmetal bullnose rebate. Auct. $120. Dlr. $225   Adjustable-style. $375

T. TILESTON, Boston, Harrison Ave. (1820-1865) Handled beech rabbet. $28-$48

J.R. TOLMAN, Hanover, Mass., ship rabbet plane 20 inches long. Auct. $45. Double iron rabbet by same maker, rosewood sole. Auct. $35. Compass bottom 9⅜ in. rabbet with double thickness iron. Auct. $45

UNION PLANE CO. No. 50 bullnosed rabbet comparable to Stanley No. 75. 4 inches long x 1 in. wide. $15-$25

VARVILL, York. Coachmaker's rabbet, tailed compass-bottom T-type. Auct. $46

WARD & FLETCHER, New York (1852-53) 2 inch skew rabbet. $35

WAY & SHERMAN, New York, (1849-1852) beechwood rebate 9½ inches long. $12

STANLEY No. 10 Bench or Carriage maker's rabbet. Iron bottom 13 inches long. Rosewood handle and front knob. 2⅛ in. cuter. (an inch longer prior to 1887). Discontinued in 1957. Auct. $85-$135. Prelateral, $110-$175.

No. 10¼ same as No. 10 except that handles tilt. First offered in 1911, discontinued at beginning of WWII. Auct. $550-$800

No. 10½ Carriage maker's rabbet 9 inches long with 2⅛ in. cutter. Auct. $110-$200 No. 10½ C with corrugated bottom. Auct. $125-$275

No. 75 Bullnose rabbet by Stanley sold for nearly a century after its introduction in 1879. Painted with polished sides, 4 inches long. $15 Mint in box. $25 up.

No. 78 Duplex rabbet and filletster in iron, 8½ in. $17-$35 Aluminum. $145 – $200

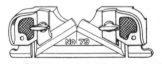

No. 79 Combination side rabbet for right or left hand work. Sold for about 50 years after introduction in 1926. Nickel plated, 5½ inches overall. Auct. $40 Dlr. $75

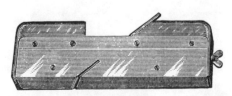

No. 80 Steel-cased rabbet plane 11 inches in length. Appears in catalogs from 1877 to 1888. Auct. $45-$50 Dlr. $75 No. 90 (with spur). $75-$90

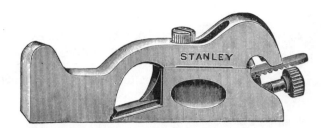

No. 93 Cabinet maker's Rabbet (sold from 1902 to 1965). Nickel plated, 6½ inches in length with 1 inch wide cutter.

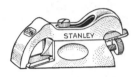

No. 90 Nickel plated bullnose rabbet 4 inches long x 1 in. wide. Fine cabinet maker's plane first sold in 1898. Discontinued in early 1970's. $40-$60

No. 92 Cabinet maker's bullnose rabbet 5½ inches long, also discontinued in the early 1970's. $55-$95

No. 93 Longer 6½ inch version. $45-$75

No. 94 Nickel plated 7½ inch size. Auct. $125-$225

Nos. 98 & 99 Nickel-plated side-rabbet planes 4 inches long. Sold from 1897 to start of WWII. Auct. $85 a pair, to $150 in original boxes.

No. 180 Iron rabbet plane 8 inches in length with 1½ inch cutter. Sold from 1886 to end of WWI. Currently selling for $20-$35.

No. 181 is ¼ in. narrower. $35

No. 182 is exactly 1 inch wide. $35

No. 190 is similar, but can be used with either hand and was sold for a much longer period (until 1962). $15-$25 Nos. 191 & 192 are the same but of narrower width. $15-$25

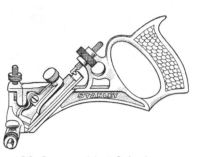

No. 196 Curve rabbet 9 inches overall. Very rare; offered for upwards of $1,000 Discontinued in 1930's

No. 278 Rabbet and filletster plane in painted iron with nickel-plated trim. 6¾ inches long. Auct. $150-$240

No. 289 skew rabbet, with fence and depth gauge. 8½ inches overall. $60-$75 avg. price with exceptional examples bringing up to $150 at auction.

No. 378 Weatherstrip rabbet plane made from 1930 to 1958. Market is very thin. We have seen them offered only twice. One with no fence for $15 and another mint in orig. box for $125. Auct. $70

American made Raising plane, Panel plane, or Raising jack with 2½ to 4 inch wide skew angle cutter (circa 1860 - 1915).

Doors, walls, chests, desks and cupboards all have one thing in common, their panels. Raising the center portion of a panel is just a matter of lowering, or leveling, its outside edges. The wide sloped edge of a panel requires a 2 to 4 inch cutter, set at a skew angle to prevent splitting and cross grain chattering. Some panel raisers also have dual knicker blades to assist in this function.

ARROWMAMMETT WORKS panel raiser 15 inches in length by 4 in. wide. (fence gone) $175

ATHERTON (1816-1829) finest quality panel raiser with 2 inch cutter. $175

BARNES, Worchester. Wooden panel raising plane with side and sole filletsters. Auct. $120

JOHN BELL, Phila. (1829-1851) Clean and shiny, raising jack 5 x 15 inches. $150

BEWLEY, Leeds. 9⅞ in. x 3½ in. panel raiser with side fence. Ward iron. $180

BUTLER, Phila. Handled panel raiser 14 inches long with adjust. fence. Auct. $160

CAULDWELL 18th Cent. panel raising plane with Mitchell blade. Offset tote. $375

R. DABBS 18th-Cent. panel raiser, handled, 14 inches long. Auct. $125

CHAPIN, Union Factory. Panel raising plane with open tote, cross cut knicker and full depth stop. $110 Another with extra wide 5 inch cutter, 2 fences. $85

E. CLIFFORD panel raiser with fence. Birchwood, 13 in. long, offset tote. Auct. $450

I. COGDELL (1750-1765) 18th Cent. handled panel raiser with iron by Tho Allen. Auct. $588

CONTINENTAL-STYLE panel raising plane 12 inches in length. Mellow fruitwood with screw arms and ornamental nuts. $135

CONWAY TOOL CO., Conway, Mass. Beechwood 16 inch panel raiser with knicker blade and fence. Fine cond. $140

M. COPELAND raising jack 14 inches in length. (replaced wedge & cutter) Auct. $75

I. COX handled 18th Cent. panel raiser with depth stop and side boxing. (tote repair) Auct. $85

DUTCH Bossinschaaf or panel-fielding plane, Heart-shaped throat with decorative carving of Goodman "type C." 18 in. x 2½ inches (some worming). Auct. $1,400

FULLER & FIELD birch panel raiser with open tote. Auct. $375

GARDNER & MURDOCK, Green Street, Boston. Beechwood panel raiser 14⅝ in. long. Sole fence, brass side stop, steel spur. Open tote. $140

THO. GRANT, New York. Panel raising plane (with replaced handle). Auct. $325

GREENFIELD TOOL CO. No. 509 factory fresh mint cond. panel raising plane 14 inches in length. Auct. $250 No. 689 with side and bottom fences and spur cutter. Auct. $175

JOHN JENNION (London 1732-1769) unhandled 8½ inch panel fielding plane with round-topped cutting iron. Auct. $590

S. KIMBAL light beech panel raiser with open tote. Excellent, all orig. Auct. $225

MATHIESON pair of stubby little panel raisers in very good cond. Auct. $180 pr.

MELVILLE short 8⅝ in. panel raising plane with 2 boxwood fences. $165

A. MILLER, New York. Close handled panel raiser 16 inches long. Usable. $200

OHIO TOOL CO. No. 114 handled panel raiser 14 in. long. Auct. $200 No. 115 (with repaired handle) Dlr. $200

PELLER, 18th Cent. style birchwood panel raiser in extra fine condition. $450

PHILLIPSON (London 1740-1760) beechwood panel raising plane with bottom fence. Dingly iron. $175

M. READ, Boston. Open handled panel raiser with boxwood corner, fence and wear strips. Multiple owner's stamps. Excellent condition. Auct. $300

I. SLEEPER panel raiser with offset handle and added walnut corner boxing. Auct. $250

J. N. TOWER, Mass. (18th Cent.) birchwood panel raising plane. (chewed handle) Auct. $225

ROBERT WOODING (1717-1728) panel fielding plane 8½ inches long. Roundtopped iron by William Crosbe. (illus. on page 74, Goodman) Auct. $740

UNMARKED panel raising planes of American make. Common woods. $55 - $75

(Below, left to right) Moving filletster by J. Buck, London. Note nicely dovetailed boxwood wear strip insert. (2nd from left) Adjustable compass smoother with a boxwood stop on nose. (3rd from left) Mahogany toothing plane with 2 inch wide upright serrated cutter. (3rd from right) Small, narrow 1865 pat. smoothing plane marked Taber Plane Co., New Bedford, Mass. 6 inches overall with large knurled brass screw holding blade. (Far right) Pair of panel planes by Alex. Mathieson & Sons, Glasgow. Both are 8¼ inches long and have moveable sole fences.

Courtesy the Mechanick's Workbench

Scottish "Turning Plane" of the 1890's
by Alex, Mathieson & Sons, Glasgow.

ROUNDER, WITCHET, TURNING PLANE, TURK'S HEAD, & PUMP LOG TAPER are all wooden planes of a type made specifically for turning or tapering huge dowels such as tool handles, wagon axles & spokes, and even the end joints in hollow logs used in pump and pipe making. These tools were commercially made in Europe and remained in British catalogs until the beginning of World War I. We found none in American tool literature of the period although a few were produced here.

ATKINS & SONS, Sheffield Works, Birmingham. Rounder, 11½ x 4⅜ inches. $175

BEECHWOOD rounding plane (or Witchet) with chamfered ends. Boxwood screw arms inserted thru large brass washers. Brass lined mouth. $155

BOXWOOD rounder of typical 2 handled shape. Brass trim and lining. $150

CHERRY dowelling box, pre 1800, looks like a giant pencil pointer with dowell-shaped handles on each side. $140 Another cherry witchet. Oval shaped, 12 inches long with 4⅝ in. wide wedged-in blade and 2 hand-carved handles. $225

D.R.P. No. 13202 scarce factory-made witchet or adjustable rounder. Resembles a cabinet maker's clamp. Complete with holding clamp. Auct. $200

DOWEL ROUNDER, British made rounding plane of solid Ebony. 2 inches wide. Brass sole, walnut wedge. Forked iron shank attached for use in brace. Auct. $330

CHARLES GREEN signed rounder approx. 3½ x 8 inches. $100

KING & COMPY, Hull. Super deluxe witchet or turning plane with brass lined mouth. Thos. Ibbotson cutter has 2 screw slots. Auct. $132 Dlr. $190

W. MARPLES & SONS, Hibernia, Sheffield. Beech rounding plane of ¾ circle shape with 2 turned handles. Size 1¼ inch. Auct. $50 - $100

MAPLE turk's head or male pipe joint tapering plane, 19½ inches long. Dlr. $195

MARPLES & SONS, Sheffield. Adjustable 2 piece rectangular shaped rounder with 2 boxwood screw handles. Auct. $90 Dlr. $145-$175

NICHOLSON (with fish touchmark) initials L.M. struck twice. Fine rounding plane. Auct. $400

PUMP LOG TAPER for outside joint turning. Handles pegged into block. Ancient and worn. Auct. $80 Another with handles that are an integral part of the main body. Auct. $120

TURK'S HEAD with hand-forged iron fittings. 22 inches overall, for pipe joints up to 5 inches in diameter. $225

UNMARKED oak rounder 9½ inches long. Size 1⅛ in. $50

UNMARKED dark beech rounder 13 inches long with 1¼ in. hole. $60

VARVILL & SON witchet or wheelwright's tail engine. Brass mouth, large wedge. Auct. $65

WITCHET, unsigned 2 pc. rectangular shape with 4 sliding stems thru blocks. 2 turned handles. Auct. $100 Another with no stem-slides, brass lined throat. $115

WHEELWRIGHT'S or Ladder rung rounder. Early handmade oak piece from England. Auct. $65

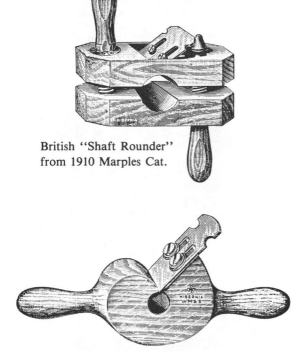

British "Shaft Rounder" from 1910 Marples Cat.

Wheelwright's Rounder, English

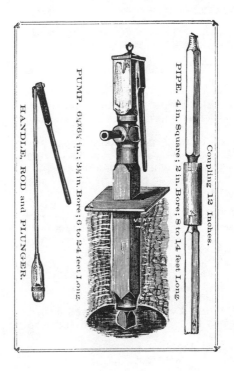

HANDLE, ROD and PLUNGER.

PUMP. 6¾x6½ in.; 3⅜ in. Bore; 6 to 24 feet Long.

PIPE. 4 in. Square; 2 in. Bore; 8 to 14 feet Long.

Coupling 12 Inches.

◄ 1850 advertisement for wooden pipe and pumps. Water pipes made of wood were still in use in some townships as late as 1880.

Wheelwright's Rounder, Scottish

Scottish self-regulating Sash Plane cuts ovolo stick & rabbet. (circa 1899)

SASH PLANES were used to cut the ornamental inside window moulding bar while at the same time rebating a lap for the outside window pane to be puttied against. English sashes were generally made in 2 steps. A sash filletster was used first to cut the rabbet and then a sash moulding plane was used to form an ornamental profile on the opposite side of the bar. Eventually the two functions were combined in one adjustable plane.

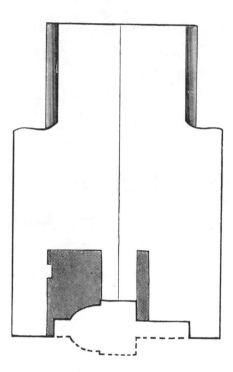

Cross Section View of 2-bladed Ovolo Sash Plane.

European style Circular Sash Plane circa 1900. (Value $40-$50)

Twin-ironed Fixed Sash (circa 1870)

AUBURN TOOL CO. No. 166 sash plane. Auct. $35

A & E BALDWIN, N. York. Beautiful beechwood plane, cuts ½ of a 1½ inch sash profile. $30

A. C. BARTLETS Ohio Planes. Adjustable twin-ironed beech sash plane with applewood screws and knobs. 2¼ in. wide. $75

JOHN BELL, Phila. Fruitwood screw arm sash plane. Auct. $35 -$50

H. BROWNING, Rowe, Mass. Adjustable beechwood sash plane with boxwood screws. Auct. $55

E. W. CARPENTER, Lancaster (circa 1859) adjustable sash plane with 2 wedges and 2 cutters. Chestnut screw knobs. $95

EDWARD CARTER, Troy, N.Y. Adjustable double-ironed sash plane with closed handle. $40

H. CHAPIN No. 190 adjustable sash plane with 2 wedges and cutters. Auct. $25

CIRCULAR beechwood sash plane with opposed wedged irons and curved bottom. Auct. $112

COPELAND & CO. (circa 1850) Two piece wooden sash plane with 2 irons. $40 Another with boxwood wear insert. $50

D & M COPELAND, Hartford (1822-1825) fixed sash plane in orig. cond. $28

COTMAN'S PATENT sash filletster. Wedge arm plow with ivory inlaid rules. $250

M. CRANNELL deluxe sash ogee with diamond-shaped brass plates around adjust screws. Twin blades and boxwood inserts. $58

H. DAVIDSON adjustable screw arm sash plane with boxwood nuts. Auct. $105

J. L. DENISON, Saybrook. Twin-ironed 2¼ in. sash ovolo, beech with boxwood knobs. $55

V. A. EDMOND, Quebec. Adjustable wood screw type sash plane. Auct. $30

L. GARDNER, Green St., Boston (1846-1854) adjustable sash plane 2¼ in. wide. Clean and shiny birchwood. $35

GREENFIELD TOOL CO., Greenfield, Mass. Very fine ebony sash plane with boxwood screw arms and ivory trim. Auct. $1,100

Screw-arm Sash with flat disc nuts.

H. L. JAMES, Wmsburg, Mass. Twin ironed rustic or bevel sash plane. Recessed brass washers. $40

KENNEDY, Hartford. Beechwood 1½ inch wide sash cutter. $28

KENNEDY & WHITE, New York (1822-1840) fixed sash plane with 1⅞ in. iron. $22

JOSIAH KING, 373 Bowery, New York. Adjustable sash ovolo. Twin irons & wedges, recessed brass washers, 2 pc. stock. $40 - $50

LAMB & BROWNELL, New Bedford. Beautiful beechwood, handled, twin-ironed reverse ogee adjustable-sash plane with boxwood arms and nuts. $95

I. LINDENBERGER, Providence. Sash plane with throat wear insert. Auct. $325

MANNERS, Glasgow (1792-1822) unique 4-ironed sash plane, solid stock, non-adjustable. Fine condition and patina. Dlr. $600

J. W. MASSEY, Phila. (circa 1820) 2 piece sash plane with applewood screws. $50

MATHIESON twin-ironed sash ogee 1¾ in. wide. $45 No. 9 side-arm sash filletster, Auct. $70 Pair of No. 1 & 2 sash ovolos plus 2 sash templates and a scribing gauge. (5 pcs.) Auct. $126

OHIO TOOL CO. double-bladed adjustable Gothic sash plane. $45 No. 133½ adjustable ogee sash plane, boxed. $45

OWASCO TOOL CO. No. 176 narrow screw-arm sash plane. Auct. $40

PRATT & CO. unhandled screw-arm sash plane. $40

A. REID circular sash ovolo for cutting arched window rails. $100

J. J. STYLES pair of adjustable sash planes in nearly mind condition. Auct. $210 pr. Another pair of fixed-style non-adjustable sash planes by same maker. $210

T. TILESTON, Front Street, Boston. Sash ovolo. $25 Adjustable sash plane by same (1820-1865) maker. Dual cutters. Auct. $55

W. VANCE (Baltimore) early wedge-arm sash plane with 2 cutters. $75

VARVILL & SON double-ironed sash in lambs tongue and rebate style. Auct. $48

Wm WILLIAMS adjustable wooden sash plane 2 in wide. $30

Stanley Cabinet Scraper

The Cabinet Scraper is used for the final smoothing before sandpapering. It removes the slight ridges left by the plane. It is also used to smooth surfaces that are difficult to plane because of curly or irregular grain.

To Adjust and Use the Cabinet Scraper. Loosen the adjusting screw and the clamp screws. Insert the blade from the bottom with the bevel side toward the adjusting screw.

Stand the scraper on a flat board. Press the blade lightly against the wood and at the same time tighten the clamp screws (a a). Bow the blade by tightening the adjusting screw (b).

Try the Scraper and change the adjustment until it takes a thin even shaving. Hold it turned a little to the side to start a cut. Dust, instead of a shaving, indicates a dull scraper.

Instructions for use of No. 80 double-handed iron scraper.

(illustrations from 1900-1929 catalogs)

STANLEY No. 81 Cabinet Scraper

RAMS HORN Handled Scraper. Misc. brands in this style were factory made from 1880 to 1925.

STANLEY No. 83 Wood Scraper with roller bottom.

E. C. ATKINS CO., Ind., Ind. Ram's horn-style handled wooden scraper. $16-$35

ELLIS brass scraper plane with wooden side handles. Fine cond. $35

FOX MFG. CO., Milwaukee, Wisc. Wood handled cabinet scraper plane with metallic lever cap. Orig. red finish. $85

KEEN KUTTER No. 79 nickel plated 2-handled iron scraper. $16-$30

RAMS HORN-STYLE beechwood scraper. Unmarked example with ebony sole. $60 Another in mahogany 12 inches wide with 3 in. cutter. Bone style ⅛ in. thick. $145

SARGENT No. 53 twin-handled japanned iron scraper with beechwood face. $25-$35 No. 52 adjustable iron floor scraper with turned wooden handles. $10 Sargent VBM iron veneer scraper same as Stanley No. 12½. Auct. $30

STANLEY "Bailey" No. 12 adjustable iron veneer scraper. $25-$38 (early & fine) $65

No. 12¼ with narrower 2 inch blade. Auct. $175-$200 Dlr. $150-$250

No. 12½ with 3 inch blade and hardwood bottom. Auct. $30-$45

No. 70 maple handled box scraper. Dlr. $15-$20 Auct. (U.S.A.) $5 (London) $34

No. 80 iron cabinet scraper 11 in. wide. Dlr. $8-$15 Auct. (London) $25

No. 81 nickel plated 10 in. wide cabinet scraper. Sold from 1909 til WWII $20-$30

No. 82 single handled adjustable scraper 14½ in. long. $12-$20. (mint) $30-$40

No. 83 roller bottom scraper with 4 in. wide cutter. $30-$50

No. 85 rabbet plane style scraper 8 in. long. Tilting rosewood handle and knob. Auct. $450-$700 Dlr. $600-$900

No. 87 (1905-1917) cabinet makers scraper plane. (scarce) $600-$900

No. 112 scraper plane 9 inches long with rosewood handle and knob. Auct. $55-$70 (London) $95-$112

No. 212 very rare scraper plane only 5½ inches long. Auct. $850-$990 Dlr. $1,000 $1,250. (Made from 1911 until 1934)

SARGENT No. 53 Scraper Plane

STANLEY No. 82 Scraper

STANLEY No. 12½ Scraper

STANLEY No. 212 Scraper Plane

STANLEY No. 70 Adjustable Box Scraper for removing brand names and labels from boxes, 13 inches long X 2 in. wide. Pat. April 4, 1876, discontinued production 1958.

STANLEY No. 85 Scraper

STANLEY No. 112 Scraper Plane

STANLEY Nos. 40 & 40½ Scrub Planes, 9½ to 10½ inches in length (1907 illus.)

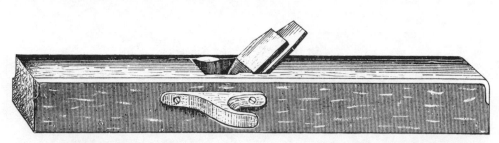

EDWARD PRESTON & SONS No. 380 Shoot Board (Mitre Shooting) Plane with thumb grip. 22 inches long, 2¾ inch wide cutter. (circa 1900)

SCRUB PLANES were used to quickly and efficiently dimension rough timber. The convex, gouge-like cutter literally sliced wood off and actually worked best when used across, rather than with, the grain.

FOREIGN-Made 6⅜ in. scrub plane with convex bottom. $15. Dutch, 5½ in. $35

GERMANY-Marked horn-style scrub plane 9 x 2 inches overall. Auct. $25-$35

SARGENT No. 160 (all-metal) scrub. $110

STANLEY No. 40 scrub plane 9½ inches long. Japanned black iron with beech handle & knob. Auct. $25-$55 Dlr. $25-$45 No. 40½ 10½ inches long. (1902-1948) Auct. $70-$95

J.H. HALL, Nashua, N.H. Iron shoot board plane 31⅞ in. long (fixture missing) Auct. $90-$100. Dlr. $125-$425 (early model). Complete with 12 x 28 in. jig board. $600

HUTCHENS PATENT shooter fixture with 28 inch double-ended plane, lever handle. $145-$195

LANGDON MITER BOX CO., Miller Falls, Mass. Pat. Sept. 19, 1882. Large metal mitre plane with 4 inch cutter at each end. Frame is a giant metal protractor shape. Auct. $400-$875

ROGERS MITRE PLANER, Size 4. (Same as above.) Auct. $600 Dlr. $1,175

MANNEBACH BROS., N.Y. large wooden shoot board plane in excellent cond. Auct. $550

EDWARD PRESTON & SONS shoot board plane 22 in. long with steel sole plate. Auct. $105

JOHN VEIT, Cor. New Market & Green Street, Phila. Wooden shoot board plane with 19 inch close handled plane. Dlr. $750

STANLEY No. 51 shoot board plane only, no fixture. 15 in. long, rosewood handle. Auct. $200-$500 No. 52 Plane & Shoot Board Fixture. Auct. $800-$1,000 (perfect). Dlr. $600 up, Avg. cond.

A. J. WILKINSON, Boston. Shoot board and plane. (no descript.) Auct. $325

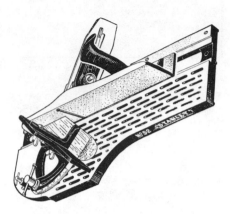

STANLEY No. 52 Shoot Board & Plane, (sold from 1905 to 1945). No. 51 refers to plane only, without board fixture.

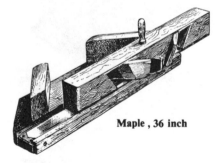

Maple , 36 inch

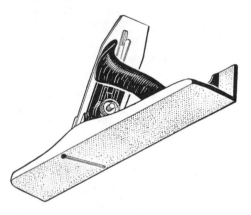

SHOOT BOARD, Mitre Shuteing, Mitre Box, or Chute Planes are all picture frame type Mitre planes that slide back and forth on a wooden or metal fixture which holds the moulding stick at a 45 degree angle for trimming. These precision angle cutting tools were also used extensively by cabinet makers and in pattern shops.

CLEGG, 15 Uxbridge Rd. W. (England) 22 inch long beechwood shoot board plane with handle mounted on side. Includes mahogany board 24 inches long with slotted brass fence. $275

JOHN VEIT, Phila. Shoot board and plane. (No descript.) Auct. $500

M. CRANNELL, Albany, N.Y. Early 28 in. long double-throated shooting plane with 4-inch wide skew angle cutting irons. Auct. $200 (no board)

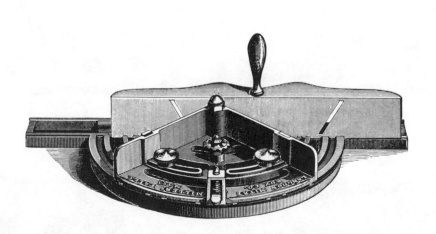

ROGERS MITRE PLANER, Langdon Mitre Box Co., Millers Falls, Mass. Various other distributor names may also appear on this 1880 patent Shoot Board Plane which was offered in three sizes.

The SMOOTHING PLANE is generally the final tool used on flat-surfaced woodworking projects. Its 6 to 10 inch length allows it to move in areas not accessible to larger tools. The smoother is designed to produce a mirror-like finish when used in the direction of the grain. Early smooth planes had straight parallel sides but 18th Century versions became more coffin-shaped (round sided).

Horned smoothers originated in Germany. Rosewood-filled metal box-style smoothing planes were first produced in Scotland around 1845. The modern Stanley "Bailey" type metallic smoother was first conceived by Hazard Knowles of Colchester, Conn. in 1825. Leonard Bailey began production of his own metal smoothing planes in 1855. The Stanley Rule & Level Company bought Bailey's patent rights and machinery in 1869.

The Dutch smooth plane (at right) is dated 1755. 8 inches long by 2 5/8 inches wide. Value approx. $1,550.

Courtesy the Mechanick's Workbench

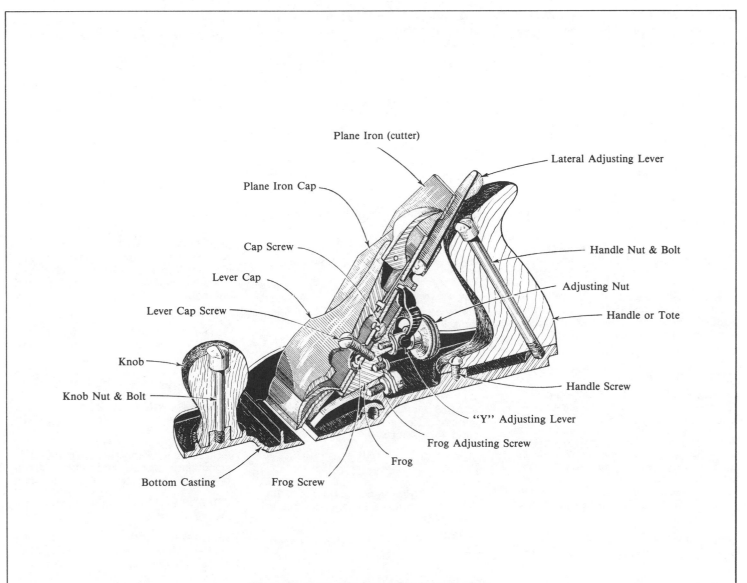

Plane Iron (cutter)

Lateral Adjusting Lever

Plane Iron Cap

Cap Screw

Lever Cap

Lever Cap Screw

Knob

Knob Nut & Bolt

Handle Nut & Bolt

Adjusting Nut

Handle or Tote

Handle Screw

"Y" Adjusting Lever

Frog Adjusting Screw

Frog

Bottom Casting

Frog Screw

(Illustration From 1926 Sargent Hardware Catalog)

ASSORTED sizes of beechwood smoothers by the more common English makers. All in good condition. (140) at $7 each in dealer lots.

AUBURN TOOL CO. handled smoothing plane 8½ in. long, dble, thick blade. $18

D. B. & AUSID, P.A., Primus No. 01248 horned smoother, slightly used. Auct. $65

AUSTRIAN smooth made of white hornbeam wood. 9 in. long, chip carved design on sides. Horn shaped front handle. Circa 1890. Auct. $75

AUXER & REMLEY coffin – shaped smoothing plane. Auct. $65

BAILEY _____ & CO., Boston, 8-31-58 pat. Transitional, wood bottom, iron top smoother with conventional tote and lever cap. Auct. $325

L. BAILEY'S "Victor" No. 3 iron smoothing plane 8½ in. long. Solid iron handle. Auct. $250 (We have no record of any other Bailey Nos. 2 thru 4½ "Victor" iron smoothing planes appearing at auction or in dealer catalogs.)

BAILEY TOOL CO., Woonsocket, R.I. "Defiance" No. 20 iron smoother. Auct. $50 No. 4 circa 1875. Auct. (1985) $80

L. BAILEY'S "Victor" combination Rabbet, Filletster and Smooth. No. 11 model of 1880-1888. 9 inches long, 2 in. cutter, embossed iron knob. $70 - $85

N. L. BARRUS (Warren, R.I. 1849) beechwood smoothing plane 9½ in. long. $25

D. R. BARTON & CO., Rochester, N.Y. Beechwood razee style smoother with open tote (cracked) $25

BIRMINGHAM PLANE CO. solid iron 9 in smoother with open work-style handle and ring knob. Auct. 1985 $400

BIRMINGHAM PLANE CO. "B" Plane, pat. Oct. 22, 1889. Similar to Stanley No. 35. $50 - $60

BOSTON METALLIC PLANE CO. all metal smoothing plane. Nickel plated wedge /lever cap has shield design. $165

J. BRADFORD, Portland, Maine (circa 1860) beechwood smoother 7 in. long. $20. Solid boxwood coffin-shaped smoothing plane by same maker. Near mint. Auct. $120

BALINESE-made unhandled pull-type smoother 10 inches long. Dark tropical wood with lizard carved in top. Auct. $45

BRATTLEBORO TOOL CO. Steer's patent iron smoothing plane circa 1883. 8¼ in. long, 2⅛ width. Rosewood handle, knob, and inlay strips in sole. Auct. $120

BUCK & CO. 281 Whitechapel Rd. Early dovetailed iron smoothing plane. Unhandled, 7⅜ x 2½ in. overall, hardwood infill. (very pitted cond.) Auct. $56 Another Buck smoother, coffin – shaped with bronze cross bar. Dlr. $150

EDWARD CARTER, Troy, N.Y. rosewood smoother 1¼ x 4¼ inches. $85

H. CHAPIN, Union factory, Warranted, (1829-1866). Beechwood closed tote smooth plane 9⅛ in. long. $30 Another in solid boxwood, 10 inches long. $100

CHAPLIN'S PATENT, Tower 7 Lyon, New York. No. 4 iron smoothing plane with adjustable throat. Orig. early plastic handle. $55 No. 75 handled transitional style with beech base and full length 9 in. iron top. $80 - $140

CHAPLIN'S IMPROVED patent No. 1203 iron smoother with hard rubber handle. $125

O. R. CHAPLIN'S Patent nickel plated iron smoother with steel handle and front knob. $100

GEO. CHICK, Maker, Bathe, ME. Rare ebony smoothing plane from ship building area. 10 inches long (shows hard use). $95

COATES, Manchester. Compass bottom smoother. Beech with adjustable boxwood nose. Auct. $70

D. COLTON, Phila. (1835-1875) rosewood smoothing plane. Auct. $50

J. E. CHILD (Providence, R.I., circa 1860) beautiful smoother 8 in. long, adjustable throat. $30

CRAFTSMAN No. 4 metallic smooth plane. $8

J. DENISON coffin-shaped 7 inch smoother, boxwood. $35

C. H. DENISON, Freeport, Me. Round bottom lignum vitae smooth plane 7 inches long. Auct. $65

J. DURGIN, Dover, N.H. Wooden smoothing plane sold at auction for $45

DUTCH "Shaftaaf" whale-shaped wooden smoothing plane 8 in. long. Auct. $130

EASTERLY & CO.,N.Y. smooth plane 8¼ in. long. $23

EAGLE MNG. CO. (company owned?) 8 inch smoothing plane. $15

EAYRS & CO., Makers, Nashua, N.H. oval-sided 9 inch smoothing plane. Auct. $50

ECONOMY MFG. CO., Phila. Transitional wood-bottom smoother, size of Stanley No. 22. $30

FM initials on Dutch smoothing plane dated 1755 on top. 8 in. long, heart-shape throat, spiral decor. Round topped wedge, 2 in. iron. Dlr. $1,550

FENN'S PATENT Improved Smoothing Plane. Registered 12 November, 1844. Beechwood with metal wedge and adjust mech. Auct. $910

FOSTER'S PAT. Jan. 29, 07 iron smooth plane. Turn-table blade hldr. Dlr. $3,000.

FIRESTONE "Supreme" iron smooth $18

FULTON TOOL CO. transitional smoother, same as Stanley No. 35 $15-$25

FULTON No. 2 iron smooth plane with mahogany handle and knob. Same as Sargent No. 407. Nearly mint cond. $100

GAGE TOOL CO., Vineland, N.J. rare No. 1 wooden smooth plane. Asking $275. No. 2 transitional smoother. $75-$85. No. 4 wood smoothing plane with metal top plate on handle. Dlr. $45-$90 No. 4½ scarce size, wooden Dlr. $90 No. 10½ beechwood razee smooth. Dlr. $48 No. 4 iron smoother 10 inches long with wooden tote and front knob. $65-$95 Early transitional model with uncapped oak handle and applewood stock, 9¼ in. $55

GLADWIN'S PATENT beechwood smooth plane with razee-style closed handle. Circa 1858. Lever/disk blade holder is mounted inside throat. Plane has no identifying mark. Auct. $500

P. A. GLADWIN & CO. beechwood unhandled smoother 8 inches long. 2 in. cutter. $15

GOODALL No. 8 inexpensive iron bodied smoothing plane. Resembles Gage brand. $25 No. 35 transitional. Auct. $45

GREENFIELD boxwood smooth plane 8 inches with oval sides. $52

W. GREENSLADE, Bristol (1862-1865) coffin-shaped beechwood smoothing plane with adjustable throat, brass plate. $65

GUNMETAL smooth plane, 7 in. long, Scottish style with walnut handle and infill. Heart-shaped pierced lever cap. Finest quality. Auct. $490

FACTORY MADE Beachwood Smoothing Plane. Millions of manufactured between 1860 and 1925 (Value $8 - $12)

FACTORY MADE Razee-style smooth 10 inches long. (circa 1860 - 1925)

IMPROVED—STYLE right hand smoothing plane with 2¼ inch wide cutter.

OHIO TOOL CO. No. 300 coffin-shaped Smooth (circa 1900)

OHIO No. 304 Razee handle Smooth 9⅝ in. (circa 1900)

STANLEY No. 122 Transitional Smoothing Plane. (1877-1918)

STANLEY No. 135 Transitional Smooth. Liberty Bell style. (1877 - 1918)

STANLEY "Bailey" Nos. 21, 22, 23 & 24 and Nos. 7, 8 & 9 Transitional style smoothing planes, first offered in 1870.

KEEN KUTTER No. KK35 Transitional Smooth. (1911 illus.)

STANDARD RULE CO. No.s 21,22,23 & 24 Smooth. (Pat. 1883)

STANLEY "Bailey" Nos. 35 & 36 Transitional Smoothers (1870-1943)

SARGENT Nos. 3408 & 3409 8 inch Smooth. (circa 1900-1926)

GERMAN horned smoothing plane with iron sole. (circa 1900)

MARPLES No. 3125 Close-handled Iron Smooth (1909 illus.)

EDWARD PRESTON Nos. 1336 & 1337 Smothing plane. (circa 1915)

MATHIESON No. 842 Unhandled Smoother, parallel sides. (1899 illus.)

EDWARD PRESTON Nos. 1341 & 1342 Smoother. (circa 1915)

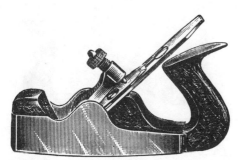

MATHIESON No. 843 Improved Smoothing plane. Round sides. (circa 1899)

L. BAILEY'S "Defiance" No. 24 Iron Smoothing Plane. (1879 illus.)

DAVIS LEVEL & TOOL CO. No. 19 Smooth Plane 9 in. (1875-1884)

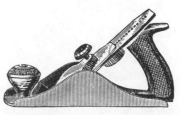

L. BAILEY'S "Victor" Nos. 3 - 4½ Smooth, 8½ inch. (1879 cat.)

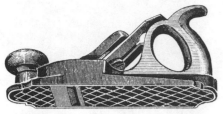

MORRIS PATENT (1870) 10 inch Iron Smoothing Plane.

STANLEY No. 104 Steel Smoothing Plane. (1879 catalog)

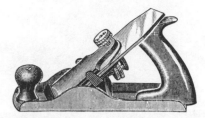

STANDARD RULE CO. Nos. 2, 3, & 4 Iron smooth. (Patented in 1883)

CHAPLIN'S PAT. Nos. 233 - 235 Smooth with hard rubber tote. (1888 illus.)

STEER'S PAT. Nos. 303 & 304 Smoother with rosewood inlaid sole.

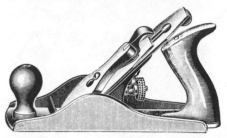

SARGENT "Hercules" No. 1409 Iron Smoothing Plane. (1926 cat.)

OHIO TOOL CO. No. 04 Iron Smoothing Plane (1910 cat.)

KEEN KUTTER No. KK4 Iron Smoother. (1911 catalog)

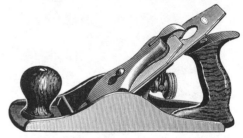

SARGENT Nos. 407 - 409 Iron Smoothing Plane (1884 catalog)

STANLEY "Bailey" Nos. 1 -4½ Prelateral Style (prior to 1885)

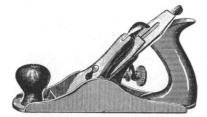

STANLEY "Bailey" Nos. 2 to 4½ Iron Smoother (ca. 1900 illus.)

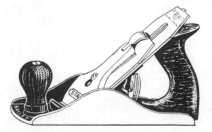

STANLEY "Bailey" Nos. 2 - 4½. (Tall front knob, 1919 onward)

STANLEY "GAGE" Nos. G3 & G4 Self-setting Smooth. (1929 illus.)

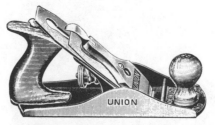

UNION Iron Smoothing Plane. Style of Nos. 2 thru 4½. (1929 illus.)

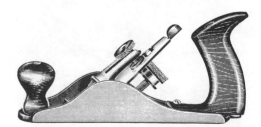

SANDUSKY TOOL CO. No. 3S Smooth. 9 inches long, (1925)

JACOB. HEISS early wooden smoother with original blade and clear stamp. $165

HOLLY'S PATENT (July, 1852) unmarked iron smooth plane 9¼ inches overall. Bottom is dimpled with spherical holes to cut friction. No front knob. $500

ITALIAN made 19th Cent. hand carved smoothing plane 9 inches long. Front knob is a scroll carving. Lignum vitae sole. $150

JORDAN No. 3 DRPA German made iron smoothing plane with tall wooden knob. Dlr. $35. (Rusty cond.) $20. Fine. $75

KEEN KUTTER No. 3 iron smoothing plane $25-$35 No. 120 Smoother. Auct. $25 No. KHS beechwood coffin shaped model. Auct. $35 No. 35 transitional smooth. Dlr. $30

KELLOGG oval sided smoother with whalebone wedge, pin and mouth insert. Auct. $55

MARPLES & SONS 7½ in steel smooth plane with rosewood infill. Unhandled type Dlr. $145

T. J. McMASTER, Auburn, N.Y., with eagle and stars imprint. 8 inch coffin shaped smoother. Iron is stamped W. Butcher, Auburn state prison. $55

MARSH No. M2 iron smoothing plane with corrugated sole. No. M3 iron smoother showing normal wear. $30. Resembles Stanley No. 2. Auct. $100 Dlr. $350

MATHIESON No. 4 Stanley-style iron smoothing plane with tall front knob. Auct. $46 Common beechwood smooth with lignum vitae sole. Auct. $48 No. 843 wrought steel smoothing plane 8 inches long with curved sides, rosewood handle and infill. Gunmetal lever cap. $130-$180 in very fine cond. No. 844 parallel sided version, circa 1899. $100-$125 Unhandled, steel-cased 8 inch smoother with walnut infill and rectangular front knob. Brass lever cap. Curved rear has short bib. Auct. $200

METALLIC PLANE CO. tiny 5 inch iron smoothing plane. $30 Rarer 8 inch size with palm rest built into top of cutter. $100 Iron smoothing plane 9⅞ inches long with faucet-handle style adjust. Auct. $130 Dlr. $165 Palmer & Storkes patent May 14, '67 corrugated bottom style. 9½ in. long. Auct. $125-$160 Three-lever adjusting style 9½ inch iron smoother by Metallic Plane Co. Dlr. $225

MILLER FALLS No. 9 metallic smoothing plane 9 inches in length. Rosewood handle and knob. Circa 1935. $20-$26 late model, stained red handle. Mint. $55

MONTGOMERY WARD "Eclipse" metallic smoother 9½ inches long. $20

MORRIS PATENT Nov. 9, 1870 metallic smooth plane with diamond pattern bottom. Closed beech handle. 10 inches in length. Dlr. $750

JOHN MOSELY & SON, London. Hefty old wooden smooth plane with adjustable steel plate on sole. $25 Thumb-sized coffin-shaped 3¾ inch smooth in beechwood, by J. Mosely. Auct. $39

NORRIS No. A2 dovetailed steel smoothing plane with patent adjust. rod. 7½ in. long, 2⅛ in. cutter. Beechwood handle and infill. Dlr. $175 Another with rosewood filling. Auct.$210-$350.

NORRIS No. 2 dovetailed steel smoothing plane with curved sides, rosewood handle and infill, gunmetal lever cap. Auct. $250-$300

NORRIS No. A5 improved steel smoother with dovetailed iron case. Hardwood infill exposed at open toe. Closed style handle. Dlr. $275 Another with patent adjust. Auct. $320 Very recent model with machined finish. $115 Rosewood filled 7⅝ x 2⅝ inch size. Auct. $300-$425

NORRIS No. A6 parallel sided steel-cased smoother with patent adjust. Rosewood infill and closed handle. Auct. $225-$345

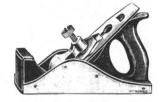

NORRIS No. A12 annealed iron smoothing plane 9 inches long with rosewood closed-style handle and a patent adjust. rod. Auct. $140-$170

NORRIS No. A14 annealed iron smoothing plane. Auct. $126 No. 14 malleable iron cased smoother with parallel sides and tapered rear. Auct. $110-$235

NORRIS No. A16 unhandled annealed iron smooth with rosewood filling. One of the rarest Norris planes. (pitted condition). Auct. $196

NORRIS No. 50G steel-soled gunmetal smoothing plane with patent adjust. Round sided model with closed rosewood handle, Auct. $288

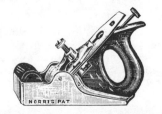

NORRIS No. A51 annealed iron smoother with straight or parallel sides. Mahogany handle and infill. $175-$225 No. 51G gunmetal model with steel sole, patent adjust. and closed handle. Auct. $280

NORRIS No. A61 annealed iron smoother with mahogany handle and infill. pat. adjust. rod. Auct. $112

NORRIS "Unbreakable" unhandled small smoothing plane with 2 in. cutter and rosewood infill. Auct. $105

NORRIS Gunmetal unhandled smoother with ebony infill, gunmetal blade cap. Ibbotson iron. Dlr. $450

OHIO TOOL CO. No. 01 iron smoothing plane 5½ inches long. 1¼ in. cutter, hardwood handle and knob. (These are rarer than Stanley No.1.) $800 - $900 No. 4½ iron smoother with corrugated bottom. Auct. $35-$40

OGONTZ TOOL CO. No. 3 smooth plane 8 inches long. $40

OWASCO TOOL CO. smooth plane 3x3x9½ inches. $30

PALMER & STORKES PATENT, Metallic Plane Co., Auburn, N.Y. Corrugated sole, 8 inch iron smoother. Circa 1870. $195-$225. (see Metallic Plane Co. listing.)

PECK, STOWE & WILCOX made this 10 inch iron smoothing plane in 1920 for a Boston hardware store. Front knob and rear handle varnished red. $16

J. PEARCE, New York. No. 8 coffin sided smoother 7¾ inches long. $12

PRESTON'S Patent No. 1340 malleable iron adjustable smoothing plane 10 inches long. Modern lever cap, rosewood handle and knob. Auct. $80 Dlr. $150

EDWARD PRESTON & SONS No. 1341 malleable iron smoother with parallel sides. Rosewood handle and infill. $110-$175 No. 1372 dovetailed steel smoothing plane with parallel sides. Gunmetal lever cap. $135

SANDUSKY TOOL CO. No. 3SC semi-steel 9 inch smoothing plane with 2 in. cutter. Stained maple handle, circa 1925. $125 Unmarked early iron smoother by same maker. Wooden handle and knob. Large tulip cut-out design on lever cap. Auct. $175

SARGENT No. 407 iron smoothing plane 7 inches long. Polished trim, mahogany handle and knob. Pat. Feb. 3, 1891 also advertised in 1925 catalog. $65-$125 No. 408 with inlaid brass name plate, hardwood handle and knob. $35-$45
No. VBM 409 iron smooth with rosewood handle & knob. $25-$45. No. 410C. $95 No. 600 Sargent smoothing plane with aluminum body. $95
No. 710 "Auto-Set" pat. Jan. 12, 1915. Iron body 10 in. long, mahogany handle and knob. $28-$55
No. 710C with corrugated bottom. $55 Sargent "Hercules" No. 1409 iron smoother of the 1940's. Green and gold pt., varnished handle and knob. $25-$45 Transitional style No. 3408 wood bottom smoothing plane 8 in. long. $15-$25 No. 3409 made without a rear handle. $12-$18. No. 3412 transitional. $30

SCOTTISH steel smoothing planes (6) of the Norris style and quality but unmarked and not alike in every detail. Rosewood, walnut or mahogany filling and handles. Auct. $105 - $175 ea. London, 1984.

H. SLATER (London 1873-1877) cast iron smoother with ebonized handle and infill. Auct. $75. Another with no handle, has raised rosewood infill. Auct. $70 Another unhandled smooth in rosewood. Gunmetal body, steel sole. Auct. $175 Dealer asking $500 for same plane, near mint.

E. SMITH Warranted. Solid boxwood smooth plane. Auct. $35

A. SMITH, Rehoboth, Mass. (1700's) beechwood smoothing plane 7¾ in. $70

SPIERS, Ayr. Early unhandled smoothing plane with screws thru dovetailed steel body into the exotic wood infill. Nicely engraved with owner's name. Auct. $300 (Another in pitted condition. $70) No. 6 Improved dovetailed steel smoother 7¼ inches long, 2 in. wide. Rosewood infill. Auct. $125-$225 Another No. 6 but rarer 6¾ inch length. Has raised rosewood heel instead of handle. Auct. $315 No. 7 with either curved or straight sides. Auct. $150 No. 14 "Empire" model iron smoothing plane. Auct. $47- $65

STANLEY SMOOTHING PLANES

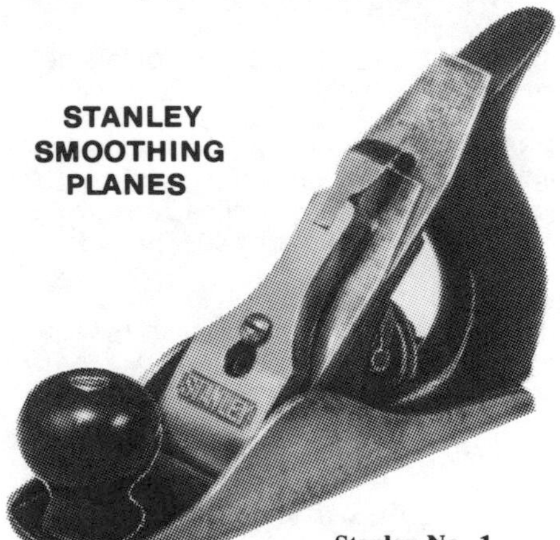

Stanley No. 1

STANLEY "Bailey" No. 1 iron smoothing planes are among the most sought after tools the company ever produced. At the turn-of-the-century these wonderfully small (5½ in.) smothers were often displayed in hardware store windows to attract curious customers in from the sidewalk. In the early days of tool collecting a No. 1 was not all that scarce and could be picked up from flea market tables (in the 1950's) for four or five dollars. By mid 1960 the supply had dried up and prices suddenly escalated to $250. Today we find them selling in the $450-$750 range at tool auctions. First offered in 1874 the No. 1 was discontinued in 1943. Weighs 1⅛ lbs. and does not have a lateral adjustment lever or number marking. As this book went to press a mint condition No. 1, in its original box, with wrapper, was sold at auction in London for $1,500. (1985)

STANLEY "Bailey" No. 2 japanned iron smoothing plane with rosewood handle and front knob. Auct. $130-$160 No. 2C with corrugated bottom. Auct. $250-$350 (Some dealers tell us they see more No. 1's than the 2C style. The No. 2 was phased out in the late 1950's while the rarer 2C was discontinued with the advent of World War II.)

STANLEY "Bailey" No. 3 japanned iron smoothing plane 8 inches long with 1¾ in. cutter. Sold for over 100 years after its introduction in 1870. Prelateral models and pre 1870 patent dates command a premium over the current average price of $30 - $40 for models produced from 1885 - 1945. An 1858 No. 3 with vertical post sold for $250 last year. An 1867-69 version was offered at $125. Undated prelaterals start at $65 in dealer catalogs. A No. 3C with corrugated bottom sold for $65 at auction. Avg. Dlr. price. $35-$50

STANLEY "Gage" No. G3 iron bench plane of the 1920-1940 period. 8¾ in. $65 up.

STANLEY No. A 4 aluminum smooth plane 9 inches long. Introduced in 1925 and dropped from the line in 1938, these planes don't show up very often. Auct. $140 Dlr. $200-$275 with original decal on handle.

STANLEY "Gage" No. G4 self-setting iron smoother 9 inches long with 2 in. cutter. Conventional rosewood handle and knob. Auct. $45-$85 Dlr. $90 No. G4C with corrugated bottom. $95

STANLEY No. S4 steel smoothing plane 9 inches long. A really tough plane with conventional parts and a forged steel bottom. Sold from 1925 to 1942. Auct. $95 Dlr. $150-$200

STANLEY No. OH4 "Two Tone", colorful iron smoother manufactured for National Hardware Sales Campaign 1941-1942. Grey bed, blue frog, yellow blade cap, etc. Dlr. $35-$40

STANLEY "Bailey" No. 4 japanned iron smooth plane 9 inches in length. Sold for 103 years. First offered in 1870 catalog, worth $20-$25 in nice shape, less if handle chipped or cracked. No. 4C with corrugated bottom has sold at recent auctions for $20-$30 No. 4½ is an inch longer (at 10 inches) and has a 2⅜ in. wide cutter. $40-$60 No. 4½C sells in $55 $110 range.

STANLEY "Bailey" No. 21 unhandled transitional wood-bottom smoother 7 inches long with full length iron top plate upon which front knob is affixed. Sold from 1870 to beginning of WWI. Dlr. $125-$195

STANLEY "Bailey" No. 22 transitional smoother similar to above but 8 inches in length. Lots of these around as they were produced until 1943. $15-$25 each, with prelateral models bringing 3 times the money.

STANLEY "Bailey" No. 23 a 9 inch version of the above wood bottom smoother. Discontinued in 1919. Auct. $25 Dlr. $15 to $40 depending upon the amount of original finish remaining intact.

STANLEY "Bailey" No. 24 wood bottom 8 in. smooth with 2 inch wide cutter. In production til 1944. Dlr. $15-$25

STANLEY "Gage" No. 22 wood bottom smoothing plane with metal plate on handle top. 10 inches overall with 1¾ in. cutter. Sold by Stanley from 1919 to 1935, earlier by Gage Tool Co. Dlr. $30-$45 No. G35 with 2 inch cutter, same length stock. $30-$45

STANLEY "Bailey" No. 35 transitional smoother with razee-type handle which extends beyond rear of stock. 9 inches long with 2 in. cutter. Full length metal top plate, chamfered wooden nose corners. Auct. $30. Dlr. $25-$50 with prelaterals bringing the higher end of price range. No. 36 is 10 inch version with 2⅜ in. cutter. (Same general pricing)

STANLEY "Bailey" No. 37 Jenny smooth plane, wood bottom, metal top. 13 inch length puts it just shy of a jack plane. 2⅝ in. cutter. These were available from 1870 to 1924 but few show up on collector market today. One was offered for $200 by a dealer in 1982 (in much altered condition). Another was sold at auction in 1983 for $150. (prelateral)

STANLEY No. 104 pressed steel smoothing plane 9 inches long with 2⅛ in. cutter. Rosewood handle and knob. Patented in Oct. of 1875, these scarce models were discontinued in 1918. Auct. $95 Dlr. up to $200

STANLEY No. H104 modern smoother 10 inches long with very short blade and a machine-screw lever cap. Dark blue bottom, polished sides, low profile. Made only in 1964. Dealer offered one recently at $125.

STANLEY No. 122 smooth plane, unhandled, metal top palm rest over butt. Wooden bottom is 8 inches long. Sold from 1877 until 1918. $25-$40

STANLEY No. 135 transitional smooth with razee handle and metal blade surround. Offered from 1877 thru 1918. Most have Liberty Bell lever cap emblem. $35-$55

STANLEY "Bed Rock" No. 602 iron smoothing plane 7 inches long with 1⅝ in. cutter. Rosewood handle and knob. Bedrock cast in toe. These extra strong planes had a special frog and cutter design that minimized slipage. They were popular from the early 1900's until World War II. Auct. $240-$440 No. 602C. Dlr. $300-$500 No. 603 is 8 in. version, 1¾ in. wide cutter. They were produced until 1934 and are less scarce. Auct. $45 Dlr. $55-$85 No. 603C with corrugated bottom sells for $50 to $100. No. 604 is 9 inches long with a 2 inch wide cutter. Dlr. $45-$85 A No. 604C sold at auction for $55 recently. No. 604½ is heavier version with 2⅜ in. cutter. Auct. $65-$140. No. 604½C. Dlr. $55-$150.

STANLEY "Victor" inexpensive modern-type smoother with red varnished handle & knob. (Not the L. Bailey Victor of 1880) 8 inches overall. $15-$25

Courtesy Roger Smith "Patented Transitional & Metallic Planes In America, 1827-1927"

Photo by Joseph Szaszfai

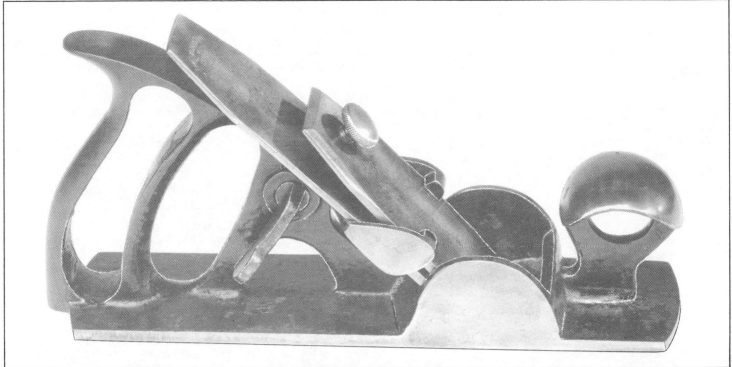

Solid iron 8 inch smoother made by the Birmingham Plane Mfg. Co., circa 1887. (A similar example sold at auction in 1985 for $400.)

STANLEY No. 1104 "Four Square" smooth plane made in 1934. Grey paint with red frog and red varnished handles. $15-$25

STANLEY "Defiance" No. 1203 cast iron smoother with red knob and hardwood handle. Circa 1939-1954. 8 inches long with 1¾ in. cutter. Low priced model intended for household use. $15-$25 No. H1204 is the 9 inch version and sells in same range.

No. 1243 "Defiance" smooth plane of 1940-1962 is 8 inches long and has frog cast into base. Red finished handle. $15-$25 No. 1244 is 9 inch long version of above. Discontinued in 1950. $15-$35

THE STANDARD RULE CO., Unionville, Conn. No. 36 transitional smooth plane. Auct. $90 No. 23 unhandled $75

WILLIAM STEERS No. 303, patented Sept. 11, 1880. Sherbrooke, Quebec, Canada. Iron smoothing plane 8⁵/₁₆ in. long with rosewood handle, knob and inlaid sole strips. Auct. $300

SUMMERS VARVILL compass-bottom smooth in beechwood with ebony nose block. Auct. $98

T. TILESTON, Boston (circa 1790) beechwood smoothing plane 8 in x 3⅛ in. $30

J. R. TOLMAN, Hanover, Mass. Beechwood smoother 2⅜ x 9 inches, round sides. $25 Another in lignum vitae with beech wedge. $100

TOWER & LYON, O. R. Chaplin's pat. Iron smoothing plane with nickel plated knob and tote. $90 Another in wood, pat. May 7-72. Auct. $65 Dlr. $100

TUCKER & APPLETON (Boston 1868-1871) 8 inch smoother in worn cond. $10

UNION MFG. CO. New Britain, Conn. No. 3 iron smoothing plane 8 inches long with mahogany handle and knob. (Circa 1900-1920) Auct. $25 Dlr. $45 (Union sold its plane manufacturing division to Stanley in 1920 and several models appear in Stanley catalogs.)
UNION No. 4 iron smoother 9 inches long. Auct. $45 Dlr. $100 No. X3 . $130 No. X4 (cracked handle) Dlr. $40 - $75 Auct. $30-$65 No. 4 ⅜ $40-$70
No. 4½ smooth 10 inches long with 2⅜ cutter. $25-$75 No. X4½ circa 1903 $85 No. X4G with 9 inch corrugated bottom. $35 No. 22 pat. Oct. 22, 1889 transitional wood bottom smooth 8 inches in length, unhandled type. $20
No. 23 ditto No. 24 wood bottom smooth. Auct. $17 No. 36 razee handled 10 in. smoothing plane. $25 No. 515 razee style transitional smooth (Missing knob) $28 (X prefix on Union planes denoted identical size to Stanley of same number.)

UPSON NUT CO. No. 21 wood bottom, iron top, transitional smoothing plane similar to Stanley smooth of 1890. $55

VAUGHN & BUSHNELL, Chicago No. 904 metallic smoother with hardwood handle and knob. Resembles Stanley "Bed Rock". Dlr. $50 No. 704 VB Auct. $30

VARVILL & SON beechwood compass smoothing plane, coffin-sided with metal sole. Thumbscrew thru top of toe. Auct. $56

JOHN VEIT, Phila. corner New Market & Green Street. Solid mahogany smoothing plane. $45 Another in rosewood, coffin-shaped. $50

H. WELLS, Wmsburg, Mass. Coachmaker's beechwood smooth, 6½ inches long. $20

WHALE-SHAPED Dutch "Schaff" smooth plane with 1⅝ in. cutter. Crown and JM embossed on toe. Auct. $75 Dlr. $95 Another with pegged-maple sole. $135

WINCHESTER W-4 metal smoother 9 inches long. $35 Corrugated model. $55 No. 3004 iron smoother (with repaired handle). Dlr. $80 No. 3005 Auct. $80 No. 3041 wood bottom smoothing plane also by Winchester. Auct. $95 No. 3204-C adjustable iron smooth similar to Stanley No. 3C. Dlr. $98 Auct. $70 No. 3205 with corrugated bottom. $40-$85 No. 3006 (size 4½) Dlr. $55-$165 (mint)

WORRALL'S PATENT (June 23, 1857) wood bottom smoothing plane 10 inches long, 2⅝ in. wide. Unmarked beechwood stock, open style maple handle, walnut front knob. Metal casting covers entire top surface. Screw type lever cap holds blade. Auct. $90 - $350 Dlr. $165-$210

UNMARKED Beechwood smoothing planes sell for $8 to $45 each. Curved bottom compass types are sometimes worth more. Boxwood smoothing planes made in America often fetch $50 and up. Elaborate handle or squirrel tail will add to value. Smaller sizes are more desirable than larger examples. Unmarked carriage maker's smoothing planes are the most valuable, fetching up to $195. Cocobolo and other exotic grained hardwoods sometimes bring $75 in unhandled curved-sided types. Lignum vitae is valuable but not a great rarity. The same is true of Rosewood.

UNMARKED GUNMETAL Scottish-style smoothing planes have been offered for as much as $400 by specialist dealers. A round heeled, unmarked circa 1895 gunmetal smoother 9½ inches long with a scroll-carved front knob sold for $777 at auction recently.

TABLE HINGE moulding planes cut hollow and round profiles on the edges of drop leaf table leaves and tops.

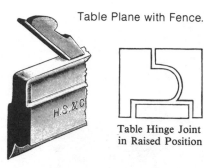

Table Plane with Fence.

Table Hinge Joint in Raised Position

D. R. BARTON, Rochester. Table hinge moulder 1 in. $15 . Matched pair of Barton ¾ in. table hinge planes. $60

JOHN BELL, Philadelphia. Table hinge plane 1⅝ inches wide. $15

E. W. CARPENTER, Lancaster. Table hinge moulder with ½ inch cutter. $25

KELLOGG wooden drop leaf table moulding plane. $10

OHIO TOOL CO. No. 136 pair of table hinge cutters in mint condition. $60 Pair of No. 138 planes as above, but with applied fences. $60

W. PENNELL, West 225 Arch Street, Phila. Table hinge moulder, round. $16

SPAR, OAR & MAST planes are usually short, unhandled, wooden planes of the Smooth or Jack style, but with concave soles and blades for cutting any cylindrical shape from a 2 in. diameter pole or an 8 inch diameter yard arm.

B. BARNES (Orange, Mass.) spar plane. Dlr. $12

BIRCHWOOD concave bottom 8 inch long spar plane with heavy chamfer, no maker. $18

CASEY KITCHEL & CO., Auburn, N.Y. spar plane with 1¼ in. cutter. $18

HIGGS 3⅛ in. long spar plane with 2½ inch cutter. $59

J. KELLOGG, Amherst, Mass. Beechwood spar plane 9 inches in length and 1⅞ in. wide. $18

PETER MACKAY & CO. Glasgow, Warranted. 8 in. long spar plane with flared sole. $40

MINIATURE T-bottom coffin-shaped spar plane with 1½ inch Sorby iron. 5 in. overall. $60

MUTTER (London 1766-1812) open handled spar plane 13 inches long with 1⅞ in. concave iron. $55

OAR PLANE unmarked 7 inch boat builder's wooden plane with double-thickness iron. $18

OAR MAKER'S hollow-bottom apple-wood plane with concave copper wear plate. 2 in. wide x 7¾ inches long. $45

S. ROWEL, Albany. Hardwood mast plane which resembles a 21 inch long fore plane with a convex curved bottom. $20

J. M. TABER, New Bedford. Unusual 1⅝ in. wide spar plane. $25

T. J. TOLMAN, Hanover, Mass. (circa 1849) rectangular-shaped spar plane 9¼ inches long. $30

SPAR plane in miniature sizes 3 in. to 5 in. long. $60 - $70 ea.

SPILL PLANES produce long curled, or straight, shavings expressively for the purpose of lighting a pipe or cigar from the fireplace. Most are home-made from hardwood but some commercially produced cast iron spill planes were offered in British tool catalogs of the late 1800's.

O. BARNES moulding-plane-shaped spill plane. Choice example. $75

BEECHWOOD 3 section laminated const. spill plane with raised decorative side panels, 10 inches long. $110 Another in beechwood, 4 x 1 x 11 inches with grooved bottom and brass side plate. Auct. $75 Dlr. $115 Beech spill plane shaped like a conventional moulder. 1⅞ inches wide. $85

BENCH HOOK-shaped table model wooden spill plane 10 inches long. Metal plated top has center groove that accepts ⅜ in. stock. $65

BIRCHWOOD rectangular 7 inch long spill plane with a perpendicular wedge. Auct. $40

CHAMFERED spill plane 9½ inches in length. Auct. $50

HOME-MADE from work shop scraps. Folk art spill plane. $50

MAHOGANY spill plane 7 inches long, slotted bottom, glued-up halves. $75 Another made from pegged halves. Auct. $105 Unusual mahogany spill plane with round end wedge. Shaving exit hole located in side. $85 Rabbit plane-shaped mahogany spill plane 9 inches long with groove for 1 inch wide board. $95

OAK spill plane 8 inches long. Auct. $45 Another oak plane but in bench hook-style. Auct. $55 Track-type oak spill with groove for ½ inch stock. $85 Coffin-shaped oak spill plane with ⅝ inch channel. Auct. $115

British table-top model Iron Spill Plane. Takes ½ inch board.

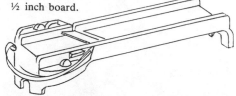

PRESTON PATENT Iron Spill Machine from 1901 catalog. Black Japanned finish. 7 inches long. Auct. $65-$145 Dlr. $120

PRESTON purpose-made beechwood spill plane in moulding plane pattern. Auct. $60

STREAMLINE-shaped beechwood spill plane 11 inches long with edge guide and front sole plate. Auct. $95

TABLE MODEL hardwood spill plane with non-slip iron points on bottom and iron bands on top. Groove for 1 inch stock. (Makes tightly curled shaving.) $165

VARVILL & SON, York. Box-shaped handled-spill with slitter to cut two tapered spills at once. Auct. $263

THUMB PLANES are miniature versions of larger rabbet, moulding, smoothing and carriage maker's planes. They were used for fine detailing in ship's cabins, coaches and carriages, instrument making and almost anywhere else where space was restricted to the width of a "thumb". Any plane under 5 inches in length can be lumped into this miniature category.

CHARIOT-STYLE Thumb Plane circa 1899.

AUCTION LOT of (6) exceptionally fine boxwood compass-bottom thumb planes from 2 inches to 5 inches long. $150 Another lot of (5) beech smoothers from 2¼ to ¾ inches in length. Good evidence of age and use. $250

BADGER PLANE in miniature beech 3½ inches long. Skew mouth & blade. Auct. $66

BRASS bullnose thumb plane 3½ inches long. Hardwood infilling. Auct. $90 Another brass rebate with oak wedge. $115

BEECH bullnose with reverse slope front. 4¼ inches long. $45

BOXWOOD coffin-shaped smoother 4⅝ inches overall. Auct. $63 Unmarked British boxwood adjustable 5 inch compass plane with T-shaped ebony front stop. Dlr. $185 Set of (10) miniature boxwood planes with an average length of 2½ inches, ⅜ to 1 in. wide. Nearly mint set. Auct. $750 3 matching pairs of boxwood thumb planes of compass hollow and round type. 3 inches long including tailed handles. (6) planes. $420 Pair of rectangular boxwood ⅝ in. hollow and rounds 1¾ inches in length. Auct. $200

J. BUCK, 124 Newgate St., London. Boxwood smoothing-style thumb plane 3½ inches long, coffin sides. Auct. $84

BRASS instrument-maker's thumb plane mounted on end of a 3 inch steel rod with turned wooden handle. Dlr. $60 - $100

R. DIX, British-made boxwood rebate 1 inch wide. $65

G. EASTWOOD, York (England) miniature bullnose in beech with 1½ inch wide brass toe plate / wedge holder. $110

I. GRIFFITHS, (Norwich) straight tailed beechwood compass hollow 4⅝ inches long. Auct. $35

GUNMETAL chariot plane of British make. 3 inches long. Owner's name and thistle decor on dark rosewood wedge. Dlr. $225 Gunmetal rebate 3½ inches long. Gunmetal bullnose rebates with round ears on top, fore and aft. Ebony wedges. 1⅞ in. overall. Pair sold at auction in 1983 for $700 Set of (4) British finger planes, bullnose gunmetal with ivory wedges. 2 to 3 inches long. Dlr. $980

HULL, Warranted. Birch smooth thumb plane 4 inches in length. Auct. $25

INSTRUMENT-MAKER'S nickel plated 2 inch thumb plane mounted on end of a 12 inch rod with turned wooden handle. Dlr. $100 Another tiny 1 inch metal plane mounted on 3 inch push rod with ball handle. Auct. $80 - $90

MAHOGANY-filled 2½ inch steel bullnosed block plane. Auct. $110

W. MARPLES tiny iron bullnose thumb plane with rosewood wedge. Auct. $45

MATHIESON, Glasgow. Late version of No. 854 dovetailed wrought steel thumb plane 5 inches long with rosewood infill. Auct. $735 No. 855 gunmetal bullnose thumb plane with ebony wedge. Auct. $87

J. MOSELEY & SON, Bloomsbury. Miniature moulding plane, ⅜ in. hollow style, 2¼ inches tall x 3½ inches long. Grained beechwood. $65

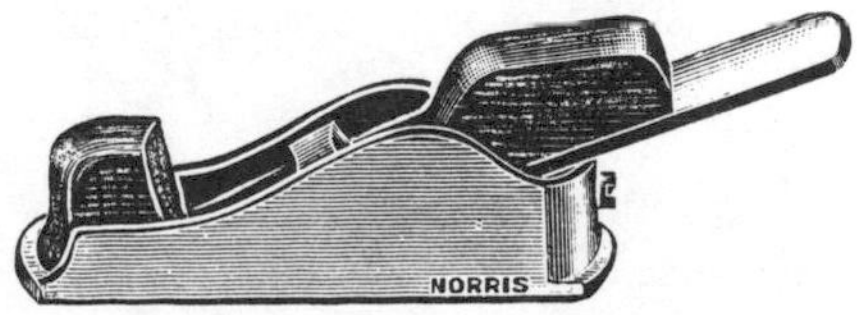

NORRIS No. 32 Thumb Plane was sold in iron or gunmetal. (Circa 1900-1938)

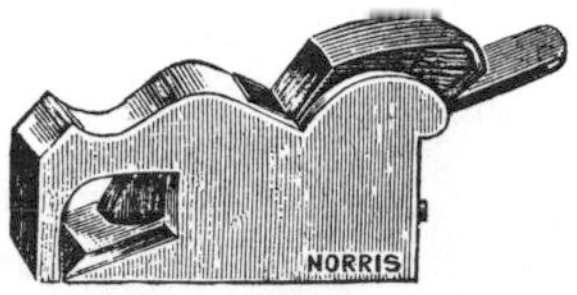

NORRIS No. 25 iron bullnose plane with rosewood wedge, 3¾ inches long. Auct. $52 Norris No. 27E gunmetal bullnose rebate with steel sole and ebony wedge, 1⅛ in. wide. Auct. $166

EDWARD PRESTON & SONS iron bullnose 3½ inches long with scrolled sides. $65 Nickel plated iron bullnose 3⅞ in. overall. $45 - $60 No. 1366 miniature iron bullnose rebate, circa 1914. 3 inches long, ⅜ in. cutter. Dlr. $75 - $125

ROUTLEDGE, Birmingham (England) beech bullnose 3⅝ in. long with brass front plate. Auct. $65 Beechwood compass rebate with sole stepped-down to half of plane's width. 3 inches long. Auct. $44

SCRIMSHAW engraved cherubs on miniature boxwood 2¼ inches long moulder of rectangular shape. Auct. $210

H. SLATER, Maker, London. Mallable iron bullnose rabbet 5 inches long. Auct. $60 Another in gunmetal 1⅛ in. x 3½ inches with steel sole, rosewood wedge. Auct. $100 Another 3¾ inches overall with iron frame and 1¼ in. mahogany wedge. Auct. $50 Dlr. $100 - $175 (in orig. cond.)

STEEL bullnose thumb planes of British manufacture 3½ to 4 inches long. $45-$85

TIGER MAPLE compass-bottom lowngle 3 inch long wedge-shaped thumb plane. Auct. $100

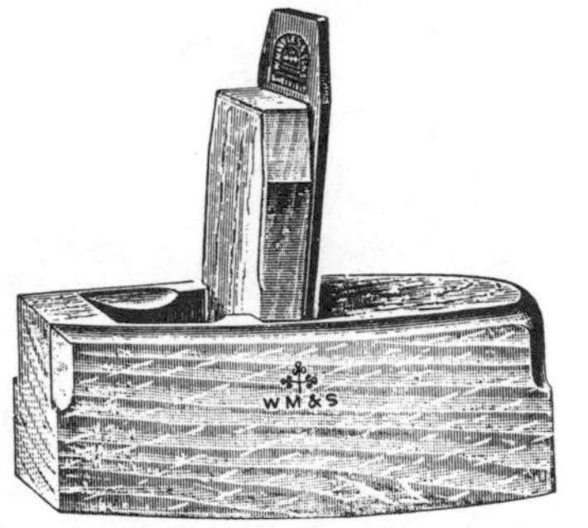

TOOTHING PLANES resemble smoothing planes but they have an almost vertical cutter with a serrated edge. These tools were used to remove saw marks from the backs of veneer boards and to prepare smooth or irregular surfaces for veneer application by a simultaneous roughing and leveling out process.

A. C. BARTLETT'S Ohio Planes, beechwood toothing plane (circa 1895-1899) $38

JOHN BELL (Philadelphia circa 1840) mont cond. toothing plane. $25

BUCK & CO., White Chapel. 7 inch toothing plane. Auct. $30

C. CARTER, Syracuse, N.Y. Wooden toothing plane. Auct. $55

CASEY & CO., Auburn, N.Y. toothing plane in mint condition. Dlr. $45

MARTIN DOSCHER, New York. Short, coffin-shaped toothing plane with 2⅛ in. wide cutter. Perfect. Dlr. $40

GABRIEL 18th-Cent. English toothing plane with Sorby iron. $35

GREAVES & SONS boxwood toothing plane with ebony strike button. $90

GREENSLADE coffin-shaped toothing plane with 2 in. cutter. $30

J. H. LAMB, New Bedford coffin-shaped beechwood toothing plane in perfect cond. $32

N. S. PAULDING McLEAN coffin-shaped toothing plane $44

D. MALLOCH, Perth. Hardwood toothing plane with 3 cutters. Coffin-shape 7 inches overall. $55

JOHN MOSELEY & SON, 54-55 Broad St., Bloomsbury, London. Toothing plane with 2 inch wide cutting iron. $26

OHIO (early mark) No. 30 beechwood toothing plane in mint condition. $40

SANDUSKY TOOL CO. coffin-shaped beechwood toothing plane. $39 No. 36 (circa 1925) in excellent cond. $45

T. E. SMITH, Pawtucket, R.I. coffin-shaped beech toothing plane 2⅛ inches wide. $27

A. J. WILKINSON, Boston. Coffin-shaped beechwood toothing plane with 2 in. cutter. $40

UNMARKED toothing planes are offered in the $15 - $45 range by tool dealers.

TRYING PLANES According to Alvin Sellens only two American makers are known to have ever used the term "Trying Plane". It is often loosely applied, by Europeans, to any jointer-type bench plane of 20 to 30 inches in length.

VIOLIN MAKER'S planes also fall into the Thumb Plane grouping. The one below is less than 1¾ inches long and was sold in five sizes with choice of flat or convex sole.

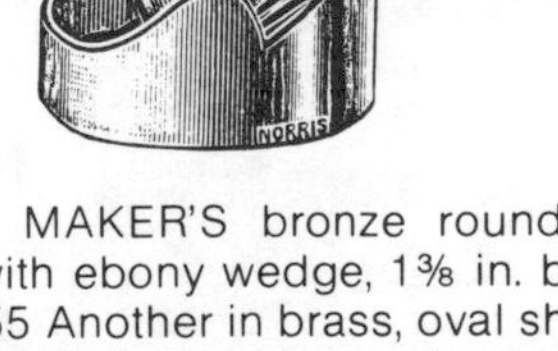

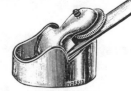

VIOLIN MAKER'S bronze round-sided plane with ebony wedge, 1⅜ in. bottom. Auct. $55 Another in brass, oval shape, 2 inches overall. German-made. Auct. $75 "Preston" gunmetal, round bottom & sides. 1¾ in. long. Auct., London, 1985 $350

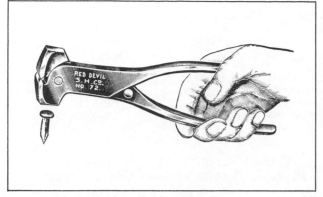

Cutting Nipper & Hammer

PLIERS (spelled "Plyers" in 19th century tool lists) have not yet caught the fancy of tool collectors and can still be picked up at bargain prices. They are usually lumped together in box lots at tool auctions and often go for less than a dollar per item. The exceptions are Keen Kutter and Winchester brands which have appeal to specialist collectors willing to pay from $15 - $30 for nicely imprinted items in fine condition. Our advice to beginning collectors is to seek out pliers in unusual sizes and shapes and those with 3 or 4 functions, such as a combination plier, hatchet, screwdriver and hammer. Also be on the lookout for early handmade examples, especially those which have been forged from old files or bear a distinctive hallmark.

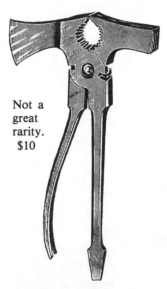

Sargent & Co. Gas Pliers, 6 to 12 inch, cast steel. (circa 1884)

Lamp Carbon Pliers   (circa 1900)

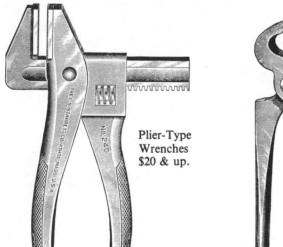

Plier-Type Wrenches $20 & up.

Starret Patented Expansion Pliers (circa 1913)

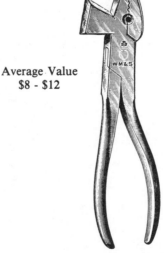

Average Value $8 - $12

Carpenter's Pliers (circa 1880-1910)

Leatherworker's Pliers British made

Not a great rarity. $10

Combination Hatchet, Hammer, Pliers, Wirecutter & Screwdriver

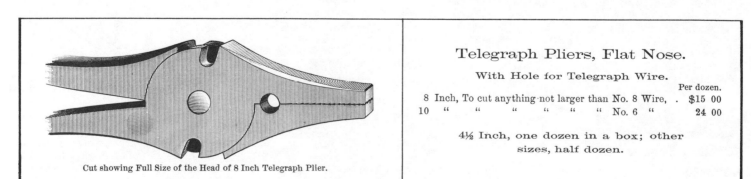

Cut showing Full Size of the Head of 8 Inch Telegraph Plier.

Telegraph Pliers, Flat Nose.

With Hole for Telegraph Wire.

		Per dozen.
8 Inch, To cut anything not larger than No. 8 Wire, .		$15 00
10 " " " " " " No. 6 "		24 00

4½ Inch, one dozen in a box; other sizes, half dozen.

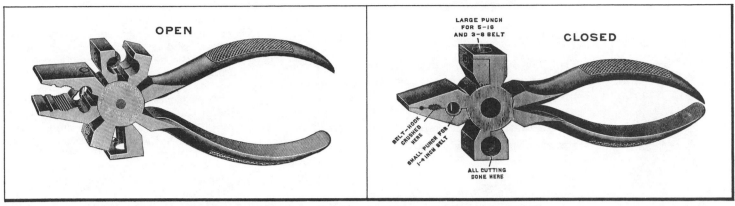

OPEN

CLOSED

LARGE PUNCH
FOR 5-16
AND 3-8 BELT

BELT-HOOK
CRUSHED
HERE

SMALL PUNCH FOR
1-4 INCH BELT

ALL CUTTING
DONE HERE

Combination Machinery Belt Punch, Cutter and Pliers, (circa 1900).

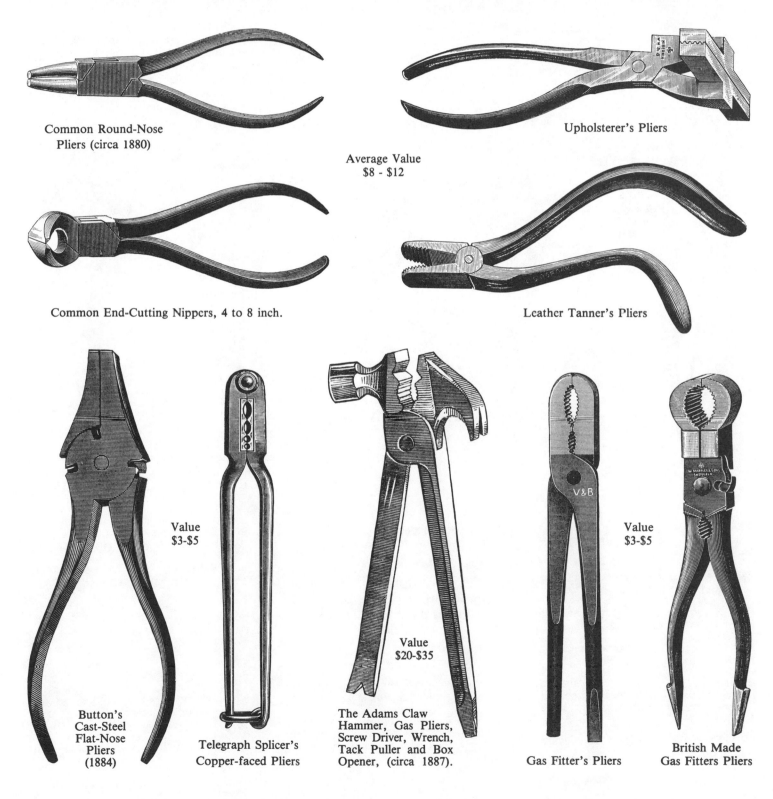

Common Round-Nose
Pliers (circa 1880)

Upholsterer's Pliers

Average Value
$8 - $12

Common End-Cutting Nippers, 4 to 8 inch.

Leather Tanner's Pliers

Button's
Cast-Steel
Flat-Nose
Pliers
(1884)

Value
$3-$5

Telegraph Splicer's
Copper-faced Pliers

Value
$20-$35

The Adams Claw
Hammer, Gas Pliers,
Screw Driver, Wrench,
Tack Puller and Box
Opener, (circa 1887).

V&B

Value
$3-$5

Gas Fitter's Pliers

British Made
Gas Fitters Pliers

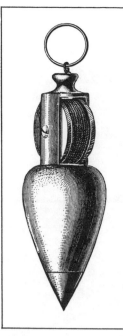

ADJUSTABLE PLUMB BOBS.

These Plumb Bobs are constructed with a reel at the upper end, upon which the line may be kept; and by dropping the bob with a slight jerk, while the ring is held in the hand, any desired length of line may be reeled off. A spring, which has its bearing on the reel, will check and hold the bob firmly at any point on the line. The pressure of the spring may be increased, or decreased, by means of the screw which passes through the reel. A suitable length of line comes already reeled on each Plumb Bob.

PRICES.

No.					Each.
1.	(Small) Bronze Metal, with Steel Point			....	$1 50
2.	(Large)	"	"	"	....	1 75
5.	(Large) Iron	"	"	"	....	1 00

1879 Advertisement by The Stanley Rule & Level Co.

Vintage PLUMB BOBS are avidly sought after by tool collectors of every stripe. What display of old carpenter's tools would be complete without a polished brass bob hanging overhead?

As you can see by the catalog cuts below, plumb bobs came in many shapes and materials. Sizes vary from as small as a thimble to as large as a turnip. Cast-iron, steel, lead, brass, bronze, wood, and pottery specimens all abound.

Dating precisely is almost impossible. Stanley's adjustable reel-top model first appeared in catalogs of the 1870's and was sold for half a century. Many European and English designs remained unchanged for just as long.

Pricing, at first, seems a hit-and-miss proposition, but careful observation bears our the fact that fine, intricately-turned brass examples of British make usually bring top dollar.

Most collectors are looking for plumb bobs in mint condition.

Value
$10-$20

Value
$4 - $8

Cast Lead
12 to 18 oz.
(Sold for 50¢
ea. in 1903)

Value
$20-$40

20th Century
Nickle Plated
Iron. 6 to 18 oz.

Brass, All Purpose Type.
2 to 24 ounce sizes
were produced

"Perfect" Surveyors
3 to 8 oz. Bronze
(Circa 1880)

"Perfect" Mechanics
3 to 8 oz. Bronze
Plumb Bob (1880)

BRASS pencil-shaped plumb bob 13 inches long with steel point. Weighs 4 lbs. Auct. $65

BRASS plumb bob with reel built into top, unmarked. Auct. $65

BRASS turnip-shaped 14 oz. mason's plumb bob. Auct. $65 Dlr. $85

BRASS acorn-shaped giant 4½ lb. plumb bob 6 inches long. Dlr. $100

BRONZE 18th-Century cone-shaped plumb bob with turned knob at each end. 5 inches long, moss green patina. Auct. $35 Dlr. $195

DIETZEN brass plumb bob in surveyor's leather case, 5½ in long Dlr. $15 - $25

IRON pear-shaped 3¾ inch plumb bob with brass screw-top. $45

JAS. A. GAFFNEY & CO., New York. Hexagonal brass 3¾ inch plumb bob. $15

GOODELL PRATT cylinder-shaped nickel plated brass plumb bob 5 inches long. $15

GUNMETAL acorn finial type, decorative British plumb bob 4¾ in. long. Auct. $95

IRON utility-type, conical-shaped, cast iron plumb bob 6 inches in length. $15

MASON'S 74 oz. brass turned-milled ornate beet-shaped Victorian plumb bob, Sold at auction in London recently for $210

POTTERY redware plumb bob from Pennsylvania, 4¾ inches tall. Dlr. $350

POSTS No. 12 brass screw-top plumb bob, long and narrow tapered, 5¾ inch. $15

SARGENT No. 206 hexagonal steel plumb bob with brass screw-top. 3½ in. overall. $10

STANLEY No. 1 reel-top bronze 3½ inch plumb bob with steel point. Auct. $110

STANLEY No. 2 polished bronze adjustable 4¼ inch reel-top plumb bob, with 1874 patent date. Auct. $85

WOODEN plumb bob in shape of a toy top with steel point. Acorn finial. 3½ in. $20

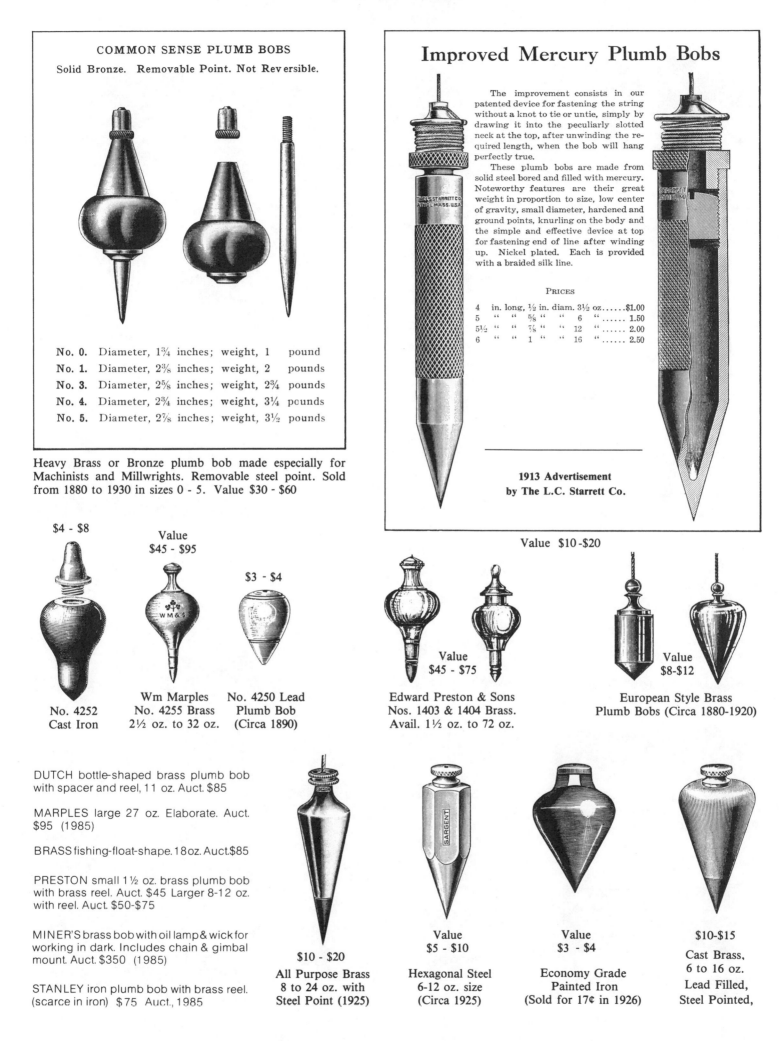

COMMON SENSE PLUMB BOBS
Solid Bronze. Removable Point. Not Reversible.

No. 0. Diameter, 1¾ inches; weight, 1 pound
No. 1. Diameter, 2⅜ inches; weight, 2 pounds
No. 3. Diameter, 2⅝ inches; weight, 2¾ pounds
No. 4. Diameter, 2¾ inches; weight, 3¼ pounds
No. 5. Diameter, 2⅞ inches; weight, 3½ pounds

Heavy Brass or Bronze plumb bob made especially for Machinists and Millwrights. Removable steel point. Sold from 1880 to 1930 in sizes 0 - 5. Value $30 - $60

Improved Mercury Plumb Bobs

The improvement consists in our patented device for fastening the string without a knot to tie or untie, simply by drawing it into the peculiarly slotted neck at the top, after unwinding the required length, when the bob will hang perfectly true.

These plumb bobs are made from solid steel bored and filled with mercury. Noteworthy features are their great weight in proportion to size, low center of gravity, small diameter, hardened and ground points, knurling on the body and the simple and effective device at top for fastening end of line after winding up. Nickel plated. Each is provided with a braided silk line.

PRICES

4	in. long, ½ in. diam. 3½ oz	$1.00
5	" " ⅝ " " 6 "	1.50
5½	" " ⅞ " " 12 "	2.00
6	" " 1 " " 16 "	2.50

**1913 Advertisement
by The L.C. Starrett Co.**

$4 - $8

Value $45 - $95

$3 - $4

No. 4252 Cast Iron

Wm Marples No. 4255 Brass 2½ oz. to 32 oz.

No. 4250 Lead Plumb Bob (Circa 1890)

Value $10 -$20

Value $45 - $75

Edward Preston & Sons Nos. 1403 & 1404 Brass. Avail. 1½ oz. to 72 oz.

Value $8-$12

European Style Brass Plumb Bobs (Circa 1880-1920)

DUTCH bottle-shaped brass plumb bob with spacer and reel, 11 oz. Auct. $85

MARPLES large 27 oz. Elaborate. Auct. $95 (1985)

BRASS fishing-float-shape. 18 oz. Auct. $85

PRESTON small 1½ oz. brass plumb bob with brass reel. Auct. $45 Larger 8-12 oz. with reel. Auct. $50-$75

MINER'S brass bob with oil lamp & wick for working in dark. Includes chain & gimbal mount. Auct. $350 (1985)

STANLEY iron plumb bob with brass reel. (scarce in iron) $75 Auct., 1985

$10 - $20

All Purpose Brass 8 to 24 oz. with Steel Point (1925)

Value $5 - $10

Hexagonal Steel 6-12 oz. size (Circa 1925)

Value $3 - $4

Economy Grade Painted Iron (Sold for 17¢ in 1926)

$10-$15

Cast Brass, 6 to 16 oz. Lead Filled, Steel Pointed,

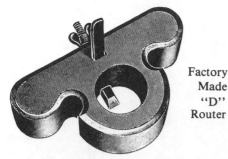

Factory Made "D" Router

ROUTERS came in many sizes and shapes in both wood and metal versions. Their basic function was to clean, or plane, the bottom surface of recesses or grooves.

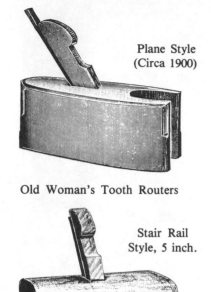

Plane Style (Circa 1900)

Old Woman's Tooth Routers

Stair Rail Style, 5 inch.

Most factory-made wooden routers are from Europe or the British Isles. American craftsmen usually fashioned their own routing tools, often from a scrap of stair rail moulding.

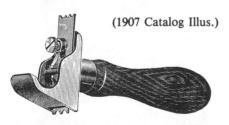

(1907 Catalog Illus.)

Stanley No. 69 Hand Beader. This very scarce model appears only in catalogs issued between 1898 and 1917.

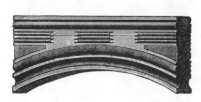

Typical example of work done by Stanley Hand Beader

A. F. BAILEY draw knife-shaped router 16 in. wide. Center portion U-shaped with right and left hand cutters on either side. Turned wooden handles. $89

J. BRADFORD (Portland, Me. 1849-1875) beechwood stair rail router/moulder with 2½ inch wide blade and plane-style wooden wedge. Dowel turned handles. Auct. $220

BRASS casting, resembles Stanley No. 71½. Twin turned handles. Dlr. $30 Another with open throat, probably reproduced from factory-made variety. $38 Brake pedal-shaped closed-throat brass router. $40 Loop-handled coachmaker's brass router. Auct. $50-$70

BUCK, 242 Totenham Ct. Rd. spoke shave-shaped 15 inch wooden double side rebate router with cast iron fence. $75. Carriage moulding router. Auct. $15

CARRIAGE MAKER'S unmarked wooden grooving routers, common single-blade style without fence. 16 inches long. Auct. $15 With fence. $17-$20 Double cutter type. Dlr. $45 up.

COACHMAKER'S dark beechwood snaggle-tooth router with iron sole and fence. Dlr. $37

COACHMAKER'S straight handled wooden routers with brass wear plates and adjustable fences. Auct. $30-$35 ea. With two cutters. Dlr. $65-$100

COACHMAKER'S yoke-style double router with 6 inch throat, 16 in. overall. Auct. $40-$400 Dlr. $100-$185 with brass trim.

COACHMAKER'S fine and early Pistol handled beechwood or mahogany routers with gunmetal fences, unmarked English. Auct. $400-$480 per matched pair.

D-STYLE small closed-throat wooden routers $25-$35 Larger, more elaborate D-routers up to 10 inches. $50 - $60

German Made D-router. Hand carved fruitwood with 2 circular knobs. Auct. $85

DRAW KNIFE Style routers with 1 or 2 inch wide blade at center of wrought bar with draw knife-type pull handles. $35-$65

G. EASTWOOD coachmaker's pistol router (see illus. pg. 165) Auct. London, $180

R. FAIRCLOUGH & CO., Liverpool. Boxwood handrail shave/moulder, 12 in. long. Dlr. $135

J. & J. GIBSON, Albany. (3) pc. set of coachmaker's routers in light oak. Includes 1 yoke type. Dlr. $345

GLEAVE, Oldham St., Manchester. Factory-made old woman's tooth router 5¾ in. wide. $40

W. GREENSLADE, Bristol. 6½ inch wide old woman's tooth type router. $40

GRIFFITHS rail-shaped router. Auct. $21

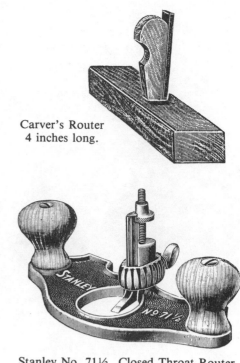

Carver's Router 4 inches long.

Stanley No. 71½ Closed Throat Router (1907 Catalog Illus.)

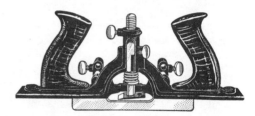

Stanley No. 171 Door trim Router. Scarce tool, produced from 1911 to 1935.

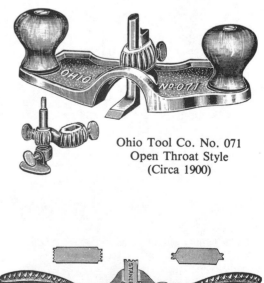

Ohio Tool Co. No. 071 Open Throat Style (Circa 1900)

Stanley No. 66 Universal Hand Beader. 11½ inches long. Offered continuously from 1886 to 1942 with 6 double-end cutters.

Double Pistol or Yoke Shape

GREENSLADE rail-shaped old woman's tooth router. Auct. $21

F. HAWKINS straight-handled oak double-ogee router. Dlr. $50

JIGGER or Side Router, lawn mower handle shape, 20 inches long. $48

KEEN KUTTER flat bed twin-handled metallic router in style of Stanley No. 71. KK Nos. 171 & 171½ Dlr. $60-$90

KING & COMPANY, Hull. 5½ inch old woman's tooth router. $35
Another King router, but in plane-shaped coffin style with open front. $50

JOSIAH KING, N.Y. 373 Bowery. Carriage maker's double pistol grip yoke-shaped beech router with 2 irons and adjustable fences. Perfect original condition. Auct. $175

W. MARPLES & SONS old woman's tooth round-front beechwood router. Auct. $15

MATHIESON rail-shaped old woman's tooth router. Auct. $21

MATHIESON Nos. 1 & 2 double-bladed iron ovolo-style routers along with a pair of brass tipped sash templates and a scribing gauge. (5 pcs.) Auct. $125

MILLERS FALLS No. 67 Black japanned router with red hardwood handles. $22-$37 No. 77 nickel plated, flat bed type, closed throat router, wooden knobs. $45

JOHN MOSES, London. Old woman's tooth router. Auct. $21

C. NURSE & CO., London. Old woman's tooth router. Auct. $20 Dlr. $45

OHIO TOOL CO. No. 071 nickel plated slab-style iron router with twin knobs. $23

OLD WOMAN'S TOOTH routers in elephant foot or rail style. Unmarked. $15-$35. Signed $25-$45. Boxwood $75.

EDWARD PRESTON & SONS single-handled iron stringing router 10½ inches long. Auct. $45. With dble. fence & 4 cutters $75. Wooden routers w/fence. Auct. $22

PRESTON'S No. 1386 Improved iron circular rabbeting and fillister router. $40-$60 No. 1387A iron sash router with twin blades, ovolo. Auct. $16-$30 No. 1388P iron quirk router 12 inches in length, has knurled top adjusting screw. $50-$90 Other Preston quirk-style routers: With 2 fences $65 With 3 fences $75 No. 1389 circular bead router. $49 No. 1393P adjustable hand reeder. $55 ($75 with all 3 orig. fences). No. 1399P flat bed-style with twin wooden knobs. Auct. $56 No. 2500P flat rectangular-framed metal router with 2 wooden knobs, 3 cutters, 2 fences and a depth stop. Auct. $65

Coachmaker's routers were sometimes used to actually form certain moulding shapes, such as beads, as well as for clean-up chores. The yoke-shaped double pistol router could cut on either the push or pull stroke.

Pistol Router

Scratch Tool with Fence

Improved Square Router

Beading Router, double-iron

Fence or Grooving Router

London Pattern Fence

Preston's Iron Sash Router, Lamb's Tongue

Preston's Iron Quirk Cutter

PRESTON'S IMPROVED circular rabbeting and fillister router. Japanned iron, 11 inches long with ¾ in. wide flat end blade. 2 fences. Auct. $30 Dlr. $60

PRESTON'S PATENT iron moulding tool 5 in. with mouse ear handles cast in. Dlr. $45

D. P. SANBORN, Worcester, Mass. double-bladed carriage maker's router with straight rectangular wooden stock, 2 wedged cutters on either side of nose type fence. $45

SARGENT No. 62 nickel plated router with two wooden knobs. Circa 1915. $25-$35

SCRATCH STOCK Pat 1885 nickel plated steel router with turned rosewood handle and egg-shaped front knob. Really a scraper blade holder for simple mouldings. $35

G. E. SPARKLIN cast iron D-router with twin wooden knobs. $25

SPEIGHT old woman's tooth router of British make. Auct. $20

SQUIRREL TAIL coachmaker's 8 inch long grooving router with steel wedge. Auct. $175

STANLEY No. 66 Universal hand beader with one fence missing. $35-$45

STANLEY No. 69 single-handled hand beader. Dlr. $695-$850 Auct. $500-$1,200

STANLEY No. 71 nickel plated cast iron slab-style router with 2 turned beechwood knobs. In production from 1885 thru 1973. $35-$45 No. 71½ closed throat model. $25-$40

No. 171 Door trim router. Auct. $170-$200

No. 271 rectangular shaped nickel plated router about 3 inches overall. Made from 1926 to 1975. Average specimen brings $15 to $25. Near mint, in orig. box. $55-$65

STRINGING ROUTER English made adjustable iron router for cutting narrow inlay band recesses in cabinet work. One iron handle is raised. $32

CHARLES TAYLOR scratch stocks. Set of (3) mahogany moulding routers 6 inches long, for cutting bead & cove pattern. Dlr. $275

ULMIA closed throat beechwood D-router. Auct. $25

VARVILL & SON, York. Beechwood lambs tongue ovolo router for circular work. Brass fence. Auct. $52

WINCHESTER No. 3070 metallic router, advertised recently for $90

WINDSOR, (Vermont) 1885 patent Beading Router, lawn mower handle shape with brass protractor-style center section. Black stained beechwood handles. $100-$165

ROUTERS, SCRAPERS, SHAVES & PLANES SOLD BY J.P. BITTNER AT KEENE, NEW HAMPSHIRE TOOL AUCTION.

1. TIGER MAPLE and Scroll Carved wooden routers. (2) pcs. $140

2. WITCHET or ROUNDER. Factory made, stamped D.R.P. No. 13202. Original and complete with matching wood clamp. $200.

3. MITER JACKS of superior grade, in tropical woods. (3) pcs. $220

4. WOOD SCREW BOXES & TAPS. Lot of (5) pieces, ½ in. to 1 inch. $135

5. DOUBLE PISTOL ROUTER. Couch-builder's yoke-shaped style. Unblemished. $400

6. COACHBUILDER'S ROUTERS. Set of (4) in birch and beech, one with wheel guide. $80

7. LOT OF (6) more Coachmaker's wooden routers. Clean assortment. $195

8. SPOKE SHAVES by D. Flather & Son, Sheffield and Irving How Co., N.Y. (2) $60

9. SCRAPERS. Fruitwood with bone wear inserts. Lot of (3) $60

10. INSTRUMENT MAKER'S CLAMP, stamped J. Stamm, Mount Joy, Lan. Co. Pa. $130

11. GROOVING PLANE WITH J.N. Crown stamp. Closed handle. Cuts 2½ in. depth. $75

12. BENCH ACCESSORIES Lot of (3): square stop, adjustable stop, and round shank hold down. $45

13. SHOOT BOARD & PLANE. Craftsman-made unmarked 34 inch plane & fixture. $105

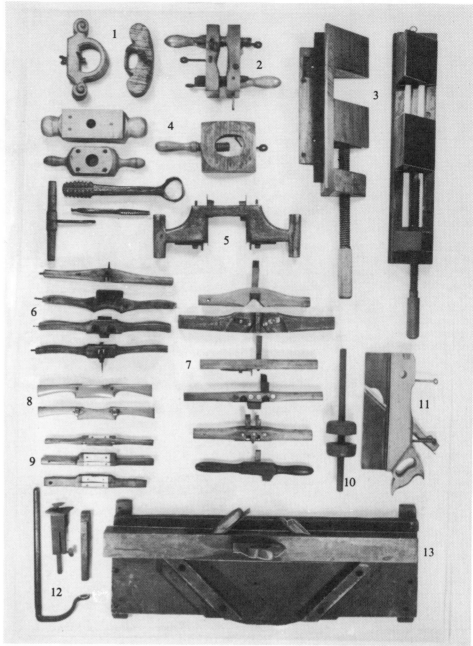

J.P. Bittner Antique Tool Auctions

Williams Pattern Improved Jiggers and Side Routers.

Hockley Abbey Works
BIRMINGHAM, England.
ESTABLISHED 1784 • NEW WORKS 1870

JOHN RABONE & SON was established in 1784 and formally adopted the above name in 1852. A second son apparently came into the firm in 1883 when the name was changed to John Rabone and Sons. Most importantly however is the fact that this family business soon became the world's largest and most respected producer of rules. Spirit levels were also manufactured at the factory which was merged with Chesterman Co. Ltd. in 1963. Tools produced since then are marked Rabone Chesterman.

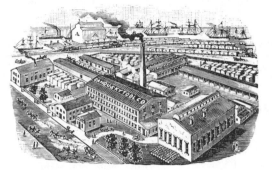

The SANDUSKY TOOL COMPANY of Sandusky, Ohio was founded in 1868 and rapidly overtook the Columbus based Ohio Tool Co. in plane production. By 1885 a full line of wood and metal planes was being produced by Sandusky which could be cross referenced with those of the Ohio, Auburn, Chapin, and Greenfield tool companies. An extensive variety of hoes and farm machinery helped the company survive until 1926 when it was purchased by American Fork & Hoe. (Now True Temper Inc.)

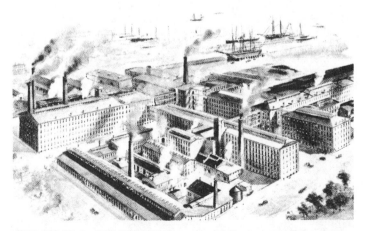

SARGENT & COMPANY first operated as a small hardware jobber out of New York City under the ownership of Joseph Sargent and two brothers. When their major Connecticut based source folded with the panic of 1857 the brothers left New York and eventually established a hardware and lock manufacturing plant of their own in New Haven. Planes and rules were purchased from outside suppliers (such as H. Chapin of Pine Meadow) until the 1880's when Sargent had grown to employ over 1,700 workmen. By the year 1925 Sargent had matched Stanley's output plane-for-plane and even managed to add a few new models of its own design. World War 2 brought an end to hand tool production by Sargent & Company but they continue to this day as one of the largest producers of locks, keys & builder's hardware.

The STANLEY RULE & LEVEL COMPANY was the result of an 1854 partnership agreement between Thomas Conklin, a rule manufacturer of Bristol, Conn. and hardware business veterans Augustus and Timothy Stanley of nearby New Britian. The fledgling firm was first named A. Stanley and Company. 36 short months later The Stanley rule and Level Co. was officially capitalized at $50,000 and merged with Thomas Hall and Francis Knapp's 4 year old plumb and level firm. Another Stanley brother, Henry, engineered this acquisition and was named president. Within 24 months an impressive trade catalog was issued by the new firm featuring an array of folding ivory and boxwood rulers as well as an extensive selection of levels, squares and marking gauges. An agressive acquisition program followed and in 1863 Stanley bought E.A. Sterns, a Vermont rule maker.

In 1869 Stanley made its wisest purchase, exclusive rights to manufacture Leonard Bailey's patented bench planes, spoke shaves and scrapers. At the turn-of-the-century Stanley was acknowledged as the world's largest producer of woodworking planes, having sold over three million units. Further lines were added and prices were lowered as production increased. Agressive advertising and acquisition soon eliminated all important competitors. Union Manufacturing sold Stanley its plane division in 1920. Gage Tool's self-setting plane was purchased the year before. Other firms acquired over the years include Hurley & Wood (screwdrivers), Roxton Tool & Mill (handtools), Humason & Beckley (hammers), Atha Tool (hammers). Eagle Square (steel framing squares), Hiram A. Farrand (steel tape measures) and North Brothers (Yankee drills).

SHEFFIELD, in Northern England, is still one of the most important industrial centers in all of Great Britain. Its riverfront location and ample fuel sources have contributed greatly to its pre-eminence as a cutlery manufacturing center since as early as the 14th century. The Cutler's Guild was organized there in 1624 and the first Bessemer process steel works was erected in Sheffield in 1859. American Indians were known to favor Sheffield-made butcher knives for scalping purposes and would willingly trade a good pony for such a useful tool. Merchants, jobbers, and common peddlers from all over Europe made at least an annual foray to Sheffield for all manner of metal trade goods. Knives, files, scissors, nutmeg graters, and edge tools were staple items as well as a vast array of silver and nickel plated notions.

When L.S. STARRETT began his little machinists' tool manufacturing venture in 1880 he had no idea that his Athol, Mass. firm would become the world's largest producer of precision hand tools within 2 decades. Starrett's 1913 catalog featured 320 pages filled with steel rules, squares, tapes, scales, calipers, micrometers, gauges, hack saws, wrenches, levels, speed indicators, and even a small builder's transit.

STEWART SPIERS of Ayr, Scotland invented the dovetailed construction steel plane. His deluxe, rosewood filled, metallic planes were produced from 1845 until well after Mr. Spiers death in 1899. His daughters and a former factory foreman continued operations until 1926. Spiers designs were widely copied on an individual basis and commercially acquired by another manufacturer, Thomas Norris, (who apparently purchased the rights in 1899).

(Top) Ivory Architect's Rule, signed JAMES GARGORY, 41 Bull St., Birmingham. German Silver trim. Bevelled inside edge. Two foot, two-fold ($200-$250). (Left center) E. A. STEARNS & CO. No. 57 ivory one foot, four-fold ($125-$175). (Center right) STEPHENS & CO. No. 91 ivory one foot, four-fold with German Silver trim ($100-$175). (Bottom left) E. M. CHAPIN No. 74 ivory caliper rule six inches in length ($150-$195). (Bottom right) J. RABONE & SONS, Birmingham. Ivory four inch caliper rule with German Silver fittings ($175-$220).

INTRODUCTION TO RULE COLLECTING

Jointed rulers have been around since the days of ancient Pompeii where a bronze example was recently unearthed. An Italian architect by the name of Scammozi made a two foot folding scale for his own use in the late 1500's. Thus began a professional fad which continued for almost 400 years.

England was the first commercial center of rule manufacturing. Over 250 firms are listed in 19th century Birmingham directories. John Rabone & Sons, established in 1784, was the largest of these concerns.

Belcher Brothers of New York City (1822-1877) was the first American firm to undertake the mass production of measuring sticks. Brass and German Silver (a copper alloy) were the most popular binding materials of the 19th century. Only a scant few presentation pieces were ever bound in actual sterling silver. Ivory was the most expensive material used in rule making but it had definite drawbacks because of a tendency toward shrinkage, staining and cracking with age. Boxwood has long been the favorite lumber of rule makers. Mature boxwood trees are harvested when they reach 6 or 7 inches in diameter. Most of the early supply came from Turkey and Russia, but by the turn-of-the-century Stanley Rule and Level was importing a Venezuelan variety with great success.

Automated production of folding rules was achieved in the 1860's by Stephens and Company at Riverton, Conn. (Lorenzo Stephens and his son had left the employ of H. Chapin to establish their own firm in 1853. The business flourished for 48 years before being sold to former employer Chapin, in 1901.)

A Stephens-designed machine dressed and marked eight inch boxwood slabs "Faster than the human eye could behold" reported Horace Greeley in 1872. Another contraption rolled out the cylindrical brass joints while yet another machine cut and spit out 40 binding pins in a single stroke. In 1870 Stephens was manufacturing 100 different rulers for a world wide market which it shared with The Stanley Rule and Level Company.

Stanley featured about 80 different boxwood and ivory folding rules in its 1860 catalog. Seven decades later, in 1929, Stanley purchased Chapin-Stephens and discontinued their ruler line while at the same time narrowing its own selection to 40 boxwood styles and eliminating ivory rules forever. By 1939 fewer than 2 dozen folding boxwood rules remained in the Stanley catalog. Inexpensive zig-zag rules (introduced in 1903), and push-pull steel tapes (1922), rapidly cornered the mass market for measuring devices.

Today you can still purchase a brand new brass-fitted boxwood carpenter's 3 foot, four-fold rule by Rabone Chesterman Ltd. for about $15.00 . . . but hurry, the company has threatened to stop making them because they are just too labor intensive to produce for a profit.

AMERICAN WOOD TYPE MFG. CO. brass typesetter's agate rule with T-top. Dlr. $12

J. ARCHBUTT & SONS, Lambeth (London) one foot, two-fold ivory sector rule. Auct. $75   Ivory parallel rule/protractor combination, 6 inches long. Auct. $185

J. ASTON, Birmingham, England (circa 1854) two foot, two-fold boxwood rule with slide and Routledge scale. Hand engraved figures. $95   Another by same maker, 3 foot, four-fold boxwood ironmonger's scale. Auct. $155   Carpenter's boxwood slide rule, brassbound two foot, two-fold. Auct. $50

BARADELLE, Paris. 18th-Cent. one foot, two-fold ivory rule with engraved silver joint. Dlr. $500

BASSET, New Haven, No. 53 two foot, four-fold boxwood rule with brass arch joint. $18

T. & W. BELCHER, New York rule makers (circa 1825-1850) no transactions reported.

BELCHER BROS., Makers, N.Y. (1850-1877) two foot, two-fold arch joint rule with slide. Auct. $45   Ebony parallel rule by same makers. $65   Shoe measure $25

BLACKSMITH'S folding brass rule 1 inch wide, two feet long. Washer/rivet hinge. $35

BLISS, N.Y. Brass parallel rule for nautical charts. Dlr. $125

BOARD STICK in form of walking cane, hand-stamped, 31 inch. $40

BOARD MEASURE, no maker's mark, square maple rod 24 inches long. $12-$24

N. E. BOX CO., Greenfield, Mass. Two foot, four-fold board scale. $38

T. BRADBURN & SONS, Birm., England (1862-1890) caliper rule 3 inches long, brass & boxwood. $35 Ivory scale, 6 inch, draftsman's. $90 Folding 1 ft. rule. $170

BRASS RULE, British Army blacksmith's two foot, one-fold. $30

BRASS RULE with Crown mark and 1889 date. ten-fold, 100 meter. $48

BUCK & HICKMAN, LTD., London, Improved Contraction Rule. Boxwood, two foot, three scales, brass tips. $120 Boxwood combination rule, level, plum with 2 enclosed vials. Auct. $100

J. BUCK, London. Architect's 6 inch ivory scale with inscribed protractor. Dlr. $72 Another by Buck, three foot, six-fold ivory architect's rule with German silver arch top and joints. Dlr. $565 One foot, four-fold ivory rule with German silver mounts. Auct. $87

H. CHAPIN, Union Factory. Brass-tipped beechwood yardstick. $18

CHAPIN STEPHENS No. 036 combination boxwood rule, level, square and bevel with protractor arch. Brassbound. In original tattered box, near mint. Auct. $225

CHAPIN STEPHENS CO. No. 36½ one foot, two-fold boxwood caliper rule. Brass square joint, tips and slide. Dlr. $18-$40

H. CHAPIN No. 39 two foot, two-fold boxwood rule. $25

THE C.S. CO. No. 55 one foot, two-fold boxwood rule with brass arch joint & tips. $35

E. M. CHAPIN No. 61 ivory two foot, four-fold rule with architect's scales. Auct. $210 No. 74 6 in. ivory rule. Auct. $300

CHAPIN STEPHENS No. 61 boxwood two foot, four-fold with square joint. $20-$25 No. 62 two foot, four-fold brassbound boxwood rule with sliding aluminum triangle attachment, dated Oct., '07. $42 Same rule minus attach. $15-$18 No. 62½ two foot, four-fold brassbound rule. $26

C. S. CO. No. 65½ one foot, four-fold, square joint brassbound rule. $22 No. 70 boxwood two foot, four-fold, brass square joint. $18 No. 79½ two foot, four-fold board measure, brass square joint. $90 No. 65 one foot, four-fold. Dlr. $24-$45

CHAPIN STEPHENS No. 84 two foot, four-fold boxwood rule, brass square joint and one side bound. $15 No. 88 ivory rule ⅝ in. wide, German silver arch joint, (sold for $32 a dozen in 1914). Dlr. asking $245 No. 96½ six inch, two-fold, one ivory and one brass leg. $55

H. CHAPIN No. 47 two foot, two-fold boxwood rule with brass slide. Auct. $85 Union Factory, walking stick/board measure 36 inches long, brass tips. Auct. $90 Pine Meadow, square rod 36 inch lumber rule in like new condition. Auct. $40

CHESTERMAN leather-cased surveyor's cloth measuring tape. Auct. $12

WEBSTER CLEGG'S 9-10-67 patent 18 in. paper cutter/rule combination. Auct. $25

E. G. COCKRELL & CO. Ltd., Manchester. Fine two foot, four-fold ivory architect's rule with German silver trim. Auct. $236

R. CHATTAWAY, Ivory Hatmaker's measure, 5 inches long plus extension slide. Dlr. $140

THOMAS CONKLIN, (circa 1854) New Britian, Conn. rule maker. No transactions reported.

DRING & FAGE, London. "Makers to The Customs." Wooden 48 inch telescoping Cotton-Bale bar caliper rule with brass fittings. Auct. $130 Timber slide rule, two foot boxwood with brass fittings. Auct. $66 Rule, boxwood two foot, four-fold with brass slide. Auct. $75 Hogshead measure in boxwood and aluminum, for Customs tax. Auct. $25

EBONY RULE, unsigned two foot, three-fold. Brass hinges and tips, raised white graduations. $65

W. ELLIOT, 268 High Holbron, London. Ebony parallel rule with center roller. Outer edges are ivory. Brass fittings. Auct. $110

E. S. & CO., Rockford, Ill., Pat. Oct. 24, 1876. Expanding inside measure, brass-bound boxwood, 12 inch. Dlr. $95

V. FABIAN, Milo Jct., Me. "Maine Log or Holland Rule," 52 inches long including handle and hook end. Auct. $65 36 inch calibrated log caliper with tally pegs. $40 Log rule with orig. paper label. 51 inches overall. $34 Fabians Saw Log Caliper with cribbage board holes in lower jaw. Mint condition. $125 Cordwood or Bark rule, 1 inch square by six feet long, hand-stamped with brass tips. $70

JAMES GARGORY, 41 Bull St., Birm. One foot, two-fold ivory sector rule with nickel silver arch joint and divider inserts. Mint. Auct. $200 Architect's rule with German-silver trim, two foot, two-fold. Dlr. $155

KERBY & BRO., New York, The Hydraulic Press Mfg. Co., Mt. Gilead, Ohio. Wooden barrel gauging rod, three feet seven inches long. $35

J. GLEAVE & SON, Manchester (British planemaker) ivory one foot, four-fold rule with brass fittings. Dlr. $195

Wm. H. GODFREY, rare Cork measure, all standard diameters. Auct. $210

F. M. GREENLEAF, Maker, Belmont, Mass. Wooden log caliper with heavy brass-lined jaws and sleeve joints. Auct. $200 Another with Cord measure, 48 inches overall. Auct. $525

GREENLEAF, Littleton, N.H. Log caliper with ten point spoked wheel. Brass trim on caliper jaw braces has diamond-shaped cut-outs. Auct. $500-$700

GUNTER, EDWARD. Seventeenth century inventor of a logrithmic slide rule for solving mathematic problems with a graduated scale.

W. & L. E. GURLEY, Troy, N.Y. Brass rule ¼ inch thick by 36 inches long. In fitted case. Auct. $150

HATMAKER'S RULE, boxwood 5 inches long plus brass extension slide, no maker. $32

HAZELTON, Contoocook, N.H. (1847-1924). Brass-tipped yard stick calibrated in ⅛ yd. increments. Auct. $65

R. B. HAZELTON, Maker, Contoocook, N.H. Iron jawed log caliper, hardwood bar with brass fittings. Auct. $140-$200 Lumber scale 24 inches long with tally holes and pegs. Auct. $85 Square board measure with eagle stamp. $20-$40

A. HOLTZAPFFEL & CO. Two foot, four-fold ivory rule with German silver trim. Dlr. $195 One foot, two-fold Sector rule with silver round joint. $150

R. HOOD, HAGGIE & SON, Newcastle. 4 inch boxwood and brass caliper rule for measuring diameter and circumference of rope. Auct. $100

H. R. HOYT, Goffstown, N.H. Solid cherry log caliper dated 1869. Auct. $50

NELSON & HUBBARD, Middleton, Conn. (circa 1851) rule makers. No transactions recorded.

HUBBARD HARDWARE CO., Middletown, Conn. (circa 1873-74). No transactions recorded.

HUBBARD & CURTIS, Middletown, Conn. (circa 1873-1874). No transactions recorded.

INTERLOX (also see Master Rule Co.) Auction lot of (3) sliding carpenter's rules in four, six and eight foot lengths. $75

JOHNSON'S No. 44 solid German silver four inch folding caliper rule. Pat. Jan. 8, 1907. Fine condition. $89 Six inch, two-fold with protractor joint. $45

W. S. JONES, London. Ivory sector rule, one foot, two-fold. Auct. $175

S. A. JONES & CO., Hartford, Conn. (circa 1841) two foot, two-fold boxwood rule with brass square joint. $25 Arch joint. $30

JORDON, Germany. Solid brass inside/outside caliper rule 4 inches long. $25 6 foot folding steel rule by Jordon $7

JUSTUS ROE & SONS, Patchogue, N.Y. Steel surveyor's tape on X-frame with handle. $30

KEEN KUTTER No. K610 two foot, four-fold boxwood ruler with brass square joint. $18-$22 No. 680 two foot, four-fold, round joint. $12-$18 K840 two foot, four-fold boxwood rule with brassbound outside edge. Orig. finish. $40

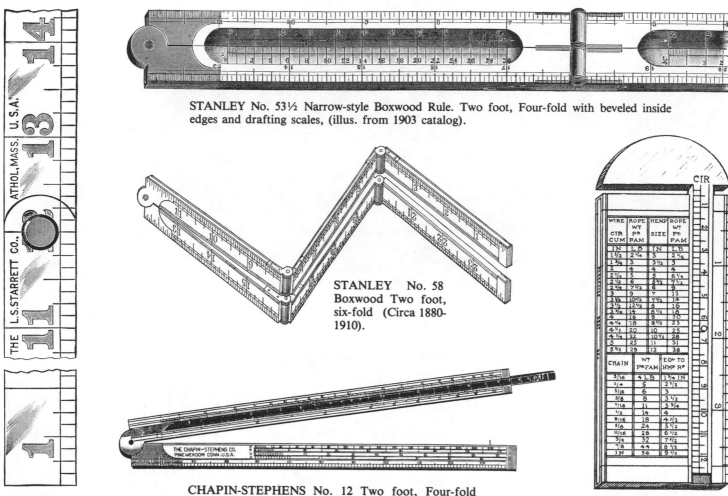

STANLEY No. 53½ Narrow-style Boxwood Rule. Two foot, Four-fold with beveled inside edges and drafting scales, (illus. from 1903 catalog).

STANLEY No. 58 Boxwood Two foot, six-fold (Circa 1880-1910).

CHAPIN-STEPHENS No. 12 Two foot, Four-fold Boxwood Rule with Brass Arch joint and Gunter Slide.

BLACKSMITH'S Two Foot Folding Brass Rule (Circa 1900).

British Made Rope Gauge (Circa 1890).

KERBY BROS., 51 Fulton St., N.Y. Boxwood shoe measure with U.S. & Paris scales. Ivory inlaid plates. Auct. $90

KEUFFEL & ESSEER CO., N.Y. No. 1758 parallel rule, brass, 18 inch with ivory center roller. Dlr. $125 "The Home Tape," leather cased steel tape. $24

KIRBY & BRO., N.Y. Boxwood and brass 5 inch caliper rule with wire and rope calibrations. Auct. $85

KUTZ, Maker, 164 Water St., New York. Two foot, two-fold boxwood rule with hand-stamped numbers. Brass trim and slide. $45

E. S. LANE, Upton, Maine. Greenleaf-style log caliper with matching measuring wheel. Complete, fine condition. Auct. $450

LOG CALIPER primitive handmade wedge-adjusted type 42 inches long. Scales are scratched on. Auct. $25 Maple log caliper dated 1880. Hand-stamped, no brass trim. Auct. $65 Another with bird's beak style narrow jaws and brass plates. Hand stamped. $75 Solid cherry wedge-arm log caliper with curved jaws and unusual 20 to 41 foot increment marks. $160 Spoked-wheel-type unmarked log caliper. Auct. $300-$450

LOWELL RULE CO., Lowell, Mass. Pat. 1884. Combination two foot, two-fold rule and bevel square, with Gunter slide. Auct. $95

LUFKIN tinsmith's "Magic Pattern Rule" circa 1890. In original box with labels and chart. Auct. $115 Lufkin two-foot, four-fold combination rule /level /inclinometer. Brass trim. Dlr. $95 No. 014 four inch caliper rule circa 1950. Like new. $9 No. 42 combination rule and ship carpenter's bevel square. Blades fold into handle. Brass tips. Mint condition. $22-$32 No. 171 six inch, two-fold caliper rule. Auct. $50 No. 281 Oil gauger's 33 foot steel tape measure on frame. Includes plumb bob. $30 Lufkin No. 372 one foot, two-fold boxwood and brass caliper rule. $15-$32 No. 373 one foot, two-fold boxwood and brass caliper rule. $20 No. 386 one foot, four-fold boxwood brass caliper Dlr. $25 -$45 English made Lufkin No. 651 two foot, four-fold boxwood rule. $18 No.703 two foot, two-fold boxwood rule. $25 No. 751 two foot, four-fold, pat. 1918. $12 No. 771 two foot, four-fold, brass bound rule, circa 1910. $15 Lufkin No. 781 two foot, four-fold boxwood and brass rule. $25 No. 861A two foot, four-fold draftsman's rule, circa 1925. $16 Lufkin No. 873L two foot, four-fold combination rule/scale/ protractor with built-in level. Brassbound. Auct. $75-$125 No. 873L two foot, four-

fold brassbound boxwood rule with protractor hinge and built-in level. $40 Lufkin No. 1085 two foot, one-fold brass blacksmith's rule. $26-$38 No. 1176 folding metal rule, 72 inches long. $15 Lufkin No. 1206 aluminum six-fold accordian-hinged brass-jointed rule. $20 No. 2062 two foot, three-fold combination level & rule with the word "Lufkin" visible inside the bubble vial. Auct. $75 No. 7135, six foot maple measuring stick. Auct. $15 No. 8205 patternmaker's ⅛ in. shrink rule. $12-$16 No. 8207 two foot shrink rule, ¼ inch scale. $10-$15 No. 8223, shoe measure, boxwood. $18 Lufkin No. 8632 two foot, four-fold boxwood combination rule/level/protractor, etc. Auct. $85

D. LYON, London. Four foot, four-fold boxwood drafting rule with double arch joints and brass tips. Dlr. $95

MASTER RULE MFG. CO. No. 106 Interlox folding zig-zag rule in fine cond. $20 Another, expansion-style, 60 inches long. $15 Brand new 72 inch slide model in original 1950's wrapper. Auct. $35 1906 Patent, 60 incher. $16

A. MATHIESON & SON two foot, four-fold ivory rule, German silver trim. $148-$295

J. B. MERRILL hand-stamped fruitwood board measure 26 inches long. Auct. $45

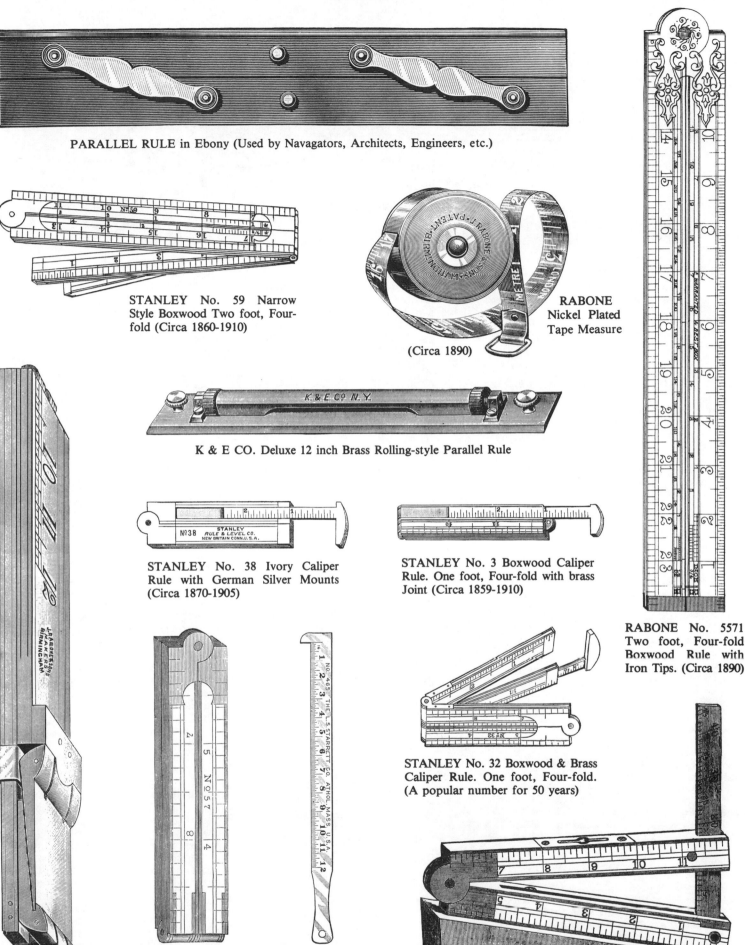

PARALLEL RULE in Ebony (Used by Navagators, Architects, Engineers, etc.)

STANLEY No. 59 Narrow Style Boxwood Two foot, Four-fold (Circa 1860-1910)

RABONE Nickel Plated Tape Measure

(Circa 1890)

K & E CO. Deluxe 12 inch Brass Rolling-style Parallel Rule

STANLEY No. 38 Ivory Caliper Rule with German Silver Mounts (Circa 1870-1905)

STANLEY No. 3 Boxwood Caliper Rule. One foot, Four-fold with brass Joint (Circa 1859-1910)

RABONE No. 5571 Two foot, Four-fold Boxwood Rule with Iron Tips. (Circa 1890)

STANLEY No. 32 Boxwood & Brass Caliper Rule. One foot, Four-fold. (A popular number for 50 years)

SHOEMAKER'S Stick (Circa 1890)

STANLEY No. 57 Deluxe Brass-bound Boxwood One footer.

BLACKSMITH'S Handled-style Hook-end Brass rule.

STEPHENS & CO. 036 Combination Rule and Level. One foot, Four-fold. Brassbound Boxwood. 1870 illus. Worth $1,000 in ivory with German Silver trim.

NARRAGANSETT MACHINE CO., Providence. Board caliper with sliding maple saw. Auct. $80

T. S. & J. D. NEGUS (New York, circa 1900) brass parallel rule 18 inches long with protractor scale. Dlr. $160

OCTAGONAL SCALES on rules are for use in laying out 8-sided projects up to 34 inches in diameter. On Stanley brand rules the middle scale is usually marked "M", and the edge scale "E".

PEABODY, Maker, New York. Two foot, two-fold boxwood rule with steel arch joint and tips. Auct. $37

B. PIKE & SONS, 166 Broadway, New York. Draftsman's ivory proportional rule 1 inch wide by 6 inches long. Scalloped ends. Dlr. $70

PRESTON tiny 3 inch boxwood and brass caliper rule. Dlr. $25 Shrinkage rule for foundry work, brass tips. Auct. $26 Caliper rule in boxwood and brass, 4 in. $35 Ivory two foot, four-fold. Auct. $247

E. PRESTON & SONS, England. Two foot, four-fold combination rule/spirit level and protractor. Boxwood with brass arch joint. Auct. $65 Steam Cylinder calculating rule, two foot, two-fold with slide. Auct. $135 Ivory one foot, four-fold with brass trim. Dlr. $150 Brass rule two feet long, two-fold. Auct. $20

JOHN RABONE & SONS leather cased cloth tape measure. Auct. $12 No. 1034 tailor's dowel-shaped 3 foot brass-tipped measuring rod. $15 Rabone No. 1 PM 11 solid brass Ullage rule. Auct. $53 No. 1167 two foot, four-fold boxwood Blind man's rule with extra large numbers. Brass trim. $29 Boxwood 10 inch rule with level inset. $60 Another 12 inches long. Auct. $65 No. 1190 combination rule and level with protractor scale. Two foot, four-fold. (Lots of this model offered in $65 - $90 range.) No. 1206 rope and chain gauge in boxwood and brass caliper-style 4 in. long. Dlr. $60-$75 No.1207, made in 1955, six and a half inch length. $50-$60 No. 1243 folding 24 inch brass rule dated 1943. $25 No. 1378 three foot, four-fold boxwood rule (darkened) $30 No. 2547 two foot, four-fold boxwood rule with brass

arch joint. Circa 1900. $25 Drafting rule with decorative Vulcan-pattern brass hinge. Two foot, two-fold. $80 Ivory one foot, four-fold by Rabone. Auct. $145-$195 Ivory architect's two foot, four-fold with German silver fittings, 7 different scales, beveled edges. Nearly mint cond. Dlr. $315 No.1119 boxwood four-fold. $70

RICHARDSON & CO. Makers, Middletown. Ohio. Madison's patent. Brass-tipped birchwood rule with rectangular cut-out near right end. Auct. $225

JOHN A. ROEBLING'S SONS CO. caliper rule 5 inches in length, wire rope scale. Auct. $225

ROOK & WINN, Boston. Boxwood straight rule 24 inches long, multiple scales, both sides. Auct. $155

G. B. SANBORN, Bristol, N.H. Log scale with peg-hole tally, 24 inch. $35

L. B. SARGENT, Lincoln, N.H., Maker. Deluxe 48 inch log caliper with brass fittings. Mint condition. Dlr. $175

S. SAVAGE, Middletown, Conn. (circa 1855) Boxwood two foot, two-fold with brass arch joint and Gunter scale. Auct. $155

The SECTOR, or French "Compas de Proportion" was invented in the 16th century. First used for surveying purposes it was later adopted by the Navy for navigation and gunnery calculation. The sector consists of a two-legged rule hinged at the top by a large round disk-joint. Each leg is engraved with graduated scales, tables, sines, tangents and secants. Sectors are used in combination with a pair of dividers to solve problems dealing with angles and ratios.

A. STANLEY & CO. rare early Stanley nearly identical to later No. 15 two foot, two-fold, brassbound with Gunter slide. Auct. $300 Another A. Stanley (pre 1857) two foot, four-fold ivory rule, brassbound with arch joint. Outside worn but readable. Auct. $600

STANLEY, London, 1885. Two foot, four-fold ivory rule with architect's scales. Auct. $275

STANLEY No. 1 boxwood two foot, two-fold with brass arch joint. First offered in 1859 catalog. This one is circa 1909. $50 Stanley No. 2 two foot, two-fold boxwood rule with octagonal scales. (circa 1870-1900) No transactions reported. Stanley No. 3 one foot, four-fold boxwood caliper rule with brass square joint and outside edge binding. Marked in ⅛ths & 1/16ths. (circa 1859-1910) No recent sales reported. Stanley No. 4 extra thin boxwood two foot, two-fold with brass square joint and frame plates. Appears in 1859 catalog, discontinued prior to 1929. None offered at auction, or by dealers. No. 5 two foot, two-fold, brassbound. Dlr. $30 No. 7 Blind man's large numeral boxwood two foot, four-fold with brass square top joint. (worn cond.) $12 Avg. $20 Near mint. $30 up. No. 12 two foot, two-fold boxwood rule with brass trim and Gunter's slide plus drafting and octagonal scales. (circa 1860-1910) $40-$60. No. 13 six inch, two-fold with caliper slide. (phased out prior to 1929 in favor of wider No. 13½) $20 Stanley No. 13½ two-fold, (appears in catalogs of late 1930's) $20-$40 No. 15 boxwood two foot, two-fold with brass trim and Gunter slide. Also has drafting and octagonal scales. (sold for half a century) $25-$45 No. 16 weights and measures scale on brassbound two foot, two-fold. (Near mint). Rare. Auct. $250 No. 17 blacksmith's brass two foot, two-fold pat. 7/31/06. Auct. $65 Another circa 1920-1935. $25 Stanley No. 18 manual training school-type boxwood two foot, two-fold with brass square joint. $20 No. 22 board measure, two-fold with brass square joint. $35-$55 No. 26 boxwood two foot, two-fold with octagonal scale. $35 Stanley No. 27 engineer's boxwood two foot, two-fold with Gunter's scale and octagonal & drafting calibrations. $40-$65 (Note: a No. 27 untrimmed maple economy two foot appears in late 1930's catalog for 20 cents retail) No. 30 thru 30½ A,B,C,D,E,F & G are two foot shrinkage rules with brass tips and assorted scales that allow for the cold-set shrinkage of various metals after casting. (sold for over 50 years) $15- $25 No. 31 is a much scarcer folding style pattern maker's shrinkage rule 24½ inches overall. (circa 1898-1910) Auct. $95-$100 No. 32 was popular for over 60 years. One foot, four-fold boxwood caliper rule with brass arch joint and caliper slide. $20-$35

Stanley No. 32½ one foot, four-fold arch joint, fully brass bound. 1 inch wide when folded. $20-$28   No. 34 brass-tipped maple manual training bench rule. $10-$18   No. 36 six inch, two-fold caliper rule with brass square joint. $19-$30   No. 36½ one foot, two-fold boxwood rule with caliper $20-$30   No. 38 ivory caliper rule six inches long. German silver trim. Dlr. $145   No. 39 one foot, four-fold ivory caliper rule. $175-$195 in fine condition. No. 40 one foot, four-fold ivory and German silver caliper rule sold for $3.70 retail from 1877 thru 1910. Recent auction price $160   Stanley No. 40½ six inch, two-fold German silver bound ivory caliper rule. Dlr. $150   No. 42 ship carpenter's bevel and rule combination with blades at either end was offered as late as 1929. $28-$48   No. 45 gauging rod for liquid measure to 120 gal. Maple, three feet long. $35-$45   Stanley No. 46½ board stick two feet in length with brass caps. Like new. Dlr. $25   Unmarked early example sold at auction for $75 (Mint cond.)   No. 47½ 3 foot long board stick. $25   No. 48 hickory octagonal board cane 3 feet long with hand-stamped numbers. $75-$100   Stanley No. 51 common two foot, four-fold boxwood rule with brass arch joint and middle plates. (sold thru late 1930's) $15   No. 52 two foot, four-fold with one side brassbound. Drafting scales. $35   No. 53 two foot, four-fold with brass arch top, unbeveled drafting scale. (circa 1859-1929) $22   Stanley No. 53½ two foot, four-fold, narrow-style boxwood rule with inside bevel drafting scales. $20-$35 (popular for 60 years).   No. 54 deluxe fully brassbound two foot, four-fold with inch and metric scales. Auct. $37   Stanley No. 57 one foot, four-fold brassbound boxwood rule phased out in late 1920's (mint cond.) Dlr. $75   No. 58 scarce six-fold two footer (circa 1880-1910) Auct. $180   No. 60 deluxe brassbound two foot, four-fold with double arch joint. $40   No. 61 economy model with square joint. $15-$25   No. 62 very popular model, full bound. Many of these offered by dealers from $15 to $35 depending upon condition.   No. 62C caliper version of No. 62, $35-$50   No. 62½ narrow, fully bound, square joint four-fold. 1880 model in fine cond. $75. 1920 type $20-$30.   No. 63 four-fold boxwood rule with brass square joint. Has drafting scales. (recent model). $28)   Stanley No. 64 four-fold with 8ths & 16ths graduations, was phased out in 1920's and sells at auction today for about $10.   No. 66½ three foot, four-fold was being produced as late as 1950 at the Shaftsbury Vt. plant. $10-$27   No. 66¾ fully brassbound three foot, four-fold. $25-$40, mint cond. Dlr. $95   No. 67 four-fold sold for $3.50 a dozen in 1910. $30-$40   No. 68 isn't worth much. Sells for $5-$15 today, (a big seller at 25¢ each in 1939).   No. 69 one foot, four-fold retailed at 15¢ each in 1909 catalog, $10-$20 by dealers today.   No. 70 two foot, four-fold with drafting scales was a popular model for over fifty years. Worth about 9 bucks on today's market.   No. 72½ fully bound version has been produced since the late 1800's. A 1920-35 version with sweetheart trademark might fetch $20-$30.   No. 75 appears in 1859 thru 1929 catalogs and was offered

recently for $26.   No. 76 two foot, four-fold fully brass-bound brought a dollar in 1929 and $20-$35 recently. Stanley's No. 77 is an extra strong double arch four-fold which was first offered in 1859 and phased out before 1929. Dlr. $75.   No. 78½ was advertised as Stanley's finest and longest wearing boxwood rule and sold for $1.40 during the depression years. $35-$65 today if you can find one.   No. 79 two foot, four-fold also had a board measure scale and was discontinued prior to 1929. fine $125-$175   No. 84 brass-bound. Fine. $25   No. 85 is ivory 2 ft. 4-fold $165-$295   No. 86 ivory Sold recently at auction for $250 Calibrated in 100ths of a foot.   No. 88 ivory four-fold is ⅝ in. wide when closed. $125-$175   No. 89 ivory rule has double arch top in German silver and full binding. Auct. $500   No. 92½ ivory rule sold for a dollar in 1900 and brings about $135 at auction today. Stanley No. 94 carriage maker's boxwood four foot, four-fold, fully brass bound, (circa 1898-1930). Auct. $50 Dlr. $65-$95   No. 95 ivory two foot, four-fold German silver bound arch joint rule with drafting scales (sold for $8.50 new in 1879). Auction, 1982. $450   No. 97 super-deluxe ivory two foot, four-fold with full German silver binding and double arch joint. Calibrated in 10ths, 12ths, 16ths and drafting scales. (circa 1859-1900) No transactions reported.   No. 136 boxwood inside/outside 4 inch caliper rule with brass jaws & slide, (circa 1935-1950). $15-$20   No. 136½ boxwood rule 5 inches long with caliper slide and brass tips. (circa 1950) $15 . Mint. $30   No. 163 boxwood two foot, four-fold $20   No. 170BE blindman's three foot, four-fold boxwood rule with bold numbers. (No transactions reported)   No. 173E three foot, four-fold circa 1929. This one marked "Damaged" by factory. $12   Stanley No. 240 maple extension stick with brass lugs. Set-screw slide allows adjustment to 4 feet. (Circa 1910-1939). Auct. $20 Dlr. $25-$35   No. 413 aluminum folding 3 foot rule patented in 1922. $15   No. 425 five footer, folds at 6 inch intervals. Alum. w/black enamel finish, brass trim. $22   No. 480 maple extension rule in 2 sections which expand to 8 feet. Auct. $45   No. 510 maple extension rule with two 5 ft. sections. $30.

L.S. STARRET No. 368 steel patternmaker's shrink rule 24 in. long. $15   No. 462 brass two foot, two-fold rule in mint condition. $26   No. 465 brass blacksmith's 12 inch hook end rule. Auct. $35 Dlr. $45

E.A. STEARNS (1838-1861, Brattleboro, Vt.) one foot, four-fold ivory rule. Auct. $170   No. 3 brassbound boxwood two foot, two-fold with arch joint and Gunter scale. Dlr. $50   Stearns No. 4 two foot, two-fold boxwood rule, as above but not bound. Auct. $40   No. 5 two foot, two-fold boxwood rule with brass slide, arch top and tips. Auct $150   No. 13 ironmonger's six inch boxwood caliper rule. $60   No. 14 builder's boxwood two foot, four-fold, fully brass bound. Has board foot scale (worn) Dlr. $65   No. 22 brassbound boxwood four foot, four-fold with arch joint. $60   E.A. Stearns No. 50 ivory two foot, four-fold (age yellowing) Auct. $130   No. 50B ivory two foot, four-fold with full German silver binding. (Near mint). Auct. $475   No. 51 $175

STEPHENS & CO., Riverton, Ct. (1864-1901) No. 17 two foot, two-fold brass-bound boxwood rule in fine condition. Dlr. $95   No. 22 brassbound boxwood two foot, two-fold with arch joint. Has board foot scales. Auct. $60   No. 26 boxwood two foot, two-fold slide rule with brass arch joint, plain tipped slide. Dlr. $40   No. 27 Gunter's scale, brassbound boxwood two foot, two-fold. Auct. $40   No. 28 engineer's brassbound boxwood two foot, two-fold with slide. Fine. Dlr. $120   L. C. Stephens & Co. No. 32 presentation-type tailor's boxwood three foot, four-fold with brass square joint and tips, (circa 1860-1864) $85   Stephens Co., Riverton, Ct. No. 036 combination rule/level/protractor, etc. One foot, two-fold with steel blade which folds out of one brassbound boxwood leg. Auct. $225 (Fine). Average cond. with some pitting and stain. $75-$150 (in ivory & silver. Auct. $1,000).   No. 65 board measure. Boxwood with brass binding. $40   L. C. Stephens & Co. No. 66 boxwood lumberman's rule with board feet on inside face. Two foot, four-fold. $60   No. 72½ brassbound boxwood two foot, four-fold. $25-$35   Stephens & Co., Riverton, Conn. No. 84 ivory and German silver two foot, four-fold. Dlr. $325   No. 89 ivory one foot, four-fold, narrow-style with brass mounts, (worn) Auct. $70

TAPE, MEASURE. Cloth tape 50 ft. long in brass-trimmed leather case. Common and not yet highly collectable. You will find these in the $5 to $15 range.

TEN FT. POLE carpenter's framing rule, six-sided with hand-marked increments. $150   Another 10 ft. rule. (You can't touch this one with less than $200.) Mid 19th-Cent. single-fold maple with a sliding brace on one leg. Brass fittings. Auct. $225

UPSON NUT CO., Unionville, Conn. (1889-1922) No. 15 brassbound boxwood two foot, two-fold rule with Gunter slide. Dlr. $85   No. 54 two foot, four-fold, brass-bound boxwood rule with arch joint. $20   No. 61 two foot, four-fold with brass square joint. (worn) $10   No. 63 ditto, (excellent) $16-$18   No. 70 ditto, $15   No. 84 ditto, $16   Un-numbered three foot, four-fold boxwood rule with brass arch joint. $22

J. WATTS, Boston. Two foot, four-fold boxwood rule with hand-stamped markings (very old, tired and worn) $15   A much nicer Gunter slide rule in boxwood with brass arch joint and stem. Auct. $115   A circa 1850 wine gauging rod by J. Watts, Boston. Four feet long. (3) offered in $50 to $100 range.

WILLIS THRALL, Hartford, Conn. (1844-1860), & SON (1860-1884). No trans-actions reported.

WINCHESTER No. 9532 one foot, four-fold boxwood caliper rule with brass arch hinge. Dlr. $35

YOUNGLOVE, Fitchburg, 1877. Hand-stamped maple, birch and cherry log caliper. Auct. $95   Another maple log caliper, walnut jaws, 44 in. overall. Dlr. $72

Sawyers of 1750 work with a pitsaw, bow-type crosscut and a framed ripping saw.

ACCORDING TO GREEK LEGEND the first saw was invented by Talus, a nephew of Daedalus who was the 1,200 B.C. equivalent of Leonardo DeVinci. (Uncle Daedalus was also credited with the invention of the hatchet, wimble brace, and level.)

Talus obviously inherited a good deal of his uncle's tool making talent. After creating the saw he went on to develop a woodworking lathe and later invent the first compass. Talus discovered the sawtooth principle while severing a soft tree limb with the jawbone of a large serpent. Legend goes that he reproduced the snake's teeth on a sheet of hammered iron—the rest is history.

From archeological excavations we know that saws were highly refined tools even in the days of Egyptian tomb builders. Early Roman saws had the "set" teeth of today's crosscut. In the late 1600's some types of wooden frame saws began to be replaced with wider-bladed saws whose hammer-hardened steel did not need the support of a stretcher frame. By 1750 modern back saws, with deep thin blades, reinforced by a heavy brass or steel back bar, had been developed.

Water and wind-powered saw mills, producing an up-and-down action, first appeared in France during the 12th-Century. Power saw mills were introduced in New England in the 1630's, but Great Britain's labor force would not allow such machinery in lumber mills until about 1820. (A mill built at Limehouse in 1760 was destroyed by an irate mob of sawyers soon after construction was completed). Steam-powered saws were finally put to use in 1793 and within fifty years giant circular blades were invented which whirled thru even the largest logs at 2,400 revolutions per minute. Old traditions do not die quickly among craftsmen however. Hardware catalogs of the 1880's offered circular saw blades side-by-side with the pitsaw variety of 100 years earlier.

C. A. ADAMS, Manchester, N.H. Hand saw. Auct. $25

E. C. ATKINS & CO. of Indianapolis, Indiana was founded in 1857 by Elias Atkins, a 3rd generation saw maker who left his family's Bristol, Conn. operation to head west where millions of acres of virgin forest were waiting to be felled. Young Elias started his humble venture in the trading post village of Indianapolis with little more than a shed, anvil, forge and hammer to his name. Within a few short years Atkins saws rivaled those of Henry Disston and Sons.

E. C. ATKINS steel backed saw with closed, carved, handle. 15 inches overall. Dlr. $20   Cross-cut hand saw 26 inches long (chipped handle). $12 Combination "93" pattern hand saw with widely spaced teeth for cutting green wood. $15   No. 54 "Silver Steel" 26 inch hand saw, comparable to Disston's best. $40   Stair builder's saw. $38   No. 51 sway-back hand saw, 5½ point, 28 inch. $22 No. 590 Docking saw with metal handle . $15

GEO. H. BISHOP, Flying horse trademark. 9 pt. hand saw marked "Hand Made". Dlr. $20   Double-sided back saw with depth gauge. Auct. $50 Comb. dovetail, rip & crosscut. $46

BOW SAWS are H-framed with a thin blade fastened between lathe-turned handles. The top of the frame is surmounted by a tension cord or threaded rod which tightens the blade. Medium and small examples have freely rotating handles that allow the blade to turn at any angle. These are also referred to as TURNING SAWS or WEB SAWS.

BOW SAWS, unmarked): Beech frame & octagonal handles, 10 in. blade. Dlr. $50   12 inch with round handles. $55 Ditto, but more graceful style. $65   Finer English examples with 12 to 20 inch blades and octagonal handles which are often boxwood. Dlr. $90 and up. Solid boxwood British made bow saw with carved loop tops and an ebony toggle stick. $175-$290 Cherry framed example with turned center span, brass ferrules and tension rod, 24 in. overall. Dlr. $150 Hickory lyre-framed bow saw with 16 in. long slotted tension stick. $65   Conventional American-made medium size bow saws with cord tops, various light hardwoods. $35-$50   Carved walnut with turned handles, 13 inch blade. Auct. $100

BUCK SAWS are rigid-type bow saws of rather plain, heavy, construction; usually with a rod and turnscrew type stretcher. They were made for the task of cutting small logs into firewood. Older varieties with side-mounted lever-blade tension-adjustment sell in the $20-$35 range.

BUCK stamped on tiny frame of Lancashire pattern hack saw with 4½ inch long blade. $75   Brass back saw with 1 x 2½ inch fine-toothed blade and 4 in. turned handle. $50 Mahog. fret saw. $195

BUCK & HICKMAN 1896. Lancashire pattern hack saw with 5¾ in. blade. $49

CHARLES BUSH, N.Y. Pat. Jan. 10, 1882 compass saw with pivot handle mounted at center of tapered and cupped blade. $75

CHAIN SAW four feet long with maple handles at each end. Dlr. $20

COLAMORE, Boston, Pat. 1852. Nice early buck saw. Auct. $17

CHAMPION one-man crosscut nearly 5 feet long, like new cond. Auct. $12

COLQUHOUN & CADMAN open handled 12 in. brass back saw. Dlr. $35

COMBINATION only mark on this combination hand saw, square, and straight edge rule. Dlr. $45

CONNEENCO, New Rochelle, N.Y. patented hack saw frame with turned wooden handle. Auct. $30

COPPER-BLADED Salt saw with coarse teeth and conventional open carved handle. Dlr. $55

CROSSCUT Timber saw 5½ feet long, two-man. Auct. $15 (Thousands available at this price.)

DELTA SPECIALTY CO., Milwaukee, Wisc. American Boy Scroll Saw, pat. Aug. 21, 1926. Cute little hand-crank table-top scroll saw, 8 x 11 inches overall. Dlr. $80

HENRY DISSTON began his saw making career as a 14 yr. old immigrant orphan boy, who bound himself over as a saw-maker's apprentice and became his employer's shop foreman 4 years later. In 1840 Henry was producing his own line of handmade saws and by 1856 "Henry Disston & Son" were winning gold medals in world wide competition with other manufacturers. The company's 1874 Keystone Saw Works plant covered 8 acres of ground in Philadelphia and employed 600 workers.

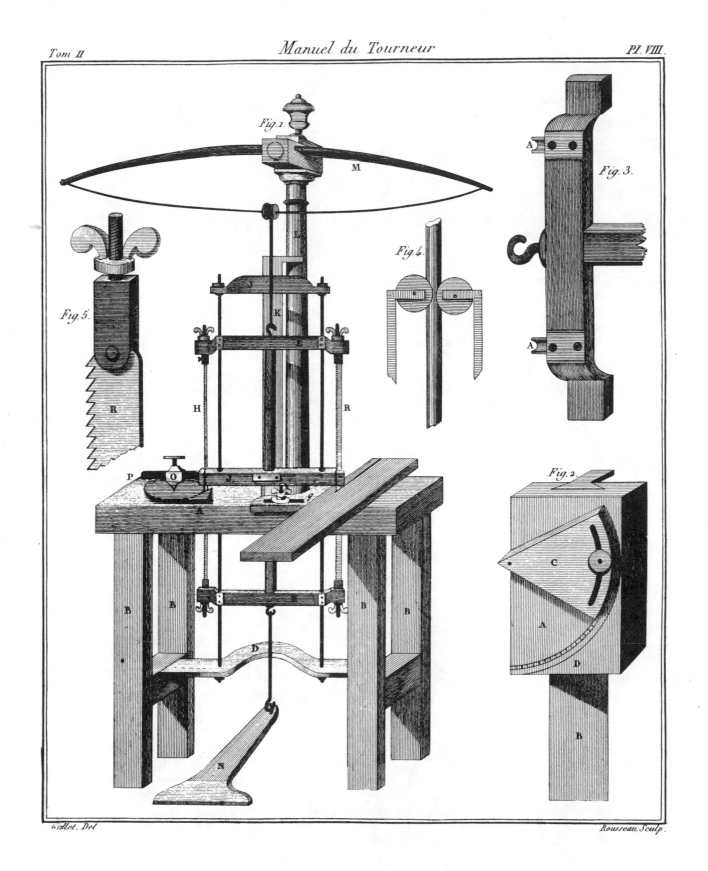

Tom II

Manuel du Tourneur

Pl. VIII.

Gillet. Del

Rousseau. Sculp.

A Double Bladed, Foot Operated Jigsaw of 1816

My friend Henry Aldinger and his collection of vintage foot-powered jigsaws.

(From left to right)

1. DEMAS COMBINATION LATHE AND SCROLL SAW. Mfg. in 1880 by A. H. Shipman.
2. FLEETWOOD No. 3 made by Trump Bros., Wilmington, Del. (1880-1900).
3. W. F. & J. BARNES No. 6 tricycle-style pedal machine, patented Mar. 1876.
4. MILLERS FALLS No. 387 sold for about $8.00 from 1895 to 1915.
5. HOBBIES No. A1 (which sold in England as late as 1930).
6. HOBBIES "O.K." another 20th century British jigsaw.
7. STAR BRAND (Millers Falls) circa 1885-1915 jigsaw with grinding wheel and bellows-type blower.
8. NEW ROGERS No. 1 also made by Millers Falls and probably the most popular Boy's saw of the era. Sold for $3.37 in Montgomery Ward's 1895 catalog.

JIGSAWS or SCROLL-SAW-MACHINES were extremely popular in the gadget crazed 1880-1900 era. A leading hardware dealer of the period wrote that most of these novelties were sold to parents to be used as holiday gifts for mechanically inclined offspring. An 1896 tool catalog dismisses them as "Toys that were gotten up to sell to boys and ministers of the gospel." Some of the heavier machines such as the Challenge, Empire and Victor brands, were designed for cabinet men, model makers, printers, jewelers, and similar craftsmen who needed jigsaws of larger capacity which were also suitable for close, accurate work on wood, bone, shell, and soft metal. Some of these pedal-powered wonders could slice thru three inch thick wooden slabs at 800 strokes a minute.

W. F. & J. BARNES, 1876 patent "Velocipeds" jigsaw with bicycle pedals mounted on flywheel. Mounted on cast iron floor stand. Light duty type with 18 inch throat. Auct. $80-$100   Dlr. $175

CRICKET foot-treadle and belt-powered cast iron tripod-mounted jigsaw sold by Millers Falls Co. (1886 price $2.50) Dlr. $145

DEMAS For 1880, by A. H. Shipman. Combination lathe and jigsaw. Complete with original tools, instruction book and patterns. Dlr. asking $600

EMPIRE heavy duty 1885 patent jigsaw with walking-action wooden foot pedals. Heavy cast iron stand and flywheel (good working cond.) Auct. $275

FLEETWOOD No. 3 Deluxe filigree-framed cast iron jigsaw (in near new cond.) Dlr. $400

LESTER IMPROVED Jigsaw and lathe combination, circa 1886. Cast iron frame and 15 inch flywheel. Ash arms, green and red orig. finish. Dlr. $250   (illus. below)

MILLERS FALLS cast iron jigsaw and lathe combination, 25 inches wide x 31 inches tall, on sewing machine-style base. Black with red pinstriping. Pedal and tool rest table are rectangular iron plates. Frame is filligree type. Dlr. $285

NEW ROGERS floor model pedal-powered jigsaw with iron frame and wooden blade arms. Auct. $65   Dlr. $125 (illus. below, left, with grind wheel attach.)

SEARS ROEBUCK unmarked single pedal foot-operated jigsaw on three-legged cast iron frame. Wooden blade bar, round work table. Auct. $100

STAR No. 387 by Millers Falls, circa 1885-1915. With grinding wheel attachment and built-in bellows on upper arm. Auct. $200

SENECA MFG. CO. "Rival" treadle powered, belt drive jigsaw on blue-trimmed, black cast iron stand 37 inches tall. Pat. June 12, 1877. Dlr. $150

TABLE MOUNTED tiny unmarked cast iron jigsaw with screw clamp. Approx. 8 x8 inches overall. Dlr. $25

TRUMP BROS. Wilmington, Del., pat. Dec. 12, 1876. Clamp-on table-top cast iron jigsaw with wooden arms. Dlr. $89

UNMARKED combination jigsaw and lathe, 20 inches wide. Large treadle plate is rectangular with circular filigree pattern. Cast iron sewing machine-style A-frame base. Wooden saw arms. Large flywheel, belt drive. Auct. $225

BARNES TOOL CO., Mfrs., New Haven, Ct. Hand-cranked table saw with foot treadle and jigsaw attachment. 30 inch dia. flywheel, cast iron frame.   Dlr. $850

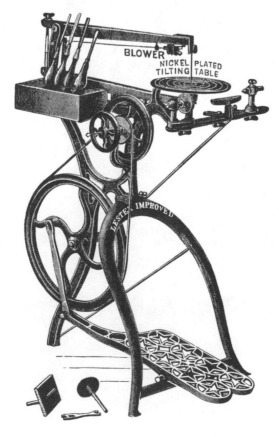

COLLECTABLE SAWS SOLD AT AUCTION

1. CORTLAND WOOD & CO. Double Eagle Kitchen Saw. Rosewood-handled meat & bone. $65

2. W. & H. HUTCHINSON, Sheffield. 11 inch steel back saw with checkered horn handle. $35

3. HACKSAWS (2) one with handforged English Lancashire pattern frame, the other has homemade wooden frame. $45

4. PISTOL-HANDLED hacksaw with very crude old handmade blade. $65

5. COOPER'S bellied saw for cutting crooze groove in repair staves. Walnut handle. $45

6. R. GROVES & SONS, London. Brass backed saw with 14 inch blade. Excellent. $25

7. DOVETAIL SAWS, lot of (3) brass-backed fine tooth variety in 4, 5, & 8 inch sizes. $50

8. SLACK, SELLARS & CO., Sheffield. 33 inch coarse timber saw (front handle gone.) $95

9. FRET SAW in solid walnut with 15 inch throat. Brass thumbscrews. Like new cond. $85

10. HENRY DISSTON & SONS fruitwood-handled shallow back saw with 16 inch blade. $40

11. STAIR SAWS, lot of (2), with applewood tailed-handle and oak closed-handle. $90

12. STAIR SAWS, another lot of (2) similar to above but in different woods. $120

13. FRAME SAW with center blade, chestnut frame, 8 x 32 inches. Brass fittings. $155

14. FRET SAW in Shaker-style with beautiful rosewood frame. $130

15. POCKET SAWS, lot of (3) folding-type, patented Feb. 19, 1889. Like new. $60

16. JEWELER'S SAWS, lot of (4) similar to one pictured, (as is condition). $25

17. FRET SAW in birch, Shaker-style. Near new condition. $55

18. CLASSIC BOW SAW in maple and birch. Excellent condition. $75

19. PAD SAW HANDLES, lot of (3) assorted styles with brasss sockets. $25

20. ROSEWOOD BOW SAW, the ultimate in collectable saws. 11 inch blade. Mint cond. $400

21. HEAVY-DUTY FRAME SAW (not pictured) finest we've ever seen. 32 x 41 inches with ram's head wing-nuts and high-posted handle. $600

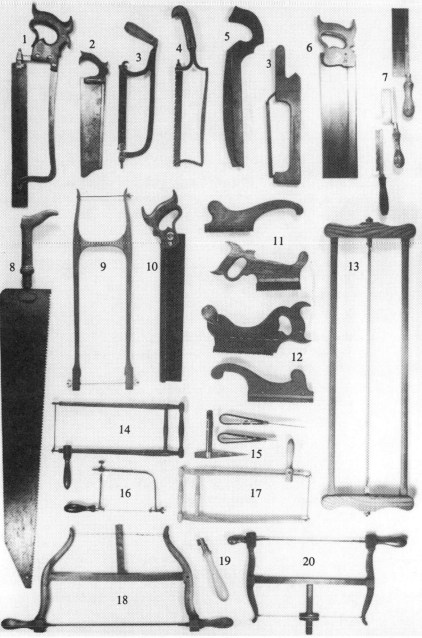

J.P. Bittner Antique Tool Auctions

HENRY DISSTON, Phila. steel backed saw with 11 pt., 14 inch blade. Circa 1840-1869. $35 Another "pre-Son" logo on this Gentleman's panel saw, circa 1840-1869. $25-$40.

DISSTON & SON rare 1870 mark on 16½ inch panel saw. $65 (Mrs, Disston produced a 2nd son in 1871). A 26 inch, 10 point hand saw of the same year. $40

HENRY DISSTON & SONS back saw with 14 to 16 inch blade and closed applewood handle. $18-$25 No. 4 back saw with contoured handle and blued steel back. $20-$25 No. 4 mitre saw, 5 inch x 24 inch backed blade. $45 No. 5 keyhole and pad saw, cast iron with screw driver end. $5 No. 7 Patent Ground panel saw, 10 pt. $15-$25

DOVETAIL SAWS are simply small back saws with extremely thin blades, used for cutting dovetail joints. Unmarked pistol-handled, brass backed, dovetail saw with 6 inch blade. $35

HENRY DISSTON & SONS No. 7 back saw with cast steel blade 14 inches long. $15-$25 No. D7 lightweight 8 point panel saw. $15 No. 8 cast steel, 28 inch rip saw. $25-$30 No. D8 cross-cut with 6 point, 26 in. blade. Circa 1914, near mint. Auct. $25

Fancy 1874 patent sway-back 8 pt. hand saw. Carved applewood handle has separate thumb hole. Auct. $48 No. 9 London Spring Steel hand saw. $35 No. 9 "Improved" 14 inch back saw with super-carved applewood handle and curve-front blade. $60 No. 10 plumber's or nail saw. Closed cherry handle fastened by single pivot at one end of 18 inch blade. $10-$15 No. 12 London Spring Steel 28 inch rip saw with carved handle and 4 brass screws. "The finest hand saw ever manufactured." Circa 1899 (Fine cond.). $50-$60 (Chipped handle) $25. No. 14 two-edged blade, rip and cross-cut . $40 D15 etched "Proclaim Liberty" (mint). $165 D16 hand saw with carved applewood handle. $20 No. D23 cross-cut hand saw with 24 to 26 in. blade. Auct. $20 No. 43

(Rare) combination hand saw, square, plumb, and level. All built into handle. Dlr. $125 No. 68 dovetail saw with brass back and turned handle. 1930 model, (new in box). $28 No. 71 offset brass-backed dovetail saw. Dlr. $45 D76 Bicentennial Limited Issue, 26 inch hand saw with walnut veneer plaque. (1,000 produced). Auct. $75 No. 80 double-edged cabinet saw, 1909 patent. $20 No. 106 docking saw 30 inches long with metal handle. $15

No. 107 gentleman's panel saw (lite rust) $15 No. D115 (top of the line in 1915) 26 inch hand saw with rosewood handle (good cond.) $35 Ditto, fine condition with custom etched Eagle & Liberty Bell blade. $95 No. 240 metal-cutting hand saw. $18 No. 342 special metal-cutting hand saw with tempered teeth which can not be reset. $25 Kitchen Knife-saw $5 Pruning saw, California style. Like new cond. $25 Another pruning saw with copper-braced handle, circa 1914. $28 Disston ship carpenter's custom-etched "Victory" rosewood handled hand saw . $40

Disston's Special Hand Saws.

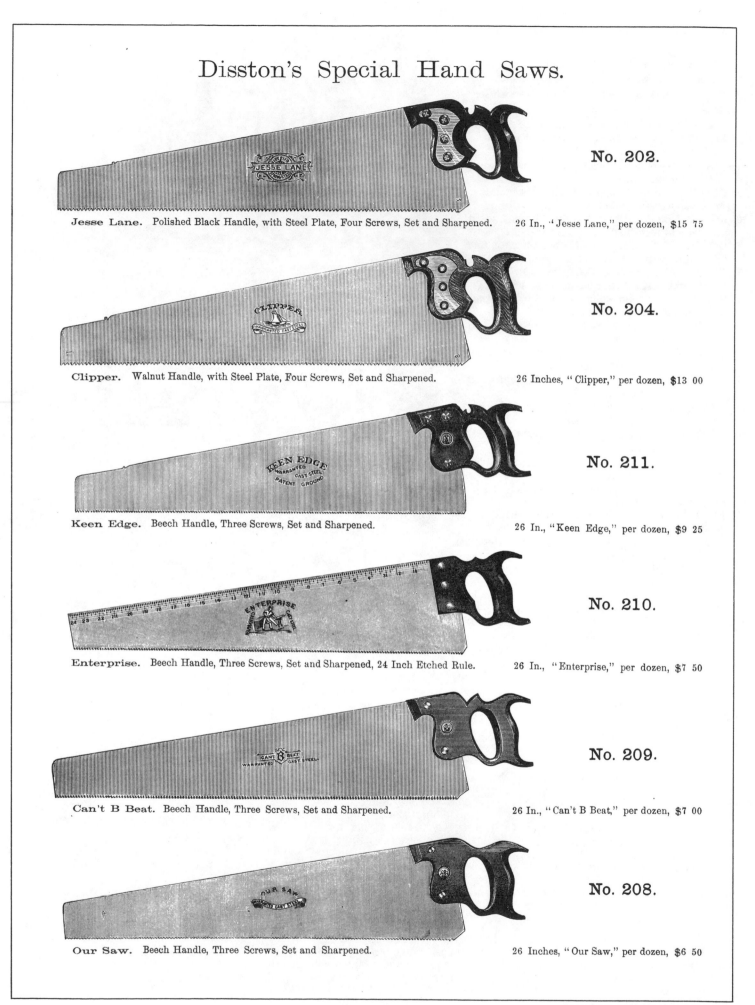

No. 202.

Jesse Lane. Polished Black Handle, with Steel Plate, Four Screws, Set and Sharpened.   26 In., "Jesse Lane," per dozen, $15 75

No. 204.

Clipper. Walnut Handle, with Steel Plate, Four Screws, Set and Sharpened.   26 Inches, "Clipper," per dozen, $13 00

No. 211.

Keen Edge. Beech Handle, Three Screws, Set and Sharpened.   26 In., "Keen Edge," per dozen, $9 25

No. 210.

Enterprise. Beech Handle, Three Screws, Set and Sharpened, 24 Inch Etched Rule.   26 In., "Enterprise," per dozen, $7 50

No. 209.

Can't B Beat. Beech Handle, Three Screws, Set and Sharpened.   26 In., "Can't B Beat," per dozen, $7 00

No. 208.

Our Saw. Beech Handle, Three Screws, Set and Sharpened.   26 Inches, "Our Saw," per dozen, $6 50

EXCELSIOR hand saw. Handle forms a tri-square with back of blade (which is a 24 in. rule). $45

FLOORING SAW, unmarked curved-back, knife-shaped. Blade pivots on carved handle. $45

FRAME SAW, unmarked 35 x 42 in. with wood-pegged frame wrought hardware. $35-$45 Another in oak with 2½ in. wide center-mounted blade, hand-forged wing nuts. Auct. $40 Larger, chamfered frame saw, 36 x41 inches with mortise and tenon corners. $50-$75 Another, 30 x 40 in. Dlr. $65 Handle-bar top extension on 26 x 40 example. Auct. $95 Coachmaker's 2-man frame saw with heavy 10 in. x 57 inch frame and 4 in. blade. $100 Superb quality 46 inch frame saw with 3½ inch wide fine-toothed blade and double mortised joints. Ram's horn adj. nut. $400

FRET SAW, unmarked factory made with metal frame and 12 in. throat. $6 English script-signed fancy metal-framed fret saw with ebonized handle. $35 Shaker-style fret saw with 12½ in. throat and maple handle. $40 Another with cherry frame. Auct. $85 Shaker-style in beechwood, 22 inches deep. $85 Rosewood-framed Shaker-style Auct. $95-$125 Sorrento Wood Carving Co. 1870 patent. $100

R. GROVES & SONS, Sheffield, (1824-1889). Dovetail saw, backed elastic spring temper 8 inch blade (rusty) $20, (mint) $40 Brass backed 14 inch saw with closed carved handle. Excellent . $28

LANCASHIRE Pattern, circa 1800. Iron frame. Lond. Auct. 1985 $35-$45

HACK SAW with Star touchmark. Brass frame, file-type handle. $50 Eagle's head carved handle on 14 inch wrought and twisted iron frame. 18th Cent. European, (clean but deeply pitted). Dlr. $525 French 18th Cent. hack saw with notch top decorative ⅜ inch thick x 14 inch frame, turned wooden handle. Dlr. $525 Gun-smith's double-bladed hack saw with center rod tension adjustment. $45 Early blacksmith-made 21 inch hack saw with wrought frame and turned handle. $60 Brass framed hack saw, circa 1830. Lancashire pattern, 15 inches overall. $65 Miniature Lancashire pattern hack saw with turned boxwood handle and 3 inch long blade. Auct. London, 1984 $100. Another with cocobola handle and 3½ in. blade. 8 inches overall. Dlr. $125

HAND SAWS in the form of conventional cross-cut, rip, and the smaller panel variety, are not nearly as collectable as earlier back or framed-bow saws. Most carpenter-carried hand saws lost their blade-etched trademarks within a few days after they were purchased. Many more have multiple handle repairs, bent or dull blades, and other defects which turn collectors off. A typical auction lot of 5 or 6 sound, but dirty, old hand saws might fetch in the neighborhood of $35. Un-usual multiple-use types and those with fancy-carved exotic wood handles com-mand much higher prices.

HOBBIES Patent fret saw with deep U-shaped metal throat and decoratively turned handle. $25 (Other Hobbies saws are listed under jigsaw heading.)

JAMES HOWARTH, Sheffield (1872-1939). Pad saw with turned ebony handle and long brass ferrule. 2 set screws hold tapered blade, (Mint cond.) Dlr. $65

HUDSON TOOL CO. Pond ice saw No. 587, (Like new). Auct. $30

W. & H. HUTCHINSON, Sheffield. Navy surgeon's horn-handled, pistol grip, steel back saw. Auct. $115 Another with checkered grip and no Navy mark. $35

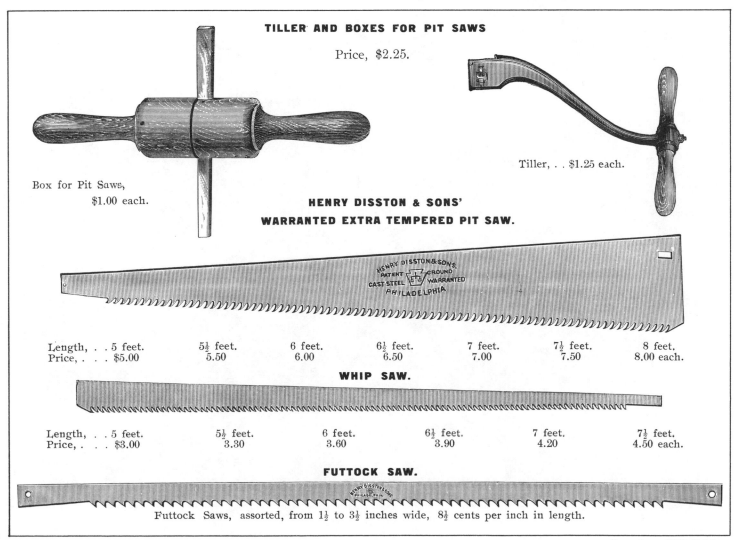

TILLER AND BOXES FOR PIT SAWS

Price, $2.25.

Box for Pit Saws, $1.00 each.

Tiller, . . $1.25 each.

HENRY DISSTON & SONS'
WARRANTED EXTRA TEMPERED PIT SAW.

Length, . .	5 feet.	5½ feet.	6 feet.	6½ feet.	7 feet.	7½ feet.	8 feet.
Price, . . .	$5.00	5.50	6.00	6.50	7.00	7.50	8.00 each.

WHIP SAW.

Length, . .	5 feet.	5½ feet.	6 feet.	6½ feet.	7 feet.	7½ feet.
Price, . . .	$3.00	3.30	3.60	3.90	4.20	4.50 each.

FUTTOCK SAW.

Futtock Saws, assorted, from 1½ to 3½ inches wide, 8½ cents per inch in length.

Page from 1899 Catalog.

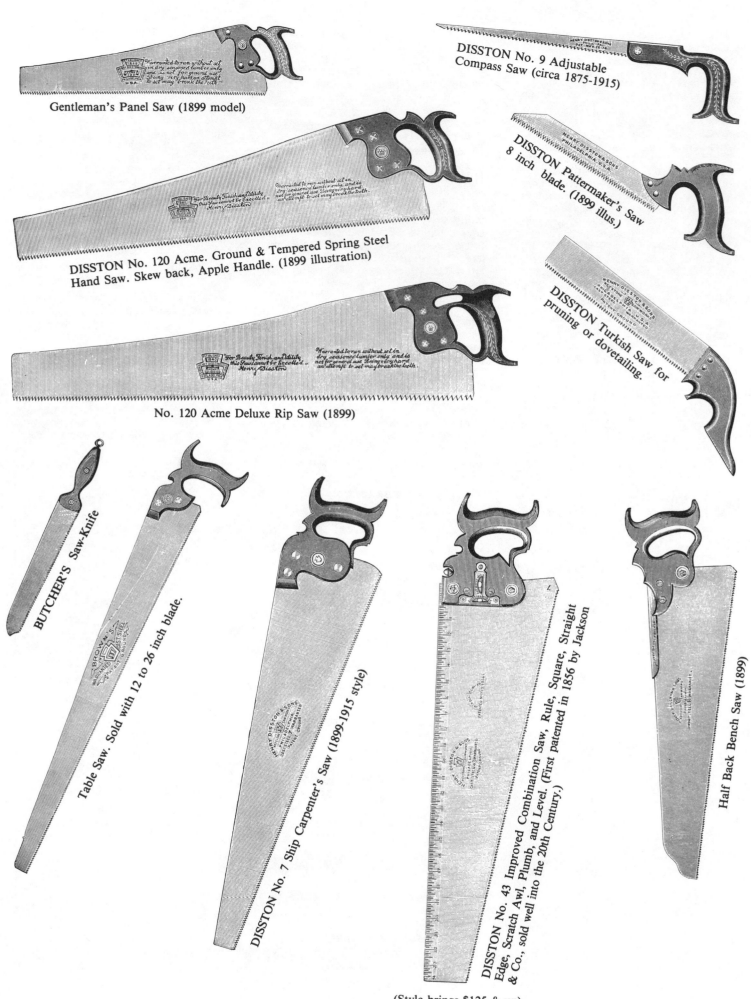

Gentleman's Panel Saw (1899 model)

DISSTON No. 9 Adjustable
Compass Saw (circa 1875-1915)

DISSTON No. 120 Acme. Ground & Tempered Spring Steel
Hand Saw. Skew back, Apple Handle. (1899 illustration)

DISSTON Patternmaker's Saw
8 inch blade. (1899 illus.)

No. 120 Acme Deluxe Rip Saw (1899)

DISSTON Turkish Saw for
pruning or dovetailing.

BUTCHER'S Saw-Knife

Table Saw. Sold with 12 to 26 inch blade.

DISSTON No. 7 Ship Carpenter's Saw (1899-1915 style)

DISSTON No. 43 Improved Combination Saw, Rule, Square, Straight
Edge, Scratch Awl, Plumb, and Level. (First patented in 1856 by Jackson
& Co., sold well into the 20th Century.)

Half Back Bench Saw (1899)

(Style brings $125 & up)

SAWS (continued)

EUROPEAN Backless Hand Saw
(Circa 1790)

DISSTON Steel backed Dovetail
Saw, 8 or 10 inch blade.

DISSTON Joiner's Saw 16 inch
(1899-1915 mod.)

DAVIS Open handled Back Saw
10 to 14 inch cast steel back

DISSTON Plumber's Saw (Sold
from 1875 onward)

GEO. H. BISHOP No. 10 Patent
Back Saw (Circa 1904)

DISSTON Duplex Saw with
12 to 22 inch double sided blade

DISSTON No. 77 Non-set Mechanics'
Back Saw (1899 illustration)

GEO. H. BISHOP No. 75 Flooring
Saw (1916 catalog illus.)

DISSTON No. 9 Improved Back Saw
10 to 18 inch blade length (circa 1900)

DISSTON Stair Builder's Saw
(1899 illustration)

EUROPEAN Backless Hand Saw
(Circa 1860-1910)

ICE SAW, extremely rare, two-man, crescent-shaped with rough dowel handles. Auct. $500 Conventional factory made ice saws sell in the $20-$35 range.

JACKSON back saw with closed-style beech handle, 14 inch blade. Auct. $18 2¼ x 10 inch open-handled variety. Dlr. $20 Brass-backed sash saw. $35

JACOBS PAT. buck saw with cast iron and steel frame, circa 1894. $15

C. E. JENNINGS & CO., New York. Rare hand saw with (6) interchangeable blades of various brands. Cross-cut and key hole types. Auct. $155 C. E. Jennings Circa 1885 brass-backed saw with 6 inch blade. $35

JEWELER'S SAWS are fine examples of functional beauty, but they do not yet command high prices. $8 to $16 will purchase most any factory made type today.

KEEN KUTTER No. KK88 applewood handled 26 inch hand saw. Dlr. $30 Stair saw by same maker (near mint cond.) $50 Keen Kutter 14 inch back saw with E. C. Simmons Cutlery etched on blade. $30 No. K816 cross-cut hand saw 26 inches long, cherry handle. $35 Floor layer's saw. Auct. $40

KEYHOLE or PAD SAW, unmarked factory made, 14 inches overall, new blade. $15-$30 English made with rosewood or ebony handle, brass ferrule. No Maker's mark. $20-$50

LANGDON MITRE BOX CO. Millers Falls Pat. 1869, 73 & 74. Saw and mitre box. Auct. $65 Another with 20 inch Disston brand saw. Dlr. $40

Wm MARPLES & SONS, Sheffield, Eng. Brass backed modern dovetail saw. 8 in. blade, turned handle. $18 Beechwood turning saw with 12 in. blade, cord top. $45 Marples No. 2400 small bow saw with 7 inch blade. Paddle & cord incl. Auct. $42 Salt saw with wooden handle and zinc blade. Auct. $45

A. MATHIESON & SON, Glasgow (1822-1894). Brass backed saw with either open or closed style handle. Dlr. $30-$40

MILLERS FALLS No. 14 rail-cutting saw, hack saw style. $25 Fret or coping saw. $5 - $10 No. 41 portable mitre box. $32

MOULSON'S, Sheffield (1824-1912) brass backed dovetail saws 10 - 14 inches overall. Dlr. $60-$85

J. M. MARSTON & CO. Boston, No. 3672 foot and hand-powered table saw. Pat. 1889. Complete with drilling attachment and other accessories. Auct. $500 - $700

MUSICAL SAW with colored glass stones set in ivory rings on handle. $68

PEG SAWS are quite collectible and sell in the $45 - $90 range. Often only 6 or 7 inches long, their wooden-backed blade has teeth pointing from each end toward the center.

PIT SAWS were popular in Britain from the 15th century onward. Wooden framed styles predate the broad-bladed tiller and box type which became popular in the 1750's and remained in use through the early 1900's. Auction prices vary from $150 - $350 with a premium placed on handwrought examples.

POST HOLE SAWS are a narrow-bladed Pennsylvania version of the Buck saw with long ratchet lever on handle for quick release of blade (which had been inserted in a pre drilled hole in the post). $50 - $75

PRESTON brass backed tennon saw. Auct. $35

RICHARDSON saw/knife for kitchen use. $5-$10

RICHARDSON, Newark, N.J. Bow saw, beech frame, 29 in. blade. $25-$45 Brass backed dovetail saw. Dlr. $40

SALT SAW with corroded zinc or copper blade and carved wooden handle. $75-$95

E. C. SIMMONS (Keen Kutter) double edge, adjustable back saw. $40

SIMONDS MFG. CO. mitre box saw with 25 in. blade. "Made expressly for Stanley Rule and Level Co." $20 No. 71 "Simondsteel" 26 in. cross-cut hand saw. $35 Simonds, G. W. Sites Pat. 1902 removable-handle-type hand saw. Auct. $55 Common 8 point hand saw. $12

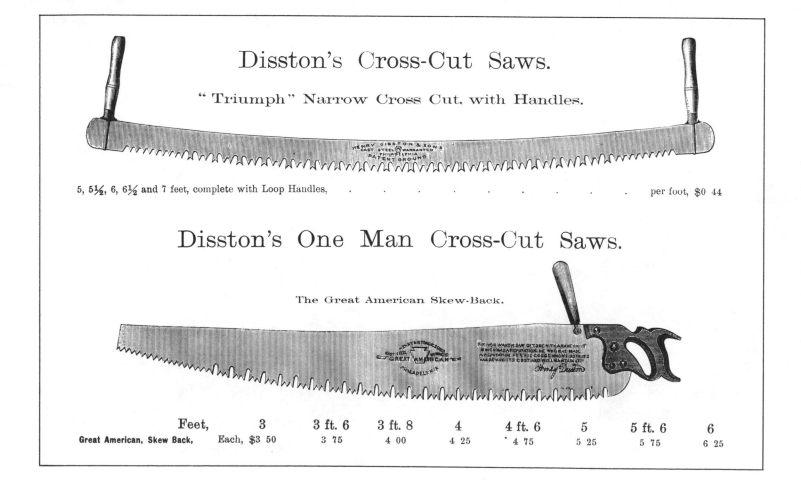

Disston's Cross-Cut Saws.

"Triumph" Narrow Cross Cut, with Handles.

5, 5½, 6, 6½ and 7 feet, complete with Loop Handles, ... per foot, $0 44

Disston's One Man Cross-Cut Saws.

The Great American Skew-Back.

Feet,	3	3 ft. 6	3 ft. 8	4	4 ft. 6	5	5 ft. 6	6
Great American, Skew Back, Each,	$3 50	3 75	4 00	4 25	4 75	5 25	5 75	6 25

I. SORBY (Circa 1810) brass backed dovetail saw with turned handle and 1 x 5 in. blade. Perfect condition. Dlr. $60

I & H SORBY (1824-1881) miniature beechwood bow saw, 8 in. blade. $50

ROBERT SORBY (1833-1859) beechwood turning saw, 12 inch frame. $55

SORRENTO WOOD CARVING CO., Temple Pl., Boston. Pat. Dec. 18, 1870. Fret saw with 22 inch carved H-shaped frame, 15 in. throat, rosewood handle. $85-$100

SPEAR & JACKSON, Sheffield (1819-1976) brass backed saw, closed handle. $35-$40 Rip saw with 28 inch blade. $25-$35 Hand saw with 26 in. blade. Like new. Auct. $35

SUDBURY Pat. Mar. 24, 1902. Double-faced hand saw with crosscut teeth on one edge and rip on opposite. Fine teeth on round nose. Nail slot in tip. Auct. $65

SURGEON'S vintage Bone Saws sell at auction for $100 and up.

STAIR BUILDERS wooden backed saws have been fetching an average of $35-$45. Exceptionally graceful styles in exotic woods bring more.

STANLEY "Victor" No. 50½ mitre box with Simmons back saw. $75-$85 No. 358 mitre box, made for Stanley by Disston. $40-$75 incl. saw. Stanley No. 39-240 dovetail saw. Like new. $15-$20

TOY SAWS of good quality, in bow saw style sell for $25-$50 each. A 3 foot long miniature crosscut timber saw in boy's size recently sold for $65 at auction.

THOS. TURNER & CO., Sheffield (1841-1845) back saw. $35-$45

W. TYZACK SONS & TURNER back saw with closed handle. Auct. $35

VULCAN SAW WORKS, Brooklyn, New York. 1885 pat. hand saw with novel handle. $20

WELLS W. AYER & CO., Northhampton, Mass. (Est. 1796). Hand saw, 6 point. Near new. $37

WINCHESTER hand saws and crosscut timber saws sell for about $30 at auction, and twice the price at Gun Shows.

One of several styles of the common Buck ▷ Saw. Still popular today. Used primarily for cutting firewood. Factory made examples sell in the $15-$25 range.

◁ **Every farmer owned a Cross-Cut Timber Saw, hence today's low market value of $15-$30.**

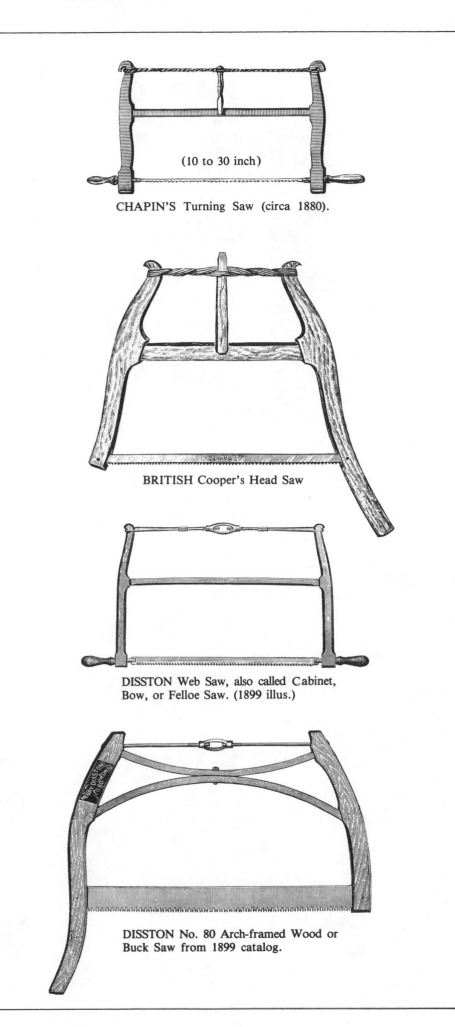

CHAPIN'S Turning Saw (circa 1880).

BRITISH Cooper's Head Saw

DISSTON Web Saw, also called Cabinet, Bow, or Felloe Saw. (1899 illus.)

DISSTON No. 80 Arch-framed Wood or Buck Saw from 1899 catalog.

SAWING IS A BREEZE with a sharp, correctly set blade. The "set" or splaying outward of the teeth is what keeps a blade from freezing up or binding. As illustrated below, a needle will slide freely in the direction it is pointed when a properly set blade is tilted downward. Plier-type setting tools were used to achieve a uniform tooth pitch on crosscut saws.

Note how the teeth of a crosscut blade are sharpened knife-like on alternating sides . . . while rip saw teeth are sharpened like chisels, on the back, in straight-across fashion. Rip saws are set with a die-type hammer-blow swage which widens the tip of each tooth as it turns it slightly to provide a slightly wider kerf than the blade.

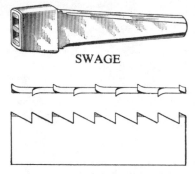

SWAGE

RIP SAW BLADE

L. A. SAYRE No. 103 Morrill Pattern Saw Set for cross-cut & circular blades, (Circa 1900).

BRITISH STYLE, Beechwood Handled "Wrest", or slotted saw set. This one is factory made, (Circa 1900).

MORRILL No. 95 with graduated wheel-adjusted anvil set for hand saws. (Sold for over 50 years to the Trade)

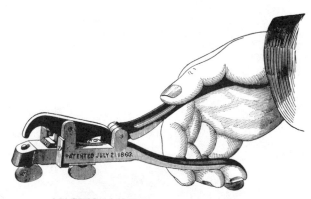

NASH'S 1863 Patent Lever saw set.

No. 1 IMPROVED Saw Set for both Hand, Band, and Jig Saws. (This low priced model sold for $1 in 1905).

EDWARD PRESTON & SONS Beechwood Handled Saw Set, (Circa 1900).

SAW SETS are currently sold for their utilitarian value and have yet to attract much attention from serious collectors. Hammer struck types retail for $5 or $10 each. British-style wrests with wooden handles fetch from $8 to $12 in shops. American made plier-type saw sets sell in the $6 to $10 range.

Rube Goldberg contraptions with cranks, pedals or levers may bring $30-$50. Common factory made grooved-plate sets start at 3 bucks and sometimes hand-forged examples don't bring much more. Brass trim often adds value to any tool, including saw sets.

SAW CLAMPS or **VISES** of the bench mounted variety average $15 to $20 each. Floor models are very scarce. Jigs and guides made for the purpose of holding a saw-sharpening file in the correct position on a saw blade are occasionally offered in the $15 to $30 range.

IMPROVED ADJUSTABLE SETTING STAKE FOR CIRCULAR SAWS.

Price, ... $6.00 each.

This valuable tool can be adjusted to set any saw from six to thirty inches in diameter. The cone *A* is moved in or out to suit the diameter of the saw, and raised or lowered, as may be required. The movable anvil at *B* is made of hardened steel, and some portions of the face being beveled more than others, the operator can regulate the amount of set as desired.

1899 Advertisement by Henry Disston & Sons.

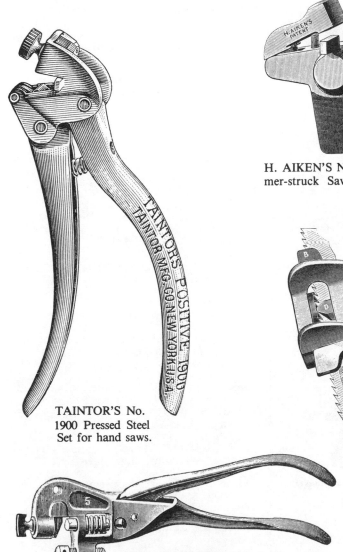

TAINTOR'S No. 1900 Pressed Steel Set for hand saws.

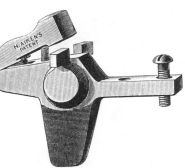

H. AIKEN'S No. 2 Common Hammer-struck Saw Set (1890's illus.)

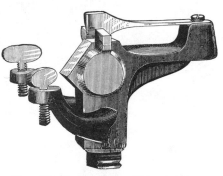

No. 23 Spring set. Hammer-type (Circa 1904 illus.)

MONARCH No. 1 by Disston. For Hand or Band saws. (Circa 1890-1920)

CHAS. MORRILL No. 5 Giant 15 inch Saw Set for 6 to 14 gauge timber cutting blades.

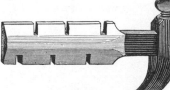

Basic Groover-plate "Wrest" for Cross-cut saws. 20th-century factory made example.

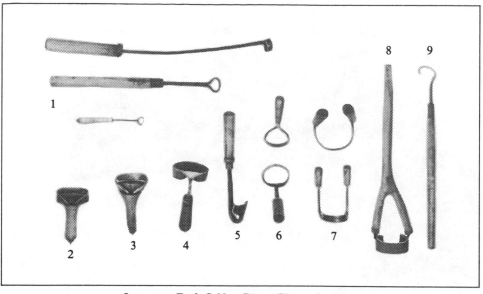

Scorp-type Tools Sold at Recent Bittner Auction.

1. Lot of (3) early closed scorps with small dia. cutters. $100

2. Chair Seat Shave with gauge handle. $75

3. Another fine early example, as above. $40

4. Cooper's type hand-forged scorp. $45

5. Open pull-style scorp, hand-forged. $110

6. Pair of (2) old closed scorps. $75

7. Two bent U-shaped, double handled. $50

8. Home-made type mounted on forked branch. $55

9. Lot of (4) Sabot Maker's hook-style scorps. $60

P.L. MFG. CO. No. 18 Box Scraper, (for removing trademarks)

COOPER'S One-handed Inshave (Circa 1890)

SCOTCH-PATTERN Cooper's Inshave (circa 1910)

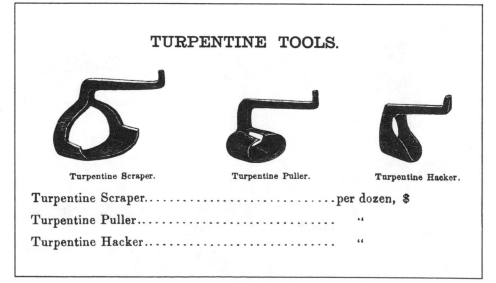

TURPENTINE TOOLS.

Turpentine Scraper.   Turpentine Puller.   Turpentine Hacker.

Turpentine Scraper.........................per dozen, $

Turpentine Puller.................................   "

Turpentine Hacker................................   "

Scorps from an 1865 Hardware Catalog.

THE WORD "SCORP" IS NOT IN ANY DICTIONARY nor could we find it among our vintage catalogs.

Old-tool-dealers and auctioneers both use the term scorp to identify any circular, or hook-bladed, knives or shaves which do not have a plane-like bottom to regulate the depth of cut.

AUCTION LOT of (4) deluxe cooper's scorps, assorted styles with brass ferrules. $145

BOWL SCORP. 3 finger & 4 finger, pull-type. Primitive, British made. Square handles. Dlr. $120 ea.

CHAIRMAKER'S scorp. Shovel-bladed type, wooden palm-sized block. Auct. $65

C. DREW & CO., Kingston, Mass. Pull-type box scraper with braced H cutter. $30

JO FULLER, Providence. Circa 1800 sap bucket scorp. Plane-like tool with attached birch handle. Auct. $125

GEO. B. ELLIS open scorp with two brass-ferruled maple handles. Dlr. $18

GREAVES open C-type 3½ in. dia. blade with two turned, ferruled, handles. $35

SABOT MAKERS scorp for hollowing out wooden shoes. Mounted on end of 24 inch iron rod with file-style wooden handle. $25

SHOVEL MAKERS closed scorp mounted on end of 14 in. bent wood handle with another cross bar handle mortised in 5 inches from end. $95

STORTZ & SON, Phila. Pa. Cooper's scorp-like two-handled draw shave. Dlr. $20

TWO HANDLED factory-made open-style scorp, 5 x 8 inches. $15-$30

TURPENTINE HACK or square-bladed scorp with nicely turned long wooden handle. $35 Another with U-shaped blade on end of a 15 inch long, weighted handle. $40 Handwrought turpentine hack with 4 inch closed triangular blade. $40

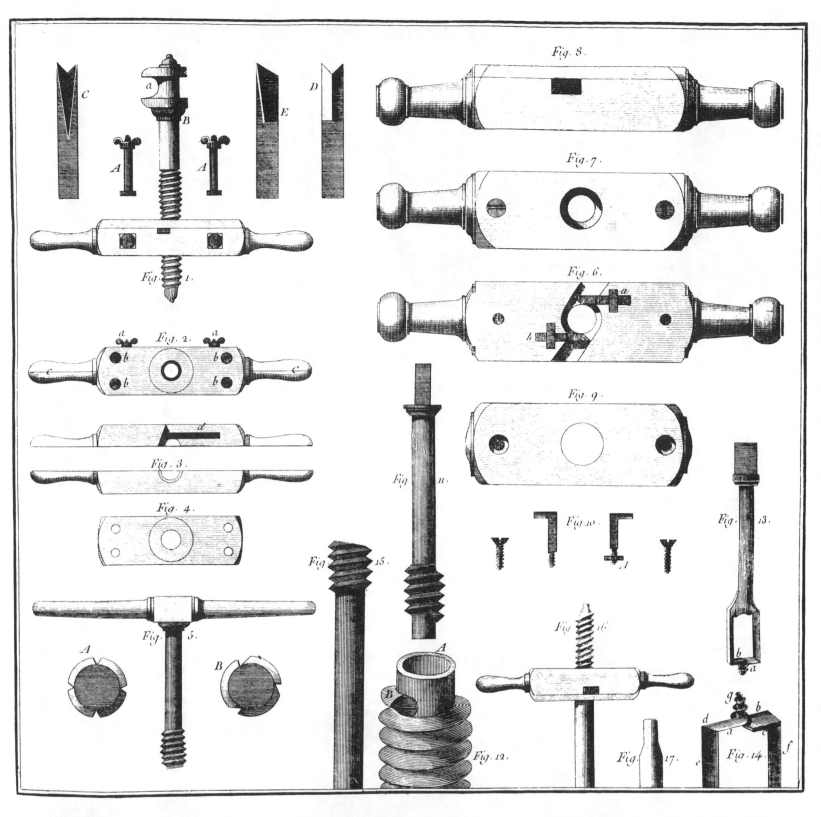

SCREWBOXES & TAPS have not changed much in appearance from those illustrated in the circa 1816 engraving above. Basically a screwbox is just a two piece wooden block which contains one or two V shaped cutters positioned inside a threaded opening.

UNMARKED Beechwood factory made screwbox and tap. Under one inch size. $35-$55

AUCTION LOT of (4) boxwood screwboxes, assorted makers. Sizes 7/32, 1/2, 5/8 & 3/4 in., all with taps. $125

BIRDSEYE MAPLE, handcrafted 1¼ in. dia. screwbox. (4) piece 6 x 12 x 3½ inch rectangular body is joined by four large wooden thumbscrews. Auct. $225

BELGIAN 18th-century rectangular screw box, cuts 1 in. dia. Held together by two turned wooden pegs. Full length carving of decorative cartouche border on front. Includes tap. Dlr. $265

BUCK, London. Wooden screwbox and matching 1 in. dia. steel tap. Auct. $45

CHERRYWOOD screw box with ash handled tap. Conventional style. $150 Another in cherry, 18th-century vintage, 20 inches long. 2 in. dia. tap. $295

EUROPEAN made, massive 13 x 3 x 3 inch ancient worm eaten screwbox with fancy scroll carving and date 1862. Cuts 2 inch eia. threads. Rectangular shape, held together by two wooden thumbscrews. Dlr. $425

HOME-MADE oak screwbox 2 x 5½ in. $20

MAHOGANY screwbox with circular body between conventional turned-type handles. Probably British. Auct. $56

MATHIESON, Edinburgh. Boxwood & beech 1 in. dia. screw box and wood handled tap. Auct. $52 Unhandled boxwood screwbox by same maker. ⅞ in. size, 5 threads per in. Dlr. $40 Beechwood model with conventional handles. Incl. ⅞ in. steel tap. $65

W. MARPLES & SONS, Hibernia. Unhandled Boxwood screwbox and steel tap ¾ in. (Mint). $55 Extra large 1⅞ dia. screwbox by Marples. Tap has its own container. $145

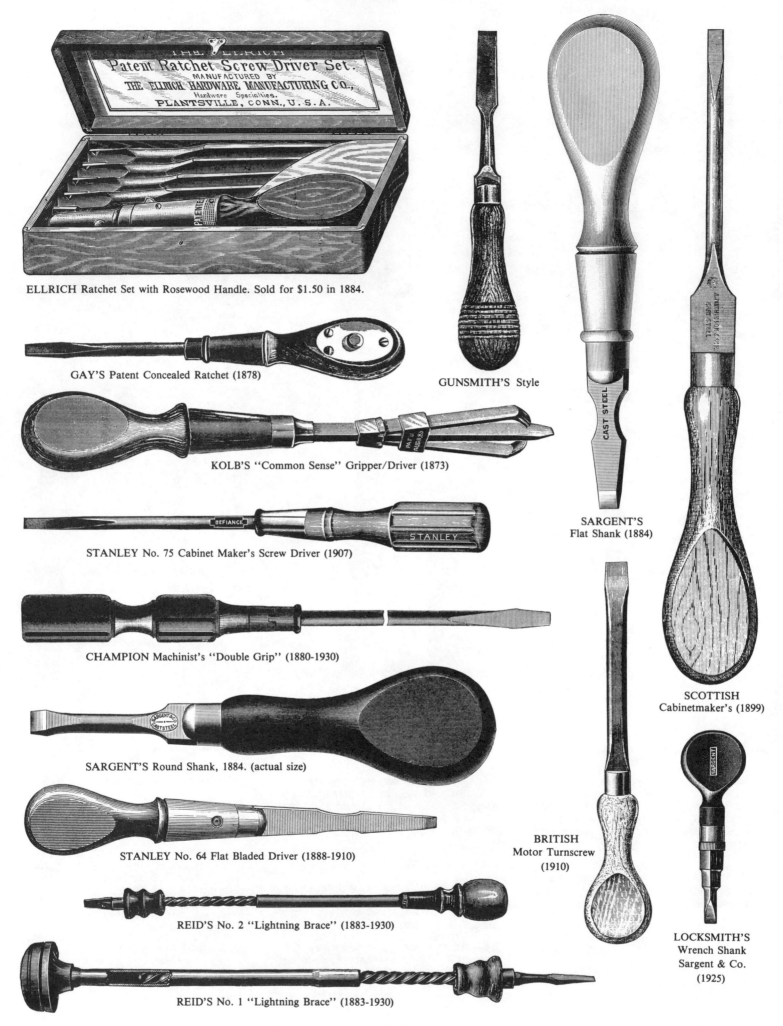

ELLRICH Ratchet Set with Rosewood Handle. Sold for $1.50 in 1884.

GAY'S Patent Concealed Ratchet (1878)

GUNSMITH'S Style

SARGENT'S
Flat Shank (1884)

KOLB'S "Common Sense" Gripper/Driver (1873)

STANLEY No. 75 Cabinet Maker's Screw Driver (1907)

CHAMPION Machinist's "Double Grip" (1880-1930)

SCOTTISH
Cabinetmaker's (1899)

SARGENT'S Round Shank, 1884. (actual size)

STANLEY No. 64 Flat Bladed Driver (1888-1910)

BRITISH
Motor Turnscrew
(1910)

REID'S No. 2 "Lightning Brace" (1883-1930)

LOCKSMITH'S
Wrench Shank
Sargent & Co.
(1925)

REID'S No. 1 "Lightning Brace" (1883-1930)

SCREW DRIVERS started showing up in joiner's tool boxes around the year 1750. Prior to then only clockmakers and gunsmiths had much use for the "Turnscrew".

Flat blades and narrow waists are design characteristics of early screw drivers, but this style carried over well into the 20th Century. Collectors value extremely large and very short turnscrews. Gunsmiths used the stubby variety, preferring rosewood handles. Undertakers, motorists, and sportsmen also carried undersized versions of this tool.

AUCTION LOT of (6) nice screwdrivers, 4 with flat blades, one "Six-Sixty". $20

BILLINGS & SPENCER CO., Hartford, Conn., Pat. Feb. 4, 1896. Wood handled "Magazine" screwdriver, awl-shaped, 4⅝ in. long when closed. Dlr. $30

BOOTH MILLS & CO., Phila. "Premium Awarded". Cherry handled, flat-bladed type. $25 Another with flat-sided apple-wood handle. $15

BRITISH Blacksmith made screwdrivers. Assorted lots in flat-bladed, double-waisted styles. Early 1800's vintage. $12 per tool. Deluxe quality British turnscrew with oval boxwood handle and 21 inch, triple-waisted, decorative blade. Dlr. $50

DECATUR COFFIN CO., Unmarked arch-median-style with wooden handle. $10 Another with Oct. 7, 1884 patent. Solid brass spiral drive. $12-$19

DRUMMOND'S PATENT screwdriver dated 1870. Shaft has brace-like steel elbow and egg-shaped wooden handle. 12 inches overall. $15

EBONY handled flat-blade type screwdriver with octagonal handle. $16

GEO. GAY, Augusta, Me. Dec 17, 1878 Pat. Ratchet Screwdriver, 18 in. Auct. $55

GOODELL-PRATT ratcheting screwdriver 1908 pat. $8 1880-1890 dates. $12-$24

GUNSMITH'S stubby little 3½ inch screwdriver with round handle. $12

Wm. JOHNSON, Newark, J.J., flat-bladed conventional screwdriver in new cond. $15

MILLERS FALLS No. 610A ratcheting screwdriver 18 inches long. Red handle. $25 (mint). No. 185A. Dlr. $10-$15

HAND-FORGED giant 22 inch long flat-bladed screwdriver with fancy turned handle. Made from an old file. $35

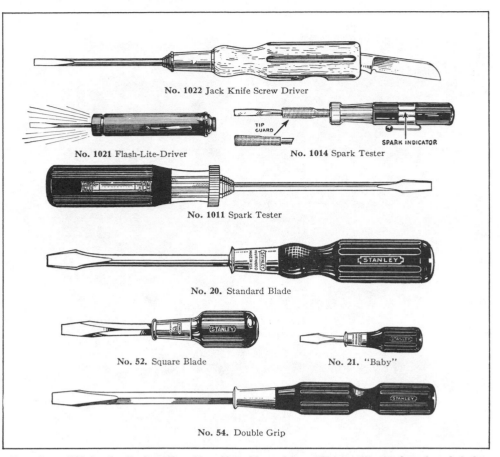

No. 1022 Jack Knife Screw Driver

No. 1021 Flash-Lite-Driver

No. 1014 Spark Tester

No. 1011 Spark Tester

No. 20. Standard Blade

No. 52. Square Blade

No. 21. "Baby"

No. 54. Double Grip

Page from 1939 Stanley Tools catalog. Nos. 20 to 54 are deluxe "Hurwood" with forged steel shafts which pass all the way through the black hardwood handles. This line was introduced around 1905.

H. MUELLER Pat. July 30, 1889. Automatic screwdriver with brass shaft. $25

C.A. MUNN & CO. patented gripper-style screwdriver dated 1893. $10

ODD FELLOWS imprint and 1892 date on stubby applewood-handled screwdriver. $35

PERFECT HANDLE beechwood inlaid steel. 1903, Plantsville, Conn. Fair. $6 Very Good. $12

NORTH BROS. No. 41 & 42 and a MILLERS FALLS. Ratchet push drills. Lot of (3). Auct. $60

A. REID, 1881 Patent, non-reversing, ratcheting 18 in. spiral screwdriver with mushroom-shaped knob. Auct. $70 1882 model with enclosed spiral Nickel plated housing with wood runner. Auct. $20 (See Drill section for more examples by this maker.)

H.D. SMITH & CO. triple lever, T-handled, metal framed screwdriver. $28

SNELL MFG. CO. flat-bladed screwdriver with turned maple handle. 18 in. $12-$15

STANLEY No. 45 "Hurwood" electrician's screwdriver with insulated head. Auct. $5

STANLEY No. 86 flat-bladed screwdriver circa 1898-1910. Brass ferrule, polished wooden handle is flat on side. $12- $14 1871 Pat. Flat blade, 14 in. overall $10-$15

TUCK rosewood handled screwdriver, 6 inches long. $4

WINCHESTER brand Mechanic's screwdriver. $15-$20

WINCHESTER No. 7160, one and a half inch screwdriver in excellent condition. $27

YANKEE No. 15 fine ratcheting screwdriver with round wooden handle. $8 No. 11 $7 Yankee by North Bros. No. 31 non-spring spiral screwdriver. $15 No. 130A springloaded spiral screwdriver. $13 - $18 No. 31 in home-made wood box $18 No. 33H (short style). $12 No. 44 Dlr. $10

YANKEE No. 30 Ratchet Screw Driver (1910 model)

Author's Collection

From the number of old engravings we have found that are related to tool sharpening it would appear to have been a steady, if not lucrative, trade! There are not many grindstone collections extant, but the possibilities are intriguing. A lot of good old stones are laying about on weed covered homesites all over the country. The axle and hardware will usually be found attached or buried nearby. Any skilled carpenter can reconstruct a simple oak frame.

SHARPENING TOOL PRICES

CHARNLY FORREST British made oil stone in decorative box. Auct. $35

CHISEL SHARPENING JIG Solid brass frame with steel idler wheel. Dlr. $28

DENGELSTOCK, Hammer, Whetstone and Knopf (horn case). Set of (4) items carried in the field for sharpening scythes. $38-$50

GRINDER, hand-cranked, high speed, bench-mounted household and shop-type sharpening wheels. $20-$30

HONING MACHINE for various curve sweeps of carving chisels. Hand-cranked spindle takes any of 20 different wheels. Mounted on rectangular wooden pumice receptacle. Comes with oak dovetailed box. Dlr. $150

MILLERS FALLS No. 240 plane iron sharpening jig. Screw clamp with roller bottom. $18-$25 Model No. 569 in orig. box. $22

NORTON boxed sharpening stone, 2 x 8 in. Like new. $8-$10

OAK-FRAMED FARMER'S grinding stone with foot treadle. 75lb. size. $75-$150

METAL-FRAMED style farmer's grindstone with sheetmetal pedals & seat. $25-$50 (A cast iron framed machine would bring much more).

SHARPENING STONES: India, Arkansas, Carborundum, etc. $5-$12 in wooden box. Patented oil stone with oil reservoir. Auct. $22 "Spencer" white stone 2 x 8 in., boxed. $20

STANLEY No. 200 Plane Blade Sharpener. Pat. 12-10-12. $32

PIKE DISPLAY CASE, Hardware store wetstone fixture in curly maple with glass door. 28 x 14 x 32 inches. Auct. $200

Dover Publications

INDIA OIL STONES "SHARP AND QUICK"

MILLERS FALLS CO.

All items this page are circa 1880-1920.

20   16   17   19   21   18

These Oil Stones are made of the best grade of emery, and do not glaze. They are made of different grades of emery to adapt them to the following work:

Nos. 16, 20, 24, and 36 are for cleaning castings, and other rough work.

No. 60 is for sharpening machinists' tools. In finishing metals it is equal to the second cut file.

No. 80 is for sharpening carpenters' and wood working tools, and is invaluable for outside jobs, where a grindstone is not available. In finishing metals it is equal to the smooth cut files.

Nos. 80 and 100 are well adapted for planer knives in place of a grindstone.

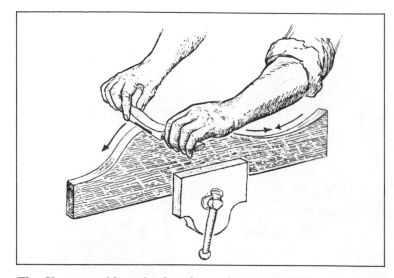

Barrel Spokeshave, also called a Plucker or Downright. Used on outside surfaces. (Auction prices range from $35 - $50)

The Shave combines the functions of a woodworking plane and a draw knife. This handy tool can be used to plane or shape concave, convex, and flat surfaces where a plane or draw knife would be impractical to maneuver. There is a special shave for almost every branch of woodworking. Wheelwrights were the first to make widespread use of this tool and folks have been calling most forms of it a "Spokeshave" ever since.

Boxwood spokeshaves are scarcer and more delicate than the common beechwood variety. Ebony and rosewood examples also bring a premium price from collectors. Brass and bronze spokeshaves are the hardest to come by. Iron has been used by spokeshave manufacturers since the 1870's when Leonard Bailey's efforts first popularized metallic planes.

Most of the examples illustrated on this page are from tool catalogs of the 1880-1910 era.

Cooper's Bent Shave with curved bottom and cutter. (Dealers ask from $35 to $40)

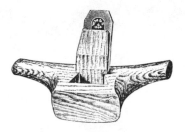

Cooper's Tub Shave, or small Inshave with convex iron and sole. Used mainly for clean up work on fouled casks. (A $20 - $35 value)

Bronze loop-type-frame Carriage Maker's Moulding Shave. (Auction price range $35-$45)

Beechwood Spokeshave with 3 inch cutter and unplated bottom. (Average value $5 - $10)

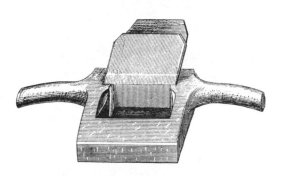

Cooper's Heading Float, also called a Plucker or Swift. Has slightly convex cutter for cross-grain work. (These sell in a wide range from $40 to $75)

Beechwood Spokeshave, factory made example with brass sole plate. (Good examples are worth from $10 - $20)

Brass wear plate combined with brass depth adjusting screws. (Price range $15 - $35)

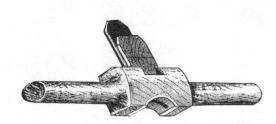

Wheelwright's Shave or Jarvis. A heavy duty tool. (Dealers asking up to $90. Auct. $35 - $75)

AUCTION LOT of (5) very nice beech wood spokeshaves, Sheffield type with brass wear plates. $55

A.C.T. CO. Round-style spoke shave with metal center section and turned wooden handles. Dlr. $35

G.L. ANDERSON, Fraserburgh, Scotland. Cooper's downright or plucker with dovetailed handles. Auct. $35-$50 Dlr. $65-$75

BAGSHAW & FIELD, Philadelphia (Circa 1881) Applewood spoke shave 11 in. long. Dlr. $22

BAILEY TOOL CO. iron spoke shave with battle axe imprint. Dlr. $65
Another with July 26, 1870 patent date and lever blade lock. Auct. $150

Bailey, Boston. Cooper's iron spoke shave 18½ in. long. Auct. $20 Dlr. $70
L. Bailey, Boston, No. 56½ iron spoke shave (pitted) Dlr. $45

D.R. BARTON -1832- Rochester, N.Y. Cooper's downshave with 3 in. cutter and 5½ inch long turned walnut handles. $35
Heavy straight-handled iron shave with "Flour City" cast into frame. $22

BATCHELDER double-bladed, concave & straight, iron spoke shave. Auct. $5

JOHN BOOTH & SON, Philada. Cherry spoke shave with whalebone wear plate. Dlr. $45
Another with brass wear plate. $35

BOWL MAKER'S primitive, unhandled, round bottom shaves. Auct. $30 ea.

BRASS spoke shaves: Unmarked, straight or curved handles, cast from factory made models. $25-$35 Carriage maker's open loop handle type, 9 inches. Auct. $35-$45

Massive 14½ inch long with 2¼ in. slotted plane blade. $100 Brass-framed, but inlaid with other materials such as wood or pewter. $75-$150 Miniature bronze spoke shave, 3 in. to 4½ inches wide. $20-$45

BUCK, script-signed ebony spoke shave with heart-shaped brass thumbscrews and brass wear plate. 11 inches overall. Dlr. $125 J. Buck, boxwood, plain. Dlr. $20

CHAIR-MAKER'S shaves: Large 11 inch example carved from single piece of hardwood. 8 inch convex blade held by peg wedges. Dlr. $85 Primitive palm-shaped slab with curved blade. Leather hand strap intact. $50 Banana-shaped 12 inch hardwood shave with inset tang-less cutter. $50 11 in. boxwood by David Flather. $60

CIN'TI TOOL CO. iron shave with wood handles. Hollow (concave) sole. Dlr. $30 Round (convex) sole. Dlr. 1985. $55

COOPERS shaves: Unmarked bottle shave, smallest of the inshaves. Auct. $45
Cooper's buzz or scraper 14 inches wide with 3 in. blade Dlr. $28-$35
Bucket shaves in birch. $30-$35 Head floats in largest sizes, from 13 to 15 inches wide. Dlr. $60-$80 Common inshaves. $20-$35

STEARNS No. 13 Universal Spokeshave (Pat. 1900)

STANLEY No. 67 Universal Spokeshave (1896-1940)

STANLEY Nos. 72, 73, 57, & 76 "Razor Edge" (1905-1910)

E. PRESTON & SONS No. 1373 Iron Spokeshave (1900 Illus.)

E. PRESTON & SONS No. 1377 Embossed Iron Shave

MILLERS FALLS No. 1 Circular Spokeshave (1884 Pat.)

Iron Spokeshaves.

Single Cutters.

No. 11, Single Irons, ...   per dozen, $2 00
No. 12, Double "   .   .   .   .   .   "   2 50

Nos. 11 and 12.

Double Cutters.

No. 13, Concave and Straight, .   .   .   per dozen, $3 50

No. 13.

No. 11, one dozen in a box; Nos. 12 and 13, half dozen.

Stearns' Iron Spokeshaves.

No. 3, 2⅛ Inch Cutter, Straight Handle, .   per dozen, $3 50
No. 4, 2⅛ "   "   Raised   " .   "   3 50

No. 3.   No. 4 is same with Raised Handle.

Adjustable Cap.

No. 5, 2⅛ Inch Cutter, Straight Handle, .   per dozen, $3 50
No. 6, 2⅛ "   "   Raised   " .   .   "   3 50

No. 6.   No. 5 is same with Straight Handle.

Adjustable Cap and Throat.

No. 7, 2⅛ Inch Cutter, Straight Handle, .   per dozen, $4 50
No. 8, 2⅛ "   "   Raised   " .   .   "   4 50
No. 9, Concave Spokeshaves, .   .   .   "   3 00

No. 7.   No. 8 is same with Raised Handle.

Circle Spokeshaves.

No. 10, 2½ Inch Cutter, Straight Handle, .   per dozen, $6 00

This Shave is suitable for either Straight work or for cutting the inside of Circles that have a diameter of 3½ inches or larger.

No. 10, Circle Spokeshave.

Half dozen in a box.

Stanley's Patent Chamfer Spokeshaves.

Adjustable.

No. 65, 1½ Inch Cutter, Raised Handle, .   per dozen, $6 00
Extra Cutters, ...   "   75

Half dozen in a box.

Easily adjusted by Thumb Screws attached to the Guides. It will chamfer an edge any width up to 1½ inch.

Wood Spokeshaves.

No. 80, Beech, Plain.

Inch,	2½	3	3½	4
Per dozen,	$3 25	3 75	4 25	4 75

No. 80, Plain.   Brass Plated is No. 85.

No. 85, Beech, Brass Plated.

Inch,	2½	3	3½	4
Per dozen,	$4 25	4 75	5 25	5 75

No. 95, Screw Iron, Beech, Plated.

Inch,	2½	3	3½	4
Per dozen,	$9 00	9 50	10 00	10 50

No. 95, Screw Iron, Brass Plated.

(Page from 1884 Sargent & Co. Hardware Catalog)

A. FALES cherry spoke shave with hollow cutter. $15

GREAVE, Manchester. English stair rail shave with block-shaped fence on bottom. Auct. $115

W. GREENSLADE, Bristol. Rare twin-handled 14 inch coachmaker's shave with movable iron fence. Cuts a 2¼ in. ogee. Dlr.$90 Another in boxwood, ogee hand-rail shave with adjustable fence. Asking $140

GRIFFITHS, coachmaker's jarvis with concave brass mouth plate. Auct. $70-$80

D. FLATHERS & SONS, Solly Works, Sheffield. Boxwood spokeshave, plain. Dlr. $12-$20

GOODELL-PRATT No. 36 patternmakers black enameled iron spoke shave. Dlr. $22

BENJ. F. HORN, E. St Louis, Ill. Cooper's wood handled shave with metal blade holder, brass cap. $35

HUMPHREY TOOL CO., Mass. 1882 patented cylindrical, nickel plated iron shave with turned rosewood handles. Dlr. $25

W. JOHNSON, Newark, N.J. Wooden spoke shave 9 inches long. $19

KEEN KUTTER double-bladed, concave & straight, iron spoke shave Auct. $12 Beechwood shave 11 inches long with 2¾ in. cutter. Brass adjust. thumbscrews. $20-$35

LIGNUM VITAE slender, graceful 10½ inch spoke shave. Dlr. $22

A. McKENZIE, Aberdeen. Copper's downright or barrel jarvis. Auct.$40 Dlr. $55-$60

J. MANNABACK, 112 Stanton St., New York. (1858-1898) Massive head float with great patina. Auct. $100

W. MARPLES & SONS common boxwood or beech, spoke shave. $15-$20 Miniature 6 inch size. $25-$50
Radius shave with V-shaped frame. Auct. $70 Cooper's bent style, 4 inch cutter. $35 Wheelwright's unplated jarvis. Auct. $35

MARTINS round bottom iron spoke shave. Dlr. $12 Larger, earlier, adjustable iron spoke shave with 2¼ in. blade. $20-$30. Auct., 1985 $35

MAST SHAVE (See Draw knife section)

MILLERS FALLS No. 1 circular spoke shave with 1884 patent date. Rosewood handles. $20-$30

JOHN MOSELY & SON, London. Heavy wheelwright's jarvis 12 in. long with brass wear plate. Dlr. $90

ONIONS & CO. boxwood spoke shave with brass bottom plate. Dlr. $20

C.S. OSBORNE rosewood spoke shave with simple tanged blade. $20
Another with brass thumbscrew adjustments on tang ends. $40-$50

PHELPS BROS., Pillston, Pa. Pair of miniature brass shaves 2⅜ wide including stubby wing handles. Auct. $95

PRESTON No. 1373 embossed iron 7 inch spoke shave. Dlr. $50 No. 1374 embossed iron spoke shave with cut out handles. $30-$50 No. 1379 Improved iron spoke shave. $25 No. 1392 Adjustable stop-chamfer shave with V-bottom, Auct. $49 No. 139OH iron spoke shave. $25 No. 1391 nickle plated adjustable spoke shave 10 inches long. $35-$45 # 322021 round bottom iron type with embossed handles. Auct. $30 RD. No. 356040 nickle-plated round-bottom iron spoke shave 6 inches long. Auct. $30 Double-cutter ovolo pattern in cast iron. $25 Beechwood curved-bottom spoke shave with brass wear plate. 11½ inches wide. $46

P. QUIGLEY, Newark, N.J. (1849-1852) Conventional boxwood spoke shave with brass sole plate. Auct. $30

ROSEWOOD spoke shaves: Classy model with brass wear plate. Belonged to royal Whipmaker. $50 Concave bottom shave with ivory wear plate $35 Auction lot of (3) adjustable type with brass thumb-screws. All for $51. Another adjustable type, 11 in. long. $25 Ornamental brass blade-surround on gull wing handled non-adjustable type. $25

A.L. SANBORN maple bannister shave. Auct. $50

D.P. SANBORN, Worcester, Mass. Ogee stair-rail shave with brass sole. $55

SORBY solid ebony spoke shave 10 inches long Dlr. $45

STANLEY RULE & LEVEL began offering Bailey's iron spoke shaves in its 1870 catalog. Numbers 51 thru 55 remained in sales literature right up until WWII, (where our research ended). 1909 seems to have been the peak of Stanley's spoke shave production...24 different models were described in that year's catalog. By 1939 the line had dwindled to 15 items.

STANLEY No. 51 with raised handles, 10 in. long. $8-$20 No. 52 light weight model with straight handles. $6-$12
No. 53 adjustable iron. $10-$15 (with much higher prices asked for 1858 patent date).
No. 54 straight handled version. $10-$15 No. 55 hollow faced with raised handles. $15-$30. No.56 cooper's style 18 in. long. $20-$25. No. 56½ heavy iron 19 in. long. $45-$55. No. 57 cooper's iron with 2⅛ in. cutter. $35-$40 No. 58 with finish gone. $5 No. 60 double cutter with hollow and straight blades. $10-$18. Lond.1985. $26

STANLEY No. 62 Iron spoke shave with raised handles. Made from 1877 to 1910. Reversible 2⅛ in. double cutter can be used in either direction. Dlr. $35-$45 Nos. 63 & 63X $22, introduced in the late 20's. No. 64 black iron 9 inch model began production in 1884 and was still being sold in the 1960's. $5-$12 No. 65 adjustable chamfer V-bottom iron spoke shave, 10½ in., twin thumbscrews. Scarce. $45-$75. No. 67 "Universal", nickel plated cylinder with rosewood handles & 2 soles. $35-$85 No. 68 rare iron rabbeting share. Dlr. 1985. $95 The equally scarce No. 71 does not appear in any except 1929 cat. 3 of the bronze shaves have been offered; One at $50 another at $120 and the latest sold at auction for $155. Nos. 72 to 76 are Razor Edge iron shaves made around 1910. In 1980 an 11 inch model with 2½ in. cutter sold at auction for $40. (No other sales reported since) Nos. 81 & 82 are also called Razor Edge, but are made of rosewood instead of iron. (Circa 1910) Dlr. $65-$95. 84 & 85 are boxwood Razor Edge, made from 1909 to 1929. Dlr. $35-$50. Nos. 151 & 152 are black iron 10 inch shaves with 2⅛ in. cutter. Produced since 1929, they sell in the $10-$20 range.

No. 55

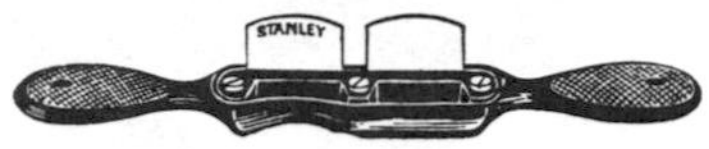

No. 60

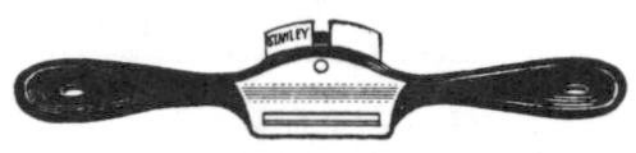
No. 63

STEARNS adjustable throat, iron spoke shave. $12 No. 73 Razor Edge, 9½ in. iron spoke shave. $16-$20 Scarce flexible-sole Stearns shave. Auct. $80

TILLOTSON, Columbia Place, Sheffield. (1837-56). Straight-bottom boxwood tang-type spoke shave. Auct. $15

U.L. CO. No. 1 solid brass gull-winged spoke shave with 2 inch wide plane-type blade. Dlr. $75

UNION MFG. CO, New Britain, Conn. Round-bottom iron shave with raised handles. Dlr. $10. Another with 1876 patent date, by George Mosher. $20 Union No. 111 iron spoke shave with chamfering gauge attachment. Dlr. $28

P.W. WALKER & CO., Burton. Cooper's head float, 13 inches wide. $20-$35

F. WALTER & CO., Solly Works. Hardwood with brass wear plate. $12-$18

G.H. WESTON iron spoke shave. Dlr. $20

WHALEBONE SOLE on typical beechwood spoke shave. Dlr. $30

L & I.J. WHITE, Buffalo, N.Y. wood handled shave with iron center section which holds 2⅝ in. blade. 16 inches overall. Dlr. $30

WILCOCK, Manchester. Boxwood 12 inch banister shave with lawnmower style handles. Sliding fence, dual direction. Auct. $105

WINDSOR CHAIR SEAT Shave with 4½ inch cutting edge. Tang adjustment. Dlr. $25 Windsor chair rung shave (or scraper) in dark mahogany. Graceful, 12 inch. $14

For those readers not familiar with shipbuilding methods employed in the 19th Century, we reprint here a page from Horace Greely's account of 1872. "A ships architect makes a model of the hull about 3 feet long. From the finished and approved model he makes 3 working drawings. Enlarged patterns are then rendered from which workmen select and shape every timber for the ship. At the launching site blocks are set on a slight incline at the waters edge. Upon these blocks a keel is laid. Its timbers, 20 inches square, are doweled together until the proper length is achieved. The stern is then mortised into the keel by way of an upright post to which other stern section members are bolted. The bottom most cross members, inletted into the keel, are called floor beams. Yet another keel, called the keelson, is laid across the top of this assembly and bolted thru to the bottom keel for a solid foundation upon which to frame the rest of the ship. Now the first curved ribs are doweled into the floor beams and the futtocks rise up the side of the hull forming a skeleton to which side planking is pegged with auger and mallet. Upright posts, resting on the keelson, provide stanchions to support the decks. L-shaped hangers or brackets, called knees, provide additional bracing between the sides and deck beams."

Most of the hull's overall strength was actually formed by the outside planking, or skin, which was made up of 4 to 10 inch thick oak boards pegged to the futtocks with locust wood pegs called treenails. Caulking is the process of making all seams watertight by driving in tarred oakum (hemp fibre) with blunt chisel-like caulking irons and covering the recess with pitch.

With the exception of some specialized items on the facing page, most shipcarpenter's tools were adaptations of those commonly used in over 30 other woodworking trades. Some very general price guidelines are: Adze ($25-$35), Auger ($10-$35), Axe ($20-$45), Caulking iron ($6-$8), Oak Mallet ($35-$65), Draw Knife ($18-$40), Razee Jack Plane ($25-$100), Razee Jointer ($95-$195) and Spar planes ($18-$55).

Captain Adrian Block built the first American yacht in 1614 at Manhattan River in the Dutch settlement of New York. Massachusett's shipbuilding industry was launched in 1631 by Gov. Winthrop's 4th of July christening of his own ship, "Blessing of The Bay". In 1641 a fifty-ton bark was built at Sandwich, near Cape Cod, by a small group of American speculators. At Plymouth, in 1642, there arrived a carpenter/salt-maker from England who quickly constructed 4 sturdy sailing craft.

Other colonies were inspired by these examples and public subscriptions were soon solicited for construction of commercial sized shipping vessels. So successful were colonial shipwrights that by 1771 more than a third of all British sailing ships were being launched from American waters.

A century later, in 1871, the tide had again turned. A heavy tariff on critical materials nearly sank the entire United States shipbuilding industry. British vessels, chiefly ironclads, again ruled the seas. In the interim period of lower production, U.S. naval architects sought speed and beauty beyond that of the most advanced English and French designs of the day. Ignoring conventional construction methods, American shipbuilders set standards of speed with their clipperships that were unbeatable by even contemporary steam powered vessels. The famous "Flying Cloud" achieved a 24 hour average speed of nearly 18 miles per hour.

The Launching of a Packet ship. Circa 1870.

This chest full of British shipwright's tools, comprising over 80 items, sold for $575 at auction in London last year.   (photo courtesy Reg Eaton)

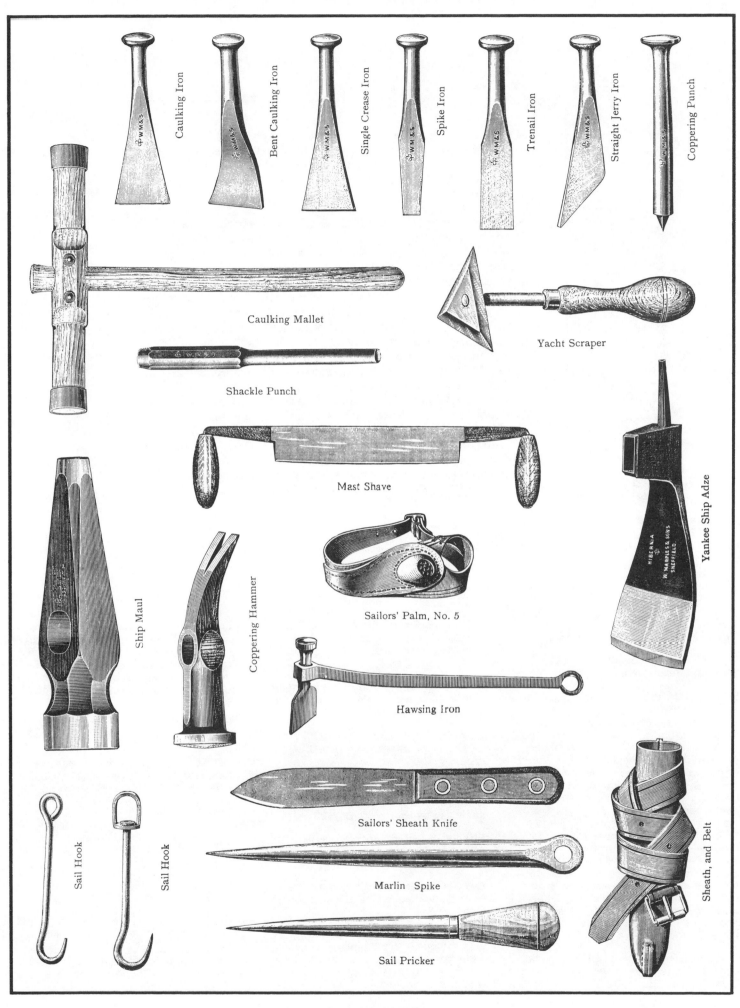

Caulking Iron

Bent Caulking Iron

Single Crease Iron

Spike Iron

Trenail Iron

Straight Jerry Iron

Coppering Punch

Caulking Mallet

Yacht Scraper

Shackle Punch

Mast Shave

Yankee Ship Adze

Ship Maul

Coppering Hammer

Sailors' Palm, No. 5

Hawsing Iron

Sail Hook

Sail Hook

Sailors' Sheath Knife

Marlin Spike

Sail Pricker

Sheath, and Belt

(Circa 1880 - 1910)

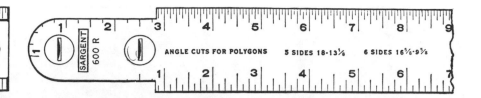

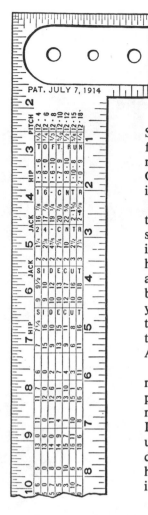

SQUARES were made of solid wood in early times. Metal reinforcement hardware was gradually added and in the mid 1700's metal-bladed try squares were produced in small factories in England. Ornamental decorations such as brass rivet surrounds were added in the late 1800's.

The steel carpenter squares pictured on this page are two-piece take-down models from a 1914 catalog. Solid steel roofing or rafter squares were invented by a Vermont blacksmith named Silas Hawes in 1817. Mr. Hawe's good fortune began when he traded a quick horse-shoeing job for a pile of rusty saw blades, (scrap steel was a scarce commodity in those days). Our blacksmith friend had broken more than his share of flimsy roofing squares over the years, and decided to make up a batch of indestructable ones from these old saw blades. While he was at the task the thought occured to add inch-mark increments along one edge...and behold a new American industry was born.

By the year 1823 Mr. Hawes and a partner named Briggs had moved their operation into a stone mill complete with water-powered machinery. For the next decade the pair had a virtual monopoly on steel square production and became quite wealthy. In 1834 Silas Hawes' patent finally expired and every rule manufacturer in the country got in on the action. Over the next two decades Hawes' square continued its evolution from a pair of hammer-welded saw blades into a highly sophisticated layout tool inscribed with 1,900 scales, tables and measurements.

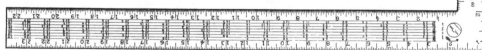

L. BAILEY'S Patent Flush T-Bevel, March 19, 1873. Cast iron handle. Dlr. $60

J. BARTONS, Philadelphia. Huge 22 inch bevel square, conventional design. $45

BEVEL SQUARES: Auction lot of (5) ebony & brass, British made. $70 all. Fancy brass stock with 2 section ebony inlay on each side. Auct. $50-$70 ea. Brass-handled beveled square with inlaid level bubble, Pat. Nov. 5, 1867. Dlr. $95
Cherry-wood ship carpenter's 20 inch bevel. $25. Double-end brass-capped bevel with knurled adjusting nuts, wooden center section. Auct. $115
Ebony and brass bevel squares with 12 to 15 in. blades, factory made. Dlr. $20-$25
Stanley-type rosewood and brass 8 to 10 inch bevel squares $6-$10 Mahogany ship carpenter's 14 inch bevel. $55
Maple sliding T-bevel with 16 in. blade. Auct. $8 Miniature brass sliding T-bevel with 2 in. slotted blade. $22 Rosewood and brass English made bevel squares. Lot of (5) Auct. $42

THOMAS BRADBURN & SONS (England) large boat builder's bevel square with brass blades. Auct. $30

BROWN & SHARPE iron and steel combination square. Dlr. $8 B & S Mfg. Co., Prov. R.I. Solid steel 6 inch try square. Perfect cond. $15

C.G. BULLARD, Ipswich. Ebony try square with 2 brass wear plates and frog's foot inlay. 8 inches overall. Auct. $35

CHAPIN STEPHENS (1901-1929) No. 3 folding steel rafter square with 1894 pat. date. Dlr. $80

Another, (lacking locking screw) Auct. $22

CRAFTSMAN nickle-plated angle divider, same as Stanley No. 30. Dlr. $22

FRANK H. COE, Boonton, N.J., "Pat. Allowed." Double arm Y-shaped bevel square. Auct. $95

C.W.S. CO., Chicago. Solid brass bevel, both blades slotted. "A Dozen Tools in One" Dlr. $17

CHAPIN-STEPHENS No. 42 shipwright's wood-stocked, double-bladed, folding bevel. Auct. $20-$30 No. 036 combination boxwood rule, level, square, and bevel, with protractor. Auct. $150-$225 (in box).

H. DISSTON (1840-1869) 6 inch rosewood and brass bevel. $15 Newer, Disston & Sons rosewood and brass 7½ inch try square. $5-$8 Scarce 4 inch try-and-mitre combination steel square with level bubble attached to side. Circa 1880. Dlr. $45

DUBY & FINN, N.Y. Universal square, 5 X 9 inches. Auct. $25

EAGLE in large letters embossed on handle of iron T-bevel with 12 in. blade. $25-$35 2 ft. take-down framing sq. $95

EAGLE SQUARE MANUF'G CO. rare U-shaped bridge square 14 x 14 x 14 in. with adjustable walnut and brass cross bar, Pat. Jan. 3, 1870. Auct. $300-$400 (Mint)

J. ESTEY Organ Factory, Brattleboro, Vt. Brass L-square 10 x 6 inches. Auct. $50-$100

DAVID FLATHER, Sheffield. Ebony and brass 4½ inch try square. (light rust) Dlr. $25

Very elaborate, etched-brass and rosewood, 17 inch try square made for the American Market. Auct. $375

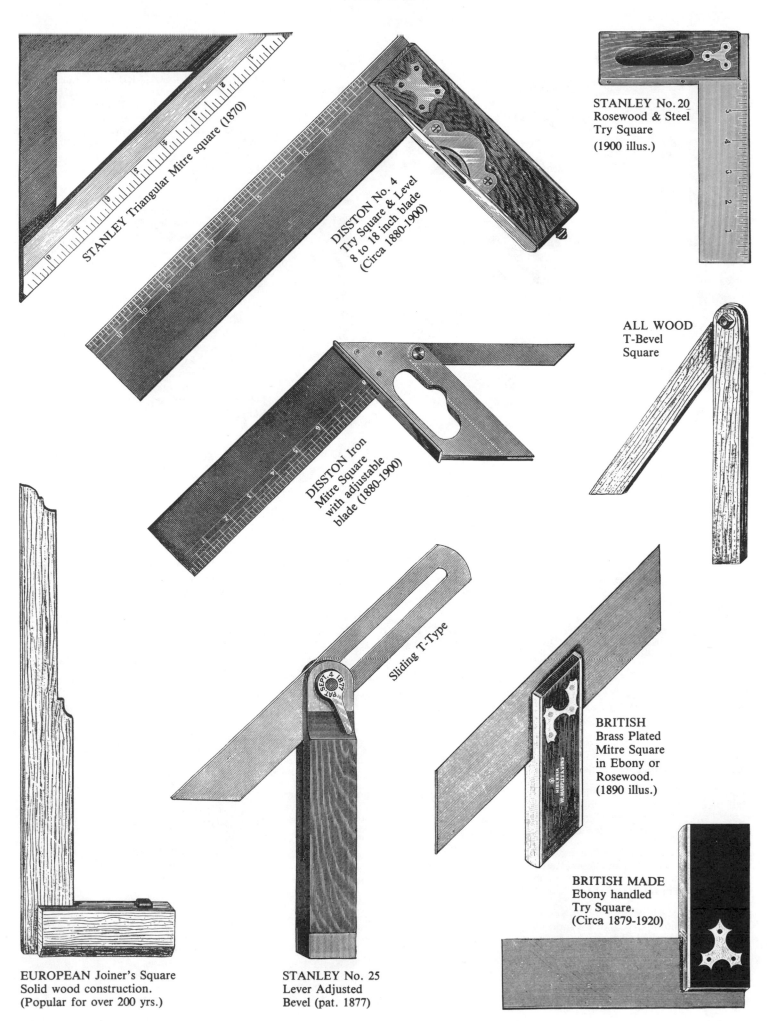

STANLEY Triangular Mitre square (1870)

DISSTON No. 4
Try Square & Level
8 to 18 inch blade
(Circa 1880-1900)

STANLEY No. 20
Rosewood & Steel
Try Square
(1900 illus.)

DISSTON Iron
Mitre Square
with adjustable
blade (1880-1900)

ALL WOOD
T-Bevel
Square

Sliding T-Type

BRITISH
Brass Plated
Mitre Square
in Ebony or
Rosewood.
(1890 illus.)

EUROPEAN Joiner's Square
Solid wood construction.
(Popular for over 200 yrs.)

STANLEY No. 25
Lever Adjusted
Bevel (pat. 1877)

BRITISH MADE
Ebony handled
Try Square.
(Circa 1879-1920)

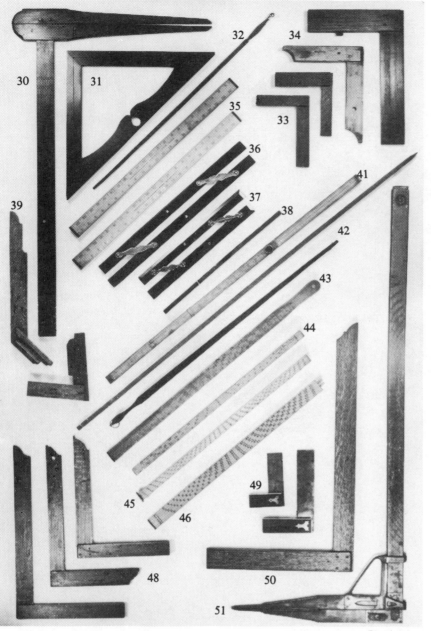

J.P. Bittner Antique Tool Auctions

30. H. R. HOYT, Goffstown, N. H. Cherry log caliper dated 1869. Paper label with instructions barely legible. $50

31. COMBINATION SQUARE heavy example in rosewood, fancy base. 16 x 24 in. $110

32. WANTAGE ROD in steel with simple scale and brass knob. JH stamp, dated 1874. $65

33. TRY SQUARE wooden with double mortise and peg joint. Scale marked on two sides. $5

34. WALNUT & MAPLE try squares. Lot of (3) early ones with no graduations. $30

35. STANLEY No. 30½ Shrink Rules. (2) items. 3/16 in. and ¼ in. per foot. $45

36. PARALLEL RULE ebony 21 inch with brass fittings, (corner chip). $25

37. PARALLEL RULE in horn-like composition material, 15 inches long, brass fittings. $30

38. WANTAGE ROD unmarked small size with Bar L, Hogo, Punch and Tierce scales. $15

39. BEVEL SQUARES, lot of (2) early fixed-angle type. Well made. $20

41. E. SMITH, Rockford, Ill., Pat. Oct. 24, 1876. Inside Measure, brassbound maple with regular and shrink scales. $55

42. WANTAGE ROD, lot of (2): Birch 48 inch wantage rod with Wine, Inch, Bb., and other scales. Also an unknown use quartered-oak tapered stick with brass inserts. $80

43. BOARD SCALE in maple with tally holes on edge, unmarked, shop-made. $20

44. R. B. HAZELTON, Maker, Contoocook, N.H., Eagle stamp, square board measure. Scales 6 in. to 20 inches long. Near new condition. $20

45. STANLEY unmarked No. 46½ maple board measure in like new cond. $75

46. R. B. HAZELTON, Maker, Contoocook, N.H. Flat board measure with tally holes and pegs on both edges. $85

48. WOODEN SQUARES, lot of (3) with scrolled tips, in birch, walnut and beech. $37

49. HALL & KNAPP Eagle brand try squares, rosewood, steel and brass. (2) $25

50. OAK CARPENTER'S SQUARE nicely pegged, 16 x 27 inches. $25

51. F. M. GREENLEAF, Belmont, Mass. No. 1036 timber calipers (wheel missing). $275

GENERAL angle divider, all metal, 8 inch. Dlr. $20　No 829 adjustable bevel with rosewood handle. $6

J. GLEAVE & SON, 8 Oldham St., Manchester (England) Ebony and brass try square with 18 inch steel blade. Dlr. $95

GOODELL PRATT CO., Greenfield, Mass. Pat. Dec. 27, 1904. Combination-style roofing square with sliding metal head, 18 in. steel blade. 2 level bubbles. Dlr. $95

GREBLE TURNER & CO. Hamilton, Ohio and Orange, Mass. Set of (4) machined steel try squares in fitted oak box with owner's name in script on lid. Dlr. $60

HALL & KNAPP (Sold out to Stanley in 1858) New Britian, Conn. Tiny 3 inch try square in rosewood and brass with eagle touchmark. $35

HASELTON, Contoocook, N.H. Large adjustable roof framing square with brass arc. Auct. $1,550

HAWES PATENT hand-stamped steel framing squares, 16 x 24. Auct. $12-$25

L.O. HOWARD, Pat. Nov. 5, 1867. Rosewood & brass stocked adjustable T-bevel square. St. Johnsbury, Vt. (well worn) Auct. 1985, $150

T. IBBOTSON & CO., large rosewood and brass try square with 6 diamond rivet washers and blued steel 24 inch blade. Dlr. $125

IDEAL TOOL CO. pat. 1914 steel rafter square. Triangle with hinged arm at apex. $20-$40

ST. JOHNSBURY TOOL CO. (Vermont) 7 to 12 in. steel try squares with rosewood inlay. Auct. $45 to $65　4 inch example $40

THE KELLOGG French tailor System. Pat. Dec. 25, 1883. Battle Creek, Mich. Folding lite weight wood and brass 12 x 24 inch square. $35

KEEN KUTTER try square with wood or cast iron handle. Small sizes. $15-$20 Sliding T-bevel square with brass and wood handle. $20-$24　With cast iron handle and embossed lettering. $25-$35 Steel framing square 16 x 24 in. $20-$25

KIRBY & BROS., Makers, N.Y. Maple L-square with brass trim. Auct. $75-$95

LUFKIN metal combination try & mitre square with 4 in. blade. Dlr. $15 No. 42 shipwright's double-end 12 inch calibrated bevel square. $30 No. 8130 light weight tailor's square. $35

TRY SQUARES sell in a very broad range. Ebony & brass examples sell at auction in London for $15 & up. U.S. dealers ask $20 to $60 for them. Rosewood & brass, British-made, common sizes. Auct. $8-$15 (Mahogany brings less). 14 in. & larger sizes bring more, as do 3 in. & smaller. Uncommon shaped escutcheons and full brass framed stocks are the most valuable.

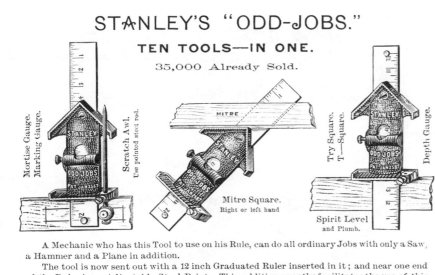

COACHMAKER'S All Metal
Spider Bevel Mortise
Popular from 1800-1920.

MARPLES rosewood & brass try square 14 in. $16. 20 in. $35 Ebony & brass 9 in. Dlr. $25 Registered ebony & brass 15 in. Auct. 1985. $140 Recently made mitre with round rivet washers. $15 Shipwright's 12 in. bevel. with brass blades at both ends. $65

MELHUISH, London. Ebony mitre square with brass wear plates. Auct. $40-$45

MILLERS FALLS try square with 4 inch metal blade, wooden handle. $7

MITRE SQUARES: English-made ebony with brass wear plate on both sides and Z-shaped rivet surround. $25-$50 depending upon quality and amount of original finish intact. Rosewood brings less.

NELSON & HUBBARD, Middletown, CN. Rosewood and brass try square with tab. $45

NICHOLLS MFG. CO., Ottumwa, Ia. Steel take-down square 16 x 24 in. $20 Another in case. $40 18 x 24 in. size. Auct. $32

OAK cabinet maker's solid wood square with French curve template. $45-$55 Another with plumb level and cut-out for bob. $149

PATTERN MAKER'S quarter-sawn oak try square with brass trim and blade, 10 x 22 in. $75

PECK, STOWE & WILCOX steel take-down framing square. $28

PLUMB BOARD level in mahogany, 27 inches long with gunmetal plumb bob. Owner initials inlaid in ivory. auct. $84

PLUMB SQUARES: unmarked mahogany 12 inch traingle with brass plated vial in each section. Auct. $325 Oak plumb square 20 x 24 in. with mortised diagonal brace. Complete with plumb bob. $140 Oak plumb square in triangle shape with 3 plumb bob cut-outs. 17 x 23 in. $70-$85

E. PRESTON & SONS machinists' small 3¾ in. steel square. $12 Tailor's square boxwood with brass hinge and tips. $48 No. 1400 brass stone mason's shift stock, or bevel square, 10½ inches long. Auct. $49 No. 1490 brass framed coach-maker's "spider" mortise bevel with 3 legs mounted on triangle. Auct. $56

I.J. ROBINSON, St. Johnsbury, Vermont. Bevel square, brass and rosewood with steel blade. Pat. 6-14-1873. $60 up.

SARGENT VBM steel carpenter's square 18 x 24 in. $8 Steel bevel, pat. July 22, 1873. Dlr. $15

I. & D. SMALLWOOD, British-made brass-stocked 5 in. try square. Auct. $26

STANLEY SQUARES: No. 1 "Odd Jobs" nickle-plated combination tool 4 inches tall. $45-$85 No. F6 steel square 12 inches overall. $12 No. 10 iron-framed try square rosewood inlay. $15-$20 No. 12 nickle-plated try square, red lettering. $5-$10 No. 16 iron-framed mitre square, walnut inlay. $16-$28 (nickle plated after 1909 and no wood trim). No. 18 adjustable bevel. all metal. $8-$12 No. 20 rosewood and brass try square, pat. 12-29-96. $10-$15 No. 21 combination try and mitre square in cast iron, nickle plated blade. $10-$15 No. 24 combination try and bevel square with slotted rosewood handle and L-shaped steel blade. $35-$45 No. 25 rosewood and brass sliding T-bevel with blued steel blade. $8-$10
Stanley No. 30 plated angle divider. $25-$50 No. 42 shipwright's bevel in boxwood with two blades. $28-$45 No. R100B fixed blade steel framing square. $10 R100TD blued steel framing square, take-down style. $40-$55 Stanley "Four Square" black handled try and mitre square with slotted nickle plated blade. $20-$25

STAR TOOL CO. lignum vitae and brass try square. $15 Star combination try & mitre square with decorative iron head. $20

L.S. STARRETT steel try square in smallest 4 inch size. $8-$15 No. 9 combination square set with 2 heads and protractor. Circa 1913. Dlr. $25 No. 14 tool maker's sliding-scale square. $7 No. 16 combination square with patent protractor and 24 inch steel blade. Auct. $35 No. 360 universal bevel-protractor made from sheet steel Dlr. $30 No. 433 combination square and accessories. $25 No. 439 builder's combinationl level and pitch protractor with sliding blade. $95-$125 No. 61 try sq. $10

E.A. STEARNS & CO., Brattleboro, Vt. No. 73 boxwood & brass shipwright's 12 in. bevel with 2 folding arms. $35

STEEL CARPENTER'S SQUARES, (10) assorted 18 x 24 inch, various makers: Eagle, J. Essex, Hart Mgf., Thomas Douglas, Southington Hardware, Perks, A. Whatley, H. Elwell & Smallwood. Auct. $10 each. Dealer lot, assorted brands, 16 x 24 in, hand stamped, tapered steel blades. Dlr. $8 ea. Collection of (65) early metal squares. All major manufacturers represented, several hand punched variety. Includes custom display and storage box. Auct. $750 Hand-forged and hand-stamped 16 x 24 & 18 x24 inch framing squares, Circa 1820-1840. $25-$40 each.

TAILOR'S combination boxwood rule & square, 3 foot, 3 fold with 18 in. arm. Brass joints and tips. Auct. $80 English-made 2 fold boxwood tailor's square. $50

UNION TOOL No. 4 combination try mitre square, fancy cast iron head. Auct. $80

UNIVERSAL bevel square with degree calibrations, 5 inch. Dlr. $10

UPSON NUT CO., Unionville, Conn. Nickel plated steel square, 4½ x 10 inches with wooden knob on corner. Dlr. $20

WITTER patent 2-22-87 double-end bevel square. Brass-clad mahogany with steel blade at each rounded end. Auct. $130

Sailmaker's Curved Roaching Shears

Artist's or Banker's Paper Shears

Horse Clippers   (Circa 1886)

Pruning Shears   (Circa 1880)

Horse Tail Shears

Household Straight Trimmer

Challange Lamp Trimmer

Household Bent Trimmers

Sheep Shears

Tailor's Shears (1863 Patent)

SCISSORS or SHEARS such as the 20th century examples illustrated above often turn up in box lot purchases and present a puzzling contrast to other tools in an accumulation. A pair of common household scissors are worth a few dollars if still sharp. Add a Keen Kutter logo and the price jumps an extra five or ten bucks. A Winchester trademark could up the ante to $25 or more. TAILOR'S shears look expensive, and they are. A century old pair of A Heinisch 14 inch shears realized $50 at a recent tool auction. SAILMAKER'S shears are hard to come by. A pair of brass handled ones by T. Wilkson & Son of Sheffield was offered by a dealer for $150 last year. SEWING scissors with figural stork handles are still being manufactured today. Vintage examples command from $12 to $25 at antique shows.

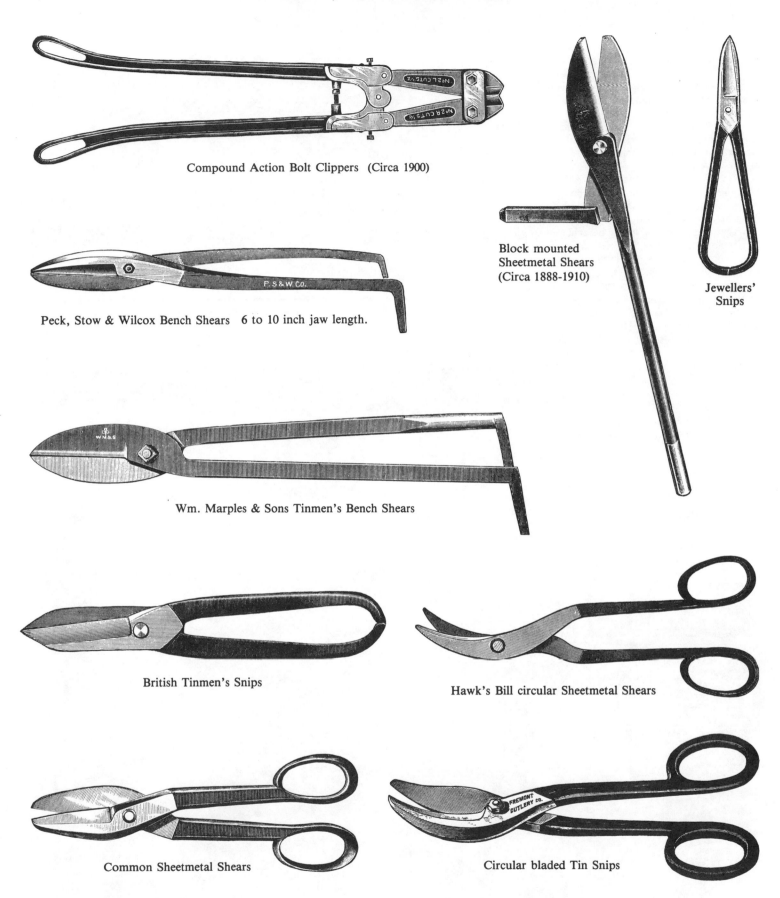

Compound Action Bolt Clippers (Circa 1900)

Block mounted
Sheetmetal Shears
(Circa 1888-1910)

Jewellers'
Snips

Peck, Stow & Wilcox Bench Shears   6 to 10 inch jaw length.

Wm. Marples & Sons Tinmen's Bench Shears

British Tinmen's Snips

Hawk's Bill circular Sheetmetal Shears

Common Sheetmetal Shears

Circular bladed Tin Snips

The average pair of factory made hand-held tin snips has more utilitarian value than collector appeal. They are virtually indestructable and rarely thrown away. Bench-mounted shears run from 14 to 48 inches in length and commonly sell for less than a dollar an inch. Double-action or compound-types fetch more. At a recent tool auction in the Midwest a 4 foot long tinsmith's compound-action bench shear brought a winning bid of $55. A 35 inch conventional-style bench shear sold for $20 at the same event. Be on the lookout for hand-forged examples of ancient appearing sheep shears. You just might discover a pair of 17th Century tapestry weaver's scissors or a Venetian glassblower's cut-off snips.

Almost every turn-of-the-century factory operation had a maze of belts and pulleys hanging from the rafters. Giant shafts powered long leather belts which ran down to each piece of grinding, boring, shaping, sanding, or sawing machinery. Each of these functions was performed at optimum speed. Some machines might fly apart if run too fast, while others (like polishing wheels) could not do their intended jobs at slow speeds.

Factory engineers had to be able to compute the horsepower and speed each motor or shaft was putting out and determine how the best combination of function and economy might be achieved. A simple hand-held tachometer called the speed indicator was developed for this purpose in the 1890's. The instrument usually came with 3 separate tips and could be thrust against the center of a rotating shaft or held on the periphery of a pulley to obtain the number of feet traveled per minute by each belt. When used with a pocket watch the number of revolutions per minute could be quickly determined.

These little jewels could prove to be very sound investments at today's collector prices of $10-$20 each. Even exceptionally complex models rarely sell for more than $35.

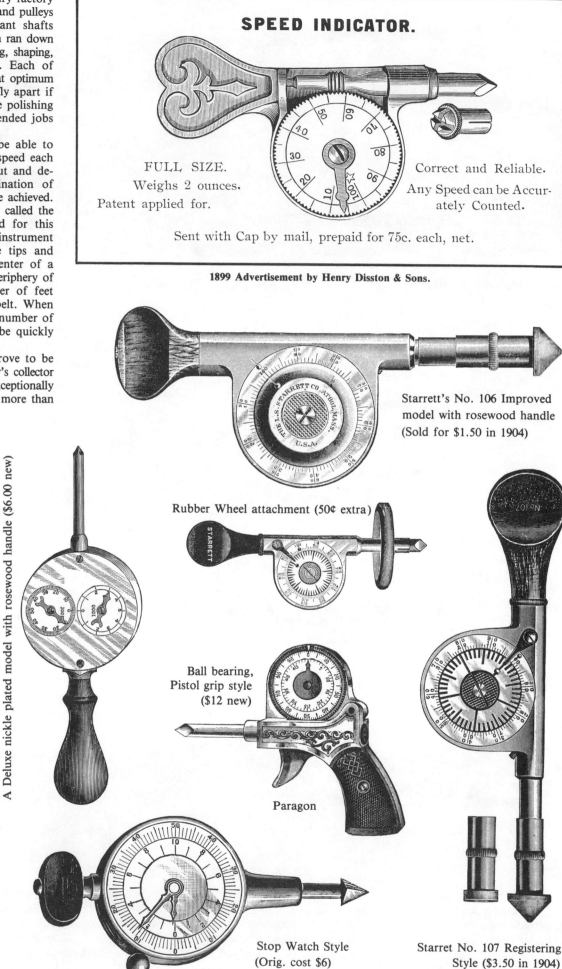

SPEED INDICATOR.

FULL SIZE.
Weighs 2 ounces.
Patent applied for.

Correct and Reliable.
Any Speed can be Accurately Counted.

Sent with Cap by mail, prepaid for 75c. each, net.

1899 Advertisement by Henry Disston & Sons.

Starrett's No. 106 Improved model with rosewood handle (Sold for $1.50 in 1904)

Rubber Wheel attachment (50¢ extra)

Ball bearing, Pistol grip style ($12 new)

Paragon

A Deluxe nickle plated model with rosewood handle ($6.00 new)

Tachometer Type was the most expensive ($60 in 1904)

Stop Watch Style (Orig. cost $6)

Starret No. 107 Registering Style ($3.50 in 1904)

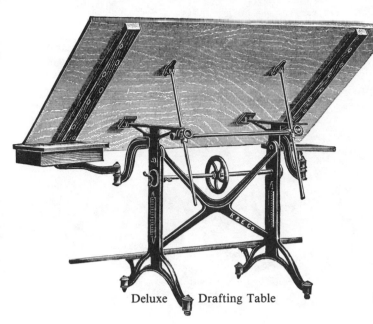

Deluxe   Drafting Table

Surveyor's Steel Measuring Chain

(circa 1900)

DRAFTING INSTRUMENTS: Ivory and brass 14 pc. set in mahogany box. Includes 2 small triangles and a French curve. Ivory handles, brass shafts, steel points. Dlr. $145

English made set in sharkskin case of the 1800's. 5¾ in. tall with hinged lid. Contains ivory sector rule and an architect's scale. Also brass protractor, dividers, inking compass and attachments. Dlr. $285
Ivory handled nickel silver set in velvet lined rosewood and mahogany case with 2 trays. 14 inches long. Auct. $120   Sharkskin covered 7 inch tall wooden box with 8 early brass drawing instruments and a boxwood sector rule. Circa 1770-1800. Auct. $200 Solid silver British made set, 5 in. tall pocket case dated 1820. 2 dividers with steel tips, plus pencil and inking attachments. No protractor. Dlr. $550. Individual steel-tipped brass drafting instruments Circa 1800-1900. Unmarked, brass-handled compass, ruling pens, dividers, etc. $4. to $8. each in mixed lots. German silver, 20th century drafting inst. set in rosewood veneered case. 20 pcs remain including ebony parallel rule. Auct. $70

W.H. HARLING, London, 1895. Mahogany cased drafting set. Contains 2 ivory handled ruling pens, 6 in. ivory scale, boxwood scale & folding sector, 6 in. ebony & brass parallel rule, 3 in. brass protractor, compass with attachments. Dlr. $165

STANLEY, London. 66 ft. surveyor's chain with brass handles and tags. Dlr. $55

Wm ERWIN. Baltimore (Circa 1850). Brass surveyor's compass, 4½. dia. face. Screw-on sight cover and tripod. Auct. $350 Dlr. $700

L. MASON, Dublin. Small old surveyor's theodolite with 11 inch telescope. Precise geared adjustments and fine scales. No. plumb bob or tripod incl. As found condition. Auct. $925

PROTRACTOR in brass with 6 inch beveled bottom edge. $20-$40 German Silver example, hand engraved, 4⅝ in. Dlr. $65 18th century brass protractor with ornamental center arches. Hand engraved. 5½ in. $250

TABLE, DRAFTING. Cast iron tripod base, 22 x 26 in. tilting top. 7 x 26 in. back shelf, 2 drawers. Auct. $275-$375

KOLESCH, N.Y., Circa 1890 Wye level in solid brass. Serial No. 545. $375

EDWARD SPICER, Dublin. Early brass surveyor's compass with mahogany tripod Auct. $600

TROUGHTON & SIMMS, London, (Circa 1850). Dumpy level 17 inches long. 2 inch diameter scope mounted on leveling base. Mahogany case. Dlr. $395

EDWARD WEIR, 142 High Holborn, London. Surveyor's level on mahogany tripod. Auct. $175

(circa 1920)

"Favorite" Farm Level. Economy model for Farmers, Landscape Gardeners and Carpenters.

20th Century Sextant

20th Century Surveying Compass with folding leaf sights.

Dumpy Level with 12 inch Telescope (Circa 1900-1925)

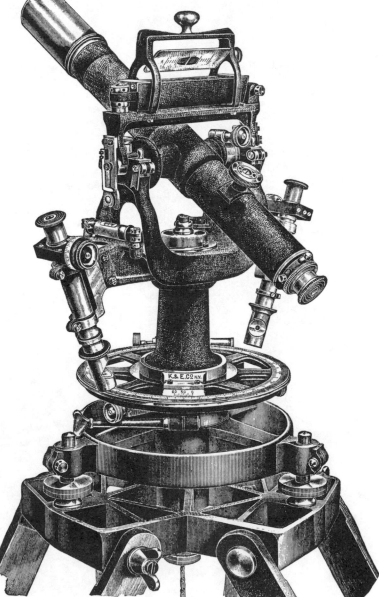

Keuffel & Esser Co., New York. No. 5089 Precision Theodolite

SURVEYOR'S INSTRUMENTS have been hailed as "The Tools That Won the West". Brave and rugged surveying crews preceeded every wilderness army from the French and English in 1755, to the Continental Army of 1776. In the year 1785, Congress deemed that a surveyor from every state in the Union be appointed to a group assigned to map and mark the entire Northwest Territory. Wild Indians and quick tempered rattlesnakes made being a member of this party a hazardous occupation. The project was extended on into the 19th century when Western and Midwestern states and territories were included, thereby enabling an orderly sale of public lands.

Some of the first surveying instruments made in America were the work of clockmakers. Today the most sought after examples are the solid brass sighting compasses of the 18th and 19th centuries. English made pieces have historically commanded higher prices than those produced by American craftsmen, but a rapidly growing group of Domestic collectors could alter future market conditions. The standard 2 volume reference for this field is "The Makers of Surveying Instruments in America since 1800" by Charles Smart, 1962.

A.S. ALOE, St Louis. No. 6707 brass transit, Circa 1900. 12 in. tall with 11 inch scope. Double 6 inch dia. half-circle German Silver verniers. 3 level bubbles. Dlr. $630

BECKMANN CO., Toledo, Ohio. No. 4557 vernier compass, 15 in. overall. Dlr. $350

BLATTNER & ADAMS, St. Louis. No. 5690 Surveyor's transit with telescope. Solid brass with all lettering in script. Unpolished. Dlr. $500

T.S. BOWLES, Portsmouth, N.H. Circa 1821 wooden-cased surveying compass on 14 inch long board with elevated sights at each end. 6 inch dia. dial. No staff or tripod. Auct. $600

F.E. BRANDIS, SONS & CO. (1890-1916) No. 2502 surveying level (scope) with box, no tripod. Auct. $275

BROWNING, Boston, Circa 1825 brass surveying compass. Dlr. $580

BUFF & BUFF No. T129 surveyor's transit and tripod. Patented 1900. Auct. $500

GOLDSMITH CHANDLEE (1746-1921). Winchester, Virginia. Brass sighting compass. Auct. $4,400

ISAAC CHANDLEE of Nottingham, Pennsylvania. Engraved brass surveyor's compass (sights missing). Auct. $3,410.

CHESTERMAN, Sheffield. 100 ft. surveyor's chain with brass handles. Dlr. $65

CHAIN, SURVEYOR'S Unmarked extra long 175 foot example with brass tabs every 5 yards and brass handles. Dlr. $75 Another, 50 link surveyors chain with center swivel and full set brass tags. Auct. $95

L. COLTON, N.Y. (1803-1885) Brass surveyor's compass 14 inches long including folding sights at each end. 4 ¾ inch needle, 2 level vials. No. box. Auct. $375 Another by same maker, 12½ in. original mahogany case. Dlr. $550

ANTHONY DAVENPORT, Portland, Maine, (19th century). Wooden compass with leaf sights, on rectangular board. Auct. $275

DIETZGEN World War II alidade & compass for field map making. Leather case. Auct. $65 Circa 1910 surveyor's pocket omnimeter with aluminum frame 5 x 2¾ x

½ in. Includes a compass and a gravity clinometer with folding brass sights. Dlr. $195 Eugene Dietzgen Co., No. 6166 surveyor's transit. Flat black on brass. Complete with mahogany case, plumb bob, tripod and 3 segment sighting rod. Auct. $225

FRYE & SHAW, 222 Water Street, New York. Heavy brass 6 in. dia. surveyor's compass in orig. mahogany box. Auct. $650

W. & L.E. GURLEY, No. 201161 builder's 24 in. telescope level complete with tripod, target rod and mahogany case. Auct. $275 No. 12 engineer's transit with brass frame and compass base. Circa 1900. includes tripod & box. Auct. $450 Surveyor's vernier compass, 6 in. dia. with 9 inch removable telescope. Hinged brass leaf sights. No tripod. Auct. $600

J.W. HARMON, Boston, Pat. Nov. 23, 1880. Surveyor's sighting level approx ⅝ in. dia. x 11 in. long. 2 bubbles, ebony stock. Dlr. $95-$150 1883 dated artificers level with bubble mounted on top of a 10½ in. long sighting tube. Dlr. $290

T. KENDALL, Jr., New Lebanon, N.Y. (Circa 1800). Brass faced surveyor's compass in original dovetailed box. Dlr. $1,400

KEUFFEL & ESSER No. 5102 builder's level (scope type) in orig. box. Dlr. $75 Wye level with box. and tripod, black finish. $185 K & E transit dated 1905. $465 1910 dated Wye level. $275 Surveyor's transit dated 1910. Incl. carring case. $500

C.G. KING, Broad Street, Boston. Brass surveying compass with 5 in. dial. Auct. $500

KNOX & SHAIN, Philadelphia. Variation transit consisting of 12 in. brass scope mounted on A frames over a 5 in. dia. compass with 2 outboard level bubbles. $975

A. LIETZ CO., San Francisco. 4 in. dia. surveying compass with attached fold-up sights. Auct. $65

MENEELY & OOTHOUT, West Troy, N.Y. No. 847 surveyor's compass in orig. mahogany box. (sights missing) Dlr. $450

PATTEN, New York (Circa 1825). Brass surveying compass with 6 in. tall sights. In original case with Water Street label. Dlr. $950

PHELPS & GURLEY (Circa 1800). Surveyor's transit & tripod in factory labeled box. Auct. $825

B. PIKE'S SON & CO. 928 Broadway, N.Y. Beautiful 7½ in. dia. surveyor's compass. Auct. $750 Circa 1840, 5½ in. dia. surveying compass with 2 bubble vials mounted on brass base. Original wooden box. $575 B. Pike & Sons, 166 Broadway. Circa 1875 black enameled brass telescope transit with vernier, 6½ in. dia. compass on German Silver base. Dlr. $950

J. POOL & COMP., Easton, Mass. Surveyor's compass with brass leaf sights. Comes with tripod in original labeled case. Auct. $500 H.M. Pool surveyor's chain, Circa 1818-1879. 33 feet long, 50 links, 4 brass tags. Dlr. $285

H. SAWYER, Yonkers, N.Y. Heavy brass engineer's transit with 18 inch telescope. Gurley brand tripod. Auct. $350

THAXTER, Boston, (1792-1822). Surveying compass with 2 level vials mounted next to 6 in dia. face Includes tripod and box. Auct. $525

J.C. ULMER, "Makers of high grade engineering instruments," Cleveland, Ohio. Brass surveyor's telescope level, stand and box. Dlr. $275

DAVID WHITE CO. Milwaukee. Surveyor's transit level (scope), on stand. Auct. $175

GEORGE WHITEHOUSE, Farmington, N.H. Wooden compass and level, Circa 1870. 11 inches overall with 5 in. compass and 4 sight vanes. Complete with tripod and mahogany case. Dlr. $950 Another, mounted in 10 in. frame Minor repairs. Auct. $500

T. WHITNEY, Maker, Phila. (Circa 1800). No. 321 surveyor's compass with cover plate, but no staff. 14 inches overall. 5¼ in. needle. Auct. $425

T.B. WINTER, Newcastle upon Tyne. No. 284 heavy brass miner's surveying compass 11 inches long. 2 folding 6 in. lever sights. Dlr. $650

WOODEN THEODOLITE from Maine, Circa 1835. Six inch diameter compass is set in a mahogany arch attached to a circular mahogany block which is in turn mounted to a rectangular mahogany sighting tube 12 inches in length. Invented by James Eames of Newry. Dlr. $1,350

Courtesy Dover Publications   Denis Diderot, 1752

Above we find a French tinsmith's family of the year 1750 hard at work producing coffee pots. Father rounds the body using a wooden mallet and a stake anvil while his young son files the burr from a rim. Another youth solders a spout in place using a charcoal fired brazier to heat his iron. Strips of soldering tin lay in front of him on the table ready for instant use. On display are other family made products including pots, pans, food warmers, rain gutters and lighting devices.

Great Britian was the ancient world's sole source for tin. Phoenician and Carthaginian traders had a monoply on the metal until Romans under Julius Ceaser arrived on the island. In those times tin was used to plate iron implements, to alloy copper in the production of bronze, and also for the purpose of making scarlet and purple textile dyes which were the most expensive colors of the period. Cornwall tin miners of the 1800's reported finding old Roman shoring timbers and mining tools at depths of up to 300 feet below the surface.

American mass production of tinplated household items did not begin in earnest until the 1830's. Irish immigrants had introduced the craft in Connecticut in 1730 but the British monoply on sheet iron production delayed domestic development by a hundred years.

Yankee tin peddlers are a fascinating study in American folklore. After purchasing a wagon load of inventory from an urban tinsmith, a brave peddler would head into the countryside to live by his wits. Some villages outlawed such traveling merchants from entering town. Highwaymen and thugs of every stripe preyed upon them, even though few were known to carry money. An 1830's account reported "Tin-pedlars receive in payment for their goods, rags, together with feathers, hog's bristles, old pewter, brass and copper, and sometimes ready cash."

A close examination of antique tinware will reveal rolled over edges and interlapping seam joints, as well as heavy iron wire reinforcement. The solder provided watertight joints but contributed little to structural rigidity. Between 1805 and 1860 a rash of hand-cranked folding, shaping, creasing, beading and burring machines were invented in New England. Prior to 1805 these functions were performed with anvil and mallet.

STOWE'S UNIVERSAL STAKE HOLDER (Circa 1900)

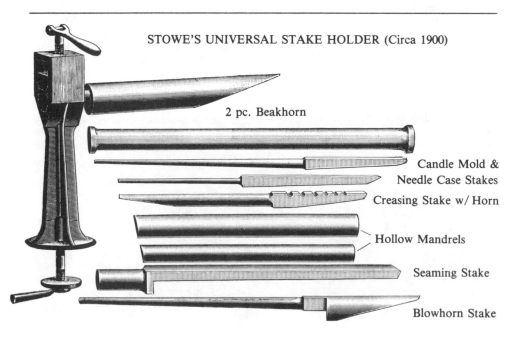

2 pc. Beakhorn

Candle Mold & Needle Case Stakes

Creasing Stake w/ Horn

Hollow Mandrels

Seaming Stake

Blowhorn Stake

BARTLET MFG CO., Detroit, Mich. Pat Oct. 1909. Double-action sheetmetal shears with lever linkage. Dlr. $22

E.W. BUCKLEY, Berlin, Conn. Tinner's beakhorn stake, 41 inches long, 45 lbs. Auct. $65

BEADING MACHINE or hand-cranked swage. ⅞" wide shaping head rollers. Dlr. $60 Another with brass gears and open-style cast iron frame. Post mounted. $95

BENCH PLATE, tinworker's socket-style, 8 x 37 inches. For holding stakes or shears Auct. $80

BENCH SHEARS, tinsmith's heavy-duty compound-type, 48 inches long. Auct. $55

FLUX BOX, tinsmith's cast iron 3 x 5 inch slab-like bowl with 2 in. dia. recess. $18

FOLDING MACHINE, hand-operated 30 inch bar folder, heavy duty, weighs 150 lbs. Auct. $100

HAMMER, Stubb's type metal-working hammer with long pane. $18

HICKORY MALLET, tinner's 2½ inch diameter. $5-$8

PEXTO stove pipe crimper, Circa 1920. Hand-held plier-type with 2 gears. $18

STAKES, anvil mounted: 2½ x 8 in. $25 2½ x 5 in. $5 11 x 1 x 7 in. T-style $35 Beakhorn type 27 inches long $45 Another 40 inches long. Auct. $35 Hardwood bench stake, rectangular shaped 3 x 11 inches. $20 Another tapers from 5 to 2 inches in dia, 32 inch long cone shape. $65 Iron blow horn stake 26 inches long inc. funnel end. $90 Candle mold stake 28 in. Auct. $85 Conductor stake. $25 Creasing stake, 14 inches long. $35 Hollow mandrell, 40 inches long. Auct. $90 Needlenose, 20 in. $40

Sheet Metal Soldering Iron Heater

PEXTO bench plate with a series of square and rectangular openings. 8 x 29 inches. Dlr. $100

PECK, STOWE & WILCOX bench shears 28 inches overall. Dlr. $26 Burring machine by same maker. pat 1867. hand cranked. $35-$50

P.N. & CO., Southington, Conn. (1834-1845). Hand-cranked burring machine. Post mounted with brass gears and spacers. Dlr. $125

ROUNDING HAMMER, tinsmith's 2¼ in. diameter handwrought head 7 in. long. $22-$35

ROYS & WILCOX, Berlin, Ct. Tinsmith's turning machine. Brass top and gears, wood handle. Dlr. $45

F. ROYS & CO., Berlin, Ct. Blown horn stake, 26 in. long cone. $85 Beading swedge by same maker. Hinged hammer-on-spike design with ram's horn nut and handwrought fence. 15 inches overall. Dlr. $150

SETTING DOWN MACHINE patented in 1860. Hand-cranked right-angle wheels turn over pail tops, cans, etc. $60

STOVE, sheetmetal tinker's stove 13 in. high. Cast iron door, removable top and inside tray. Dlr. $145

SOLDERING IRONS with large solid copper head on iron rod with wooden handle. $5 to $15 ea. (many of these are hand made).

SPOUTING CREASER, pat. Jan. 25, 1898. Flutted iron block 4 inches long. $40

A.W. WHITNEY, Woodstock, Vt. Burring machine, wood handle, metal gears. Auct. $50-$70

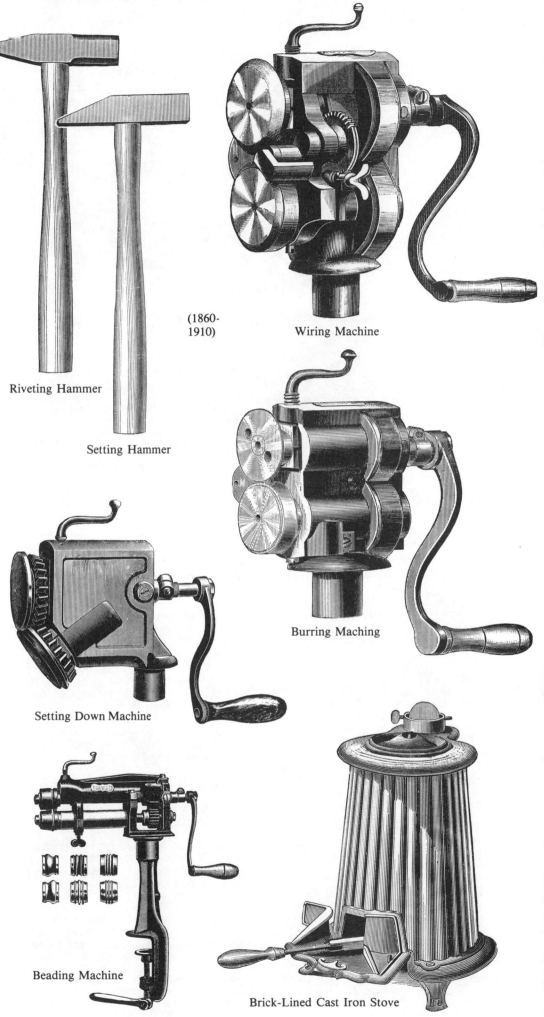

Riveting Hammer

Setting Hammer

(1860-1910) Wiring Machine

Burring Maching

Setting Down Machine

Beading Machine

Brick-Lined Cast Iron Stove

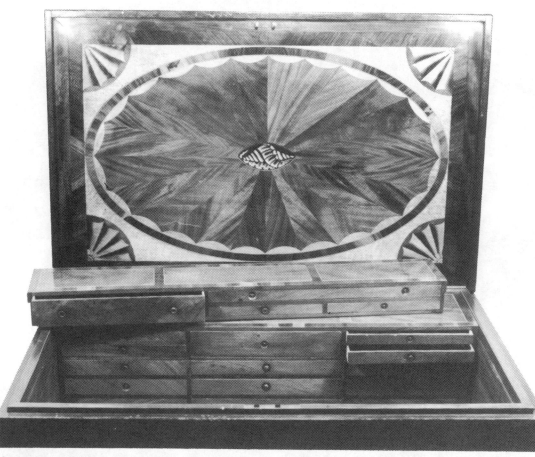

Elaborate tool chests have gone the way of the buggy whip and surviving examples often command prices comparable to those of good antique furniture. Above is an exceptionally fine English cabinet maker's chest of the 1780-1890 period. It's heavy pine exterior boards protect a finely fitted mahogany interior consisting of 4 sliding tills with false fronts and 13 dovetailed drawers. Three lower compartments have sliding lids and the open top displays bird's eye maple, satinwood, rosewood, ebony, and boxwood decorations. This 41 x 27 x 26 inch box brought a winning bid of $2,625. at a recent tool auction in London conducted by Tyrone R. Roberts. Less elaborate tool boxes of 1880-1930's vintage are showing up in antique shops stripped of their battleship grey enamel, refinished in pumpkin pine, and sold as "blanket chests".

BIRD'S EYE MAPLE tool chest 38 x 24 x 23 inches. Dovetailed ¾ in. maple construction throughout. Panelled top. Typical immigrant chest design. Auct. $850

BOY'S TOOL CHEST. Union No. 60 with inside lid label intact. 6 x 12 x 4½ inches overall. dovetailed. Dlr. $50 Elite Tool chest For Boys No. 620 printed on colorful inside label. Stained, oak grained 10 x 7 x 18 in. box. (no tray) $150 Boys Favorite No. 3000 tool chest complete with all jr. sized tools except the hammer. Large inside paper label. $175 Boys Tool chest 9½ x 6½ x 17½ in. with only 12 of original 34 tools listed on colorful inside label. $85

CABINENT MAKER'S chest with 11 dovetailed sliding trays which are mahogany framed with sycamore fronts and brass handles. Teak framed top has inlaid sunburst star. 39 x 26 x 27 in. overall. Auct. $480 British pine chest 22 x 39 x 25 in. Polished interior has 3 cherry wood trays. Inside top lid inlaid with crotch walnut and bird's eye maple with 2 stars. Dlr. $1295 Decorative cabinet maker's tool chest from England. 25 x 24 x 39 inches. 4 sliding compartments 12 dovetailed drawers. Lots of veneering in mahogany, rosewood and boxwood. Ebony knobs. Flat black exterior. Auct. $1,450 Another

British chest. Black exterior with Cuban mahogany interior. Burl and satinwood inlaid lid. Three sliding drawers lift out. Plain interior but very fine. 34 in. wide x 22 high x 21 in. deep. Dlr. $1,800 Superb quality inlaid tool chest 41 x 27 x 26 inches. Circa 1800 with mahogany lined interior, 4 sliding tills and 13 dovetailed drawers. Recessed ebony knobs. 3 lower compartments. Top inside lid inlaid with oval Sheraton design in 5 diferent exotic woods. Auct. $2,625

COLQUHOUN & CADMAN gentlemen's tool chest in solid oak. 9½ x 18 inches, 5 in deep. brass handles and estuchean. Mint condition. Dlr. $150

GILBERT No. 707 Boy's tool chest including some tools. Auct. $35 Gilbert Big Boy, 13 x 21 inch box complete with 15 original tools. Auct. $55 Dlr. $95

GOODELL PRATT No. 712 Home Companion tool set with orig. label and tool list. Solid walnut, finger-jointed box, 8½ x 16 x 6 inches overall. Hinged top, single drawer. Auct. $175 complete with all tools.

HAMMACHER, SCHLEMMER & CO. wall hung cabinet with lower drawer. Measures 7½ x 17 x 25½ inches. Dlr. $135

JAMES HOWARTH & SONS, Broom Springs Works, Sheffield. Gentlemen's chest in dovetailed oak with brass handles Lift out tray. 18½ x 10 x 5½ inches overall. Original paper labels intact. Dlr. $150

C.E. JENNINGS & CO. 71-73 Murray Street, New York City. Side-opening dovetailed pine carrying case. Pat. 1908. 16 x 17 x 34 inches. Hinged front and lid. Orig label. Dlr. $55

KEEN KUTTER wall-hung style oak tool cabinet with 2 large logos inside. Measures 19 x 27½ x 8 inches including bottom drawer. Empty. $150-$200

MACHINIST'S TOOL BOX, standard factory-made drop front oak chest. Auct. $85-$110., Dlr. $150 up. Another with eleven freshly relined drawers in green felt. 9 x 26 x 16 in. Exterior also refinished. Auct. $170 Dlr. $250. Mahogany machinist's tool box with panelled exterior. 27 x 14 inches. 4 drawers and lift lid. Brass corners and recessed ring pulls. Auct. $200 Another in mahogany, 21 x 13 x 14 in. overall with 4 drawers and top compartment. Decorative brass and cast iron handles. Dlr. $225

MASON PARKER MFG. CO. Boy's tool chest in original red paint. 7¾ x 20 in. $25

British made Gentleman's Wall Mounted
Tool Cabinet. Oak, Pine or Mahogany (Circa 1910)

American Style Machinists' Chest or Jewelers' Case.

Machinists' Tool Chest in Oak or Chestnut
with Black Walnut Trim. (1902 price $6.00)

OAK ROLL-FRONT cabinet maker's tool chest 33 x 28 x 23 inches. 2 large moulding plane drawers and 13 smaller drawers plus 2 more full width bottom compartments. All have mahogany veneered fronts. Flat black exterior. Auct. $588

PINE TOOL BOX, crude construction. contains 50 assorted moulding planes. Auct. $200   Another pine chest 33½ x 17½ x 14 inches. 2 sliding interior trays. 6 board style but not dovetailed. $75   Dovetailed pine carpenter's box 18 in. tall by 38 in. long. Auct. $80 Stained pine tool chest in immigrant style. Lift out top tool tray 35 in. long. $95-$150 Pine chest in old green finish with the usual interior sliding trays and lidded boxes. Panelled on 4 sides. Auct. $150 Fine paneled pine chest 22 in. high by 36 in. long. Dovetailed boards are inlaid and inside top lid is decoupaged with period trade cards and stick-ons from 1880's. Dlr. $350   Another panelled pine box as above but with 5 mahogany trays and recessed handles. 24 x 24 x 37 in. $350

SHEFFIELD WORKS, gentleman's dovetailed oak tool box Circa 1900. Size 7 x 4 x 13 in. Old paper label in lid lists original factory packed contents. $90

STANLEY No. 850 wall-hung tool cabinet in oak or walnut. 1939 model has roll front. (1929 catalog shows side-hinged doors.) 8½ x 25½ x 29½ inches overall. Original sold with 49 Stanley tools for $95 total. Today's price with no tools $375. No. 861 dovetailed oak wall-mounted unit 12 x 29 x 7½ in. with Stanley logo affixed inside. $110-$150 No. 904 oak tool cabinet 11¼ x 20 x 4½ in. when closed. $60

WALNUT tool chest 42 x 26 x 25 in. Dovetailed construction. Auct. $425   Walnut and pine carpenter's chest 38 x 22 x 23 in. with 4 dovetailed walnut drawers. Partitioned and hinged well flap. Dlr. $425

I.F. COLE dovetailed tool box with normal array of cherrywood interior trays and boxes. Offered as found, with 40 moulding planes and 2 plows, all with I.F. Cole owner's stamp. Auct. $900

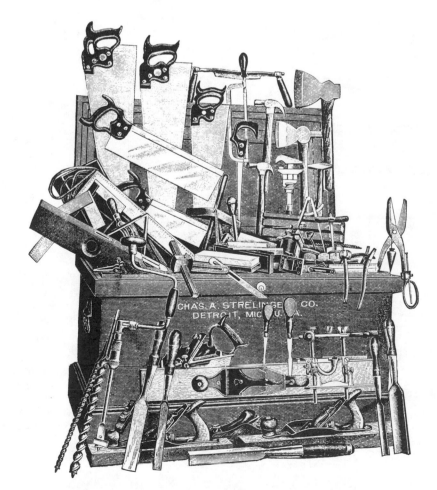

Factory-made 39 inch Carpenter's Tool Chest. (1897 price $9.00)

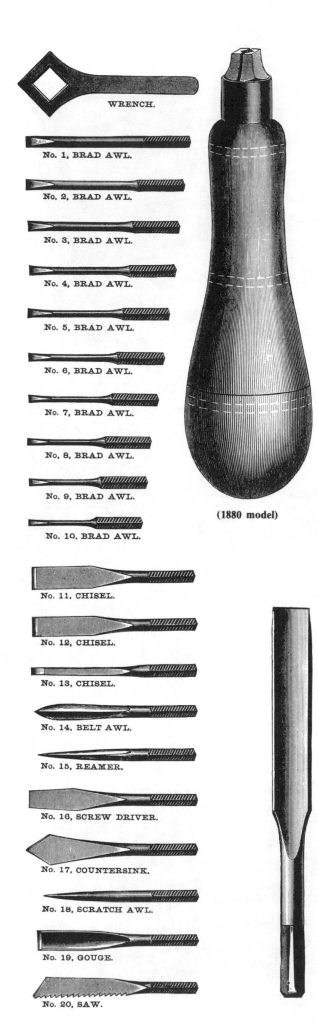

WRENCH.

No. 1, BRAD AWL.

No. 2, BRAD AWL.

No. 3, BRAD AWL.

No. 4, BRAD AWL.

No. 5, BRAD AWL.

No. 6, BRAD AWL.

No. 7, BRAD AWL.

No. 8, BRAD AWL.

No. 9, BRAD AWL.

No. 10, BRAD AWL.

No. 11, CHISEL.

No. 12, CHISEL.

No. 13, CHISEL.

No. 14, BELT AWL.

No. 15, REAMER.

No. 16, SCREW DRIVER.

No. 17, COUNTERSINK.

No. 18, SCRATCH AWL.

No. 19, GOUGE.

No. 20, SAW.

(1880 model)

TOOL HOLDERS evolved from changeable-point-type cobbler's awls to their modern form in about 1860. The first versions, like the Aiken's Patent tool at left, required a chuck wrench. Stanley offered an "Excelsior" model in 1867 which featured a handle-tightened chuck. Hollowed-out Rosewood and Cocobolo handles were the most popular. These "Poor Man's Tool Kits" sold by the millions in the $1.50 to $2.50 range over a 75 year period. Today's prices run from $10 or $15 for a small-handled 5 tool set, to $35 for the deluxe quality version (below) complete with woodcarving gouges and a saw blade. An interesting find might be an advertising imprint such as Arm & Hammer Soda.

(1904 engraving)

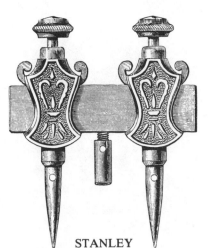

STANLEY

Nos. 1, 2 & 3 Bronze Trammel Heads, steel points. (This pattern 1872-1908)

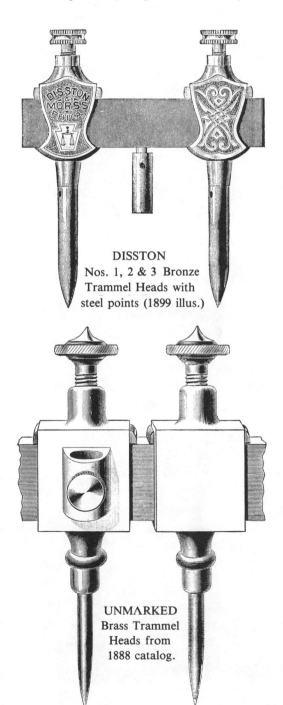

DISSTON

Nos. 1, 2 & 3 Bronze Trammel Heads with steel points (1899 illus.)

UNMARKED
Brass Trammel Heads from 1888 catalog.

TRAMMELS were used by Millwrights, Machinists, carpenters and others having occasion to strike arcs or circles larger than could be done with dividers.

Some had an extra pencil clamp affixed while others had removable points which could be replaced by a pencil or holder.

BRASS trammel points in unmarked pairs from 4 to 6 inches long sell in a general price range of $25-$50 Finely turned or extra large examples will command a higher price. A 7 inch pair, Circa 1880, sold for $100 at auction recently. A (3) piece set with 4 inch heads and a 6 inch double-pointed center head brought $150.

J.B. CHACE pair of 7 in. brass trammel points, one with offset pencil holder, on rosewood bar. Dlr. $85

EBONY wood trammel points with elegant turned boxwood screw-tops and brass ferrules. 5¾ inches tall incl. steel points. Dlr. $110

ENGINEER'S huge pair of keg-shaped cast iron 9 inch trammels. Auct.$35

E.S. CO. tiny pair of 2⅜ in. brass points which also hold a pencil. Dlr. $40

GUNMETAL trammel points, British made. Various sets from 4½ to 6 inches long with decorative cut out designs in sides. Auct. $50-$95 German Silver in orig. box. $105

MAPLE trammel points 9 inches long including brass ferrules and steel points. Dlr. $125

PRESTON & SONS brass trammel heads with rectangular bodies, turned ferrules and tops. Various sizes from 5 to 6 inches long. Auct. $35-$55 Dlr. $65-$85 pair

SHAKER-STYLE walnut trammel bar with 1 fixed and 1 sliding walnut head. Auct. $25

E. SMITH & CO., Rockford, Ill. 10-24-1876 Pat. Combination sliding inside measure, board rule, and trammel bar with points. Auct. $95

STANLEY No. 1 smallest size bronze trammel points approx. 3½ in. tall Sides are decorated. (These became plain in design Circa 1909). Auct. $25-$35 No. 2 size approx. 4½ in. tall with removable steel points. $35-$50 No. 3 largest size, approx. 5½ in. $35-$50 Stanley No. 4 nickel plated iron trammel points 4½ inches tall. Have socket for pencils. Auct. $18-$30 No. 5 japanned iron trammels with 4 adjusting screws (no transactions reported). No. 99 brass trammel set, for use on carpenter's rule. 3 pcs. Dlr. $55

L.S. STARRETT No. 50 trammel pts. $28 No. 51 beam set with curved legs. Dlr. $45

TAYLOR & DURBY Cleveland, Ohio. pair of brass trammel points mounted on a 33 inch beam. Auct. $20

WALNUT trammel points mounted on 38 inch beam. Auct. $40

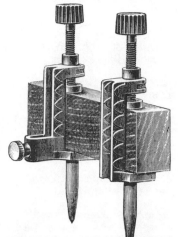

STANLEY No. 4 Nickel Plated Iron Trammel Points . (1905 illus.)

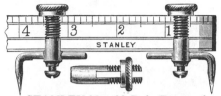

STANLEY No. 99 Rule Trammel Brass incl. pencil holder. (1888-1930)

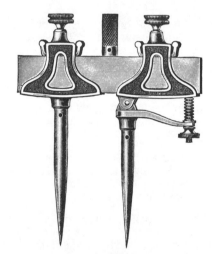

L.S. STARRET No. 50 Adjustable Nickel Plated Bronze Trammel Heads .(Circa 1915)

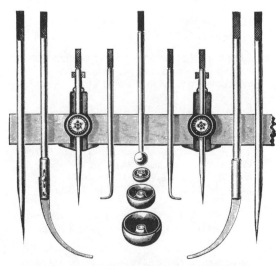

L.S. STARRET No. 59 Trammel Point Set with Centering Buttons and Caliper Legs.

BLACKSMITH'S LEG VISE, also called a Solid box, or Staple vise. With 4-5 in. wide jaws. Approx. 40 inches to floor. $40-$50. Larger models are scarcer.

BROOM MAKER'S vise, Pennsylvania, circa 1860. Auct. $85

CARVER'S BENCH SCREW, a large threaded iron woodscrew which is tightened from under the bench by a giant wing nut. 11/16 in. x 12 in. $20-$30

CHAIN DRIVE bench vise with parallel wooden jaws. Auct. $55

CLOCKMAKER'S hand-forged, screw-on, table-top vise with large wing nut clamp. 6 in. overall. $16-$25

COMMON BENCH-TOP utility vises with 2 to 3 inch wide jaws and no anvil. $8-$12 ea.

COLUMBIAN cast iron vise with anvil and hardy hole. 3½ in. wide jaws. Dlr. $15

DISSTON saw vise. No. 1 $10-$15 No. 5, near new cond. Dlr. $20

EMMERT Pattern maker's deluxe revolving vise. 18 inches wide jaws pivot in all directions. $225-$325

FISHER No. 2 heavy duty blacksmith's chain-drive vise with 4½ inch jaws. Asking $150

GOODELL-PRATT No. 96 hand held vise 4⅞ in. long. Dlr. $15

HAMMACHER SCHLEMMER polished steel hand vise, 5 inches in length. Circa 1896. $22

HAND VISES by various makers, 3 to 6 inches long with 1 to 1½ in. wide jaws. $7-$15 ea. (Brass trim or exotic wood handle might increase the price).

HANDWROUGHT bench-top vise with huge ram's horn wing nut clamp, 2½ in. jaws. $45 Another, finer quality. Dlr. $95

HOBBY SIZE or Jeweler's clamp-on table-top vise with anvil end. $8-$15

LEG VISE, hand-forged example with 6 in. wide jaws. Auct. $65

RAM'S HORN handle and screw clamp on this early and fine hand-forged 6 x 8 inch vise from Conn. Asking $175

SARGENT No. 95 saw vise, circa 1925. $15

STANLEY "Marsh" No. 400 faucet-handled picture framer's vise. $95 No. 700 inexpensive portable woodworker's vise with 4⅝ in. jaws. $20-$30 No. 743 clamp-on portable vise with 2 inch jaws. $35

STEPHENS PATENT lever action cam-lock, quick-acting, heavy duty 4½ in. wide vise. $125

WOODWORKING bench vises with up to 11 inch jaws, wooden dowel handle. $35-$50 in good working condition.

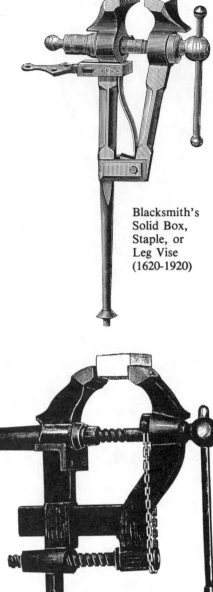

Bonney's Swivel Jaw Bench Vice with Anvil (Circa 1880)

Blacksmith's Solid Box, Staple, or Leg Vise (1620-1920)

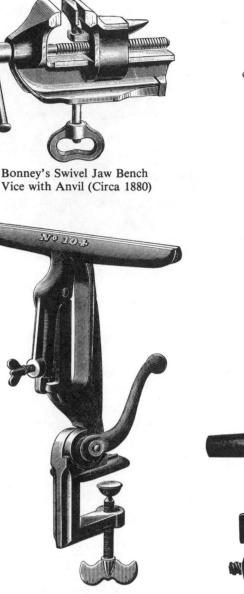

Sargent No. 104 Adjustable Angle Saw Filer's Vise (Circa 1884)

Blacksmith's Chain Vise (Circa 1865)

Alford's Hand Vise. (1880-1920)

Came with screw driver & awl inserts.

Deluxe Jeweler's Vise (1865)

British Clock Maker's Vise (1900)

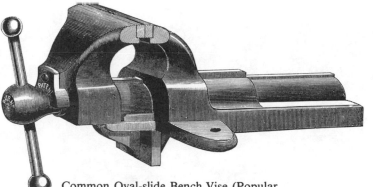

Common Oval-slide Bench Vise (Popular
from 1860-1930)

Sargent No. 34 Saw Filers
Parallel Vise (1864–1884)

Woodworker's Vise in steel & iron with
swivel base. (Circa 1900)

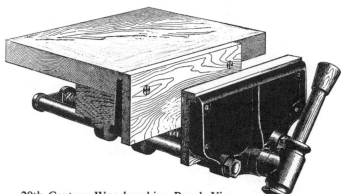

20th Century Woodworking Bench Vise

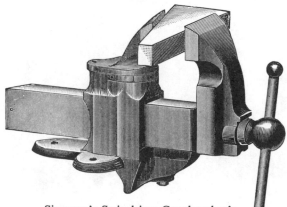

Simpson's Swivel-jaw Coachmaker's
Vise (Circa 1899)

Sargent No. 63 Swivel Vise
with Anvil (Circa 1880)

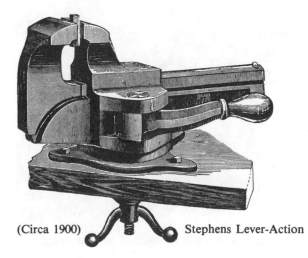

(Circa 1900)   Stephens Lever-Action

TOOLS OF THE WHEELWRIGHT

Denis Diderot, 1752

Above: 16th century wheelwright apprentices plying their 3,000 year old trade. The workman at far left mortises felloes which have been shaped with side axe and adze. At center we see spokes being driven home in a hub which had been aged for 10 years before being turned and mortised. In the background an apprentice uses a spoke shave to round off square edges. At right a skilled workman measures and trims oversize spokes before doweling the felloes together.

Below: A frantic looking crew of French wheelwrights hammer and pry a red hot iron rim into place. Afterwards they will plunge the whole thing into a water trough to shrink fit. At right, glowing nails are driven through the rim into each felloe section. A hundred years later, in 1850, one man might mount and shrink 4 carriage rims in half an hour using the newly invented hydraulic tire-setter. By the year 1865 every phase of wooden wheel construction had become a machine assisted operation.

Another type of wagon tire called Strakes made it possible for only one or two men to assemble a wheel or complete on-the-spot repairs. Strakes are short, curved lengths of tire iron about a foot long. They were hammered on hot...over each felloe joint. The last section was pulled together with a screw clamp, called the Sampson, just before a glowing red strake was nailed in place. The sketches above and below were rendered between 1802 and 1807 by the British artist W.H. Pyne.

TRAVELERS were used in many occupations to measure curved surfaces before accurate steel or cloth tapes were invented. The wheelwright's version was usually numbered from 1 to 24 inches. By counting the number of revolutions the tool turned as it traveled around the circumference of a wagon wheel, one could reproduce the dimension upon a flat length of tire iron before cutting to fit.

BLACKSMITH made, hand-forged travelers with 2 to 6 iron spokes. Up to 9 inch diameter. $25-$50. (Serpentine-curved spokes bring slightly more.) Handles may be wooden or forged loop variety.

BRASS or BRONZE travelers command a premium over iron ones. A three spoked model with pointer, wooden handle, iron frame. Near mint. $125 - $170

CLOCKMAKER'S hand-forged, two spoke traveler, 4¾ inches in diameter, Dlr. $80 Another, but with solid metal wheel, no spokes. Auct. $75

J.W. & T. CONNOLLY LTD., London. Brass 7 inch solid disk-type with advertising on both sides. 5 inch wooden handle. Dlr. $149

FACTORY MADE iron traveler with serpentine spokes and a pointer. 8 in. dia. Yoke frame, wood handle. Orig. red and black finish. $35

GALVANIZED IRON sheet metal traveler. Home-made. $10 - $12

STAR SPOKE design, wheelwright's 8 in. dia. traveler with crude wooden handle. $50

SHEETMETAL, solid, unspoked 8½ in. dia. early traveler from New Hampshire. Auct. $70

WELLS BROS. & CO., Greenfield, Mass. "Little Giant" iron traveler with indicator. $35-$50

WOODEN TRAVELERS, crude to fine examples. Auction range: $28-$85

AXLE GAUGE, aligns wheel at correct angle with axle. 6 foot long wooden bar with sliding iron bracket-like points. Some have protractor-type end piece. $40-$75

AUGER, hook-end 18th-century hub auger 30 inches long with 27 in. T-handle. Dlr. $140

BRUZZ or wheelwright's V-shaped parting chisel. $35

CHISEL, wheelwright's socket mortise, size ⅝ inch, 15 inches long. $28 Gooseneck style, 20 inches long. C. Whitehouse & Sons. $55

CONESTOGA wagon jack, dated 1855. Iron-straped wooden base, 24 inches tall. Auct. $110 Another with iron top section. Early orange and red paint. Dated 1858. Dlr. $150

HUB RING CUTTER, for cutting groove inside axle hole. 7 in. dia. cylinder with handles on sides. 16 inches overall. Dlr. $180

HUB SHOULDER CUTTER, Doles pat. July, 1854. Auct. $55

HUB BORING ENGINE by Silver & Deming, Salem, Ohio. Pat. 1854. Auger-type tool with large self-centering chuck. $95

JARVIS or wheelwright's axle shave. English-made model with brass sole. Dlr. $120-$140 10 inch long American made jarvis with 2 inch cutter. $40 13 inch lawnmower-style handled oak jarvis. $57

REAMER, blacksmith-made 8 inch long tapered reamer, no handle. $8-$12 Hand-wrought tapered-nose type, 23 in. overall, wooden handle. $34 Hooked reamer, 24 inches long, no handle. Auct. $75

SPOKE DOG with hand-forged hook near top of wooden handle. $18-$26 All metal variety. $30-$60

SPOKE POINTER, Hargrave cast iron funnel 3 inches across. $8

TROUGH, cast iron quenching container, curved bottom, 4½ x 4 x 24 inches. Signed Medina, N.Y. $45 Another 3 inches wide by 29 inches long D.R. Sperry & Co. $40

Courtesy Dover Publications

Webster's defines the wainwright as a wagonmaker, often working in conjunction with a wheelwright. Wainwrights were kept busy well past the turn-of-the-century building all forms of farm wagons, mining, and freight vehicles....long after carriages had disappeared from public roadways. In the United States wainwrights were responsible for manufacturing thousands of Conestoga freight wagons produced between 1725 and 1850. Originating in Pennsylvania's Conestoga region, these wide-wheeled prairie schooners were indeed our inland ships of commerce. For more than a hundred years wagon trains criss-crossed America's mountains and plains carrying everything from complete households to commercial freight. A six horse Conestoga could comfortably move 8 tons of cargo over a thousand miles of trackless prairie sod. The wagon's bottom, a long narrow box, hung bow-shaped between front and rear axles and kept heavy loads centered when traveling over rough mountain terrain.

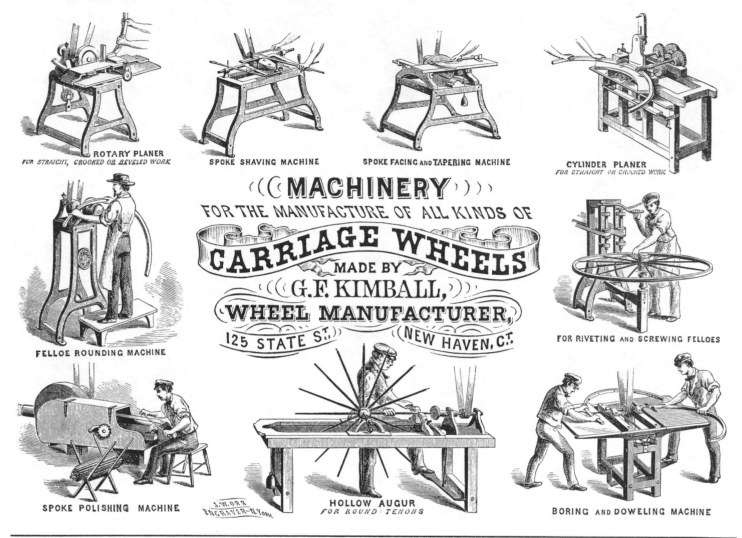

1866 Business Directory Advertisement

Advertisement from 1902 edition of The Blacksmith & Wheelwright Magazine.

"STEEL CHAMPION"

"STEEL CHAMPION" REVERSIBLE ROAD MACHINE"

The Steel Champion is so simple in construction that any man can do good work with it. It has very few parts to break or get out of order. This machine is extremely light in draft. Four good horses are all that are ordinarily required, although in heavy work six should be used. In smoothing city streets or country roads where the soil is light the machine is sometimes used with but two horses. This machine is frequently used by municipalities for scraping into windrows the dirt and trash that collects on stone, brick or wood streets; for scraping snow, ice and slush from streets and gutters, or for cutting down weeds in outlying streets or alleys. One of its most important uses, however, is that of a ditch or drain builder; for this purpose it is very largely used in South America, Australia and certain parts of the United States.

Gravel Spreader

Capacity 2 cubic yds.
Weight 1,900 pounds

Sprinkler Wagon

Capacity 1,000 gallons
Weight 3,600 pounds
Price $820

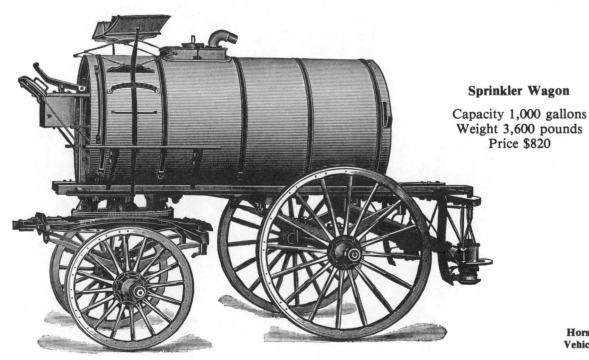

Horse Drawn Contractor's Vehicles from 1902 catalog.

The first wrenches were used during the heat of battle to twist bars out of castle windows. The next designed were for the purpose of bolting together wagons and boats, or perhaps even stone-throwing war machines. So far we have been discussing only fixed-jaw tools. The metal wedged jaw of the first shifting-type spanner, or "monkey" wrenches (1790-1835), provided only a partially successful method of adjustment. In 1835 Solyman Merrick of Springfield, Massachusetts patented the first sleeve/screw adjusting feature. In 1841 the brothers A. & G. Coe refined the screw closing principle further by replacing Merrick's handle-wrapped design with a smaller knurled-rosette nut on a shaft parallel with the handle. This modification made it possible to adjust the jaws with the same hand that held the handle. By 1860 Coe's Patent wrenches were in world wide distribution.

AUCTION LOT of (10) collector-quality adjustable style wrenches assorted brands, circa 1863-1900. $178 Another lot consisting of (10) old cast iron implement wrenches in both open and closed-end types. $10 Box of (30) assorted wrenches from tool collector's estate. $50 Lot of (5) hand-forged wagon wrenches. One is adjustable and dated 1898. $20 Group of (3) Coes-type monkey wrenches, 10 to 15 inches long. $5 Lot of (4) wood-handled pipe wrenches from 6 to 14 inches long. $5

ACME tiny twisted-loop-handle 4⅞ in. adjustable wrench. Dlr. $8 Another 8 inches long, dated 1883, rope twist metal handle. Dlr. $18 15 inch size. Dlr. $15

ALLIGATOR style jaws on double-end pocket wrench, unmarked. $3-$6

THE ALL RIGHT, pat. Feb. 28, 99. Cute little nickle plated pocket-sized monkey wrench $30

AMERICAN BEAUTY monkey wrench with wooden handle, 8 in. overall. $10

AMPCO Berillium steel 10 inch crescent wrench. $15 Solid brass open end 12 inch wrench by same maker. $14 No. W-17 bronze crescent wrench. $23

ATWOOD & CO., Boston, Mass. Round-headed, wood-handled, wrench with adjustment in form of knurled ring around head, rare. Asking $125

BAXTER style double end adjustable S-wrench. 8 inches long. Dlr. $15

BARWICK plier-type wrench, pat. Jan. 1915 Resembles water pump pliers. $7

BAY STATE TOOL CO., pat. June 7, 1904. Quick-action monkey wrench, wooden grips. $15 Iron handled type 10 inches long. $30 12 in. spring latch. Dlr. $50-$65

BEMIS & CALL, Springfield, Mass. Wood handled monkey wrench 8 inches long. $8 No. 45 combination pipe and monkey wrench, 15 inches overall. Like new condition. $30 No. 48A adjustable open-end S wrench, adjustable. $15 Combination pipe and buggy wrench 12 inches long, wooden grips. $20 Common 10 inch wood handled monkey wrench. $8-$15 No. 90 all metal monkey wrench 15 in. long. $5

BICYCLE WRENCH, no maker's name. 5 inches long, adjustable. $5

BILLINGS & SPENCER, Hartford, Conn., Sept. 29, 1896. Pocket wrench with flat center adjustment. $8 Another dated 1879. $8 Monkey wrench, 8 in., iron handle dated 1879. $12 Nickel plated 7 inch monkey wrench with adj. nut in center of handle. $12 No. 0 nickel plated pipe wrench 9 inches long. Pat. June 6, 1871. Parrot-shaped head. $25 Locking lever-handled quick adjust. 5¼ inch wrench dated 1894. $35

BLACK HAWK No. 151 adjustable T-head double-jawed wrench, 9 inches overall. $25

BOOS TOOL CORP., Kansas city, Mo. adjustable wrench 8 inches long, knurled cylinder handle. $10-$20

BUCKEYE double-end adjustable S-wrench 10 in. long. $25

L & S BUCKEYE side adjusting bicycle wrench, 5½ inch. $5

BUGGY WRENCH with wooden crank on handle. Pat. Feb. 1, 1898. $20

BULLARD Pat. Oct. 27, 1903. Lever-handled, quick-adjust, pipe wrench. Came in 9½ to 17 inch lengths. $15-$30

C.W. CHENEY, Athol, Mass. Aug. 4, 1891. No. 2 adjustable wrench with ratchet handle $47

COCHRAN Speed Nut, pat. May 2, 1916, Chicago, Ill. Adjustable open end style, 8 in. long. $8-$12

L. COES & CO. Worcester, Mass. Circa 1869 to 1882 patent wooden handled monkey wrenches in 4⅞ to 20 inch lengths. Smallest size has been quoted as high as $40-$60. 6½ inch $8-$16 12 in. $12 21 inch $20 Metal handled "Key" model 40 inches long. $125 asking price.

THE CRAFTSMAN TOOL CO. Pat. Nov. 1907. Quick adjust. 12 inch pipe wrench with wheel-shaped lower jaw. $20-$30

CRAFT TOOL CO., Conneaut, Ohio. Gear-type 12 inch long pipe wrench. $25

CRESCENT FORGING CO., Oakmont, Pa. "Cresco" pivoting jaw pipe wrench, 10 in. $12

CRESCENT TOOL CO., Jamestown, N.Y. Adjustable double-end 10 inch wrench. $12

CRESSY, Pat. Mar. 7, 1876. Adjustable wrench with parrot-shaped head. $35

DIAMOND WRENCH MFG. CO., Portland, Me. Buggy wheel wrench with adjust. ring at center of handle. $12 Another in brand new, mint condition. $45

W. DICKS, Nov. 21, 1893. Pocket wrench with screw driver inside handle. $10

EATON COLE & BURNHAM CO. N.Y. Pat. July 20, 1886. Offset-handle, adjustable pipe wrench 10 inches long. $20

EIFEL GEARED PLIERENCH with 3 interchangable jaws. Mint condition in orig. leather pouch. $30 Another with single head, and wrench-like parallel jaws, screwdriver handle end. Mint condition. Auct. $80

ELGIN, Pat. June 8, 1887. Adjustable alligator wrench with built-in bolt threading die. $20

FITZALL wedge-jaw 6 inch long wrench. $12

FORD Script signed automobile wrenches. Open end. $4-$8 Monkey wrench. $12-$18 Lot of (5) Ford Model-T era open end and box wrenches. Auct. $10 Dealer lot of (10) assorted Ford marked wrenches. $30

G.M. CO., L.I. City, N.Y. Combination monkey wrench and hammer with tack puller. $15

GOODELL CO., Antrim, N.H. Pat. May 19, 1880. Spring-loaded, wood-handled adjustable buggy wrench. A beautiful tool. $28 Another dated 1861. Auct. $35

GREENFIELD "Little Giant" 4-way pipe wrench, pat. Feb. 4, 1913. Dlr. $25

GRIP n STICK, 707 Dover, O. Pat. Apr. 13, 1924. Plier-type quick adj. wrench. $15

HAND-FORGED wedge-lock wrench with sliding lower jaw that opens to 7 inches. Hanger ring in end of handle. 23 in. overall. Dlr. $100 Another 26 in. long. $75

HANDEE WRENCH CO., New Bedford, Mass. 1921 patented buggy or monkey wrench with collar adj. on slotted steel handle. Like new cond. $25

H & E WRENCH CO., New Bedford, Mass. Pat 1923. All metal pipe wrench with knurled adjustment on handle. Original bluing. $40

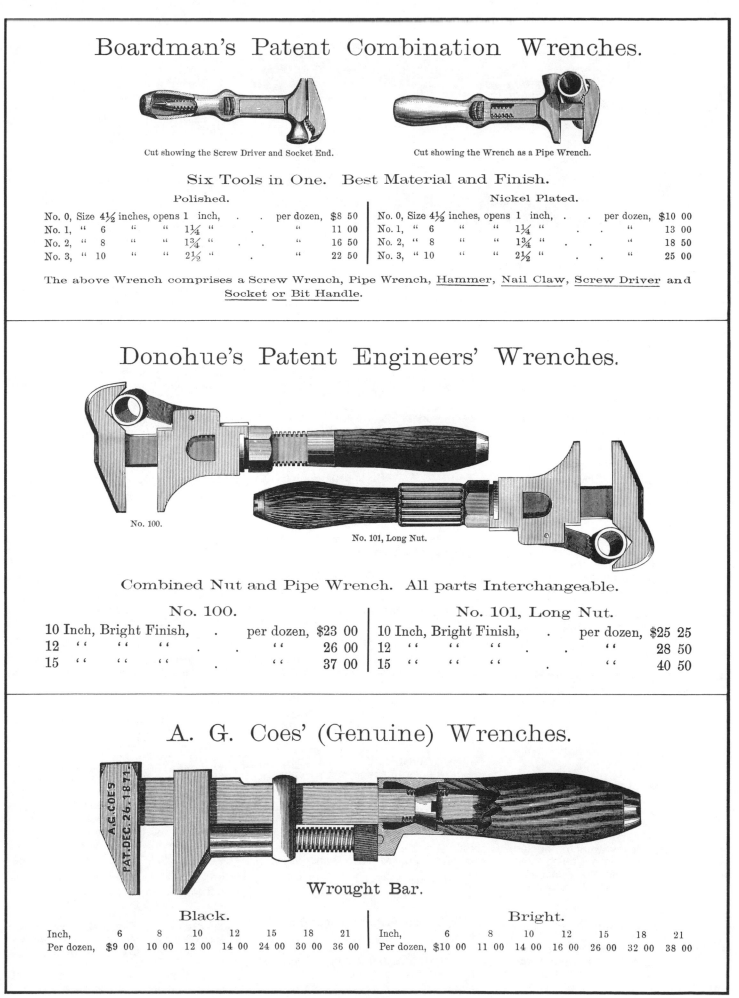

Boardman's Patent Combination Wrenches.

Cut showing the Screw Driver and Socket End.

Cut showing the Wrench as a Pipe Wrench.

Six Tools in One. Best Material and Finish.

Polished.		Nickel Plated.	
No. 0, Size 4½ inches, opens 1 inch, . . per dozen, $8 50		No. 0, Size 4½ inches, opens 1 inch, . . per dozen, $10 00	
No. 1, " 6 " " 1¼ " . " 11 00		No. 1, " 6 " " 1¼ " . . " 13 00	
No. 2, " 8 " " 1¾ " . " 16 50		No. 2, " 8 " " 1¾ " . . " 18 50	
No. 3, " 10 " " 2½ " . " 22 50		No. 3, " 10 " " 2½ " . . " 25 00	

The above Wrench comprises a Screw Wrench, Pipe Wrench, Hammer, Nail Claw, Screw Driver and Socket or Bit Handle.

Donohue's Patent Engineers' Wrenches.

No. 100.

No. 101, Long Nut.

Combined Nut and Pipe Wrench. All parts Interchangeable.

No. 100.		No. 101, Long Nut.	
10 Inch, Bright Finish, . per dozen, $23 00		10 Inch, Bright Finish, . per dozen, $25 25	
12 " " " . . " 26 00		12 " " " . . " 28 50	
15 " " " . " 37 00		15 " " " . " 40 50	

A. G. Coes' (Genuine) Wrenches.

Wrought Bar.

	Black.								Bright.						
Inch,	6	8	10	12	15	18	21	Inch,	6	8	10	12	15	18	21
Per dozen,	$9 00	10 00	12 00	14 00	24 00	30 00	36 00	Per dozen,	$10 00	11 00	14 00	16 00	26 00	32 00	38 00

Page from 1884 Hardware Catalog

COE'S STANDARD

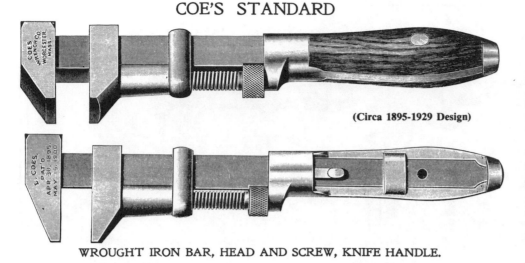

(Circa 1895-1929 Design)

WROUGHT IRON BAR, HEAD AND SCREW, KNIFE HANDLE.

H. HAWKINS, Derby, Ct., W. Baxter pat., Dec. 1, 1868. Double-end 8 inch crescent-type wrench with single adjustment in center of handle. $20

HELLER BROS. Masterench, Pat. 7-25-27. 8 inch size. $12 10 in. $6-$9

HOE CORP., Poughkeepsie, N.Y. Pat. FEB. 21, 1922. Vise grip style wrench 19 inches long with coil spring and lever on top jaw. $15-$30

INTERNATIONAL HARVESTER farm implement wrenches in 7 to 12 inch sizes. $6 to $8 ea.

JARECKI MFG. CO. Erie, Pa., 1879 dated pipe tong, 12 in. long. $14

H. JENKS, Pawtucket, R.I., J.S. Barden pat. 1891. Polished steel pipe-jawed 6 in. long wrench with folding handle. Mint cond. $20 8 inch pipe wrench. Dlr. $18

A.P. JOY, Rockingham, N.H. No. 1 buggy wheel wrench. Pat. Feb. 1, 1898. Nickel plated frame with wooden side handle, lever on back of head. $25

KEEN KUTTER No. K93 pocket wrench 4 in. $8 Alligator style wrench, like new. $20 6 to 8 inch crescent wrenches with Keen Kutter imprint. $15-$20 Wooden handled monkey wrench. $20-$35

KING DICK adjustable pocket wrench, 4⅛ in. Mint cond. $35

L & S CO., Cleveland, O. Rare wood handled bicycle wrench, 5 inches overall. Mint. $45

P. LOWENTRAUT, Manuf'r, Newark, N.J. Dec. 25, 1877. Much sought after wrench-brace. Half a monkey wrench mounted where chuck would normally be on a carpenter's type brace with elbow. Made for wagon wheel use. Auct. $60-$80 Dlr. $90

R.A. MANN & CO. Buffalo, 1888. Brass plated miniature pipe wrench. Auct. $95

D. McFARLAND, Worcester, Mass. Pat. Dec. 1874. Adjustable buggy wrench with a thumbscrew lock on spiral nut behind lower jaw, Dlr. $30

MILLERS FALLS No. 900 rim wrench. Drill brace type with wooden elbow and small top knob. $75

FRANK MOSSBERG, Attleboro, Mass. (circa 1895) Pocket wrench 5 in. long, flat handle, center adj. $6-$8 No. 50 hollow handled 10 in. monkey wrench, all metal const. $15 No. 13 (15 pc.) socket wrench set in wooden box. Auct. $5

NUT GEARRENCH, Houston, Tex., 6-1-26. 8 inches long. $25

PARK METALWARE, unusual double-end adjustable socket wrench, 8 in. $20

PEXTO wood handled 6 inch long pipe wrench. $8 Iron handled 7 in. monkey wrench. $7 No. 10 maple handled Stillson type, 10 inches long. $8

PLATTINA No. 3 adjustable lever-action pipe wrench. $20

POCKET WRENCH made in USA. Miniature 3 inch side-adjusted, screw driver end. $10

RECORD, pat. applied for. Double-end adjustable monkey wrench. $30

REED MFG. CO., Erie, Pa. Pat. Aug. 10, 1897. Quick adjust. pipe wrench with crescent-shaped lower jaw. 11 inches overall. $28

RINO WRENCH CO., Denver. Solid iron pipe wrench in shape of an Elephant's trunk. $35

RICHARDS MFG. CO., Aurora, Ill., Pat. Dec. 13, 1904. "Wizard" adjustable socket-like wrench. $28 Another, dated 1907. Ratching type with 2 knurled worm gears behind round head. Loop handle. $60

SHAW WRENCH, pat. Apr. 26, 1910. 9¾ in. long with V-shaped mouth. $12

SHELLY brand bicycle wrench 6 inches long. $15

F.H. SIMMONS, 1883 buggy wrench with brass adj. collar on threaded handle shaft. $32

SMITH "Perfect Handle" open end 13/16 size wrench 10 inches long. $15 Crescent wrench by same maker. 8 inches overall. $20

SPECIALTY BRASS CO., Kenosha, Wisc. Open end wrench 16 inches long. $8

SPEEDNUT WRENCH CORP., Chicago, pat. May 2, 1916. Pivoting head open-end quick adjust 8 in. wrench. $25

STANDARD TOOL CO., Athol, Mass. Quick opening iron handled wrench 6 in. long. $10

STANDARD WRENCH & TOOL, Providence, R.I. Wedge adjusted wrench with tire iron. 9 & 10 inch. $15 Scarce 6 inch length. $35

JOHN J. TOWER, New York, Pat. 1866, 1882. Unusual combination buggy and pipe wrench. Auct. $50

TRIMO, June 18, 1889. Convertable angle pipe wrench, 2-way adjust. $25

UNIVERSAL WRENCH CO., Detroit-Windsor. Pat. 6-3-19. Quick adjust crescent wrench with plier-type hand lever. $15-$30

UTILITY WRENCH CO., New York, pat. Aug. 13, 1878. Quick adjust. monkey wrench with rosewood handle, 7 inches overall. $35

THE VICTOR, Pat. May 26, 1903. Adjustable alligator jaw wrench approx 7 in. long. $10 Quick adjust pipe wrench, Pat. 8-25-03. $25

WAGON WRENCHES: Handwrought 17 inch with square socket. $5-$10 Double-end 23 inches long with 2 & 2½ in. square sockets. $17 Eliptical loop socket on end of hand-forged 11 in. wrench. $20 Drill brace type with square socket instead of a chuck. Metal elbow, wooden handle. $25

WAKEFIELD No. 3 bicycle wrench. $5 No. 8 patented Sept. 4, 1900. $5 Wakefield Wizard No. 120 double-end 8 inch wrench. Dlr. (1982) $10-$12. Dlr. (1985) $45

WEEKS & WHITNEY weird monkey wrench with furniture-clamp-style wooden handles. One adjusts lower jaw. Made in Sebago Lakes, Maine. $50

WINCHESTER, Coes-type monkey wrench pat. 1922. Wooden handle, 6 in. overall. Auct. $45 Forged steel 8 inch long pipe wrench. Dlr. $25 Socket wrench. $25 No. W39 open end wrench 13 in., original red paint. $35 Set of (3) open end wrenches. $65 No. 1022 pipe wrench with wooden handle, 11 inches overall. $45

WINDSOR MANUF'G. CO., Windsor, Vt. pat. January 24, 1860. Adjustable monkey wrench. Auct. $35

E. WRIGHT, Pat. Oct. 3, 93. Plier handled quick-release wrench with pipe grip jaws. 8½ in. overall. Dlr. $22

WRIGHT WRENCH, Tacoma, Wash, thumb pressure adjusted monkey wrench. $25

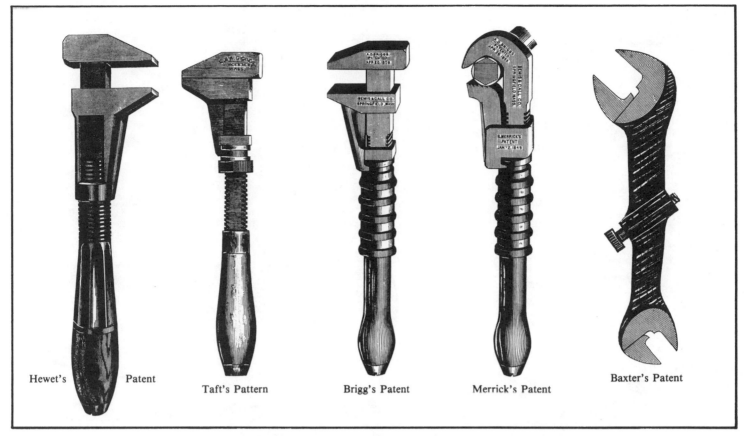

Patented "Screw Wrenches" featured in Russell & Irwin's American Hardware Catalog of 1865.

Hewet's Patent　　Taft's Pattern　　Brigg's Patent　　Merrick's Patent　　Baxter's Patent

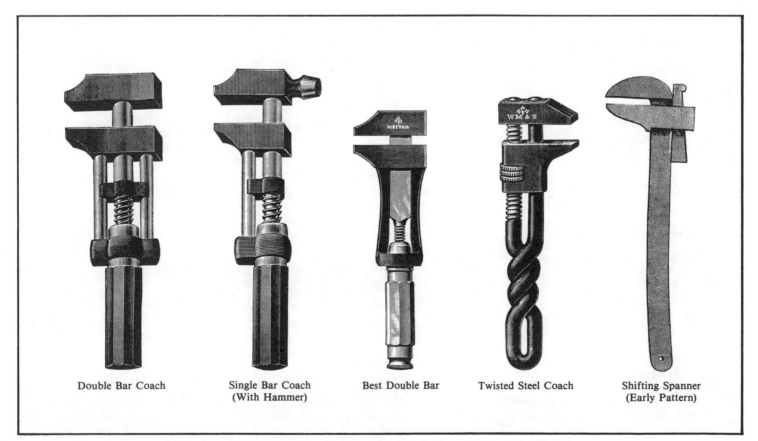

Double Bar Coach　　Single Bar Coach (With Hammer)　　Best Double Bar　　Twisted Steel Coach　　Shifting Spanner (Early Pattern)

A Selection of British Made Wrenches from the 1909 Catalog of William Marples & Sons.

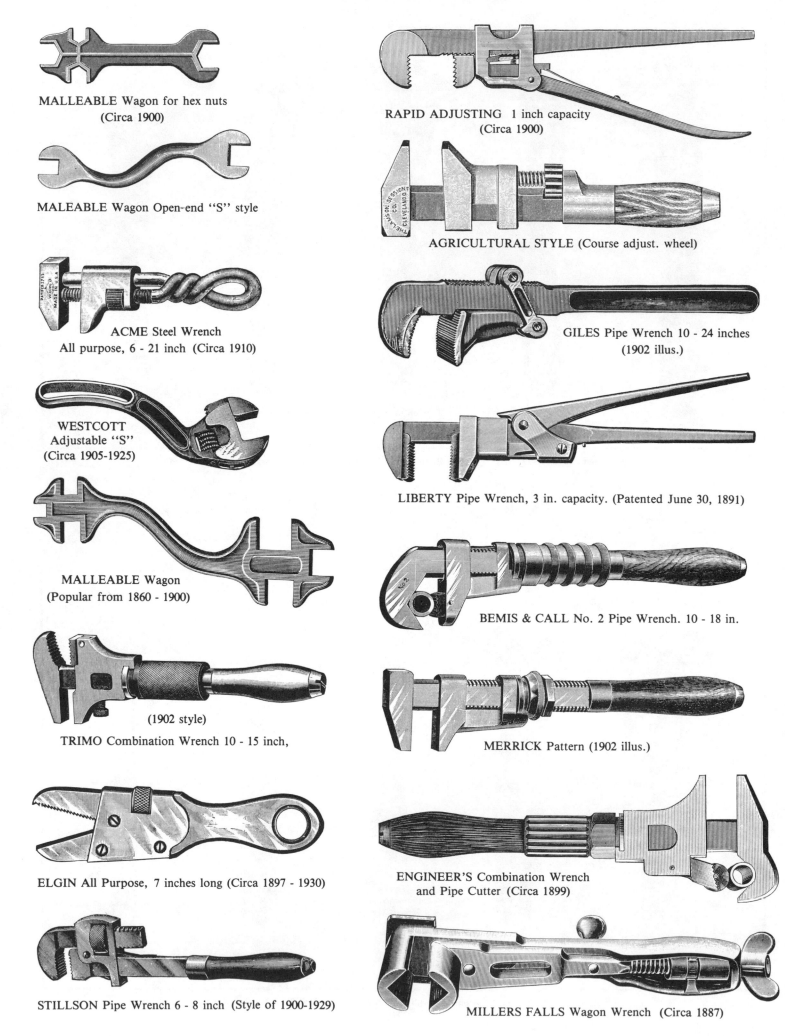

MALLEABLE Wagon for hex nuts
(Circa 1900)

MALEABLE Wagon Open-end "S" style

ACME Steel Wrench
All purpose, 6 - 21 inch (Circa 1910)

WESTCOTT
Adjustable "S"
(Circa 1905-1925)

MALLEABLE Wagon
(Popular from 1860 - 1900)

(1902 style)
TRIMO Combination Wrench 10 - 15 inch,

ELGIN All Purpose, 7 inches long (Circa 1897 - 1930)

STILLSON Pipe Wrench 6 - 8 inch (Style of 1900-1929)

RAPID ADJUSTING 1 inch capacity
(Circa 1900)

AGRICULTURAL STYLE (Course adjust. wheel)

GILES Pipe Wrench 10 - 24 inches
(1902 illus.)

LIBERTY Pipe Wrench, 3 in. capacity. (Patented June 30, 1891)

BEMIS & CALL No. 2 Pipe Wrench. 10 - 18 in.

MERRICK Pattern (1902 illus.)

ENGINEER'S Combination Wrench
and Pipe Cutter (Circa 1899)

MILLERS FALLS Wagon Wrench (Circa 1887)

Pocket Wrenches.

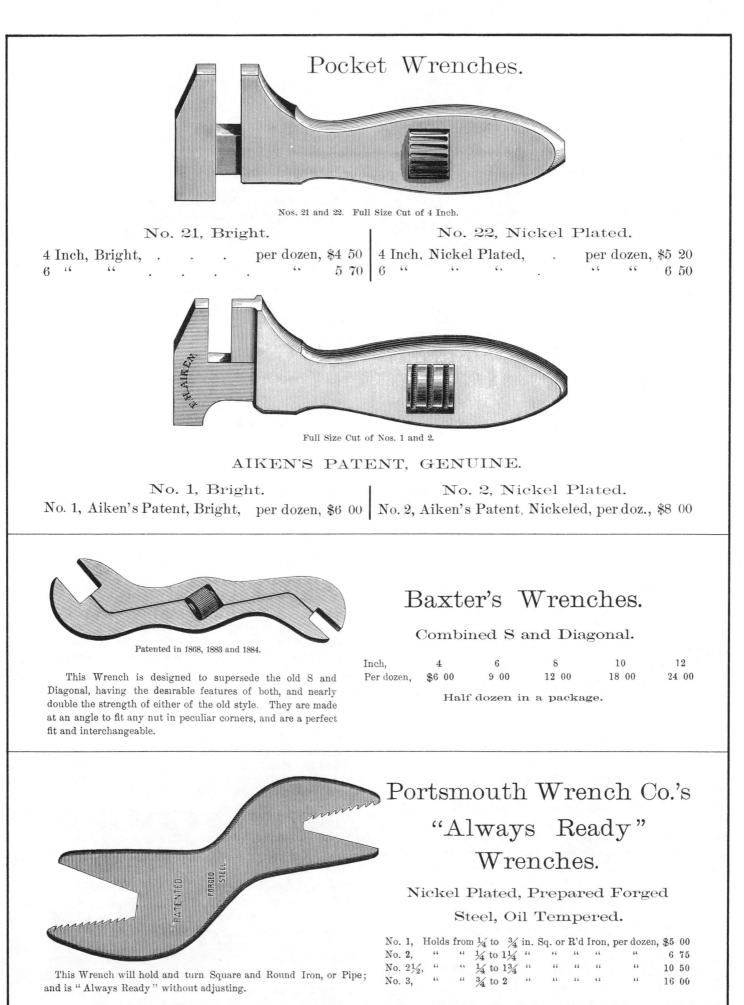

Nos. 21 and 22. Full Size Cut of 4 Inch.

No. 21, Bright.	No. 22, Nickel Plated.
4 Inch, Bright, . . . per dozen, $4 50	4 Inch, Nickel Plated, . per dozen, $5 20
6 " " . . . . " 5 70	6 " " " . " " 6 50

Full Size Cut of Nos. 1 and 2.

AIKEN'S PATENT, GENUINE.

No. 1, Bright.	No. 2, Nickel Plated.
No. 1, Aiken's Patent, Bright, per dozen, $6 00	No. 2, Aiken's Patent, Nickeled, per doz., $8 00

Patented in 1868, 1883 and 1884.

This Wrench is designed to supersede the old S and Diagonal, having the desirable features of both, and nearly double the strength of either of the old style. They are made at an angle to fit any nut in peculiar corners, and are a perfect fit and interchangeable.

Baxter's Wrenches.

Combined S and Diagonal.

Inch,	4	6	8	10	12
Per dozen,	$6 00	9 00	12 00	18 00	24 00

Half dozen in a package.

Portsmouth Wrench Co.'s "Always Ready" Wrenches.

Nickel Plated, Prepared Forged Steel, Oil Tempered.

No. 1,	Holds from ¼ to ¾ in. Sq. or R'd Iron, per dozen, $5 00
No. 2,	" " ¼ to 1¼ " " " " " 6 75
No. 2½,	" " ¼ to 1¾ " " " " " 10 50
No. 3,	" " ¾ to 2 " " " " " 16 00

This Wrench will hold and turn Square and Round Iron, or Pipe; and is "Always Ready" without adjusting.

(Page from 1884 Hardware Catalog)

BIBLIOGRAPHY

Auction Catalogs

J.P. Bittner. Photo illustrated catalog of antique woodworking tools and related items. Current and back issues available. RFD 3, Putney, Vermont 05346

Christie's South Kensington. Periodic sales of craftsman & carpenter tools. Illustrated catalog. 85 Old Brompton Road, London, England SW7 3JS

Richard Crane, Your Country Auctioneer Inc. Photo illustrated catalog of antique woodworking tools & related items. Hillsboro, N.H. 03244

Early American Industries Association. 50th Anniversary Benefit Tool Auction catalog. Illustrated 27 page edition available from: The Mechanick's Workbench P.O. Box 544, Front Street, Marion, Mass. 02738

Tyrone R. Roberts. Important sales of quality British, American and European woodworking and craft tools. Auctions held at Kensington New Town Hall. Catalog from consignor, Reg Eaton. 35 High Street, Heacham, King's Lynn, Norfolk, United Kingdom PE31 7DB

Note: Other non-specialist auction events covered on a partial basis are not listed. Prices reported are from a four year review of auction catalogs issued by the above firms. In case of duplication prices are averaged or latest figure is shown within the range quoted.

Dealer Catalogs

Any prices not prefaced by the term "Auct." were taken from over 150 retail catalogs issued during the past 48 months by the dealers listed below. (Be sure to include a large stamped, self-addressed, envelope when writing to these sources.)

Birchland Antiques. Box 94, Landsville, Penn. 17538

Chucknives. P.O. Box 6196 Sta. A, Daytona Beach, Fla. 32022

Dan Comerford. Box 271 Stony Brook, New York 11790

Harry's Hardware. Chris & Ruth Kaldor, Cabot, VT 05647

Heritage House Antiques. 6 South George Washington Road, Enfield, Conn. 06082

Iron Horse Antiques. RD #2, Poultney, VT 05764

Bob Kaune. 511 W. 11th, Port Angeles, WA 98362

The Mechanick's Workbench. P.O. Box 544, Front St., Marion, Mass. 02738

Hap Moore / Corbe Feeney Antiques. Waterside, South Berwick, Maine 03908

Arthur Risdell. P.O. Box 104 Malverne, New York 11565

Roger K. Smith. 1444 North Main Street, Lancaster, Mass. 01523

Bud Steere. 110 Glenwood Drive, North Kingstown, Rhode Island 02852

Tesseract (Scientific instruments) Box 151 Hastings-on-Hudson, New York 10706

The Tool Box. John A. Moody, 8219 Old Petersburg Road, Evansville, Indiana 47711

Tom White's Antiques. P.O. Box 399 Mattawan, Mich. 49071

Two Chiselers. 1864 Glen Moor Drive, Lakewood, Colo. 80215

Ye Olde Tool Shed. Box T, Rt. 32, Cornwall, New York 12518

Primary Works Consulted

The Book of Trades, Frankfurt, 1568. Reprint by Dover Publications Inc. New York

British Planemakers From 1700. Roy Arnold. 77 High Street Needham Market, Suffolk, England IP6 8 AN

Dictionary of Tools Used In Woodworking and Allied Trades, 1700-1970. R.A. Salaman. Charles Scribner's Sons. New York

A Diderot Pictorial Encyclopedia of Trades & Industry, 1751. Denis Diderot. Reprinted in two volumes by Dover Publications. 180 Varick Street, New York, N.Y. 10014

The Great Tool Emporium. David X. Manners. Popular Science/E.P. Dutton. New York

The Great Industries of The United States, 1872 Edition. Horace Greely and others. J.B. Burr, Hyde & Co. Chicago

Malleable Casting, Brass Founding, Blacksmithing and Forging. 1905 Editon. International Textbook Co. London

Manuel du Tourneur, 1816 edition. Hamelin Bergeron. (From the collection of Edward W. Warren, II)

A Museum of Early American Tools. Eric Sloane. Ballantine Books, and Funk & Wagnalls. New York

Panorama of Professions and Trades, 1837 edition. Edward Hazen. Uriah Hunt, Philadelphia

Patented Transitional & Metallic Planes In America, 1827-1927. Roger K. Smith. North Village Publishing Company. 1444 No. Main Street, Lancaster, Mass. 01523

Rural Occupations in Early 19th century England. 641 illustrations by William H. Pyne. Reprint by Dover Publications, Inc. New York.

The Stanley Plane, A History and Descriptive Inventory. A. Sellens. 134 Clark Street, Augusta, Kansas 67010

Wooden Planes in 19th Century America. Kenneth D. Roberts. Roberts Publishing Co. Box 151 Fitzwilliam, NH 03447

Woodworking, Patternmaking, Moulding, Core making, Mixing, Cast Iron. 1905 edition. International Textbook Co. London

Woodworking Planes, A Descriptive register of Wooden Planes. A. Sellins. 134 Clark Street, Augusta, Kansas 67010

Periodicals Reviewed

Tools and Trades Journal and *TATHS Quarterly Newsletter* Winston Grange, Stowmarket, Suffolk, IP14 6LE, U.K.

Antiques And The Arts Weekly A weekly tabloid of the eastern antiques scene. Articles, photos, auction and show announcements. Good coverage of important tool sales. Bee Publishing Co., Newton, Conn. 06470

The Chronicle. Current quarterly magazine of The Early American Industries Association. P.O. Box 2128, Empire State Plaza Station, Albany, New York 12220

The Fine Tool Journal. Monthly newsletter and advertiser for tool collectors. R.D. #2, Poultney, VT. 05764

Fine Woodworking. Monthly "How-To magazine" written and illustrated by a group of master craftsmen. Taunton Press. 52 Church Hill Road. P.O. Box 355, Newton, CT 06470

Maine Antique Digest. "The Marketplace for Americana". Thick monthly tabloid, often featuring advertisements and articles about old tools. Box 358, Waldoboro, ME 04572

Woodworking Crafts. Bimonthly publication of The Guild of Master Craftsmen. Parklands House, Keymer Road, Burgess Hill, Sussex, England RH15 OBA

Trade Catalogs Consulted

Benj. Allen & Co. Chicago, 1891. Watches, Clocks, Tools & Materials.

Champion Blower & Forge Co. Lancaster, Pa., 1896. Every conceivable style.

Collins & Co. Collinsville, Conn., 1921. Axes, Hatchets, Picks, Hammers, etc. Reprint by The Early Trades & Crafts Society, Long Island, New York

Davis Level & Tool Co. Springfield, Mass. 1880. Reprint by North Village Publishing Co. 1444 North Main Street, Lancaster, Mass. 01523

Disston, Henry & Sons. Philadelphia, 1899. Keystone Saw, Tool, Steel & File Works.

Goodell - Pratt Co. Greenfield, Mass., 1917. "1,500 Good Tools" Cat. No. 13.

Feron of Paris. At The Royal Forge, 1927. Woodworking tools. Reprint by The Early American Industries Association. P.O. Box 2128 Empire State Plaza Station, Albany, N.Y. 12220

Hirth & Krause. Leather & Findings, 1896. Reprint by Midwest Tool Collectors Association.

Hammacher, Schlemmer & Co. New York, 1896. Tools For All Trades. Reprint by Mid-West Tool Collectors Assoc. Distributed by E.A.I.A., New York

Hofman Supply Co. Columbus, Ohio, 1890. Watchmaker's Tools & Supplies.

Hynson Tool & Supply Co. St. Louis, 1903. Cooper's Tools. Reprint by Mid-West Tool Collectors. Dist. by E.A.I.A., N.Y.

Keuffel & Esser Co. Hoboken, N.J., 1927. Draftsman, Engineer's and Surveyor's Supplies.

Manning, Maxwell & Moore. New York, 1902. Giant catalog of Railway, Steamship, Machinist, Factory, & Mill Supplies, plus Woodworking Tools.

Marples, William & Sons. Sheffield, England, 1909. "Tools For All Trades" The most comprehensive tool catalog of the period. Profusely illustrated. Reprint by The Early American Industries Association.

Millers Falls Tools. Greenfield, Mass. 1916 & 1935 editions.

Montgomery Ward & Co. Spring & Summer of 1895. Reprint by Dover Publications Inc., New York

Joshua Oldham. New York, 1880. Saw catalog with an illustrated history of saws, their manufacture and use. Reprint by The Early American Industries Association.

C.S. Osborne and Company. 1880's. Leather Working Tool Catalog. Reprint by E.A.I.A., New York

Geo. A. Rubelmann Hardware Co., St. Louis, Mo., 1923. Mechanics and Carpenter's Tools.

Russell & Erwin. 1865 Illustrated Catalog of American Hardware. Reprint by The Association For Preservation Technology. Dist. by The E.A.I.A.

Sargent & Co. New Haven, Conn., 1884 & 1926 editions. Trade catalog of Planes, Tools, Locks and Hardware.

Sears Roebuck & Co. 1902, 1908, & 1927. General Merchandise Catalogs. Reprints by Bounty Books, New York, and DBI Books, Northfield, Ill.

J.B. Shannon. 1873 Illustrated Catalog of Carpenters' Tools. Reprint by William C. Cavallini. Berry Lane. Box 267 West Harwich, Mass. 02671

Simmons Hardware Company. 1880 Catalog of Tools and Hardware. (From the collection of Edward W. Warren, II)

E.C. Simmons Hardware Co. St. Louis, Mo., 1906. Keen Kutter brand Tools, Hardware, and Gen. Mchdse. 4,200 page edition. (Courtesy of Michael Armstrong)

Stanley Rule & Level Co. Various editions of Catalog No. 34 dating from 1907-1939. (Authors collection)

Stanley Tools. Catalog No. 129. (Largest and most complete of all Stanley catalogs) Reprint of 1929 edition by North Village Publishing Company. 1444 North Main Street, Lancaster, Mass. 01523

Starret Tools. Athol, Mass., 1913. Machinists' Hand Tools, Cat. No. 20

Chas. A. Sterlinger & Co. Detroit, Mich., 1897. Woodworking Tools Catalog. (Courtesy Edward W. Warren, II)

Union Hardware & Metal Company. Los Angeles, Ca. 1903. Giant Catalog of Tools, Hardware, Mining, Oil Drilling, & Mill Supplies.

Wm. P. Walter's Sons. Philadelphia, 1888. Illustrated Catalog of Woodworker's Tools. Reprint by North Village Publishing Co., Lancaster, Mass.

Joh. Weiss & Sohn. Wien, 1909. Austrian Catalog of Tools For Cabinet Makers and Carpenters. Early American Industries Assoc. reprint.

Reprints by Ken Roberts Publishing Co.
Box 151, Fitzwilliam, New Hampshire. 03447 :

Arrowmamett Works. Middletown, Conn., 1857. Baldwin Tool Catalog of Bench Planes and Moulding Tools.

Auburn Tool Co. Auburn, New York, 1869. Catalog of Planes and Skates.

Leonard Bailey & Co. Hartford, Conn., 1876. Illustrated Catalog and Price list of Iron Bench Planes.

D.R. Barton & Co. Rochester, New York, 1873. Mechanics' Tools.

Buck Brothers. Millbury, Mass., 1890. Chisels, Plane Irons and Edge Tools.

Chapin-Stephens. Pine Meadows, Conn., 1901. Catalog No. 114. Rules, Planes, Levels, etc.

Greenfield Tool Company. Greenfield, Mass., 1874. Illustrated Catalog of Bench Planes.

I. Lufkin Measuring Instruments. 1880-1940 Catalog Excerpts & History.

Alex Mathieson & Sons, Ltd. Glasgow, 1899. Catalog of Planes, Levels & Hand Tools.

Millers Falls Company. Mass., 1887. Tool Catalog and History.

Ohio Tool Company. Columbus, Ohio, 1915. Illustrated Catalog of Woodworking Tools.

Edward Preston & Sons. Birmingham, England, 1901 & 1914. Combined reprint of both catalogs. Planes, Spirit Levels, Rules.

John Rabone & Sons. Birmingham, England, 1892. Colorful reprint. Rules, Tapes, & Spirit Levels.

Sandusky Tool Co. Ohio, 1925. Catalog No. 25 Metal & Wooden Planes.

Spiers & Norris. 1914 & 1925. Combined catalogs of Scotch and English-Made Metal Planes.

Stanley Rule & Level Company. Catalog reprints for the years: 1859, 1867, 1870, 1872, 1874, 1879, 1884, 1888, 1892, & 1898

Collector Organizations

British-American Rhykenogical Society. Elliot Sayward 60 Harvest Lane, Levittown, N.Y. 11756

Early American Industries Association. P.O. Box 2128 - Empire State Plaza Station, Albany, N.Y. 12220-0128

EAIA-West. Roger B. Phillips, Pres. 8476 West Way Drive, La Jolla, Calif. 92038

Mid-West Tool Collectors Association. Tom Ward, Pres. P.O. Box 11, Avondale Estates, GA 30002

Ohio Tool Collectors Association. George Woodard, Box 261, London, OH 43140

Society of Workers in Early Arts & Trades. Fred Bair Jr. 606 Lake Lena, Auburn Dale, FL 33823

Southwest Tool Collectors Association. Ed Pitcher, Pres. 7032 Oak Bluff Drive, Dallas, TX 75240

Three Rivers Tool Collectors. Robert Kendra 39 S. Rolling Hills, Irwin, PA 15642

Tools and Trades Society. Winston Grange, Stowmarket, Suffolk, United Kingdom IP14 6LE

The following 300 listings are from the 1991 auction of the A.M. Beitler Tool Collection by Barry Hurchalla, Auctioneer, 343 High Street, Pottstown, Pennsylvania 19464.

PA/German GOOSEWING AXE, D. Lighty, 12½ in. Blade. $275

4 in. SLICK, W. Brady. $65

Early TWIBILL, Signed? $325

GOOSEWING AXE, W. Brady. $250

44 in. WOOD REAMER Sample, Walnut. $95

HAT STRETCHER. $110

Wagon Maker's AXLE SHAVE. $75

The Greatest BOWL ADZE, 7 in. Cut. $150

BRICK AUGER. $150

Conestoga Wagon AXE HOLDER, Iron, Star Design. $325

⅜ in. DADO PLANE, w/stop, Kieffer & Auxer, Lancaster, PA. $65

Wedge Arm PLOW PLANE, M. Long, Reading. $165

MOLDING PLANE, F. Nicholson, Wrentham. $1,100

COFFIN PLANE, Dbl. Wedge, E. W. Carpenter, Pat. March 27, 1849, Lancaster. $100

COFFIN PLANE, Dbl. Wedge, Sam Auxer, Lancaster. $130

Pair of 5 in. Brass TRAMMEL POINTS. $150

PLUMB, Official "Tomascout" B.S. of A. (new, no box). $65

Mahogany STAIR SAW with Great Style. $350

Combination ROUNDER w/5 Interchanging Size Dies, All Wood. $80

Brass SURGEON'S SAW, Pilling, Phila. 11½ in. $150

BACK SAW, Spear, Engraved, "James Lock, New York, 1818." $300

Rare, Basket Weaver's REED SIZER, Iron. $210

Dbl. CLAW HAMMER, Pat. 1902. $225

BACK SAW, Harvey Peace, Brooklyn, NY. $55

BACK SAW, Henry Disston, Dbl. Eagle, Phila. $30

COOPER PLANE, Screw Arm, 1890, Ezra. $125

SMOOTH PLANE, Transition WB, Chaplin's Pat., Tower & Lyon, 10 in. $90

COMPASS PLANE, Classic Style Carved, 7½ in., 1¾ in. Iron. $180

1 in. BEAD PLANE, Auxer & Remley, Lancaster. $325

¾ in. BEAD PLANE, E. W. Carpenter, Lancaster. $60

MOLD PLANE, 2 in. Cut, Sam Auxer, Lancaster. $100

MATCH PLANE, D. Heiss, Lancaster. $260

Great FLUTER PLANE, 1½ in. Iron, Philip Reber, Eastern PA, Early. $800

BEADER PLANE, Boxed, E. W. Carpenter, Lancaster, ⁵⁄₁₆ in. $55

BEAD PLANE, D. Heiss, Lancaster, Worn. $60

SHOOT BOARD PLANE, J. Mannebach, NY 34 in. x 5½ in. $200

18th C. VENEER SAW w/Nice Rams Head Nut. $350

MATCH PLANE, E. W. Carpenter's Pat. Adj. Width Iron, Lancaster. $200

SCREW ARM GROOVER, J. Stamm, Mt. Joy, Lancaster Co. $85

HOLLOW AUGER, Swan's Imp. No. 6001, (new, no box). $120

Windsor HAND BEADER, Pat. 1885, (in orig. box). $225

Great Little MONKEY WRENCH/Screwdriver. $105

Pistol SPEED INDICATOR, Harvey Hubbell, Pat. 94. $150

Cased RACE KNIFE w/Extra Blade. $150

BACK SAW, Henry Disston, Phila. Dbl. Eagle. $25

Bagshaw & Field, Phila. TOOL HOLDER w/21 Bits, Cased (in orig. box). $375

2½ in. Brass "LEGS" CALIPERS. $55

Round Bottom PLANE, Palm Size. $90

3 in. Cut DRAWKNIFE, Keen-Kutter. $175

SUNPLANE, E. W. Carpenter. $275

4½ in. MINIATURE RABBET PLANE. $65

Miniature 8 in. WOOD BRACE. $150

Early WOOD BRACE, Ryley. $250

BEVEL, Brass & Rosewood, I. J. Robinson, Pat. 1870, St. Johnsbury, VT, 6 in. $275

FOLDING RULE, Gentleman's, 12 in. Sterling Silver. $100

CLAPBOARD GAGE, E. W. Carpenter, Lancaster. $475

Pair Horse Collar STUFFING MALLETS, Lignum Vitae Heads, 18 in. Handles. $300

Great Mahogany PANEL GAGE w/Brass Wedge. $210

SCREWDRIVER/BRACE Combination. $125

Sheffield BRACE, Fenton & Marsdens, No. 986, Reg. 1847. $300

No. 71 & No. 271 ROUTER, Stanley Works, England (in orig. box). $45

STANLEY No. 36, 9 in. Level (in orig. box). $55

STANLEY No. 67 Spokeshave, w/Fence & Round Sole Plate. $125

STANLEY No. 610 Hand Drill (in orig. box). $140

STANLEY No. 1 Odd Jobs w/Original Rule w/Point (in orig. box). $200

STANLEY No. 386 Fence (2), One Black/One Nickel (both in orig. box). $175

STANLEY No. 20 Compass Plane (in orig. box). $100

STANLEY No. 271 Router & No. 22 Dowel Sharpeners (2) (both in orig. box). $80

STANLEY No. 79 Side Rabbet (in orig. box). $50

STANLEY No. 138 Level Sights, 2 Styles (in orig. box). $65

STANLEY No. 208 Level Glasses, 2 Box, & No. 44 Bit & Square Level (in orig. box). $85

STANLEY No. 42X Saw. Set w/Directions, & No. 59 Dowelling Jig (both in orig. boxes). $45

STANLEY No. 95½ Butt Gage, & No. 4 Trammel Points (in orig. box). $50

STANLEY No. 200 Chisel & Cutter Grinders, One Black, One Nickel (in orig. box). $75

STANLEY No. 35, WB Plane (in orig. box). $375

STANLEY No. 71 Router w/Instruction Sheet (in orig. box). $25

STANLEY No. 50 Beader (in orig. box). $125

STANLEY No. 95 Edge Plane (new, in orig. box). $200

STANLEY No. 77 Dowel Machine w/⅜ in. Cutter Head, Filed Base. $300

STANLEY Cutter Heads, ½ in. ¼ in. ¾ in. ⅝ in (in orig. box). $200

STANLEY No. 45, Nickel w/Instructions (in orig. box). $125

STANLEY Catalog, 1905. $65

STANLEY Catalog, 1907, 2nd Edition. $70

STANLEY Catalog, 1912. $65

STANLEY Catalog, 1914. $50

STANLEY Catalog, 1920. $50

STANLEY Catalog, 1921. $50

STANLEY Catalog, 1927, 7/1/1927 Edition. $45

STANLEY Brochures, 1874, 1876, 1886. $260

STANLEY Brochures (3). $25

STANLEY Brochures (5). $55

STANLEY Manual for No. 55 in French. $75

STANLEY Dealer Catalog No. 134. $175

4 Asst. Tool BROCHURES (Metallic Plane Co., Sargent, Chaplin). $800

3 Tool Maker BILL HEADS (Bibighaus, King, Farr). $500

BOOK Carpenter Rules, Published 1728. $125

BOOK, 2 Vol. "Practical Builder," Nicholson. 1823. $175

BOOK, "Ancient Carpenter Tools," 1st Edition, 1929, Signed by Mercer. $410

PHOTO, TINTYPE, C. W. Era, Man w/Goosewing Axe. $375

PA/German GOOSEWING AXE, W. Brady. $375

Saw TRADE SIGN, Richardson's Saws, 53 in. Fantastic. $850

PANEL RAISER, 3½ in. Cut, E. WCarpenter, Lancaster. $400

COFFIN PLANE, Dbl. Wedge, E. W. Carpenter, Pat. 1849. $300

BEAD PLANE, Jacob Heiss, Boxed. $250

BEAD PLANE, J. F. Bauder, Manheim, Lancaster Co., PA. Boxwood wear insert. $150

ROUND PLANE, Sam Auxer, Lancaster, PA. $50

BEAD PLANE, J. F. Bauder, Manheim, Lancaster Co., PA, Boxed. $150

Wedge Arm PLOW PLANE, M. Martin (Phila.). $475

COFFIN PLANE, E. W. Carpenter, Lancaster. $70

SCREW ARM Sash Plane, Spayd & Bell, Phila. $70

PLOW PLANE, E. W. Carpenter's Improved Arms Pat., Lancaster. $900

SHEFFIELD BRACE, Tillotson. $175

TRAMMEL POINTS, 5 in. Brass. $150.

Universal "STAR" LEVEL. $210

LEVEL, Davis & Cook. $450

Folding RULE w/Level, Lufkin No. 2072, 2 ft. 3 Fold. $150

Folding RULE w/2 Levels, Lufkin 2 ft. 4 Fold. $250

24 in. 2 Fold RULE, Gunter's Slide, Biddle Co., Phila. $100

24 in. 2 Fold RULE, Gunter's Slide, Stephens & Co., No. 27. $125

RULE, 1 ft. 3 Fold, 2/Level, Lufkin No. 2051. $200

RULE, 4 Fold, Ivory & German Silver, No. 57B (Stanley) E. A. Stearns. $175

6 Fold, No. 58 STANLEY RULE (see pg. 170). $200

Board Ft. RULE, A. I. Diffenbacher. $150

2 Fold, 2 Level RULE, Thomas Foulds. $800

RULE, 4 Fold w/Caliper, Ivory & German Silver No. 99½, Chapin-Stevens? $100

CLAPBOARD GAGE, J. F. Bauder, Manheim, Lancaster Co., PA. $1,200

Brass Bound LEVEL, Rosewood, 2 Bubble 12 in., Millers Falls No. 10. $200

"Legs" CALIPERS (see page 35). $110

TRAMMEL POINTS, Cased Draftsman Drawing, Harling, London. $105

Cast Brass Double CALIPERS, Caron. $270

Wheel Wrights TRAVELER, w/Pointer, Brass (see page 19). $75

Davis No. 1 LEVEL, 6 in. Pag. 1867 (see page 90). $325

Push DRILL, Johnson & Tainters, Mass., Pat. 1869 w/Bits (in orig. box). $275

STANLEY Butt & Rabbet GAGE No. 92 (see page 74). $75

Cased DRAWING SET, Looks Complete. $260

Eclipse SCRAPER PLANE, Ohio. $325

Birmingham SMOOTH PLANE, 9¾ in. (Iron Plate Clamp Variation). $250

Iron LOW ANGLE PLANE 8 in., Cast in Heart Design in Front. $140

Morris Pat. Iron PLOW PLANE, Missing Wedge. $600

Lewis CORE BOX PLANE, Unmarked, Small Break. $100

Bayley Pat. CORE BOX PLANE, Marked G.I. Co., Nice w/Irons. $250

SAW, Disston & Sons, Phila. $25

BACKSAW, Johnston & Conaway, Phila., Dbl. Eagle. $110

Speed DRILL, 7½ in., Decorated (Millers Falls?). $55

DRAWKNIFE, Applewood, Carved, Booth & Mills, Phila. $200

Brass Bound LEVEL, Rosewood, 6½ in. Stratton Bros., No. 10. $450

Brass Bound LEVEL, Rosewood, 2 Bubble, 10 in. Stratton Bros., No. 10. $275

Brass Bound LEVEL, Rosewood, 2 Bubble, 12 in. $125

Brass Bound LEVEL, Rosewood, 2 Bubble 30 in., Stratton Bros. LEVEL, No. 1 w/Eagle Mark. $125

Melick LEVEL, Pat., 1889, Grade Scale. $325

LOG RULE, A. Nutting. $190

2 Interesting RULES. $80

2 in. Hook REAMER, J. Dubs. $170

Iron LEVEL, STANLEY 24 in. Nicholson Pat. Style (see page 98). $150

Handled PLOW PLANE, Sandusky, No. 132. $300

SMOOTHING PLANE, 11½ in. Mahogany, Brass Faced, Pull Handles. $90

Nice CROWN MOLDER, 3 in. Cut, E. W. Carpenter, Lancaster. $400

BEAD PLANE, Thomas Napier, Phila., Boxed. $300

ROUND PLANE, Thomas Grant (NY/NJ). $150

COPING PLANE, N. Norton, Camden, NJ. $250

BEAD PLANE, Israel White, Phila., Boxed, 6 in. Long. $375

HOLLOW PLANE, W. Martin, Phila. $125

CROWN MOLDER, W. Raymond, MA, 18th C., 15 in. x 6 in., 4¾ in. Cut, Rare. $900

PANEL RAISER, E. W. Carpenter, Lancaster, 2½ in. Cut. $225

Fantastic "D" ROUTER, 13 Inlays, Hearts, Acorns, etc. (a work of art). $650

PLANES, 2 Miniature 3 in., 1 Flat, 1 Convex. $150

IVORY RULE, 3 in. x 12½ in., W. Elliott, London. $300

Sheffield BRACE, James Bee/Henry Brown Pat. $200

BRACE w/Ebony Inlay Work. $550

ROUTER, Carriage Maker's Dbl. Pistol Grip, Auxer & Remley, Lancaster. $600

SASH PLANE, Screw Arm, B. Sheneman, Phila. $200

Plate & WIRE GAGE, Ivory Cased, Stubs. $425

4½ in. Davis LEVEL. $300

6 in. Davis LEVEL, Pat. 1883, 3 Bubble (see page 90). $400

Brass & Rosewood BEVEL w/Level, 9 in. J. D. Howard, Pat. Nov. 5, 1867. $225

PLOW PLANE, E. W. Carpenter's Improved Arms, Lancaster. $900

PLOW PLANE, Ohio Tool, No. 103, Ivory Tipped. $600

BRACE, Marples, Ultimatum. $550

ADVERTISING Saw Blade, National Hardware Banquet 1896, Phila., Henry Disston & Sons. $200

TRY SQUARE & BEVEL Combination, Wm. McNiece, Phila. Pat. Applied For. $500

DRAWING INSTRUMENTS, Cased. $275

BEAD PLANE, Dbl. Blade Convex, Wm. Goldsmith, Phila. $1,100

Mechanic's RULE, 2 fold, Gunter Slide, Thomas Bradburn, Birmingham. $200

"Legs" CALIPERS. $175

BRACE, Booth & Mills, Phila. $650

Framed SAW. $160

Coopers STAVE PLANE, 60 in., E. W. Carpenter, Lancaster. $475

30 in. LEVEL, Disston & Morss, Phila., No. 112. $100

LOG CALIPER, T. R. Hoyt, 1874 w/Original Label. $250

MATCH PLANE, E. W. Carpenter, Lancaster. $130

Wedge Arm, MATCH PLANE, E. W. Carpenter, Lancaster. $80

ROUND PLANE, Donoho, Phila. $50

MOLDING PLANE, W. Martin, Phila. $160

MOLDING PLANE, M. Martin (Phila.). $170

SASH PLANE, Screw arm, Israel White, Phila., Eagle Mark. $200

FRET SAW, Millers Falls (w/Manual, in orig. box). $180

CORE BOX PLANE, G., Wohler. $250

CARRIAGE MAKER'S RABBET PLANE, Brass, 7½ in., Laminated Infill. $375

E. Walker Adjustable Face PLANE, Erie, PA (Missing Fence). $100

(a) CROWN MOLDER, T. Napier, Philadelphia, 18 in. long x 10 in. wide, 6⅞ in. Iron, Apprentice Pull.

(b) CROWN MOLDER, T. Napier, Philadelphia, 18 in. long x 10 in. wide, 6½ in. Iron, Apprentice Pull. (Similar to page 131, except tug bar is on top.) The Pair. $11,250

3 in. L. Bailey/Victor PLANE, No. 51. $100

Bullnose PLANE, Edward Preston & Sons. $50

Birmingham CARRIAGE MAKER'S RABBET PLANE, 6 in. $375

Block PLANE, 6½ in., Boston, Metallic. $60

PLANE, Miniature 4 in. Smoother (like an Erlandsen). $325

Phillips Improved PLOUGH PLANE, Nice Original Paint. $450

BOWL ADZE, Early. $130

AXE, Early PA COOPER'S (Rehrig), P. RE RIG. $200

STIRRUP ADZE. $100

PANEL RAISER, E. W. Carpenter, Lancaster, 2¾ in Cut. $225

GOOSEWING AXE, Mr. Beitler's Favorite, 19 in. Blade. (Similar to No. 11 on page 11, but longer, narrower blade.) $1,200

BUTCHER AXE, Iron 29½ in., 14 in Cut, D. Hoffman, Lancaster. $325

RULE, 2 Fold 24 in. Belcher Bros., NY, Ivory, German Silver. $600

RULE, 3 Fold 12 in. Ivory Scale, Sliding Caliper, Scales for Iron Weight, German Silver. $375

Davis LEVEL No. 4, Pat. 1888, 24 in. (see page 90). $325

Davis LEVEL No. 4, Pat. 1867, 24 in. $200

Davis LEVEL, 3 Bubble, Pat. 1883, 24 in. $625

Davis LEVEL, No. 3, Pat. 1867, 18 in. $250

Davis LEVEL, Pat. 1867, 12 in. (see page 90). $150

Davis LEVEL, Pat. 1867, 7 in. $300

Davis LEVEL, No. 1, Pat. 1867, 6 in. $325

RULE, 24 in. 2 Fold, L. Hedge, Hartford, Conn. (Rare). $1,500

RULE, 24 in. 2 Fold, Stephens & Co. No. 28. $150

RULE, 4 Fold, 24 in. Ivory, Stephens & Co. No. 83. $125

Stevens No. 38 INCLINOMETER, Ivory & German Silver. $3,750 (See page 171 , $2,750 price increase.)

Disston & Sons No. 43, 2 Bubble Level SAW w/Scribe. $375

LEVEL, Edward Helb Railroad, York, PA, Pat. 1904. $550

30 in. LEVEL, H. Disston & Sons, Phila., Brass Bound. $100

BRACE, Booth & Mills, Phila. $350

Handled PLOW PLANE, Kieffer & Auxer, Lancaster. Beautiful. $5,000

CROWN MOLDER, John Bell, Phila. 15 in. x 6 in., 4 in. Iron. $500

BRACE, T. E. Wells & Co. $400

Mortise CHISEL AXE, J. Dubs. $1,850

CROWN MOLDER, Thomas Napier, 14 in. x 5 in., 3 in. Iron. $800

ROUTERS, Pr. L. & R. Carriage maker's. Fine Workmanship (see page 37 lower right, French style). $1,500

PANEL RAISER, Israel White, Phila., 2¾ in. Iron. $350

CROWN MOLDER, Dbl. Blade, B. Sheneman, Phila., 15½ in. x 6¼ in. (purchased 4 years ago for $2,050). $4,000

BRACE, T. E. Wells & Co. $200

CROWN MOLDER, W. Martin, Phila. 14 in. x 5⅝ in., 3¾ in. Iron. $850

INCLINOMETER, L. C. Stevens, June 12, 1858 Patent, Brass & Ebony (similar to page 171). $4,000

COOPERS AXE, Great Style, Signed? $150

20 in. Bit BRACE, E. W. Carpenter, with 9 Bits (only example known). $5,000

Pair Carriage Maker's Right & Left BEAD PLANES, Boxed. $375

Fantastic PLUMB & LEVEL INDICATOR, R. Porter. Engraved outdoor scene on round face, shows brick layers using this instrument. $2,800

PLOW PLANE, E. W. Carpenter's Improved Arms, Lancaster. $2,500

Miniature 3½ in. Apprentice Toy HORNED PLANE. $225

CIRCULAR ROUTER. $375

Early TWIBILL, Signed? $425

Board Foot RULE, J. S. Carpenter, Maker, Philadelphia. $250

3 ARM PLOW, Ivory Tipped, Outer Arms are Ebony, NEW AUCTION RECORD PRICE FOR AN AMERICAN PLANE. $8,500

STANLEY No. 11, Beltmaker's Plane. $50

STANLEY No. 12¼ Veneer Scraper. $150

STANLEY No. 1 Smooth Plane (see page 156). $750

STANLEY No. 2 Smooth Plane (see page 154). $125

STANLEY No. 9½ Type 4 (see page 107). $50

STANLEY No. 72 Chamfer Plane. $200

STANLEY No. 72½ Chamfer Plane, 5 Cutters & Bull Nose Attachment (see page 108). $475

STANLEY No. 85 Cabinetmaker's Scraper Plane (page 108). $450

STANLEY No. 62 Low Angle Plane (see page 108). $250

STANLEY No. 97 Cabinetmaker's Edge Plane (see page 108). $275

STANLEY No. 131 Double End Block Plane (see page 107). $200

STANLEY No. 144 Corner Rounding Plane ⅜ in. (see page 111). $150

STANLEY No. 239 Special Dado Plane, Missing Spur (see page 111). $100

2 Fold Boxwood Rule, A. STANLEY, 24 in. Brass Bound, with Gunter's Slide. $700

4 Fold STANLEY Rule, Ivory No. 86, German Silver. $325

4 Fold STANLEY Rule, Ivory No. 86½, German Silver. $150

4 Fold STANLEY Rule, Ivory No. 87, German Silver. $200

STANLEY No. 96 Chisel Gauge (see page 42). $150

STANLEY No. 340 Furring Plane (see page 114, lower left). $800

STANLEY 2nd Model No. 42 Millers Pat. Combination Plane in Gun Metal & Irons (see cover photo). $1,500

STANLEY 2nd model No. 41 Millers Pat. Combination, Iron, Cased & Irons (see page 140). $2,300

STANLEY No. 101½ Bull Nose Toy Block Plane (see page 108). $350

STANLEY No. 212 Scraper Plane (see page 149). $850

STANLEY No. 1 SW, New Britain, in orig. box w/Paper (see page 156). $1,250

STANLEY No. 1, Single Irons (3), New, no box. $100

STANLEY No. 444 Dovetail Plane, in orig. box (see pg. 112). $800

STANLEY No. 196 Curved Rabbet (see page 141). $900

STANLEY 2nd Model No. 42 Miller Pat. Combination Plane in Gun Metal (see cover photo). $1,250

STANLEY No. 32 Pat. Adjustable & Graduating Level, Sights Added. $400

Millers 1872 Pat. Combination Plane, Manufactured by STANLEY for one year only (1872). $5,500

2 MINIATURE PLANES, One Handled. $240

Cased Set Plow IRONS (12 blades for a plow plane). $90

PANEL RAISER, E. W. Carpenter, Lancaster, 14 in. x 5 in. x 3 in. Iron. $250.

SCREW ARM SASH PLANE, E. W., Carpenter, Lancaster. $175

8 Pt. Henry Disston & Sons SAW, No. 43, 2 Level & Scribe (see page 180). $600

CROWN MOLD PLANE, E. W. Carpenter, Lancaster, 14 in. x 5½ in., 3½ in. Iron. $725

Curved STAIR PLANE, I. White, Phila. $1,000

CROWN MOLD PLANE, 13½ in. x 4 in., 3 in. Iron, Henry G. White, Phila. $600

Circular STAIR PLANE, Goldsmith, Phila., w/Eagle, no Iron but a Great Plane. $500

MOLD PLANE, T. Donoho, Phila. $150

MOLD PLANE, Butler, Phila. $170

BEAD PLANE, Mockridge & Francis, Newark, NJ. $25

PA/German GOOSEWING AXE, J. M. Strause. $325

Dutch Emigrant TOOL CHEST, M. Streenlan, Amsterdam, to N. America, 5 April (S. S. Caland, Slant Top, Fall Front Chest, Painted Dark Green, Yellow Script, COMPLETE WITH 30 MOLDING PLANES, 2 Panel Raisers, 1 Mast Plane, 2 Bevels, 1 Marking Gauge, Brace w/16 Bits, Plus other Small Tools; an Early Rare Piece). $3,000

HOOK REAMER, G. Rohbach. $150

BACKSAW, W. Toland, Phila. $150

BACKSAW, W & C Johnson, Phila., Double Eagle. $195

BACKSAW, Dilworth Branson & Co., Phila. $85

BACKSAW, Wm. McNiece, Phila. $65

PA/German GOOSEWING AXE, G. Sener. $450

Israel White, Phila.

3 ARM PLOW, Ivory Tipped, Outer Arms are Ebony, NEW AUCTION RECORD PRICE FOR AN AMERICAN PLANE. $8,500

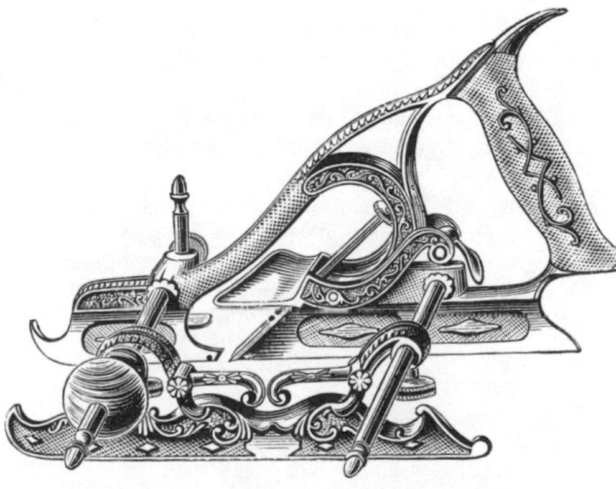

Millers 1872 Pat. Combination Plane, Manufactured by STANLEY for one year only (1872). $5,500

AMERICAN WATCH, TOOL CO. jeweler's lathe with cross-feed, face plate, 25 collets and other assorted attachments. Auct. $225

THOS. APPLETON, Boston, handled rosewood plow plane with boxwood screw-arms. Auct. $375

THOS. L. APPLETON, Chelsea, solid boxwood smoothing plane, 7 inches long. Auct. $145

ALFORD, New York, hollow moulding plane. Auct. $75

J.S. ALLEN, Vernon, Ohio, panel raising plane with handle. 14 inches overall. Auct. $160

ALLEN & CO., New Haven, Conn. Pat. applied for. Unique ratcheting bit brace. Auct. $55

D. AMSDEN, Lebanon, N.H. complex wooden moulding plane by scarce maker. Auct. $375

ARNOL & SON, London, brass surgeon's brace, only 8 inches overall, breakdown design. Auct. $225

ARROWMAMMETT WORKS, Middletown, (Ct.), crown moulding plane, 14½ in. x 6 in., with 4½ inch cutter. Auct. $650. A solid boxwood screw-arm plow plane by same maker brought $100

ASHTON & JACKSON. Sheffield style brace with brass plates and stem. Auct. $125

E.C. ATKIN Co., Ind., sawmaker's hammer, 7lb. size. Auct. $45

ATKINS & SONS coffin-sided mini boxwood smoothing plane, 3½ inches in length. Auct. $150

AUBURN TOOL CO. solid boxwood plow plane with ebony wedge. Handled, screw-arm style. Auct. $350. A No. 30 toothing plane by same maker brought $15

BAILEY TOOL Co., Woonsocket, R.I., rare iron block plane with maker's name cast over entire length of bottom surface. Auct. $700. (see pages 105-107 for other Bailey block planes.)

BAILEY TOOL Co., Woonsocket, R.I., No. 6, iron jointer plane with Battle Axe trademark. Rosewood handle and knob. Auct. $600. Another iron jointer by same maker, No. 8, 24 inches long $300

L. BAILEY, Boston, (5) spoke shaves in wooden box with paper label, "One doz. No. 52 Bailey's patent spoke shaves." Auct. $110. (Also see STANLEY "Bailey")

A & E BALDWIN, 22 inch wood jointer plane with Palmer's patent, Feb. 3, 1857 blade & holder. Auct. $70. Boxwood screw-arm plow plane with ivory tips (missing). Auct. $250. Complex moulder, 2¼ inch cutter, by same maker. Auct. $45

A. & E. BALDWIN and E. BALDWIN, two complex moulding planes, unhandled style. Auct. $65 pair

JON BALLOU, Providence (1723-1770) hollow moulding plane. Auct. $900

W.F. & JOHN BARNES catalog No. 39 of 1894, soft cover, 44 pages, foot-powered machines. Auct. $85

W.F. & J. BARNES bench saw, Pat. 6-20-1874. Foot operated treadle, hand crank handle sheared off. Auct. $300

W.F. & J. BARNES, Rockford, Ill., Pat. Feb. 1876. Foot-powered jigsaw, iron frame, restored & pinstriped. Auct. $475

D.R. BARTON, Rochester, N.Y., cooper's sun plane, Tiger Maple, curved stock. Auct. $225

N.L. BARRUS handled panel raising plane 14 inches long with 1¾ in. skew angle blade. Very nice cond. Auct. $700

E. BASSETT, rabbet plane with fence. Auct. $350

E.Z. BAXTER moulding plane, round, 9⅞ inches long. Auct. $425

L. BECKMAN, Toledo, Ohio. Surveyor's vernier transit, 11 in. telescope, 6 in. limb, 5 in. needle, (dirty, no box). Auct. $400

JOHN BELL, Philda. handled raising panel plane, 15 in. x 4 in. with 3 inch skew blade. Auct. $85

BENSEN & CRANNELL coffin-shaped smoothing plane, 4 inches long. Boxwood with 1 in wide cutter. Auct. $70. Adjustable sash plane by same maker brought $45. Pair of narrow complex moulders fetched $65. Two tongue and grove match planes, No. 14, sold for $45

E.A. BERG MFG., Eskilstuna (Sweden). Matched set of shark brand bevelled finishing chisels, 11 pcs. in two cartons. Auct. $300

E. BERRY, "V" groove plane. Auct. $130

G. BERRY, 193 Old Street, London, bead and groove moulding plane, double boxed, twin bladed. Auct. $150

W. BINGHAM Co. Hardware catalog, Jan. 1894. Hard cover, 7 in x 9 in., thousands of illustrations. Auct. $190

BIRMINGHAM PLANE CO., group of (3) iron block planes, from 6 in to 6½ inches long, 1¾ in blades. Auct. $75 all. An iron smooth plane 6½ in in long (photo pg. 157) brought $575. 14 inch jack planes, with mushroom knobs, fetched from $100 to $125. An iron jointer 22 inches in length sold for $200 (in chipped condition) and another by same maker, with ring front handle, brought $500

BODMAN & HUSSEY, Pawtucket, R.I., wooden jack plane with razee handle, 15 inches overall. Auct. $10

BORING MACHINE (see pg. 7) solid iron, adjustable base has bit storage area. Auct. $190

BOSTON METALIC PLANE CO. iron block plane, 8⅞ in. length, 1¾ in. blade. Shield design on cutter cap. Auct. $200. A 15 inch long jack plane by same maker, with diamond design on lever cap and seethru sole, brought $350. An 18 inch fore plane with slotted sole fetched $575

S.F. BOWSER & CO., Ft. Wayne, Ind., ratcheting brass screw driver with wooden handle. Auct. $25

BOYS UNION TOOL CHEST, No. 700B 8 x 16 x 6 inches, empty. Auct. $45. (Other examples on page 210.)

J. BRADFORD, Portland (Maine), wooden cooper's howell. Auct. $75. Cooper's crooze by same maker. $65. A complex moulding plane with 1¾ inch blade brought $75 and a very large cooper's combination croze and howell with brass head sold for $125.

HENRY BROWN, Patentee, brass plated bit brace, framed on burlap mount board with 3 bits. Auct. $150

BROWN TOOL CO., John Brice Patent, Feb. 8, 1887, wooden jack plane, 16 in. long, with Auburn Tool Co. Thistle Brand cutter. Auct. $225

BUCK BROS., matched set of (17) gouges, 3/16 in. to 2 in. wide, and a set of (5) bevel edge chisels. Auct. $275

CHARLES BUCK, wood chisels, (2) sets, (13) pcs. total, half are gouges, all have bevelled edges. Auct. $260

CHARLES BUCK draw knife, 7 inches overall, 4 inch cutting edge. Delicate shape. Auct. $55

BUCK, Whitechapel (London, 1840), matched set of beading planes, 7 pcs. Auct. $175

BUFF & BUFF, Boston, Patent July 11, 1916. Surveyors transit, verniers, 11½ in scope, 4½ in needle. Model No. 16754. Auct. $450

BUCKEYE MFG. CO., Union City, Ind., doubleheaded boring machine (see page 7). Auct. $185

E.T. BURROWES, Portland, Me., Pat. Mar. 24, 1891. Inside rule, 24 in. to 48 in. that folds to 12 inch. Auct. $75

BUSH, hollow moulding plane, 7/8 in. x 9 9/16 in., with wide, flat chamfers and distinctive wedge profile. Auct. $150

H. BUSH, beading plane with heavy chamfer. Auct. $65

C. & CO. PATENT, Brattleboro, VT. (Am 1835 pat. rule mfg'd. by S. Morton Clark.) boxwood two foot, two fold, rule with brass slide. Auct. $200

CARPENTER CLAMP CO., Cleveland, Pat. Nov. 6, 1900. Special clamp for holding doors while planing. Auct. $50

EDWARD CARTER, Troy, N.Y., large cornice moulding plane, 16 inches long with 3½ in. blade. Auct. $450. A handled rosewood screw-arm plow plane by same maker fetched $125

R. CARTER, Troy, boxed and adjustable sash plane. Auct. $30

R. & C. CARTER, Troy (N.Y.), plow plane with boxwood screw-arms. Auct. $55. An adjustable wooden sash plane by this maker also brought $55

CASEY & CO., Auburn, N.Y., wooden tongue & groove combination match plane with two cutters. Auct. $30

CENTURY cast iron base wood-carver's bench. 3 legs, 1 adjustable. Hand cranked table top is 14 in. x 28 in. Auct. $225

CHALLENGE, iron jack plane, 15 inches long. pat. 1883 & 1884. Embossed logo on sides. Auct. $700-$875. An iron fore plane with distinctive handle shape, 18 inches overall, brought $275. A smooth plane, 9 inches in length, by same maker, fetched a winning bid of $375

H. CHAPIN wooden panel raising plane, 14½ inches long, with adjustable fence and depth stop. Auct. $150-$200. A coffin-shaped, tiny 3½ in. boxwood instrument maker's plane, brought $165. Complex moulding plane with 2 inch blade fetched only $50. Matched set of (2) ⅞ in. tongue and groove planes. Auct. $20. No. 238 beechwood, center screw, plow plane sold for $500. Another plow plane by H. Chapin, No. 240, sold in the $100-$175 range at recent auctions. (See pg. 136 for other models.)

H. CHAPIN No. 37, two foot, four fold, arch joint rule. Auct. $40. No. 66, two foot, four fold, ivory board measure, German silver bound, sold for $450. A yellowed ivory No. 95½ two foot, four fold, brass bound rule brought $160

CHAPIN STEPHENS No. 036 combination brass bound rule. Auct. $150. No. 162½ panel raising plane, 5½ in wide by 15 inches long, brought $300

CHAPLIN'S Improved, Pat. 1888-1902 iron jointer plane, 24 inches long, corrugated top and bottom. Auct. $55-$65. No. 207 iron jack plane 14⅞ inches overall. Auct. $45. No. 255 iron smoothing plane with adjustable throat brought $75. An 18 inch iron fore plane sold for $45

ORRIL R. CHAPLIN Patent, Corrugated bottom iron smoothing plane, 9 inches long with 2 in. cutter. Auct. $350

C.E. CHELOR, Living in Wrentham. Hollow-style moulding plane in good condition. Auct. $2,000 (previous prices brought by this maker are listed on pages 126 & 130.)

J.E. CHILD (Providence, R.I.) complex moulding plane with 2 inch cutter. Auct. $95

J.E. CHILD, larger complex moulder, 14½ inches long by 4 in. wide, with 3 inch blade marked Providence Tool Co. Auct. $300

E. CLARK, Middleboro, complex moulding plane nearly 10 inches long. Auct. $800

H.H. CLEVELAND, Boston, Bailey;s Patent, June 22, 1858. Wooden jointer plane, 26 inches long. Auct. $175

E. CLIFFORD, also marked S. NOYES, wooden moulding plane, unhandled, 10 inches long, heavy wide chamfered stock. Auct. $950

GERAL COACH is the marking on this iron, wood and brass coachmaker's double router. Auct. $100

G.W. COFFIN (Freeport, Maine) early crown moulding plane 16½ inches long. Only mark is on 2¾ in. blade. Auct. $475

C. COLE, early yellow birch, closed handle, plow plane with wooden thumb screws and ivory depth stop. Auct. $300

W. COOLEY, Blackstone St., Boston. Wooden toothing plane. Auct. $90

COOPER'S rare stave plane, 15 in. x 4½ in. with James Cam (1787-1838) blade. Auct. $150

COOPER'S flagging iron and bung mallet. Auct. $65

M. COPELAND, moving fillester plane, 14 inches long, 5 in. wide, with adjustable fence. Auct. $100

CORE BOX plane, V-shaped trough, 6¼ in. x 6¾ in., Birds Eye Maple. Auct. $145

I/COX, narrow beading plane. Auct. $15

M. CRANNELL, Albany, handled rosewood screw-arm plow plane with boxwood fence. Auct. $325

CRESCENT ice saw, 7 feet long with 8 inch tall blade. Auct. $500

J. CROSBY imprint on Yankee-style 18th century plow plane with octagonal arms. Auct. $400. A hollow moulder with heavy chamfer and same imprint brought $300

A. CUMMINGS, Boston, "V" groove plow plane, unhandled, slide-arm, wood thumb screws. Auct. $300

D. & S., Bangor, Me., pat. 1857, iron try square with rosewood infill, 8 in. x 5 in. Auct. $60

S. DALPE handled crown moulding plane, 15 in. long. Blade marked Roxtons Pond (Quebec). Auct. $450

L.L. DAVIS No. 1 clock-shaped 6 in. level, in original box, (see illus. pg. 90) Auct. $275

DAVIS LEVEL & TOOL CO., No. 9 ornate cast iron level 24 in. long with adjustable brass vial. Exceptional quality. Auct. $375

DAVIS LEVEL & TOOL CO., Springfield, Mass., No. 6 six inch long iron level, three vials, (illus. pg. 90). Auct. $325

M.J. DAVISON, New York, brass trimmed 18 inch level. Auct. $45

B. DEAN, cherry wood sash moulder with double irons, 9½ inches overall. Auct. $450

S* DEAN, Dedham, Early hollow moulding plane, 9⅝ inches long. Auct. $1,450

S. DEAN, crown moulding plane with tow bar thru nose. Exceptional design & workmanship, with off-set handle, size 3⅝ in. x 13 in. Auct. $1,000

J. DENISON, unhandled solid boxwood plow plane with screw-arm fence. Auct. $125

DIRIGO, J.W. Penney, Pat. July 3, 1877, Mechanics Falls, Me., rugged foot-powered, ornate iron jig saw. Auct. $375

DISSTON ice saw with tiller handle, 48 inches long. Auct. $15

DISSTON croscut hand saws 26 inches long, No. D8, in orig. boxes, circa 1940. Auct. $45 ea.

DISSTON No. D-115 Victory, hand saw, 8 point crosscut, with eagle and liberty bell TM. Auct. $325

HENRY DISSTON & SONS, Phila. No. 340 special high temper, metal-cutting handsaw. Auct. $30

HENRY DISSTON & SONS, try square, 18 in. x 10 in., rosewood, brass trim, built-in level and scribe, with tab support, (illus. on page 199). Auct. $350

S. DOGGETT (Dedham, Mass.), round moulding plane, 10 inch length. Auct. $450

DUCKWORTH & SMITH, Springfield, Mass., iron bevel square, 9 inch, Pat. Aug. 14, 1883. Auct. $85

DUTCH Schaff plane, whale-shaped, compass-bottom smoother. Auct. $175

ECLIPSE PANEL CO., Coshocton, Ohio, adjustable iron scraper plane, 9 inches long, 2⅞ in. blade. Auct. $300

FABIANS Saw-Log-Caliper with tables. Brass hardware, paper label still readable. Auct. $125

ISAAC FIELD, Providence, unhandled wooden 2 in. complex moulding plane. Auct. $150

FILE MAKER'S heavy hammer and one chisel. Auct. $175-$225

G. FISHER early 10 inch moulding plane with heavy flat chamfering. Auct. $325

D. FLATHERS & SONS, Sheffield. Wrought iron bit brace, brass neck, ebony head. Auct. $45

FORD TOOL CHEST No. 13, set of miniature auto tools in cardboard box. Auct. $45

FRANKLIN, Pat. May 6, 1873. Heavy iron surfacing plane. Auct. $45

FRANKLIN'S square & bevel attachment for wood planes, pat 1861, mfd. by Geo. A. Rollins, Nashua, N.H. Auct. $200

G.E. FRANKLIN, Natic, Mass., pat. 1873, iron shoe makers surfacing plane. Auct. $30

FROE, basket maker's small size, 5 inch edge. Auct. $55

B. FROGATT (18th Cent. English maker), moulding plane 9¾ in long, boxwood wear insert. Auct. $25

C. FULLER, Boston, Causeway St. (also located at Pine St.), 3 wooden moulding planes. Auct. $85

D. FULLER (West Gardiner, Me.) complex moulding plane. Auct. $225

JO FULLER, Providence, unhandled complex moulding plane, 10 inches in length. Auct. $375. A rabbet plane and a common moulder. Auct. $350 the pair. Another complex moulding plane by this early maker brought $500. A plain round-moulding plane, 10 inches long fetched $150. An ovolo style, ⅜ in. with relieved wedge and early fluting $325.

GAGE TOOL CO. wood bottom smoothing plane, 9¾ inches long. Auct. $35. Another by same maker, 10¼ in. $20. (See page 152 for additional examples)

GAGE TOOL CO. wood bottom jack plane, 14 inches long. Auct. $85. Another, 16 inches $45

GAGE TOOL CO. wood bottom jointer plane, 30 inches overall. Auct. $120

J.R. GALE wooden plow plane with slide arms and brass set screws. Auct. $45

NAT GAMBLE (London, 1730). Rare 18th century moulding plane, (wedge not orig.). Auct. $500

L. GARDNER, Boston, wide moulding plane, 9¼ in. long, 2¼ in. cutter. Auct. $250. Pair of coping planes by same maker brought $225. A slide-arm wooden plow plane fetched $50

GARDNER & MURDOCK, Green St., Bst. (Boston). Crown moulding plane 14½ inches long with 3½ inch wide cutter. Auct. $400

T.J. GARDNER, Maker, Bristol, set of 3 complex moulding planes. Auct. $75

GAYLORD'S Patent Mar. 3, 1885 picture frame moulding plane, in iron with wood handle. Auct. $1050

GENERAL HARDWARE No. 800 brass plumb bob with removable point. Auct. $35

GLADWIN'S Pat. 1878 combination plane and tool handle with 1 inch wide blade. Auct. $275-$300

P.A. GLADWIN tiny, ring handle-socket, iron body, smoothing or block plane, only 3 inches overall. Auct. $275

GOODALL CO. No. 35 Phila., PA. stamped on toe of this 8⅝ inch wood bottom smooth plane. Auct. $45

GOODELL-PRATT, nut wrench, brace & bit-style, with four nut sizes. Auct. $45

GOODELL PRATT No. 279 breast drill, large heavy duty model with leather strap end. Auct. $55 (other examples on page 62.)

THO GRANT unhandled plow plane with wedged slide arms. Auct. $300

I. GREGG, hollow moulder, 9½ inches long, chamfered stock. Auct. $235

JOHN GREEN handled panel raising plane. Wide chamfer, adjustable fence, depth stop, (excellent cond.) Auct. $200

GREENFIELD TOOL CO. No. 518 rosewood plow plane with boxwood screw arms, handled. Auct. $250. (See page 136 for other plows by this maker.)

F.M. GREENLEAF, Littleton, N.H., log caliper with St. Croix paper Co. Imprint. Auct. $650 - $775. (Several sold in this price range.) Another by same maker, with wheel, marked "Conn. Valley Lumber" and "Carey Standard". Deluxe quality. Auct. $850

GREENLEE, Rockford, Illinois. Carpenter's slick with 6 inch wide blade. Auct. $200

W. & L.E. GURLEY, Troy, N.Y., sighting level with vertical angle readings. Bubble in level can be observed while sighting. Complete with custom-made wood box. Auct. $175

W. & L.E. GURLEY, Troy, N.Y., transit with tripod, telescope and two verniers. Auct. $400

W. & L.E. GURLEY, Troy, N.Y., surveyor's vernier compass, 4½ inch needle, 9 in. telescope, collapsable tripod. Auct. $1,025

GRIFFITHS, Norwich. Matched pair of English handrail planes, short wooden stocks. Auct. $135

EDWIN HAHN No. 14 iron jointer plane, 23¾ in., (other sizes have brought more money). Auct. $50

HALL CASE & CO., Columbus, Ohio, handled screw arm plow plane (with some threads damaged). Auct. $75

HAMMACHER, SCHLEMMER & CO., Tools for all trades catalog of 1896. Soft cover, 7 x 10 in. Auct. $180. Catalog No. 500 of 1917, hard cover, 1111 pgs. Auct. $160

HAMMER, combination hammer, nail puller, pliers, etc. Early patent (1866), makes this one worth more than average. Auct. $70

T.W. HARRIS, Portland, adjustable sash plane, by unlisted maker. Auct. $75

HARTFORD PLANE CO., Pat. 1869, No. 1141 stamped on heel. Brass hardware. Double dado plane, Duval patent. Auct. $500

C. HARWOOD, 18th century panel raising plane with open handle. Birch, 12 7/16 in. overall, 1 13/16 in. cutter. Auct. $1,700. Lot of (3) moulding planes by same maker, avg. ⅝ in. x 10 in. Auct. $950. Another, hollow moulding plane. Auct. $85

R. HARWOOD, single bladed sash plane, 18th cent., round top blade, chamfered stock. Auct. $170. A plow plane by same maker, slide-arm with thumb screws. Auct. $360

R.B. HASELTON, Contoocook, N.H., lumber rule with eagle trade mark, brass tips, 36 inch. Auct. $95

R.B. HASELTON, Groton, H.H., lumber rule, 36 in. long. Auct. $100

R.B. HASELTON, log caliper with wheel. "Improved, caliper, cubic, measure". Auct. $550

HATHERSICH (Manchester, England, 1820-1861) matched set of 20 hollows and rounds. Auct. $500

HATHERSICH matched set of 8 beading planes. $150

HATHERSICH 2 pair of snipe bill and side snipe planes. Auct. $100

HATMAKER'S tool box full of Hatter's tools. Auct. $310

EDWARD HELB, Railroad, York, PA. combination level & grade finder, with compass and sighting tube. Auct. $250

HERMITAGE WORKS, Sheffield, brass plated wooden bit brace. Auct. $80

S. & H. HILLS, Springfield, unhandled beechwood screw-arm plow plane with set of (7) cutters. Auct. $100

HILLS & WINSHIP, Springfield, MS., adjustable sash plane with boxwood wear insert. Auct. $45

I.P. HOLMES, Berwick, ME., shoot board plane. Auct. $125

HOLT MFG. CO., Hartford, Conn., Pat. July 1898. Bit brace set with (3) braces, (8) bits, (2) screwdrivers, adaptor, etc. All are threaded at ends. Auct. $100

HOLTZAPFFEL, ebony handle, hack saw-shaped, dovetail saw with 4 inch long blade and a wide brass ferrule. Auct. $80

HORNED-style smoothing plane, hardwood stock, brass sole, hand carved decorations. Auct. $55-$100

HORNED handle smoothing planes. Auct. $20-$30 ea. (decorated).

L.D. HOWARD (St. Johnsbury, Vt.) Patent Nov. 5, 1867. Combination bevel square and level. Brass bound stock with steel arm. Auct. $600

J. HOWARTH steel smoothing plane, 8 inch, with rosewood infill, 2 in. blade, brass lever cap. Auct. $250

J. HUMPHREY, Keene, NH, log caliper with 21 inch arms, 48 inches overall. Auct. $30

H.W. HUNT (circa 1821, 78 Wall St., N.Y.) brass scope and level, 17 in. overall. Breaks down to fit in box. Auct. $450

I. IONES, Living In Holliston, crown moulding plane, 13 inches long, 3½ in. iron, (scars and wormholes). Auct. $900

IRWIN, unusual oak bit holder and set of 13 bits, cylinder-style container. Auct. $205

JAMES MFG. CO. Williamsburg, Mass., rosewood plow plane with closed handle, boxwood screw arms and nuts (minor damage). Auct. $275

C.E. JENNINGS ornamental cast iron level, 24 in., (corners chipped). Auct. $55

C.E. JENNINGS & CO. No. 307 Steer's Patent iron jointer plane, 22 inch long, rosewood inlaid sole. Auct. $175. Another, No. 304, iron smooth plane, 9 inches long, slight damage. Auct. $75

RUSSELL JENNINGS matching set of (13) metal brace bits in special-made oak box labeled T.B. Rayl Co., Detroit. Auct. $110

JEWELLER'S lathe in wooden box with hand operated drive wheel. Auct. $75

JEWELLER'S pedal-operated grinder, polisher, with drill. Iron base, wooden platform has drawers with attachments. Auct. $100

JEWELLER'S stake set. 'INVERTO" Kendrick & Davis, Lebanon, N.H. Complete with wood case. Auct. $125

S.E. JONES, unhandled complex moulder, 10 in. long. Heavy flat chamfer. Auct. $775

K & E CO. brass plumb bob, 12 ounce with removable point. Auct. $30

KEEN KUTTER No. K-4 iron smooth plane in orig. box with label. These were made for Simmons Hardware Co. by Stanley, circa 1910. Auct. $100. The same plane in average "used" condition brought a winning bid of $25. (See page 155 for more Keen Kutter smoothing planes.)

KEEN KUTTER Nos. KK120 & KK220 small iron block planes. Auct. $25 pair. (See page 105 for other block planes by this maker.)

J. KELLOGG, Amherst, MS., complex moulding plane with 2 inch blade. Auct. $145

KERBY & BRO., makers, U.S. Standard wantage rule, 36 in. long, with ivory and brass inlays. Auct. $300

J. KILLAM, panel raising plane, 2½ inches wide by 14½ in. long. Auct. $275

D. KIMBERLY & SONS, England, wooden wedge-arm plow plane with brass trim and boxwood sole. Auct. $75

C.G. KING (Boston, 1808-1858) surveyor's transit with tripod. 10½ inch telescope, 5½ in. limb, 4 in. needle. Auct. $800

JOSIAH KING, 373 Bowery, N.Y., snipe bill moulder with double boxed wear strip. Auct. $225

S. KING (American), 10 inch nosing plane, wooden moulder, Auct. $250

HAZARD KNOWLES Patent iron jointer plane, 19¾ inches long, 3⅛ in. wide, with maple handle. Auct. $350

E.S. LANE, Upton, Me., log caliper with spoked wheel on one end. Brass fitting is marked Greenlief. Auct. $700

J.H. LAMB, New Bedford, rosewood plow plane with boxwood screw arms. Auct. $325

LATHE (See watchmaker, clockmaker)

LEATHER WORKER'S and shoemaker's tools, over 450 items including awls, hammers, shares, cutters, knives, draw gauges, etc. Some rosewood & brass. Auct. $850

J.F. & G.M. LINDSEY, Huntington, Mass., tongue and groove combination match plane. Auct. $45

I. LINDENBERGER, ten inch moulding plane in excellent condition. Auct. $150. Beading plane by same maker, boxwood wear insert. Auct. $175-$20

I. LINDENBERGER, Providence. Yankee-style slide-arm plow plane with brass tips and depth stop. One of the first American plow planes to have brass trim. Auct. $1,000

I. LINDENBERGER, Providence (Circa 1800) slide-arm plow plane with wooden depth stop. Auct. $625-$650. (3 years ago a similar plane brought $900.)

A. LIETZ & CO., surveyor's transit, vernier. 11½ in. telescope, 3½ in. needle. Box marked Buff & Buff, Boston, No. 3646. Auct. $350

N. LITTLE wooden panel raising plane, 15 inches long with offset handle. Auct. $225. A 10 inch long moulding plane by same maker brought a bid of $175

I. LONG., Hopkinton, N.H., crown moulding plane, 15 in. long, 4½ in. wide, 3⅜ in. cutter. Heavy flat chamfered stock, offset handle, hand forged blade, marked D.K. Auct. $1,300

LUFKIN, open-reel steel tape measure, 200 ft. Auct. $30. (The Lufkin company has been in the measuring tool business since 1869 and is today a division of Cooper Industries of Apex, NC.)

LUFKIN, lot of (3) two foot, four fold rules. No. 48 maple, No. 651 boxwood, and No. 851 boxwood. Auct. $45

LUFKIN No. 95 sheetmetal worker's steel rule. Auct. $45

LUFKIN No. 590 cylinder shaped brass plumb bob. Auct. $15

LUFKIN No. 863L, two foot, four fold, combination rule with built-in level and protractor. Auct. $60

LUFKIN No. 2051, one foot, three fold rule with built-in level. Auct. $75

LUFKIN No. 2071 brass bound, one foot, three fold rule with built-in level. Auct. $300

LUFKIN "Gro-tape Keepsake Rule". Specialty advertising tape for recording growth of house apes, circa 1940 with orig. box. Auct. $55. (Lots more Lufkin rules on page 170.)

LUTHER GRINDING MFG. CO., "Hummer" grinder, foot-operated, with a cast iron seat. Auct. $45

LYNCH SKATE PLANE, Tacony, Pa., Pat. July 17, 1894. Auct. $45-$95

MALLET, BRASS, with wooden stuffing. Auct. $55

MALLIN, Maker, warranted. Two foot, two fold, arch joint rule with many tables. Auct. $45

MANNEBACH BROS., 112 Stanton St., New York. Beautiful large coopers croze and howell with brass wear strips. Auct. $225

MANNEBACH BROS., N.Y.C., large cooper's croze with inlaid brass wear plates. Auct. $50

MARBLES ARMS & MFG. CO., Gladstone, Mich., safety axe with hinged blade cover Auct. $75-$110

MARDEN'S Patent 1872 marking gauge. Auct. $100

WILLIAM MARPLES, by Her Majesty's Royal Letter Patent. Ultimatum-style brass bit brace with boxwood infill. Auct. $1,000. Another, by same maker, with Rhinoceros Horn infill, (cracked). Auct. $600. Still another, this one with beechwood infill Auct. $425. (See pages 31 and 32 for illus. and more prices.)

W. MARPLES & SON, Hibernia, Sheffield, 2 complex moulding planes. Auct. $65

MARSH No. 2C, corrugated bottom smoothing plane, 7 inches long, resembles Stanley brand. Auct. $300

W. MARTIN, Philad. wooden chamfer plane with skew angle blade. Auct. $100

C.R. MASON & CO. handled screw-arm plow plane. Beech with boxwood arms, nuts and fence. Auct. $90

MATHEWS, Dayton, Ohio, "Never Stall" 10 inch combination monkey wrench, screw driver, etc. Auct. $35

A. MATHIESON & SON, Glasgow, No. 11 steel bridle handled plow plane with triangular arms of ebony. Auct. $325

JAMES McCOSKRIE, Cambridge Port, MS. (1848-1850), rosewood level, heavy, 1⅝ in. x 3½ in. x 28 inches, with brass trim. Auct. $100

ALEX MEGAREY, New York, early brass surveyor's compass, 14 inches long. Auct. $300

MELHUISH, London is the stamp on brass lever cap of this 22¾ inch iron jointer with rosewood infill. (Mint cond.) Auct. $400

METALLIC PLANE CO., iron block plane, 6⅞ inches long with 1⅞ in. blade. Auct. $425. Smooth plane by same maker, 9½ inch corrugated bottom. Auct. $55. Iron jack plane of same design, 15 inches overall. $75-$85. Jointer plane, Palmer's pat. 1867, 20½ inch. Auct. $55-$65. Early plow plane, in iron, with rosewood handle, 11 inches long, 6 in. wide. Auct. $300. Filletster plane with decorative bottom, 10½ inch. Auct. $675-$750

MILLERS PATENT No. 42 combination plane with gun metal frame, (fillester missing). Auct. $1,000. (See STANLEY planes listing for other examples.)

MILLER FALLS cast iron level, 24 in., with 8 large circles, 2 vials. Auct. $20

MILLER FALLS No. 3, wood carving chisel set (12 pcs.) in oak box. Auct. $110

MILLER FALLS No. 18 mitre box and saw, Langdon mark, Disston saw. Auct. $55

MILLERS FALLS No. 87 iron block plane in orig. box. Auct. $20. (See pg. 105 for more.)

MILLERS FALLS No. 831A carpenter's brace (2), and a Pexto No. 8010E brace with art deco plastic handle & head. (3) pcs. Auct. $35

MILLERS FALLS "Shaker-style" rosewood H-framed fret saw, 5½ in. x 11½ in., circa 1880. Auct. $100

G. MOORE, New York, triangular carpenter's square, maple, 24 in. x 36 in. Pat. Jan 14, 1873. Auct. $70-$105

B. MORRILL, Bangor, (Maine), sash plane with boxed insert. Auct. $125

MORRIS PATENT iron jack plane 15¼ inches long with 2⅛ in. Sandusky blade (and some possible replacement parts). Auct. $450

MORRIS PATENT scissor-arm-type iron plow plane, circa 1871, wooden handle. Auct. $1,300

MOSLEY, boxwood fillester plane with brass trimmed slide-arm fence. Auct. $70

MULTIFORM moulding plane set. (3) planes with double slot for removable handle. Bead plane and tongue & groove set with adjustable fence. Includes double slot master handle. Screw heads on heel are floral decorated. Auct. $2,250. Set of (5) 1854 patent, hollows and rounds with a single master handle. Auct. $300

MULTIFORM Moulding Plane Co., pat. 1854, pair wooden planes, a fillester, and a bead plane. One has removable handle. Auct. $400 pair. Wooden tongue plane with adjustable fence and removable handle. Auct. $100. (See page 139 for others.)

A. MURDOCK (early Boston maker) handled spar plane, 14 inches long. Auct. $375

E. NEWELL match plane, tongue, 9⅞ inches in length. Auct. $375

WM. T. NICHOLSON iron level, 19½ in. long, ¾ in. wide, Providence, R.I., pat. May 1, 1860. Brass bubble plate marked Stanley. Auct. $210

M. NORTON, wooden compass plane, slightly rounded bottom, 9 in. long, heavy chamfers. Auct. $175

SIMON C. NOYES, Lisbon, N.H., lumber caliper with tables. Auct. $175-$200

F. NICHOLSON, Living in Wrentham, complex moulding plane. Auct. $800

I. NICHOLSON, In Wrentham. 10 inch moulding plane, also marked GH. Auct. $1,000

P. NICOL, Roxton Pond (Quebec), wooden 26 in. jointer plane, 1888 patent date. Auct. $180

NORRIS, London, Patent Adjustable, is the stamp on this mint condition 9 inch smooth plane's brass lever cap, (Pat. No. 11526-13). Auct. $600. (See page 155 for average prices on used Norris planes.)

THE OHIO TOOL COMPANY began operations in Columbus, Ohio, in 1823, and used prison labor (200 inmates) from a nearby State Penitentiary from 1841 to 1880. In 1899 the firm merged with The Auburn Tool Co., and in 1900 received a first place award for carpenter tools entered in The Paris Exposition. Power tools and pre-cut mouldings undoubtedly contributed to the firm's decline and demise in 1920.

OHIO TOOL CO. pat. 10-13-81, wood bottom plane, 8 inches long with 2 inch wide blade. Auct. $160

OHIO TOOL wood bottom plane, 24 inches overall. Auct. $25. Two other wood bottom planes by same maker, one 15 inch and one 8 inch. $25 pair.

OHIO TOOL CO. No. 03 iron smoothing plane. Auct. $30

OHIO TOOL CO. No. 08 iron jointer plane, 24 inches overall. Wooden handle and knob. Auct. $30. Shorter, 22 inch, No. 07 by same maker. Auct. $30

OHIO TOOL CO., large 2 handled smoothing plane, 16 in. long. 2¼ inch blade. Auct. $45

OHIO TOOL CO., complex moulding planes, Nos. 43, 43½, and 62. Auct. $15 ea.

OHIO TOOL CO. No. 60 wooden moulding plane 2¼ inch size. Auct. $55

OHIO TOOL CO. No. 75 wooden tongue & groove combination match plane. Auct. $25

OLIVER, railroad track setter's level with gage. Auct. $100

RICHARD F. PALSEY, "Ne Plus Ultra" ultimatum-style brass bit brace with rosewood infill. Auct. $250

R.A. PARRISH, Philada., is the mark on the 4¼ inch wide blade of this handled crown moulder, 15 inches long by 6 in. wide. Auct. $400

PECK, STOW & WILCOX CO., catalog of 1905, hard cover, 456 pages. Auct. $115

E.W. PENNELL, 90 Callowhill St., Phila., pair of tongue and groove match planes, handled, screw arms, 14 inches long. Auct. $65

PERFECT AXE, Kelly Axe Mfg. Co., Louisville, Ky. Engraved message on head tells how good the product is. "Once you have tried it you will use no other." Auct. $155

PHILLIPSON, (London, Circa 1760), bead plane. Auct. $150

PHOENIX COMPANY - Hitchcockville, handled plow plane with boxwood screw-arms, (slight damage). Auct. $275

PIANO MAKER'S bit brace, rosewood, 10½ inches long with only a 1¾ in. throw, ivory head, German silver side plates. Auct. $550

PIANO TUNER'S TOOLS, set of 40 mixed tools in leather case. Auct. $125

PILKINGTON, PEDIGOR & STORR, improved Sheffield-style bit brace with heavy brass side plates and crown finials. Brass stem has ivory ring. Framed on burlap mount with 4 bits. Auct. $1,600

PLOW PLANE, unmarked, ebony wood with ivory tipped boxwood screw-arms and nuts. Auct. $1,300

PLUMB BOB, narrow cylinder shape with inlet grooves, 10 oz. brass. Auct. $65

PLUMB BOB, solid brass, rocket shape, (no fins). One foot long, weight eleven lbs. Auct. $200

PLUMB BOBS, group of plain iron plumb bobs (6) pcs. from 5 oz. to 4½ lbs. Auct. $45. Another group of (4) pcs. 6 oz. to 12 oz. Auct. $55

PLUMB BOBS, Brass, plain, (7) pcs. Auct. $80. Another group of (6) from 5 oz. to 13 oz. Auct. $90. (See pages 162 and 163 for other examples.)

H.M. POOL, Easton, Mass. brass trimmed mahogany level, 24 inches in length. Auct. $50

W. POWEL, moulding plane, 10 inches long, heavy chamfer. Auct. $1,100

PRATT & CO., Buffalo, wide moulding plane with 2⅝ inch cuter. Auct. $60

RABONE No. 1185, four foot, four fold boxwood coachmaker's rule. Auct. $105. (Other examples on page 172.)

W. RAYMOND unhandled plow plane with wedged slide-arms. Auct. $175. A 15 inch jack plane by same maker brought $105 and a double-slotted beading plane fetched $105. At another auction a wooden rabbet plane with adjustable fence and depth stop commanded a winning bid of $225.

W. RAYMOND, reverse ogee moulding plane, 9¼ inches long, 1½ in. wide. Auct. $225. (See page 133 for other moulders by this maker.)

REED, Utica, solid boxwood screw-arm plow plane in nearly mint cond. Auct. $275

C.F. RICHARDSON & SON, Athol, Mass., pat. Aug. 16, 1887. Builders transit and level with tripod and instructions. Auct. $275

RITCHIES Patent, Aug. 19, 1884 combination rose-wood square with built-in levels and bubble pro-tection feature. German silver trim. Auct. $250-$300

ROBINSON, adjustable brass bevel square with rosewood infill, 4 in. x 6 in., pat. 1870. Auct. $275

RODIER'S PATENT iron smooth plane, 9¼ inches long with 2⅛ inch Buck Bros. cutter. Applewood handle. Auct. $425

JOHN A. ROEBLING, rule, rope caliper with brass slide. Trenton, N.J. maker. Auct. $65

RODIER PATENT, iron jack plane with faucet-handled blade adjust., 14½ inches overall. Auct. $450

ROPE MAKER, The Wonder, Pat. App'd. for. 4-strand twisting machine. Auct. $115-$250

SANDUSKY TOOL CO., set of (4) ogee moulding planes, ½ in. to 1¼ in. Auct. $100

SANDUSKY TOOL CO., "Special" miniature round bottom plane, 4 inches long, ¾ in. blade. Auct. $95

SANDUSKY TOOL CO. No. 122 beechwood plow plane with boxwood screw arms. Auct. $125

SANDUSKY No. 126, applewood plow plane with boxwood screw-arms. Auct. $100. (Many more examples on page 139.)

SANDUSKY TOOL CO., No. 140 self-regulating plow plane with brass center wheel. Auct. $2,100 in repaired condition.

SARGENT & CO. Mechanics' Tools catalog of 1911, hard cover, 250 pages. Auct. $115

P. SARGENT, Concord, N.H., wooden moulding plane. Auct. $50

SARGENT No. 74 circular bottom metal plane. Auct. $70-$95. No. 76 by same maker, $110

SARGENT No. 160 iron scrub plane with iron handles. Auct. $110-$135

SARGENT No. 316 iron block plane with removable tail handle, wood ball grip. Auct. $175. (Other block planes by this maker on page 106.)

SARGENT No. 409 scrub plane. Auct. $40

SARGENT No. 414C jack plane with corrugated bottom. Auct. $45

SARGENT No. 514, low angle metal block plane with adjustable mouth. Auct. $375

SARGENT No. 718C fore plane with auto-set blade and corrugated bottom. Auct. $55

SARGENT No. 722 iron jointer plane, 22 in. long. Mahogany handle and knob, auto-set blade. Auct. $65

SARGENT No. 1508 bull-nose rabbet plane, iron, beetle shape, removable front. Auct. $205

SAWMAKER'S HAMMER, Auct. $65

BOW SAW small, fine, 12 in by 4½ in frame with 9 inch blade. Auct. $120

BOW SAW, boxwood, 18 in x 11 in. x 10 in. Auct. $150

BOW SAW, rosewood with brass bound outer edges, 27 in. x 18 in. x 16 in. Auct. $150

PIT SAW early framed example, 24 in. x 75 in. Handles at each end. Auct. $250

VENEER SAW rugged style, 16 in. x 60 in. with 4 inch wide blade and cover. Auct. $50

MICHAEL SAXBY, (London, 1756) hollow moulding plane. Auct. $400

SCIENTIFIC PATTERN CO., Boston Mass., Tailor's L-square & ruler. Auct. $20

SCISSORS, steel with brass handles. Auct. $35

SHEPLEY (England, circa 1800) pair of hollow moulders. Auct. $30

B. SHENEMAN, 297 Market St., Phila., adjustable sash plane with boxwood wear insert. Auct. $45

SHOEMAKER'S peg-cutting tools on long handles. Lot of (3). Auct. $15

SIEGLEY No. 2 iron plow plane. Auct. $50. Another in original wooden box with all accessories. Auct. $120

SIEGLEY Patent plow plane, iron with wooden fence. Auct. $50. Another model with decorative iron fence, wooden faced. Auct. $350. (See page 139 for additional examples.)

SIEGLEY No. 4 smooth plane, metallic with cor-rugated bottom, (dirty). Auct. $40

SIEGLEY No. 8 corrugated bottom fore plane, 18 in. length. Auct. $30

SIEGLEY No. 12 iron jointer plane, 24 inches long with corrugated top and bottom. Auct. $120

SIGN BOARD, Collins Axe Co., figural axe head, 12 in. x 18 in. cutout. Auct. $75

SIGN BOARD, over 6 ft. long, 11 in. high, in shape of a crosscut saw with handles at each end. Disston Tool Co., Philadelphia, in red letters. Auct. $225

SILVERSMITH'S box of 100's of Repousse'e tools (as found). Auct. $85

SIMON & SKIDMORE Mfg. Co., Santa Ana, Ca., Pat. 7-8-19 try square & bevel. Auct. $25

ARAD: SIMONS (Lebanon, N.H. moulding plane by scarce maker. Auct. $1,000

D. SIMMONS & CO., Cohoes, N.Y. shovel-handled carpenter's slick (chisel). Auct. $65

H. SLATER, maker, Meredith St., Clerkenwell, London. Steel smoothing plane with rosewood infill. 7½ in. long, 2⅓ in blade, brass lever cap. Auct. $225

I. SLEEPER, rosewood beading plane 9⅞ in. long. Heavy chamfer. Auct. $150. Unhandled complex moulding plane by same maker. Auct. $175. A sash coping plane by same maker brought $75

I. SLEEPER, astragal moulder, 9 13/16 inches long. Auct. $200. (See page 133 for other moulding planes by this maker.)

S. SLEEPER, round botom plane, 21 inches long. Auct. $175

A. SMITH, Rehoboth (1769-1822) early decorative touch-mark, round moulding plane. Auct. $325. Another, narrow example, $300. A hollow-style moulder, 9 7/16 inches long. Auct. $300

A. SMITH, Rehoboth, wooden plow plane with slide-arm fence and thumb screws. Auct. $525

E. SMITH, Rehoboth, (The son of A. Smith). Hollow moulding plane 1¾ in. size, 9½ inches long. (Fine cond.) Auct. $90. By same maker, a complex moulder with 2¼ inch wide cutter, boxwood wear insert. Auct. $40

SORENTO Wood Carving Co., Pat. Dec. 13, 1870. Another beautiful woodframed coping saw from this famous maker. Auct. $200

L.S. SOULE, Waldoboro, ME, double bladed ship-builder's rabbet plane, 1 in. wide, 4 in. high, (excellent cond.) Auct. $250

A.C. SPICER, beading plane with boxwood wear insert and relieved wedge. Auct. $175

W. SPRATS, two complex moulding planes in yellow birch, with heavy chamfers, 10⅛ inches overall. Auct. $475 pair

B. SPRING & CO., Sheffield. "Ultimatum" metallic, brass framed, bit brace with ebony wood infill. Auct. $300

SQUARE, 1882 pat. combination brass bodied square, bevel, rule and level, with slotted blade & circular mouth, approx. 10 inches overall. Auct. $625

STEER'S patent, iron fore plane, (see page 113) over 17 in. long. Auct. $170

STALEY, Sheffield. Rare metallic frame, patented bit brace with boxwood infill. Auct. $1,400

STANDARD RULE, wood bottom plane, 9 in. x 2½ in. Auct. $125

STANDARD RULE CO., iron bodied smoother, 9¼ in. x 2 inches. Auct. $275

STANDARD RULE CO. No. 3 iron smoothing plane, 8 inches long. Auct. $175

STANDARD RULE CO. No. 6 iron fore plane, 18 inches long. Auct. $100

STANDARD RULE CO., Unionville, Ct., No. 38 ivory caliper rule, 6 inch, two fold. Auct. $125

STANDARD TOOL CO., Athol, Mass., Chaplin's Pat. (1880) combination machinist's square with iron scroll-shaped V-head & 12 inch steel rule. Auct. $125

L.S. STARRETT two-way, table top level, 2 in. x 3 in. Auct. $20

L.S. STARRETT No. 515C cylinder type plumb bob. Auct. $15

E.A. STEARNS No. 50B ivory rule, two foot, four fold, inside and outside scales, (mint cond.). Auct. $600

E.A. STEARNS, maker, Brattleboro, No. 23 boxwood rule, two foot, four fold, fully brass bound. Auct. $45 (See many more examples on page 173.)

E.A. STEARNS No. 48B, two foot, four fold ivory rule, German silver binding & arch joint. Auct. $225

E.A. STEARNS No. 57, one foot, four fold ivory rule with square joint. Auct. $125-$150. Also sold in same price range were slightly yellowed ivory rules, Nos. 52B & 54, and a No. 16 folding boxwood rule.

E.A. STEARNS & CO., Makers, Brattleboro, VT., No. 73 shipbuilders double bevel square. Boxwood with 4 in. and 7 in. brass arms. Auct. $135

STEPHENS & CO., boxwood rule, two foot, four fold, with brass arch joint, slide, scales. Auct. $85

STEPHENS & CO., U.S. Standard, ivory rule. Two foot, four fold, (near mint cond.) Auct. $375

STEPHEN'S Pat. 1909, unusual open-end wrench, 7½ inches long. Auct. $25

STEPHENS No. 36 boxwood combination rule, inclinometer & level, brass bound. Auct. $100

STEPHENS No. 65 boxwood board measure. Auct. $55

J. STEVENS, Pat. Feb. 14, 1888, two wood boxed divider and caliper sets, 5 in. to 12 in. Auct. $100

IONAH STETSON complex wooden moulding plane (broken wedge) unhandled style. Auct. $325

STEYRISHER STAHL No. 16, goosewing hewing axe with 16 inch edge, sunburst mark. Auct. $150

J. STILES, Kingston (N.Y.) round moulding plane and a bead plane. Auct. $125 pair

J. STILES, 1782, wooden "V" groove plane. Auct. $475

J. STILES, 1802. Bead plane, 9⅜ in. long. Auct. $135

J. STILES, 1818, gun-barrel-stock inletting plane. Auct. $225. Gutter plane and a tongue plane with Eagle trademark, by same maker (2) $85

J.P. STORER, Brunswick, Me., mahogany smooth plane, 9 in. long with 2¼ in. blade. Auct. $150

STRATTON BROTHERS, Greenfield, Pat. 1870, rosewood level, 8 in. long, brass bound, vertical bubble is in one end. Auct. $250

STRATTON BROTHERS, Greenfield, Mass., tiny 8 inch brass bound rosewood level. Auct. $300. 10 inch example, fully bound. Auct. $200-$225. (See page 99 for larger sizes.)

J.J. STYLES, Kingston, N.Y., unhandled complex moulding plane. Auct. $25

A.J. SYMES, group of 3 wooden moulding planes, 6 inches or smaller, 1 with tail. Auct. $50

STANLEY "Bailey" No. 1 smooth plane. Auct. $450-$700

STANLEY "Bailey" No. 2 smooth plane. Auct. $95-$205

STANLEY "Bailey" No. 2C smooth plane. Auct. $275-$400

STANLEY "Bailey" No. 3 smooth plane. Auct. $35-$55

STANLEY "Bailey" No. 4 smooth plane. Auct. $20. Dlr. $40

STANLEY "Bailey" No. 4C smooth plane. $20-$40

STANLEY "Bailey" No. 4½ smooth plane. $25-$45

STANLEY "Bailey" No. 4½C smooth plane. $25-$75. Auct. (in orig. box) $145

STANLEY "Bailey" No. 4½H smooth plane. $300-$375

STANLEY "Bailey" No. 5 jack plane. $20-$25. Auct. (in orig. box) $45

STANLEY "Bailey" No. 5C jack plane. $20-$30

STANLEY "Bailey" No. 5¼ jack plane. Auct. $25-$45

STANLEY "Bailey" No. 5¼C jack plane. Auct. $150

STANLEY "Bailey" No. 5½ jack plane $25-$45

STANLEY "Bailey" No. 5½C jack plane. $25-$65

STANLEY "Bailey" No. 5½H jack plane. $425-$600

STANLEY "Bailey" No. 6 fore plane. Auct. $30-$45

STANLEY "Bailey" No. 6C fore plane. $25-$45

STANLEY "Bailey" No. 7 jointer plane. Auct. $25-$65

STANLEY "Bailey" No. 7C jointer plane. $35-$55

STANLEY "Bailey" No. 8 jointer plane. Auct. $45-$65

STANLEY "Bailey" No. 8C jointer plane. Auct. $50-$105

STANLEY No. 9 cabinet maker's block plane. Auct. $600-$900

STANLEY No. 9¼ general purpose block plane. $10-$20

STANLEY "Bailey" No. 9½ block plane. $15-$30

STANLEY "Bailey" No. 9¾ ball-handled block plane. Auct. $225. (Earliest model. Auct. $200. Dlr. $425)

STANLEY No. 10 carriage maker's rabbet plane. Auct. $95-$130

STANLEY No. 10C carriage maker's rabbet plane. $200-$350

STANLEY No. 10¼ carriage maker's rabbet plane. $300-$700 (Auct. near mint)

STANLEY No. 10½ bench rabbet plane. Auct. $80-$160

STANLEY No. 10½C bench rabbet plane. Auct. $150. Dlr. $350

STANLEY No. 11 beltmaker's plane. Auct. $45-$90

STANLEY No. 11½ floor plane. Auct. $250-$300

STANLEY No. 12 veneer scraper plane. Auct. $30. Dlr. $55

STANLEY No. 12¼ veneer scraper. Auct. $150-$250

STANLEY No. 12½ scraper. Dlr. $25-$50

STANLEY No. 12¾ with wood bottom. $300-$500

STANLEY "Bailey" No. 13 circular plane. Auct. $45-$130 (earliest model).

STANLEY "Bailey" No. 15 block plane. $15-$30

STANLEY "Bailey" No. 15½ wood handled block plane. Auct. $160 up

STANLEY "Bailey" No. 16 block plane. $10-$25 (with 90% of orig. nickel plate. Dlr. $40

STANLEY "Bailey" No. 17 block plane. Dlr. $18

STANLEY "Bailey" No. 18 block plane. $15-$35 (near mint, in orig. box. Dlr. $65)

STANLEY "Bailey" No. 018 block plane. Rare model, lacks nickel plate, blued metal finish. $100-$225

STANLEY "Bailey" No. 18¼ block plane. $40-$70

STANLEY "Bailey" No. 19 block plane. $15-$35

STANLEY "Bailey" No. 019 block plane, blued metal frame and lever cap. $100-$250

STANLEY "Victor" No. 20 circular bottom plane. Auct. $45-$65

STANLEY "Victor" No. 20½ circular plane. $75-$100

STANLEY "Bailey" No. 21 wood bottom smooth plane. Auct. $95-$150

STANLEY "Bailey" No. 22 wood bottom smooth plane. Auct. $15-$30

STANLEY "Bailey" No. 23 wood bottom smooth plane. $20-$30

STANLEY "Bailey" No. 24 wood bottom smooth plane. Auct. $15-$30

STANLEY "Bailey" No. 25 wood bottom block plane. Auct. $90 and up.

STANLEY "Bailey" No. 26 wood bottom jack plane. Dlr. $15-$25

STANLEY "Bailey" No. 27 wood bottom jack plane. Dlr. $15-$25 (pre-lateral, Auct. $35)

STANLEY "Bailey" No. 27½ wood bottom jack plane. Auct. $25-$40

STANLEY "Bailey" No. 28 wood bottom fore plane. $15-$25

STANLEY "Bailey" No. 29 wood bottom fore plane. Auct. $15-$30

STANLEY "Bailey" No. 30 wood bottom jointer plane. Auct. $10-$40

STANLEY "Bailey" No. 31 wood bottom jointer plane. Auct. $20-$50

STANLEY "Bailey" No. 32 wood bottom jointer plane. Auct. $20-$30

STANLEY "Bailey" No. 33 wood bottom jointer plane. $30-$45

STANLEY "Bailey" No. 34 wood bottom jointer plane. Auct. $45-$65

STANLEY "Bailey" No. 35 wood bottom smooth plane. Dlr. $15-$35

STANLEY "Bailey" No. 36 wood bottom smooth plane. $15-$25

STANLEY "Bailey" No. 37 Jenny smooth plane, (a Jenny is slightly smaller than a Jack plane). Auct. $125-$225

STANLEY No. 39 dado planes in sizes ¼, ⅜, ½, & ⅝ in. average $50 ea. (Auct. set of (4) $150 . No. 39¾ is a bit scarce and has brought $60-$85

STANLEY No. 39 dado plane 13/16 in. size (in original box) $1,000-$2,500. The larger ⅞ in. and 1 inch sizes average $75 each. A set of (5), excluding the rarer 13/16 size, brought $220 at auction recently.

STANLEY No. 40 scrub plane. $25-$35. No. 40½ brings $65 to $125 (near mint cond.)

STANLEY No. 41 "Millers Patent" plow plane was the first in an evolving line of metal combination planes which began in 1871. The following prices include some models missing cutters or fillester attachment, and others in nearly mint condition, with all accessories and an extra fence.
No. 41 Auct. $225-$1,300
No. 42 Auct. $1,000-$3,700
No. 43 $150-$250
No. 44 $750-$1,000
See page 140 for complete descriptions.

STANLEY attachments for use with No. 45 plane. Pair No. 8 hollow and round in original carton which also contains a 1¼ in. nosing attachment, all blades included. Auct. $140

STANLEY No. 45 combination plane. Auct. $45-$150 (in orig. box with all access.)

STANLEY No. 46 "Traut's patent" combination plane. Auct. $40-$175 (orig. box). No. 47, without fence, averages $95-$150

STANLEY No. 48 tongue and groove plane. Auct. $20-$65 (pre 1898). No. 49 averages $50 from dealers.

STANLEY No. 50 adjustable beading, our combination plane. Avg. Dlr. $55. Mint in orig carton, Auct. $150-$225

STANLEY No. 51 chute board (plane only) $200-$300. No. 52 chute board with plane attached. Auct. $700-$900

STANLEY No. 54 plow and rabbet $400-$600

STANLEY No. 55 universal combination plane. Auct. $250-$450 (in orig. carton w/accessories).

STANLEY No. 56 core box plane, only 4 inches long. Auct. $750-$1,550

STANLEY No. 57 core box plane. Auct. $135-$220

STANLEY No. 60 block plane. $18-$25. No. 60½ $18-$25

STANLEY No. 61 block plane. $75-$125

STANLEY No. 62 low angle jack or block plane. Auct. $150-$350. No. 62C with corrugated bottom. Auct. $500

STANLEY No. 63 (same as No. 61 except longer) $75-$125

STANLEY No. 64 butcher's block plane. Auct. $900, Dlr. $1,500

STANLEY No. 65 block plane. $10-$25 (earliest 1898 model) $75-$125. No. 65½ $10-$25

STANLEY No. 66 universal hand beader, $20-$30. Auct. $80 (mint with fences & cutters).

STANLEY No. 69 hand beader with wooden handle, avg. $450-$650. Mint in box $1,000 and up.

STANLEY No. 70 box scraper. $10-$25. "Bailey" model, with 1870 patent. Auct. $55

STANLEY No. 71 router. Dlr. $15-$25. Auct. $35 with fence. No. 71½ with closed throat. $15-$25

STANLEY No. 72 chamfer plane. Auct. $200-$250. No. 72½ with beader. $250-$350

STANLEY No. 74 floor plane with handle. Auct. $350-$600. Without its handle, $100-$200

STANLEY No. 75 bull nose rabbet plane. $10-$22

STANLEY No. 78 duplex, filletster and rabbet plane. $15-$25 Auct. (2) for $45

STANLEY No. 78W door rabbet plane. $400-$600

No. 79 side rabbet plane. $25-$40. Circa 1926 model with nickel plate intact. $65-$10

STANLEY No. 80 steel cased rabbet plane. Dlr. $65-$100

STANLEY No. 80 cabinet scraper. $8-$15

STANLEY No. 81 cabinet scraper with wood bottom. $15-$30

STANLEY No. 82 single handled scraper. $12-$20

STANLEY No. 83 roller bottom scrapper $35-$75

STANLEY No. 85 cabinet maker's scrapper plane with tilt handle. Auct. $375 (no blade) to $700 (near mint). Dlr. $845 (98% orig. finish).

STANLEY No. 87 cabinet maker's scrapper plane. Auct. $1,000. Dlr. $1,200-$1,500

STANLEY No. 90 steel cased rabbet plane, (same as No. 80, except has a spur.) Auct. $45-$65. Dlr. $95-$110

STANLEY No. 90 bull nose rabbet plane $30-$50

STANLEY No. 90A cabinet maker's rabbet plane. $200-$400

STANLEY No. 90J cabinet maker's rabbet plane. $25-$40

STANLEY No. 92 cabinet maker's rabbet plane $45-$65. No. 93 which is an inch longer $60-$80

STANLEY No. 94 cabinet maker's rabbet plane. Auct. $125. Dlr. $250

STANLEY No. 95 edge trimming block plane. Auct. $115-$150

STANLEY No. 96 chisel gauge. Auct. $150-$170

STANLEY No. 97 cabinet maker's edge plane. Auct. $200-$375

STANLEY No. 98 and No. 99 side rabbet plane. Dlr. $30-$50 each.

STANLEY No. 100 toy-size block plane. $20-$30. No. 100½ with curved bottom. Auct. $60-$75

STANLEY No. 101 tiny household block plane. $5-$10

STANLEY No. 101½ bull nosed, toy-size, block plane. Scarce. $500-$750

STANLEY No. 102 non-adjust. block plane. $10

STANLEY No. 103 common block plane. Dlr. $15. (Earliest models, circa 1880, bring much more.)

STANLEY No. 104 "Liberty Bell" smooth plane. $75-$125. Dlr. (mint) $275

STANLEY No. 105 steel bottom jack plane. Auct. $75-$135

STANLEY No. 110 block plane. Modern version, (circa 1900-1973) $5-$15. Star cap models, (1877-1888) $30-$55. Earliest mfg. (circa 1876) with filigree cap. $400-$500

STANLEY No. 112 scraper plane. Auct. $65-$80

STANLEY No. 113 circular plane. Auct. $55-$105

STANLEY No. 118 school block plane. $15

STANLEY No. 120 block plane. Early models with star cap. $30-$55. Modern plain-cap version (1893-1950) $5-$10

STANLEY No. 122 smooth plane. $20-$30

STANLEY No. 127 wood bottom jack plane. $25

STANLEY No. 129 wood bottom fore plane. $25-$35

STANLEY No. 130 double-end block plane. $15-$30 (earliest models bring twice the price).

STANLEY No. 131 double-end block plane. Auct. $120-$150

STANLEY No. 132 wood bottom jointer plane. $30-$45

STANLEY No. 135 wood bottom smooth plane. $20-$35

STANLEY No. 140 rabbet and block plane. Auct. $75-$100

STANLEY No. 141 bull nose plow, filletster and matching plane. $175-$275 (with all cutters)

STANLEY No. 143 bullnose plow and matching plane. Auct. $200-$250

STANLEY No. 144 corner rounding plane. Auct. $150-$200

STANLEY No. 145 double-end match plane. $60-$100. No. 147 $60-$100. No. 148 $35-$85 (near mint).

STANLEY No. 164 low angle block plane. Auct. $1,500-$2,400

STANLEY No. 171 door trim and router plane. Auct. $150-$180

STANLEY No. 180 rabbet plane. $25-$40. No. 181 and No. 182 are narrower. $25-$40

STANLEY No. 190 rabbet plane. $15. No. 191 and No. 192 are narrower. $15. No. 190W is rare (only sold for 24 months during WWII), has removable bottom. $400-$600

STANLEY No. 193 fibre board cutter. $45-$60. No. 193A and No. 193B have more attachments and sell for $70 and up.

STANLEY No. 194 fibre board beveler plane. $35

STANLEY No. 195 hard board beveler plane. $75

STANLEY No. 196 curve rabbet plane. Auct. $650-$1,300

STANLEY No. 201 toy size, block plane. $100-$200

STANLEY No. 203 manual training block plane. $30-$55

STANLEY No. 212 scraper plane. Auct. $600-$800

STANLEY No. 220 block plane $5-$15

STANLEY No. 238 weathestrip plow plane. $75-$150

STANLEY No. 239 special dado plane. $80-$120. No. 239 pre-fence model, circa 1915. $90-$170. No. 239½ with fence, circa 1920. $150-$250

STANLEY No. 248 plow plane, with 2 cutters. Auct. $45-$100. No. 248A (came with 7 cutters) Auct. $55-$165

STANLEY No. 271 router, 3 in. square. $10-$15

STANLEY No. 278 rabbet and filletster plane. Auct. $75-$180

STANLEY No. 282 fixed-angle floor scraper. $5-$10

STANLEY No. 283 adjustble scraper. $150 & up

STANLEY No. 289 filletser and rabbet plane. $70-$145

STANLEY No. 292 floor scraper. $8

STANLEY No. 340 furring plane. Auct. (damaged) $700. Dlr. $1,200 (fine cond.)

STANLEY No. 378 weatherstrip rabbet plane. Auct. $80 $150 (near mint)

STANLEY No. 444 dovetail plane. Auct. $600-$1,200 (mint in orig. box).

STANLEY "Bed Rock" smooth planes: No. 602 $250-$400. No. 602C $400-$500. No. 603 $35-$75. No. 603C $40-$70. No. 604 $20-$40. No. 604C $25-$45. No. 604½ $100-$200. No. 604½C $150-$250

STANLEY "Bed Rock" jack planes: No. 605 $20-$40. No. 605C $35-$45. No. 605¼ $350-$700. No. 605½ $35-$90. Mo. 605½C $45-$85.

STANLEY "Bed Rock" fore plane, No. 606. Auct. $30-$65. No. 606C. Auct. $35-$85

STANLEY "Bed Rock" jointer planes: No. 607 $40-$70. No. 607C $45-$75. No. 608 Auct. $70. Dlr. $90. No. 608C $75-$100

STANLEY No. OH4 "Two-Tone" smooth plane $30. No. OH5 jack plane $30-$45. No. OH20 block plane $25

STANLEY No. 1120 "Four Square" block plane $20-$35. No. 1104 smooth plane. Auct. $36. No. 1105 jack plane. Auct. $20. Dlr. $45

STANLEY No. H1247 "Handyman" block plane. $15-$20. No. H1204 smooth plane. $18-$20

STANLEY No. A4 aluminum smooth plane. Auct. $100. Dlr. $150. No. A5 jack plane. Auct. $95-$110. Dlr. $175. No. A6 fore plane. Auct. $120-$150

STANLEY No. A18 aluminum block plane. $75-$125

STANLEY No. A45 aluminum combination plane. $1,200-$1,800

STANLEY No. A78 aluminum duplex, filletster, and rabbet plane. Auct. $155-$175

STANLEY No. S4 steel smooth plane. $125. No. S5 steel jack plane. Auct. $55-$80. No. S18 steel bloc, plane. $30-$55

STANLEY "Gage" metal smooth plane. No. G3 $35-$90. No. G3C $45-$80. No. G4 $35-$50. No. G4C $40-$65

STANLEY "Gage" metal jack plane. No. G5. Auct. $35-$70. No. G5C $75-$150

STANLEY No. G6 "Gage" metal fore plane. $40-$60. No. G6C with corrugated bottom. $50-$70

STANLEY No. G7 "Gage" metal jointer plane. $65-$95 No. G7C, corrugated. $75-$100

STANLEY No. G22 "Gage" wood bottom smooth plane. $25-$50

STANLEY No. G26 "Gage" wood bottom jack plane. $30-$55. No. G27½ $75-$150

STANLEY "Gage" wood bottom fore plane No. G28. $35-$65

STANLEY "Gage" No. G30 wood bottom jointer plane $40-$75. No. G31 $75-$150

STANLEY "Gage" No. G35 wood bottom smooth plane. $30-$55. No. G36 $75-$150

STANLEY "Bailey" Victor, metal block plane, circa 1880. No. 0 Auct. $150. No. 0½ Auct. $150-$200. No. 00 $175-$250. No. 000 $200-$275. No. 1 (in original carton, with 1876 pat. date) Auct. $1,700. Normal price range $200-$300. No. 1¼ $400-$700. No. 1½ $500-$800. No. 1¾ $250-$350

STANLEY "Bailey" Victor No. 2 block plane with wooden ball handle. $200-$300. No. 2¼ $400-$750. No. 2½ $500-$800. No. 2¾ $250-$350

STANLEY "Bailey" Victor smooth plane with conventional handle. No. 3 $200-$350. No. 3½ $200-$350. No. 4 Auction. $200. No. 4½ $200-$350

STANLEY "Bailey" Victor, No. 5 jack plane. $200-$350. No. 5½ $200-$350

STANLEY "Bailey" Victor No. 6 fore plane (circa 1880-1888) Auct. $270-$375. Nos. 6½ thru 8½ sell in same range.

STANLEY "Bailey" Victor No. 10 circular bottom plane with adjustable sole. Auct. $275. No. 10½ was sold as early as 1877 and has brought $1,000 to $2,500 when offered on today's market.

STANLEY "Bailey" Victor No. 11 metal combination rabbet and filletster plane. $1,000-$2,500. No. 11½ is harder to come by at $1,500-$3,000

STANLEY "Bailey" Victor No. 12 pocket block plane (circa 1880-88) Auct. $300-$350. No. 12½ should sell in same range, but No. 12¼ was offered for a short 48 month period, is nickel plated, and has brought from $400 to $600

STANLEY "Bailey" Victor metallic combination plane, circa 1880-1884, with movable fence. Auct. $500-$1,000

STANLEY "Bailey" Victor metallic circular plane, sold for 78 years. Auction $410-$575

STANLEY "Bailey" Victor box scraper. $40-$75

STANLEY "Bailey" Little Victor, all metal, 3¼ inch long block planes were sold from 1880-1884. Nos. 50 thru 52 sell in a broad range from $100 to $300 depending upon the amount of original black paint or nickel plate remaining intact.

STANLEY "Bailey" Defiance metal block plane, circa 1879-80. Auct. $425. Small variations in models B, D, E & F have enticed crazy collectors to pay from $500 to $900 for these 6½ to 7½ inch planes with a battle axe trademark, no wooden parts.

STANLEY "Bailey" Defiance No. 3 smooth plane, iron body, rosewood handle, circa 1880. Auct. $75-$260. Dlr. $200-$350. Nos. 4 thru 27 are from 8½ to 24 inches long and all seem to fall in the same general price range.

STANLEY No. 00 rare, two fold, six inch ivory rule. Auct. $400

STANLEY No. 4, two foot, two fold, arch joint rule. Auct. $260

STANLEY No. 13½, two fold, caliper rule, 6 inch length. Auct. $55

STANLEY No. 15, two foot, two fold, brass bound, Gunters scale, slide rule. Auct. $55

STANLEY No. 22 two foot, four fold, boxwood rule with brass trim and board measure tables. $110

(Please see pages 172 and 173 for hundreds of other Stanley rules.)

STANLEY Nos. 38 and 40 ivory rules, 6 inches and 1 foot lengths. Auct. $100 each

STANLEY No. 39 ivory caliper rule, one foot, four fold, (near mint). Auct. $275. Another, with original leather case. Auct. $450

STANLEY No. 40, ivory rule, one foot, four fold, with caliper slide. Auct. $125

STANLEY No. 40½, two fold, six inch, ivory caliper rule in near fine condition. Auct. $375

STANLEY No. 58 boxwood two foot, six fold, rule with brass arch joint. Scarce model. Auct. $220

STANLEY No. 62C, folding boxwood two foot rule with brass caliper, circa 1930. (Fine cond.) Auct. $75

STANLEY No. 66 scarce model, three foot, four fold boxwood rule. Auct. $140

STANLEY No. 76 two foot, four fold, brass bound rule. This one is English made, so...$150 Auct.

STANLEY No. 81, two foot, four fold, arch joint rule with scales. Auct. $110

STANLEY No. 87, rare two foot, four fold ivory rule, bound on all sides, arch joint, (near mint cond.) Auct. $475. Another, (age-stained) Auct. $75

STANLEY No. 88, one foot, four fold, bound ivory rule with arch joint, near mint cond. Auct. $275

STANLEY No. 92 one foot, four fold, ivory rule in mint condition. Auct. $325

STANLEY No. 97 ivory rule, 2 foot, 4 fold, (faded but readable). Auct. $150

STANLEY No. 98 (2) school rules made into a parallel rule by a patented device mfd. by W. Miller, Boston. Auct. $210

STANLEY No. 106 box of (6) zig-zag rules in orig. carton, circa 1939. Auct. $40

STANLEY No. 1193 brass bound 12 inch wooden level. Auct. $135

STANLEY No. 7506 push-pull rule in orig. carton, circa 1939. Auct. $30

STANLEY No. 1093 fully brass bound 12 inch mahogany level. (Excellent cond.) Auct. $125

STANLEY "Special" rule, 11/16 in. square stick, 32 inches long. Auct. $50

STANLEY No. 1 "Odd Jobs" combination square, scribe, level, etc., with correct 12 inch maple rule, fine condition, original box with instructions. Auct. $100-$160. In average shape, with rule only $50-$85

STANLEY No. 2 "Excelsior" iron tool handle with (3) tool bits, 1867 patent date. Dlr. $35

STANLEY No. 6 trammel points with (9) points and a roller-marker. Auct. $250

STANLEY No. 12 iron handled try square with 2 inch blade, circa 1911, rare size. Dlr. $75

STANLEY No. 18, iron handled T-bevel square with 8 inch blade, circa 1915. Dlr. $15

STANLEY No. 19 "Victor" plumb and level, rosewood with brass trim, 26 inches long. Near mint, and in original carton. Auct. $275

STANLEY No. 20, rosewood handled T-bevel square, circa 1925, with 10 inch blade, brass trim. Dlr. $9

STANLEY No. 34 Tool Catalogs: 1917 edition $45, 1922 ed. $35, 1929 ed. $35, 1935 ed. $30, 1941 ed. $25. No. 120 Stanley dealer's, large, hard cover catalog, 1919 edition, $125-$165. Circa 1888 catalog, 65 pages. $120. 1902 Stanley hardware catalog, $110

STANLEY No. 50 "Everlasting" chisel, 7½ inches long. Dlr. $18

STANLEY "Bailey" No. 54, adjustable iron spoke shave. Early model, circa 1885, with adj. screw inside brass cone. Dlr. $20

STANLEY No. 63X, circa 1920, spoke shave. Auct. $30

STANLEY No. 71, brass spoke shave. A rare find. Auct. $160

STANLEY No. 77 Dowel & Rod turning machine. (illus. pg. 39) Auct. $200-$325. Set of (8) diff. cutter-heads for above, unused, in orig. boxes. $560

STANLEY No. 77 and No. 172 marking gauges. Lot of (2). Auct. $65. (See page 74 for other marking gauges by this maker.)

STANLEY No. 85½ rosewood and brass panel gage. Auct. $105

STANLEY No. 86 box of (6) flat-bladed screwdrivers, circa 1915. Auct. $50-$60

STANLEY No. 93 brass bound mahogany plumb & level in average used condition. Auct. $45. (See page 98 for more Stanley levels.)

STANLEY No. 95, iron butt gage. Early model, circa 1898, only 1¾ inches long. (Later models are 3 in.) Dlr. $65

STANLEY, educational charts Nos. 100-122, with extra blueprints. Auct. $130

STANLEY No. 181 two-way level, 1¼ in. x 1¼ in., for cameras, clocks, etc. Auct. $20

STANLEY No. NH15 screwdriver with jacknife blade in handle, No. 1021 screwdriver with flashlight brass handle. (2) pcs. Auct. $50. (Both are illustrated at top of page 189).

STANLEY ratcheting screwdrivers, lot of (3): Nos. 215, 5 inch and 6 inch, plus a 3 inch No. 216. Auct. $60

STANLEY RULE & LEVEL CO., pair of cabinet screwdrivers, circa 1880. Auct. $40

STANLEY No. 313 aluminum plumb & level with all of its original orange and silver paint intact. Auct. $10

STANLEY No. 610 pistol grip hand drill with sweetheart trademark and 98% of original black and orange paint intact. Auct. $135

STANLEY Victor No. 935 ratchet brace, plus a Goodell-Pratt circa 1905 corner brace, and a John Fray & Co. No. 146 brace. Lot of (3). Auct. $35

STANLEY No. 850 oak wall tool cabinet with roll-up front, few tools. Auct. $200. (See page 211 for more Stanley tool chests.)

STANLEY No. 984 corner ratchet bit brace, cocabolo wood head & handle, circa 1936. (Fine Cond.) Auct. $90

STANLEY Nos. 1220 & 1265 "Defiance" hand drill, and a breast drill, (2) pcs. Auct. $30

STANLEY No. 6020 "Atha" upholsterer's magnetic tack hammer with No. 605 claw attachment, circa 1939. Dlr. $27

STANLEY set of (13) Russell Jennings auger bits in wooden box. Auct. $55

STANLEY WORKS presented this oak machinists tool box to an apprentice graduate in 1919. Auct. $175.

WING H. TABER, slide arm plow plane with brass thumb screws. Auct. $120. (Boxwood brings much more).

T. TILEFTON wooden dado plane, 3/16 in. Auct. $75

I.C. TITCOMB, N.P. (1813-1859, Newburyport, MA.), crown moulding plane 14 inches long, 4 in. wide. Auct. $500

I.C. TITCOMB, N.P., massive crown moulder, 16 inches long, 6 in. wide, double throat, twin blades. Auct. $2,100

C. TOBEY, Hudson (N.Y.) bead plane 9 5/16 inches long, birch with lignum vitae boxwood wear insert. Auct. $300

J.I. TOBEY, Hudson, N.Y., adjustable sash plane. Auct. $100

J.R. TOLMAN double-bladed shipbuilder's rabbet plane, 20 inches long Auct. $110. Another, 1 in. x 22 in. Auct. $125

J.R. TOLMAN, Hanover, Mass. "V" groove plow plane with wooden thumb screws. Auct. $225

TOOL BOX, inside cover inlays form sunburst. Rosewood and birdseye maple. Six drawers, owner's initials and Masonic emblem. Auct. $775

J.N. TOWER, Grecian ogee moulding plane 9⅜ inches long, ⅝ in. wide. Auct. $225. Bead moulder. Auct. $175

TOWER & LYONS iron fore plane, 18 inches long, corrugated top and bottom. Auct. $35

TUCK MFG. CO., Brockton, Mass., group of (8) screwdrivers in two cartons. Auct. $45

TUCKER & APPLETON, handled rosewood plow plane, boxwood screw-arms & nuts. Auct. $675

UNION MANUFACTURING CO., New Britain, CT. Incorporated in 1866 by several other related firms, to produce grey iron castings, subassembly parts, hardware and tools. Stanley Rule & Level, and also Davis Level & Tool, were among the original stockholders. Stanley purchased the plane manufacturing division in 1920, perhaps to offer a lower priced line. Siegley made some plow planes for Union before 1905.

UNION No. X4½, Pat. 12-8-03 iron smoothing plane, 10 inches overall. Mahogany handle and front knob are perfect. Auct. $225

UNION brand, chamfering spoke shave. Auct. $130

UNION No. X0, tiny 6 inch metal smoothing plane with perfect cond. mahogany handle and knob, 98% of original japanning remains. Auct. $2,500

UNION MFG. CO., No. 0 iron smoothing plane, only 5½ inches long. Auct. $1,900

UNION MFG. CO. No. 2 metal smoothing plane. Auct. $125

UNION No. 2, corrugated bottom metal smooth plane 7⅞ inches long. (Top of wooden handle has been sheared off, otherwise good cond. Auct. $300

UNION No. X2, Pat. 12-8-03 metal smooth plane, 8½ inches overall, perfect handles and finish. Auct. $950

UNION No. 3, iron smoother, 9½ inches long. Black bed with original red lever cap. Auct. $50

UNION No. 5A iron jack plane with wooden handle and knob. Auct. $25

UNION No. 7 corrugated bottom iron jointer. Auct. $45. No. 8 fore plane by same maker. Auct. $30

UNION No. 31 transitional wood bottom jointer plane, 24 inches long. Auct. $25

BENJ. VAN AMRINGE, Oakland, Cal., Pat. 1887, combination saw, bevel square, level & rule, with ebony handle. Auct. $125

VARVILL & SONS, York. English plow plane with simple wedge-arm fence. Auct. $30. (Also see pg. 140)

VICTOR (See STANLEY "Bailey")

JOHN VIET, Corner Newmarket and Green St., Phila. Wooden clamp-shaped cooper's plane with 3 screw arms. Auct. $350

J. & G. H. WALKER, wooden level with brass trim. Political adv. for WHIG Candidate, presidend 1852. Auct. $105

WM. P. WALTERS, Market St., Phila., 1888 Woodworking tool catalog with (3) advertising broadsides. Auct. $220

I. WALTON, Reading, is the very faint mark on this round bottom 10⅛ in. moulding plane. Auct. $150.

WATCHMAKER'S Lathe. Brass with 4 inch stock, 13 inches overall. Auct. $225

EMERY WATERHOUSE & CO., Portland, Me. (1871 mark), No. 148 beading plane. Auct. $45

M. WATKINS & CO., Bristol, CT., rare iron sighting level, 19½ in. long. Patented in 1847. Auct. $300

WARD set of (10) gouges, plus flat chisel, and parting tool. Auct. $70

WARD & FLETCHER, 513 8th Ave., New York, rosewood plow plane with boxwood screw arms. Auct. $400

SL WARD, skew rabbet, birch with spur on each side, 1⅛ in. cutter, 9 15/16 in. long. Auct. $175

J. WATTS, Boston, 48 inch wantage rule with brass tips and several tables. Auct. $200

WEBB, Pittsfield, complex moulding plane, unhandled style, Tiger Maple. Auct. $145

J & W. WEBB, New York, pair of complex moulding planes with boxwood wear inserts. Auct. $75

Wm. H. WEED, Cohoes, N.Y., well worn hewing axe with 13 inch applied steel edge. Auct. $175

H. WETHEREL, Chatham (with two T.M.'s). Narrow round moulding plane, 9¾ in. long. Auct. $375. Another moulder by same maker, Auct. $200. Group of (4) moulders, (2) with double crown mark. Auct. $100 for all. (1) hollow moulding plane. Auct. $50-$70. (3) moulding planes by H. Wetherall. Auct. $130

F.W. WHITCHER & CO., Boston, Mass., iron surfacing plane, 17 inches long. Franklin patent, 1873. Auct. $75

L. & I.J. WHITE, cooper's leveling plane, No. 239-L, in Lignum Vitae wood. Auct. $125

WHITE & SPEAR, Warren (Oh), panel raising plane, 4 inches wide by 13¾ in. long. Auct. $150

A.J. WILKINSON, Bost., rosewood bit brace, only 11 inches overall. Auct. $175

WINCHESTER No. W5, iron jack plane, 14 inches overall. Auct. $45-$55. (Another, rusty cond.) $35

WINCHESTER No. 9605 take-apart framing squares, (2) with 1914 patent dates. Auct. $45 pr.

WINDSOR Beading Tool, Windsor, VT. Pat. 1885 router-shaped beader with brass center section. Auct. $75-$100. Dlr. $125

WINSTED PLANE CO., (Winsted, Ct.) is the mark on 2¼ in. cutter of this complex moulding plane. Auct. $75

THE WONDER ROPE MAKER, pat App'd for. Hand-cranked, cast iron. Auct. $115-$250

WRENCH, Pat. May 16, 1871. Multi-purpose 5-jaw wrench, pliers, screwdriver, etc., no brand name. Auct. $50

YANKEE No. 100 ratcheting screwdriver set in original wooden bos. Auct. $95-$135 (fine) and $25 (worn cond.) Stanley Tools division purchased North Brothers, who manufactured "Yankee" drills, in 1946.

YANKEE No. 131A, by North Bros., spiral ratchet screwdriver in orig. box with (3) bits. Auct. $60

YOUNG & M'MASTER, Auburn, N.Y., large moulding plane with 2¼ in. blade. Auct. $75

YOUNG & SONS, Phil., No. 860 precision level in 6 inch wooden box. Auct. $45

ZENITH, large and heavy hewing axe with 13½ inch edge. Auct. $150
